WARS OF THE 20th CENTURY

WARS OF THE

20th CENTURY

derbibooks

First published in the
United States of America by
Derbibooks and distributed by
Book Sales Inc., 110 Enterprise Avenue
Secaucus, N.J. 07094

Reprinted 1976

Parts of this book have appeared previously in
World War I and *World War II*, both published
by Octopus Books Limited

Designed by David Eldred
Cartography by Arka Graphics
Picture Research by Robert Hunt

© 1973, 1975 Octopus Books Limited

ISBN 0 7064 0434 3

Produced by Mandarin Publishers Limited
22A Westlands Road, Quarry Bay, Hong Kong

Printed in Hong Kong

Contents

Introduction by S.L. Mayer

The turn of the century was a watershed in world history. Victoria still reigned in Britain; Kaiser Wilhelm II was calling for a 'place in the sun' for Imperial Germany; Czar Nicholas II was at the start of his ill-fated reign in Imperial Russia. Austria-Hungary, the Hapsburg Empire, dominated parts of Central and Eastern Europe along the Danube as she had done for centuries; the Ottoman Empire, with its Sultan in Constantinople, claimed suzerainty over most of what is now called the Middle East and even part of the Balkans. Africa and Asia were ruled by a few Western European states, notably Britain and France. The sleeping giant, the United States, had just entered the imperial race in the Spanish-American War, and was beginning its expansion in the Caribbean and Latin America. There were none who questioned European hegemony over the world. Europe, in fact, was the center of the world. It was only a matter of which power or combination of powers would dominate the other.

All this today seems far away. The history of the 20th century has been a stormy one, with many small wars, two world wars, and the threat of a third world war omnipresent. Europe is no longer the center of the world. Europe no longer rules Africa and Asia. Russia and the United States, with all their nuclear and industrial power, are increasingly less able to do their will anywhere in the world. Western Europe is in disarray, despite its attempts to unite. China, the new nuclear threat, is growing as an industrial power and is developing delivery capabilities for her nuclear weapons that soon could pose a threat to both Moscow and San Francisco. Korea and Vietnam have tested America's ability to cope with brush-fire wars, and attention in recent years has focused on the Middle East, which contains much of the oil necessary to continue industrial growth in Europe and America. One thing emerges clearly from this vastly altered picture: the power centers of the world have proliferated. Not only are they no longer exclusively in Europe; they are the monopoly of no continent or nation.

These changes have emerged first slowly, then rather suddenly as the world wars of one of the most violent centuries in history accelerated change and encouraged it. A world war could not break out because of the assassination of anyone today. This is a far cry from 1914, when the assassination of an Austrian archduke of whom few Europeans or Americans had heard caused a worldwide conflagration. The issues in 1914 were, of course, complex, but after we have discussed the rise of nationalism, the arms race after 1900, the conflicting and interlocking alliances and alignments of European states before the First World War, rising industrialization and urbanization, the impact of socialism on the rise of the labor unions and the growing intellectual ferment which characterized those halcyon Edwardian years, we are left with one irreducible fact which more than any other probably caused World War I; Anglo-German rivalry.

By 1900 the Germans had passed the British in industrial strength, especially if one turns to the most vital indices of industrialization of the time. In coal, iron and steel production Britain had already been outstripped. Her markets on the Continent were slowly being taken over by Germany. Even her naval hegemony in the world, unchallenged for almost a century, was now being threatened as Germany entered the naval construction race. Britain controlled much of the world. Reverberations in the City of London were felt everywhere. The Union Jack flew over a quarter of the earth's surface. Germany had enormous economic and military strength, but few colonies and little prestige. When Kaiser Wilhelm tried to assert Germany's influence in British areas, such as South Africa, or French areas of interest, like Morocco, the British became nervous and began to look for allies in France, Russia and Japan. Across the Atlantic the American industrial machine was rapidly outstripping both Britain and Germany. America was unaware of the enormous potential she could bring to bear if she entered European affairs. Russia was industrially backward, tottering on the brink of revolution.

When World War I broke out, everyone thought it would be short, sharp and decisive. After four years of the most massive conflagration the world had yet seen, the results were diffuse and indecisive. Britain had checked Germany's attempt to dominate the Continent, but had brought herself to the verge of bankruptcy and military defeat in order to do it. The American entry in the war in 1917 helped tip the balance in Britain's favor, but almost as quickly as she entered European affairs, the United States tried to withdraw into isolationism once again.

Germany was severely weakened, but not sufficiently to prevent a resurgence of the imperial will in Berlin. Russia underwent a revolution and civil war which effectively isolated her from European power-making for two decades. Above all, European confidence in itself was shaken irreparably. Britain and France were the apparent victors in World War I. Through the mandate system of the newly constructed League of Nations, each had expanded her empire, so that the two Western European democracies dominated even more territory than before the war. But this expansion of power was more apparent than real.

Britain and France had become debtor nations. The United States was the world's leading creditor. New York became the financial capital of the world, not London. Above all, the nationalism which was spreading throughout Europe now was filtering into the colonial world. Intellectuals in Delhi, Batavia, Peking and Shanghai, Cairo and Nairobi were beginning to agitate for self-rule, to control for themselves the vast economic potential that the Afro-Asian world possessed. For Asian nationalist leaders, Japan was the model. Of the African and Asian nations only Japan had emerged as a great power in the 20th century. Her defeat of Russia in 1905 was an inspiration to Afro-Asian nationalism. Japan not only had maintained her independence at the high tide of European imperialism, but she also had asserted her own imperial claims in Korea, Formosa, Manchuria and China. The supposed invincibility of Europe was a myth, and Japan was proving it. When the stock market crash in New York in 1929 signalled the beginning of a worldwide economic slump, Japan was one of the first nations to feel it and react by seizing Manchuria and threatening China proper. Dictatorships proliferated in Central and Eastern Europe. Britain and France, holding both the torch of democracy and the banner of imperialism in Europe, tried in vain to deal with the rise of Hitler's Germany and Mussolini's Italy, but refused to allow Stalin's Soviet Union to help them keep the Fascist powers in check. By 1939 the treaties which brought peace to Europe after World War I were a back number, most of their clauses having been bartered away by Britain and France or seized by Germany and Italy. Japan had conquered most of coastal China, and the Western Powers had been unable to prevent the erosion of much of their power in Europe and Asia.

When World War II broke out in September 1939 Germany hoped to re-establish the position she had in Europe during World War I. In one sense, World War II in Europe was a rematch between the two superpowers of 1914, Britain and Germany. But unlike 1914, Europe no longer had the power individually or collectively to dictate policy to the rest of the world. Although Germany soon overran most of Continental Europe by 1940, neither Russia nor America had entered the conflict. Britain was again on the verge of bankruptcy, and needed American intervention to restore even a semblance of her former imperial strength. In 1941 the reality of European weakness in the face of Russian and American strength came as a shock to Hitler as well as Churchill. Germany claimed that it would take six weeks to defeat Russia when the Soviet Union was invaded in June 1941. By the end of the year, although Germany held huge gains in European Russia, the defense of Leningrad and Moscow convinced even Hitler that his victory would not come easily. Japan's daring gamble to wipe out American naval strength at Pearl Harbor in December 1941 brought the greatest industrial power into World War II. What had begun as a European power struggle between Britain and France on the one hand and Germany and Italy on the other, now had become, in effect, two quite different struggles: the US versus Japan for control of East Asia and the Pacific; and Germany versus Russia for hegemony in Europe.

The wars in Europe and the Pacific were linked basically by one factor after Pearl Harbor; both involved the United States in a significant way. But until 1944 the Americans were only peripherally involved in the European war. Although the Americans helped land troops in North Africa in Operation Torch in 1942, and fully participated in the conquest of Sicily and southern Italy in 1943, neither operation made a real difference in defeating the principal enemy in Europe, Nazi Germany. During the 1941–43 period Russia bore the brunt of the fighting against Hitler, and it was the Soviet Union that finally broke the back of the Wehrmacht, at Stalingrad and later at Kursk. When it became obvious to even Nazi leaders that the war was lost, the US and its allies, notably Britain, stepped in at D-Day and in Operation Anvil, the two invasions of France, to make certain that Communist armies did not establish a European hegemony as unpalatable as the one they were extinguishing.

In the Far East the balance of strength lay even more clearly in the Americans' favor. The US stopped the Japanese at Midway, and Nimitz and MacArthur conducted two separate, yet curiously linked campaigns in New Guinea, the Philippines and across the islands in the Pacific toward Japan so that, when the atomic bombs were dropped on Hiroshima and Nagasaki, there was little for Russia to do except sweep through Manchuria into Korea after the war was over. Of course a chiefly British campaign cleared Burma of Japanese soldiers by the end of the war. Australia, New Zealand, and to a lesser extent, Britain and Holland made contributions to the conquest of Japan in the Pacific. But the American contribution was the most significant, like Russia's role in Europe. This is not to minimize or denigrate the participation of Australia, New Zealand and particularly Britain in the Desert campaign. But the Desert war, like the Burma campaign, was essentially a sideshow to the main action. Of course, the Anglo-American conquest of Western Europe in 1944–45 hastened the end of the war in Europe. But by that time the German war machine was grinding to a halt. Allied bombing of German cities, much of it directed from the British Isles, slowed the German economy. But the fact remains that the conquest of Germany ended Europe's role as decision-maker on a world scale.

World War II, which, like World War I, started as a struggle over who was to rule Europe, Britain or Germany, ended with Russia and America dominating Europe, dividing it into spheres of influence. It was similar in some respects to the way Europe, in the 19th century, had divided other parts of the world into spheres of influence. In short, the two world wars turned European affairs into local rather than global significance. Bismarck once remarked that his concept of Africa was France on one side, Russia on the other, and Germany in the center. After 1945 it was the position of Russia and America which was critical in every part of the globe. The European civil wars which the two world wars represented ended with the eclipse of British, German and all other purely European nations in world decision-making.

Of the two superpowers the United States had predominance in 1945. The Americans possessed a monopoly of nuclear weapons and the only major economy which had come out of World War II unscathed. In fact the war stimulated the economy so that over half the world's industrial production and almost half its production of foodstuffs came from the United States. The Russian economy, on the other hand, was stultified after the German occupation of much of European Russia stripped the country bare of essentials. The Russians lost an estimated 25 million people during the war. Industrial capacity that remained was exhausted. Nevertheless, the Russians had one advantage over the Americans; the determination to extend their power, at the same time when American public opinion dictated a rapid demobilization of the fifteen million in uniform at the end of the war. Although incapable of waging war against the United States, the Soviet Union saw to it that Eastern Europe was firmly in their camp and then sought to undermine governments in Central and Western Europe. In 1948 both France and Italy almost voted the Communists into power. In Czechoslovakia the Communists seized it. The American reaction slowly began to form when

the Marshall Plan was announced and the Truman Doctrine helped send military and economic aid to Greece and Turkey, both of which were in danger of falling into Communist hands. By 1949 American public opinion was determined to prevent Communism from winning more territory after China was taken over by Mao Tse-tung. The NATO Pact was organized to give American protection to Western Europe as the US began to rearm once more. This rearmament was given an injection of enthusiasm when the US decided to resist the North Korean attempt to take over South Korea in 1950 by sending ground troops to the continent of Asia. The Cold War was hotting up. Stalin realized that direct confrontation was ineffective in subverting the Americans' will to maintain their global authority.

Despite the fact that the Soviet Union was able to develop its own atomic capability, the 1950's were a period of continued American global ascendancy. The US possessed the only credible delivery system and the only viable defenses against atomic attack. Thus, in the Suez Crisis of 1956 when Russia threatened London and Paris with bombardment, this threat was not taken seriously, as Khrushchev would never have risked nuclear confrontation with the United States and certain obliteration of Russian cities unless he was sure that Britain and France would be forced out of Egypt by the United States anyway. When the Russians attempted to gain influence in the Lebanon in 1958, Eisenhower sent American troops to Beirut beaches and the Russian threat was withdrawn. But by the 1960's Russia was testing the American will to maintain this belligerent posture. Khrushchev was not impressed when he met Kennedy in Vienna in 1961, and the construction of the Berlin Wall was a challenge which Kennedy did not meet forcefully. The Wall remained standing, and the Bay of Pigs invasion and the backdown in Laos in the same year convinced the Russians that Kennedy could be bluffed. During the Cuban missile crisis of 1962, however, the Soviet Union was forced to back down before Kennedy's challenge. The Soviet Union quietly built their navy to match the American fleet above and below the seas while their nuclear and missile strength developed massively. By the mid-1960's the Russians possessed a strength equal to or in some areas superior to Western combined forces. The Vietnam War, however, was the test of American will against the wrong enemy in the wrong place at the wrong time. It was the breaking of America's world hegemony.

In the wake of the Vietnam débâcle the Americans willingly accepted the illusion of détente with Russia at a moment when the strength of the Soviet Union was at its peak. Meanwhile, China had developed its own nuclear capability and power in the world began to proliferate once again. By the 1970's the bipolarization of world power was at an end. Although Russia and America still are the greatest of the world powers, China's missiles with nuclear warheads presented a growing threat to both Russian and American clients in the Far East. The legacy of Vietnam convinced the Americans that their power was over-extended. Europe began to develop ideas of independence from American economic domination as the dollar devalued twice and with it, American prestige. India created its own atomic capability and the nuclear club now includes six nations, with more to come in the foreseeable future. The oil producing nations of the Middle East, after the Yom Kippur War of 1973, were well on their way to becoming the world's creditors. If the two world wars determined that Europe's days as a power center were done, the 1970's indicated that bipolarization of world power was equally over. Perhaps the Mediterranean world is beginning to reassert its authority as the fountainhead of civilization and economic might over 1500 years after the first sack of Rome. Is this the renaissance of ancient hegemonies or the rise of a new barbarism?

WORLD WAR I
David Shermer

CHAPTER ONE

The Conflagration Begins

NO. 4,438.

HEIR TO AUSTRIAN THRONE MURDERED.

ARCHDUKE AND HIS WIFE SHOT DEAD IN THE STREET.

DETERMINED PLOT.

BOMB FIRST THROWN AT THEIR CAR.

MURDERED

The Archduke Francis F

SECOND ATTEMPT WITHIN AN HOUR.

BOY ASSASSIN.

the burgomaster and the m town council, and it was that he was then in a fu and bitterly resentful of a pened.

The burgomaster stern

Above: News of the assassination made headlines, but few grasped the significance of this event. **Opposite, top left:** Sarajevo, 28 June 1914. Archduke Franz Ferdinand and his wife arrive for their triumphal procession. **Top centre:** After the first assassination attempt, the princely pair continued along the parade route. **Top right:** They arrive at the City Hall to be greeted by the Mayor. **Left:** The second attempt was all too successful.

The incident that provoked World War I was the assassination of the heir to the Habsburg throne, Archduke Franz Ferdinand, and his wife, Duchess Sophie. The underlying causes of the war were, of course, more complex and of longer standing. As Sir Basil Liddell Hart wrote, 'Fifty years were spent in the process of making Europe explosive.' Yet on 28 June 1914, the day of the double murder, a crisis began which seemed to lead inexorably to war.

The fact that Habsburg royalty were on that date in Sarajevo, capital of the Austrian province of Bosnia-Herzegovina and neighbour of independent Serbia, was a needless provocation. Serbia's greatest national festival, commemorating St Vitus and the medieval battle of Kosovo, was held on 28 June. But 28 June was also the fourteenth wedding anniversary of the Archduke and his morganatic wife. Franz Ferdinand's visit to Bosnia in his capacity of inspector general of the Austro-Hungarian armed forces gave him the chance to appear in public ceremonially with his beloved Sophie. In Vienna, on the other hand, the Duchess led a socially withdrawn life under the shadow of imperial disapproval of their marriage, since Sophie's rank was considered too low for marriage to the heir to the throne. So, ironically, it was Sophie's wedding anniversary treat that led her to death beside her husband.

Vladimir Dedijer, the leading historian of the Sarajevo incident, has noted that Duchess Sophie had arrived in Bosnia with forebodings of what was to come. She recalled that one of the leaders of the Bosnian assembly or *Sabor* had warned that the visit should be cancelled because of pan-South Slav feeling in the province, provoked by Serbia. Despite this and other warnings, the visit had to take place. Cancellation would have seemed an admission of Austrian nervousness. Yet the police protection of the imperial party was minimal, and but for the haphazard arrangements the badly-organized assassination attempt would never have succeeded.

Sunday, 28 June, was a bright and sunny morning in Sarajevo as the royal train pulled into the station. On hand to greet the royal couple was General Oskar Potiorek, military governor of Bosnia. Confusion occurred almost immediately. The first car in the procession was intended for security detectives, but somehow all but one of them was left behind at the station and only three local police officers were present. Security arrangements were bungled from the beginning.

The Archduke, his consort, and General

Potiorek travelled in an open Viennese sports car. As they drove along the Appel Quay, the Archduke, whose attitude towards attempts on his life was rather fatalistic, requested that the car be driven slowly so that he could have a good look at his surroundings. Although the crowds were thin, a few cheers rang out as the procession passed. Near the central police station, as General Potiorek was pointing out a new army barracks, a tall young man, Čabrinovič, suddenly hurled a hand grenade directly at the sports car from a nearby group of onlookers. The grenade bounced off the folded roof of the car and fell into the street, exploding under the next car in the procession and wounding several officers and about twenty of the crowd. As the Archduke's chauffeur accelerated towards the town hall, however, Franz

Right: Gavrilo Princip, who wiped out two lives and an era.

Otto von Bismarck, the Iron Chancellor of the Second Reich.

At that very moment a short young Bosnian, Gavrilo Princip, took out his revolver. A policeman tried frantically to grab his hand, but was struck by someone nearby. Emerging from the crowd at a distance of only four or five paces, Princip fired twice into the car. The first bullet mortally wounded the Archduke in the jugular vein. The second bullet entered the Duchess's abdomen. Duchess Sophie sank to the floor, her face between her husband's knees. The Archduke murmured, 'Soferl, Soferl, don't die. Live for my children.' Then he passed into unconsciousness. The car raced towards the Konak, Governor Potiorek's official residence, but the bumpy drive only worsened their condition, and the royal couple were pronounced dead shortly after arrival. As the bells of Sarajevo began to toll, none could have realized that their mournful clamour heralded four years of bloodshed and the death of millions.

Franz Ferdinand was far from popular in Vienna; but his death raised issues of far-reaching significance. Investigations eventually showed that the assassinations at Sarajevo had been organized by the Black Hand, a Serbian secret society headed by 'Apis', a shadowy figure who was also chief of Serbian military intelligence. The Serbian Prime Minister, Pasič, and possibly others in the Serbian government heard rumours of the existence of a plot against the Archduke; but Pasič had made only a half hearted attempt to warn Vienna against the Bosnian visit. The collective and direct complicity of the Serbian government was not proved, and after two Balkan wars in recent years, the Serbians were probably not anxious for further fighting. However, the responsibility for the murders was not assigned quickly or accurately enough to satisfy the Austrians. Serbian territory had been the base from which the assassinations were carried out, and there was a case for strong Austrian measures against Serbia.

The motives behind the double murder will probably never be fully known, but extreme Serb nationalists regarded Franz Ferdinand with fear because he advocated concessions to the South Slav minority of Austria-Hungary. The Black Hand felt that these concessions might detract from Serbia's position as a rallying point for South Slav discontent and as the nucleus of a future South Slav state. Thus the Archduke had to be eliminated. Furthermore, 'Apis' at least may have intended the killings to provoke war between Austria and Serbia, calculating that Russia, traditional patron of the small Slav nations, would ally with Serbia to force concessions from Austria. The Serbian press and public hardly bothered to conceal their pleasure at the murder of two members of the hated Austrian royal house. Thus, with tempers strained on every side, Austrian reprisals against Serbia could be expected.

In fact, the assassinations at Sarajevo could not go unchallenged if Austria-Hungary was to continue as a great power. The implications of the crisis were manifold. If Austrian reprisals resulted in Habsburg domination of Serbia, this would bring Austria-Hungary too close to the Dardanelles for Russia's comfort. For generations the

Ferdinand ordered a halt to see who had been injured by the attack. Until this was ascertained, the imperial car was a sitting target for a further assassination attempt. It was now discovered that Duchess Sophie's neck had been grazed, but she was otherwise unhurt.

The Archduke arrived at the town hall in an outraged mood. His wife's celebration had been spoiled. He immediately decided to visit one of the officers wounded by the grenade, who had been taken to a military hospital. The visit to a local museum would then proceed as arranged. Duchess Sophie had not originally intended to visit the museum, but now she insisted on remaining with her husband.

Setting out again, the imperial procession drove along Appel Quay at high speed. At this point another curious error occurred: evidently the chauffeurs had not been informed of the unscheduled visit to the hospital, for the first car turned right at the corner of Appel Quay and Franz Josef Street, and the second car followed. Potiorek shouted angrily to the driver of the third car that he was making a mistake. The chauffeur braked sharply, and the car stopped.

Straits had been the principal Russian interest in the Near East, for they were Russia's lifeline to much of the world beyond her borders. If, on the other hand, Serbian independence could be maintained, a decisive step would have been taken against the growing German and Austrian influence in the Balkans and Turkey.

Austria-Hungary was allied to Germany, Serbia was the protégé of Russia, and Russia was the ally of France. Italy and Rumania, although formally allied with Germany and Austria-Hungary, had shown signs of undependability. As for Britain, she had ententes – but not alliances – with France and Russia. These inter-relationships meant that potentially the Sarajevo crisis might escalate into a European war.

The Rise of Nationalism

In addition to the power manoeuvres of the great alliances, the Sarajevo incident took place in a period of virulent nationalism. Britain and France were powers that on the whole were sated and secure as a result of their colonial expansion. Their empires had brought them markets, raw materials, and prestige. Part of Russia's growing energies had been devoted to eastward expansion. Germany was different. She had become a nation only in 1871, too late to gain a share of the richer colonies. To Germany, as a young nation flexing its muscles and seeking its fortune, the situation was bitterly unjust. Germans thought that Britons and Frenchmen were denying them their rightful share of colonial influence. This was a situation that the Reich did not intend to tolerate indefinitely. Austria-Hungary was also in a sullen and confused mood, as pressures for change mounted among the minorities of her polyglot empire, and as Russian strength became a growing challenge to her Balkan policy. By 1914, many in Vienna had concluded that only a decisive move against Serbia, the stalking-horse of Russia, would sufficiently discourage South Slav disaffection and provide a unifying cause which might prolong the life of the enfeebled Habsburg empire. To such men, Sarajevo was a golden opportunity. The situation was the more fraught with danger because Germany and Russia also possessed influential factions which looked to war as a safety valve for national emotions, ambitions, and frustrations.

Kaiser Wilhelm II and Emperor Franz Josef led the Central Powers. Neither believed that military action against Serbia would lead to world war.

Left: British naval strength in 1914. **Right:** Germany's challenge to British naval hegemony was a major cause of the war.

'A Nightmare of Coalitions'

A closer look must be taken at the position of Germany. The outstanding issue in Europe for a generation had been a deadly-paradox, described by Cyril Falls as 'the arrogance which disguised Germany's anxieties.' Many would have judged the German future rich with promise, but Germany's anxieties'. Many would have judged as A. J. P. Taylor has noted, economic might in peacetime 'must have brought Germany the mastery of Europe within a few years', Germany saw only the fact of her 'encirclement' by the Franco-Russian alliance. Ironically, her reactions to her neighbours fed the very fears that had caused them to combine against her. To understand how this came about, we must examine the history of the preceding four decades.

The Rise of Germany

In 1871 Prussia defeated France and united the other German states into an empire. The German chancellor, Bismarck, felt the containment of a seething France was vital, and with this aim in mind in 1873 he associated Germany with Austria and Russia in the Three Emperors' League. By 1882 Italy had joined the alliance formed between Germany and Austria-Hungary in 1879, followed by Serbia in 1881 and Rumania in 1883. Then in 1887, Russia, by now estranged from Austria, negotiated her own treaty with Germany. France watched impotent as she was isolated from Europe by these manoeuvrings.

However, in 1890 the arrogant and unstable Kaiser Wilhelm II became jealous of Bismarck's prestige and dismissed him. Swiftly all Bismarck's worst fears were realized. Russia, rejected by the Kaiser in favour of Austria, allied herself with France, and at a stroke the Bismarckian policy of containment of France was destroyed.

It has been said of Bismarck that his aim toward Britain was to keep her 'in friendly isolation from Germany and unfriendly isolation from France'; but after his departure from office, Anglo-German relations soon deteriorated. This mounting ten-

Opposite above: The British battle cruiser *Inflexible* was ready to fight in 1914. **Below:** Britain's feared dreadnoughts lead the fleet out to sea: 18 July 1914.

sion resulted in Britain and France reconciling their major differences in the 'entente cordiale' of 1904. No formal alliance was established, but especially after the 1907 Anglo-Russian 'arrangement', France, Russia, and Britain became known as the Triple Entente, and formed an alliance in fact if not in name.

In 1905, Japan, already allied to Britain since 1902, defeated Russia in a war begun in 1904 over rival claims to influence in Korea. This momentarily strengthened Germany's position in the balance of power. However, in the same year German strong-arm threats to France over the future of Morocco drove the British and the French into a closer relationship. The next increase in tension occurred in 1908 when Austria annexed Bosnia and Herzegovina, thereby risking an Austro-Russian war by outraging Russian sensitivity on the subject of the Balkans. Germany, however, backed Austria and deterred any aggressive move by Russia. At this point, with France having been alienated in 1905 and Russia in 1908, with Britain still in disagreement with Berlin, and with Italy's attitude still uncertain, Austria remained Germany's only friend in Europe. Relations with Vienna assumed crucial importance if the Germans were not to be totally isolated.

In 1911 Germany increased her pressure on France by dispatching a gunboat to the Moroccan port of Agadir, but she was forced to climb down by British support of France. Between 1908 and 1911 German naval strength had been increasing faster than ever, and despite a degree of outward friendliness, Britain, traditional bastion of naval power, viewed these developments with suspicion.

The Arms Race

The level of armaments was now increasing throughout Europe. Haunted by fears of a sudden outbreak of war, politicians allowed their generals to formulate ingenious but fatally rigid war plans and mobilization procedures. Flexibility and manoeuvre took second place, and by 1914 Europe was a powder keg awaiting a spark.

Nun bin ich wieder gerne Soldat.

Laurence Lafore wrote of Austria and the crisis of July 1914: 'In a situation where coolness and skill were needed, alarm and clumsiness took their place and brought about the fatal steps to catastrophe.' In fact, heavy-handedness and bungling were not the prerogatives of Austria alone.

The initial reaction of Conrad von Hötzendorff, Austro-Hungarian Chief of Staff, to the Sarajevo murders was to move swiftly against Serbia. 'The hour has struck for the Monarchy,' he said, though he realized that immediate action was not feasible, since the necessary mobilization of forces would take about sixteen days. Conrad was opposed on practical grounds by Count Tisza, the Hungarian Prime Minister, who asked if German support would be forthcoming. Berchthold, the Austro-Hungarian Foreign Minister, was in urgent need of some bold measure to bolster his own sagging prestige. He decided to obtain advice from Berlin.

The Blank Cheque

The Sarajevo crisis was greeted in Berlin with conflicting counsels. Many Foreign Ministry personnel, seeing a potential chain of disaster, took a more moderate line than the military. However, on 5 July the Kaiser, seconded by Chancellor Bethmann-Hollweg, gave Vienna a 'blank cheque' for action against Serbia. As Szögyény, the Austro-Hungarian ambassador in Berlin, reported: 'Action against Serbia should not be delayed . . . Even if it should come to a war between Austria and Russia, we could be convinced that Germany would stand by our side . . .' Germany would be sorry to see Austria miss 'the present favourable moment' for strong measures.

Those who spoke thus in Berlin apparently felt that Austrian inaction, vaccillation, or delay would so reduce the prestige of the Dual Monarchy as to lead to severe repercussions, even the break up of the empire. The Kaiser himself was outraged at the shedding of royal blood, parti-

cularly that of the Archduke, a personal friend. He may have thought that Tsar Nicholas, similarly indignant, would keep Russia aloof from the crisis. Nevertheless, at the beginning of July the Kaiser had commented, 'The Serbs must be disposed of, and soon.' The German historian Fritz Fischer has suggested that the actions of the German government in early July perhaps show that Germany was using Sarajevo as an excuse to launch a preventive war against Russia; but this interpretation is highly controversial, and one can argue with equal success that Germany, feeling herself and Austria surrounded by hostility, saw Sarajevo as a fortunate chance to reassert her support for her ally. For even though Austria was a partner of dubious strength, Germany wanted to keep her away from the Franco-Russian alliance system.

Many historians have argued that the Germans, either naïvely or disingenuously, thought that the approaching conflict might be confined to Austria and Serbia. Russia, Berlin reasoned, might be in a position to do little more than bluff ineffectively, though her strength was growing daily. It was widely felt that Russian ambitions in the Balkans and elsewhere made war with Germany inevitable sooner or later. The question was: could Germany wait until the Russian colossus turned on her?

By 14 July Tisza had substantially agreed to Conrad's arguments for a forward policy. Discussions in Vienna on 7 July showed that there was considerable fear on the part of Austria that if she did not now settle accounts with Serbia, German support in future was problematical. Some even feared a German-Russian settlement at Austria's expense. From Berlin Szögyény emphasized that Russia was preparing for eventual war and, as the German Foreign Secretary, Jagow, reiterated, that in a few years Russia would 'overwhelm us if she is not forestalled'.

If Austria allowed herself to become enmeshed in diplomatic negotiations over the assassinations, her enemies would have time to out-manoeuvre

The Austrian cavalry was an extravagant echo of a glorious past.

her. Thus it was decided to send Serbia an extremely stiffly-worded memorandum. If, as Austria expected, Serbia were uncooperative, an excuse for war would be provided. Despite Berlin's impatience toward the leisurely pace of Austrian preparations against Serbia, it was decided to lull foreign suspicions by allowing the usual annual holidays to be taken: Moltke, the German Chief of Staff, remained at Karlsbad until 25 July, and the Kaiser enjoyed his customary summer cruise.

The Austrians elected to delay their memorandum to Serbia until the completion of the state visit to Russia of the French President and Prime Minister, lest their presence in Saint Petersburg be used to stiffen the Russian position at the moment of crisis. On 22 July, perhaps acting under the influence of the French, the Russians had warned Austria not to present Serbia with unacceptable demands.

On 23 July the French state visit to Russia was completed. Immediately Vienna sent a strong memorandum to the Serbs. The note contained ten demands; the most important required that Serbia allow Austria to suppress local agitation against Austria-Hungary and take action herself

Austrian army uniforms were romantic and splendid.

against those involved in the Sarajevo crime. Emperor Franz Josef said on reading the terms: 'Russia cannot accept this . . . this means a general war.' He spoke prophetically, but no one listened. Sazonov, the volatile Russian Foreign Minister, echoed these sentiments when he learned of the contents of the Austrian note. The note was to be answered within forty-eight hours, although the Russians tried unsuccessfully to get the limit extended by another two days. But on 25 July, just before the time limit expired, Belgrade accepted most of the Austrian demands and offered to submit to arbitration those which infringed her sovereignty. Thus the Serbs had very cleverly put Vienna in the wrong by appearing in the guise of sweet reasonableness. As Lafore drily put it, 'Butter remained visibly unmelted in their mouths.' Yet they did not expect their reply to satisfy Vienna, for three hours before the reply was given, they had ordered mobilization.

Mobilization

On receiving the Serbian response, Austria-Hungary immediately broke diplomatic relations, and planned to commence war on 10 August, when mobilization would be completed. The Kaiser, however, returned from his cruise, and on 28 July learned the full story of events during his absence. Whether from sober second thoughts, or merely panic, his reaction was that Belgrade's compliance with most of the demands meant 'every reason for war disappears'. He suggested that in order to satisfy her honour, Austria should occupy the Serbian capital and then negotiate. However, his attempt to restrain Vienna was negated by the officials in Berlin. Bethmann-Hollweg did not relay the message until the evening of 28 July, and he omitted the crucial sentence that war was no longer necessary. By this time, Austria had already declared war on Serbia.

After the Serbian reply of 25 July, Ambassador Szögyény had telegraphed to Berchthold that Bethmann-Hollweg and Jagow were still advising the Austrians to act immediately and confront the world with an accomplished fact. Later, as British intervention in the dispute became more likely, Bethmann panicked and sent a series of telegrams to Vienna urging restraint. But Moltke was urging Vienna to push forward! Divided authority in Berlin assured recklessness in Austria, her junior partner.

The Serbian mobilization strengthened the hands of extremists everywhere. Only a few hours later, on 25 July, Austria ordered partial mobilization on the Serbian front, to begin on 28 July. On 25 July both Germany and Russia themselves began to prepare for mobilization. When her mobilization began on schedule on 28 July, Austria declared war on Serbia. War had come at that moment because Vienna felt in danger of being diverted into unwanted negotiations with Serbia.

Meanwhile, a double miscalculation had been made. Just as Austria expected Germany to neutralize a threat from Russia, the Russians hoped that their alliance with France, and British diplomatic pressure, would isolate Vienna. In fact, though Serbia was sometimes a nuisance and an embarrassment, Russia could not see her

President Poincaré visits Tsar Nicholas II and the Russian fleet: 25 July 1914.

protégé eliminated without in effect abdicating as a great power. However, the Russians had advised Belgrade to conciliate the Austrians and rely on the justice of the great powers, but little notice was taken of this counsel. The Serbians were aware of their influence on Russian attitudes; and indeed, Sazonov warned Pourtalès, the German ambassador in Saint Petersburg, that 'if Austria swallows Serbia we will make war on her'.

France was prepared to fulfill her treaty commitments to Russia, but on the whole she played a moderating influence throughout the crisis. In a sense, she could do little else, for although the French state visit to Russia lasted only from 20–23 July, the French leaders, Poincaré and Viviani, were away from Paris from 15–28 July, during which time policy-making machinery was paralyzed.

The British Commitment

Although there was no alliance between the two countries, the British had a strong moral commitment to France, more especially because of secret negotiations in recent years. Yet throughout the crisis, the British government was preoccupied with the domestic issue of Irish Home Rule. Given the mood of the times, neither government, Parliament, nor the people would have sanctioned an announcement that Britain stood firmly behind France and Russia in the event of general war. Grey, the Foreign Secretary, hoped that this very lack of commitment would weaken the forces pulling towards war in both Germany and Russia. What made British entry into the war unavoidable was the unprovoked German violation of the neutrality of Belgium, which Prussia, Britain, France, Austria, and Russia had guaranteed some seventy-five years earlier. The country was able to unite behind this total disregard of treaty obligations. For centuries a vital British interest had been to prevent the Low Countries from being dominated by a great power. German conquest of Belgium and France would have made this likely if not certain.

Between 24 and 26 July, Grey made various proposals for mediation of the Austro-Serbian dispute. Again, the temporizing effect of Berlin and Paris on Saint Petersburg and Vienna was overestimated. To add to the confusion, Britain warned that she might not stand aside from the conflict. Yet as late as 1 August, Grey refused a definite commitment to France on the grounds that the terms of the Franco-Russian alliance were unknown to the British government.

There is evidence that the German General Staff expected British participation in the war; but they did not worry much about it, influenced in part by the British Army's difficulties in the Boer War. More important, Germany expected to be able to knock France out of the war before British aid, if it were given, could be effective.

War with Serbia

The Austrian declaration of war against Serbia was followed on 29 July by the bombardment of Belgrade. Russia was deeply affected. Already, on 28 July, the Tsar had ordered partial Russian mobilization on the Austrian front, in this way trying to make it clear that Russia would not stand

aside if Austria attacked Serbia. The previous day, 27 July, Messimy, the French Minister of War, attempted to persuade the Russians to proclaim general mobilization and take the offensive, but the Tsar had restricted himself to bringing pressure to bear by partial mobilization. Meanwhile, the Russian generals themselves were also persuading the Tsar that any measures short of full mobilization were impracticable. Russian mobilization would take many weeks; and the generals argued that it must be started during the crisis in order to be effective if war later ensued. Tsar Nicholas agreed to commence general mobilization on 31 July; but later on 29 July, as a result of a message from the Kaiser, the Tsar reverted to his policy of partial mobilization. Nicholas was a man of naturally vaccillating temperament, and as the crisis gathered strength, he reversed himself once

more on 30 July, in the belief that German general mobilization would begin at any moment. The French government had called on Russia to present a cautious and non-provocative attitude towards Germany, but the transmission of this message may have been bungled or deliberately misinterpreted by Paléologue, the French ambassador to Russia. At this point the Russians lost their nerve and ordered mobilization before the Germans, who in turn ordered their own mobilization. Austrian general mobilization then followed on 31 July.

In fact, on 31 July Germany only declared a state of war emergency and demanded that Russia 'suspend every war measure against Austria and ourselves within twelve hours'. Falkenhayn, the Prussian Minister of War, felt that because German mobilization would be so much quicker than that of Russia, Germany could afford to wait a few days. But Moltke was adamant. Having received no satisfaction from Russia, Germany declared formal general mobilization and war against Russia on 1 August.

By now French involvement was certain. On 31 July, Germany sent an eighteen-hour ultimatum demanding that France define what her position would be during a German-Russian war. On 1 August, Vivani replied that 'France will act in accordance with her interests'. Meanwhile, the French General Joffre had been pressing for mobilization, and on the afternoon of 1 August the cabinet yielded. As it happened, even if the French had agreed to neutrality, the Germans had decided to demand the occupation of the French fortresses of Verdun and Toul as a pledge of good conduct – a humiliation which they knew no French government could tolerate.

The Schlieffen Plan

Why was it necessary for Germany to pick a quarrel with France? The answer lay in the rigidity of the German offensive plans. Moltke related in his memoirs that when the Kaiser questioned whether Britain would enter the war if Germany attacked only Russia, the general replied that war with Russia alone was impossible. Germany had only one war plan, and it could not be changed. This was the famous Schlieffen Plan, and it called for a swift knock out blow against France via a German sweep through Belgium, followed by a rapid transfer by rail of the victorious troops to the eastern front for the expected longer campaign against the Russians, who would take the six weeks required for victory in the West to complete their mobilization. On 2 August, therefore, Germany demanded passage through Belgium for her armies, a demand which was firmly refused. On 3 August, Germany declared war against France. The German war on two fronts had begun.

By 4 August, the threat to Belgium was uniting the British, and Grey issued an ultimatum demanding that Germany respect Belgian neutrality. When the ultimatum expired without result, war between Britain and Germany began at midnight, German time.

Why did the War Break Out?

How the war broke out is a subject for endless discussions and limitless conclusions.

After the Balkan wars, Austria's military men were afraid of Serbia's increased population and military might. In Germany, the soldiers looked with apprehension on Russia's swift recovery from her 1905 defeat by Japan. The feeling grew that war, if it had to come, would be more favourable to Germany and Austria now than later. Russia, for her part, was more and more concerned at increasing German influence over Turkey; if the 'sick man of Europe' were rejuvenated in the Balkans, Russian ambitions would be thwarted. Thus mutual fears and rivalries helped to create a situation in which swift escalation to war was possible.

Divided interests accelerated the advent of war. In Germany, for example, the desires of military, business and governmental circles conflicted in

Von Falkenhayn, the Prussian Minister of War. He wanted to wait. The Kaiser didn't.

many ways. As A. J. P. Taylor wrote, 'it was easier. . . to drift with events' than to take positive action. To make matters worse, in 1914 each of the great powers lacked a statesman who could see beyond the immediacy of events and pull his country back from the abyss. Emperor Franz Josef was almost senile, and both the Kaiser and the Tsar were unstable and impetuous. The British were preoccupied, and the French were without a leader through much of the crisis. Sir Edward Grey, the British Foreign Secretary, spent most of the month of July bird watching, and, with regrets, had to give up his pastime to return to London when the crisis deepened.

In addition, the sudden nature of the July crisis made improvisation necessary. Grey and Sazonov in particular confused the issue by making repeated suggestions before all the other powers had

had the opportunity to consider their previous proposals. Perhaps most remarkable of all, a mood of fatalism overcame many in the summer of 1914. It was as if men knew that peace in Europe was too happy a state of affairs to last.

Was Germany at Fault?

Although she felt that time was working against her and considered a preventive war more and more seriously, Germany had no long-term war plan timed for 1914. Such specific planning would have required an assertiveness and consistency which was lacking in both Bethmann-Hollweg and Moltke, not to mention the Kaiser. Underwriting Austrian grievances was an easy alternative. Even so, German support for Vienna was a crucial influence on the coming of war, for without the backing of Berlin, Vienna could never have acted as she did. Not all of this support was conscious, however, and Austria knew exactly how to play on divisions within the German ruling elite to get her own way.

Germany's situation was bitterly ironic. The Franco-Russian encirclement, which drove her on to war, was probably far less solid than she imagined. There were plenty of influential people in both countries who opposed the alliance. Russian strength might well have faltered due to revolution, as in fact occurred in 1917. Domestic affairs in France would soon have weakened her military strength.

Rivalries for trade and colonies had been important causes of the tensions which eventually snapped in 1914. However, by the actual year these issues had ceased to be predominant since, for example, Britain and Germany were developing markets in different parts of the world.

Despite the build-up of alliances and armaments, few men expected a long war, and hardly anyone envisaged the more than four years of relentless bloodletting and upheaval which lay ahead. This revealed an amazing collective lack of responsibility, imagination, or foresight. At the same time, many saw war as a means of reweaving the tattered social fabrics of the nations, or of achieving the aims of subjugated nationalities; few thought of the vast social changes that 'total' war itself would bring about.

Pacifist and internationalist forces were overwhelmed by the sudden upsurge of patriotism in every country on the eve of war. Fostered by popular education, nationalism was a force stronger than men realized – until it was too late. Also important, particularly at a subconscious level, were ideas of irrationalism, violence, and nihilism. Men such as Sorel and Nietzsche, as well as Darwin and Freud, saw their ideas applied or distorted to serve the cause of war.

No single explanation can account for the outbreak of war. The complex problems and suspicions combined with the immediacy of the crisis finally overwhelmed both politicians and generals.

Opposite: Kaiser Wilhelm II and von Moltke during the mobilization. They knew that speed was necessary if the Schlieffen Plan was to succeed.

Uhlans, the elite of the German cavalry, were to prove powerless in the face of the machine gun.

CHAPTER TWO
The War Unleashed

The outbreak of war was greeted by cheering crowds in every belligerent capital. The popular mood in every country was one of nationalistic self-righteousness, and everywhere the war was expected to be short, glorious, and victorious. By 4 August 1914, all but one of the great European powers was at war; Italy had declined to enter on the side of her erstwhile allies, Germany and Austria.

The Great War was one of mass armies. In 1914 the German army numbered 856,000 men in peacetime, rising to 3,800,000 when trained reserves were mobilized. If necessary, almost 4,000,000 additional men could be made available. The French army consisted of 736,000 men in time of peace, but upon mobilization this could rise to a maximum of over 3,500,000. In fact, about 1,650,000 French troops were engaged in the opening campaigns. In all, millions of men were placed in uniform in the service of the elaborate war plans, which each side possessed.

The war had opened according to plan for Germany. As her war blueprint, the Schlieffen Plan, had instructed, five armies, the *crème de la crème* of German military might, were hurled through Belgium into northern France. The French eastern fortresses were thereby circumvented, and the Germans now supposed that they could fall on the French armies west of Paris and inflict a quick and crushing defeat. But Moltke could not resist adjusting the Schlieffen Plan. The eventual result was that the plan misfired, and with it collapsed the German dream of lightning victory.

To meet the German threat, the French war plan, Plan 17, called for an offensive regardless of cost (*l'offensive à outrance*). The French were to strike into Alsace-Lorraine and east of Metz. Another French force under General Lanrézac, and the British Expeditionary Force (BEF) under Field Marshal Sir John French, was to move into Belgium if, as happened, Germany violated the neutrality of that country; otherwise they would have proceeded straight towards Metz.

Toujours Chic

In placing inordinate emphasis on offensive action, the French forgot the principle that superiority in numbers at any point must be paid for by adopting defensive positions elsewhere. The French also feared that their infantry, previously whipped up to an enthusiasm for attack, would be unable to stand on the defensive against the German army, which they considered more highly trained than their own. The result was that the French rushed forward, heedless of the consequences. General, then Lieutenant, Spears observed:

The sense of the tragic futility of it will never quite fade from the minds of those who saw these brave men, dashing across the open to the sound of drums and bugles . . . The gallant officers who led them were entirely ignorant of the stopping power of modern firearms, and many of them thought it chic to die in white gloves.

If only the French had reinforced the Belgian defences, they might have been able to hold the Germans along the Namur-Antwerp line of fortresses. Instead, the two armies which they threw across Lorraine were repulsed; and when they tried to break through the German centre in the Ardennes, the French were again defeated. Indeed, from 20–23 August, in the Battle of the Frontiers – in Lorraine, the Ardennes, the Sambre, and at Mons – the Allies were decisively routed. The French alone suffered well over 300,000 casualties, which included many of the bravest soldiers or those with greatest initiative. More than one officer in ten was already a casualty, and at Flaxon on 19 August, the French Twenty-sixth Division lost two-thirds of its officers. Without the promotion of many able men from the ranks, these losses would already have been irreparable.

The BEF at Mons

The British Expeditionary Force was by now fully involved in the campaign. Under Field Marshal Sir John French, the BEF had crossed the Channel between 12 and 20 August. Almost 90,000 soldiers took part. Their mood was mainly one of optimism; they had no idea that slaughter was their destiny.

After concentrating near Maubeuge, on 22 August the infantry dug itself in and prepared for action in the pit headgears and slagheaps of the drab little Belgian mining town of Mons. British reconnaissance planes had reported many German troops moving towards Mons; and the British waited with a 'keenness whetted by the first sight of the enemy', in the words of John Terraine. The twenty-third of August was a Sunday, and as they hurried to Mass, the inhabitants of Mons eyed the British troops with amiable curiosity.

French had placed his men along the line of the Mons-Condé canal. The position to be defended was a salient to the north east of Mons itself. The

The outbreak of war was greeted jubilantly in every belligerent capital. In Vienna the cheering began even before the war, when Austria-Hungary broke off diplomatic relations with Serbia.

General Joffre led French forces in China and Africa and was appointed Chief of the General Staff in 1911.

overall defensive position was far from easy, for the canal, while providing no real obstacle to the German advance, was difficult to defend in view of its shallowness and the many bridges which crossed it.

Early on 23 August, the Germans under Kluck moved in. About thirty thousand British faced nearly ninety thousand Germans. The focus of the German attack was the bridge at Nimy, the northernmost point of the salient. After a short but fierce bombardment, the Germans attacked frontally, suffering heavy casualties from British musket fire, which was so accurate and rapid that the Germans mistook it for machine gun fire. The Germans were 'the most perfect targets' because of their method of advancing in close order. As a British sergeant described it, the Germans advanced 'in solid square blocks, standing out sharply against the skyline, and you couldn't help hitting them'. Another soldier reported that the first company of Germans 'were simply blasted away to Heaven by a volley at seven hundred

Above: In Germany even the weapons were bedecked with flowers. **Right:** Not every German soldier was as enthusiastic about the war as his Kaiser would have wished.

yards, and in their insane formation every bullet was almost sure to find two billets'. In fact, Mons became a series of strong German attacks being met with equally strong British defences. A German account emphasized that the enemy, 'Well entrenched and completely hidden . . . opened a murderous fire . . . finally the whole advance stopped . . . with bloody losses the attack gradually came to an end.' Nevertheless, under the pressure of a prolonged German attack, in early afternoon the British forces were driven back to new positions south of Mons, and by late evening a new British line had been established. Due to their exhaustion, the Germans had been unable to force their passage across the Mons canal, and this inconclusive result was typical of the day's fighting.

At 11:00 p.m. on 23 August, as the British prepared to dig in before the next day's battle, word reached them that, in a supremely uncoordinated move, the French Fifth Army under Lanrézac was breaking off fighting to the right of the British positions and had decided to withdraw. The success of the German advance and the failure of the French offensives had bred caution, and the BEF, finding it futile to stand alone, now retreated to the Maubeuge-Valenciennes line. Many of the troops were confused, for they had seen Mons as a great victory and knew nothing of the dire warnings coming in of a superior German concentration of forces. Kluck's army had been held up for a day at the price of sixteen hundred

Crown Prince Rupprecht of Bavaria was the son of King Ludwig III of Bavaria. He commanded the German Sixth Army in 1914.

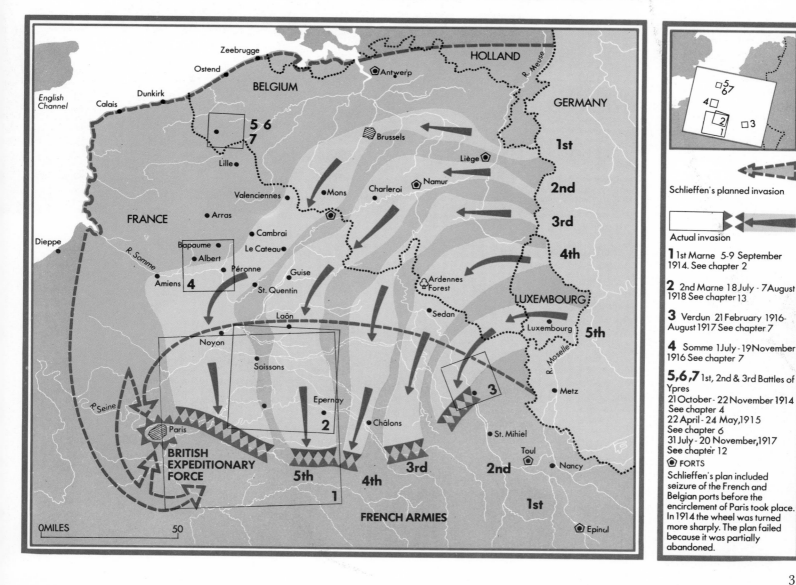

Schlieffen's planned invasion

Actual invasion

1 1st Marne 5-9 September 1914. See chapter 2

2 2nd Marne 18 July - 7 August 1918 See chapter 13

3 Verdun 21 February 1916- August 1917 See chapter 7

4 Somme 1 July - 19 November 1916 See chapter 7

5,6,7 1st, 2nd & 3rd Battles of Ypres 21 October - 22 November 1914 See chapter 4 22 April - 24 May, 1915 See chapter 6 31 July - 20 November, 1917 See chapter 12

⬡ FORTS Schlieffen's plan included seizure of the French and Belgian ports before the encirclement of Paris took place. In 1914 the wheel was turned more sharply. The plan failed because it was partially abandoned.

33

Right: British recruits march to Waterloo Station, led by a brass band from Doctor Barnardo's Orphans' Home. **Far right above:** The cream of French manhood feared no one. **Far right centre:** The first British volunteers arrived in Le Havre less than a fortnight after the outbreak of war.

Left: Field Marshal Sir John French led the BEF across the Channel. **Right:** The German juggernaut rolls through Belgium. **Centre above:** The Germans met heavy resistance at Mons, but pressed the Allies back into France. **Below:** The British cavalry retreat from Mons. **Far right:** Many French prisoners were taken.

Right: In memory of the 1,000 English and 300 Belgians who were captured near Antwerp, October 1914.
Below: The battle of the Yser Canal near Ypres.

Gedenkblatt zur Erinnerung an die Gefangennahme von 1000 Engländern und 300 Belgiern bei Moerbeke westl. Antwerpen 9/10. 10. 1914. durch II. Batl. bayr. Landw. Inf. Regts. Nr. 1.

Der europäische Krieg 1914.

Nr. 16.

Nr. 10160.

Neuruppin, bei Oehmigke & Riemschneider.

Die Schlacht am Yser-Kanal bei Ypern.

Die nach Eroberung der Festung Antwerpen geflüchteten belgischen und englischen Truppen sammelten sich an der Küste des Kanals auf der Linie Ostende - Dünkirchen, wo sie Unterstützung durch französische und frische englische Truppen fanden, ferner durch die aus Afrika und Indien herangezogenen Spahis, Sikhs, Gurkahs, Afridis und Patkans. Unsere Armee rückte sofort hinterher und es entspann sich in der Gegend von Ypern ein mörderischer Kampf. Englische und französische Kreuzer beschossen vom Kanal aus den rechten Flügel unserer Truppen, wurden aber durch verschiedene Volltreffer unserer schweren Geschütze zum Rückzug gezwungen. Die Schleusen bei Nieuport wurden von den Engländern zerstört und dadurch ein Teil des Geländes unter Wasser gesetzt; es konnte dies den Vormarsch unserer Truppen vielleicht etwas verzögern, aber nie aufhalten, die Pioniere hatten sehr bald Brücken geschlagen. Unter schweren Verlusten an Mannschaften und auch an Geschützen wurden die Verbündeten fortwährend zurückgedrängt, feindliche Vorstöße brachen in sich selbst zusammen, was auf ein Erschlaffen der Truppen schließen läßt. Ein vollständiger Sieg unsererseits dürfte nahe bevorstehen.

British casualties. The total German losses are not known, but must have been much higher.

An aura of mystique surrounds Mons, the opening British engagement of the war. According to legend, the BEF was even aided by the intervention of angels! The significance of Mons for the Allies was that, as Cruttwell wrote, the battle was 'neither a victory nor a defeat, but a delaying action which achieved its purpose'.

Despite his many faults, General Joffre, the French Commander in Chief, was an indomitable and unflappable man. His armies had suffered grievous defeat and immense losses, but his soldiers maintained a surprisingly high morale. Now Joffre decided to take a defensive position and reduce the enemy by attrition. He would regroup his forces in retreat, while looking for an opportunity to take the offensive when the Germans least expected it. To act prematurely, however, 'would have run the risk of being turned into a hopeless rout', as Joffre himself wrote later.

The Long Retreat

Thus, from 24 August to 5 September, the Allied armies retreated. Along the way, the British engaged the enemy at Le Cateau, and the French at Guise-Saint Quentin. Yet Joffre's stolid optimism might have been misplaced, if not for the fact that the German supreme commander, Moltke, received exaggerated reports of German successes on every battlefront. Moltke became overconfident; indeed, he deluded himself that final victory was within his grasp. Thus he drastically reduced the strength of the German right wing. Although he could therefore no longer make an encircling movement west of Paris, in the euphoria of his mood, this hardly mattered. On 25 August, he decided to send four western divisions to the eastern front. These successive weakenings of the German western position had a decisive influence on the outcome of the Battle of the Marne some twelve days later.

At the end of August, Moltke felt ready to try to envelop the French by means of Crown Prince Rupprecht's army on the left and those of Bülow and Kluck on the right. Now fate took an ironic hand. The German armies had advanced so swiftly that their supplies had failed to keep pace. The armies were too big to live off the land, and the troops, already exhausted from incessant fighting and marches, faced hunger as well. Sir Basil Liddell Hart observed that now 'so much grit had worked into the German machine that a slight jar would suffice to cause its breakdown'. This jar was to be administered at the Marne.

Suddenly, Moltke became concerned at reports of ominous French troop movements. At the same time, and in the absence of adequate communications, Kluck interpreted the spirit of his orders in the way he thought best, and he advanced across the Marne. Prompted by General Galliéni, the military governor of Paris, Joffre moved to take advantage of this overreaching movement. The French Sixth Army under Maunoury was sent against Kluck's right, while the BEF and the Fifth Army, now commanded by Franchet d'Espèrey, attacked in the north.

By 5 September, when it was already too late, Kluck realized that German successes had been

General von Kluck, whose lack of courage to carry out the Schlieffen Plan led to disaster for Germany at the Marne.

exaggerated, and that the Allies were recuperating more quickly than he had dreamed possible. Meanwhile Maunoury continued to advance, and when he encountered German forces under Gronau on a line extending from Vincy to the Marne, the Battle of the Ourcq ensued. This fierce display of fighting marked the first engagement in the Battle of the Marne. The results were inconclusive, since the German advance by day was countered by their withdrawal from exposed positions by night. However, Cruttwell assesses the significance of the Ourcq as being that 'the sting . . . had been partially drawn by the vigorous and unexpected initiative' of the Allies.

The Marne

Much of history is decided by luck and timing, and the Marne was no exception. On 7 September, Bülow decided to utilize two of Kluck's corps to complete a wheeling movement. But Kluck, by now seriously concerned about the fighting north of the Marne, instead decided that the corps would retire behind the Petit Morin river. The result was a widening gap between Bülow's right and Kluck's left, and into it moved the BEF, now six divisions in strength, and the French forces of Conneau and Franchet d'Espèrey. The advance of the BEF was snail-like in its slowness and caution. This was due to the shock of previous casualties, the suspicion that the Germans were preparing a giant ambush, and the lack of imagination or resolution on the part of the high command. Nonetheless, this steady advance was crucial to the coming Allied victory.

Maunoury was pressing his attack with vigour, and a division was brought from the east to help

Above: French reinforcements were called up to defend Paris at the Marne. **Right:** The BEF rests before digging in at the Marne.

Left: A transport brigade is hit by shrapnel near the Marne.

Below left: The 1st Cameronians cross a pontoon bridge at la Ferte: 10 September 1914. Below: The Germans were stopped at the Marne. This time it was their turn to be taken prisoner.

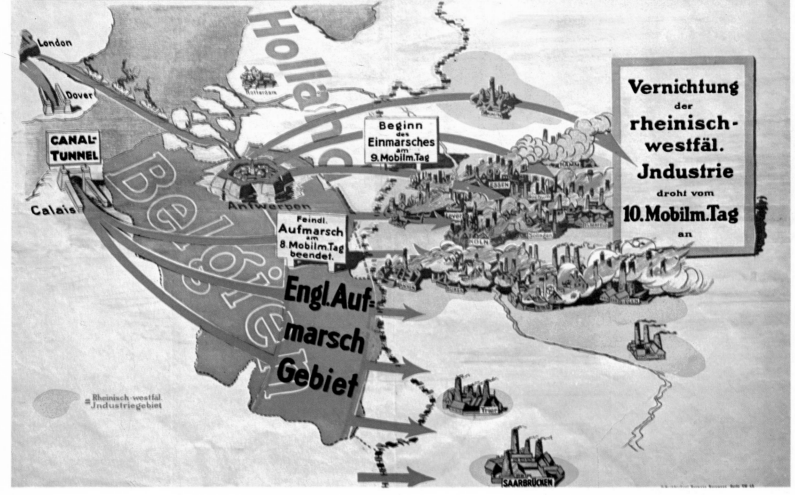

Darf Belgien Englands Aufmarschgebiet werden?

Above: German propaganda claimed that Belgium would be occupied by Britain and used as a launching pad against Germany's Rhine cities and the Ruhr Valley, the industrial heartland of Germany. This excuse was used to convince Germans that their invasion of Belgium was pre-emptive and therefore justifiable. Although such a ploy was never considered since the Germans occupied most of Belgium so quickly, it was seriously discussed by Britain during the early stages of World War II.

Right: A German artist's impression of the savage hand-to-hand fighting which took place in the early stages of the war.

him. On 7 September, the resourceful Galliéni swiftly conveyed two of these needed regiments to the battlefield in an armada of more than one thousand commandeered Parisian taxicabs. This stroke, although it captured the public imagination, had no important influence on the fighting, but was significant for its demonstration of the potentialities of motorized transport in war.

Between 6 and 8 September the Allies were unable to gain a decisive victory. On 7 September the BEF forced its way across the Grand Morin river, and the next day the British crossed the Petit Morin and advanced to within four or five miles of the Marne. Franchet d'Espèrey and his cavalry also crossed the Petit Morin, but without encountering the Germans. Meanwhile Foch's Ninth Army was driven back and lost control of the passages of the Marshes of St Gond.

However, cumulative forces were telling on the German position. By 8 September, Bülow was despondent and tired, and his troops were more exhausted and ravenous than ever. Bülow reported that the German Second Army was 'no longer capable of forcing a decisive victory'. Moreover, the anticipated breakthrough in Lorraine had failed. Now Moltke sent Hentsch, head of intelligence for France, to tour the German armies, to assess the situation and to order retreat if necessary. Hentsch found Bülow badly shaken; and on 9 September, influenced by the French capture of Marchais-en-Brie and reports of British columns advancing to the Marne, Bülow decided to pull back his forces. The same day, the battle with Maunoury was broken off, and on Hentsch's order the First Army also retreated. By 11 September a German general withdrawal to the Noyon-Verdun line along the river Aisne was in progress, and here the Kaiser's forces regrouped among their prepared defences. The German retreat had also been hastened by rumours that forty thousand British and eighty thousand Russian troops were landing on the Belgian coast; ironically, only three thousand British marines had arrived.

On 11 September, Joffre wrote that 'the advance must be pursued energetically, leaving the enemy no respite'. Yet, having summoned their last strength to meet the clash of armies, the Allied infantry, debilitated by their arduous retreat, were incapable of further extensive effort. In addition, on 9 September the weather, previously hot, had turned to cold and rainy mists. Munition supplies were low or non-existent. Many

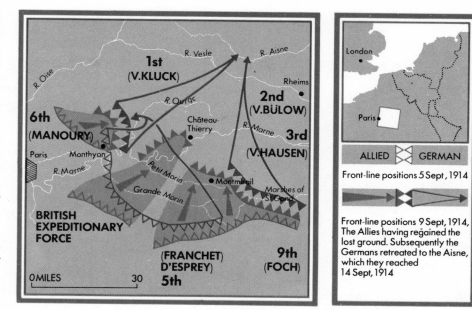

ALLIED ⬦ GERMAN

Front-line positions 5 Sept, 1914

Front-line positions 9 Sept, 1914. The Allies having regained the lost ground. Subsequently the Germans retreated to the Aisne, which they reached 14 Sept, 1914

bridges over the Marne had been destroyed, and the roads were clogged with traffic. But the main victory, a strategical and psychological hammering of the Germans, had been achieved.

Moltke is alleged to have told the Kaiser on 13 September that as a result of the Marne episode, 'Germany has lost the war'. Whether or not this statement was actually made, it was true to the extent that Germany had seen the irrevocable failure of her most basic strategic concept, that of quickly winning the war in the west in order to turn east with all her might. The Marne was only a partial tactical success for the Allies. Few German prisoners were taken. As Sewell Tyng, an historian of the Marne, has noted, the battle 'left the victors masters of the field, but did not impose on the vanquished the sense of hopeless inferiority that is the mark of decisive defeat'. Even so, the Marne ranks as the premier strategical victory of the war, for with their success the Allies had made a long and costly war on two fronts unavoidable for Germany.

Thus ended the opening phase of the war on the western front. Churchill was to capture its significance exactly when he wrote:

The measured, silent drawing together of gigantic forces, the uncertainty of their movements and positions, the number of unknown and unknowable facts made the first collision a drama never surpassed. Nor was there any other period in the War when the general battle was waged on so great a scale, when the slaughter was so swift or the stakes so high.

Prisoners from the Battle of the Marne.

CHAPTER THREE

Eastern Clashes- Tannenberg and Serbia

In accord with the demands of the Schlieffen Plan, the Western front had seen the main initial concentration of German forces. While Moltke's armies expected to overwhelm France in six weeks, Austria-Hungary and East Prussia would have to bear the brunt of the Russian attack. Conrad, Austria's chief of the general staff, commented that he hoped Moltke would not leave him too long 'in a nasty mess'.

In the east each power seemed bent on taking the offensive. For Conrad in particular, the offensive was a veritable obsession. Austria expected to remove the Serbian thorn from her side in about two weeks; Vienna was not unduly worried over dealing with a 'kingdom of pig-breeders'. Certainly the Serbian campaign was expected to be finished before the Russians hacked their way through Galicia. However, when put into action, the Austrian plans bogged down. In addition, because Russian mobilization was swifter than had been expected, Conrad had to transfer troops from the Serbian front to face the more formidable foe.

Because the Serbian capital, Belgrade, lay along the frontier with Austria-Hungary, the Serbs half expected the first Austrian attack in this direction. Elaborate defensive preparations were made, and even before the outbreak of war, the government and the royal court were evacuated inland. As it happened, however, the Austrian war plan called for attack from the west and northwest. The intention was to create a movement of envelopment which would strike a deathblow at the heart of the enemy.

A Serbian Disaster

As war began, the Austrians were optimistic. Their troops were fresh for battle, but those of Serbia were already dog-eared from two recent Balkan campaigns. Austrian equipment was also superior. On the other hand, Serbian morale was also high as the tiny nation steeled itself to defend its hearths.

On 11 August the Austrian Second Army crossed the Sava river and easily took the town of Šabac. But next morning, as the Fifth Army crossed the Drina, it encountered heavy fire from two Serbian divisions. Next day, Serbian harassment from high defensive positions brought the Austrian offensive to a temporary halt, but it subsequently moved forward, sustaining enormous losses.

The Austrians were led by Potiorek, the mismanager of the archducal visit to Sarajevo. On 19 August, after Serbians under Putnik launched a counteroffensive, Potiorek unsteadily withdrew his forces back across the Drina, and by the twenty-fourth the Austrians had completely evacuated Serbia.

On 7 September, Potiorek was able to cross back into Serbian territory. This time he inflicted severe casualties on the enemy. In one horrendous disaster, a Serbian division, which had entered Hungary, was trapped as it tried to recross into Serbia. Five thousand men were mown down in a few hours. Even so, Putnik managed a counterthrust at Sarajevo, causing Potiorek to pursue him for seven weeks in an effort to ensure the safety of the Bosnian capital.

By 25 October Bosnia had been cleared of Serbian forces, and Austrian predominance in men and supplies had had its effect. Yet as Potiorek drove back the enemy, his pursuit was so relentless that it reduced his own forces to physical and spiritual wrecks. Somehow he managed to take the offensive again in the first week of November, and his task was helped by the heavy rain and ice which played havoc with the Serbian supply lines. On 2 December, by a happy coincidence the sixty-sixth anniversary of the accession of Franz Josef, Belgrade was captured. Austria now became overconfident. Though Serbia was practically destitute of reserves of ammunition, the courage of her men endured. Next day, 3 December, the Serbs threw themselves with suicidal abandon at the Austrians – and the Austrian lines caved in. By 13 December, Potiorek was once more driven back across the Sava; Belgrade was relieved on 15 December.

Austria had sustained over one hundred thousand casualties; in addition, her troops had abandoned countless weapons which were invaluable to the Serbs. Yet Serbia was unable to press forward her advantage. The oncoming winter, the ravages of typhus, and the loss of more than half of her crack troops (including one hundred and seventy thousand dead and injured) produced a stalemate which was to last for many months.

The Eastern Front

From the beginning of the war, the Russians had received a stream of French demands and pleas for an attack on East Prussia as soon as possible. The French emphasized that every thrust in the east was a relief of pressure from the west. Finally, yielding to their ally, the Russians attacked before their armies were fully concentrated.

Left: The tenacity of the Serbs was tremendous.

Right: Serbian infantry put up a stout defence against overwhelming odds.
Far right: A Montenegrin infantryman. Montenegro supported Serbia when war broke out.

Although thousands of Serbs were taken prisoner, their comrades in action fought on.

East Prussia was the site of numerous estates of the Prussian aristocracy. Germans regarded the territory with fierce pride as a bastion of the Teutonic way of life against the hordes of barbaric Slavs beyond. These atavistic feelings made the Germans determined to hold the province at all costs. Fortunately for them, although they were greatly outnumbered by Russian forces, the Germans were much superior in the education and training of their men, in the excellence of their command, and in their logistical support. Germany also had the advantage of better transportation facilities. In Fuller's picturesque description, the Russian soldier was 'a big-hearted child who thought out nothing and was surprised by everything'. Less appealingly, Russian troops were a reflection of their own corrupt and inefficient society.

East Prussia Invaded

On 17 August the Russian general Rennenkampf led the First Army in force westwards into East Prussia in the direction of Königsberg. Three days later he defeated the Germans at Gumbinnen, about ten miles inside the frontier. Mackensen's Seventeenth Corps took to their heels 'in fearful panic', as one observer tells us, and the Russians captured over seven thousand German prisoners. Yet this was only a tactical incident in the overall picture, and the fumbling Rennenkampf was

about to order a retreat himself, when he heard that the Germans were withdrawing instead.

Because of failure of nerve and general bungling, the German Eighth Army commander, Prittwitz, popularly known as 'Fatty' because of his legendary girth, was now replaced by his brother-in-law, Hindenburg. Ludendorff was brought in as chief of staff. By now the Germans had decided to concentrate against the Second Russian Army under Samsonov, which had crossed the German frontier on 20 August. In this the Germans were taking the calculated risk that they could deal with Samsonov before the cautious and slow-moving Rennenkampf could intervene. Cruttwell suggests that Rennenkampf's incompetence may have reflected a covert sympathy for Germany, the land of his ancestors. His inaction can also be explained, however, by his dislike of Samsonov and his unwillingness to cooperate with his rival. In any case, the German plan was aided by the fifty-mile chain of the Masurian Lakes, which formed a natural barrier between the two Russian armies.

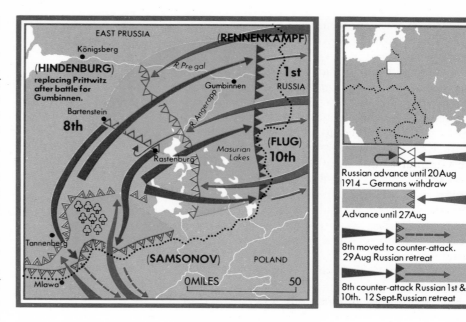

Hindenburg Takes Command
When Hindenburg arrived to take command, the First Corps, led by a German general with the unlikely name of François was already detraining to the west of Tannenberg. For a considerable time François was heavily outnumbered by the Russians, but in the end the latter played into German hands. Samsonov, thinking that the German Eighth Army was routed, and hurried along by Jilinsky, commander of the North-western Army Group, pushed forward faster than ever, but then stopped to rest on 25 August. Actually, by 22 August the fighting capacity of Samsonov's men had already been drastically reduced by their marching in scorching heat through desert terrain without proper food. According to one German eyewitness, 'Whole army corps advanced . . . without bread or oats, and had to have recourse to their reserve rations . . . the march discipline was bad . . . Nerves were so shaky that the troops fired at every airman . . .'

On 25 August, Ludendorff, who was still worried about Rennenkampf in the background, ordered François to attack Samsonov and envelop his left wing. Lacking full artillery support and ammunition supply, François demurred. Ludendorff angrily insisted, but just in time, intercepted Russian communications revealed that his fears about Rennenkampf were unfounded.

The Russian Lines Crack
The twenty-sixth of August was a day of fierce fighting. Samsonov had resumed his advance, but Mackensen and Below drove him back. By the evening, the Russian position was becoming untenable. Contact between the two Russian divisions was broken, and during the night the situation deteriorated into complete chaos. Orders

were issued and countermanded as crisis followed crisis. One Russian corps, the Twenty-third, was described as 'terribly exhausted . . . they had been three days without bread or sugar'. Though he was trying to save himself from envelopment rather than to envelop the enemy, Samsonov decided to continue the battle as a holding action until Rennenkampf could arrive to turn the tables on the Germans. However, although on 26 August the German troops were themselves too tired to press their advantage and pursue Samsonov with vigour, part of one Russian division had been pinned down around Lake Bössau. In a state of utter exhaustion and panic, many Russians drowned. This incident was a portent of the slaughter to come.

On 27 August, François was ready for action. Relentlessly battered by his heavy artillery, the Russians, pitifully hungry and now lacking any will to fight, were hurled back from their positions, suffering horrendous casualties in the process. Seeing the full gravity of their situation, on the evening of 27 August Jilinsky ordered Rennenkampf to move forward. The order came too late and carried an insufficient note of urgency.

On 28 August Ludendorff ordered François to relieve the pressure on Scholtz's Twentieth Corps, but François again disobeyed orders, being determined to cut off Samsonov's line of retreat. The Germans were fortunate that François acted as he did, for otherwise a large part of the Russian forces would have escaped the trap into which they were forced on the following two days. As it was, Samsonov was hemmed in on three sides, and as Cyril Falls remarked, for the Germans 'it was like heading stock into a corral . . .' Meanwhile Ludendorff was again haunted by the spectre of Rennenkampf. He wrote, that Rennenkampf's 'formidable host hung like a threatening thunder cloud to the northeast. He need only have closed with us and we should have been beaten'. In reality, Ludendorff greatly overestimated Rennenkampf's strength; no coup de grace was ever to come from that quarter.

The Tannenberg Triumph

Samsonov's position was nonetheless desperate. Rennenkampf was moving forward so ponderously as to be useless. Only two of Samsonov's corps, the Thirteenth and Fifteenth, were any longer able to fight with any effect. His communications were badly disrupted. In desperation he moved to take personal control at the front. It was too late. Defeat stared at him unblinkingly, and Samsonov was gripped by a fathomless melancholy. A general retreat on 29–30 August developed into a cataclysmic disaster. Many troops were surrounded in forests and marshes, where they wandered helplessly about, some despondently trying to regroup. Countless soldiers starved to death or were killed by German troops who were combing the forests. In places, Russians in sufficient numbers and with the strength born of desperation managed to break through the German cordons; but the overall picture remained unchanged. One Russian column met a typically gruesome end: 'From two directions searchlight beams shone forth . . . Immediately after there followed machine gun

Paul von Hindenburg takes command after the retreat in East Prussia. General von Below stands third from the right, next to Hindenburg.

Samsonov led the disastrous Russian attack.

46

Left: Germany's heroes. From left to right: Field Marshal von Mackensen, General von Ludendorff, Hindenburg, and General von Seeckt, subsequently Head of the Reichswehr and Architect of the Wehrmacht. Oskar von Hindenburg, the Field Marshal's son, stands behind Ludendorff.

fire and a few rounds of rapid shrapnel fire . . . Five times the Germans repeated the same manoeuvre and each time the column melted and melted.' The Germans had taken ninety-two thousand prisoners; François' corps alone captured sixty thousand. At least thirty thousand Russians were dead. German losses numbered between ten and fifteen thousand. Their booty included a vast supply of guns which the Russians could ill afford to lose.

An important witness was missing from the climax of the debâcle. Late on 29 August, after spending the evening walking and wandering in a forest, Samsonov slipped away from the staff officers who were accompanying him. Minutes later, a single shot rang out through the wood. Unable to face the Tsar or his men again, General Samsonov had killed himself.

Although Hindenburg had described the German netting of the Russians as 'harvesting', the victors themselves were reduced to the last stages of exhaustion by the six days of fighting. At the suggestion of either Hoffmann or Ludendorff, a name was found for the battles: Tannenberg, in verbal revenge for a defeat which in 1410 the Poles and Lithuanians had inflicted on the Teutonic Knights.

The two German corps which Moltke had inadvisedly transferred from the west had now arrived on the eastern front, and here they proved invaluable, despite the fact that their continued presence in the west would probably have reversed the outcome of the Marne. Reinforced by the new arrivals, Hindenburg was able to defeat Rennenkampf, though he failed in his primary objective of cornering the First Russian Army on the coast and destroying it as he had done with that of Samsonov. True, Rennenkampf lost between thirty and forty-five thousand men as prisoners, but he was able to evade the Germans by retreating with the bulk of his troops. Nevertheless, in the Battle of the Masurian Lakes, 8–9 September, Rennenkampf was driven out of East Prussia. His own nerve cracked, and he fled in ignominy by car to Kovno (Kaunas), eighty miles away.

Tannenberg was a great and imaginative victory for Germany, but the damage it did to Russia has been exaggerated. Although she sustained extremely heavy losses, Russia was not irreparably crippled. As it occurred, the battle was not the result of deliberate planning. The German army had sought to hurl back the Russians, not to surround them, and the idea of their envelopment emerged later, made possible by the passivity of Rennenkampf's army.

Perhaps, however, the most lasting aspect of Tannenberg was its valuable lift to German morale. East Prussia had been saved. As a result, Hindenburg became and remained a folk hero. This was ironic, for Tannenberg was planned by the brilliant young staff officer, Hoffmann, and was won in large measure because of the initiative and sure judgment of François. As for the French, they expressed their condolences to Russia because of the sacrifices made in the name of alliance; but Paris could not help but rejoice that the Russian offensive had led to a fatal weakening of the German western front. On the Marne, Moltke's pigeons came home to roost.

Above: The retreat to Tannenberg was a bloodbath for the Russians. **Left:** Tens of thousands of Russians were slaughtered at Tannenberg.

Opposite above: Russian soldiers kneeled to pray before the Tsar on their way to the front. **Opposite below:** Field Marshal Paul von Hindenburg, the victor of Tannenberg.

49

Above: Hungarian cavalry press forward on Russia's southern flank. **Right:** A wire implacement is stormed near Lemberg.

Previous page: Almost a hundred thousand Russian soldiers were captured by the Germans.

Austria and Lemberg

Farther to the south, in Galicia, Austrian troops had entered Russian territory on 10 August. Ten days later Conrad ordered a northward offensive to meet the Russian armies, which had attacked Galicia once they were certain that the major initial German concentration was to be on the western front. Immediately Conrad was thrown off balance, for he had expected a slower and more ineffective Russian mobilization than in fact occurred.

On the morning of 28 August the Austrian Twenty-seventh Division was ambushed, and over eight thousand men were lost. Conrad was now a seriously worried man. Two days previously the Russians had advanced on the Austrians in such force that a general panic had set in with many troops fleeing to Lemberg, where they demoralized the civilian population. At the same time, the Slavs in the Austro-Hungarian army showed their disregard for the Habsburg cause, many of them willingly surrendering to the Russians or supplying them with strategic information. No wonder Conrad wrote to Emperor Franz Josef that he was 'now going through the most terrible moments' of his life.

No doubt Franz Josef was too. The aging Emperor, after over sixty years in power, could envision all his efforts coming to a tragic end.

Lemberg and the Austrian Front

Fortunately for the Austrians, the Russian Southwestern Army Group under Ivanov vastly overestimated the Austrian strength facing them in the region of Lemberg, and therefore did not press the advantage of their recent victory at Zlotchow. Liddell Hart comments that had Ivanov 'pushed on at once it is likely that he would have crashed through the shaken Austrians as through a paper screen'. Although Grand Duke Nicholas, judging the situation more accurately, ordered the Russian advance to continue, the Russians had lost two precious days in dithering, in which time the jittery Austrians had had a chance to pull themselves together. Yet misinformation from aerial reconnaissance did much to undo the Austrian plans, and meanwhile on 30 August the Russians under Brusilov were victorious in breaking the line of the Austrian Second Army. Everywhere the cry was heard, 'The Cossacks are coming!' A few days later the Galician capital of Lemberg (Lwow), the fourth largest city in the Habsburg Monarchy and an important centre for communications, fell after being encircled by Russian forces from the north and east.

After several intermediary bouts of vicious fighting, on 10 September the two armies clashed along a wide front. The Russians placed great significance on the outcome of this affray. Influenced by the result of Tannenberg, Nicholas decided to concentrate on the defeat of Austria-Hungary, and only secondarily on that of Germany. On 31 August he ordered Ivanov to destroy the Austrians without regard to cost in life and limb. This was easier said than done, for though the Austrians were suffering frightful casualties from the armies of the Tsar, the Russians' slow advance allowed their armies to remain intact; and, when cornered, the Austrians

were still able and willing to engage in bloody attacks in which both sides were slaughtered with macabre impartiality. Eventually, however, the Habsburg soldiers' spirits broke under the impact of a Russian holding action from the east and an attack from the north. On 11 September Conrad had no choice but to abandon the fight and withdraw his armies beyond the River San.

The victories around Lemberg were great triumphs for Russia, and they did much to erase the shame of Tannenberg from the public mind. Austria had been left with two hundred and fifty thousand casualties, and Russia had captured over one hundred thousand prisoners. Barbara Tuchman judges that the Russians had 'accomplished a mutilation of the Austro-Hungarian Army, especially in trained officers, from which it was never to recover'. Indeed, the Austrian retreat continued in increasing chaos for more than three weeks. To the ravages of sickness and disease were added long arduous marches. Austrian morale suffered a crushing blow; their attempts to invade both Serbia and Russia ended ignominiously. In Berlin muttered complaints were heard that the Fatherland was 'fettered to a corpse'.

Thus, wracked by internal dissensions and denuded of many of its best and most reliable officers, the Austrian rout in Galicia was com-

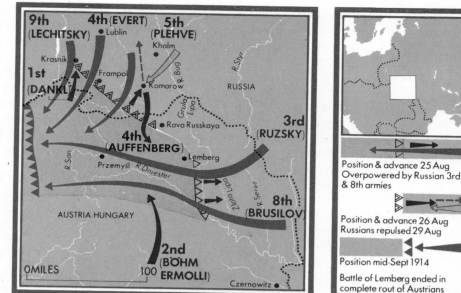

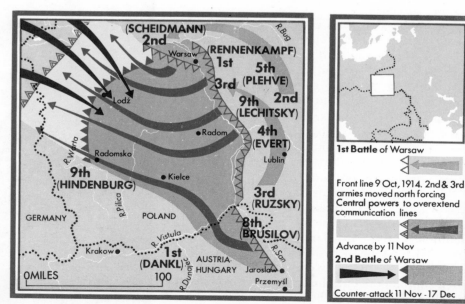

1st Battle of Warsaw

Front line 9 Oct, 1914. 2nd & 3rd armies moved north forcing Central powers to overextend communication lines

Advance by 11 Nov

2nd Battle of Warsaw

Counter-attack 11 Nov -17 Dec

Position & advance 25 Aug Overpowered by Russian 3rd & 8th armies

Position & advance 26 Aug Russians repulsed 29 Aug

Position mid-Sept 1914

Battle of Lemberg ended in complete rout of Austrians

plete. This left the Germans worried lest the coal-fields and industries of Silesia, vital to the war effort, fall to the Russians. Their fears were well placed, for in fact the French were urging exactly such an action upon their eastern ally.

The Push Toward Warsaw

As Russian armies ominously regrouped, the Germans decided to take protective measures. Hindenburg reasoned that with a surprise thrust he could cross the Vistula and capture Warsaw. A fortress city, Warsaw was an important defensive position; in addition, denying it to the Russians would remove an excellent base from which to launch an offensive into Silesia.

Meanwhile the Russians had reversed their plans and had now decided to give top priority to the destruction of German forces before taking any further measures against the Austrians. Grand Duke Nicholas planned an enveloping movement close to Warsaw. Hindenburg, he prophesied, would be driven off and into Austrian forces further south. Hindenburg knew of part of this plan via the usual Russian carelessness in sending vital radio and telegraphic messages uncoded. As a result the German advance was ploddingly careful, being slowed down further by the same knee-deep Polish quagmires of mud which had ensnared Napoleon.

On 10 October the German Seventeenth Corps encountered and defeated a strong Russian force at Grójec. It was here that the Germans discovered detailed Russian battle orders on the body of a dead Russian officer; but the Germans were unable to act fully on this information, since the Russian plan was already in full swing. Desperate fighting took place with Russian troops who were forcing their way across the Vistula. Late on 11 October Ludendorff prepared to retreat. Conrad's forces were of little help to him, for by now the Austrian communications had been severely disrupted by snow and ice. In any case, the Austrians resented German high-handedness and were prepared to assert their independence of action even if it meant failure for the common cause. Conrad was eager to place blame for defeat in any quarter but his own, and he complained that 'flighty and rambling operations' on the part of the German Ninth Army were responsible for Russian successes.

Eventually Austrian *amour propre* was partly satisfied, and as the Germans moved north, Austrian troops replaced them and prepared to face the Russians around Ivangorod. They were to attempt to push the enemy out where their German ally had failed to do so. For four days, in vicious and strenuous hand-to-hand combat, the Austrians tried their utmost to break into the Russian positions. Their failure did not detract from the outstanding bravery which they showed under appalling conditions.

Now German-Austrian bickering flared up to new heights. The Germans, more and more fearful of a Russian offensive in Upper Silesia, abandoned the Austrians to their fate and struggled back to their own territory. The Russians had once more overextended themselves. Their supplies ran out, their men were exhausted; their horses dropped in their tracks.

A New Offensive in Poland

On 1 November Hindenburg was appointed Commander in Chief of all German forces in the east. Immediately he began preparations for a new offensive in Poland. He still had hopes that a knock-out blow could be delivered against Russia, though this in itself would not end the war. Rather, the German hope was now to defeat Russia and then crush France before the new British recruits were sufficiently trained for battle. However, Falkenhayn, now chief of staff, could not spare Hindenburg troops from the West until December, by which time the second German attack on Warsaw had forfeited the advantage of surprise. Meanwhile, Hindenburg had to muddle along as best he could.

By 11 November the Germans were ready to advance. On the south bank of the Vistula, Mackensen wreaked havoc on a lone Russian corps. Communications between the Russian First and Second Armies were felled. The Second Army tried to protect the area of Lodz and deal Mackensen a glancing blow, but Mackensen caught up and shoved the Russians back on Lodz in disarray. Lodz, a city of half a million inhabitants, was an important billeting area and an industrial centre, and the Russians set great store in holding it. Yet by now the Russian Second Army was hemmed in on three sides.

From 18–25 November, a confused, whirling murderously vicious battle took place. Thousands of the injured froze to death. Somehow the Russians held on to Lodz and prepared to entrap fifty thousand Germans who were cut off from their fellow troops some twenty miles away. Characteristically Rennenkampf bungled the operation. He failed to close off the German way of escape to the north, and Scheffer was able to break out. As the savage winter extended its frozen grip, the rival armies prepared for yet more battles to come.

Above: Hungarian hussars are forced to retreat. **Far left:** Polish cavalry, under Russian command, rush to defend Warsaw. **Left:** A Russian field gun digs in to face Hindenburg's onslaught.

CHAPTER FOUR
The Widening War

In September 1914, at the First Battle of the Marne, a decisive and irreparable blow was dealt to German strategy in the west. In consequence, on 14 September Moltke was relieved and was replaced by Falkenhayn, though the change was not openly admitted until 1 November.

After the Marne, the Germans had retreated to defensive positions on the Aisne. When the Allies eventually caught up with them, they attacked these positions forcefully. Heavy but indecisive fighting lasted from 13 to 18 September. The western front stabilized, and each side tried, and failed, to envelop the other. The armies collided in a series of devastatingly fierce battles, during the course of which the BEF moved towards the Flanders town of Ypres. As the left flank of this Ypres-bound movement reached the coast, Falkenhayn decided to penetrate the position before further British troops arrived.

The Germans had considered their western flank vulnerable to attack, for to their rear was Antwerp and the 'tattered, weary and shaken' Belgian field army of at least sixty-five thousand troops. Falkenhayn resolved that the city must be captured; and although it was strongly fortified, the heavy German siege artillery made short work of the defences. In brief, as one history relates, 'the operation was a walkover', and Antwerp

fell on 9 October. Nevertheless, if the Belgians had not held out until further resistance was impossible, the German troops surrounding Antwerp would have been thrown into the general affray at least five days earlier. In that case the Allies might have been broken altogether before it was possible to hold the Germans at Ypres.

On the British side, Sir John French was full of confidence. He firmly believed that the BEF was stronger and the German army weaker than at Mons the previous month. On 10 October, the order went out that the BEF would advance to meet the enemy. Unhappily for the British, however, their estimate of German strength was highly optimistic. Similarly sanguine was Foch, the commander of the French northern group of armies. Obstinate, wilful, but exuding 'gusts of optimistic encouragement', as Liddell Hart put it, Foch was certain that the Germans would be unable to extend and secure defensive positions to the coast. German cavalry could delay, but not prevent, a general Allied thrust, and the French plan was to envelop the German flank. Foch made the further mistake of underestimating the exhaustion of the Belgian divisions. His urgings to attack had a hollow ring among men whose leadership had been decimated.

Already, however, the BEF was advancing from

Above: The 2nd Scots Guards, equally confident, test their trenches. **Left:** The Cloth Hall in Ypres in 1914 before its destruction.

Previous page: Belgian villagers watch the British move up to the front.

Ypres to the La Bassée canal. Undaunted by the failure to capture Lille, on 18 October Sir John French was still cheerfully expecting an advance on Brussels. Reality wore a different face. Though British forces were shortly to be strengthened by the Indian Corps and other reinforcements, the Germans were able to field men in even greater numbers. Already on 10 October, the first of these new German units had left for Belgium. They included large contingents of students 'flaming with patriotism and enthusiasm', as Falls describes them. These raw young recruits, sometimes called the 'schoolboy corps', were scythed down by the grim harvester of battle, and the Germans referred to their slaying as *Der Kindermord von Ypern*, or 'the massacre of the innocents at Ypres'. Nevertheless, these doomed young men fought with such fanatical fury and dedication that their inexperience at times was overcome, and they annihilated battalion after battalion of Allied troops.

By the week beginning 17 October, both French and Germans had begun to weigh each other's strength more realistically. Foch now concluded that the gap in the German line had closed and solidified, whereas previously he had sought and expected to find such a gap between Lille and Antwerp. Falkenhayn and Duke Albrecht of Wurttemberg, the Fourth Army commander, also now understood in approximate terms the size of the force opposing them. Now, counselling against manoeuvring, Foch informed Rear-Admiral Ronarc'h, commander of a brigade of French sailors, that 'Your mission is to stop the enemy in his tracks.' To Joffre, Foch appealed for reinforcements; French, he cautioned about the need for a defensive line behind the main BEF. To everyone, Foch was an inspiration.

British aerial reconnaissance was meanwhile reporting the westward advance of German troop columns. The situation was somewhat confusing, and much of French's false optimism is explained and justified by the fact that while he received a stream of reports indicating that strong German opposition was to be expected, this was counterbalanced by the numerous Allied successes in forcing back the Germans with a minimum of effort. What French did not understand, however, was that the German light cavalry or *Uhlans* was acting both as a screen and a scouting party for the columns, which were marching behind.

Early on 19 October, the German Forty-fifth and Forty-sixth Divisions encountered the enemy. Excited by this first martial experience, the new recruits prepared for action. To their intense disappointment, no thrilling engagement followed. Instead, there was skirmishing and intermittent exchanges of shell and rifle fire. The morning ended with an air of anticlimax.

In the afternoon, the two German divisions moved forward towards the villages of Kortemark and Hooghlede. The Forty-sixth Division intended to capture the ridge of Hooghe, but when the Germans arrived they found that the French dragoons had dispersed.

By the evening of 19 October the Germans had taken all the Allied positions covering the Yser and had mercilessly bombarded the remaining French and Belgian defences in Dixmude and Nieuport. Next day, the 20th, the main German offensive was to begin, with the Fourth and Sixth Armies advancing together. Albrecht was confident that the day would end in an Allied rout.

North of the La Bassée canal, Rupprecht and his men heavily outnumbered the BEF. Their intention was to break out between Béthune and Armentières, but first the British positions overlooking Lille had to be wiped out.

On 20 October, two German battalions moved towards the village of Le Pilly, where an Irish battalion faced them. As the Germans loomed up out of the morning mist, the well-trained Irish pumped their deadly fire into the oncoming Westphalian ranks. For five hours the Germans struggled continuously to enter the village. Eventually the Irish position became untenable, for they were isolated in the crossfire of Germans to the south and east. Nevertheless, in the afternoon when the German assault was resumed, the plucky Irish battalion fixed their bayonets and soldiered on at gruesome sacrifice. As the day ended, the hapless battalion was erased from the map. Two hundred and fifty-seven men were dead, and all but 50 of the remaining 290 were wounded. Only 30 men slipped out from under the German net and returned to their lines.

The Flanders Swamp

As luck would have it, torrential rains were turning the plain of Flanders into a swamp. This naturally made fighting very difficult, and air reconnaissance was prevented, so that as yet Sir John French was ignorant of the decimation of the Irish. Other reports showed that the Allied lines were generally being held, and Lieutenant General Sir Douglas Haig was able to send news that his troops were moving into the battle zone of

The 129th Baluchis on the outskirts of Wytschaete.

Ypres. Such German prisoners as had been taken were young and badly trained. These factors initially bolstered French's optimism, though his spirits soon deteriorated. As this happened, it appeared to the angry Joffre, that French's new mood of despair was due to fears that a repetition of the retreat to the Marne was getting under way.

On 21 October, Haig was disgusted to learn that British and French troops had retired from the key position of Passchendaele – later to achieve bloody immortality – with only slight resistance. To make matters worse, that afternoon the nearby French cavalry was ordered to retreat. While at first resisting such folly, its commander had to obey when the order was repeated. Gloom prevailed. Passchendaele had fallen to the Germans from sheer bungling of orders, and now the Forest of Houthulst had been yielded without a fight.

The position was better on the strategically vital Messines ridge. British forces under Allenby were attacked by Rupprecht's cavalry on the morning of the 21st, but a potentially disastrous confusion of orders was resolved in the nick of time.

Once more the Germans resumed the offensive on the ridge, but they were unable to get very far. However, they caused many casualties, and the British had partially to withdraw, because of the shortage of men and ammunition which was beginning to be felt.

At Dixmude, the French were 'having a hellish time', as British reconnaissance colourfully reported. The German Fourth Army followed the Sixth in attacking everywhere, with some tactical success but with no general breakthrough.

On the Yser, Beseler decided to attempt by stealth what he had failed to achieve by assault, and took his Germans across the river under cover of darkness. The ploy was successful, for when morning came the Allies were unable to dislodge the Germans.

By 22 October Foch, despite his dynamism and inspirational coordination, concluded that the initiative was passing to the enemy. Striving to reinforce Anglo-Belgian cooperation, he simultaneously approved a French offensive under d'Urbal. Circumstances appeared to be thwarting Foch's initial instructions, but then an Allied counterattack was victorious over the Forty-fifth Division. By 24 October, French troops had secured a line from Dixmude to Zonnebeke; yet the British defence continued over much the same ground as previously, and Foch's plans for a general counteroffensive remained unrealized. Yet neither was the campaign proceeding according to plan for Germany, which now decided to attack at three points: around Dixmude; to the east of Ypres; and between La Bassée and Menin.

At Dixmude, it seemed that the forces of nature were smiling on the Reich. Chill winds and water

Armoured cars were called up to support the British defenders of Ypres.

Top left: The Belgians fought hard in the face of the German advance. **Top centre:** The Germans brought up artillery which dated back to 1896. **Top right:** French troops (and their war dogs) held fast. **Left:** In the face of horrific devastation and carnage, the French attack . . . and attack again. **Above:** General Haig was disgusted to learn of the Allied retreat.

were as effective as German shells in weakening the French defenders. On the night of 24–25 October, artillery bombardment steadily pounded at the town, followed by wave after wave of German assaults. As dawn broke, the Germans drew back; Dixmude lay in ruins. Both sides were utterly exhausted by their exertions.

On the 25th, the Germans made repeated attempts to break through on the Yser. The Allies remained fiercely determined that they should not pass. Each side battered and hacked away, and the casualty lists grew longer.

Along the low ridge of Ypres meanwhile, the German 'schoolboy innocents' were attacking and encountering the resistance of the French. One French regiment managed to cripple the German advance, but additional German troops moved forward and retook Zonnebeke.

By 24 October, Albrecht's aim of breaking open the British line had met with success. Strangely, the Germans, as if unaware of this, failed to press home their advantage. Meanwhile the British were reinforced by French cavalry under Dubois, and the line was stabilized. Furthermore, the British somehow held the Messines ridge. Fighting raged throughout the day. The unhappy Germans began to think that a decisive break in the Allied line was impossible, while the Allies for their part were continuously suffering under an endless outpouring of German firepower, backed by seemingly limitless reinforcements of troops. The stark horror of the endless rounds of battle is captured in a description given by Brigadier Farrar-Hockley, historian of the First Battle of Ypres: 'As each body of Germans is destroyed, we surge forward and take on the next, shooting and charging alternately, bayoneting the survivors until by sheer exhaustion and losses we come to a standstill.'

On 25 October, fresh British troops began to arrive at the front; and French infantry reinforcements were not far behind. Overjoyed, French reported home, 'My anxiety is over.' Only hours later, Sir Horace Smith-Dorrien blunted French's mood of euphoria by reporting that he feared the imminent breach of his section of the Allied line. Not many men or supplies were at hand to fill the threatening gap, yet miraculously the line was still holding the next day. Subsequently two thousand additional British troops shored up the previously weakening link.

Throughout 25–26 October, the salient of Kruiseecke was hammered and pulverized by German bombardments. Scores of men were buried and smothered as earth fell in on them. Despite this ordeal, the nerve-shattered survivors somehow reassembled. French's optimism waxed again, for Foch was still his incorrigibly optimistic self, and the French reinforcements had arrived. Now the Allied attack could be resumed. But on 29 October, the Germans themselves again took the offensive, their main attack beginning the next day. Yet on the evening of the 28th, the Belgians had played their last trump by opening their sluicegates and flooding a two-mile area from Dixmude to the sea to a depth of three or four feet. In the most literal sense, the German advance was bogged down. One account relates that 'it seemed to the Germans as if the whole country had sunk

with them and behind them'. Yet for the Belgians, outwitting their enemy had been achieved at a ghastly price. Thus far in the campaign they had already lost twenty thousand casualties, about 35 per cent of their armed forces.

The thirtieth of October saw a day of incredible devastation. As night fell, however, deep dissatisfaction was registered on each side. Rupprecht, expressing himself 'profoundly disappointed' with the course of events, renewed his resolve to take the Messines ridge. The German commanders demanded an even stronger offensive. At the same time, Foch was shoring up the sagging British morale, advising his allies to 'hammer away, keep on hammering and you will get there'.

The Middle of an Earthquake

On 31 October, after prolonged bloodshed and firing so intense that, as one sergeant put it, 'The ground was literally shaking as if we were in the middle of an earthquake', the Germans assailed and later captured Messines ridge. At Gheluvelt, nearly five miles southeast of Ypres, the British position began to crumble, and for a time all seemed lost; but by a desperate summoning of Allied reserves, the Germans were again driven back. Earlier the rapid British firing had again given the impression that machine-guns were being used.

The next day, 1 November, the Allies had anticipated further horrendous German attacks. The juggernaut, however, did not materialize, and the Germans bided their time until the Allies had exhausted themselves in localized attacks. Their inactivity was, in fact, mainly due to despondency at the endless chain of sufferings and losses without decisive result. Foch's attacks on 1 and 2 November were bold and imaginative, but for eleven more days Falkenhayn refused to take no for an answer. Finally, the additional miseries of snow and flooding, added to his preoccupation with events in the east, forced him to call a halt to the slaughter.

On 10 November, the Germans finally captured Dixmude, but the gain was meaningless, because by now the flooding of the Yser bank had been completed. Next day the fighting flared up to a climax of destruction. After further skirmishing, the Battle of Ypres formally ended on 22 November.

Ypres was the last occasion in 1914 when the Germans tried to break through the Allied positions to reach and capture the Channel ports. The attempt had been made, and had failed.

Ironically, Ypres itself, the occasion of the carnage, was a poor defensive position, in fact a bottleneck. The German emplacements on the hills above were far better, as also was a north-south position just to the rear of Ypres. But the town had become a symbol of the Allied cause, just as Verdun hypnotized the French later in the war. Ypres had to be held, at no matter what price. Over fifty thousand British had been killed or wounded, and the French losses were at least as great. Between 13 and 25 October alone, Germany sustained one hundred and thirty-four thousand casualties. One historian estimated that Ypres took a toll of a quarter of a million dead and maimed.

L'INGORDO
TROP DUR

Top left: Marshal Foch.
Left: An *Uhlan* with a
captured colonial soldier.
Racist propaganda played
an important role in
convincing Germans that
the French were incapable
of defending themselves.
German *Kultur* would
triumph over French
barbarism. **Top right:**
Allied propaganda against
Germany was grotesque.
Already charged with
eating babies and impaling
them on spikes, 'the Huns'
were supposed to have
laughingly cut off the hands
of their mothers. No lie was
too great, no distortion too
bizarre. **Above:** An Italian
caricature of the Kaiser,
greedily devouring the
world.

戰慄ス=力威之砲巨我軍獨擊攻總島之青之軍本日　（四十二其）報畫亂戰大洲歐

Above: A Japanese
propaganda poster
depicting their attack on
Tsingtao. **Right:** A more
realistic impression of
Japanese armed forces
before the seizure of
Tsingtao.

By now the entire western front had become the scene of a futile, stale and repetitive struggle. Between November 1914 and the spring of 1917, at least half a million of the flower of European manhood fell – while the result was that the lines of battle varied less than ten miles in either direction. This fact, which in retrospect seems to us unimaginable in its callous irrationality, stands out as the ugliest and most senseless occurrence of a peculiarly unlovely war. Falls explains that stalemate occurred because 'The assault could never be driven through into open country fast and clearly enough to prevent new lines of resistance being established and the defence congealing about the bulge.' However, the squandering of life remains inexplicable.

Ypres itself was nevertheless an example of mass heroism. Its indomitable veterans were, as Sir John Edmonds wrote, 'tired, haggard, and unshaven men, unwashed, plastered with mud, many in little more than rags'. In the midst of a vast exercise in destruction, the human spirit of the survivors prevailed against incredible odds.

The Entry of Japan

Meanwhile, on the political front, the war had been spreading to include a number of other belligerents, the foremost of which was Japan. Both Britain and Germany made early efforts to keep the war from spreading to the Far East; and on 1 August Grey had specifically told the Japanese that if Britain joined in the approaching conflict, she did not expect to need the help of her Asian ally. Indeed, initially Japan agreed that she would observe neutrality in any war confined to Europe; she would enter the war only if a third party – in this case, Germany – attacked British interests in the Far East. This position accorded with the renewed Anglo-Japanese alliance of 1911. In addition, Japan implied that she would only go to war if Britain asked her to do so.

On the other hand, the British Admiralty had decided that Japan would be needed to 'hunt out and destroy German armed cruisers who are attacking our commerce' in the Pacific. On 6 August, Grey informed the Japanese of this. This position was of course completely contrary to the one which Grey had taken only five days earlier. After reflecting on the course of events, on 7 August the Japanese cabinet decided to join the fighting on the side of the Entente.

Japanese motives were self-interested. As the Foreign Minister, Kato, emphasized to his colleagues, Japan could exploit the situation to gain both the fortress and port of Tsingtao and certain Pacific islands at Germany's expense. Thus, on 9 August, Kato told the British that Japan would have to participate in the war on more than a token basis in order to destroy German power in the Far East. Grey, by now worried at unleashing Japanese power in China or the Pacific islands, made it clear that London wanted Japanese help to be restricted to naval operations; and accordingly the British withdrew their request for Japanese aid. But the Japanese were adamant, and in the end Grey had to admit that it was for Japan alone to decide the nature of her actions.

On 15 August Japan issued an ultimatum to Germany, calling on Berlin to agree by 23 August to withdraw her naval might forthwith from Japanese and Chinese waters, or to disarm those ships that could not be withdrawn immediately. Germany was also to hand over to Japan within a month the German leased territory of Kiaochow, in the Shantung province of China. As the Japanese nebulously put it, Kiaochow would be held by them 'with a view to' its 'eventual' restoration to China. Meanwhile, despite pressure from Britain, Japan refused to give specific assurances as to the limits of her ambitions.

No German reply to the ultimatum having been received, on 23 August Japan declared war against Germany. Almost immediately she moved against the German Pacific islands and Tsingtao, which fell on 7 November. The islands in particular were an important strategic gain. America and the Pacific Dominions, as well as Britain herself, looked with suspicion on this further accretion

General Liman von Sanders, German adviser to the Turkish army. His efforts to bring the Ottoman Empire into the war on the side of the Central Powers succeeded.

Above and opposite above: Uniforms of the Chinese army. Although the Japanese invaded China to seize Germany's colonial possessions, China did not enter the war until 1917.

His Excellency Djemal Pasha with his Chief of Staff, Fuad Bey. Djemal Pasha had no enthusiasm for fighting Britain and France.

to Japanese strength. Japan had plunged into the Great War – as an unwanted ally.

Several factors made it likely that if Turkey became a belligerent, she would do so on the side of the Central Powers. German influence over the Turkish army was strong; indeed, it had recently been reorganized under the direction of General Liman von Sanders. Moreover, Enver Pasha, War Minister, the pugnacious leader of the Young Turk revisionists and himself already of pre-eminent stature in Turkish life, was a convinced Germanophile. Strengthening ties of trade and commerce linked the two nations. The Kaiser himself was eager for Turkish support in connection with the Berlin-Baghdad railway scheme, and he loudly proclaimed his sympathy for Mohammedan aims. Above all, Russia, a member of the Entente, was the hereditary enemy of that pan-Turkish irredentism which was coming to the fore at Constantinople. Pan-Turanian expansion could only be achieved at Russian expense.

On the other hand, the Minister of Marine, Djemal Pasha, at first leaned in sympathy towards the Entente. French influence was felt through her investments in the country, and the British held a powerful position in naval circles. Furthermore, the condition of the country as a whole had been debilitated by a series of recent wars. Probably most Turks wanted either neutrality, or war against only the hated Romanovs, though popular opinion was outraged at the British appropriation of two Turkish battleships which had been constructed in an English shipyard.

As early as 2 August, Enver committed himself to a secret agreement under which Turkey would intervene on the German side if Russia took the part of Serbia. It was agreed that if Greece allied herself with the Entente, Turkey would receive the Greek Aegean islands and Crete in the event of German victory. Yet Turkey did not commit herself to immediate participation in the conflict; and, simultaneously with the secret negotiations

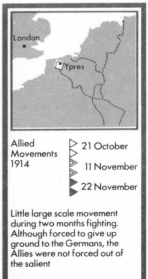

Allied Movements 1914

▷ 21 October
▷ 11 November
▶ 22 November

Little large scale movement during two months fighting. Although forced to give up ground to the Germans, the Allies were not forced out of the salient

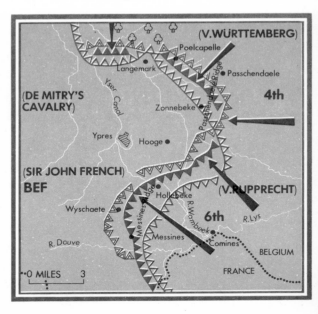

with Germany, Enver approached the Russians with an offer of alliance in return for the cession to Turkey of western Thrace and the Aegean islands. Russia, needing whatever Balkan support she could get, was unreceptive, though she proposed certain concessions which were intended to keep Turkey neutral. Instead, they merely whetted the Turkish appetite for gains. To make matters worse, Allied diplomacy towards the Turks worked at cross-purposes because of their differing interests in the Near East. For all these reasons, despite initial hesitancy because of British participation in the Entente, by early in September it became obvious that Turkey was gravitating towards the Central Powers. In August, the German cruisers *Goeben* and *Breslau* had evaded their British pursuers, entered the Dardanelles, and had been 'purchased' by Turkey complete with befezzed German crews. This transparent ruse had shown which way the wind was blowing; and the Marne and the Russian

victories in the East only delayed the inevitable. By October, Djemal had reconciled himself to an anti-Russian policy, and in return for a large German loan, Enver and Talaat Bey, the Interior Minister, had promised to stand at the side of Berlin. The pro-neutral or pro-Entente Turkish ministers were disunited and ineffectual.

On 28 October, without a declaration of war, the Turkish fleet under the German Admiral Souchon bombarded Russian ports on the Black Sea, and by 5 November all three major Allies were at war with the Ottoman Empire.

Turkish entry into the war meant that considerable Allied forces had to be diverted to defend Egypt and the Caucasus. In fact, Turkey's strategic location threatened the Russian lifeline to the Mediterranean and that of Great Britain to India and the Far East. Furthermore, it was feared that the Turkish alliance with the Central Powers would lead to the disaffection of the Mohammedan millions within the Indian Empire.

The German cruisers *Goeben* and *Breslau* enter the Dardanelles, evading their British pursuers. Their German crews were given fezzes when the ships were incorporated into the Turkish navy.

In addition, the smaller Balkan states might now be tempted to align themselves with Germany.

Nevertheless, Turkey was to pay dearly for her impetuous entry into the war. Already poor, backward, and inefficient, her price for losing was reduction to an Anatolian rump-state. Before they leaped, the Turks did not look hard enough.

Thus Japan and Turkey had joined the conflict, though on opposing sides, and the Great War had spread beyond the confines of Europe. In the meantime, however, several countries had declared their intention of abstaining from the war. Of the European nations, Norway, Sweden, Denmark, the Netherlands, Switzerland, and Spain were all successful in maintaining their neutrality throughout the war.

The Role of the Neutrals

The role of a neutral was by no means easy, the British blockade affected all their interests in varying degrees and often prevented the neutrals from taking full advantage of the increased demands for goods from warring nations. On the other hand, in the United States, which remained a neutral until 1917, the upsurge in trade with the Allies as a result of the wartime situation contributed significantly to creating a climate in which influential sections of the country felt a vested interest in an Allied victory. Though often precarious and equivocal, the position of the neutrals was not untenable. As most of them realized fully, they were fortunate indeed to escape the disastrous loss of life sustained by the belligerents.

Because they had entered the war for ostensibly defensive reasons, in one sense the absence of specifically stated British or French war aims is hardly surprising. Their first priority was to win; and because of the nature of the early course of the war, for much of the time this meant, in effect, the clearing of the enemy from occupied Allied territory. The German rape of Belgium had been the rallying point behind which the British had marched into the affray; therefore the restoration of Belgium was an inseparable part of the Allied cause. Similarly, the German armies had to be pushed out of northern France; and once the war began, if not before, the overwhelming majority of Frenchmen dreamed of the reunion of Alsace-Lorraine with France, though the territory had been German since 1871 and was an ethnic and linguistic crossroads.

Early in the war, few men agreed with Kitchener that a long struggle lay ahead before victory could be achieved. If the war were to end by Christmas, then victory itself would define specific war aims. Not until the end of 1914 did this optimism irretrievably fade before the spectre of havoc which the fighting had invoked. By then, with the chance of rapid victory irrevocably lost, all the belligerents intensified their search for allies, and in doing so were forced to clarify what they were fighting for – and against. Moreover, as the war and the concomitant suffering grew ever longer and more frightful, appropriate spoils of victory had to be found. Somehow the holocaust had to be justified, to be made worthwhile; somehow the maimed and weary soldiers had to be inspired to struggle on. As Allied resources

evaporated under the voracious demands of total war, American financial and material aid became increasingly indispensable, and the evolving aims of war were influenced in part by the desire for American approval.

Thus the British fought to restore the Low Countries to their age-old status of buffers; the French to free their territory and regain their lost provinces; and the Russians to maintain their momentum, to survive as a great power, and later merely to remain together as a political entity.

In October 1914, the Russian Ambassador in Paris, Isvolsky, asked for a statement of French war aims. He was told that German power must be destroyed. The following month, Paléologue, Isvolsky's opposite number, was received by Tsar Nicholas. Besides discussing the 'necessary' destruction of Austria-Hungary, the idea of a separate Hanoverian kingdom in northwest Germany was mooted. Paléologue also mentioned that 'perhaps' France would favour an extension of her territory to include the German Rhineland, although in fact the Quai d'Orsay remained non-committal on this point. Thus as the autumn wore on, the debate on Allied war aims did become more specific; but there was still no comprehensive or agreed list of aims, nor any concrete plan for their achievement.

In England the liberal press, once it was reconciled to the idea of participation in the war, emphasized the more righteous reasons for the conflict. Gardiner of the *Daily News* spoke of fighting to free the German masses from the Prussian yoke. As early as 14 August, H. G. Wells dubbed the affray 'The War to End War'. By November, both Asquith, the Prime Minister, and Grey had emphasized that the Allies must fight to prevent either 'continuance or recurrence of an armed brute power in Central Europe'.

As the fighting continued, with ever-lengthening casualty lists as silent witnesses to the slaughter, the propaganda services of each side harped upon the brutality of the enemy. For the Allies, the natural corollary of their image of the Germans as brutes was that 'the Huns' were unfit to be colonial masters. Gradually the idea gained strength that these German dependencies, considered unready or unable to rule themselves, should be taken in so-called trust, by the (as they saw themselves) morally superior Allies. The colonial issue illustrates well the almost imperceptible and natural emergence of certain aims. The 'realists' were also pleased with the reflections of the 'idealists' on the colonial problem, since for reasons of strategy they badly wanted areas such as German Southwest Africa. For these and other reasons, by early 1915 the British had conquered most of the German territories in Africa.

While Allied annexationism proceeded apace, it was different from the ambitions of Germany in terms of power politics. Klaus Epstein wrote that '*only* German annexations threatened the complete overthrow of the European balance of power; and *all* German annexationist plans were certain to violate the now fashionable principle of nationality'.

The emergence of war aims underlined the divisions among the Allies themselves. For example, Britain and France bickered over the

future of the German Cameroons. While France was more concerned for the future of Poland than for Serbia, Britain was relatively unconcerned about both. There were fewer French than British who worried about national self-determination. The French hoped to soothe their Russian ally by securing the principle of freedom of the Straits; the British were more dubious. However, in September 1914, by the Treaty of London it was agreed that when peace terms might be discussed, 'no one of the Allies will demand terms without the previous agreement of each of the other Allies'. Yet for all this, it must be underlined that, as A. J. P. Taylor pointed out, 'There was no serious exchange of ideas between the Entente Powers on war aims during the first winter of the war.' Allied ideas on the shape of the future world were embryonic and tentative.

On the German side, the aims of war were defined earlier and in more detail. Whether or not one accepts the Fischer-Geiss thesis that Germany was literally 'grasping at world power',

German aims were undoubtedly far-reaching. In many circles, for instance, the idea of *Mitteleuropa*, or German domination (either by outright annexation or economic control) of the Balkans and the Near East, and also of much of Eastern Europe, was expected to provide a vast area for development and exploitation, comparable to the British and French colonial empires. The paucity of German colonial holdings was also bitterly resented, and dreams arose of a powerful bloc of German territory in the centre of Africa: the *Mittelafrika* concept.

In early August, the Kaiser hinted that after the expected German victory, the Polish Kingdom would be re-established, divorced from Russia and closely linked to Germany. At the same time, Bethmann-Hollweg encouraged Finnish separatism and considered the idea of a Ukrainian buffer-state. By 21 August, the Chancellor was speaking of Belgium, Holland, and Poland as German protected states or *Schützstaaten*, and almost three weeks later, when a decisive German triumph in

Flying Officer Bruno Büchner stands before his aeroplane, one of the few the Germans left to defend their East African colony.

the west seemed imminent, Bethmann formulated his September Program, a kind of provisional shopping list of German needs and desires.

According to the Chancellor, Germany's first priority was 'to achieve security for the German Reich in west and east for all imaginable time'. To do this, it was necessary to weaken France to the point where 'her revival as a great power' would be 'impossible for all time'. Similarly, 'Russia must be thrust back as far as possible from Germany's eastern frontier and her domination over the non-Russian vassal peoples broken.' With France and Russia sapped of strength, Germany would be the dominant European power.

The September Program also listed specific war aims. France was to cede the Briey orefield and possible other pieces of territory to Germany, while French Flanders was to be joined to Belgium. Belgium itself was to make certain territorial concessions and 'must be reduced to a vassal state, . . . economically a German pro-

vince'. Holland 'must be left independent in externals, but be made internally dependent on' Germany. Luxembourg would be incorporated into the Reich. An economic association to include France, Belgium, Holland, Denmark, Poland, Austria-Hungary, and possibly Norway, Sweden, and Italy would be created under German leadership to 'stabilize Germany's economic dominance over *Mitteleuropa*'. The issues of *Mittelafrika* and Russia 'will be considered later'.

The program outlined above is an indication of the massive shift in the continental European balance of power that Germany considered necessary to her own future as a power of world stature. But the September Program was never rigidly followed; and after the definitive failure of German western strategy at Ypres, Bethmann-Hollweg seriously considered a compromise peace with Russia in order to turn westward with free hands. Although this idea was shelved because of opposition, Germany's war aims, while flexible, remained grandiose.

CHAPTER FIVE

Navies and Armies Clash

During the Great War the Japanese, seeing their opportunity, took the lion's share of the German Far East and Pacific colonies. These colonies were also important because Tsingtao, the capital of Kiaochow, was the headquarters of the German East Asiatic Naval Squadron, commanded by the formidable Vice Admiral Graf Maximilian von Spee.

During October 1914 it became evident that a major part of this squadron was heading for South America, where Germany had powerful interests. To the Germans, this course seemed prudent in view of the Japanese declaration of war against Germany. Such action brought two further advantages: it was thought unlikely that the Japanese would pursue the Germans so far afield, in view of possible complications with the United States, and the journey could be accomplished in relative ease and secrecy by journeying via the myriad islands en route.

The British were anxious lest subsequently the German fleet might round Cape Horn and cause havoc to the vital South American-European trade in meat and maize. The Admiralty resolved that this danger must be averted at all costs, for if her foreign trade and food imports were seriously disrupted, Great Britain would be brought to her knees in a matter of weeks. Thus the German vessels must be found and destroyed.

Coronel, to the south of Santiago, Chile, was the scene of the first round in a double clash of navies. On 31 October the British light cruiser *Glasgow* anchored in Coronel Bay. She had taken a battering in tremendous gales during her journey from the Falkland Islands, and was now in need of a brief respite in port for repairs. Next day, however, the *Glasgow* sailed away, aware from telegraphic signals that a German ship was nearby. Soon she joined the rest of the British fleet some forty miles west of Coronel.

As it happened, Spee had moved south to forestall the *Glasgow* at the same time that the British commander Rear Admiral Sir Christopher Cradock, had voyaged north to fight what he supposed to be the isolated German light cruiser *Leipzig*. Although both navies sought the encounter, the actual battle was full of mutual surprises.

The British ships, *Good Hope*, *Monmouth*, *Glasgow*, and *Otranto* spread out in linear formation. On the afternoon of 1 November, the German armoured cruisers *Scharnhorst* and *Gneisenau* approached on the horizon; the *Leipzig* was not, after all, alone. To this German concentration was added the *Dresden*. The British were at a heavy

disadvantage: against two elderly armoured cruisers, an armed merchant ship, and a light cruiser, the Germans pitted two modern armoured cruisers and two light cruisers, with the danger of a third, the *Nürnberg*, in the background. Moreover, the German ships were manned by expert professional sailors, whereas the British seamen were mostly recent recruits. Cradock could have avoided action by retiring southwards; Cruttwell guesses that his motive for not doing so was his hope that before his inevitable destruction he might damage the German fleet sufficiently to enable the British ship *Canopus*, 300 miles to the south, to finish the job.

Cradock was a true son of Nelson. Fearlessly he prepared for battle against overwhelming odds. As evening fell, the German guns blazed fire, and thunderously the British boomed their reply. Yet, outlined in the sunset, the British ships were doomed. In under an hour the *Good Hope* found a watery grave. Torn by an explosion, her hulk blazing like a charnel house, the British flagship disappeared from sight. Lumbering on into the darkness, the burning *Monmouth* was annihilated by the *Nürnberg*. Both British ships went down in grim defiance, with the loss of every single man aboard, 1440 in all. Somehow the *Glasgow* contrived to escape, while the *Otranto* had only played a minor role. The German ships were barely scratched, and their only casualties were two wounded. Here was a German victory at the very moment when Allied morale needed a fillip to counter Turkish entry into the war.

Britain did not sit down under the humiliation.

Opposite: The *Scharnhorst* in the foreground, with the *Leipzig*, *Nürnberg* and *Dresden*, sailing off the Chilean coast: November 1914.

Admiral Sir Christopher Cradock, who sailed into disaster in 1914.

Right: The German cruiser *Dresden*, which the British finally cornered and sank in March 1915. **Below:** The German disaster in the Falklands. The *Inflexible* and its crew assist the survivors of the *Gneisenau*.

Admiral Lord Fisher, newly reappointed as First Sea Lord, was fiercely determined to hunt down Spee wherever he went. Yet Spee had tasted victory and liked its flavour. As the French say, *l'appétit vient en mangeant*. After much delay, Spee decided to pull off another coup by attacking the Falkland Islands, a position of tremendous strategic importance due to its use as a coaling station and radio communications centre. He was partially encouraged by several reports that the islands now lay undefended.

Meanwhile, on 7 December, Vice Admiral Sir Frederick Doveton Sturdee, Commander in Chief of British naval forces in the Pacific and South Atlantic, had arrived with his squadron for coaling in the Falklands. Next day the *Gneisenau* and *Nürnberg* were sighted. The Germans had seen a tremendous pall of smoke rising from the harbour, but thinking that the stocks of coal were being destroyed on their approach, they proceeded. Too late, the German vessels spotted the British battle-cruisers lying at anchor in Port Stanley. Swiftly they and the rest of the German fleet sped south-east. Ironically, several of the British ships were still coaling, and had Spee boldly attacked, he might have done considerable damage.

Sturdee, calm and unhurried in the best tradition of Drake, but nonetheless relentless, followed in pursuit. Caution lest his ships be damaged seriously led Sturdee to fight at long range, and this considerably lengthened the duration of the battle. Nevertheless, he had it mostly his own way. In the afternoon, the *Scharnhorst*, already burning uncontrollably, was pulverized by the *Inflexible* and the *Invincible*. Rolling on her side, the *Scharnhorst* sank. Firing haphazardly to the end, the *Gneisenau* went down with flags flying and sailors cheering the Kaiser. The Germans had proved themselves as brave in defeat as they were haughty in victory. Then the *Nürnberg* fell victim to the *Kent*, and the *Leipzig* similarly to the *Cornwall* and the *Glasgow*. Only the *Dresden* escaped, to lead a charmed life as the last German cruiser at sea, until she too was cornered the following March.

Some two hundred German sailors survived the rout, but eighteen hundred died, including Spee and his two sons. British casualties were only thirty. The Falklands was Coronel in reverse, but now the threat from German surface raiders was over. Britannia once more ruled the waves.

Stalemate in the East

In the eleven days preceding Christmas, Joffre's hopes of a breakthrough in the west were once more disappointed. The Tenth Army attacked at Arras, while the Fourth Army concentrated in Champagne. Falls has stated the bald truth in describing this French offensive as 'a mere killing match', useless from every point of view; yet it was one which dragged on until 17 March. The French fought with gallantry and fortitude, but nonetheless made no strategic impact on the Germans. The resulting casualties numbered at least one hundred and eighty thousand, about evenly divided between Germans and French.

On the eastern front, the winter campaign was an anticlimax to the great clashes of the autumn. German reinforcements during December led to

Damage done to HMS *Kent* after the Battle of the Falklands.

Admiral Lord Fisher, the First Sea Lord, who was determined to hunt down Graf Spee. His friends called him Jackie. The Germans probably had another name for him.

the fall of Lodz on 6 December, for as usual the Russians were short of supplies and especially munitions. Yet Hindenburg failed in his bid to smash through the Russian fortifications to the west of Warsaw, and indeed, the line remained unyielding until the summer of 1915.

In Galicia, the Austrians were still struggling rather unsuccessfully to push the Russians back. Despite a few hopeful advances, Conrad was unable to disrupt the Russians along the line of the Dunajec, and the full force of winter now added to the difficulties of further operations. Meanwhile, Falkenhayn strongly emphasized the decisive importance of the western front as opposed to that in the east. He believed that the war could never be won until Britain and France were defeated. Apprehensive of a repetition of Napoleon's disastrous experiences in 1812, he urged a separate peace with Russia in order that the whole of German might could be swung westwards. But Hindenburg and Ludendorff pressed the argument that knocking Russia out of the war first could be achieved; and when this was done, Germany would have acquired vast supplies with which to turn fully to the west. Moreover, Germany had to bolster her Austrian ally in the east. These latter arguments were convincing to Chancellor Bethmann-Hollweg and Jagow, and in January 1915 Falkenhayn was finally forced to give way. The war in the east would continue with high priority.

On 9 February the German Eighth and Tenth Armies moved forward from their positions at Lötzen and the Masurian Lakes. Their object was to make a pincers movement and thus to encircle the Russian Tenth Army. Due in part to the now-familiar interception of Russian uncoded radio messages, the Germans were able to force a break in two places. In the Winter Battle of Masuria, they cornered at least seventy thousand Russians

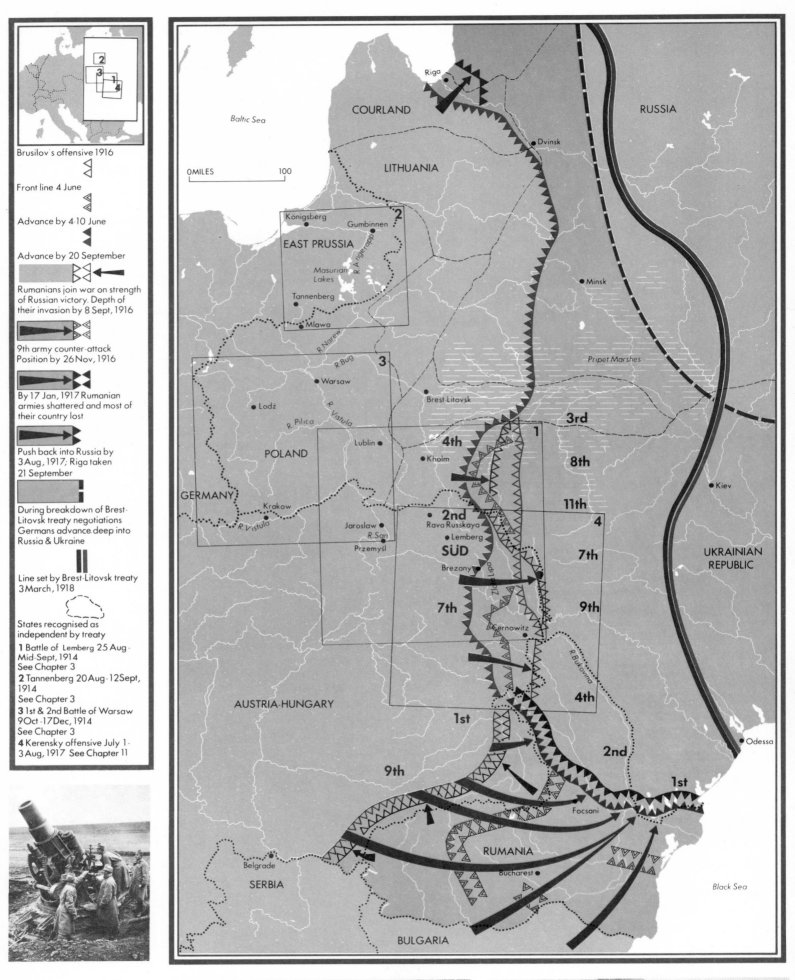

Brusilov's offensive 1916

Front line 4 June

Advance by 4-10 June

Advance by 20 September

Rumanians join war on strength of Russian victory. Depth of their invasion by 8 Sept, 1916

9th army counter-attack Position by 26 Nov, 1916

By 17 Jan, 1917 Rumanian armies shattered and most of their country lost

Push back into Russia by 3 Aug, 1917; Riga taken 21 September

During breakdown of Brest-Litovsk treaty negotiations Germans advance deep into Russia & Ukraine

Line set by Brest-Litovsk treaty 3 March, 1918

States recognised as independent by treaty

1 Battle of Lemberg 25 Aug - Mid-Sept, 1914 See Chapter 3
2 Tannenberg 20 Aug - 12 Sept, 1914 See Chapter 3
3 1st & 2nd Battle of Warsaw 9 Oct - 17 Dec, 1914 See Chapter 3
4 Kerensky offensive July 1 - 3 Aug, 1917 See Chapter 11

Above: Austrian artillery in Galicia. **Right:** Polish troops in action: December 1914. **Far right:** A German barricade dividing a village north-west of Arras, April 1915.

German trench mortars in action.

in the forests surrounding Augustovno (Augustow). However, as Edmonds points out, another Tannenberg was avoided, since the German encirclement was accomplished with only one division, and the insufficient number of German troops meant that the majority of Russians were able to escape. Furthermore, the Russians did not slide into panic as they had at Tannenberg. Yet to the Germans, the important fact was that their hallowed East Prussia was once more cleared of the enemy.

The Struggle for the Carpathians

Yet if East Prussia were free, the Carpathians were not. Vienna was by now convinced that if Italy joined the Entente, the war was lost, and Austria sought a tremendous victory in Galicia in order to prevent Italian and Rumanian entry into the war. As it turned out, no such victory came, and the expected interventions followed. For their part, the Russians believed that if Austria-Hungary could be defeated, the shock would cause German morale to collapse. Thus both sides independently decided to force an action in the Carpathian Mountains, gateway to the Hungarian heartland.

The ice-covered Carpathians provided an unenviable site for a winter offensive. Roads which now were frozen proved equally impassable later, when the thaw had made them muddy and slimy. Before this occurred, however, untold thousands, including whole companies at a time, died of exposure on the march. Finally the campaign became a series of misery-laden attacks up

sheer slopes that would have defied an army of mountain goats. In fact, the whole Carpathian episode degenerated into what the official Austro-Hungarian history admits was 'a grisly folly'.

On 23 January the Austro-Hungarian Army took the offensive by means of a general attack on the passes of Dukla, Lupków and Uzsok. The German South Army simultaneously attempted to take the passes of Verecke and Wyszków. On the defensive stood the Russian Eighth Army. The offensive lasted only a few days, then petered out, a dismal failure caused in large measure by the disruption of supply lines in the miserable weather.

Late in January, the Russians in turn went over to the attack, ran into difficulties, but made some progress. Despite this, Conrad planned a further offensive for late February, for he feared the blow to morale and the effect on the southern European and Balkan neutrals if he did nothing to relieve the Russian siege of the fortress of Przemysl. Yet again the hapless troops were defeated by the weather, by then known as 'General Winter'. Przemyśl fell on 22 March, and with it the Russians gained one hundred thousand prisoners. Slav obstructionism in the Austrian ranks reached a new peak, and Habsburg morale hit rock bottom. Furthermore, the Russian troops surrounding Przemyśl were now freed for a counterattack which gained considerable ground. They were halted and the line stabilized only by the arrival of German reinforcements in April. This in itself was symbolic. For the exhausted and demoralized Austrians, the winter fighting was their last major effort independent of Germany.

Previous page: 1500
Russian prisoners receive
bread rations in Augustowo.

The ill-fated *Lusitania*.

The Sinking of the Lusitania

On 7 May 1915, a sudden disaster broke upon a horrified and astonished world. A German submarine had sunk the steamship *Lusitania*, pride of the Cunard Line, with the loss of 1198 lives.

On the morning of 1 May the *Lusitania*, a British vessel, had left New York for the transAtlantic crossing to Liverpool. Many Americans were on board – despite a solemn black-bordered advertisement which had appeared in the New York papers.

The advertisement had caught the eye of many newspapermen and thrill-seekers, and as the mighty liner steamed out of harbour, an air of premonition hung over Pier 54. Some of the more morbid photographers present were selling pictures of the ship and proclaiming, 'Last voyage of the *Lusitania*!' Ominous telegrams warning passengers to cancel their berths added to the electric atmosphere. One which was addressed to the multimillionaire Alfred Vanderbilt cautioned, 'Have it on definite authority the *Lusitania* is to be torpedoed.' Yet few on board the powerful vessel, the largest and fastest steamer on the Atlantic run, paid heed. Vanderbilt himself scoffed at any thought of danger. After all, as many reasoned, why would anyone attack a harmless luxury liner, especially one including many Americans whose goodwill was sorely needed by the Central Powers? Who would foolishly attack a ship whose passenger-list included a gaggle of VIPs?

As the *Lusitania*'s passengers settled down to their opulent voyage, they little realized that in the hold were 4200 cases of small-calibre rifle ammunition and over 100 cases of empty shrapnel shells and unloaded fuses. Such a small amount of material hardly constituted an imminent danger to the German war effort; yet nevertheless the Germans defined these goods as contraband of war. Moreover, the passengers included a group of Canadian volunteers en route to the front.

As the *Lusitania* made its way across the Atlantic, approximately fifteen German submarines were restlessly patrolling the ocean depths. In their fear that the Allied blockade would strangle their economy, on 4 February the German government had proclaimed that the waters surrounding the British Isles constituted a war zone wherein, after

17 February, 'every enemy merchant ship . . . will be destroyed without its being always possible to avert the dangers threatening the crews and passengers on that account'. In view of alleged Allied misuse of neutral flags, 'Even neutral ships are exposed to danger in the war zone.' The *Lusitania* was sailing straight towards her doom.

On the night of 4 May, the 32,000-ton Cunarder moved swiftly through the invisible midpoint of its voyage. At the same time the German *Unterseeboote* (U-boat) U-20 appeared off southern Ireland, and during the next two days sank three ships, though without loss of life.

On the evening of 6 May the *Lusitania*'s captain, Turner, 'a seadog's seadog', as one authority called him, received a terse radio message from the British Admiralty: 'Submarines active off south coast of Ireland.' Elaborate safety precautions were undertaken; lifeboats were readied, bulkhead doors and portholes were secured, and after a further warning message, it was decided to take a mid-channel course. Meanwhile the ship's lookout had been doubled.

In the early afternoon of the following day, the Irish coast appeared on the horizon. The fog which had persisted earlier had now lifted. The *Lusitania*'s journey was nearly over. Now was sighted a familiar landmark, the Old Head of Kinsale. At that very moment – 1:40 p.m. – Kapitänleutnant Schweiger of the U-20 sighted the *Lusitania* in his binoculars. Swiftly the U-boat submerged, shortly to move in for the kill. The *Lusitania* became a sitting (or rather, moving) duck, for as he proceeded on a steady course at eighteen knots, Turner had unwittingly manoeuvred the ship into the position of an ideal target.

At two o'clock, most of the *Lusitania*'s voyagers had finished a leisurely luncheon. While some lingered in the Louis Seize dining saloon, others had adjourned for their coffee to the exquisite late-Georgian lounge. Many had emerged to take a stroll on deck, for the air was pleasant and the sun had come out. In the distance an orchestra played the 'Blue Danube'.

At 2:09 p.m., the U-20 unloosed a single of its deadly torpedoes. Heading straight for the British ship, the 290 lb missile cleaved through the water, leaving a trail of white foam in its wake.

Suddenly a lookout saw the danger to starboard. His shouted warning was superfluous. At precisely 2:10, the torpedo thudded into the starboard side behind the bridge, to the accompaniment of a terrifically powerful explosion. Suddenly the 790-foot vessel sharply lurched to starboard. Among the passengers, complacency gave way to fright. Several lifeboats, ready for launching, were thwarted because the *Lusitania* was moving too rapidly for evacuation measures to be taken safely. Already one boat had gone over the side, and its hapless occupants fell into the sea.

As the *Lusitania* listed ever more sharply to starboard, lifeboats to port crashed onto the deck in steady succession. Panicky passengers scurried about, many of them wearing their lifebelts incorrectly. As water surged onto the sinking starboard deck, several voyagers leapt overboard. By now a few of the boats had been safely launched – but not nearly enough. Amid the anguished cries of women and children, a grotesque note of black comedy was provided by a trio of Irish maidens distractedly warbling 'There Is a Green Hill Far Away'. Screams and oaths were intermingled as unanchored objects skidded and hurtled across the decks. In his ship's log, Schweiger laconically noted, 'Great confusion on board . . . They must have lost their heads.'

Now the *Lusitania*'s end was near. Suddenly her rudder and propeller heaved into the air, the bows thrust deeply into the water. Eighteen minutes after the torpedo had sunk home, as one survivor saw it, the *Lusitania* sank forever beneath the waves 'with a thunderous roar as of the collapse of a great building during a fire'. A scene of pandemonium spread across the surrounding mile of water. The sea was full of boats, some secure and some capsized. Flotsam and jetsam and hardy swimmers abounded, but the scene was rendered hideous by a steadily mounting number of lifeless floating bodies.

Eventually the roll of death amounted to 1198 of the 1959 passengers and crew. Of those dead, 128 were neutral Americans and 94 were children. The Allied press shrieked with outrage, while the *Frankfurter Zeitung* inadvisedly crowed about the German Navy's 'extraordinary success'.

Those in charge of the wheels of Allied pro-paganda quickly capitalized on the monumental German blunder, and no effort was spared to bring America into the war on a crest of passion. *The Times* stormed that the sinking 'has placed the whole German race outside the pale'. President Wilson's intimate adviser, Colonel House, urged immediate war in the absence of a full German apology. Many Americans railed against Germans and 'hyphenates' in general, but Washington kept its head. After a warning to Germany to cease unrestricted submarine attacks on merchant vessels, American neutrality was maintained for two more years. Still, the *Lusitania* incident occasioned an emotional outpouring of sympathy for the Allied cause. As such, in the words of Gaddis Smith, 'it was a sensitive barometer forecasting future American behaviour.'

The official inquiry into the disaster found that two torpedoes had fatally damaged the *Lusitania*, but German and other evidence suggests that only one torpedo found its target. The inquiry skimmed over the question of Admiralty carelessness, for one may well ask why the ship was not sent via a more northerly route when submarines were first observed off southern Ireland; why was the *Lusitania* unescorted even by patrol boats? Why did she carry war material at a time when the Germans were desperate enough to stop at nothing? Whatever the answers to these questions, the story of the *Lusitania* provides perhaps the outstanding example in the war of a misconceived policy with repercussions that besmirched Germany's good name.

Some of the few survivors of the *Lusitania*.

Disaster in Gallipoli

Liddell Hart and others have emphasized that the keynote of the Allied campaign against Turkey was one of shortsighted lethargy. In retrospect, Liddell Hart considers that an Allied attack on the Dardanelles should have been pressed home at the beginning of November 1914 – for at that time and for at least three months afterwards, the Turkish defences remained an obsolete patchwork.

In view of the long and tangled arguments that developed over the merits of a naval versus a combined land-sea operation against the Straits, it is both tragic and ironic that the chance was missed to field an army against the Dardanelles without the use of Allied troops already committed to the field. In August 1914 the Greek Prime Minister, Venizelos, had offered the Allies such forces, but they were refused because of Grey's unwillingness to offend Turkish susceptibilities.

As early as August, Churchill, as First Lord of the Admiralty, had seen the importance of forcing the Straits. On 25 November, at the first meeting of the War Council, he proposed a naval attack on the Dardanelles. The idea was shelved, but a month later the Secretary of the War Council and general *eminence grise*, Sir Maurice Hankey, urged a knockout blow against Turkey as a means of forcing her withdrawal from the war, of aiding Russia, and of influencing events in the Balkans. Indeed, by the end of 1914 many influential men, including Lord Fisher, the First Sea Lord, and Lloyd George, then the Chancellor of the Exchequer, looked for a means of breaking the deadlock, which the war had reached in the west, by use of force, particularly naval power, in another theatre of operations.

The argument for a new eastern front was immeasurably strengthened by the arrival on 2 January of a Russian appeal for a British diversionary action against Turkey to relieve the Ottoman pressure on the Tsarist positions in the Caucasus. As it turned out, however, within days the moment of greatest Russian need had passed because of the victory of Sari Kamish, and the Russians withdrew their request. Yet the Dardanelles idea had been given the fillip it needed, and the project moved forward with a momentum of its own.

Now Churchill telegraphed to Vice Admiral Carden, commander of a British squadron in the Aegean, with reference to the merits of a naval assault. Carden replied, 'I do not consider Dardanelles can be rushed. But they might be forced by extended operations with large numbers of ships.' Seizing on this last sentence, Churchill got the War Council to agree on 15 January to 'prepare for a naval expedition in February to bombard and take the Gallipoli peninsula, with Constantinople as its object'. Churchill took this provisional decision (*prepare* being the operative word in the sentence just quoted) as definite and final, and pushed aside the doubts of others such as Fisher. Robert Rhodes James has shown that Churchill took the sole initiative, pressing Lord Kitchener, the Secretary of State for War, for the British Twenty-ninth Division for use after the naval attack. However, not until 10 March did Kitchener agree to this.

Left: Australian troops on board HMS *London* heading toward their landing at Gallipoli. **Below:** French battleship in action in the Dardanelles, 1915.

Above: The Turks moved their howitzers up and down the coast to compensate for their lack of artillery. **Above right:** The *Suffren*, one of France's contributions to the Allied fleet at Gallipoli.

Below: HMS *Queen Elizabeth*. Length: 600 ft. Beam: 90 ft. 6 in. Draught: 29 ft. 7 in. Armament: 8 × 15 in. guns, 14 × 6 in. guns, 2 × 3 in. guns, 4 × 3 pdrs, 4 × 21 in. torpedo tubes. Crew: 951.

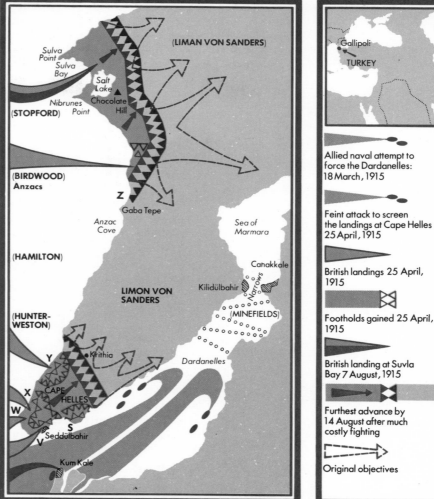

On 19 February the naval attack commenced. Bad weather then caused a delay until 25 February, but on the 26th the task of destroying the intermediate Gallipoli defences began. The results were extremely disappointing. After light opposition to a few tentative marine landings, early in March Turkish resistance became much stronger. Yet on 18 March, urged on by promptings from London, the Anglo-French assault on the Narrows began in earnest. A minesweeping operation took place simultaneously, but on 8 March the Turks had been able to lay a new set of mines, one of which now destroyed without warning the French battleship *Bouvet* and almost all her crew of over six hundred men. In the end, mines destroyed or put out of action six of the nine Allied battleships taking part.

Meanwhile, General Sir Ian Hamilton had been appointed commander of a Mediterranean Expeditionary Force of some seventy thousand British, Australian and New Zealand (ANZAC) and French troops. On 22 March he and Rear Admiral Sir John de Robeck, who had replaced Carden as naval commander in the area, agreed on the need for a combined land-sea operation. Yet with the advantage of hindsight one might argue that a further naval attack on the 18th would have succeeded; certainly the Turks, short of heavy shells and ammunition, had thought so. Indeed, if Constantinople, the Turkish capital, had fallen then, Turkey would probably have sued for peace, for in this area lay her only source of munitions.

On 25 March, worried by the recent naval assault, Enver formed an army to defend the

Top left: The Allied naval attempt to force the Dardanelles was doomed to failure almost from the outset. **Left:** The Allies bombarded the Dardanelles unceasingly in the hope of softening up the Turks.

Rear Admiral Sir John de Robeck.

Dardanelles under General Liman von Sanders. Through mismanagement and dilatory measures, the Allies allowed Sanders a month to complete his defences and bring up his troops. The entire Allied operation was bedevilled by conflict of wills at home, lack of coordination and divided command at the front, and a complete inability to know when to cut losses.

By 20 April the Allies were ready at last. The unfavourable weather, like an omen of disaster to come, caused a temporary delay. At dawn on 25 April, the Twenty-ninth Division landed at five small beaches – designated S, V, W, X and Y Beaches – at Cape Helles, on the southern end of the Gallipoli Peninsula; the ANZACs moved above Gaba Tepe, ten miles farther north on the western side of the peninsula. A British feint was made at Bulair, while the French made a mock diversion at Besika Bay and a temporary landing at Kum Kale on the Asiatic side of the Straits.

The ANZAC landing at Gaba Tepe got off to a bad start. The strong current carried the landing boats a mile north of the projected disembarkation area and to a much less favourable spot. Nevertheless the ANZACs came ashore to only light fire; but the smallness of the – evermore to be known as ANZAC Cove – led to impossible crowding and intermingling of units. The Turkish counterattack, inspired by Colonel Mustapha Kemal, later Atatürk, developed the fury of a whirling dervish, and the ANZACs were thrown back with heavy casualties.

Farther south, three of the British landings were comparatively easy. At W Beach, however, all was dark and silent as the men headed for shore, but as they clambered onto the land, Turkish rifles spewed fire, while many British were enmeshed in underwater wire as they went over the sides of their boats. Eventually the landing was made, but the strain and the decimating losses were sufficient to exhaust the troops for the rest of the day.

If the 'W' landing was difficult, the one at V Beach (Sedd-el-Bahr) was worse. As three thousand troops approached the shallow cove, its cliffs towering above, the Turks prepared their welcome. In the words of Liddell Hart, 'hell yawned'. Lying in wait, the Turks held back their fire until the boats had almost reached land. Then, their bullets ripping across the water with devastating accuracy, the Turks swiftly made the sea run red with British blood.

At S Beach, after making a successful landing, the battalion followed its orders, which were to wait for the troops from other beaches to join it before proceeding further. If these troops from S and X Beaches had instead moved to V and W sites, they could have overwhelmed the Turks. Similarly, at Y Beach two thousand men idled the day away; they sat on the cliff and, as Falls said, 'enjoyed the scenery' for want of orders or coordination. Next day, even as the Turks retreated, in a mood of alarmism the troops re-embarked. The official history acknowledges the great opportunity which was lost: 'It is as certain as anything can be in war that a bold advance from Y Beach, on the morning of the 25 April, must have . . . ensured a decisive victory.' Cruttwell sees in the wasted chances 'the most dramatic day of the whole World War'.

In the end it was passivity that triumphed. At Helles, for example, it was initially decided to rest the tired troops and await the arrival of French forces before attempting any advance. By 28 April a new attack was hazarded, but the Turks had greatly augmented their numbers, and the Anglo-French line broke close to the shore, to be

Above: The Turks, under Mustapha Kemal, conducted a brilliant defence against the Allies in Gallipoli. **Left:** British troops awaiting evacuation near Cape Helles.

Below: The ANZACs fought bravely but suffered heavy casualties at Gallipoli.

1915'de
Çanakkale'de
TÜRK

saved only by a shell from the *Queen Elizabeth* which landed smack in the middle of the advancing Turkish force and flattened it.

In the first phase of the Gallipoli campaign, Allied casualties were more than twenty thousand (of these, over six thousand were killed) out of a force of seventy thousand. The Turks were slaughtered in their turn, as when, on 1 and 3 May, they surged forward, bayonets fixed, and were sliced down by the thousand. Bravery and heroism on both sides were legendary. On 6 May the Allies returned to the attack, but, short of shells and observation aeroplanes, their position was undermined by the exhaustion of their troops. On 18 May, ten thousand more men fell in a Turkish attack of suicidal fury.

In London, public furore at the bungled campaign helped to bring down the Liberal government. After this, the new Coalition government of 25 May gave greater support to the Gallipoli project in terms of both men and supplies. Balfour had replaced Churchill at the Admiralty because of the latter's role in the campaign. Nevertheless, Hamilton continued to fight on in bursts of effort; in any case, it would have been hard to withdraw the troops because of the lack of natural cover and the shortness of the summer nights. Yet the steadily increasing Turkish build-up made an Allied defence equally difficult. Some bold new stroke was obviously needed.

During the summer a new scheme took shape. ANZAC forces, reinforced by British and Indian troops, would break forth towards the Sari Bair Mountains after diversionary thrusts had been made. New troops would be landed at Suvla Bay, three miles north of Anzac Cove, and an attack would be mounted on the Turks by an army with a 2:1 superiority in numbers.

S. L. A. Marshall notes that 'no other amphibious operation was ever floated from such an inordinately complex and unnecessarily ramified plan'. The reason for such complexity in the Suvla Bay operation remains a mystery. Still, the site itself was well chosen for a landing, for the Turkish defences were only lightly manned; Suvla provided an excellent anchorage for the fleet; the nearest ridges could not completely command the shore and thus abort the operation almost before it commenced; and the landing room available on the large sandy beaches meant that the enemy need not be presented with any concentrated target.

Despite the muddles that accompanied it, the Suvla operation almost succeeded. Early on 7 August, ANZAC forces came within an ace of capturing the commanding heights, but the Turks were saved by the disastrous inexperience of the British troops, the incompetence of their commanders, and their prostration from the merciless heat. During 7–8 August there was a breakdown in Allied supplies. On 6 August the men had come ashore with only one canteen of water each; now they lay helpless and parched while fresh water in plenty lay offshore in tankers. Cruttwell adds that 'the plague of flies was such that food was blackened by them as it was raised to the mouth'. Not surprisingly, dysentery was rampant.

On the night of 8–9 August, Kemal's reinforcements began to arrive, and when the Allied attack

On entend
le canon
Constantinople...

GERDA·WEGENER·

This French cartoon cynically portrays the Sultan cringing with his harem when the guns of Gallipoli were heard.

got under way, it was thwarted by these fresh troops. Early on 10 August, Kemal's forces hurled the Allies from their positions. Further Allied thrusts were futile because of what the German official history called 'a ring of ever-increasing strength round the British position'.

As opposition grew at home, the Gallipoli campaign faltered and subsided into the now-familiar trench fighting. By the end of the year, Allied evacuation was rendered inevitable, for the Central Powers had recaptured the Berlin-Baghdad railway project, thus enabling them to deliver supplies quickly to their Ottoman ally. Amazingly, not a single casualty resulted from the with-drawal – a weird end to a campaign in which the Entente lost over a quarter of a million men as casualties or prisoners, and in which the Turks bore losses nearly as great, including sixty-six thousand killed.

On 28 December, the British government recognized the futility of Gallipoli by formally resolving that the war would be decisively settled in the west. Fuller's summation stands as a poignant but just epitaph: at Gallipoli 'there was no judgment; no clear strategical analysis of the initial problem; no proper calculation of its tactical requirements; and no true attempt to balance the means in hand with the end in view.'

CHAPTER SIX

Italy: Egoism at War

On 3 August 1914 as the cataclysm of war struck Europe, and Italy declared her neutrality despite long-standing defensive obligations to the Central Powers through the alliance forged in the days of Bismarck, the intentions of Italy had long been in doubt; and as early as 1902 she had anticipated 1914 by an agreement of neutrality with France in the case of individual attack. The Italians justified their policy on the grounds that Austrian action against Serbia violated the alliance with Italy, since Vienna had acted without consulting Rome. Further, the entry of Great Britain on the Entente side had resulted in conditions which Italy had not envisaged and under which, so Rome argued, she was relieved of her commitments. Germany and Austria-Hungary accepted, at least outwardly, the accomplished fact of Italian neutrality, but they made anxious overtures to ensure that Italy did not go over to the Entente. In fact, in the race to acquire allies, or at least to deny them to the foe, Italy was wooed by both sides.

Thus she was able to follow a policy which Salandra, the Italian Prime Minister, contrasted with one of sentiment and aptly called *sacro egoismo*. Literally this meant 'sacred egoism'. More broadly it referred to a line of action of exclusive or innate self-interest, and to a policy which aimed at maximum acquisition of territory and prestige at minimum cost.

In Italy's pursuit of *sacro egoismo*, the Allies were from the beginning at an advantage. Italy's longings were directed primarily towards the seven hundred and fifty thousand Italian-speaking inhabitants of *Italia irredenta* ('unredeemed Italy'), an area consisting of part of the Austrian South Tyrol (including the Trentino) and Istria, along with the Habsburg Adriatic port and the hinterland of Trieste. Thus Italy's territorial ambitions were mostly directed against the Dual Monarchy; but despite pressures from Berlin and threats and blackmail from Rome, Vienna refused to cede these territories. Dubious exceptions to this refusal were a probably insincere offer of part of the Trentino in March 1915, followed by a larger concession in May – when it was already too late to keep Italy out of war. On the other hand, the Allies had less to lose (even though they had to be careful not to offend Slav susceptibilities by a magnanimous offer to Italy), so they could promise the Italians considerable gains in return for their aid in achieving victory. Moreover, as 1915 dawned, the Allies became more desperate to break the bloody deadlock in the west via a thrust

into Central Europe from the south, and their offers to Italy increased. However, there were accompanying hints that full belligerency rather than mere neutrality would be exacted in return.

At the same time, other factors drove Italy towards war. Popular Italian sentiment, though hoping for Italian non-belligerency, was firmly in favour of an Entente victory against Austria, Italy's feared and hated rival in the Adriatic and the Balkans. Further, the war faction was dominated by the articulate middle class and included important industrialists and publicists (such as Luigi Albertini of the Milanese liberal newspaper

Opposite: The war between Italy and Austria-Hungary took place largely along their common frontier, the Dolomites. This illustration exaggerates the techniques used but not the terrain over which artillery had to be hauled.

This cartoon shows Italy bravely stringing up the Austrian Eagle. The task was neither so bravely nor so easily accomplished.

Above: Italians cheer their Queen and Princess outside the Royal Palace when Italy declared war on the Central Powers in 1915.
Opposite top: An Italian peasant goes off to war.
Opposite bottom: The Italian Air Force played a limited role in the first campaigns. The pilot, Gabriele d'Annunzio, centre, was Italy's great nationalist poet. He played a crucial role in the seizure of Fiume after the war.

General Count Luigi Cadorna, the Italian Commander, who was inhibited by both circumstances and temperament.

Corriere della Sera). Finally, many leaders of government and captains of industry felt that the war provided a Heaven-sent, now-or-never opportunity for the realization of Italian ambitions. Retrospectively it is thought that as early as October 1914 Salandra had decided to join the Allies if good enough terms could be obtained, a decision provoked by nationalistic ferment.

Italy Declares War

Propelled by these sentiments, Italy declared war against Austria on 23 May, though not against Germany until 27 August 1916. In her pocket lay the Treaty (or, more correctly, the Pact) of London, signed on 26 April 1915 by Italy, Britain, Russia, and France. Though the terms were theoretically secret, their gist was widely rumoured. The Allies had promised Italy that in the event of victory she would receive all of the South Tyrol (Alto Adige) south of the Brenner Pass; Istria (including Trieste) and the northern Dalmatian littoral; the Albanian port of Valona and an Italian protectorate over that country; legalization of her position in the Dodecanese Islands, off the Turkish coast; and a loan of £50,000,000. Moreover, if victory led to a partition of Turkey, Italy would receive a sphere in Asia Minor, as well as suitable booty if Britain and France appropriated the German colonies. In return, Italy was to join the war against all the enemy within one month. In fact, however, this proviso was almost immediately violated by Italy's dilatory declaration of war against Ger-

many, a delay caused mainly by her financial problems.

Thus Italy had joined the war: but the worth of her participation was at best dubious. The Libyan War against Turkey only three years earlier had cost Italy dearly, and in 1915 her military resources were still depleted. Further, Italy lacked sufficient heavy industry and resources of investment for large-scale production of military material. Despite these obstacles, however, she managed to triple the size of her armed forces to nine hundred thousand men by the spring of 1915.

In May 1915, with the Austrian and German offensive in Galicia gaining momentum, some Habsburg divisions could be spared for the Italian front. Seven of these were facing Italy by 23 May. Four days later, General Boroević von Bojna, a Croatian whose valour had been shown at Przemyśl, took command of the Austrian Fifth Army against the Italians. A believer in the importance of solid defences, Boroević immediately ordered that the Austrian troops should construct positions, place obstacles in front of them and remain there.

Italy was poorly placed to open a campaign against her northern neighbour. The contortions of their common frontier left Austria in a position to partition Venetian provinces along the geographically convenient wedge of the Trentino. An Italian offensive into the mountainous Alpine frontier region would be, most literally, an uphill battle against the Austrians poised above her, and, even if successful, would result in no great strategic gain. In the east, the terrain was relatively (and only relatively) less difficult, but it was irregular, bleak and barren country in which any army would find it hard to make headway. As Edmonds emphasizes, Italy's single great advantage was that her lines of interior communication were shorter than those of the enemy. Yet, although troops might be swiftly dispatched between the Trentino and the eastern frontier of the Isonzo River, there was always the danger of an Austrian attack on the rear positions.

It seemed to both sides that the Isonzo front was the easiest area in which to bid for a decision. Even there, however, the Italians were acutely aware that the Austrians, controlling the river crossings and dominating the heights, were well prepared to riddle and decimate any Italian move forward. Piero Pieri notes the paradox of the Italian position: 'The river could not be crossed until the mountains had been seized, and the mountains could not be seized until the river had been crossed.'

Nevertheless, during 1915 the first four Battles of the Isonzo took place. Seven more were to occur before the war was over. For Italy, the campaign became an exercise in futility. At the loss of a quarter of a million men, she failed to prevent the Central Powers' success against Serbia and succeeded in diverting only a dozen Austrian divisions from the east.

In each case the Isonzo fighting was marked by an Italian offensive, for Austria, coping with the campaigns against Serbia and Russia, chose to stand on the defensive. The Italian aim throughout was the immediate gain of the Carso (Karst or Kras) Plateau and the town of Gorizia (Görz), though the ultimate objective remained Trieste and, beyond it, the Danubian plain via the Laibach (Ljubljana) Gap. By this means, the Italians hoped to fulfil their promise to Russia of 16 May to try to join up with the Serbs.

Cadorna's Offensive

Although General Count Luigi Cadorna, the Italian commander, showed perhaps excessive caution and therefore lost several opportunities for action, his methods were circumscribed by the strategic and political facts of life already mentioned. Falls points out a tremendously inhibiting factor: the number of men killed in the Isonzo campaign as a proportion of total casualties was very high indeed, due to the deadly effect of shell explosions disintegrating and scattering the rocks of chalky composition which littered the terrain. An additional trial was the chill mountain wind or *Bora*, to which was later added the lashing autumn rains and bitter winter.

Yet on 24 May, Cadorna launched into a general offensive along the whole front. By 16 June, when the initial phase of operations had ended, the Italians had made some gains in their positions for further tactical operations. However, it was already clear that the campaign would be one of ghastly attrition. Sure enough, the First Battle of the Isonzo 23 June–7 July and the Second 18 July–3 August were both costly and fruitless. Over one hundred thousand casualties were calculated, the majority of them Italian. In the Third

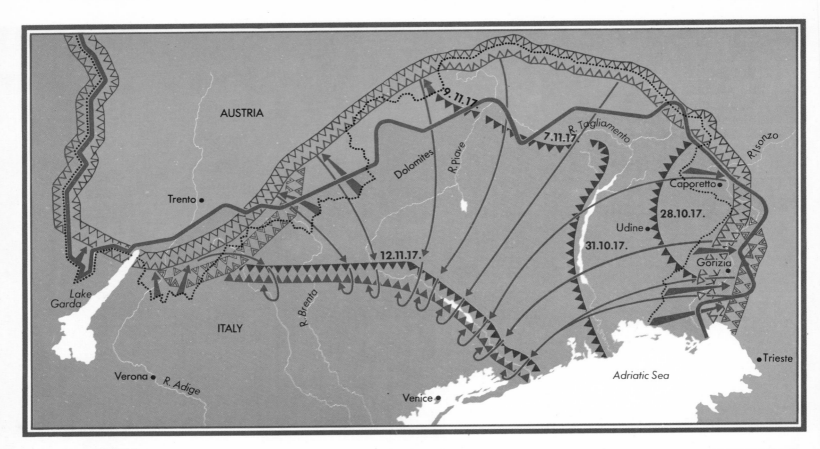

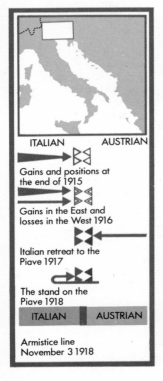

ITALIAN　　　　AUSTRIAN

Gains and positions at
the end of 1915

Gains in the East and
losses in the West 1916

Italian retreat to the
Piave 1917

The stand on the
Piave 1918

ITALIAN　　AUSTRIAN

Armistice line
November 3 1918

Above: The wide, flat
expanse of the Champagne
district was fought over
many times during the first
year of the war.

Battle, 18 October–3 November, and the Fourth,
10 November–2 December, Cadorna introduced
heavier artillery, but its support proved ineffectual against determined and strategically
fortified Austrian defenders. Thus the Italians
displayed 'magnificent valour', as their admiring
enemy termed it, to little avail. Casualties –
again predominantly Italian ones in these two
battles numbered about one hundred and ninety
thousand. The final bitter irony was that for the
Habsburg Empire, the Italian campaign proved a
rallying-point for its diverse nationalities such as
no attack against a Slav state could ever have
been. All in all, the dispassionate observer might
have remarked that in 1915 Italian egoism walked
hand in hand with folly.

Stagnation in the West

Meanwhile, undeterred by the repeated failure
of attempts to break through on the western
front, Joffre decided in March 1915 to launch yet
another offensive, this time in Artois with the
heights of Vimy Ridge as its objective. However,
to launch the attack, it would be necessary first
to have the British relieve the two French corps
north of Ypres; and this was not immediately
possible because of the exigencies of the Gallipoli
campaign and a delay in sending British reinforcements. Independently, French himself believed that the relief of Ypres would leave the
BEF with little energy to help in Artois; and he
decided to support his ally by a separate attack at
Neuve Chapelle. A further motivation was the

Taking soup to the men in
the trenches in Artois.

British commander's wish to improve the somewhat low estimate that the French had formed of British attacking capabilities.

On 10 March, after thirty-five minutes of fierce bombardment to 'soften up' their opponents, the British advanced. The Germans were routed, but soon their brave and adroit retaliation began to yield results. Now the British faltered, giving the Germans time and opportunity to prepare a counterattack which, while it did not gain much ground, at least forced a halt to the British offensive. By 13 March, when the battle ended, losses were approximately equal, with between twelve and thirteen thousand casualties on both sides. British morale remained high. Nevertheless Cruttwell emphasizes the 'short sighted extravagance' of this British 'gamble' in view of the BEF's shortage of ammunition.

On 9 May, after the dreadful interlude of the Second Battle of Ypres, the French offensive in Artois began. Joffre was fortified by the knowledge that the Central Powers' primary attention was in the east, in the major offensive of Gorlice-Tarnów. Brave and well-versed in warfare, the troops now crashed through the German defences, and the thirty-third Corps under General Pétain almost reached the crest of Vimy Ridge. But German reinforcements and a mistaken withholding of French reserves caused the whole shape of the battle to change. The scene altered to one of lengthy and wretched bloodletting which consumed at the very least one hundred thousand French and seventy-five thousand German casualties before the fighting ended on 18 June.

By now the French General Staff had decided that only when the enemy was 'so worn down that he has no reserves available' could victory be grasped. The remedy for the disease of slaughter was . . . more slaughter.

Above left: British artillery, Vimy Ridge. **Above:** A French Colonel, the battle flag of his regiment in his hand, leads an attack in Champagne in 1915. **Left:** The 1st Cameronians prepare for a gas attack.

Overleaf: Italian incursions into Austrian territory were stopped at almost every turn.

At the same time, at Aubers Ridge and Festubert the British were achieving only disappointing results. Throughout this period, especially because of the demands of Gallipoli, ammunition continued to be in short supply. Yet optimism remained unquelled, since the BEF knew that at least they had diverted German forces which would otherwise have been used against the French.

Now a long lull in major operations ensued. The western front lay in stagnation. During this time, the Germans transferred four divisions from the east after successfully concluding their summer offensive. In addition, using civilian forced labour, they rapidly strengthened their defences for the expected onslaught.

Joffre had by now decided that the spring Artois operation had failed because, large as it was, it lacked the necessary magnitude. Moreover, he concluded that the attack had been mounted too narrowly and on only a single front. Now he intended that the Allies should attack broadly on separate fronts, destroying the German power to concentrate reserves and threatening both sides of the German salient. Buoyantly optimistic as ever, Joffre exulted that this would 'compel the Germans to retreat beyond the Meuse and possibly end the war'.

After three days of preparatory bombardment, the French again attacked on 25 September in Champagne. Joffre urged his men to let the enemy have 'neither quarter nor rest until the achievement of victory'. Stirringly he told them, 'Your *élan* will be irresistible'.

As the French moved forward, Joffre described the scene as a 'whirlwind of fire and steel let loose'. Yet after a fierce initial assault, there was no great breakthrough to the Meuse and Belgium, and the Germans counteracted by a second and reinforcing line of defence two to four miles behind the first one. This entrenchment mostly remained intact. Seeing that the result was a deadlock, Joffre halted the offensive on 30 September, but he had by then taken eighteen thousand prisoners and, as Falls says, given the Germans 'a scare to remember'. Early in October the fighting was renewed, but the results were still inconclusive.

Simultaneously the French had plunged into Artois, where the results were even worse than those in Champagne. On 28 September, one division once again attained the crest of Vimy Ridge. However, bad weather ruined any further assault, and the campaign was also affected by the demands of the Salonika operation, which had been theoretically determined on 11 September. Fighting was halted 30 September and renewed 11 October, again inconclusively.

As their contribution to the Artois offensive, the British had fought bravely but unsuccessfully at Loos. As so frequently occurred in the Great War, the battle dragged on beyond its logical time limit, neither side knowing when to cut its losses. After this disappointing operation, Sir John French was relieved of his command of the BEF and replaced by General Sir Douglas Haig.

On the western front in 1915, a frightful bill for dead and wounded was presented, and paid in full. Conservative estimates place French losses at one

hundred and ninety thousand, British at sixty thousand, and German at about one hundred and eighty thousand – all for little or no strategic improvement.

In the view of the German official history, the Allied autumn offensive might have succeeded if it had been made a month or two earlier. Yet at the same time the Allies were unprepared for attack. Might-have-beens are always tantalizing, if unproductive. Whether because of destiny or miscalculation, the close of 1915 found the western front impregnable.

Gas Warfare

In the spring of 1915 the Germans introduced poison gas, in an attempt to regain the initiative in the stagnating west. In January Germany had already used gas against the Russians, but the extreme cold had practically nullified its effect. Now, however, the experts advised that at Ypres winds would be favourable for its experimental use. This fitted in well with the German desire to drive the Allies out of Ypres and its surroundings; for as long as they held positions in the area, the French and the BEF were strategically placed for an eventual offensive against Brussels. Conversely, if the Germans held Ypres, they could threaten the Allied flank and complete their conquest of Belgium.

For three weeks before the first gas attack, captured prisoners had reported that Germany had brought to the front 'enormous tubes of asphyxiating gas'. Yet at the highest level the news had been received with scepticism. As the days went by and nothing happened, no defensive preparations were made. It is possible to rationalize this dangerous neglect. The official history itself notes, 'It was presumed that the effect (of the gas) would be trivial and local.' After all, the Allies reasoned, there were Geneva Conventions prohibiting, in spirit at least, the use of such weapons.

(In discussing the ethics of gas warfare, Cruttwell reminds us that the French had burned men alive with liquid fire in the autumn of 1914. Thus behaviour which ordinary people would condemn

Above: A complex chain of tunnels linked thousands of trenches on both sides of the Western Front. **Far left:** A Russian Commander and his Cossack scout officers observe enemy positions near the wall of Cracow. **Left:** French troops drag German bodies from their trenches.

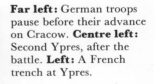

Far left: German troops pause before their advance on Cracow. **Centre left:** Second Ypres, after the battle. **Left:** A French trench at Ypres.

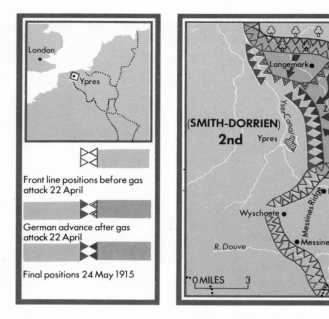

Front line positions before gas attack 22 April

German advance after gas attack 22 April

Final positions 24 May 1915

Opposite top: British wounded. A painting by Eric Kennington. **Opposite left:** Gas warfare at Ypres was no laughing matter. **Opposite right:** There was no rest in the trenches – even at night. **Below:** One of Raemaeker's most bitter cartoons, portraying the Kaiser as the friend of war and starvation.

as immoral was not confined to one side.)

On 22 April, the Germans began a formidably heavy bombardment of enemy positions near Ypres. Suddenly, French colonial troops of the Forty-fifth Algerian Division were seen reeling about, some vomiting, all with their throats and eyes burning. Some men managed to gasp the word, 'gaz'. Swinson quotes one eye witness thus: The troops came forward, 'a panic-stricken rabble . . . with grey faces and protruding eyeballs, clutching their throats and choking as they ran, many of them dropping in their tracks and lying on the sodden earth with limbs convulsed and features distorted in death'. As enveloping clouds of chlorine gas swirled about them, first greenish yellow and then blue white in colour, the troops pelted to safety across the Yser canal, or into the town of Ypres itself. Seeing the pandemonium, General Robertson remarked face-

tiously that, 'there must have been something invigorating about that gas'.

The deadliness of the gas lay in its method of scalding and destroying lung tissue. Full recovery, if at all possible, took a very long time. Moreover, the Allied protective measures were at best piecemeal. Wet handkerchiefs were used, commonly covered with bicarbonate of soda if it were available. Makeshift respirators were put together from lint and tape. In June a protective helmet was introduced, but the box respirator was not employed until August 1916.

As the Germans joined the pursuit, many of them stumbled into their own clouds of gas, while others cautiously hung behind. Meanwhile the British Second Army commander, Smith-Dorrien, undeterred, ordered the Ypres salient to be held and consolidated by available Canadian troops. On 24 April, after disastrous Allied attempts to attack on the previous day, the Canadians suffered severe casualties from a second German gas attack which reached the salient in the form of a cloud fifteen feet high. Somehow they held back the Germans, who also sustained appalling losses. Nevertheless, by the following day the Germans controlled the heights around Ypres, plus much of the salient. They were to prove very difficult to dislodge without a well-prepared offensive.

As we have seen, the French were meanwhile engrossed in preparation for their Artois campaign of early May, although their efforts to attack at Ypres were both fruitless and muddled. After a bitter quarrel between Sir John French and Smith-Dorrien, the latter was replaced. Smith-Dorrien had recommended withdrawal to the environs of Ypres. Ironically, his successor, General Sir Hubert Plumer, was instructed to pursue the very same course. After further debate produced by opposition from Foch, the retreat was successfully accomplished on 1–3 May.

On 8 May, in a terrific attack east of Ypres known as the Battle of Frezenberg Ridge, the Germans again advanced. In six days of bitter fighting, the British, once more deficient in stores and ammunition, retreated. However, the limited German success was gained so catastrophically that further advances were abandoned.

On 24–25 May, in the Battle of Bellewaarde Ridge, German infantry again attacked, using gas on a larger scale than ever, but without much gain. Both sides were now chronically lacking in ammunition, and the Second Battle of Ypres petered out.

Swinson records that 'Second Ypres' was a new kind of battle, in that materials were matched against men. Falls judges that, though the battle was for them 'the biggest success of the year in the west', the Germans could have won a much greater victory had they possessed the means to exploit to the full the strategy of surprise in their use of gas. In any case, though for the Germans the battle had diverted troops which would otherwise have opposed them in Artois, for its size 'Second Ypres' was one of the deadliest clashes of the war. The grisly toll of losses from the month's fighting numbered 60,000 from the British Empire, 10,000 French and up to 47,000 German troops. In the east, the winter Battle of Masuria had inflicted a total of 200,000 casualties (in-

Right and opposite:
Russian uniforms were
elegant and tasteful. The
men that filled them seldom
matched the quality of
their tailors.

cluding prisoners) on the Russians: and yet the
Central Powers had still failed to eliminate Russia
from the war. However, many considered that
internal forces in Russia were preparing for just
such a conclusion. By spring the Russian forces
were battered and attenuated. Ammunition and
even adequate clothing were lacking, while the
soldiers were depressed by letters from home
which could scarcely conceal news of the appalling
shortages of food and an insidious general corruption. In these circumstances, an immediate
Russian offensive was out of the question. And
seeing the state that the Russians were in, Germany and Austria decided to seize what appeared
a golden opportunity to inflict a serious, if not
fatal, blow. Moreover, Conrad for one was still of
the opinion that a successful massive thrust against
Russia would do more than anything else to
influence Italy and Rumania in favour of the
Central Powers. The Allied measures against the
Dardanelles also demanded a reply in the east.

East of Cracow (Kraków) and not far from
Lemberg (Lwów) in the Gorlice-Tarnow area,
the Germans steadily built up their offensive preparations. Unlike Hindenburg, Ludendorff or
Conrad, Falkenhayn did not believe that the
ruination of Russia in one campaign was possible;
but he did think (wrongly, as it turned out) that in
1915 the Austro-German onslaught possessed the
power to cripple Russia 'for an indefinite period'.
On 9 April Falkenhayn took the decision to
attack, and supplies and men were transferred en
masse from the west.

Now 600,000 Germans and 700,000 Austro-
Hungarians faced Russians numbering nearly a
million and three-quarters. With considerable
superiority in artillery and firepower, on 2 May
the German Eleventh Army and the Austrian
Third and Fourth Armies moved forward to the
attack on a twenty-eight mile front. The Russians,
though they expected an offensive, were never sure

where it would come. Now they retreated in dis-
order and panic, and the Central Powers achieved
a complete rout on 4 May. The next day General
Dragmirov, the chief of staff of the Russian South
Western Front, correctly assessed the disastrous
position of his forces when he decided to retreat
behind the river San. Though Grand Duke
Nicholas opposed the idea, further Austro-German
successes caused an order for withdrawal.

By 8 May progress was such that General von
Seeckt, Chief of Staff of the German Eleventh
Army, could exclaim that 'The tactical and
strategical breakthrough has fully succeeded'.
Two days later, as General Radko-Dmitriev
reported that his Russian Third Army had 'bled
to death', a general Russian retreat from the
Carpathians ensued. Grand Duke Nicholas now
pressed strongly for an Allied diversion in the west,
hoping to accelerate Italian involvement in the
war. At least one authority, Kurt Peball, has
described the Central Powers' success thus far as
'the most significant of the war'.

Between 15 and 22 May, the Russians counter-
attacked but achieved only local successes. According to some estimates, the Russians had
now suffered well over 400,000 casualties
and prisoners, and early in June their armies
were described as being reduced to 'a harmless
mob'. Yet, in contradiction to the hopes of Berlin
and Vienna, and despite challenging eastern
successes, Italy had now joined the war on the
side of the Entente.

Still the Austro-German offensive continued,
capturing Lemberg, the Galician capital, on
22 June. Relentlessly, though now more slowly,
the Central Powers moved on, taking Warsaw
4–5 August, after extremely fierce Russian resistance. They seized the charred remains of Brest-
Litovsk on 26 August. By autumn the Central
Powers' offensive had come to a halt and Falkenhayn had decided to stabilize the front – for

Germany and Austria-Hungary had outstretched their communications; Russia had counter-attacked; Italy was making herself felt; a new Allied campaign was in preparation in the west; and Serbia had to be vanquished to relieve the supply routes to Turkey. Hindenburg, however, was determined to attack further, and Vilna fell on 18 September. Still, by December the Russians had been thrown back a considerable distance, as far as Riga in the north and the extremities of the Carpathians in the east.

The end of 1915 saw the close of a year in which the Russians had lost a million casualties and a further million prisoners. In a desperate attempt to save the situation, the Tsar himself had taken supreme command of the armies in September, swearing to, 'fulfil our sacred duty to defend our country to the last'. Somehow, miraculously, the Russian giant had lurched and tottered its way through another year without collapsing. Despite their brilliant victories, the Central Powers had failed to drive the Tsar to sue for peace. Now the care worn and decimated Russian troops rested behind a green and watery barrier of lakes and forests, resolved to renew the fighting with the coming of spring.

CHAPTER SEVEN

From Verdun to the Somme

Below: General Haig, General Joffre and Prime Minister Lloyd George debate the slaughter of Verdun and the Somme.

With the opening of 1916, the Great War had crystallized. With a kind of dull fatalism and dawning realization, the nations pondered on the destruction in lives and materials that was to leave the world, and especially Europe, changed forever. All the belligerents were drawing on their last reserves of men and goods. Their financial resources were for the most part meagre or nonexistent. In the latter case, the nations went up to the hilt into debt, struggling to achieve that overwhelming victory which had as yet eluded them.

Yet still the fundamental question remained unsolved: how was a breakthrough in the west to be achieved? Almost everyone was more than ever convinced that the war would be won or lost only on the western front. The alternatives were uninviting. For the Central Powers the eastern campaigns of 1915 had been brilliantly successful, though, like a mirage, decisive victory had shimmered away from them into the vastness of the Russian hinterland. The Russians had, nevertheless, reeled back, and the Germans could afford to concentrate westward sufficient forces possibly to extort a decision in France. For the Allies, 1915 had brought the Dardanelles fiasco, and no great victory anywhere else in compensation. Furthermore, prevailing opinion was that no very suitable back door to the west was to be found in theatres such as Italy, Macedonia or the Baltic. Most important of all, neither side dared risk denuding the western front of troops to win a victory, however great, elsewhere, lest the opponent take advantage of the situation to press home a decisive thrust in France or Flanders. Fearing that the other side would take the initiative, each set of belligerents concluded that an attack was imperative. In the end, the Germans got in their blow first. Falkenhayn for one had been spurred on by the thought that only an attack would delay the Anglo-French build-up of superiority in material.

Pondering on where to attack in the west, Falkenhayn was impressed with what he saw as 'the ever-dwindling power of resistance and the limited ability of the French people to hold out'. Falkenhayn surmised that if France fell, surely Russia would finally cave in and sue for peace. Then England would be left alone – and in all probability unable to continue the fight. (In these larger calculations, Italy and the smaller powers were largely discounted.)

The Carnage of Verdun

Thus the key question was: how to deal the French a death blow? Falkenhayn decided to attack Verdun, the key fortress in eastern France. If Verdun quickly fell, the loss would shatter French prestige irreparably. As the German Crown Prince remarked, 'Verdun is the heart of France'. Yet an actual German breakthrough was not necessary (though there is some evidence that in fact Falkenhayn hoped for this). What was necessary and likely was to trap the French into making Verdun a mystic symbol. If only France would defend Verdun to the last man, the balance of manpower in the west would swing in Germany's favour. Thus Falkenhayn's motives for standing at Verdun were complex. Liddell Hart has argued that perhaps Falkenhayn was an opportunist keeping all his options open. If the French suffered a sudden moral collapse, well and good. If not, he would see what happened next, being not very clear in his own mind what to do. There may also have been the consideration that the British would panic at the threat to Verdun and launch a disastrously premature offensive on the Somme or elsewhere. Naturally the acquisition of Verdun, would strengthen the German front, for the Verdun complex linked the northern and eastern parts of the French line facing the Germans, and the outer defences came within a dozen miles of Metz and Sedan, the keys to any German effort in Champagne. It seems that above all, Falkenhayn was attracted by the idea of threatening Verdun with only a modest number of troops and then drawing the French into a snare where heavy artillery would pound them to dust. What he apparently forgot was that the symbolism of Verdun might work both ways, and that it might not be possible for Germany to decide when to withdraw from the campaign without losing her own prestige. This miscalculation was to prove disastrous for Germany – and for Falkenhayn himself.

In early December 1915, the Allies had decided that each should launch a simultaneous attack as soon as this could be coordinated. Joffre, now supreme commander of all French military forces, proposed an offensive on the Somme. The British supremo, Haig, had reservations, but finally agreed for the sake of Allied solidarity. Meanwhile, the Russians would do their best to retrieve their own position, and the Italians would renew the Isonzo struggle. Anticipating these plans, however, the Germans struck first.

In describing the Verdun campaign, Paul Valéry called it 'a kind of duel before the universe, a singular and almost symbolic tourney'. Perhaps the epic proportions of the horror of the battle made men think and hope that an issue of similarly epic moral purpose was being decided. But whatever the moral implications, Verdun in 1916 was the scene of unsurpassed carnage. The holocaust was never exceeded and seldom equalled. When speaking of the abattoir of the First World War, this description may sound extreme, but it is nonetheless justified.

In contrast with the flat terrain of Flanders or the Somme, Verdun was surrounded by hills and ridges which provided superb positions of defence. On the heights were built three concentric circles of underground forts, their guns emplaced so as to dislodge all but the most vast and relentless waves of infantry. The forts lay five to ten miles from Verdun itself, and in between was placed a veritable network of trenches, barbed wire, and other ingenious impediments. Unfortunately, however, the defences of Verdun had been badly neglected. Many guns had been removed for use elsewhere, and the relative inactivity in this area had lulled the men into a deceptive calm. Lieutenant Colonel Emile Driant made only trouble for himself when he warned the imperturbable Joffre of this.

Perhaps with undeserved luck, the French were

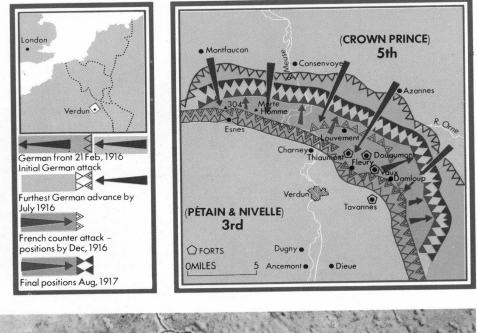

German front 21 Feb, 1916
Initial German attack

Furthest German advance by
July 1916

French counter attack –
positions by Dec, 1916

Final positions Aug, 1917

London

Verdun

(CROWN PRINCE)
5th

Montfaucon
Consenvoye
Meuse
Azannes
304 Morte
Homme
R. Orne
Esnes
Louvement
Charney
Thiaumont
Fleury
Douaumont
Vaux
Damloup
Verdun
Tavannes

(PÉTAIN & NIVELLE)
3rd

☿ FORTS
0 MILES   5
Dugny
Ancemont   Dieue

presented at the outset with a hindrance to the German plans. Bad weather caused a nine-day delay in operations. Had this been otherwise, the Germans would have opened the offensive with vastly superior odds, and the French would have had little opportunity to carry out essential repairs to roads and bridges.

On 21 February the German bombardment began. Never in history had such a formidable load of shells and firepower been unleashed. The rumbling from the pounding artillery could be heard one hundred miles away. The violence of the attack was itself enough to annihilate or disintegrate the badly prepared French trenches. One hapless regiment saw eighteen hundred of its two thousand men blown up or mown down. Countless others were buried alive.

Yet already the Germans had made a bad mistake. The Crown Prince, within whose command Verdun was to be fought, wanted to encircle the fortresses by simultaneous attacks on both banks of the river Meuse. Given the French lack of preparedness, this would probably have succeeded. But Falkenhayn decided against releasing the large number of men who would be needed, and only the right bank was attacked.

On the first day of fighting, the Germans moved forward in a probing action. Next day the incredible bombardment continued. Somehow the French held on despite their bloody losses. By the third day, whole units at a time were annihilated and confusion spread. The unfortunate French also added to their own losses by mistakenly shelling some of their own trenches. By 24 February, no amount of heroism could hold the French line. The continuing bombardment smashed it to atoms. Yet despite their gains, the Germans had already met with more opposition than they had expected, and their losses, already great, bred caution. Moreover, between the two sides a barrier intervened the chains of fortresses, including Douaumont, the strongest.

But on 25 February events took a completely unexpected turn. Fort Douaumont, negligently left ungarrisoned, was taken almost absent-

Above left: Aerial view of Fort de Vaux. **Far left:** The Germans attack at Fort de Vaux. **Left:** Lieutenant Rackow, the fanatical German officer who was the first to penetrate Fort de Vaux.

Opposite top left: Gassed in the trenches. **Opposite top right:** Crown Prince Wilhelm. **Right:** The Germans press forward at Verdun.

mindedly by a German patrol. Public opinion in France reeled with shock, while the more sober calculated that the disaster would cost the lives of 100,000 Frenchmen. Throughout Germany, church bells pealed in jubilation at the coup.

Now, at the very moment of France's unfathomable gloom, General Henri-Philippe Pétain arrived at Verdun to take command. Efficient and unhurried, he set himself to organize the men and raise their morale. His encouraging phrase, *ils ne passeront pas* (they shall not pass) became immortal. Under Pétain's inspiration the French perked up. Along the road from Bar-le-Duc, the vital lifeline of Verdun, lorries began to bring a steady stream of supplies. Men referred to this as *la voie sacrée* (the sacred road). During the first week of March alone, 190,000 men trod its path, to add their weight to the struggle.

By 28 February French artillery fire had helped to cause the German attack to falter. During a relative pause in the battle, Falkenhayn considered breaking off the offensive, but rejected the idea because German losses had not yet reached intolerable proportions. Moreover, a new offensive elsewhere would take too long to stage. He therefore agreed to extend the fighting across the Meuse after all.

By about 8 March, the Germans had carved out a holding position across the Meuse, and a titanic battle ensued for possession of the dominating positions. One of the fiercest concerned a ridge with the macabrely appropriate name of Mort Homme. Throughout the spring the battle for its crest waved murderously back and forth.

By April the French counterattacks were both fierce and frequent, but they could only circumscribe the German advance. To add to the impersonal hideousness of the fighting, men by the thousand died from long-range artillery fire, with many infantrymen never catching sight of the enemy. The French and Germans together had already lost over 160,000 men.

Right: The horror of
Verdun was matched only
by the bloodbath of the
Somme. Below right: The
landscape around Verdun
became a surrealistic scene
of twisted limbs and
ravaged earth.

air and morsel of food. The survivors betrayed in their glazed or dilated eyes the nameless horror of their experiences. Some moved about with their frames bent over with physical and nervous exhaustion. Scores of men went mad from strain; others existed in wooden or hypnotic insensitivity. Even the most stolid and brave of men were unlikely to have escaped unscathed.

The French at least had had the advantage of frequent rotation of their troops at the front line. The Germans had never adopted this policy. On the other hand, the fact that higher numbers of Frenchmen than Germans passed through the 'mincing machine' of Verdun had a disastrous effect on the French reserves of manpower. His concern at these developments was among the reasons why Joffre replaced Pétain by promoting him; another was that Pétain was suspected of being too much moved by the catastrophe. He was succeeded by Generals Robert Nivelle and Charles 'the Butcher' Mangin.

On 26 May Joffre had appealed to Haig to bring forward the date of the Somme offensive. If it were left until 15 August, said Joffre, 'The French Army would cease to exist . . '. Thus the opening of the Somme campaign was set for 1 July.

At Verdun the grisly tale continued. After a week of assaults, on 7 June the Germans captured Fort Vaux, the French northeastern bastion. The fort was surrendered only when its 600 defenders had gone two complete days without water. As they wallowed in putrefaction, their thirst had reduced them to drinking urine.

Yet at this point the Brusilov offensive in the east forced Falkenhayn to transfer needed troops to prop up the Austrians. On 21 June the Germans attacked using phosgene gas. The French held on, but they were at breaking point. Only the knowledge of the imminent Somme offensive held them together, although Verdun had already reduced the French contribution to the Somme from forty to sixteen divisions, of which only five were ready by 1 July.

By 11 July, when the final German offensive at Verdun failed, the scene of the most crucial fighting had been transferred to the Somme. Henceforth the Germans stood on the defensive, though the casualties at Verdun continued to mount.

The total bill for Verdun was between 315,000 and 377,000 French killed or wounded. These were matched by 337,000 Germans. Of the dead, at least 150,000 were never buried, but simply rotted where they lay. No wonder one distracted eyewitness croaked that 'the earth around us was literally stuffed with corpses'.

Jacques Meyer wrote that Verdun 'was a French victory only in the sense of an invincible resistance'. Neither could the Germans claim success. If they had reduced the ranks of Frenchmen, they had lost as much themselves.

In the autumn the French had been able to rally for a limited counter-attack, and Douaumont and Vaux were recaptured, with Nivelle scoring further French successes in December. Yet the futility of the sacrifice of so many lives was underlined by the fact that at the end of the year the adversaries were very nearly at the positions they had held in early 1916.

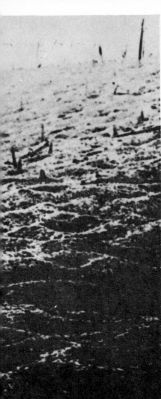

Finally the Germans overcame the defenders of Mort Homme, only to be faced with French gun emplacements on the ridge known as Côte 304. More German divisions had to be thrown in, however much this went against the grain for Falkenhayn. By May the Germans had more or less cleared the left bank of the Meuse, but at such cost that even Falkenhayn wondered if the fight should be abandoned. Yet German honour made this impossible, as he and others grimly saw upon reflection.

The landscape around Verdun had become a scene of surrealistic and nauseating horror. Deep craters gouged out by shells gaped everywhere. At frequent intervals limbs protruded from the ravaged soil, torn from torsos by the merciless artillery fire. Everywhere, wrote Jacques Meyer, were 'distended bodies that your foot sank into'. The stench of death hung over the jumble of decaying corpses like some hellish perfume. As chaos reigned, many wounded died of gangrene or exhaustion. As the weather turned warmer, the reek of the charnel house invaded every breath of

Far left: Gas burning after the capture of Fort Douaumont. **Centre left:** Fort Douaumont, after its capture. **Left:** The German onslaught at Verdun. **Below:** The Germans attack on the Somme from their positions in some ruined farm buildings.

Battle of the Somme

The Battle of the Somme raged from 1 July to 18 November, taking up all of the British energy in the west for 1916. Here, against some of the strongest German western defences, the Allied attack was undertaken, with the British for the first time bearing the brunt in a major western front offensive. At the Somme was suffered a holocaust of misery and dying equal to that of Verdun, and the casualties were even higher: 650,000 Germans, 420,000 Britons and 195,000 French-men. Together the battles marked the decimation of European manhood.

Topography played an outstanding role in the Somme campaign. The battle area was mostly devoid of important geographical features, with one exception: the Ginchy-Thiepval ridge. Here the German second positions looked down on the Allied lines. Although there was some advantage to be gained from artillery fire uphill, the exposed Allied positions meant that there could be no element of surprise against the foe. However,

Above: Wounded had to be carried off the battlefield under fire.
Right: The British trenches were to become a hell of stench and pain.
Far right: The Germans dug in and held despite heavy bombardment.
Below: The Somme gave the British a chance to go over the top to their deaths.

though they could see from preparations in the spring the battle that was to come, the Germans at that moment lacked the troops to stage a preventive attack. Instead, Falkenhayn decided to deal with the problem of Brusilov in the east, then carry out a decisive counterattack' in the west. In any case, until July Falkenhayn appeared to believe that the Allied preparations were so obvious as to constitute a red herring while the real attack would be staged further north.

Contrary to former theories, Haig fully intended and hoped for a breakthrough at the Somme. Unlike Joffre or, to some extent, Rawlinson, the British Fourth Army commander, Haig was not satisfied with attrition. Yet Rawlinson's doubts made disaster of the British plans. Liddell Hart points out that Rawlinson's advocacy of prolonged bombardment lessened the chance for that element of surprise which would have compensated for limited British artillery and the depth of the German position; while Rawlinson's wish to advance in limited stages hampered the exploita-

Below left: The attacks continued throughout the night. **Below:** Canadian troops were sent against the Germans – to no avail.

tion of successes by giving the Germans the time to recover and bring up reinforcements. Moreover, it appears that Rawlinson disastrously overestimated the destructive power of his own long-range artillery.

The Germans had been dug in on the Somme for nearly two years. During this time they had excavated trenches to a depth of forty feet, and these were impervious to damage from all but the heaviest shells. Churchill called these lines 'undoubtedly the strongest and most perfectly defended position' on any battlefield.

'Murderous Fire'

After seven days of heavy bombardment, which the Germans called 'murderous fire', the British had failed to make an impact on the German dugouts, though by weight of metal alone they had wiped out many of the enemy's front-line trenches. Worst of all, the ground ahead lay covered with barbed wire, which the bombardment had completely failed to break up. It is thus the more odd that the eve of battle found the British optimistic.

Early on the morning of 1 July, nearly 100,000 soldiers advanced shoulder to shoulder from their trenches. Moving forward at a slow walk because of their battle-kit of 66 to 90 lb. in weight, the infantry were perfect targets. German machine guns mowed them down until the ground was littered with corpses. That day, the strength of many battalions was reduced to one hundred men. In terms of losses for the British, 1 July 1916 was the blackest day of the war. Over 57,000 men fell, including nearly 20,000 dead. These casualties numbered 60 per cent of the officers and 40 per cent of the soldiers engaged; and the losses would have been higher had not many soldiers broken ranks and using their common sense, worked or crawled their way forward in small groups.

South of the Somme, and in the context of a smaller attack altogether, the French were brilliantly successful. The terrain was more favourable, their tactics were less wooden-headed, and the German defences in this area were weaker. In addition, the French had concentrated a larger amount of heavy artillery, and to a degree the French attack in this quarter had been unexpected. Troops under Fayolle had almost made a breakthrough. Yet none of this could obliterate the fact that the major attack in the British sector had been a disaster of the first magnitude. Cruttwell criticizes this attack as coming too late in the day, and cites the disadvantages of poor quality ammunition, lack of gas shells, and the spreading of the offensive in virtually equal strength along a too-wide front.

Now, by any reasonable standard, Haig might have been expected to give up the attempt at the Somme. The official history gives the opinion that if as an alternative he had pressed the assault at Messines, which was to achieve success the following year, it would have had 'a far better chance of decisive result, especially if combined with a coastal attack . . '. Only a few weeks earlier Haig had hinted at such an operation if the Somme offensive 'met with considerable opposition'. By any definition, the opposition on 1 July was 'considerable'! Perhaps obstinacy in the face of disappointment influenced Haig, but it is also certain

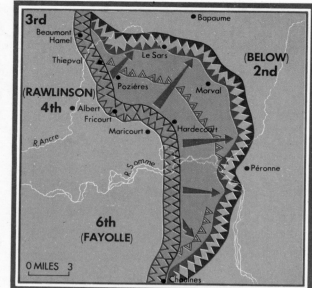

Front line positions 1 July, 1916

Allied advance by 15 Sept

Final phase (introduction of tanks) and final positions 19 November

Opposite far left: Soldier on leave to his girlfriend: 'I like your dress but isn't it a bit short?' Her reply: 'Well, in wartime we all have to cut down.' *Poilus* often doubted, with good reason, that their sufferings were shared on the Home Front. **Left:** General Rawlinson, the British Fourth Army Commander. **Opposite below:** On the art of camouflage: 'War, as far as the artillery is concerned, is developing into a fancy dress ball.' Immunity from destruction was the prize for the best costume. **Right:** A well-fortified trench, reminiscent of a coalmine. **Below:** A pause in the carnage of the Somme.

that he had not been told of the full extent of British casualties. Loyalty or sycophancy from Haig's subordinates explains a great deal of his decision to carry on fighting. When on 3 July he did finally learn of the frightful losses, Haig decided to concentrate on the right, and the battle proceeded on a smaller scale.

The second great assault of the campaign began on 14 July. Rawlinson attacked by night, with Bazentin Ridge as his objective. The French and Haig alike were sceptical, the former describing the idea as 'an attack organized for amateurs by amateurs'. But afterwards the French had to eat their words, for the British managed to breach the German second positions. A liaison officer spoke for all when he reported: '*Ils ont osé. Ils ont reussi*'! ('The British have dared; and they have succeeded'.)

This success raised the British hopes, but they were only to be dashed. The higher command reacted with maddening lethargy, and the fruits of victory fell through their fingers. Too much time was given for the Germans to rally, and Haig at least temporarily became resigned to attrition as an end in itself. But at least by this time, the Somme had relieved the pressure on Verdun.

August saw the peak of attrition, *la guerre d'usure*, with slaughter on both sides resulting in fractional gains or none at all. Sometimes the objectives of the fighting were piled high with bodies by the time they were attained. Yet Haig still entertained hopes that by mid-September the Germans would be sufficiently worn down for an Allied breakthrough to be attempted. Meanwhile several fortified positions were secured, and though their efforts to eliminate the salient around Thiepval were unsuccessful, the British were able to reduce its size somewhat during the fighting of early August.

On 23 August German losses of men and destruction of morale reached such proportions that General von Below of the First Army was forced to modify Falkenhayn's earlier ruthless order that 'It must be a principle in trench warfare not to abandon a foot of ground, and if a foot of ground be lost to put in the last man to recover it by an immediate counter-attack'. Indeed, Falkenhayn himself was forced to resign on 28 August. The ostensible reason was Rumania's entry into the war on the Entente side, but actually his departure was due to German losses at Verdun and the Somme without visible compensatory successes. Hindenburg, assisted by Ludendorff, replaced him. They found much evidence of low morale at the front, intensified by depression at Allied command of the air. In the last stages of the campaign there were some desertions and voluntary surrenders, as the Germans saw their own losses surpassing even those of the enemy.

On 4 September the French Tenth Army joined their Sixth Army compatriots in the affray, but their initial successes soon turned into a confused collapse. Meanwhile Hindenburg ordered a holding operation on all fronts, with the object of utilizing 'all other available sources' against Rumania. On the fifteenth, Haig mounted an assault along a ten-mile front from Combles to beyond Thiepval. The battle is known as Flers-Courcelette, and it lasted a week. Tanks were used

The war of attrition cost hundreds of thousands of lives on both sides.

Right: The Somme – the aftermath. **Below:** *Barrage on the Somme* – a painting by Hamlyn Reid. **Bottom:** German machine gunners who survived the intensive barrage cut down their attackers mercilessly.

in war for the first time, but to less than full effect. Subsequently a storm of criticism was directed at Haig, since by using tanks prematurely and in insufficient numbers he revealed their existence without a major gain in return. Yet it was hard to decide when to put the tanks into use, and knowledge of the new weapon might well have leaked out before the moment for their optimum employment had arisen. Moreover, Rumanian belligerency was believed to have strained the German nerves to breaking-point; and it was thought that the introduction of a new weapon might now cause them to snap altogether.

On 25 September the Allies moved forward again. Two days later, and with the help of a single tank, Thiepval fell. The defence was heroic and inflicted highly disproportionate casualties through hand-to-hand fighting. Allied intelligence reported that the Germans had now lost at least three hundred and seventy thousand men (actually an underestimate), and thus Haig was tempted into preparations for another attack towards mid-October. But on 2 October the weather threatened to defeat both sides. Incessant autumn rains brought mud, slime, and yet more mud. This made it impossible to move forward at any certain pace, and objectives had to be gained via small and very costly localized attacks. In Cruttwell's graphic description, 'The battle degenerated into a series of desperate nibbles at a medley of shell-holes hastily strung together and called a trench'. Yet Joffre doggedly insisted that the campaign continue, while Haig urged on the British.

After fighting at Transloy Ridges and Ancre Heights, in mid-November the British achieved success in the area of the Ancre river, a tributary of the Somme. The field fortress of Beaumont-Hamel was captured 'a particularly heavy blow', as Ludendorff noted. The Somme campaign ended on 18–19 November amid abysmal blizzards and torrential rain.

Like Falkenhayn, Joffre had seen his plan of attrition boomerang against his own armies. Verdun had not fallen, but neither had strategic gains been made. Indeed, the British had felt that the Somme was a battle fought in an area devoid of strategic objectives, and one which was launched before sufficient resources had been marshalled. The Allies paid dearly for deficiencies in heavy howitzers and ammunition at the Somme, even though these disadvantages were offset to a considerable extent by the heroic determination of the British Army. This stamina is the more remarkable when one remembers that the British Army had been hastily improvised to fight a highly professional German force.

Perhaps the long-term effects of Verdun and the Somme were the most significant. Certainly the French decimation led to the 1917 mutinies. Beyond this, Pétain and other Frenchmen drew the wrong conclusions from Verdun, which resulted in the postwar Maginot Line of fortifications. Most disastrous of all was the effect of the Verdun experience on the three out of every four Frenchmen under arms who passed through it. Here was born that attitude of fatalism and defeatism which came to fruition in 1940, with Pétain as its tragically appropriate instrument.

Above: A German
painting of the Somme
battlefield as viewed from
a balloon. **Left:** The
devastation of the Somme
created a crisis of morale in
the Allied armies.

CHAPTER EIGHT
Eastern Tangled Webs

In the western world, recent history has provided for a variety of vaccination against the horrors of genocide. Within the span of a single generation, mankind has witnessed the ovens of Auschwitz, and the disasters of Biafra and Bangladesh. Yet man's existence is largely made up of dealing with a succession of ordinary problems and simple joys, and in contrast both the repetition and the sheer magnitude of such disasters has made genocide for many a matter to be put aside. Our minds are incapable of grasping the extent or significance of such tragedies.

The First World War has the unenviable distinction of being the scene of the first such holocaust of modern times. Its hapless victims were the Armenians, one of the numerous minorities within the polyglot Ottoman Empire. The first mark against them was that they were Christians within a largely Islamic autocracy; the second was that they were a relatively prosperous community surrounded by backwardness and sloth. Many Turks regarded this close-knit community of go-ahead infidels as a thorn in the side of the nation. Over the centuries, their numbers had been greatly reduced by slaughter, forced conversion to Islam, or emigration. More recently, pressure from European nations had caused the authorities to agree to instigate certain reforms. In practice, however, reform was never seriously attempted, and resentment of outside interference in these matters bred in the Turks a cruel determination to put an end to such complaints by a removal of the sources of the outcry.

In 1896 at least 80,000 Armenians had been slaughtered. This was a pale shadow of what was to come. With the outbreak of the Great War, chauvinist Young Turks saw their chance to annihilate the Armenian nation. Measure of strict internal control could be taken under the guise of wartime necessity, and thus the butchery could be disguised with relative ease until it was too late for others, even if willing, to intervene.

Carefully the Turks laid down their plans. First to be eliminated would be the 100,000 Armenian conscripts within the Ottoman armed forces. Next, Armenian community leaders throughout the empire would be arrested and silenced. Finally, the remaining Armenians would be taken from their homes and deported to die in the desert of thirst, sunstroke, or starvation. Implementation of this 'final solution' was entrusted to an assimilated Bulgarian gypsy, the Interior Minister, Talaat Bey, himself the descendant of a misunderstood and persecuted minority.

The Turco-Russian campaign in the Caucasus provided an additional pretext for persecution, for now the Turks alleged that a pro-Russian Armenian fifth column had conspired in Turkey's defeat. Consequently, in early 1915 the first part of the extermination campaign, that involving Armenian conscripts, was carried out successfully and secretly in an atmosphere white-hot with murderous fanaticism. Then in April one thousand leading Armenians in Constantinople were sent away and butchered.

It is human nature not to face the unendurable,

Left: Serbian refugees crowded the roads during the retreat of 1915. **Right:** A million and a half Armenians were exterminated by 1916. The world was largely indifferent to their fate.

and the Armenians were no exception. They were unable to visualize the extent of the intended infamy, and anyway could do little to help themselves against the operations of an efficient and merciless authority. In May the community leaders were murdered, and only large numbers of women and children remained, easy prey for their tormentors. Lest officialdom feel any wince of compassion, Talaat instructed that 'the Government . . . decided to destroy completely all Armenians living in Turkey . . . An end must be put to their existence, however criminal the measures taken may be, and no regard must be paid to either age or sex nor to conscientious scruples'.

Throughout the summer and autumn of 1915, mass deportations of Armenians proceeded apace. Arshag Sarkissian, most recent chronicler of the disaster, has described the scene: The people would be told to assemble in a central locale, and there they would learn that the government had decided to move them to 'better and safer areas'. Since (so they were told) the journey would be short, the Armenians need bring only a few of their possessions. The more infirm would be transported in ox-driven carts (probably for the sake of speed, and certainly not from compassion), while

the rest would go on foot. En route, many would be disposed of to hasten the journey, though time was always at hand for interruptions in the march for rape and orgies, corruption of young girls and boys alike. Finally, in the desert, the Armenians would be cut down or left to die except for those deemed attractive enough to grace a harem.

As in other infamous slaughters, heroic resistance took place, but in uncoordinated pockets, on a relatively small scale, and in an atmosphere of utter hopelessness against superior odds. In the summer of 1915 a quarter of a million Armenians managed to escape to Russia. These were exceptions. Of the two million Armenians within the Ottoman Empire in 1914, about one and a half million of them had disappeared from the face of the earth by 1916. German and other representations against the bloodbath were at first hotly denied; afterwards most protests were shunted aside with mutterings about other nations minding their own business. Later tyrants were to mark well the indifference with which the world as a whole greeted the Armenian tragedy. As Hitler remarked on the eve of the Second World War, 'After all, who remembers today the extermination of the Armenians'?

LA JOURNÉE SERBE
25 JUIN 1916
ANNIVERSAIRE DE LA BATAILLE DE KOSSOVO

DEVAMBEZ G. PARIS

The Serbian Débâcle

On the Serbian front, 1915 found the Balkan Kingdom in an appalling state. Serbia's armies had already been decimated by successive battles with Austria-Hungary. The soldiers had been ravaged by typhus, as indeed had much of the peasantry. After the Austrian-German Gorlice-Tarnów offensive, the Serbians required more assistance than ever but little was forthcoming. The British and French were preoccupied with the western front, and their efforts to persuade Bulgaria to remain neutral were unsuccessful. For their part, the Serbs had never believed much in the possibility of Bulgarian neutrality, for the enmity caused by the Second Balkan War of 1913 was too recent to have been assuaged. As for Bulgaria herself, she was infatuated with the idea of territorial gain, and believing Berlin and Vienna to be in a better position to fulfil their promises, she sided with the Central Powers. Probably only the fall of Constantinople could have persuaded her to do otherwise, since the Bulgars harboured the fiercest of irredentist ambitions against Serbian Macedonia, and the king was a Russophobe. Now plans were formulated for a coordinated German-Austrian-Bulgar attack on Serbia, and these were carried out when the last Bulgarian reservations disappeared with the Allied debacle at Gallipoli.

Falkenhayn's original interest in the subjection of Serbia was in order to utilize the Belgrade-Sofia section of the Constantinople railway which ran through the north east corner of the country. Germany felt that until all of the route to Constantinople lay under her control, the capacity of Turkey for remaining in the conflict was under constant threat. But Italy's entry into the war and her efforts to link up with Serbian forces persuaded Falkenhayn that Serbia was a threat to be stamped underfoot completely.

The armies of the Central Powers, though they held numerical superiority, expected difficulties in moving into Serbia. Communications in the region were primitive, and the barren and semi-mountainous terrain offered meagre comfort in the way of billets or supplies. Nevertheless, on 7 October 1915 the Austrians and Germans swarmed across the Sava and Danube rivers, and Belgrade fell to them two days later. On 11 October, by prearranged plan, the Bulgarian First Army moved against Serbia from the east. Yet subsequent progress was slow, and the Serbs retreated south and southeast out of the way of defeat. Meanwhile, Bulgarian forces cut off the Serbian escape-route to Salonika, and an Allied force arrived in the Vardar valley too late and too enfeebled to be of consequence. Yet despite the onset of winter snows, the lack of food and countless other privations, 150,000 men of the Serbian Army escaped to Albania in what Esposito rightly terms 'one of the most dramatic and difficult retreats in history'. In the process the Serbs were forced to discard much of their transport and artillery. But though they had suffered 100,000 casualties and lost 160,000 men as prisoners, the remaining Serbs had lived to fight another day. The furious Austrians salved their pride by swallowing fierce but tiny Montenegro.

In 1915 the Allies had embarked on their Macedonian adventure. The origins of the Salonika expedition were complex. In the winter of 1914–15 many had thought that relief might be brought to the western front by a northwestward thrust into Central Europe via the Danube, much as the Turks had done in earlier centuries, and in France a leading exponent of this idea was the Fifth Army commander, General Franchet d'Esperey. Then on 26 January 1915 the Greek Prime Minister, Eleutherios Venizelos, had offered to commit his country's forces to the Entente if Bulgarian or Rumanian aid were also secured. In particular Venizelos urged that if Bulgaria refused benevolent neutrality or alliance with the Entente, Allied troops should be sent to the Balkans to dissuade Bulgaria from siding with the Central Powers. At the same time Lloyd George favoured a display of force at the Greek Aegean port of Salonika in order to win the support of all the Balkan states and thereby crush Austria.

The practical difficulties were great. Salonika (Thessaloniki) was a port with limited facilities, and the railway northwards to the Serbian Danube positions was only a single-line track, which could not easily handle an army of any considerable size, yet which could be widened only with great difficulty and delay. On the other hand, the very inhospitality of the country was a factor in dissuading the Germans from attempts to corner the Allies. In the interim the Gallipoli campaign was occupying the forefront of attention, and the Macedonian issue temporarily receded into the background.

In June 1915, however, Joffre's sacking of General Maurice Sarrail because of the heavy losses in the west made it necessary to find the latter a new command. At the same time Paris had been actively considering the dispatch of further forces to the east, in addition to commitments at the Dardanelles. As the Gallipoli campaign turned into an obvious failure, the French persisted in their idea of a Salonika landing, and on 11 September the British agreed to contribute two divisions. A final decision on the worth of the Macedonian operation would be made after the Franco-British autumn campaigns in the west; but before this it became obvious that an attack by the Central Powers on Serbia was imminent. On 22 September the Serbs appealed for 150,000 Entente troops to be sent to her aid via Salonika. Three days later Bulgarian general mobilization persuaded the British to stand behind the Macedonian project, both in order to aid Serbia and in the hope that Greece could be persuaded to secure the Siberian flank against the Bulgars.

Greece, however, declined to fulfil her vaguely-worded obligations to her Serbian ally. Matters were further entangled by differing interpretations of the ill-defined commitments entered into in 1829 at the time of the creation of independent Greece. The British, French, and Russians argued that as protectors of the state under the 1829 agreement, they had the right to send troops to Greek territory. The Greek king, Constantine, and the army leaders denied this. Certainly in the course of the succeeding year the Allies made grave violations of Greek sovereignty, all of which the Entente excused to themselves under the formula 'reason of state'. As for Venizelos, his

position was supremely opportunistic. By co-operating with the Allies, he believed that Greece would gain territory at Turkish expense.

On 3 October one British and one French division arrived at Salonika from the Dardanelles. Venizelos had secretly consented to the landing, even though the Greek government felt obliged to issue a formal protest against this apparent assault on its neutral rights. However, by this time the whole atmosphere surrounding the Macedonian venture had become permeated with trickery and double-dealing, and the British began to have the gravest doubts concerning the project. Yet for the moment their support continued. Early in October the British and French agreed to send five further divisions to Macedonia; and by now Serbia had been invaded. A new crisis arose when, because of new disagreements with the Germano-phile king, Venizelos again resigned as Greek prime minister. The air was electric with political uncertainty, when as we have seen, an Allied force was sent up the Vardar valley to aid the Serbs. But eventually the ambivalence of the Greek attitude, the Bulgarian threat (for Britain and France had declared war on Bulgaria on 14–15 October, and the increasingly wretched weather caused the Allies to withdraw).

Pressure now mounted once more for the abandonment of the Salonika project. The British General Staff had never been optimistic over its chances of success. Yet since the French seemed determined to treat the question as a test of British confidence in the Entente, the British could only grudgingly remain. Thus came about the vast Allied encampment at Salonika, which the Germans jeeringly referred to as a self-constructed Allied internment camp.

For their part, the Bulgars had been anxious to cross into Greece and drive the Allies into the sea. Falkenhayn forbade this, however, fearing that such a relentless pursuit would bring Greece into the Allied camp on a wave of popular sentiment against Bulgaria. There were, in addition, the considerations of poor physical communications and inhospitable terrain which applied to much of the fighting in southeast Europe. Moreover, the Germans were aware that both the Bulgars and the Austrians coveted Salonika for themselves. To avoid dissension among the Central Powers and a new extension of age-old Balkan feuds, it seemed best to do nothing. The decision was a fateful one, for at this moment the Bulgars could probably have annihilated the Allied armies and their Salonika base. Alternatively, Greek entry on the Allied side might have saved Serbia.

In the early spring of 1916, Macedonia was almost forgotten as the rival sets of belligerents carried out their main campaigns elsewhere. April, however, brought an extremely slow Allied advance from Salonika to the Greek frontier. Greek forces put up no opposition to this and in some cases cooperated in guard duties. Yet late in May, by secret agreement with Athens, a German-Bulgar force advanced some ten miles into Greece and took Fort Rupel, the major defensive position in this area. As a rejoinder the Allies made demands upon Greece, which included the establishment of a non-party government and the

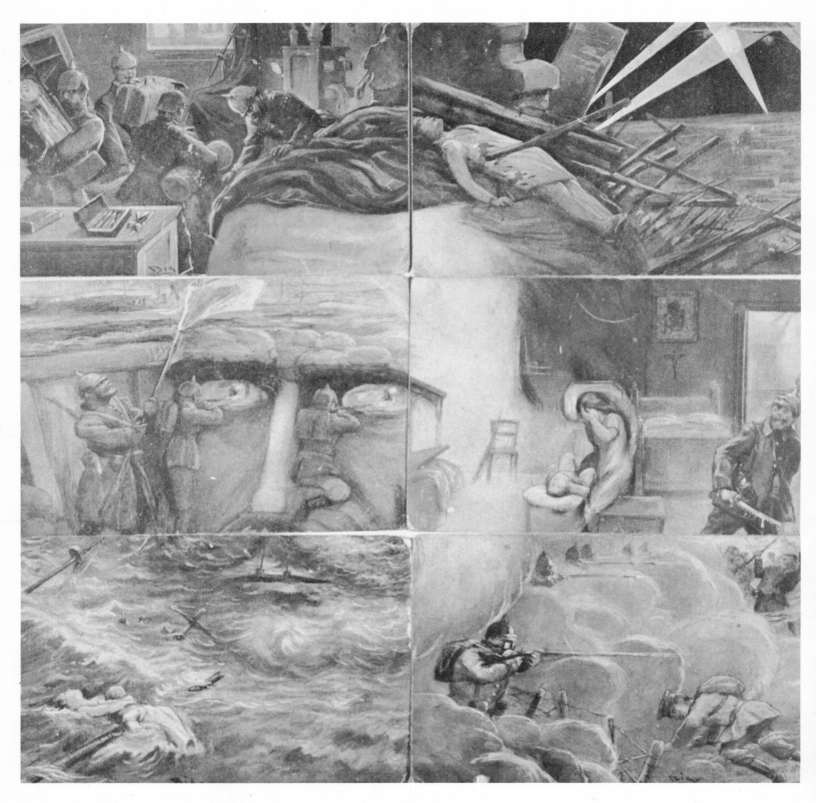

The many faces of
the Kaiser – a pastiche of
postcards.

demobilization of the armed forces. The first
demand was evaded, but the second was followed.
The gunboat diplomacy of the French in particular caused bitter resentment in Greece.

The French continued their strong support for
an offensive in Macedonia as a prerequisite for
Rumanian and possibly Greek participation on
the Entente side. During May and June the
British continued to oppose the idea, but in July
gave way when it became clear that otherwise
Rumania would refuse to join the Allies. On
27 August 1916, Rumania duly proclaimed her
belligerency; but before this, emboldened by the
ill-advised Greek demobilization, the Bulgars
launched their own attack on the seventeenth.
Though they gained considerable initial success,
by the time of Rumania's entering the war the
offensive had petered out.

On 12 September Serbian and French forces
attacked west of the Vardar river. They were
aided by Italian and Russian troops, for both
these powers were conscious of considerations of
prestige and future influence in the Balkans. The
Serbs showed supreme resilience in the light of
their earlier suffering. The British held fast to
their positions on the Struma and carried out
numerous small attacks.

Once more the wooded and mountainous terrain caused the Allied counteroffensive to move
at a slow pace. At one point two days had to be
spent in hacking a path through a beech forest by
means of bayonets. After two months, however,
the Allies had made a significant advance, and
though by now the troops were suffering griev-
ously from exhaustion and 50,000 casualties had
been sustained, the Entente troops had pushed the

A French view of what was happening to Germans in the Carpathians.

The Allied advance to the Greek frontier was agonizingly slow.

Bulgars to breaking-point and the latter were saved only by the arrival of two improvised German divisions. Bulgarian and German casualties had risen to about 52,000, in addition to the loss of 8000 men as prisoners.

Yet for Sarrail none of this was enough. He had dreamed of some great stroke which would restore his reputation. At the very least he had wanted to drive Bulgaria to the negotiating table, but he had not succeeded, and neither had the offensive helped Rumania much. By this time trouble with Greece had again caused the Allies to threaten a blockade, and despite Athens' recalcitrance its imposition forced the Greeks to capitulate to Allied demands.

In May 1917 Sarrail essayed a new offensive, but the Serbs, still nursing the grudge that they had not been properly supported the previous year, made sure that the operation stalled. By the summer the Allies had completely lost patience with Greece. They forced Constantine to abdicate, Venizelos again became Prime Minister, and on 2 July 1917 Greece finally sided with the Entente.

In 1916 the hero of the eastern front was the Russian general, Alexei Brusilov. His name was given to the extraordinary initial success which the Russians were able to gain that year against the Central Powers. Later Brusilov himself maintained that if his early victories had been correctly exploited, the war in the east, and perhaps the whole war, could have been won that year. What seems almost certain is that Brusilov's victories at least prevented the Allies from losing in 1916 no mean achievement.

Westwood and other writers have emphasized

that the great Russian retreat of the previous autumn, successful as it was in avoiding destruction at the hands of the Central Powers, merely reinforced an already strong propensity in the minds of Russian generals to regard withdrawal as a means towards achieving victory itself. In this sense the lessons of 1812 had been learnt too well, or too much had been deduced from them.

By the spring of 1916, at least superficially, the major Russian deficiencies of the previous year were on their way to being repaired. Rifles and ammunition were now available in much greater supply, partly from increased home production and partly through imports; and the lull of winter had given the opportunity for improved training of recruits, though experienced officers were still in short supply. At the highest level, the machinations of the Germanophile Tsarina and her coterie, including the new Prime Minister, Sturmer, saw to it that the ablest and most independent-minded soldiers were passed over for promotion in favour of yes-men and sycophants.

In the winter of 1915, the Allied plans for a co-ordinated offensive had called for a relatively small Russian effort, due to her earlier extremely heavy losses. The bloodbath of Verdun necessitated a revision of this scheme, and now the French asked the Russians for action which would divert some German divisions eastwards.

The first and premature Russian effort in this direction, the battle of Lake Naroch (Narocz) on the Baltic flank, was highly inauspicious. Here, in March and April, Russian armies attacked with strong artillery support, but then, inexplicably, much of the artillery and aircraft cover was withdrawn. The Germans brought in heavy firepower and once more made use of gas, while the Russians, lacking the protection of gas masks, were thrown back with the loss of over 100,000 men, five times the German casualties.

On 14 April, however, the Tsar and his generals had concluded that a larger westward offensive should be undertaken shortly. Preparations were made at several different sites along the front, so that the Germans would be uncertain where the main attack was to take place. It would be necessary to push through a very well fortified Austro-Hungarian defence, but aerial reconnaissance was of tremendous help in enabling the Russians to anticipate the location of major hazards such as machine-gun nests and deep dugouts. In the interim, in mid-May the Italians appealed for Russian action to relieve Austro-Hungarian pressure in the Trentino.

The new Russian offensive was launched on 4 June, when three of Brusilov's four armies managed an immediate breakthrough. Once again an example of Habsburg internal weakness was provided when Czech troops surrendered to the Russians in droves and welcomed them as fellow Slavs and liberators. Soon Brusilov's troops punched yawning gaps in the Austrian lines, and the latter swiftly fell back. By 9 June Brusilov had taken over 70,000 prisoners. It was the greatest Russian victory of the war.

In the meantime Ludendorff was searching diligently for German units to reinforce the crumbling Austrians. Of even greater consequence was the fact that the attack, which Evert of the Russian West Front was to have undertaken in the direction of Wilno (Vilnius or Vilna) on 14 June, was cancelled because of bad weather and, some said, because of cowardice in the face of German (as opposed to Austrian) troops in this sector. As a substitute, a paltry and unsuccessful advance was essayed further south. Moreover, despite Brusilov's objections, Evert's troops were sent to Brusilov himself to strengthen his forces instead of mounting their own attack westwards. Now the Germans, aided by superior communications, switched their troops to the south and by August prevented further significant Russian advances. The main thrust of the Brusilov offensive came to an end about 10 August, though the campaign itself was not called off until October. Austria-Hungary and Germany had lost over 400,000 prisoners of war and over 340,000 casualties, while Russian losses exceeded 1,000,000. If Vienna tottered under the strain, so did Petrograd. This time the spirit of the Russian army was irreparably damaged.

If Evert had attacked towards the west as Brusilov had planned, it is possible that Austria-Hungary would have collapsed. This might have been enough to drive Germany to sue for peace by the year's end. Despite their own heavy toll, however, the Russians had forced the Central Powers to transfer troops eastwards from the western and Italian fronts. Cruttwell is of the opinion that the Brusilov offensive 'made inevitable' the breakup of the Habsburg Empire, while historians unite in emphasizing that the dynamism behind the campaign was uniquely that of General Brusilov himself. For this reason the Russian offensive of 1916 is the only campaign of the war to have been named for its commander.

On 27 August, as was noted earlier, Rumania declared war on the Central Powers. The Russians in particular had been angling for this event since the beginning of the war, but Brătianu, Rumania's Prime Minister, had bided his time to consider what was in the best interests of his nation. As it turned out, Rumania hesitated too long and was crushed, whereas her intervention even a few months earlier might have swung the balance against the Central Powers.

Bulgarian infantry advance toward the Allied position.

General Alexei Brusilov became the Russian hero of the Eastern Front.

Rumanians had grave doubts as to the wisdom of entering the war on either side; but if neutrality were to be abandoned, it was equally difficult to know for whom. Although she hankered after the border territory of Bessarabia, Rumania had many ties with her giant Russian neighbour. Rumania was also linked with Italy, from whose Roman legions a mixture of legend and fact holds the Rumanians to be descended, and with France, like Italy a 'Latin sister' and cultural mentor. Yet Rumania had also connections with Germany and Austria-Hungary, not least because of the abiding interest which these two powers had traditionally held in the Balkans. Public opinion was almost evenly divided in its preferences. Thus under the circumstances, a policy of prudent caution and self-interest seemed called for.

In 1916, however, the initial success of the Brusilov offensive emboldened the Russians to press the Rumanians much more firmly. On 17 August, having been promised large tracts of Magyar-controlled Transylvania and also the Banat and the Bulgarian Dobrudja as the spoils of victory, Rumania signed a military alliance with Britain and France. Yet to the disappointment of the Entente, Bucharest did not press south against Bulgaria and towards Salonika, since her most immediate ambitions against Bulgaria had already been satisfied three years earlier. Instead, when she entered the war (and the actual entry had been made only after the Russians had lost patience and threatened invasion unless Rumania took immediate action), Bucharest moved against Transylvania. The regional capital, Hermannstadt, fell on 6 September, due less to the valour of the pitiably equipped and disgracefully officered Rumanian army than to the fact that the Central Powers were, or had recently been, under severe pressure on several fronts.

The Germans, now deeply concerned, somehow scraped together enough forces under Falkenhayn and Mackensen to regain control of the situation. Though Russian troops caused Mackensen a temporary setback in the middle of September, towards the end of the month the Rumanians were driven back in north and south alike. After the fall of Rumania's chief port, Constanza,

The Russian armies achieved a major breakthrough in June 1916. It was the greatest Russian victory of the war.

on 23 October, the capitulation of Bucharest itself followed on 6 December. The Central Powers had now gained control of valuable resources of oil and wheat, and their links to Turkey were more secure than ever, though Bulgaria and Turkey soon engaged in a vicious quarrel over the fate of the Dobrudja. In addition, although their eastern front had been lengthened, the Central Powers surmised that the trouncing which they had given the new belligerent would cause other neutrals to think twice before abandoning their nonalignment.

The Mesopotamian Campaign

We should now consider events yet further east, in Mesopotamia or modern Iraq. There, on 11 March 1917, the British made their triumphal entry into Baghdad. After the earlier setbacks, the fall of this fabled city furnished welcome exotic interest to the headline writers. Here was a victory over the Turks which did something, at least, to assuage the festering wound of Gallipoli.

The campaign in Mesopotamia had begun early in the war, when the India Office had suggested a British demonstration at the head of the Persian Gulf to reinforce Arab tendencies to turn against their Ottoman overlords, if not actually to rally to the Allies. Thus it was hoped to dissuade the Turks from invading Egypt, since such an expedition was considered impossible without Arab support. At the same time, the war effort made it also necessary to secure the route of the Anglo-Persian oil pipeline.

After initial operations in November 1914, British Empire forces moved inland. Basra fell on 22 November; Qurna, junction of the Tigris and Euphrates rivers, on 9 December; and Amara on 3 June 1915. A determined Turkish offensive, ironically with extensive Arab support, had intervened around Basra on 11–13 April, but had been successfully fought off. Numerous other conquests were made, including that of Nasiriya on 25 July, but a high toll of troop strength was taken by sunstroke and the many diseases endemic to Mesopotamia.

Now General Sir John Nixon, leader of the Indian Expeditionary Force, decided that he could control the *vilayet* (province) of Basra more efficiently if he captured Kut-al-Amara, junction of the Tigris and the Shatt-al-Hai. By unspoken agreement, Kut was also considered the last stage before the capture of Baghdad, which some looked forward to as almost an *ersatz* Constantinople. Accordingly Major General Townshend of the Sixth Division was set the task of Kut's capture, and after a battle against the Turks outside, he entered Kut on 28 September. Now, especially as the Gallipoli campaign was obviously failing, 'a striking success in the East . . . to . . . win the Arabs' was considered vital. On 23 October, with Kitchener dissenting, the British cabinet authorized the over optimistic Nixon to attempt the capture of Baghdad itself. But after a ferocious clash in November at Ctesiphon, sixteen miles southeast of Baghdad, Townshend decided to fall back on Kut, which he reached on 3 December.

A decision to stand at Kut was taken in the knowledge that there were present enough supplies to last for at least two months in the event of

Far left: A Turkish siege forced a British surrender at Kut. **Left:** The Austrians attack.

Far left: Field Marshal August von Mackensen helped Hindenburg encircle the Russians at Tannenberg and later succeeded him as commander of the Ninth Army. In 1915 his new command, the joint Austro-German Eleventh Army, cleared the Russians from Galicia in a fortnight, a victory which won him a marshal's baton. In November 1915 his armies overran Serbia. **Left:** The Austrian Army on the march.

Far left: German aid to the Austrians helped to stop the Brusilov offensive just in time. **Centre left:** Rumania's doubts about entering the war were confirmed by the initial casualties which she suffered. **Left:** British gunboats helped the advance up the Tigris. This river gunboat of the Insect class saw service throughout the campaign. **Below:** The British march through Baghdad with Turkish prisoners in tow.

Above: General Townshend, surrounded by his staff at Kut. Townshend must share the blame for British losses at the hands of the Turks. **Above right:** The King of Montenegro and General Allenby in November 1916. Allenby's successes later in the war forced the Turks to collapse.

Right: The British swept the Turks out of both Palestine and Mesopotamia by 1918. **Opposite left:** Soldiers from different areas of Rumania. **Opposite right:** These Turks were captured by the 38th Lancashire Brigade.

siege, after which time relief would be likely. In fact, the subsequent Turkish siege lasted almost five months and caused much hardship. But if the town could be held, it would provide a barrier to further Turkish progress towards the Persian Gulf. In any case, by the time they had fallen back to Kut the British forces were probably too exhausted to have travelled further. Townshend must be blamed, however, for insufficient attempts to ration food within the garrison or to search out new supplies, and his appeals for relief caused a premature and disastrous British attack which was three times repulsed in January 1916, after which a further opportunity for relief was bungled. Finally, on 29 April, the beleaguered British were forced to surrender unconditionally. The Turks gained well over 10,000 British and Indian prisoners, of whom the officers were treated tolerably well, but the men were beaten, murdered, sexually mutilated, or herded across the desert like animals.

By this time the War Office (now in charge of Mesopotamian operations) had decided that neither Kut nor Baghdad was an important British objective, even though 'as forward a position as can be made secure tactically' was to be maintained. In September 1916 a complete withdrawal from Mesopotamia the following spring was mooted, but later it was decided to advance to the Shatt-al-Hai to free the right bank of the Tigris of hostile forces. This was accomplished by 4 February 1917, and by the twenty-fourth Kut was retaken, even though lack of supplies caused the overall operation to be curtailed on 28 February. Nonetheless the troops were able to move forward again on 5 March, and Baghdad was occupied on the eleventh. The ancient city had fallen to its thirtieth conqueror.

The Turks laid serious plans for the recapture of Baghdad, but difficulties in Palestine caused diversion of the necessary troops. In the autumn of 1917 the British made further advances, though the following spring the intense heat caused a relative lull in operations. After Allenby's success in Palestine in September 1918 at Megiddo (the Biblical Armageddon), the British decided to exploit their increased prestige by further operations in Mesopotamia, but events in the Turkish theatre were now overtaken by Allenby's continued success. Turkey left the war under the armistice of Mudros on 30 October.

The Mesopotamian campaign cost over 90,000 British Empire casualties, including nearly 29,000 dead. The Turks lost over 45,000 prisoners and unnumbered dead and wounded. The siege of Kut and Baghdad, although to a certain extent worthwhile, could certainly have been conducted with less waste of human lives.

W.THÖNY 16.

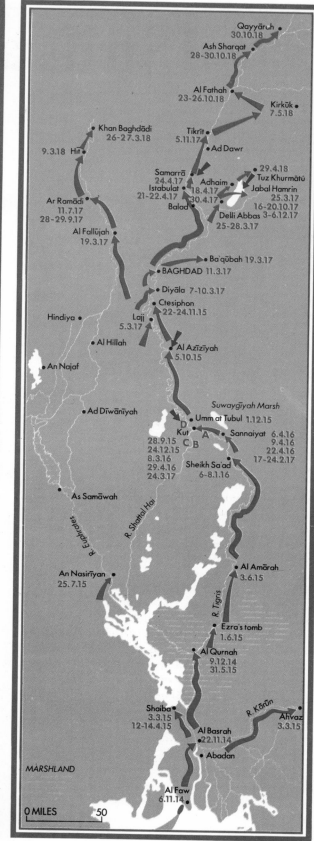

TURKEY

Baghdad

Landing of British troops
at Al Faw

Al Basrah
5.11.17

Advance and dates of capture
November 1914-October 1918

A
Khudhaira Bend taken
4 December 1916-19 January
1917

B
Hai Salient taken
25 January -5 February
1917

C
Dahra Bend taken
9-16 February 1917

D
Shumran Bend taken
23-24 February 1917

Turkish counter-attacks

Qayyārah
30.10.18

Ash Sharqat
28-30.10.18

Al Fathah
23-26.10.18

Kirkūk
7.5.18

Tikrīt
5.11.17

Ad Dawr

29.4.18
Tuz Khurmātū

Khan Baghdādi
26-27.3.18

9.3.18 Hit

Samarrā
24.4.17

Adhaim
18.4.17

Jabal Hamrin
25.3.17

Istabulat
21-22.4.17

30.4.17

Delli Abbas
25-28.3.17

16-20.10.17
3-6.12.17

Ar Ramādi
11.7.17
28-29.9.17

Balad

Al Fallūjah
19.3.17

Ba'qūbah 19.3.17

BAGHDAD 11.3.17

Hindiya

Diyāla 7-10.3.17

Ctesiphon
22-24.11.15

Al Hillah

Lajj
5.3.17

Al Azīzīyah
5.10.15

An Najaf

Ad Dīwānīyah

Suwaygīyah Marsh

Umm at Tubul 1.12.15

Kut
28.9.15
24.12.15
8.3.16
29.4.16
24.3.17

D

C B

A

Sannaiyat 6.4.16
9.4.16
22.4.16
17-24.2.17

Sheikh Sa'ad
6-8.1.16

As Samāwah

R. Euphrates

R. Shatt al Hai

An Nasirīyan
25.7.15

Al Amārah
3.6.15

R. Tigris

Ezra's tomb
1.6.15

Al Qurnah
9.12.14
31.5.15

Shaiba
3.3.15
12-14.4.15

Al Basrah
22.11.14

Abadan

R. Kārūn

Ahvaz
3.3.15

MARSHLAND

Al Faw
6.11.14

0 MILES   50

149

CHAPTER NINE

Naval Strife and Peace Moves

The Battle of Jutland (or the Battle of Skaggerak) took place on the night of 31 May 1916, in a large area some seventy miles west of the North Jutland coast. For a generation both Britain and Germany had anticipated such a meeting, but so far each had failed to bring about conditions in which a vast naval encounter could be fought on favourable terms.

Conflict at sea was inevitable in 1916; the Allied blockade was affecting Germany, but Russia was suffering from German interference with her imports even more, making it necessary for the Allies to loosen the German stranglehold on the Baltic. The British Grand Fleet bases were in a good state of readiness, and the fleet itself was concentrated in the Orkney Islands at Scapa Flow; its commander, Admiral Sir John Jellicoe, was confident that he could deal with any German threat, either by closing off the northern exit from the North Sea, or by doing battle should England's coasts be threatened.

Admiral Reinhard Scheer, commander of the German High Seas Fleet, was also ready for the offensive. He and his colleagues had been deeply perturbed, first by the effects of the Allied blockade, and then by the curtailment of the German fleet's activities after the Battle of Dogger Bank in 1915. However, by the spring of 1916 the British fleet was almost twice as strong as that of Germany, so in an attempt to force some division of British strength, Scheer planned a series of raids to goad them into sending out small detachments which, he hoped, could then be destroyed by U-boats and surface vessels.

On 24–25 April, at a time when the British were under pressure because of the rebellion in Dublin, the Germans carried out a sortie in which they bombarded several towns along the east coast of England, including Norwich, Lowestoft,

Admiral Jellico boards HMS *Iron Duke*.

The British Fleet leaves Spithead in 1914.

Yarmouth, and Lincoln. A more extensive operation was planned for the second half of May. German battle cruisers were to bombard Sunderland, and when the British squadrons put out to sea in retaliation, twelve U-boats would move in for the kill. However, bad weather intervened and prevented reconnaissance by Zeppelin airships. Without prior information there was a danger that the High Seas Fleet might be cut off by British forces, and so an alternative plan had to be devised. The German battle cruiser force under Rear Admiral Franz von Hipper would proceed north from Heligoland Bight to the Norwegian coast, where it would demonstrate its presence. Scheer would follow from a distance, hoping that the British battle cruiser force under Vice Admiral Sir David Beatty would be tempted out of its base at Rosyth, near Edinburgh. Unfortunately, he did not realize that the British were able to decode German radio messages.

On the afternoon of 30 May the alternative scheme was approved. Although the British knew that a major action was to take place, the full meaning of the German messages was unclear. Still, Jellicoe decided to move the main portion of the Grand Fleet seawards from Scapa Flow. He was joined by a further force from Cromarty Firth and the base of Invergordon; the two contingents were to rendezvous ninety miles west of the southernmost tip of Norway on the morning of 31 May, their combined forces totalling twenty-four dreadnoughts, three battle cruisers, eight armoured cruisers, twelve light cruisers and fifty-one destroyers. Separately but simultaneously a scouting force of six battle cruisers, twelve light cruisers, four *Queen Elizabeth*-class battleships, twenty-eight destroyers and a seaplane carrier left Rosyth under Beatty's command. He was to be 120 miles west of Jutland Bank by 2:00 p.m. on

31 May, while Jellicoe would be fifty miles off the Norwegian coast. If by this time he had not sighted the enemy, he was to move northwards to meet Jellicoe.

Ironically, Scheer's U-boats had already failed him on two counts. They had not been able to successfully attack any of the British ships as they moved out; and their reconnaissance was incomplete – the Germans had no hint that their rival's main fleet was now at sea.

At 1:00 a.m. on 31 May, Hipper's force of five battle cruisers, five light cruisers, and thirty-three destroyers weighed anchor and headed into the North Sea. Behind them followed Scheer's fleet of sixteen dreadnoughts, six pre-dreadnought vessels, six light cruisers, and thirty-nine destroyers.

At 2:15 p.m. Beatty was changing course to join Jellicoe, when suddenly his light cruiser *Galatea* saw smoke to the east. On investigation the ship was found to be a Danish merchant steamer, as the German *Elbing* also discovered when it came on the scene. As the *Galatea* and the *Elbing* saw each other, the order was given to fire. The Battle of Jutland had begun, and this chance encounter with the Danish vessel may have cost the British a decisive victory; if the rival fleets had met an hour later further north the Germans would have been at an even greater distance from home and shelter.

When he learned what had happened, Beatty quickly turned southeast, hoping to place himself between the Germans and their home base, but the British battleships under Rear Admiral Evan-Thomas failed to read his signal to turn and fell behind. Meanwhile, Hipper had turned south, hoping to lead the British into the oncoming German battle squadrons.

At 3:48 p.m. each side opened fire. Six British ships faced five German vessels, and Beatty went

Top: The German fleet comes out to meet them, led by the armoured cruiser *Blücher*. **Above:** Admiral Sir David Beatty.

Below: Prince Henry of Prussia (with field glasses) and Admiral von Scheer, Commander-in-Chief, of the German High Seas Fleet at Jutland.

into action without waiting for the Fifth Battle Squadron to catch up with him. At 4:04 p.m. two salvoes from the *Von der Tann* caused the British *Indefatigable* to explode and capsize with the loss of one thousand men; this was closely followed by the blowing up of the *Queen Mary* under the impact of concentrated fire from *Derfflinger* and *Seydlitz*. Twelve hundred men went down with her, and a dark pillar of smoke estimated at a height of 800 to 2300 feet, rose above the spot. In the interim, the *Lion*'s turret had been removed by a shell from the *Lützow*, and the ship would have exploded but for the heroism of a dying man, Major Harvey, who ordered that its magazines be flooded. Several other British vessels were damaged; other German ships were similarly hit, and the *Seydlitz* lost a turret. In fact, the Fifth Battle Squadron, now finally in action, would have overwhelmed several enemy vessels had they not been issued defective shells which could not penetrate the German armour.

At 4:33, just as the tide seemed to be turning in Britain's favour, Commodore Goodenough of the Second Light Cruiser Squadron saw the German battle fleet on the horizon. Goodenough's sudden encounter gave Beatty a chance to escape the trap which Hipper had set for him. He turned northwards, but the Fifth Battle Squadron was still engaged in heavy fighting, during which the British *Nestor* was sunk and the *Barham* and *Malaya* damaged. The German *Lützow*, *Derfflinger* and *Seydlitz* were also hit.

In the interim Jellicoe's battleships were moving southeast; the battle cruisers under Rear Admiral Sir Horace Hood were farther east. In an attempt to get between the German fleet and the coast, Jellicoe moved his squadrons to the left, while Beatty's battle cruisers intersected with the battleships and took up new positions.

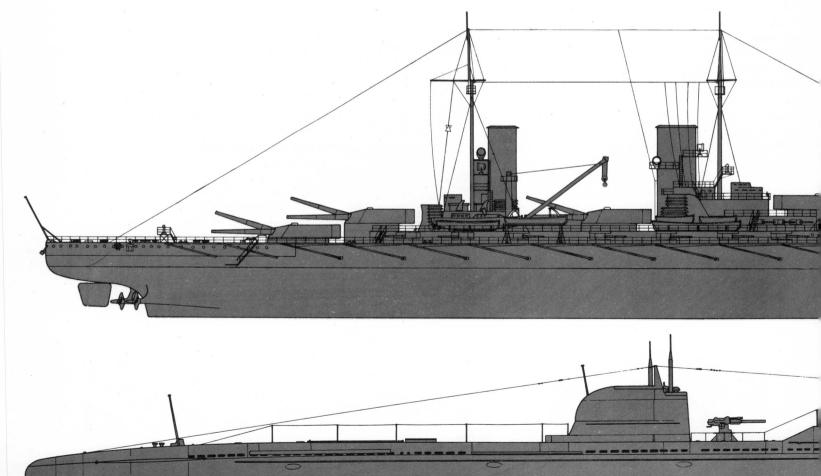

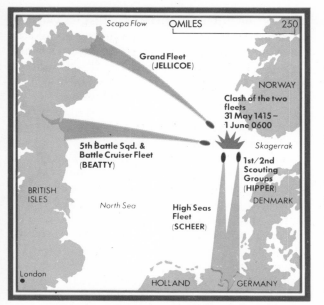

Hipper, who had turned north, suddenly sighted Beatty again at about 5:40. As he bore down on his adversary Jellicoe sent his left column on a south by southeast course. The German admiral was aghast when he saw this totally unexpected force come out of the mist, but he kept his wits and managed to execute a co-ordinated turnaway movement (*Gefechtskehrt-wendung*) to starboard. This superb somersaulting manoeuvre enabled the German ships to elude their foe in record time, if only temporarily.

The Germans had gained other impressive successes that afternoon. The British *Warspite* had been forced out of action, the *Defence* had been blown up, and the *Warrior* had to be abandoned next day because of the damage she sustained. In addition the *Derfflinger* had sunk the *Invincible*. The Germans had proved the excellence of their ship design and ammunition, even though the *Lützow*

was hit and disabled and the *Wiesbaden* wrecked. Nevertheless, Scheer was on the defensive. At 6:44 p.m., despite threatening mist and darkness, Jellicoe again turned southeast to move between the enemy fleet and their base. Scheer changed course, perhaps hoping to pass across the enemy's rear to safety, or perhaps thinking that the Grand Fleet was divided, but once more he was forced to retire in the face of the British dreadnoughts.

Meanwhile Scheer's destroyer flotillas launched twenty-eight torpedoes at the British fleet, to which Jellicoe's response was a simultaneous turning action of his own. None of the torpedoes found a target, but during the delay Jellicoe lost his chance to smash the German fleet. By 7:18 p.m. Scheer managed another turnaway, but the *Seydlitz* and the *Von der Tann* had been damaged and fire had broken out aboard the *Derfflinger*, which had lost three of its four heavy turrets. Jellicoe now decided against further interception of the enemy that night. This decision subsequently received much criticism, but visibility was failing and he no longer had accurate information on the German positions. Radar had not been invented, and he felt that further action would at best achieve uncertain results. Scheer still had to contend with a heavy enemy force between himself and home – unless he could slip through during the night. He decided to try, though fully conscious of the risks involved.

Though Jellicoe intended to renew the battle in daylight, he was hampered by inexact knowledge of German movements. Between 10:00 p.m. and 2:00 a.m., scarcely believing their good fortune, the Germans broke their way through the British line. The armoured cruiser *Black Prince* was eliminated, and their own *Pommern* was cut in half. Jellicoe had let several opportunities to cripple the enemy slip by, but many of his errors were the

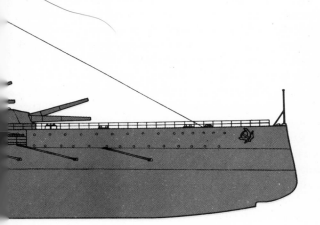

WHAT A RED RAG IS TO A BULL-

THE RED CROSS IS TO THE HUN.

To the already Long List of Outrages by the HUNS on The RED CROSS both on Land and Sea, there was added on January the 4th This Year, the Sinking without warning in the Bristol Channel of the Hospital Ship "REWA."—Fortunately owing to the Splendid Discipline and the Unselfish and Heroic Conduct of the Officers, Crew, and The Medical Staff, All the wounded, of whom there were over 700 on board were saved,—But three poor Lascar Firemen went down with the ship.

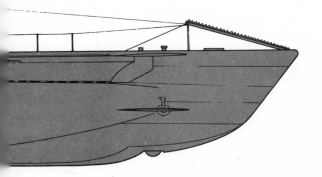

Torpedoes began to take their toll.

result of misleading or incomplete information. Now there was nothing to do but follow the German example and head for home. At 11:00 a.m. on 1 June, the Grand Fleet set course for Scapa Flow.

British losses amounted to three battle cruisers, three cruisers, eight destroyers and over six thousand men. The figures for Germany were one battleship, one battle cruiser, four light cruisers, five destroyers and three thousand casualties. The loss of the three British battle cruisers was mainly the result of inadequate armour. Moreover, the powers of British guns was greatly diminished by the poor quality of their armour-piercing shells.

Such was the Battle of Jutland which in the end had involved over 250 ships, prompting Churchill to describe it as 'the culminating manifestation of naval force in the history of the world'. Both sides claimed to have won; in fact neither did so. Jutland was indecisive, and as Liddell Hart comments, its value as a battle was 'negligible'. If anything, the naval clash decreased British prestige in Allied eyes, for the British had failed to free the Baltic; as the noose around Russia tightened, that luckless nation lurched towards its rendezvous with destiny in 1917. British overall command of the sea, however, was unaffected.

Several historians have emphasized that Jellicoe's objective was less to insure a British victory than to forestall a German success, and in this he was successful. By the late summer of 1916 the German high command had decided that a further major naval battle involved unacceptable risks. The High Seas Fleet was placed on the defensive, and morale suffered badly, resulting in mutiny in August 1917 and a major revolt in 1918. Thus it may be said that this extraordinary battle had long-term consequences which far outweighed its immediate results.

America tries to Mediate

Since before the outbreak of war, Woodrow Wilson, the idealistic American President, had desperately tried first to avert and then to end a conflict which he thought would be the ruin of civilization and the rule of law. In the autumn of 1915 it seemed that the war was reaching a deadlock, and conditions for peace occupied his mind even more. Lacking a definite plan, however, he turned to his intimate friend, Colonel Edward House for advice.

House, always an Anglophile, believed that Imperial Germany was a diehard autocracy which would find no place in the new order following a peace settlement. In October 1915, he explained to the President that Britain and France should and could be convinced of the essential identity of interests between themselves and America; a tripartite understanding should be reached, according to which the United States would call for a peace conference. If the Germans cooperated, a compromise peace might yet be achieved without American belligerency, but if they proved recalcitrant, the United States could intervene on the Allied side under the banner of a moral crusade against the Kaiser.

Colonel House thought that the war could be ended on terms that would include the establishment of a League of Nations to monitor the peace settlement, universal disarmament, and a territorial settlement which would restore the pre-war frontiers. Wilson readily agreed to the scheme, though their views on the specifics of a peace settlement differed more than either man realized. For example, House already believed that American participation on the Allied side was all but inevitable, while Wilson still hoped to use moral rather than physical persuasion.

In January 1916 House was received in London with considerable scepticism and reserve. Grey, the Foreign Secretary and a close friend of House, and Balfour, First Lord of the Admiralty, pointed out that America's efforts to settle the conflict would meet entrenched resistance from Allied governments and peoples alike. The British were fully aware that German occupation of considerable French and Russian territory meant that a return to the 1914 *status quo* was the very most that could be expected. This boded ill for Allied war aims, which by now encompassed much in the way of revision of borders and redistribution of power. Above all, the Allies still believed that they could win, and this was infinitely preferable to a compromise arranged by a government which, however friendly, appeared increasingly interfering and naive.

In Berlin, House encountered similar obstinacy, though more subtle Germans tried to convince him that Allied obstructiveness was all that prevented peace, and that in consequence the United States ought to remain neutral. In Paris he was told bluntly that his efforts were coming at an entirely inappropriate time. Still, he left the impression both in Paris and London that America would back the Allies to the hilt.

On 22 February House and Grey produced a memorandum, agreeing that some time in the unspecified future the Allies would ask America to call a peace conference. The general feeling was that German non-cooperation would *probably* result in America's entering the war on the Allied side. (It is significant that the conditional 'probably' was omitted by House, but added by Wilson.) The terms which would be put to the Germans would include the restoration of Belgian and Serbian independence and sovereignty, the retrocession of Alsace-Lorraine to France, the cession of Constantinople to Russia, and the establishment of an independent Poland. Germany would receive extra colonies in compensation for these losses. A postwar security system would be established, including the abolition of competitive armaments, and guarantees against unprovoked aggression.

To London the signing of the memorandum meant a welcome postponement of American demands, but Washington was more optimistic. As it happened, however, the Allies never invited the President to issue his peace appeal.

German peace moves

With the collapse of Rumania at the end of 1916, the Germans saw an opportunity to propose a compromise peace from a position of apparent strength, and on 12 December the German government called publicly for peace negotiations, sternly declaring that otherwise the Fatherland in its 'indestructible strength' was prepared to fight on to a successful finish. The Central Powers hinted that they had their own plan to stem the flow of blood, but the terms were not disclosed.

In fact, the Central Powers envisaged the consolidation of German *Mittelafrika* by the acquisition of all or part of the immensely rich Belgian Congo. Germany would keep the important industrial resources of the French Briey-Longwy basin, while Belgium would come under German 'influence'; failing that, Germany would retain Liège. Austria was to benefit from adjustments along the Italian frontier, and Montenegro was to be split between Austria-Hungary and Albania. The Hungarian-Rumanian frontier was to be 'rectified', Serbia would be required to cede territory to both Austria-Hungary and Bulgaria, and the Straits question would be 'examined' at length.

These demands were put forward by German moderates who believed in the peace initiative for its own sake. Their more calculating colleagues hoped that the mere possibility of peace would prevent or delay American participation on the Allied side. If peace on German terms was impossible, they reasoned, the gesture of negotiation might make the resumption of unrestricted submarine warfare by Germany more palatable. Also, many leading Germans feared that Austro-Hungarian morale would collapse without some gesture toward peace.

Just at this time, Wilson was preparing a further appeal for each side to state its minimum war aims, and on 18 December the American President called for 'soundings (to) be taken' to determine if mankind were within sight of that 'haven of peace' for which all yearned. But the Germans were reluctant to state their peace terms publicly, and the Entente, regarding German peace overtures as insincere, rejected them as lacking any positive indication that the Central Powers would return to the *status quo* of 1914 or guarantee their future non belligerency.

On 10 January 1917 the Entente replied at length to the American proposals. They claimed that Allied war aims implied:

Necessarily and first of all, the restoration of Belgium, Serbia, and Montenegro, with the compensation due to them; the evacuation of the invaded territories in France, in Russia, in Rumania, with just reparation; the reorganization of Europe guaranteed by a stable regime and based at once on respect for nationalities, and on the right to full security and liberty of economic development possessed by all peoples, small and great; and, at the same time, upon territorial conventions and international settlements such as to guarantee land

Below: The *Indomitable* and *Inflexible* move in for the kill. **Below centre:** The *Invincible* is hit. **Bottom:** The *Invincible* sinks. The torpedo boat *Badger* approaches to pick up the six survivors.

LA POTENTE FLOTTA GERMANICA ...
... A KIEL ...

KAISER WILHELM

and sea frontiers against unjustified attack; the restoration of provinces formerly torn from the Allies by force or against the wish of their inhabitants; the liberation of the Italians, as also of the Slavs, Rumanians and Czechoslovaks from foreign domination; the setting free of the populations subject to the bloody tyranny of the Turks; and the turning out of Europe of the Ottoman Empire as decidedly foreign to Western Civilization.

In order to mollify Russia, the independence of Poland was not specifically referred to, and no mention was made of the future of the German colonies. As all but the most unrealistic must have known, these terms and the aggressive way in which they were stated had no chance of acceptance until Germany faced utter defeat.

At the end of January Count Bernstorff, the German ambassador in Washington, told Wilson of his government's decision to resume unrestricted submarine warfare. At the same time he informed Wilson privately that German peace demands included the restoration of Belgium 'under special guarantees for the safety of Germany' and the restitution of German-occupied parts of France 'under reservation of strategical and economic changes of the frontier, and financial compensations'. The French would keep that small part of Alsace which they had managed to occupy. Germany and the re-established Poland would redefine their eastern frontiers in order to secure themselves strategically and economically against Russia. Freedom of the seas was to be insured. Finally, Germany expected the return of her colonies and compensation for war damage.

Other attempts to end the war
In Vienna Emperor Karl succeeded the aged Franz Josef on the Habsburg throne, and immediately started to work for an early peace settlement, via his brother-in-law, Prince Sixtus (Sixte) of Bourbon. The Emperor's hope was that in return for a separate peace, the Western Allies would allow Austria-Hungary to remain more or less intact. The ensuing series of negotiations, however, proved fruitless, mainly because of the

irreconcilable nature of Austrian and Italian war aims. France made matters worse with demands that included a reversion to the French frontier of 1814 (i.e., including Alsace-Lorraine and the Saar and Landau territories), the restoration of Belgium and of Serbia with an Adriatic outlet, and the cession of Constantinople to Russia.

The Vatican's efforts to effect a compromise in the summer of 1917 were equally unsuccessful. The Pope called for the renunciation of reparations and territorial annexations, but neither side was prepared to agree.

In November 1917 the Marquis of Lansdowne published a memorandum which he had shown to the British cabinet a year previously. The document urged that, with absolute victory becoming increasingly unlikely, concrete proposals for a negotiated peace be drawn up. Earlier, the inclination of some cabinet members to negotiate had led to a major political crisis and to the formation of a new government under David Lloyd George, champion of the 'knockout blow'. In 1917 Lansdowne's views were simply ignored. Desperation had not reduced either side to breaking-point, so the war continued.

The Blockades

From the beginning, both Britain and Germany recognized the importance of trade warfare. In conducting this aspect of the war, each side reached for the weapons that were most readily available. Thus the main British device was the blockade of Germany and regulation of the trade of her neighbouring neutrals, the Netherlands, and the three Scandinavian countries. Germany's retaliation took the form of a hard-hitting submarine campaign which for a time threatened to cripple the import of goods vital to Britain.

Until America entered the war in April 1917, the established tenets of international law still influenced the conduct of the Allied blockade. The Entente knew that it could ill afford to offend the United States, the most powerful of the neutrals and a nation traditionally sensitive about its

Above left: The heir to the Habsburg throne, Karl, decorates his soldiers. **Above:** The ageing Franz Josef, shortly before his death.

Opposite top: 'The Mighty German Fleet at Kiel' – Italian sarcasm about the inactivity of the German navy. After Jutland the High Seas Fleet never launched any serious threat to British naval supremacy. **Below left:** The Grand Fleet moves into line for the first barrage. **Below:** SMS *Thuringen* engaged a British cruiser during night action.

Above: A zig-zag sailing pattern was adopted to avoid direct submarine attack. **Far left:** Jutland during the height of battle. **Left:** The British cruiser *Queen Mary* is destroyed: 31 May 1916.

Right: The British lost more ships than the Germans at Jutland, but it is a matter of some controversy which side won the battle. **Below:** The German battle cruiser *Derfflinger* was heavily damaged.

maritime rights. However, with her participation, America's attitude changed to one of defending almost any measures deemed necessary.

Under international maritime law it was understood that a belligerent's rights included the capture of enemy merchantmen, the prevention of enemy trade in and out of its home ports by means of blockade, and the confiscation at sea of certain enemy war material. Ancillary rights included those of visit and search to determine a vessel's belligerency or otherwise and to inspect its cargo for contraband. In the latter case, goods might be subject to seizure upon their condemnation by a prize court.

Maritime law had been further codified in the sixty years preceding the war but since then the development of new weapons had drastically altered circumstances. For example, the 1856 Declaration of Paris had held that to be legal, a blockade had to be 'effective'; this was interpreted to mean that enforcement had to be at close range rather than on paper, but the use of undersea weapons and long-range guns made this sort of enforcement impossible, as well as affecting the practice of visit and search.

The British, therefore, decided to initiate their own system of controls; this was easy to do since Britain was in command of the sea and was also in a position geographically to control the entrances and exits to the North Sea and thus to Germany's ports. These controls gradually evolved into a system which was well-defined by the end of 1916.

Before the position was clarified, however, the rivals engaged in a series of moves and counter moves. A British declaration on 3 November 1914 stated that the North Sea was a military area in which ships would be exposed to mines and other hazards, and soon Britain had established contraband control stations in the Orkney Islands and near the Straits of Dover. Germany answered this on 4 February by declaring that the waters surrounding the British Isles formed a war zone in which any ship might be sunk without warning. This phase of unrestricted submarine warfare lasted only a few months, however, before it was shelved because of protests from neutral countries. The British replied in their turn on 11 March 1915 with an Order in Council declaring that goods bound for Germany might be seized even from a vessel sailing to a neutral port.

By late 1916 the Allied blockade was taking effect through the following channels:

1. Inspections in port. These replaced visit and search procedures. Besides the inspection of neutral merchantmen suspected of trade with the enemy, the ports handled a growing number of neutral vessels which called for examination voluntarily in order to keep in favour with the Allies.

2. Rationing. By means of a complex system, neutral nations bordering Germany were allowed imports sufficient only for their own needs. The aim obviously, was to prevent the re-exportation of goods to the Central Powers. In practice this measure had many loopholes and supplies did get through to Germany, but the system was still quite effective and was severely tightened after America joined the war. Although European neutrals resented British interference, more often than not it was in their interest to comply with the regulations lest they incur retaliatory measures such as confiscation of their goods.

3. Navicerts. These were letters of clearance issued for neutral cargoes, certifying their origin, contents, and destination in order to simplify subsequent processing.

4. Blacklists of firms known or suspected to be trading with the enemy. If neutrals continued dealing with them, the Allies retaliated by blacklisting the ships carrying such trade and denying them fuel facilities at sea.

5. Bunker control. Britain's coal exports and command of the major ocean routes and the coaling stations along them allowed her to regulate fuel for neutral vessels in transit.

6. Censorship and interception of neutral mails and cables.

7. Pre-emptive purchasing of neutral food surpluses to deny them to the enemy.

These and other Allied measures led Germany to revive unrestricted submarine warfare in February 1917, and this in turn led to American entry into the war. The blockade tightened still further, and as 1917 wore on very few imports were reaching the Central Powers. Many necessities of life disappeared altogether, civilian morale was undermined, and internal collapse was hastened. Several historians have concluded that without the blockade, the defeat of Germany would have been 'at least doubtful'. What is known is that widespread malnutrition, tuberculosis and other ailments resulted from the deprivations of its final eighteen months. An accurate calculation of resulting deaths is not possible, but estimates run as high as 750,000.

President Woodrow Wilson hoped for peace without victory in 1916.

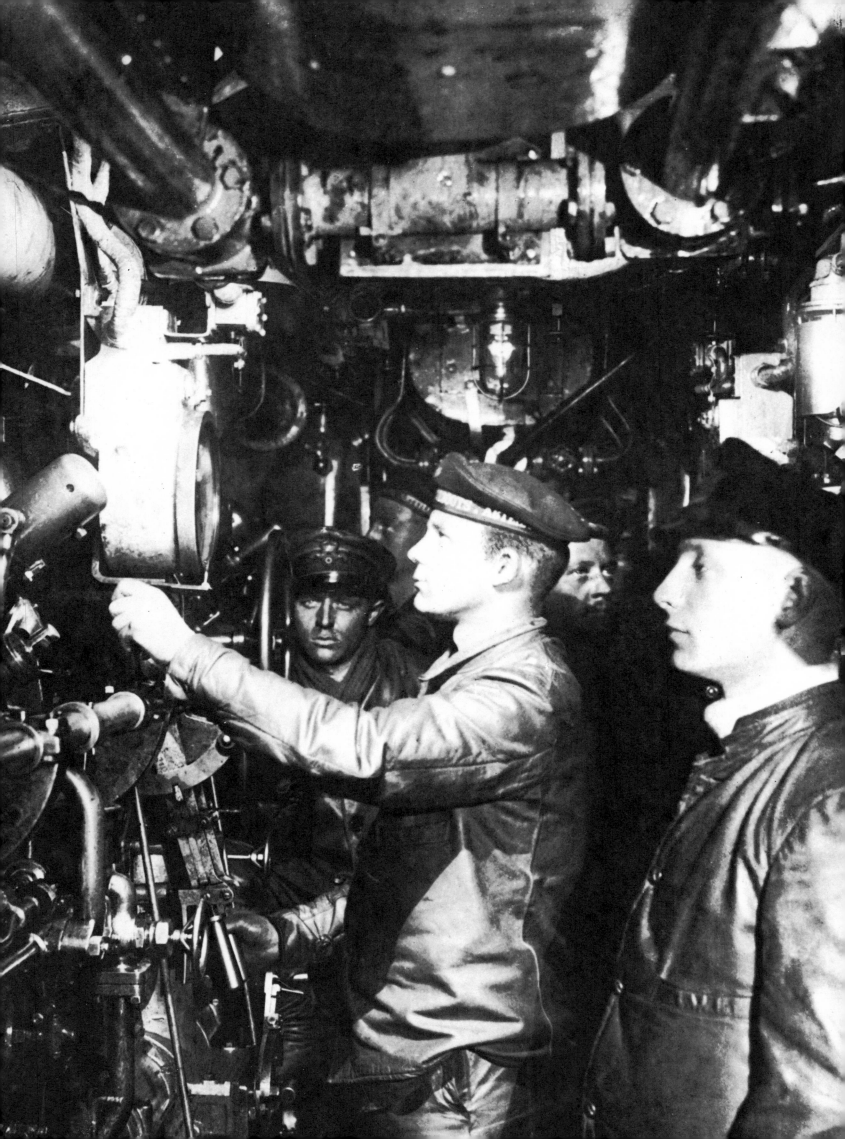

CHAPTER TEN

America Steps In

Germany's campaign of unrestricted submarine warfare was the most important immediate factor in America's decision for war. The additional and underlying causes of American belligerency were complex; but when the United States declared war against the Central Powers, the submarine issue weighed heavily on the scales.

The question of the use of submarines had become an important issue early in the conflict. It was obvious that German U-boats might have a disastrous effect against Great Britain in particular, for eighty per cent of British foodstuffs and most of her raw materials had to be imported by sea. Moreover, the Germans reasoned that unless their submarines did what they could to challenge British naval supremacy, the Grand Fleet would be able to deny the Reich access to American and other neutral resources. Then, in 1916, the Battle of Jutland had shown the great difficulties and high risks involved in challenging the British by conventional means alone. Finally, the Germans realized that their submarines were well fitted for the task of attacking shipping in the crowded sea lanes around the British Isles.

In September 1914 the German U-9 had effortlessly sunk three British cruisers. Despite this example of the submarine's efficiency, however, an all-out undersea campaign was postponed because of the possible political repercus-

sions. Yet by early 1915 it was clear that the war would be a protracted struggle, and in addition to the stalemate on the Western Front, the Allied blockade was already tightening. In these circumstances Germany undertook the initial phase of her intensive use of submarines on 18 February 1915.

The *Lusitania* disaster, described in an earlier chapter, emphasized the risk of adverse public opinion which an undersea campaign would involve. For although the Germans were correct in their assertion that the Allies had already bent the rules of international law to suit themselves, they failed to grasp that while British policy interfered with trade, German actions were leading directly to loss of life at sea among neutrals and belligerents alike.

America's moralistic attitude towards the conflict was given concrete expression in its outraged reaction to the sinking of the *Lusitania*. As we have seen, the Allies were quick to make the most of this tragedy, both in simplistic propaganda about 'the beastly Hun' as well as at a more sophisticated level. Furthermore, more realistic Americans were concerned that if Germany were to continue on the rampage at sea, America's growing and lucrative trade with the Allies in war matériel and other goods would be curtailed. At length, after three American notes on the subject of submarine

Far left: The engine room of a German submarine.
Left: A submarine takes on torpedoes.

Right: By 1916 British seaplanes helped escort convoys through the War Zone. **Opposite top:** Allied convoys were unable to stop the heavy attrition at sea caused by German submarines.

Opposite left and centre: Direct hit! A steamer is torpedoed by a German submarine . . . and sinks.
Opposite right: The German submarine fleet became increasingly more effective against Allied shipping.

Admiral von Tirpitz, the creator of the German High Seas Fleet, resigned over the submarine issue in March 1916.

President Wilson addresses Congress advising the severance of diplomatic relations with Germany, April 1917.

depredations, the Germans realized that some concessions had to be made to public opinion in the United States lest that nation commit her power against them. After a further altercation over the sinking of the British liner *Arabic* in August 1915, with the loss of three American lives, orders were issued in Berlin severely restricting submarine activities. Yet American and other lives were once more sacrificed or endangered in March 1916, when the cross-Channel steamer *Sussex* was torpedoed. The United States then threatened to break diplomatic relations with Germany unless the latter promised that ships would no longer be sunk without warning and without provision for the safety of those aboard. Although the German government had to yield, stating that it would 'do its utmost to confine the operations of war . . . to the fighting forces of the belligerents . . .', it reminded Washington that Berlin expected action to induce the Allies to curb their violations of maritime law, failing which Germany would 'reserve to itself complete liberty of decision . . .'.

In the interim the entire submarine issue had become the subject of fierce controversy within German ruling circles, with an extremist position being taken by Admiral von Tirpitz until he resigned in disgust in March 1916. By early 1917, with the Allied blockade affecting the very fabric of German domestic life, and victory on land appearing increasingly unattainable, both Hindenburg and Ludendorff threw their weight

behind the faction advocating ruthless use of U-boats. Unrestricted submarine warfare was resumed on 1 February 1917, when Germany declared that the waters around the British Isles, western France, and the Mediterranean were an area of blockade in which Germany would sink at sight any vessel of any nationality. The calculation in Berlin was that as a result, the Allied war effort could be wrecked within six months and before possible American belligerency could materially aid the Entente.

Because of its previous stand and its increasing fury at German actions, the American government broke relations with Berlin on 3 February. In March German submarine attacks involved the sinking of seven American as well as countless other neutral and Allied vessels. Thus, in an atmosphere envenomed by the interception of the Zimmermann Telegram (in which Germany proposed to enter into an alliance with Mexico should the United States enter the war), America did go to war on 6 April.

Meanwhile German submarine attacks brought Britain within sight of defeat. From October to December 1916, U-boats sent to the bottom an average of over 300,000 tons of British shipping a month. The new year brought even more disastrous losses: 250,000 tons in the first ten days of April alone, and 875,000 tons for the whole month. No wonder Admiral Jellicoe admitted that if British tonnage continued to be crippled on such a scale, peace on German terms might be

"Disavowal? Disavowal? There Is No Such Word In the German Tongue!"

necessary by November 1917 or earlier. Yet eventually the point of crisis passed, for the convoy system, antisubmarine measures, provision of more cargo space, increased home production of foodstuffs, and an excess of confidence on the part of Germany all helped to stave off disaster. Thus was possible the transportation of two million fresh and eager American troops to France, an injection of adrenalin into the Allied system which tipped the scales in favour of victory.

On 2 April 1917 President Woodrow Wilson appeared before a special joint session of the Congress of the United States. Wilson had come to ask for a declaration of war against Germany. The House of Representatives, where the president was to speak, was filled to the brim with a tense and expectant audience. Congressmen and senators, members of the Supreme Court, cabinet colleagues, and a host of distinguished visitors were present.

How had events reached this point? How had the United States, the most powerful neutral and a nation by tradition wary of Old World entanglements, taken the decision to enter the stale and blood-soaked conflict which for nearly three years had already raged across Europe and the seas?

In his address President Wilson attempted to give a personal answer. He castigated the German submarine campaign as a wanton rampage against mankind. Armed neutrality, he continued, would not now be sufficient to protect American interests and lives. Thus the United States should 'accept the status of belligerency which has . . . been thrust upon it, by the actions of Imperial Germany and her associates'.

Wilson now believed – and did not hesitate to say so – that the present German government had to be brought to terms because it was the implacable foe of liberty. Thus the president had concluded with the utmost reluctance that in order to make the world 'safe for democracy', America must now play its full part in the conflict. 'The

right is more precious than peace', Wilson declared. In sombre tones he continued:

We shall fight . . . for democracy, for the right of those who submit to authority to have a voice in their own governments, for the rights and liberties of small nations, for a universal dominion of right by such a concert of free peoples as shall bring peace and safety to all nations and make the world itself at last free . . . America is privileged to spend her blood and her might for the principles that gave her birth and happiness and the peace which she has treasured . . .

As the President reached the climax of his speech, the audience burst into wild and deafening applause. It seemed that only Wilson himself was solemn. As he later remarked sadly, his speech was 'a message of death for our young men'.

Carried away by their enthusiasm or idealism, both Houses of Congress voted for war by overwhelming majorities. The bulk of opinion throughout the country supported this decision. America had entered the fight.

Woodrow Wilson had greeted the outbreak of war in 1914 with shock and horror. During the July crisis he had been deeply involved in wrangling with the American Congress and distracted with worry over his wife's terminal illness. (Mrs. Wilson died on 6 August.) Then, once war had come, Wilson had to work within the limits set by American public opinion, which, though divided along ethnic and other lines in its preferences for the different belligerents, was basically thankful that the main theatre of war was likely to be far away, in the Old World whose intractable problems Americans had put behind them. The American people were basically agreed that Europe should settle its own squabbles; the United States would stand aloof from the fight. *The New York Times* spoke for many when it described the conflict as 'the least justified of all wars since man emerged from barbarism'.

On the other hand, as Wilson himself was

Above left: American public opinion became aroused against the destruction of neutral shipping by German submarines. **Above:** Wilson campaigned for a second term of office in 1916 under the slogan 'He Kept Us Out of War'.

aware, Americans were increasingly conscious of their growing importance on the international stage. Though they were extraordinarily reluctant to assume the status of world power to which destiny beckoned them, much less the consequences of the exercise of that power, the people of the United States would not tolerate repeated and naked violations of their rights. When such violations rose to a crescendo during the German U-boat campaign of early 1917, American opinion came to accept the necessity of military involvement to protect their national idealism.

As soon as the war began, the United States proclaimed its neutrality. Yet what did neutrality mean? Some historians have held that the overriding reason for American involvement on the Allied side was a desire to salvage or protect America's huge commercial interest in the Entente through her sales of munitions, raw materials, foodstuffs and other goods, and through huge loans. Such had been the quantity of this trade in goods and money that the United States had been pulled out of the recession of 1914–15. Yet it has been convincingly argued that the alternative, to have denied or severely restricted Allied access to American markets, would itself have been unneutral. It was not America's fault if the Allied blockade prevented the Germans from similar

access. Arthur Link, a leading historian of American involvement in the war, writes that 'Only if Great Britain had been fighting for objectives that imperiled American security would Wilson have been justified in attempting to deny to the British advantages flowing from their control of the seas'. Besides, until the moment of its own belligerency the United States made frequent and to some extent effective protests whenever Britain trod too heavily on neutral rights in the course of administering her blockade of the Central Powers.

Whatever the rights and wrongs of the matter, trade statistics speak for themselves in showing the American economic involvement with the Entente. United States trade with the Central Powers, $169,000,000 in value in 1914, almost disappeared by 1916 to $1,159,000. Yet trade with the Allies, already high in 1914 at $824,000,000, rose by 1916 to $3,214,000,000.

As 1914 closed, Wilson still expected the war to end in an Allied vistory or, at worst, a stalemate. He viewed either prospect equally, though he hoped for a just peace of reconciliation after the conflict. Yet as we have seen, the German U-boat campaign of 1915 and especially the *Lusitania* incident brought German-American relations to a low point. After two earlier protests, Wilson

'A Fast Convoy'. War material and other goods could only be shipped across the Atlantic in convoy when the U-boat campaign was stepped up.

informed Berlin that America would consider further sinkings of ships without warning as 'deliberately unfriendly'. Such language had been too strong for William Jennings Bryan, Wilson's Secretary of State, and Bryan had resigned on 8 June 1915.

Ironically, the German submarine issue forced Wilson to discount the protests of Bryan and others at American lack of neutrality in acquiescing to several Allied measures to strengthen the economic blockade. The Entente argued with much plausibility that they had little alternative. Meanwhile American pressures and the dearth of German submarines caused the U-boat campaign to be modified. German-American relations improved to some extent. Then, in October 1915, Robert Lansing, Bryan's successor, transmitted to London a strongly-worded note which termed the spreading Allied blockade 'ineffective, illegal, and indefensible'. Thus American relations with the two warring sides were fairly if uneasily even-handed as 1916 began.

However, as Wilson knew, beneath the surface all was far from well. Since the Allies had begun to arm even merchant ships, pressures were mounting in Berlin for all-out submarine warfare. As a precaution against the unexpected, in the winter of 1915–16 Wilson himself advocated limited

Left: 'Drive the Ships Out!': German propaganda supporting the attempt to sweep Allied shipping from the seas.

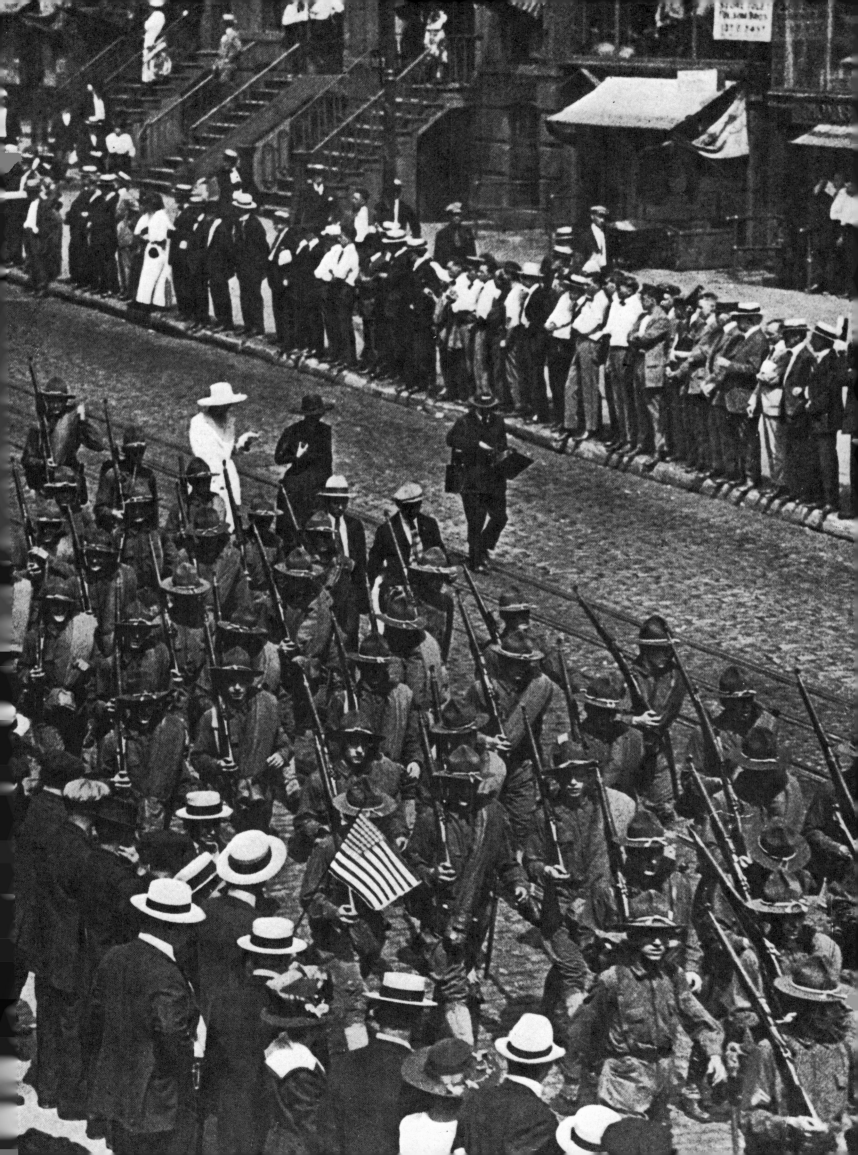

Previous page:
Conscripts and volunteers
answer the call in New
York. **Right:** So did
Tin Pan Alley.

the Allies rejected this idea outright, and Washington fell back on its earlier position that despite the dangers from Allied armed vessels, the Germans ought to refrain from sinkings without warning. Berlin, however, thought the contrary and announced the resumption of sinkings without warning as from the end of February.

Meanwhile the press had come to hear of the *modus vivendi* proposals, and a faction in Congress decided that, now that America's suggestions had been spurned, she ought to stand aloof from the defence of neutral rights. Thus the Gore-McLemore resolutions asked Congress to forbid American citizens to travel on belligerent ships in order to minimize American involvement. Playing on the fact that self-respect would not allow such an abdication of American rights, Wilson managed to oppose the resolutions successfully; but the affair was indicative of the isolationist mood of a considerable section of the populace.

Soon afterwards, the *Sussex* crisis exploded. As discussed earlier, the Germans yielded with reservations to Wilson's ultimatum that he would break relations if Germany did not abandon her ruthless submarine operations. At the end of May, Wilson announced that America would participate in a postwar League of Nations, but the announcement was tragically premature.

Despite heavy American pressures, neither Britain nor France would agree to peace talks in the uncertain state that the war had reached by mid-1916. Americans viewed this as obstinacy, and in the context of the post-*Sussex* relief of tension in relations between Washington and Berlin, Allied stock plummeted in American estimation. In addition, America viewed with a jaundiced eye Britain's fierce suppression of the Irish Easter Rising and yet further measures in the economic blockade. Wilson sent the Allies a series of increasingly reproachful notes on the latter issue. In September 1916 the President obtained powers to restrict imports and deny clearance to Allied ships, and he warned the Entente that their continued recalcitrance could force him to put these measures into practice. As the Allies made no fundamental concessions, the danger of serious friction with America grew.

Below: Wilson
campaigned for the victory
loans in 1917. **Below
right:** First American
conscripts were chosen in
this way.

measures to strengthen the American armed forces. In the meantime, Colonel House was in Europe on his latest peace mission, and in February the House-Grey Memorandum was initialled, only to be shelved. Indeed, the memorandum was partly undermined by British resentment at the American attitude on the question of armed merchant ships, an issue which also led to an American domestic crisis.

Originally the Germans had argued that since the Allies had fitted a number of their merchant vessels with large guns, which were to be used to shoot on sight any enemy submarine, the Central Powers could hardly be expected to adhere to the traditional rules of visit and search. Seeing the logic of the German position, in January 1916 Lansing had asked the Allies to consider a *modus vivendi* under which the merchantmen would be disarmed, and in return the Germans would not sink any ship without first inspecting its cargo and providing for the safety of those aboard. But

Yet America was mainly held back by the increasing mood of extremism which a determination to settle the war in 1917 had bred within the dominant faction in Berlin. Moreover, 1916 was a presidential election year, and until his re-election in November, Wilson required a minimum of controversy while campaigning under the slogan 'He Kept Us Out of War'.

Once safely reconfirmed in the White House, however, Wilson launched his peace initiative of December 1916, attempting to settle the war before America was dragged in. Then February 1917 saw the commencement of an all-out German submarine campaign, despite the earlier *Sussex* pledge. At this time the majority of Americans still clung to the hope of peace, but events rapidly shattered their illusions. In late February, even as he was requesting Congress for defensive armament for American merchantmen and emphasizing that war would come only if Germany wanted it, Wilson learned of the sinking of the British liner *Laconia* with the loss of three American lives. Almost simultaneously, an outraged American public was informed of the existence of a telegram sent on 16 January by the German Foreign Secretary, Alfried Zimmermann, to the German Minister in Mexico City. The British had intercepted and decoded this, the famous Zimmermann Telegram. Zimmermann had proposed a German-Mexican alliance in the event of the now-expected American belligerency. Mexico would attack the United States 'to reconquer the lost territory in New Mexico, Texas and Arizona'. Germany further suggested that Mexico 'should communicate with Japan suggesting adherence to this plan'. Thus a far-reaching anti-American combination was envisaged.

As Arthur Link wrote, for Wilson the Zimmermann Telegram was the last straw which 'caused him to lose all faith in the German government and to believe that the unscrupulous military masters of the *Reich* would stop at nothing in their mad ambitions'. Now a significant part of the thunder-struck American populace supported any measures, including war, which the government might find necessary. Moreover, the Russian 'February' Revolution did a great deal to influence pro-Allied sentiment in the United States. A corrupt, victorious, and parasitical autocracy had been overthrown, and the new government appeared to harbour democratic aims. As the *Nation* commented, 'A German victory now would mean the collapse of free Russia'. By the end of March, demand for war was widespread across America, given impetus by the sinking of three American ships between 16 and 18 March, the last of them, the *Vigilancia*, with considerable loss of life.

Wilson still wanted to avoid war. He saw the danger that an injection of American strength might lead to an Allied victory sufficiently overwhelming to make for a contentious peace. He feared that Americans would be brutalized by their war experiences. But on 20 March the cabinet unanimously advised him to ask Congress for a declaration of war. Wilson took their advice in the belief that at least American entry would end a war already in its final agony, and reasoning (in partial contradiction to some of his other

BRINGING IT HOME.

PRESIDENT WILSON. "WHAT'S THAT? U-BOAT BLOCKADING NEW YORK? TUT! TUT! VERY INOPPORTUNE!"

Punch took a jaundiced view of American neutrality in 1916.

thoughts) that only as a belligerent could America strongly influence the subsequent peace settlement in the direction of Wilson's own high ideals. By now he was fairly realistic concerning the extent of Allied objectives. If left to their own devices, he concluded, the Europeans would never see justice done. America must step in to redress the moral balance. So, in fact, German actions triggered off a decision for war in which the motives far transcended the scope of the original provocations.

Was the entry of the United States into the First World War inevitable from the beginning? Almost certainly not. Despite the ties of blood, culture, and ideals which bound America, and especially its Establishment, to Britain, the Central Powers might have avoided American participation if they had played their hand with greater finesse. Stupid blunders like the *Lusitania* affair and the unrestricted submarine campaign slowly convinced leading American circles that the kind of world in which American democracy could thrive was incompatible with a German victory. Until 1917 at least, this sentiment was uncertain and reversible, and it is likely that an astute German statesman could have avoided the fatal parting of the ways. Indeed, there was every chance that America might at some stage have obtained a compromise peace not unfavourable to Germany itself. Yet Germany lacked a leader of Bismarckian stature, and German politicians (wrongly, as we now see) had little or no faith in Wilson's impartiality. Events outran the power of men to deal with them, and took on a momentum of their own. In a sense, even the United States slipped into war half-unknowingly, for if the American people had thought that the step they were taking would ultimately lead to a long-term involvement in world affairs, they would have drawn back in consternation. Rather, as a whole they believed with touching naïveté that the world could be put right by victory and justice, and then America could return to her own affairs. After all, this was a war to end wars.

CHAPTER ELEVEN

Upheaval and Chaos in Russia

Many would argue that the Russian Revolution was the greatest event since the fall of the Bastille. The importance of its impact on the structure of the international community, the distribution of power in the world, and the ideas by which men live, or profess to live, can hardly be overestimated. Nineteen seventeen saw a fundamental upheaval in the world's largest state, a country which for all its backwardness and inefficiency corruption and sloth was potentially a giant among nations. The revolution also saw the rise to power of undoubtedly one of the most brilliant and formidable leaders in history: Vladimir Ulyanov, known to the world as Lenin.

The events of 1917 had roots which reached far back into the history of Russia itself. The intrigues at court and the military setbacks and hardships that accompanied the war have been frequently referred to in this narrative. No doubt this aspect of the fighting accelerated the process of internal disruption and disillusionment that led to revolution. For at least half a century, military reverses had intensified the undermining of the old order: the Crimean defeat led to the emancipation of the serfs in 1861; the Japanese victory of 1904–05 led to the 1905 revolution; and the disappointments and miseries of the Great War brought on the explosion of 1917. Yet other underlying and continuing factors had slowly but relentlessly done their work in tipping the balance against the status quo. Bad government existed independently of periodic fighting, as did agricultural penury, with millions of landless peasants, usurious landlords and profiteers, and gentry callously indifferent to the most elementary needs of those whom the system had placed at their mercy.

After the 1905 upheaval had subsided, the evils of the Tsarist regime actually increased. The decadence and obstinacy of the court completely separated it from the lives and interests of ordinary folk. In the succeeding decade, major and petty abuses of myriad varieties spread to such an extent that any incident could have sparked off an explosion whose final repercussions could not be perceived. The Duma (Parliament) was a mere travesty, its consultative powers flouted at will by the Tsar. At the end of 1916, there was still no end to the war in sight. A smouldering resentment spread inexorably throughout the land, a massive and largely inarticulate feeling which, searching in vain for an outlet, built up an inner tension comparable to the stresses beneath a geological fault which lead to an earthquake. Only a revolution from above could have staved off the revolution from below. None was forthcoming. Thus when the dam burst, the good in the system, what little there was, was swept away with the bad.

(Before discussing the revolution further, a note on dates should be added. Until the Bolshevik Revolution, the Russian calendar operated thirteen days behind that in use in the West; thus dates in the following chronicle of events will be given in both calendars.)

On the night of 17/30 to 18/31 December 1916, an extraordinary ritual was enacted. Some have called it the first concrete blow in the 1917 revolution; others have, perhaps more correctly, written that the happening only underlined for the last time the utter futility of trying to influence Tsar Nicholas in the direction of change. That evening, Prince Yussupov murdered the evil genius of the Tsarist regime, the lecherous 'monk' Grigory Rasputin, in a final effort to rid the court of the depravity and Germanophile influences which were alienating the population. Rasputin, a foul and semiliterate wolf in sheep's clothing, had become the power behind the throne through his autosuggestive treatment of the hereditary hemophilia which afflicted the young heir to the dynasty, the Tsarevich Alexei. In addition, Rasputin had spread his influence throughout the court by his assiduous cultivation of peasant manners and his equally shrewd seduction of the titled ladies of Petrograd. That day, as evening approached, Rasputin was tricked into accepting what he thought to be another assignation. Instead the witchdoctor was set upon, poisoned with cyanide, shot for good measure, and hurled

Opposite: Rasputin, the 'Mad Monk', surrounded by his admirers. It took cyanide, bullets, a knife and the icy waters of the river Neva to kill him.

Hunger was widespread before the revolution. It increased once the revolution began.

Front lines 1 July

Russian Advance by 16 July 1917

Counter-attack 19 July. Lost ground regained & further advance forced 3 August

Lenin exhorts the colonial people of the world to follow the Soviet path to freedom from the imperialists.

ПОД ЗНАМЕНЕМ ЛЕНИНА — ВПЕРЕД К МИРОВОМУ ОКТЯБРЮ!

beneath the ice of the river Neva. Yussupov and his fellow conspirators had hoped that the Tsar would be frightened into moderate reforms, which would permit the essential structure of autocracy to be maintained. Instead, however, the Tsar and Tsarina retreated behind a veil of resentful obduracy and devoted themselves to

attempts at communicating with their recently departed 'holy friend' through seances.

In January, as conditions in Russia worsened and tension rose to still greater heights, a delegation from the Western Allies arrived to lay plans for a final and victorious military onslaught. During their discussions with the Russians, the French conspired to aim for the restoration of their 1814 frontiers, a measure which the British repudiated later when they learned what had happened. In any case, the whole discussion was academic. The old order was on its last legs.

People in the capital were still going about their business in an atmosphere of uneasy peace. Few indeed recognized that an irreversible change was imminent. Later, when the revolution had begun, only a small number understood its scope or significance. Proposals to shore up the monarchy were made even after the people had rejected the Romanovs and anyone to do with them.

As February wore on, food in the capital became increasingly scarce. The heavy snows of winter had damaged many transport vehicles and had led to a shortage of the fuel that was needed to bring in supplies from the countryside. Distribution of food was inefficient; profiteering was more shameless than ever. On 23 February/ 8 March there were widespread strikes and food riots, and far from dying down, the strikes continued next day. The popular outburst apparently had no preconceived, detailed aims or central co-ordination; yet before police dispersed the demonstrators, the cry, 'Down with autocracy'! was heard. The 'February' Revolution had begun.

By 25 February/10 March the strikes had spread to include a quarter of a million workers. Factories and industries ground to a halt. Although troops and police were sent to break up demonstrations, and certain police opened fire indiscriminately on defenceless crowds, many army units refused to take part in the slaughter. Instead their members defected to the populace in their tens of thousands, many regiments butchering those officers who stood behind the old regime. Unseeing to the end, on 26 February/11 March the Tsar answered urgent appeals for reform from Rodzianko, President of the Duma, by ordering that body to disband. Yet the Duma remained assembled unofficially in Petrograd.

On 27 February/12 March, events moved to a climax. More and more soldiers joined the tide of revolt. The Tsar had ordered up troops from the front to crush the workers, but these soldiers too were either prevented from reaching the capital or were persuaded to throw in their lot with the revolution. In the afternoon, factory delegates, socialists of varying shades, and strike committee leaders formed the Petrograd Soviet (Council of Workers' Deputies). Subsequently the name was embellished to Council of Workers' and Soldiers' Deputies. On 1/14 March the Duma elected its own Provisional Committee, and a Provisional Government was nominated under Prince Lvov. Thereafter authority was divided between the Soviet and the Provisional Government; and this division of power proved to be one of the weaknesses of the first revolution.

Swiftly the rest of the country followed the lead of Petrograd. Although the overthrow of the

Above left: All the people had to do was kick in the door, and the whole House of Romanov came crashing down. **Above:** The Duma controlled events now. News sheets distributed by the Duma were issued on a regular basis to the people of Petrograd.

Romanovs was an accomplished fact, attempts were at first made to persuade Tsar Nicholas to abdicate in favour of his son Alexei, while the Tsar himself favored his brother, the Grand Duke Mikhail, as successor. With the situation still unresolved, on 2/15 March, Nicholas abdicated. Afterwards he and the other members of the royal family were arrested and, according to the accepted version, were eliminated in the Ural town of Ekaterinburg. However, certain doubts remain concerning the authenticity of this story.

The Provisional Government still made no decision either for or against the monarchy. It did not matter. The Duma whence it came was itself unrepresentative of popular forces, and instead served the interests of upper- and middle-class elements who were no match for the militantly organized workers and soldiers. Thus, because their own social and political ideas differed from those of the proletariat, the Duma and the Provisional Government were only partially effective.

At this point the German government hesitated – and lost. In the heady aftermath of liberation, confusion reigned over widespread areas of Russia. Much of the armed forces, not including those who had already left the front to work for the revolution, were demoralized by the sufferings of the war and influenced by the propaganda of the Petrograd Soviet. Under the circumstances, a German move against Russia would have had a high probability of success. Then Germany would have been free to move all her forces westwards, and might well have knocked the Entente out of the war before American help arrived. On the other hand, Berlin was anxious over events on the Western Front, and moreover thought that a hard bargain might be struck with the new Russian regime if internal chaos were allowed to progress undisturbed. Some thought that, alternatively, the warring forces might be immediately united in the face of an external threat from Germany. In any case, the Reich attempted further disruption by facilitating the entry of potential troublemakers into Russia – most significantly Lenin. The Germans allowed Lenin to pass through Germany from exile in Switzerland in a sealed train. Had those Germans who let Lenin through have imagined the successes which he would achieve in Russia and

almost in Germany itself, they might have had second thoughts.

Meanwhile the Provisional Government, egged on by Allied pressure, determined on a renewed military offensive. Dreams of the Balkans and Constantinople (Tsargrad, as Russians had once thought of it) also lured them on. Yet Lenin, leading the Bolshevik extreme left-wing revolutionaries, opposed continuance of the war; and many voices on all sides supported him. But by now, the Petrograd Soviet was being swept away by the power of the revolution. Throughout the period leading to the 'October' Revolution, the Petrograd Soviet and the Provisional Government, though they grappled for the reins of power, made repeated attempts to resolve their differences. Indeed, until May the Petrograd Soviet more or less accepted the authority of the Provisional Government; and in the matter of resuming the war, the radicals lost. Earlier the Petrograd Soviet had appealed to the belligerents for peace and the renunciation of chauvinistic war aims. Similarly, the Provisional Government had proclaimed that it desired 'not the forcible seizure of foreign territories, but the establishment of a stable peace on the basis of the self-determination of peoples'. Nevertheless the Provisional Government promised to continue the fight and respect existing Russian obligations.

On 18 June/1 July a strong Russian offensive was launched in two places, using many Siberian troops thought to have been protected by distance from revolutionary doctrines. In fact, Bolshevik propaganda and German fraternization had already effectively undermined military morale, and when the Russians attacked, their paucity of reserves quickly became evident. Meanwhile the Germans had brought in four divisions from the west in readiness for a counteroffensive. First, however, the Russian offensive of 22 June/5 July under Kornilov succeeded in pulverizing the defences of Tersztyansky's Austrian Third Army and made a considerable advance before suddenly faltering and then being stopped short by the German reserves.

After some delays and prevarications, the German counter-assault began on 6/19 July. One of its outstanding features was the brilliant use of artillery bombardment by Colonel Bruchmüller,

Grand Duke Nicholas briefly controlled the Provisional Government.

Above and right: General Kornilov, whose rivalry with Kerensky assumed the dimensions of a revolt

Below: The leadership of Kerensky (left) was ineffectual.

РАЙОННЫМЪ
Совѣтамъ Рабочихъ Депутатовъ
Фабрично-Заводскимъ Комитетамъ

ПРИКАЗЪ.

Корниловскія банды Керенскаго угрожаютъ подступамъ къ столицѣ. Отданы всѣ необходимыя распоряженія для того, чтобы безпощадно раздавить контръ-революціонное покушеніе противъ народа и его завоеваній.

Армія и Красная Гвардія революціи нуждаются въ немедленной поддержкѣ рабочихъ.

Приказываемъ районнымъ Совѣтамъ и Фабр.-Зав. Комитетамъ:

1) выдвинуть наибольшее количество рабочихъ для рытья окоповъ, воздviганія баррикадъ и укрѣпленія проволочныхъ загражденій;

2) гдѣ для этого потребуется прекращеніе работъ на фабрикахъ и заводахъ, немедленно исполнить;

3) собрать всю имѣющуюся въ запасѣ колючую и простую проволоку, а равно всѣ орудія, необходимыя для рытья окоповъ и возведенія баррикадъ;

4) все имѣющееся оружіе имѣть при себѣ;

5) соблюдать строжайшую дисциплину и быть готовыми поддержать армію революціи всѣми средствами.

Предсѣдатель Петроградскаго Совѣта Раб. и Солд. Депутатовъ Народный Комиссаръ ЛЕЕ ТРОЦКІЙ.

Предсѣдатель Военно-Революціоннаго Комитета Главнокомандующій ПОДВОЙСКІЙ.

120

TO THE DISTRICT
SOVIETS OF WORKER'S DEPUTIES AND
SHOP-FACTORY COMMITTEES

ORDER

THE KORNILOV BANDS OF KERENSKY ARE THREATENING THE OUTSKIRTS OF OUR CAPITAL. ALL NECESSARY ORDERS HAVE BEEN GIVEN TO CRUSH MERCILESSLY EVERY COUNTER-REVOLUTIONARY ATTEMPT AGAINST THE PEOPLE AND ITS CONQUESTS.

THE ARMY AND THE RED GUARD OF THE REVOLUTION ARE IN NEED OF IMMEDIATE SUPPORT OF THE WORKERS.

THE DISTRICT SOVIETS AND SHOP-FACTORY COMMITTEES ARE ORDERED:

1) To bring forward the largest possible number of workers to dig trenches, erect barricades and set up wire defenses;

2) Wherever necessary for this purpose to SUSPEND WORK in shops and factories, it must be done IMMEDIATELY.

3) To collect all available plain and barbed wire, as well as all tools FOR DIGGING TRENCHES AND ERECTING BARRICADES;

4) ALL AVAILABLE ARMS TO BE CARRIED ON PERSONS;

5) Strictest discipline must be preserved and all must be ready to support the Army of the Revolution to the utmost.

President of the Petrograd Soviet of Workers & Soldiers Deputies People's Commissar LEV TROTSKY.

President of the Military-Revolutionary Committee Chief Commander PODVOISKY.

[*Reproduction in English of the Russian text on opposite page.*]

1   121

later nicknamed 'Breakthrough' (*Durchbruch*) Müller because of the devastating effect of his weaponry on the Russian morale. As the Germans poured along the front, the Russian troops retreated in droves. Discipline and command-structure were wrecked, and the Russians' pell-mell flight through Galicia was marked by hideous assaults on the local populace. Soon all the gains of the so-called Kerensky offensive had been eliminated.

Further south, on 9/22 July, the Rumanians, their army now reorganized by the French, had launched an attack in the Carpathians, aided by the Russian Fourth Army. Though the Rumanian offensive won success at first, it was pushed back by Mackensen on 23 July/6 August and after, in a series of fights known as the Battle of Maraseti. Then this front again fell silent.

Soon after the renewed fighting on the Eastern Front, the events known as the 'July Days' took place. By this time the Bolsheviks already had strong support in Petrograd, but in the provinces the moderate socialists still prevailed. While this situation lasted, Lenin was eager to avoid a trial of strength; but the workers in Petrograd got out of hand and unsuccessfully attempted a *coup d'état*.

On 3/16 July soldiers and workers demanded that the reins of power be yielded to the Petrograd Soviet, but the Provisional Government brought in troops and put down the revolt. Now the Provisional Government turned on the Bolsheviks, accusing them of undermining tactics which were leading to the defeat of the Russian armies in the field. It denounced the Bolsheviks as traitors and Lenin in particular as a German agent. On 6/19 July Lenin fled into hiding as a warrant for his arrest was issued.

The Provisional Government never recovered

from the blows to its prestige caused by the 'July Days'. The forces represented by the Petrograd and other soviets began to assert their strength. On 24 July/6 August they demanded constitutional and land reforms, and when the government of Prince Lvov refused, it was swept away. Kerensky formed a moderate but hopelessly indecisive coalition. Soon rivalry surfaced between Kerensky and Kornilov, the new Russian commander-in-chief. First, however, the fall of Riga intervened.

Ludendorff had decided that if the Russians could be driven out of their Baltic bridgehead at Riga, the Latvian capital, Petrograd would be unnerved. Bruchmüller and his men once more put their artillery to good use, but the retreating Russian Twelfth Army managed to get away with all but nine thousand of its men. Yet on 21 August/3 September, Riga fell without noticeable effort, and afterwards the Germans occupied several islands at the mouth of the Gulf of Riga, from where, if necessary, it would be relatively easy to strike at the Russian naval base of Kronstadt and also at Helsinki (Helsingfors).

By this time the Western Allies had reluctantly concluded that Russia, awash in its own troubles, would either leave the war or cease to play any important role in its conduct. Lloyd George commented that he had, 'lost all interest in Russia as a working factor in the success of the Allies'.

In the interim, Kornilov seized on the fall of Riga to withdraw his support from the government. The details behind this incident are still far from clear, but the rivalry between Kerensky and Kornilov now assumed the dimensions of a revolt. On 25 August/7 September Kornilov ordered a march on Petrograd, but this was nullified with Bolshevik help.

The position of the moderate socialists weak-

ened yet further, as it became increasingly obvious that the Provisional Government was proving itself incompetent. The coalition government collapsed, and on 1/14 September Kerensky formed a Directory marked, as Deutscher tartly remarks, by his 'personal incapacity to rule'. Soon the Bolsheviks had obtained majorities on the soviets of both Petrograd and Moscow, as well as in most of the provinces. Thence their influence in the country as a whole mounted rapidly.

In this situation, Lenin decided that the time for the major Bolshevik Revolution was ripe. The 'bourgeois-democratic' phase of the political transformation of the country had proceeded and had served its purpose, and it was time to move on. On 10/23 October the Bolshevik Central Committee took a definite decision to prepare for revolution, despite the opposition of Zinoviev and Kamenev, two of its members.

How had conditions riped for the final cataclysm? The Provisional Government, for all its liberal measures in certain spheres, hung back in the face of the many and difficult social problems of the country. Its determination to continue the war had meant that there was less time, energy, and funds to instigate quickly a broad measure of needed reforms. The Bolsheviks were perfectly suited to exploit the situation, for they were ruthless and dynamic, with a gift for appealing to the unsatisfied hopes and needs of the general population. Above all, their guiding light, Lenin, and their organizational genius, Trotsky, towered like giants over mediocrities like Kerensky.

With supreme irony, Kerensky's final miscalculation was that he vastly underestimated the Bolsheviks' strength and looked forward to an insurrection as a chance to repress them. He had not long to wait – but his plans went awry.

Late in October (or early in November, accord-

Mutiny within the army was rife. Attempts to prevent soldiers from going home, as in this case, were futile.

ing to the Julian calendar) Kerensky decided to secure his position by sending the more revolutionary armed contingents to the front, and thus away from the capital, where they might cause trouble. The Revolutionary Military Committee of the Petrograd Soviet vehemently objected. Stung into action, on 23 October/5 November Kerensky ordered the arrest of several Bolshevik leaders. It was too late. His actions had given the revolutionaries the pretext they needed. Castigating 'counterrevolutionary conspirators' who were plotting against it, the Revolutionary Military Committee moved swiftly. On the night of 24–25 October/6–7 November the Bolsheviks took over key points throughout the capital. By morning Kerensky had fled to the front in a vain endeavour to round up support. Almost effortlessly and with little bloodshed, the initial aims of the revolution had been achieved; and though three years of bloody civil war were needed to consolidate their control, the Bolsheviks could rejoice that the world's first Marxist state had come into existence.

On the evening of 25 October/7 November, Lenin called for 'a just, democratic peace . . . without annexations . . . and . . . indemnities'. In another momentous decree, he declared that 'landlord property is abolished forthwith without compensation'. Next day a Council of People's Commissars was formed with Lenin as chairman. The establishment of the dictatorship of the proletariat, to be followed by peace, was proclaimed. Indeed, not only in the first heady moments of their success, but for long afterwards, the Bolsheviks hoped that the world revolution was at hand, and that afterwards peace would spontaneously occur as proletarian governments took power in every country.

The story of the many internal developments which took place as a result of the 'October' Revolution lies beyond the scope of this narrative. It is sufficient to say that the two major problems of the new regime were the consolidation of its power throughout the vast Russian territories and the establishment of some kind of relationship between Soviet Russia and the non-revolutionary world outside. In this sphere the first priority was some arrangement by which Russia might leave the war. To the general embarrassment of the Bolsheviks, the hoped-for immediate world revolution had not yet occurred, and Britain and France had made no response to the Soviet call for a general peace. It seemed that there was no alternative but to ask the Central Powers for a separate peace, despite the violent ideological objections of many Bolsheviks to this measure. It did not matter that under the 1914 Pact of London, the Tsarist regime had promised Britain and France not to make a separate peace; The Bolsheviks repudiated past obligations en masse, and as if to rub this in they published the texts of the Allied secret treaties, which had been concluded earlier in the war. This underlined the Marxist feeling that the war was a struggle between rival and equally loathsome imperialisms in which the working people in every country had no interest and, indeed, no place.

Eventually the Allies made known their own position. Having agreed that Russia was still bound by the Treaty of London, Britain and France declared that although there would be no separate peace, they 'would proceed to a revision of war aims together with Russia' as soon as that country was ruled by 'a government aware of its duties to the country and defending the interests of the country and not of the enemy'. The Bolshevik mood was hardly improved by this slap in the face, and arrangements to negotiate with the Central Powers proceeded.

Sir John Wheeler-Bennett, the historian of the Treaty of Brest-Litovsk (as the separate peace was called) has declared that for Russia, the capitulation was 'the greatest humiliation in her diplomatic and military history' because of the Draconian terms of the settlement.

Brest-Litovsk: A Separate Peace
Preliminary conversations between the Bolsheviks and the Central Powers had begun on 3 December at the Polish town of Brest-Litovsk, German headquarters for the Eastern Front. On 15 December agreement was reached for a twenty-eight-day truce from 17 December, during which negotiations for a settlement would be concluded. The Germans' wish for a quiet Eastern Front in order to turn westwards had overcome their distaste for negotiating with men whom they considered to be guttersnipes. However, the severity of the terms which the Central Powers demanded was partly conditioned by their realization that the Bolsheviks as yet had no indisputable claim to the right to speak for Russians as a whole, let alone the non-Russian nationalities of the former empire. In addition, there were difficulties peculiar to negotiations with the new Russian regime. Unlike governments bound by bourgeois conventions, the Communists were willing to use a remarkable array of tactical weaponry in the furtherance of their aims. For example, they would temporarily yield whole provinces at a time if by so doing they thought they could arouse the class solidarity of the working masses of the Central Powers.

Left: The revolt of the Bolsheviks was well-organized and effective. **Below:** Strong points were taken throughout the capital.

On the German side, Hindenburg and Ludendorff were anxious to exploit the opportunity of confrontation with an enemy at bay by annexing the Russian Baltic regions of Estonia, Livonia, Courland (Kurland) and Lithuania. Centuries ago these areas had been penetrated by the Teutonic Knights, and much of their aristocracy and bourgeoisie was of German origin. In addition, Germany needed the 'breadbasket' of the Ukraine to feed its people, by now in great distress because of the Allied blockade. Moreover, the more amputations of provinces from the sick and wounded body of Russia proper, the weaker Germany's opponent would be left, reasoned many of the German general staff. The Germans clearly held the upper hand; and if the Bolsheviks

proved recalcitrant at Brest-Litovsk, the German armies would drive forward to Petrograd itself to dictate terms.

The German foreign secretary, Baron Richard von Kühlmann, disagreed with the 'politics of illusion' of the German general staff. Kühlmann was less confident of Germany's ability to force a military victory; a shrewd negotiated peace with the Entente was, he felt, a better bet. Moreover, whereas Ludendorff wanted territorial and strategic gains in the east in order, as he bluntly put it, to help 'the manoeuvring of my left wing in the next war', Kühlmann wanted to obtain large territories in the east in order to use them as bargaining counters at the peace table vis-à-vis the lands which Germany had conquered in the west. Eventually, however, when it became clear that the British and French had no intention of coming to Brest-Litovsk for a general settlement, in Berlin imperialist designs carried the day.

For their part, the Bolsheviks had to weigh their desire for immediate peace against their wish to use the peace conference as a showcase for propaganda designed to undermine the will to war of the ordinary people among the other belligerents. A headlong clash of wills took place between Kühlmann and Trotsky, now People's Commissar for Foreign Affairs. Meanwhile the Austrian foreign minister, Count Ottokar von Czernin, stood by helplessly in the knowledge that the Emperor had told him that in no cir-

Above: German cavalry march in triumph through a Ukrainian town. Helpless against the German invader, the Soviet government decided to make a separate peace.
Opposite: Joffe, Karakhan and Trotsky formed the Russian delegation which is greeted by the Germans in Brest-Litovsk.

German troops pursued bands of Bolsheviks in the Ukraine when Russian lines cracked.

cumstances must he return home without that peace which, it was thought, alone could save the dying Habsburg Empire.

After weeks of negotiations, prevarications, and interminable delays, on 9 February 1918 the Central Powers reached a separate agreement with the Ukraine, which had previously broken away from Russia itself. The Ukraine became a *de facto* protectorate of Germany, while an agreement was reached for the export of a million tons of foodstuffs to the Central Powers.

Now the Bolsheviks realized that they needed peace even more than they needed propagandistic ferment. Counter-revolutionary forces were rapidly organizing on all sides. Swiftly abandoning his policy of delay, on 10 February Trotsky declared a state of 'no war, no peace' and returned to Petrograd in the belief that the opposing side would accept the situation. But instead the Germans resumed the offensive and struck within eighty miles of Petrograd, meeting hardly any resistance from the bewildered and demoralized populace or the remnants of the military. The Bolsheviks had no option but to cave in.

On 3 March the Treaty of Brest-Litovsk was signed. In tandem with later agreements, the Russians were forced to yield Russian Poland, Estonia, Litvonia, Courland, Lithuania, and certain small islands to Germany and Austria-Hungary, and to surrender Kars, Ardahan, and Batum to Turkey. Finnish independence was to be recog-

nized, in addition to that of the Ukraine and Georgia. Massive reparations payments in money and goods were to be undertaken. This amounted to a Carthaginian peace, since under its terms Russia was almost cut off from the Baltic, was entirely landlocked to the south, and lost 34 percent of her population, 32 percent of her agricultural land and 89 percent of her coal resources. Despite the harshness of these terms, Russia had no option but to ratify the treaty on 29 March.

Meanwhile, after concluding an armistice on 9 December, the Rumanians encountered the full wrath of the Central Powers. Bucharest now paid dearly for her abandonment of that grouping in favour of the Entente. In March she was forced to yield the entire Dobrudja for future partitioning among Germany, Austria-Hungary, Bulgaria, and Turkey. Austria-Hungary was to receive substantial territory on the Rumanian side of the Carpathians. The Rumanian Army was to be reduced almost to nothing, and odious economic measures against Rumania were discussed. Even worse was to follow, for in the final settlement, signed 7 May, Rumania was cut off from the sea entirely, with the use of Constanza as a free port. Her vast oil resources fell prey to Germany, and several other onerous conditions were to be enforced by an army of occupation which would leave only at a time 'to be agreed upon'. Through Rumania was to be encouraged to gain Bessarabia from Russia, this measure was evidently a further move to weaken Russia rather than one motivated by any regard for Russia's smaller neighbour. Rumania was saved only by an Allied vistory in which she theoretically participated by resuming war against the Central Powers just before the armistice of November 1918.

The Bolsheviks had signed at Brest-Litovsk with gritted teeth. Yet had they not capitulated and gained time to organize the Red Army and reinforce their power base, they might well have been destroyed by Germans or dissident internal forces separately or in collusion. Moreover, the irony of Brest-Litovsk was that far from liberating German forces for use in the west, the extent of the Central Powers' gains caused a million men to remain committed in the east in a holding-down operation. Who knows what might have been achieved in the spring of 1918 if these forces had streamed westwards?

The Allies learned one major lesson from Brest-Litovsk. Here they saw the full extent of German territorial ambition, and the experience was salutary in silencing those who still pressed for a compromise peace in the west. The effect on the United States was even greater. In April 1918 President Wilson declared that the German eastern treaties had shown that Germany demanded as arbiter 'force, and force alone'; America would reply with '. . . but one response . . .: Force, Force to the utmost . .'. The Allied and Associated Powers closed ranks as never before. Furthermore, in 1919 the German socialists were persuaded to accept the Versailles *diktat* partly in the belief that its injustices would be fought against by a world public opinion as outraged as it was by the Peace of Brest-Litovsk. Truly the repercussions of the peace negotiations of the winter and spring of 1918 were endless.

Opposite top: General von Hoffmann (with cane) helped form part of the German delegation which won so many concessions from the Bolsheviks at Brest-Litovsk. **Far left:** Stormtroops advance after a smoke bomb attack on the Rumanian Front. **Left:** Rumania was bombarded into submission by the Central Powers.

CHAPTER TWELVE
Ideals—and Continued War

In 1917, even as momentous events were taking place in the East, the Western Front was also very active.

The Allies met at Chantilly in November 1916 to plan their strategy for the year ahead. Joffre and Haig, the French and British supremos, both realized that Verdun and the Somme had worn the German armies to a thread. On the other hand, the French in particular were reaching the end of their own tether, especially psychologically. Now Joffre believed that his men had the stamina and *élan* for one more great battle. This must be decisive. Joffre looked forward to spring as the occasion for this offensive, but in the interim he was replaced by the young General Robert Nivelle. In the meantime, bad weather prevented any large-scale concerted action during the winter, though in February a somewhat larger campaign took place on the Ancre.

Nivelle was bursting with confidence. His optimism proved both infectious and misplaced. Somehow he convinced both the French and British Prime Ministers – Briand and Lloyd George – that he could break through in the west in a mere two days – although this was the key to victory sought in vain for two and a half years!

Nonetheless, Nivelle's boldness was undiminished. Relying on the twin tactics of speed and surprise, the French would mount a large-scale offensive on the Aisne, while the British would make their major diversionary attack near Arras. Before this could happen, however, several things went wrong. The Germans pulled back to strong defensive positions (the Hindenburg Line), yet Nivelle continued with his plans much as if nothing untoward had occurred. Then his security proved unreliable, and exact information as to Allied movements reached the Germans. Nonetheless the Second Battle of the Aisne, otherwise called the Nivelle Offensive, began on 16 April.

Above: General Nivelle aged twenty years in the five months he commanded French troops on the Western Front. **Opposite:** View of Oosttaverne Wood, showing trenches taken by the British in the Battle of Messines.

Below left: Dozens of French tanks were destroyed on the first day of the Second Battle of the Aisne. **Below:** The French advance under fire. **Below right:** German machine guns help to stop the French advance.

Nivelle exhorted his troops with typical verve: *L'heure est venue!* (The hour has come!) *Confiance! Courage! Vive la France!*

The attack on the Aisne was certainly not without its successes, except that, measured against the overweening confidence of its commander it was judged a failure. As had happened before, German machine guns wreaked havoc among the advancing French, and a large number of the French tank force of two hundred was destroyed on the first day. Yet on 17 April Mangin's French Sixth Army advanced two and a half miles and captured a large quantity of German artillery. As later gains became increasingly unimpressive, further efforts at progress were postponed until May, when they were unsuccessful.

On 15 May Pétain in turn had replaced Nivelle. As at Verdun, his influence quickly had a calming effect. Calm could not have been more desperately needed, for their exhaustion and frustration had resulted in widespread mutinies among the French armies. As the ill-starred Nivelle Offensive had cost the French an additional hundred thousand or more casualties, it became increasingly obvious that the tattered Gallic armies would have to stand on the defensive until American forces at last arrived on the Continent. Meanwhile the Germans had hardly escaped unscathed: their toll of dead and wounded was one hundred and sixty-three thousand.

Thus, pending the arrival of 'Uncle Sam', the British were left with almost the full burden of Allied fighting in the West. On 9 April the attack at Arras had begun, and north of the Scarpe river the troops, urged on by their own high morale, made the deepest advance achieved in a single day since trench warfare had stabilized the front. However, tanks were employed to very poor effect. By 11 April, full realization was dawning that the Germans had brought in fresh troops for which

the increasingly weary British were no match. Still, in the second phase of the battle, on 23–24 April, in the midst of particularly ferocious fighting, the British gained the upper hand. However, this achieved little long-term result, and further efforts concentrated mainly around a renewed offensive undertaken on 3 May in order to encourage and shield the French. Final casualties for Arras were 150,000 British and perhaps nearly as many Germans (though statistics for this battle are unreliable).

The British were now faced with the need for a move in Flanders. Like Sir John French before him, Haig had long sought the opportunity to clear the Belgian coast of the enemy. Indeed, he had wanted to attack in this direction instead of on the Somme or later at Arras, but various factors had contributed to his being overruled. Now, considering Nivelle's failure and events in Russia, the Germans, even though many of their troops were worn out, had somehow to be prevented from dealing a hammer-blow at either Italy or the possibly disintegrating former Tsarist empire. Attrition in the west seemed the answer. Moreover, the British Admiralty, and in particular Jellicoe, the First Sea Lord, was anxious to cripple the German submarines, some of which operated from Ostend and Zeebrugge, and to do this the British would have to break through to the coast. Subsequently it was learned that the Admiralty had exaggerated the importance of the Belgian submarine bases and that the main U-boat campaign was conducted from German ports. It is uncertain how much Haig himself believed in Jellicoe's alarmism, but the latter's arguments tied in neatly with Haig's ideas on a Flanders offensive. In any case, in a final bitter irony, by the time the attempted breakthrough was launched, the adoption of the convoy system for merchant vessels had mitigated the worst of the submarine damage.

Haig knew that it would be necessary first to secure the southern approach by capturing the strategically vital Messines Ridge, whence he hoped to break through at Ypres and proceed northeast. An advance along the coast and an amphibious landing near Ostend would also be required for this plan to achieve maximum effect. Control of the coast would outflank the German northern line before Berlin could transfer more troops from the East; and the new Allied flank would itself be protected by its contiguity to neutral Holland. On the other hand, the actual staging of the operation became increasingly difficult in the absence of French support except for an elite force of six divisions. Still, Haig remained confident, despite the warnings of Robertson and the scepticism of Lloyd George. Haig seems to have been motivated by a wish to continue to protect the tottering French, but more importantly, by a desire to make his mark with a great victory in Flanders that would bring the British into clear pre-eminence in the Allied coalition and push Germany over the brink into defeat. The French, in fact, thought very little of Haig's projected clearing operation, and Foch, their chief of the general staff, sneered that the campaign would become 'a duck's march'.

The Battle of Messines took place on 7–8 June.

Top: Canadian troops of the 19th Infantry Battalion consolidate their positions. **Above:** An eight-inch Mark V howitzer in action near Arras. **Left:** Scottish troops advance to the attack. **Opposite:** British soldiers regroup near an abandoned tank.

Its most interesting and memorable aspect was the detonation of almost a million pounds of explosive, which had previously been placed under the German positions. Nineteen mines were fired simultaneously, and the entire top of the hill was blown away. The explosion could be heard across the Channel. Then a tremendous artillery barrage began, under cover of which Plumer's Second Army advanced across the crest of Messines, and the Germans pulled back to positions behind the Ypres-Comines (Komen) Canal, where they found themselves too debilitated to counterattack. Their morale, not to mention their health, had been further undermined in the interim by gas and boiling oil. At the cost of at least 17,000 casualties, the British had succeeded in closing the salient south of Ypres. German losses were 25,000, including 7,500 prisoners.

After a delay of over seven weeks, caused among other things by cabinet debates as to the advisability of the Flanders project, at the end of July the new offensive began. The Third Battle of Ypres, also known collectively and inaccurately as 'Passchendaele' (after a village near Ypres), began after an Allied air offensive commencing 11 July and involving 700 aircraft.

Lasting until 6 November, Third Ypres was plagued with inordinate bad luck. The fatal delay between the Messines and Ypres operations had given the Germans the chance to bring up reinforcements and provide a new and efficient system of defences. Nevertheless, in fact Haig had himself planned a considerable delay between the two battles.

Third Ypres saw the German use of mustard gas, the effect of which was to create on all parts of the body burns and huge blisters which were slow to heal. In July 1918 the French in turn made use of this atrocious weapon, and no doubt would have done so earlier if they had had the means to produce it.

To return to the battle itself: the preliminary bombardment of a fortnight's duration was counterproductive, for its 65,000 tons of shells destroyed the surface drainage of the area and turned the soil into a sticky, soggy entrapment which badly hindered the Allied advance. In fact, the entire area was unsuitable for fighting purposes, because a level plain stretching for twenty miles made all the British preparations obvious to the enemy and made excellent targets of both men and supplies after the battle had begun.

Above left: An eighteen-pounder is pulled out of the mud. The territory around Passchendaele became an unspeakable quagmire.
Above right: A wounded Canadian being carried to a dressing station on the back of a comrade, followed by two German prisoners.
Opposite top left: Grenades were taken to German soldiers on the front by messenger dog.
Opposite top right: Slaughtered Germans; Third Battle of Ypres, 31 July 1917. **Opposite bottom:** Near 'Clapham Junction', looking towards Sanctuary Wood: 23 September 1917.

Haig's original plan had been for the Fifth Army under General Sir Hubert Gough to advance fifteen miles and seize control of strategic communications in the region, after which the Fourth Army would attack on the coast with the aid of troop landings. The British Second Army would move northeast to gain control of Passchendaele. However, the actual outcome was quite different. Third Ypres became essentially a battle for control of a vital plateau, and no breakthrough to the sea occurred.

Despite all setbacks, the first day's fighting was marked by British successes. But the previously balmy weather broke, and heavy rains added the finishing touches to the developing quagmire. Thousands of shell craters filled to the brim with mud and water. Earlier warnings that this would happen were made in plenty – but ignored. The Royal Engineers worked magnificently, constructing roads of planks and boards over which men and matériel had to travel. Often, however, all but the most surefooted found themselves up to their waists in mud and slime, and many men drowned.

The first part of Third Ypres involved the Fifth Army primarily, and was marked by the opening Battle of Pilckem Ridge, as well as those of Gheluvelt Plateau (10 August) and Langemarck (16 August), in both of which the Germans fiercely and successfully counterattacked. Already Gough had concluded that no worthwhile success could be achieved, and he so informed Haig. But Haig refused to call off the battle, not only on account of his wish to aid the French, but because otherwise his forces might have been diverted to the Italian Front and the Allied lines might have collapsed in the West.

At the end of August Haig transferred the main burden of operations from Gough to the more cautious Plumer. Yet Plumer spent too much time in September carefully preparing his next moves. In this he failed to take advantage of a period of relatively more favourable weather. Finally, however, the second phase of Third Ypres opened with the Battle of Menin (Menen) Road Ridge on 20 September. Brilliant use of artillery contributed greatly to the British Empire forces' success. Six days later, the battle fought at Polygon Wood was a similar triumph, as was Broodseinde (4 October), even though the troops were plagued with dust clouds of sandstorm-like intensity. By October, in fact, the weather had worsened again;

and despite all tactical successes, there was no strategic innovation. Furthermore, the amphibious coastal operation had by now been given up.

The third and final phase of the campaign centred around control of the village of Passchendaele, which finally fell on 6 November. Pouring rain drenched everything in sight. Ludendorff called the living and fighting conditions 'mere unspeakable suffering'. Indeed, the Passchendaele phase of Third Ypres became an exercise in futility. Passchendaele neither prevented the Russian collapse, nor the Central Powers' victory at Caporetto. Attrition was severe – but it affected both sides.

Casualties for Third Ypres are difficult to estimate. Beyond doubt, the cost was horrifying; the question is only one of the quantitative extent of the slaughter. British losses were certainly 245,000, but may have been up to 300,000. German casualties were somewhere between 175,000 and 400,000. In contrast, the small French army under Antoine suffered less than 9000 dead and wounded. The campaign had continued beyond all usefulness because of Haig's obstinate belief that Germany was near to collapse. He was sustained in this illusion by the sycophancy of many of his staff. Thus it was that Third Ypres came to epitomize the tragedy and waste of heroic effort for indifferent strategic results, and in retrospect its importance has been denigrated and its short-term successes eclipsed by the accompanying suffering and misery.

British reserves were now virtually nonexistent; thus the subsequent Battle of Cambrai was doomed before it began. Moreover, Lloyd George began to distrust both Haig and Robertson, and concentrated more on his pet diversion of a brilliant victory to be gained in Palestine.

The Fourteen Points

In January 1918, Woodrow Wilson made his first definitive statement of war aims. For some time, various sources had been urging the American president to clarify the ideals and objectives for which Americans, at least, were fighting. After consultations with Colonel House and certain experts known as The Inquiry, Wilson enunciated his famous Fourteen Points.

Wilson spoke at a crucial moment for the Allied cause. The Bolshevik Revolution in Russia, its leaders' call for a peace based on neither annexations nor indemnities, and its publication of the Allied secret treaties all caused grave embarrassment to the Allied and Associated Powers (as the Western coalition was known after American entry into the war, the United States being an 'associate' rather than an ally of the others). The need was urgent for a high-minded formulation of war aims, not only to counteract the Soviets and their accusations as to Allied cunning and duplicity, but to still the strident objections to the secret treaties which liberal and progressive opinion made within the Allied camp itself. On the other hand, Wilson was temperamentally inclined to excessive idealism, whereas the Allies themselves never had any intention of renouncing those territorial acquisitions which they felt vital, and for which their populations clamoured as a reward for the misery and destruction of the war. To complicate matters further, in late December 1917 the pronouncements of Czernin, the Austro-Hungarian Foreign Minister, led to speculation that a renewed peace initiative by the Central Powers was in the offing. It was now clear that Russia needed immediate encouragement if she were not to sign a separate peace with Germany and Austria (which, as we have seen, is what subsequently took place at Brest-Litovsk).

In drafting the Fourteen Points, as well as to consider Russian susceptibilities two other major considerations were kept in mind. On the subject of Alsace-Lorraine, the former French province which the Second Reich had annexed as a result of the Franco-Prussian War, Wilson was determined to make a statement. The President favoured restoration of Alsace-Lorraine to France, although the case for doing so was not clear-cut; a large part of the population was ethnically and linguistically

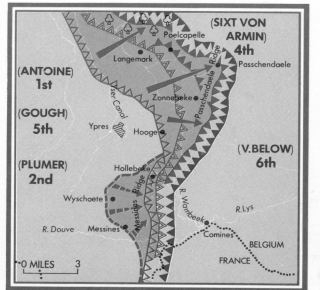

(ANTOINE)
1st

(GOUGH)
5th

(PLUMER)
2nd

(SIXT VON ARMIN)
4th

Poelcapelle

Langemark

Passchendaele

Zonnebeke

Ypres

Hooge

Hollebeke

Wyschaete

Messines Ridge

R. Douve   Messines

R. Wambeek

R. Lys

Comines

BELGIUM

FRANCE

(V.BELOW)
6th

Iser Canal

Passchendaele Ridge

0 MILES 3

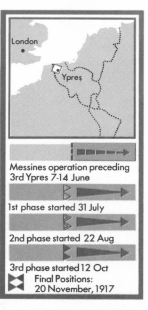

London

Ypres

Messines operation preceding
3rd Ypres 7-14 June

1st phase started 31 July

2nd phase started 22 Aug

3rd phase started 12 Oct
Final Positions:
20 November, 1917

193

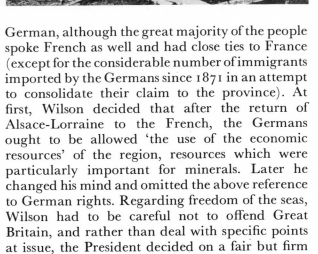

Above: The Duke of Aosta, whose Third Army was destroyed, poses with his son, Amedeo of Savoy.
Above right: Austrian mortar in action. Bombardment of Italian positions was heavy.

Heavy artillery fire at Caporetto.

German, although the great majority of the people spoke French as well and had close ties to France (except for the considerable number of immigrants imported by the Germans since 1871 in an attempt to consolidate their claim to the province). At first, Wilson decided that after the return of Alsace-Lorraine to the French, the Germans ought to be allowed 'the use of the economic resources' of the region, resources which were particularly important for minerals. Later he changed his mind and omitted the above reference to German rights. Regarding freedom of the seas, Wilson had to be careful not to offend Great Britain, and rather than deal with specific points at issue, the President decided on a fair but firm statement.

Just before the Fourteen Points were announced, Washington received news of Lloyd George's personal statement of British aims. Britain, the Prime Minister declared, was not involved in an aggressive war or a vendetta against the German nation. The peace settlement ought to be based on the principle of 'government with the consent of the governed', he continued. However, Britain expected Belgium to be restored and Alsace-Lorraine to be given up. Germany was not to receive back her colonies. The legitimate claims of the Poles for independence and the Italians for 'unredeemed' compatriots should be met; indeed, all the minorities of the Habsburg Empire had a right to 'genuine' and 'democratic' self-government. Some kind of postwar international organization was essential to preserve peace without an armaments race.

After an initial reaction of some consternation, Wilson persuaded himself that Lloyd George's statement was sufficiently close to his own to make it all the more necessary to speak out. A few finishing touches were added to the President's speech, including a modifying clause in Point 2 (see below) which sought to make it more acceptable to the British, and the omission of reference to German economic interests in Point 8.

On 8 January 1918, Woodrow Wilson delivered his Fourteen Points before a joint session of Congress. On Points 6 and 7, no compromise would be possible; however, Points 8–13 inclusive were, it seems, negotiable, for the President declared that they 'should' rather than 'must' be realized. Point 14, Wilson's prescription for a League of Nations, was the most important of all, and it was his personal tragedy that the United States turned her back on this experiment in international organizations.

President Wilson's Fourteen Points were as follows:

1. 'Open covenants of peace, openly arrived at . . . diplomacy shall proceed always frankly and in the public view.
2. 'Absolute freedom of navigation upon the seas, . . . in peace and in war . . .
3. 'The removal, so far as possible, of all economic barriers and the establishment of an equality of trade conditions among all the nations . . .
4. 'Adequate guarantees given and taken that national armaments will be reduced to the lowest point consistent with domestic safety.
5. 'A free, open-minded, and absolutely impartial adjustment of all colonial claims, based upon a strict observance of the principle that . . . the interests of the populations concerned must have equal weight with the equitable claims of the government whose title is to be determined.
6. 'The evacuation of all Russian territory . . .
7. 'Belgium . . . must be evacuated and restored. . .
8. 'All French territory should be freed and the invaded portions restored, and the wrong done to France by Prussia in 1871 in the matter of Alsace-Lorraine . . . should be righted . . .
9. 'A readjustment of the frontiers of Italy should be effected along clearly recognizable lines of nationality.
10. 'The peoples of Austria-Hungary . . . should be accorded the freest opportunity of autonomous development.

11. 'Rumania, Serbia and Montenegro should be evacuated; occupied territories restored; Serbia accorded free and secure access to the sea; and the relations of the several Balkan states to one another determined by friendly counsel along historically established lines of allegiance and nationality; and international guarantees of the political and economic independence and territorial integrity of the several Balkan states should be entered into.

12. 'The Turkish portions of the present Ottoman Empire should be assured a secure sovereignty, but the other nationalities which are now under Turkish rule should be assured an undoubted security of life and an absolutely unmolested opportunity of autonomous development, and the Dardanelles should be permanently opened as a free passage to the ships and commerce of all nations under international guarantees.

13. 'An independent Polish state should be erected which should include the territories inhabited by indisputably Polish populations, which should be assured a free and secure access to the sea . . .

14. 'A general association of nations must be formed under specific covenants for the purpose of affording mutual guarantees of political independence and territorial integrity to great and small states alike.'

Arthur Link, historian of the Wilsonian era, describes the Fourteen Points as 'incomparably the greatest liberal manifesto of the war'. American opinion was overwhelmingly behind the President. British and French left-wing support was assured.

However, those who thought in a less lofty and more realistic vein soon pointed out the flaws in the President's declaration. In Germany, opinion on the Fourteen Points was generally unfavourable at the time; only later, when the war was clearly lost, did moderates and left-wing thinkers support Wilson's plan. By the time the Treaty of Brest-Litovsk was signed on 3 March, it was clear to Wilson and most others that the war would continue to the bitter end. There would not, indeed could not, they realized, be a negotiated peace because of the irreconcilable aims of the opposing sides. Bitter but unshakeable in his beliefs, Wilson determined to fight on with all of America's might until victory was won. His last hope was that justice and reason would prevail at the postwar peace conference.

In retrospect we see that the Fourteen Points were loaded with anomalies and contradictions. For example, it was simply unrealistic to declare, in the middle of a war replete with detailed and secret Allied commitments such as the Treaty of London with Italy in 1915, that semipublic diplomacy ought to be the rule in future, as was implied in Point 1. Point 5, calling for colonial justice, ran counter to British, French, and Japanese intentions to retain the ex-German colonies which they had occupied during the war. Similarly, Point 9 was in opposition to Italy's grotesquely inflated territorial ambitions. Point 10 was, in a sense, an exercise in naïveté. One example will suffice: a fair and democratic case could be made out for Czechoslovak independence, but it proved impossible to establish the

Above left: Italian soldiers desert to the enemy at Caporetto. **Above:** Austrian reserves press forward when Italian morale collapsed.

state with viable borders and yet exlude a huge German minority and smaller minorities of Hungarians, Poles, and Ruthenians. Central Europe was too much a patchwork quilt of nationalities for it to be possible to draw any new borders with anything approaching complete fairness. Point 13 was used as the point of departure for the establishment of a Polish state whose chauvinism and intolerance towards all minorities verged on lunacy. Such were some of the inconsistencies and distortions which emerged from Wilson's well-meaning efforts.

Showdown in Italy

In 1915, as we saw earlier, the Italian Isonzo offensives achieved indifferent results. Little further was gained in the six subsequent battles of 1916–17, although in the Eleventh Battle of the Isonzo (19 August–12 September 1917), staged to coordinate with Third Ypres in the West, General Luigi Capello's Italian Second Army broke through to the Bainsizza Plateau and rendered the Austrian positions precarious. The Italian success was only limited, however, since among other reversals the Duke of Aosta's Third Army was vanquished. Yet the Austrians doubted that they could withstand a Twelfth Isonzo, and thus they decided to forestall this by attacking the Italians themselves.

Above: Gas masks were used by the French in the trenches throughout most of the war.
Right: The Austrians won their greatest victory in what they called 'The Miracle' of Caporetto.
Opposite top: A Canadian six-inch howitzer.
Opposite bottom: The Austrians constructed their defences by night on the Italian Front. **Below right:** Mark IV Tank (Male). Crew: 8. Overall length: 26ft. 5in. Height: 8ft. 2in. Width: 12ft. 10in. Armament: 2 ×6pdr., 4 ×Lewis 303 machine guns. Maximum armour: 12 mm. Engine: Daimler 6 cylinder, 105 b.h.p. Performance: 3·7 m.p.h. Range: 35 miles.

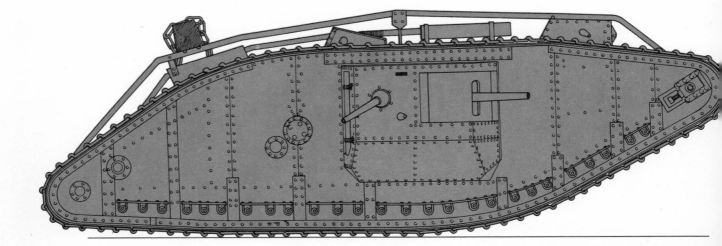

While he was chief of the Austrian general staff, Conrad had been obsessed with dealing a knock-out blow against Italy. In early 1917, Conrad was replaced and sent to command the Trentino sector of the Italian Front. Here he reflected further on his plan for an Austrian attack on the Caporetto (Karfreit; now Kobarid) sector of the Isonzo region, where, it seemed, the Italian lines were least ably defended. At the end of August Conrad sought German assistance for this move. Austrian motives were complicated, and they did not seek inordinate help from their ally, since they feared that as a result, Italy might gain equivalent Anglo-French support. Escalation of the conflict might then shatter Vienna's hopes of a compromise peace. Yet on the recommendation of Lieutenant General Krafft von Dellmensingen, the Germans finally decided that since 'success lies only just on the border of possibility', they would assume direction of a limited offensive in the Caporetto area, keeping largely clear of what Ludendorff in particular considered to be Austria's bungling methods.

In September 1917 six German and nine Austrian divisions, newly grouped into the German Fourteenth Army, assembled some sixty miles east of Caporetto. The equipment and the troops themselves were of generally high quality. Three more Austrian formations and six additional German divisions were also available.

Krafft von Dellmensingen, now chief of staff of the Fourteenth Army, reasoned that two simultaneous thrusts meeting near Caporetto would isolate a contingent of Italians, and allow the Germans and Austrians to advance to the Stol and Colovrat ridges and beyond, thus taking in flank much of the Italian Second Army and leading to a general enemy retreat. Meanwhile Cadorna, the Italian commander, heard rumours of an enemy offensive and ordered defensive preparations in depth, though actually such precautions as were finally taken were rather haphazard. Later Czech and Transylvanian deserters from the Austrian forces gave the Italians more detailed news. Ironically, Cadorna himself had abandoned for the moment that Twelfth Isonzo which the Austrians feared, for he was short of ammunition.

Cadorna has been characterized as an autocrat and a bully, and military historians agree on his lack of empathy with his troops. Certainly neither he nor Capello took sufficient note of low morale among their men. Rather, Capello had spent too much time dreaming of an Italian counter-offensive in the Tolmino (Tolmein) area, an idea that Cadorna rejected.

On 24 October, under cover of misty, rainy weather, the Austrian bombardment opened on a vast scale. Thus began Caporetto (the Twelfth Battle of the Isonzo). The Austro-Germans used gas and high explosive shells, and panic spread as the Italians found that their gas masks were ineffective. For the most part the Central Powers were able to push forward with little difficulty, their success increased by bad leadership in the Italian ranks. The Austrians, somewhat astonished at their own prowess, now referred to *Das Wunder von Karfreit*. Many Italians simply deserted and ran, due to a mixture of fear of German military might and apathy or active hostility towards the war itself. The Italian troops were also influenced by the opposition of the Vatican to the conflict, the example of Bolshevism in Russia, and resentment at the deprived conditions under which they had to live as soldiers. Moreover, not until Caporetto did the enemy invade Italian soil; thus previously an important ingredient in patriotic appeals to fight had been missing.

By the morning of 25 October the Italian situation was poor. In the previous afternoon the enemy had made a fifteen-mile breach in the Italian line; by the evening of the twenty-fifth a retreat to the Tagliamento River became necessary. Everywhere Italian morale had caved in, and Capello was desperately ill and thus unable to use much influence to exhort his troops to greater efforts.

Throughout 26 October, as the Germans and Austrians continued to press forward, Cadorna was the victim of garbled information and mismanaged reports. Early on the twenty-seventh, however, the orders for retreat at last went out – not that the disorganized troops had bothered to wait for them. As they streamed away in their hundreds of thousands, the Italians stopped to enjoy themselves en route, eating, drinking, and carousing. The roads were cluttered with fleeing civilians, and any reinforcements of men or supplies were hopelessly entangled by this mass defection.

By the night of 2–3 November, despite confusion and indecision in the Austrian command structure, the Central Powers had made a passage north of the Tagliamento, across which Cadorna and his troops had retreated by 31 October. On 4 November Cadorna ordered a further pullback to the River Piave, behind which his armies stood by 9 November. Paradoxically, morale and discipline were already beginning to improve, and this process was accelerated by General Armando Diaz, who now replaced Cadorna as commander

Below: Men of the 11th Royal Irish Fusiliers with German prisoners.
Opposite Top: British machine gunners operate out of a captured second-line trench.
Opposite bottom: French tank passing captured German guns in the Battle of Cambrai.

and whose beneficial effect on his troops was similar to that of Pétain in France.

Caporetto was over. The Italians had lost 10,000 killed, 30,000 wounded and up to 293,000 prisoners, in addition to the countless numbers of deserters. Strangely, the realization of the dimensions of this disaster pulled the Italians together as never before. In a concerted drive to support the war effort, artillery and munitions were manufactured in vast quantities. Finally, in October 1918, Caporetto was avenged in the victory of Vittorio Veneto.

Tank Warfare

Our attention must now return briefly to the Western Front. Here, between 20 November and 3 December 1917, was fought the Battle of Cambrai, most remembered for a British dawn attack on the opening day of battle, which used almost four hundred tanks in a bold attempt to seize the initiative in the West before the arrival of German reinforcements from the Russian Front.

As the battle was originally conceived, tanks were to be used to 'demoralize and disorganize' the enemy 'and not to capture ground'. A tank raid of eight to twelve hours' duration would be completed before the Germans had time to group for counterattack. However, the Third Army commander, General Sir Julian Byng, was inclined to escalate the project into a large-scale offensive which aimed at a breakthrough to Cambrai and thrusts beyond to Valenciennes. Yet the objections of General Kiggell, Haig's chief of staff, were sufficient to persuade the British supremo to delay the Cambrai project pending the outcome of the Third Battle of Ypres, by which time British reserves had been wiped out in the Passchendaele slaughterhouse and decisive results were no longer feasible. Under the circumstances, by the time the Cambrai action was approved, Byng's objectives were over-ambitious.

At 6:20 a.m. on 20 November, without the customary warning of a preliminary bombardment and with the added advantage of concealment in heavy mist, the British tanks rolled forward. For the first time, tanks were being employed as their architects had intended: in conditions of surprise and in large numbers. On the first day of battle alone, the tanks advanced over three miles. Next day, bells pealed in London in anticipation of a great triumph. Although, as it turned out, the self-congratulation was premature, the new tactics used at Cambrai were employed to good effect the following year and again in the Second World War.

The British had calculated that their tanks could surmount the formidable barriers of the Hindenburg Line by flattening its massive barbed-wire defences instead of taking time to cut through them by means of artillery fire. In addition, brushwood would be dropped from the front of each tank and laid across the massive trenches to provide ersatz bridges. The success of these ploys changed the conduct of trench warfare.

In the early stages the British received an unpleasant setback. At Flesquieres, three German batteries wreaked havoc among the advancing tanks; one alone destroyed sixteen of the new weapons. This had the effect of delaying the

Above: 'Howitzer Firing' by Paul Nash. **Above centre:** General Cadorna, Chief of Staff of the Italian army. **Top right:** An Italian bomb thrower. **Far right:** An Italian poster portrays a light infantryman with one of his most important defences – the shovel.

Right: Ordnance BL 912 Howitzer Mark 11. Total weight of gun and carriage: 16·4 tons (it must have 11 tons of earth). Maximum elevation: 50°. Minimum angle: 15°. Height: 8ft 11in. (loading position). Overall length in working position: 17ft. 6in. Crew: 14. Performance: maximum range 13,935yds. **Right centre:** Ordnance QF 4·5 Howitzer Mark 1. Total weight of gun and carriage: 1·33 tons. Maximum elevation: 45°. Maximum depression:—45° Height: 5ft. 9in. Overall length in working position: 13ft. 6in. Performance: maximum range 7,300 yds. crew: 10.

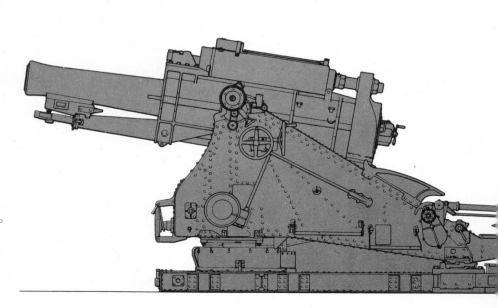

advance of the infantry, which had been utilizing the tanks as an essential advance auxiliary.

On the evening of the twenty-first, only inconclusive results had been achieved, whereas by this time Haig had hoped to have won the battle. Unwilling to give up, he spent the next week pursuing limited objectives, handicapped by the dearth of his reserves and the weariness of his men.

After the initial fighting, the most important clash of Cambrai took place on 30 November. In a clever counterstroke, which employed their skill and enthusiasm to the utmost, the Germans pounded away with gas and smoke shells; then their aircraft, flying low, riddled the exhausted British with machine-gun fire. Meanwhile the German infantry was brought forward. For a time the issue seemed in doubt, but soon the Germans were able to continue their advance. Tired and inexperienced troops and, more importantly, overcautious senior commanders accounted for much of the British losses, which amounted to 37,000 men, besides 6000 prisoners. German casualties numbered 30,000, in addition to the loss of 11,000 prisoners; but Berlin was satisfied, feeling that it was regaining the initiative.

CHAPTER THIRTEEN
Each Side Bids to Win

Top left: Germans march forward as the Kaiserschlacht opens. **Top centre:** Middlesex men hold a street barricade in Bailleul, 15 April 1918. **Top:** A German mortar position. **Above:** Ludendorff, who hoped to break through in the West before the Americans arrived. **Left:** German tactics were successful, but a terrible price was paid.

Below: General (later Marshal) Foch, who became overall commander-in-chief of the Entente forces on 26 March 1918. On his left is General Weygand, who held the same position on the Western Front in the disastrous spring of 1940. **Far right:** General von Hutier, who attacked and faltered south of the Somme.

The war was now three and a half years old. It had taken a frightful toll in human lives, reflected in the acute shortage of skilled and experienced fighting men from which the British and French Empire forces were suffering by early 1918. Moreover, bleak despondency and frustration gripped and numbed the many who asked: when and how would the carnage end?

As if there were not enough difficulties on the Western Front, in the autumn of 1917 the Italian rout at Caporetto had made it necessary for the Western Allies to send eleven divisions to prop up their crumbling colleague. Furthermore, the long-awaited injection of new American blood at the front was proving slow to materialize, for by March 1918 only six rather inexperienced divisions had arrived in France. The battered armies resolved to cling to their present positions somehow until 'the Yanks' arrived in sufficient numbers to make a fresh offensive possible.

Meanwhile, the Allies braced themselves for a renewed German offensive, although, the plight of the Germans was hardly much better than that of the Entente. On the German home front, cynicism grew apace with the desperate lack of food. Politically, the situation was equally grim. Bulgaria was exhausted; and Austria-Hungary and Turkey, surviving only by a miracle, lurched on from crisis to crisis. However, by the summer of 1918 German troops were being transferred in large numbers from the East, and had the Americans not arrived in force by then, the Germans would have been at a distinct advantage.

Yet earlier, Ludendorff, by now the kingmaker in German life, had concluded that a spring offensive was vital to pre-empt American gains and encourage Germany's reeling allies. After being tempted to attack in Flanders, where a break-through to the sea would cut off the British from the Channel ports, Ludendorff decided that the rain-soaked terrain precluded the quick success for which he strove, and instead determined to thrust into the lightly-defended region of the Somme.

Once again Ludendorff concentrated on tactics which had proved their worth the previous year at Riga and Caporetto. These included a short preliminary bombardment of gas and smoke shells, to be followed by a strong artillery barrage. The difficulty was, however, that whereas in the above-mentioned battles the Germans faced opponents of very low morale in operations on a restricted scale, in the West a huge offensive would be needed against troops of greater resilience.

The German Somme offensive (referred to as the *Kaiserschlacht* or 'Emperor Battle') opened on 21 March 1918. Its ultimate objective was to separate the British from the French and to corner the British on the coast. Some thought Ludendorff's fatal mistake was to become obsessed with the fate of the British instead of concentrating against the weaker French in the sector farthest from the British lines. However this may be, under cover of thick fog, the Somme attack commenced with a fantastically powerful artillery barrage from 6000 guns, the greatest bombardment yet seen by history. On the first day of battle the Germans scored heavy successes. By 23 March Gough was forced to pull back his British Fifth Army behind the Somme; Byng's Third Army, though heavily pressed, did not fare as badly. A few days later, land communications between the British and French were in danger, but fortunately for the Allies, when the Germans moved towards Arras they were thrown back and the British lines held.

South of the Somme, though Hutier's German Eighteenth Army took Montdidier on 27 March, both his men and supplies were beginning to falter. Subsequently several German attacks proved futile, and on 4 April, despite the tremendous tactical success achieved, Ludendorff called off the offensive.

The Allies had sustained almost 200,000 casualties and had lost up to 90,000 prisoners. Their consolation was that their armies had neither been separated nor destroyed. German losses were approximately 200,000, but from now on they could ill afford casualties which were even remotely equal to those of the Entente, for the Americans were beginning to arrive in even greater numbers.

By this time the Allies had felt the situation sufficiently serious to create a long-overdue uni-

Right: General Sir Hubert Gough, Commander of the Fifth Army, which covered much of the Allied sector of the front. **Below:** The Yanks arrive! The march through Paris on the way to the front. **Below right:** One of the 305,000 British casualities. **Opposite top:** The Americans at Chateau-Thierry. **Opposite bottom:** A street barricade at Chateau-Thierry. The arrival of fresh American soldiers was an incalculable boost to the morale of the Allies.

fied command. Thus on 26 March General Foch had become overall commander-in-chief of the Entente forces.

In the interim Ludendorff made one more effort to smash the BEF once and for all. This, the Lys offensive, lasted from 9 to 29 April, but although the German tactics were brilliantly successful, strategic gains were once more non-existent. Both sides paid a terrible price for these three weeks of battle: 350,000 German and 305,000 British casualties. The Germans were gambling for high stakes; they could not possibly afford to sustain losses on this scale. Meanwhile American troops continued to pour into France, bringing new hope. Foch, as usual, remained buoyantly optimistic, exclaiming *Bon!* whenever he was told of news from the front, whether good, bad, or indifferent.

Despite the realities facing him, Ludendorff doggedly maintained that 'one more' blow would wipe out the British. With this in mind, on the morning of 27 May his First and Seventh Armies attacked on the Aisne at the oddly-named location of Chemin des Dames. Smashing through the Allied defenses, by the end of May the Germans had reached the Marne. In desperation Pétain called on General John Pershing for an American division to stem the German onslaught. The American Third Division reached Château-Thierry by 1 June, and their efforts enabled the Allies to meet and withstand repeated enemy thrusts. Similarly the American Second Division held back the Germans further west. Bitterly disappointed, Ludendorff called off the Aisne offensive on 6 June.

Ludendorff had manoeuvred himself into an unfavourable position. His troops were located in a salient which was vulnerable to counterattacks, yet if he withdrew, his soldiers' morale would undoubtedly suffer. Searching around for a means of deliverance, Ludendorff determined to make two further thrusts against the Noyon-Montdidier and Soissons sectors, in this way exposing Paris itself to danger. He calculated that the threat to the French capital would induce the latter to pull back and leave Flanders less adequately defended. This, he reasoned, would give him a chance to pulverize the British. However, between 9 and 13 June the French under Fayolle

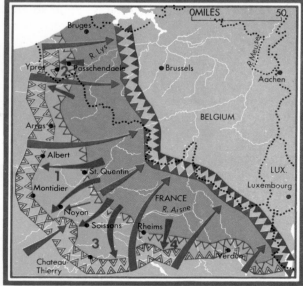

foiled this scheme. Once more the Germans suffered heavy casualties to little effect, whereas the French got away lightly.

Champagne–Marne offensive

In the succeeding month, while Foch laid his plans for a counter-offensive, German morale weakened and discipline suffered dramatically. By now many of Ludendorff's crack troops were dead, and in their place to a large extent stood men past their prime, inexperienced youths, or those at best marginally fit for battle. Yet Ludendorff managed to strike once more, in the Champagne-Marne offensive of 15–17 July. Foch, having gained advance information as to Ludendorff's plans, was well placed to inflict a heavy setback. The German *Friedensturm* (peace offensive) was finally checked, for after the loss of 800,000 men in a period of four months, Ludendorff was in no position to launch further attacks, for Germany the war was already lost.

The Second Marne

The Allied Aisne-Marne counteroffensive of 18 July–6 August, which together with the preceding German drive is commonly known as Second Marne now took place. Foch's objective was to reduce the German salients of Marne and Amiens, created during the previous enemy offensives, and that of Saint-Mihiel, which had remained quiescent since the first autumn of the war.

Above: Bridge across the Marne blown up by the French. **Right:** Kansas troops in a tight spot.

Below: A French mess near the front lines. Rolling kitchens such as these provided the only hot meals available to front line troops . . . except for a tin heated by matches in a trench.

First to be dealt with was the Marne salient. The Allied attacking force consisted of the French Fifth, Sixth, Ninth, and Tenth Armies, in which were already incorporated four British, two Italian, and eight American divisions. The initial day of the assault, 18 July, proved highly successful, outstandingly so for the French tank force. Next day Mangin's Tenth Army raced on towards Soissons, and the Germans found themselves obliged to conduct a fighting withdrawal. Thus the Marne salient was eliminated – an extraordinary victory for the Allies and the French in particular, and the first major Allied success that year. Foch, meanwhile, had received his just reward, having been created *Maréchal de France*.

By now the Americans were playing a truly vital role on the Western Front. In the Aisne-Marne offensive they had fielded eight divisions, whose value was tremendously enhanced by their containing twice the infantry strength of either Allied or German divisions. By this time, although the Germans had not been annihilated, they had definitely lost the psychological initiative. The American performance, exceeding British and French expectations, spurred the Entente on to greater efforts, tired and exhausted though they were.

Meanwhile an Allied operation against the Amiens salient was in preparation. Rawlinson underlined the secrecy which was vital to the offensive by having included in the soldiers' pay-

books a small notice which stated baldly: 'Keep Your Mouth Shut.' The most elaborate precautions enabled secrecy to be maintained up to the opening of battle.

The Battle of Amiens (or, as the French called it, Montdidier) was of tremendous importance. Fuller called it 'the most decisive . . . of the First

Above: General Pershing receives an honour guard upon his arrival in Boulogne.

World War', while Liddell Hart praised Amiens as 'the most brilliant (victory) ever gained by British arms' during the war. The German official history admits that the battle was 'the greatest defeat which the German army . . . suffered' in the Great War. Moreover, such a gain was achieved with relative economy: British casualties numbered under 9,000 on the first day's fighting. Whereas, after Second Marne, the German armies had not yet lost hope, after Amiens they were in a state of psychological collapse. The long Western stalemate had been broken, and the Germans gave up hope of a renewed offensive.

In the early hours of 8 August, in conditions of zero visibility due to a dense mist, Rawlinson's British Fourth Army moved against the enemy, employing the tactics earlier proved at Cambrai and using a formidable array of weaponry which included hundreds of tanks, many of the latest type. Without a preliminary bombardment, suddenly the tank armada struck. Two thousand guns pounded and hammered in unison against the German defences. Soon the British Empire forces, in which Canadian and Australian troops formed a *corps d'élite*, were joined in the affray by the French First Army under Debeney. The Third Army (Humbert) was also to be included. Facing them were von der Marwitz's Second Army and Hutier's Eighteenth Army.

As the British tanks rolled effortlessly forward, the German infantry proved unable to defend

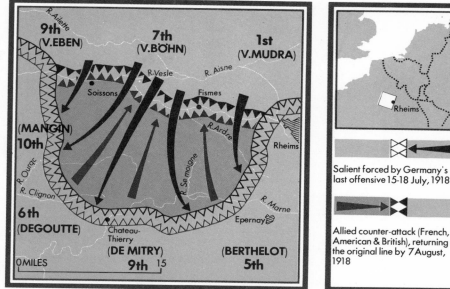

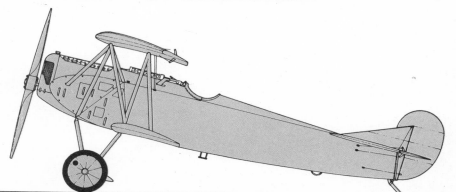

Salient forced by Germany's last offensive 15-18 July, 1918

Allied counter-attack (French, American & British), returning to the original line by 7 August, 1918

themselves against these behemoths. Not that the tanks were responsible for mass slaughter; rather, the suddenness of their appearance and the scale of the attack led to a kind of moral caving-in. Many men simply took to their heels. Almost immediately the British captured 16,000 prisoners, while the French made good progress.

As whole units at a time disintegrated, Ludendorff was moved to call 8 August 1918 'The black day of the German Army in the history of this war'. Even though artillery fire managed to cripple 109

Opposite top left: General John J. ('Black Jack') Pershing, the American Commander-in-Chief. **Opposite top right:** Manfred von Richthofen, the Red Baron, Germany's greatest air ace. **Far left:** Dog fight in the skies. Air warfare made a significant impact on the Western Front in the latter stages of the war. **Left:** 'The Blind Spot.' by N. G. Arnold. A Sopwith Camel closes in under a German tailplane.

Far left: S.E.5a. Engine: 200 hp Wolseley W4a Viper. Span: 26ft. 7.5in. Length: 20ft. 11in. Armament: one fixed ·303 in. Vickers machine gun, one ·303in. Lewis machine gun on Foster mounting. Maximum speed: 130 mph at 10,000 feet. **Left:** Spad XIII. Engine: 220 hp Hispano-Suiza 8BA.

Span: 26ft. 3.75in. Length: 20ft. 4in. Armament: two fixed, ·303 Vickers machine guns. Maximum speed: 133·5 mph at 622 ft. **Right:** Fokker DVII. Engine: 175 hp Mercedes D3. Span: 29ft. 3·5in. Length: 22ft. 11·5in. Armament: two 7.92mm Spandau machine guns. Maximum speed: 118·1 mph at 6549ft.

British tanks on the first day, Amiens was the greatest Allied triumph since the Marne in 1914, although neither Foch nor Haig was aware of this at the time. However, as the attack reached the scarred battlefields of the Somme, it faltered in a welter of derelict impediments; and, as earlier at Cambrai, lack of reserves began to tell. By 11 August, the first phase of the offensive was over. French casualties were over 24,000; those of the British were 22,000; and German losses were 75,000, including prisoners, of which the French took over 11,000 and the British over 18,000.

After lengthy argument between Haig and Foch over how best to exploit an extremely favourable situation, Haig got his own way, and on 21 August his armies once more thrust forward. At first the Germans retreated under the impact of Byng's Third Army, but by 22 August they were counterattacking, without greatly disrupting the Allied progress. By the end of August the Germans had been forced to evacuate their previously strong position at Roye-Chaulnes, Mont-Saint-Quentin had been taken, and the enemy had retreated to its spring positions on the Hindenburg line (*Siegfried Stellung*). Such was the German despair that at a Crown Council on 14 August the Kaiser said that 'a suitable time must be chosen to come to an understanding with the enemy'. If possible, negotiations with the Entente would be initiated through the mediation of the Queen of Holland and the King of Spain. As for Ludendorff, he stated simply: 'The war must be ended.' Meanwhile the Reich forces would attempt to stage a fighting retreat and to remain on French soil as long as possible. In practical terms, however, the German lack of strategy devolved into mere passive resistance. At the same time the Austrians' almost blind belief in German military supremacy had been dealt an irremediable body blow. Seeing the psychological results of their offensive, Haig and Foch came to the conclusion that the war could be won in 1918 after all.

What had led to *Der Schwarze Tag*, to Germany's 'Black Day'? Undoubtedly the brilliant employment of tanks and the exploitation of the element of surprise had played an important role in events. Yet military success alone is insufficient to explain the disproportion of the German inner collapse. Perhaps the foremost additional reason for the Reich's collective nervous breakdown was the throttling effect of the Allied economic blockade. Even with massive imports of food from the Ukraine and Rumania, Germany was living at the borderline of starvation. Already depressed by tales of woe from home, the German soldier saw that the costly 1918 offensives had

Left: The Big Parade . . . forward. **Above:** Another parade . . . back; 750 German prisoners go into French custody.

Bottom right: French
tanks move up to stem the
German tide. **Opposite
top:** 'The Red Door' on
'The Black Day'. **Opposite
bottom:** A French
armoured car moves
forward to the front.

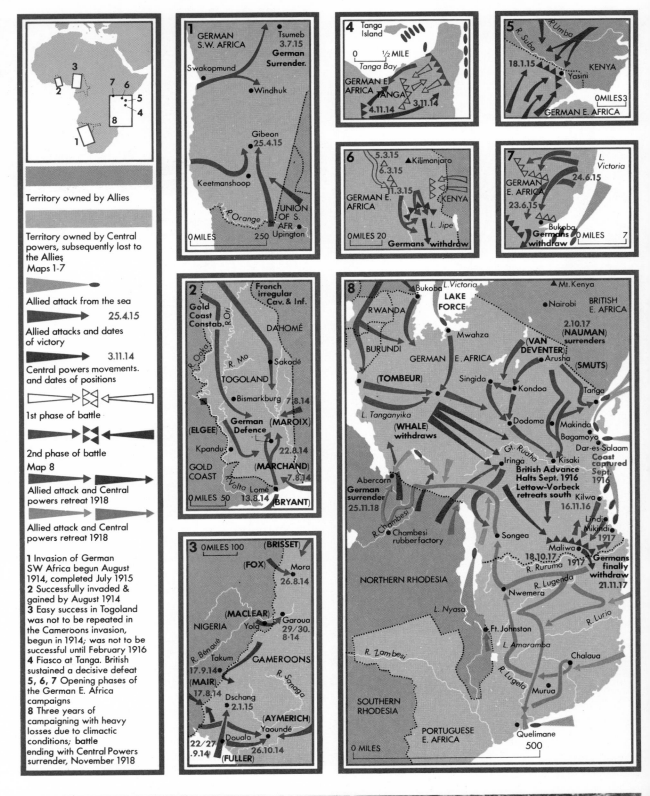

Territory owned by Allies

Territory owned by Central
powers, subsequently lost to
the Allies
Maps 1-7

Allied attack from the sea
25.4.15

Allied attacks and dates
of victory
3.11.14

Central powers movements.
and dates of positions

1st phase of battle

2nd phase of battle
Map 8

Allied attack and Central
powers retreat 1918

Allied attack and Central
powers retreat 1918

1 Invasion of German
SW Africa begun August
1914, completed July 1915
2 Successfully invaded &
gained by August 1914
3 Easy success in Togoland
was not to be repeated in
the Cameroons invasion,
begun in 1914; was not to be
successful until February 1916
4 Fiasco at Tanga. British
sustained a decisive defeat
5, 6, 7 Opening phases of
the German E. Africa
campaigns
8 Three years of
campaigning with heavy
losses due to climactic
conditions; battle
ending with Central Powers
surrender, November 1918

merely led him into a hopeless position, a defensive blind alley. Several sources including Ludendorff have recorded that as German reinforcements arrived at the front, those whom they replaced abused them with catcalls and cries of 'Blacklegs, you're prolonging the war!' It was a far cry from the glorious and unsullied days of the summer of 1914.

Influenza

One of the most self-evident observations concerning the First World War is that it is a tale of unrelieved military casualties. Less well known is the fact that, even as the war was drawing to a close at last, a worldwide influenza pandemic infected and in many cases killed countless civilians and soldiers alike. Indeed, it is thought that at least twenty-seven million people died of virulent influenza in 1918–19; and in India alone, deaths from the flu exceeded the total casualty lists for 1914–18.

The great influenza pandemic may have originated in Spain or France in early 1918; other theories hold that *la grippe* began its journey of devastation in places as far apart as China and Kansas. Possibly the disease had been germinating in several areas simultaneously, and rose to epidemic proportions when the deprivations of war had caused a widespread decline in health. Certainly the pandemic found a comfortable breeding-ground in the unsanitary trenches of northern France and the crowded metropolises of Europe, Asia, and America.

The course of the disease ran approximately from the spring of 1918 until the following year, reaching its height in the last autumn of the war. In its wake the influenza carried complications such as pneumonia, and its debilitating effects led or contributed to tuberculosis, heart disease, miscarriages and other complaints; thus the true total of its casualties is impossible to estimate. Everywhere a large percentage of the population contracted the illness; at least twenty million in the United States alone.

Countless pathetic tales of misery accumulated as the pandemic took its course. ANZAC troops in Britain were decimated by its effects, and special cemeteries on Salisbury Plain were laid out to accommodate the fatalities. In the second and most severe wave of the 'flu, six to eight per cent of the population was wiped out.

Perhaps the most saddening aspect of the pandemic was its high incidence among youth.

Right: A captured German tank, Elfriede. The first major tank battles took place during the spring and summer of 1918. **Far right:** Americans move through Chateau-Thierry.

Left: A contemporary painting shows horses killed by battery fire. Millions of animals were slaughtered on all fronts during the course of the war.

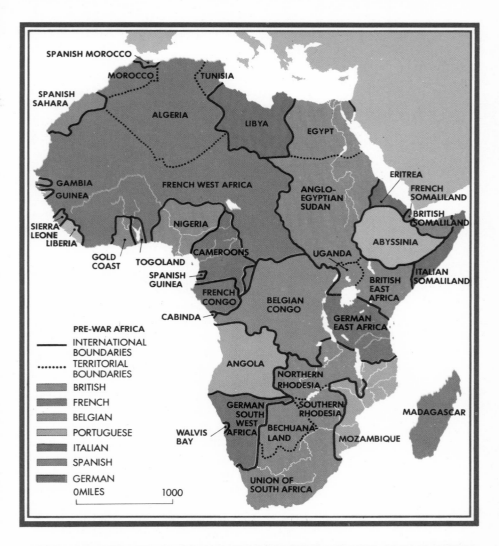

PRE-WAR AFRICA
INTERNATIONAL BOUNDARIES
TERRITORIAL BOUNDARIES
BRITISH
FRENCH
BELGIAN
PORTUGUESE
ITALIAN
SPANISH
GERMAN

0 MILES   1000

SPANISH MOROCCO
MOROCCO
TUNISIA
SPANISH SAHARA
ALGERIA
LIBYA
EGYPT
GAMBIA
GUINEA
FRENCH WEST AFRICA
ERITREA
FRENCH SOMALILAND
BRITISH SOMALILAND
SIERRA LEONE
LIBERIA
NIGERIA
ABYSSINIA
GOLD COAST
TOGOLAND
CAMEROONS
UGANDA
ITALIAN SOMALILAND
SPANISH GUINEA
FRENCH CONGO
BELGIAN CONGO
BRITISH EAST AFRICA
CABINDA
GERMAN EAST AFRICA
ANGOLA
NORTHERN RHODESIA
GERMAN SOUTH WEST AFRICA
SOUTHERN RHODESIA
MADAGASCAR
WALVIS BAY
BECHUANA-LAND
MOZAMBIQUE
UNION OF SOUTH AFRICA
ANGLO-EGYPTIAN SUDAN

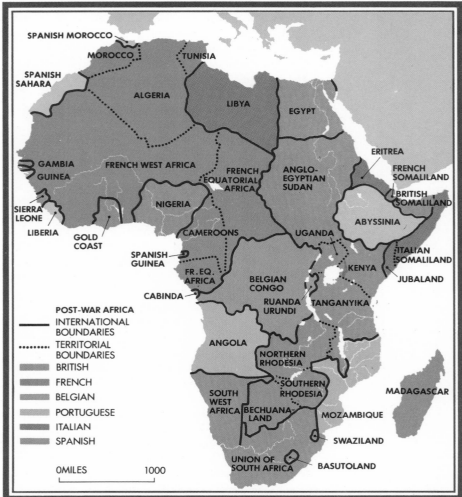

POST-WAR AFRICA
INTERNATIONAL BOUNDARIES
TERRITORIAL BOUNDARIES
BRITISH
FRENCH
BELGIAN
PORTUGUESE
ITALIAN
SPANISH

0 MILES   1000

SPANISH MOROCCO
MOROCCO
TUNISIA
SPANISH SAHARA
ALGERIA
LIBYA
EGYPT
GAMBIA
GUINEA
FRENCH WEST AFRICA
FRENCH EQUATORIAL AFRICA
ANGLO-EGYPTIAN SUDAN
ERITREA
FRENCH SOMALILAND
BRITISH SOMALILAND
SIERRA LEONE
LIBERIA
NIGERIA
ABYSSINIA
GOLD COAST
CAMEROONS
UGANDA
ITALIAN SOMALILAND
SPANISH GUINEA
FR. EQ. AFRICA
KENYA
JUBALAND
CABINDA
BELGIAN CONGO
RUANDA URUNDI
TANGANYIKA
ANGOLA
NORTHERN RHODESIA
SOUTH WEST AFRICA
SOUTHERN RHODESIA
MADAGASCAR
BECHUANA-LAND
MOZAMBIQUE
SWAZILAND
UNION OF SOUTH AFRICA
BASUTOLAND

217

The flower of European manhood had already been killed or maimed at the battlefront; now, on top of this 45 per cent of influenza fatalities occurred among the 15–35 age group. One doctor commented fatalistically: 'The disease simply had its way. It came like a thief in the night and stole treasure.' It was an undeserved end to more than four years of worldwide suffering and carnage.

The German Colonies

As mentioned earlier in this narrative, in the course of the World War, the German colonies in Africa and the Pacific fell to the Allies. Though the final fate of these possessions was not yet to be determined, the Entente quickly saw the necessity for eliminating the excellent German naval and communications bases; besides, Britain, France, and Japan in particular coveted several of these colonies for themselves.

In Africa, the German colony of Togoland fell to a combined Anglo-French attack in the first few weeks of the war. The Allied objective, the destruction of the radio communications complex at Kamina, was quickly achieved.

Kamerun (the Cameroons) was considerably harder to capture. In early September 1914, the British attacking mission failed completely, and though an amphibious Anglo-French expedition met with some success, it was hampered by difficult terrain and intense heat. Eventually, in February 1916, the last of the German opposition was worn down, and, as in Togoland, a joint British-French administration was set up.

Farther south lay the large colony of German Southwest Africa. Besides its mineral resources, the territory was important for the radio station at the capital of Windhoek. South African troops bore responsibility for operations in this theatre, but the project was impeded by disaffection on the part of two South African military leaders. In January 1915, however, operations recommenced, and by July South Africa was in control of its northwestern neighbour.

To the east lay the largest and richest of Germany's colonies: Tanganyika or German East Africa. Here the Allied forces encountered their most determined colonial opposition under the leadership of the legendary Lieutenant Colonel (later Major General) Paul von Lettow-Vorbeck. By a combination of wiliness and military skill, Lettow-Vorbeck held out against his opponents throughout the war. By this means he bottled up 300,000 Allied troops who were needed elsewhere. Only on 25 November 1918 did Lettow-Vorbeck accept the *fait accompli* of the armistice.

In the Far East Kiaochow and the German Pacific Islands, including the Carolines and the Marshalls, fell to various Allied forces, among them troops of Japan, Australia, and New Zealand.

After the war, when the Treaty of Versailles deprived Germany of her former colonies, France and Great Britain reached an arrangement over division of the Togoland and Cameroons mandates. Britain also received Tanganyika, Belgium gained Ruanda and Urundi, while South Africa retained control of Southwest Africa; and the Pacific Islands were divided by the equator between Japan in the north and Australia and New Zealand to the south.

Right: Thousands of German prisoners were taken after the 'Black Day'.

CHAPTER FOURTEEN

The Bitter End:
The Central Powers Cave In

In addition to the Mesopotamia campaign described earlier in this narrative, important operations also took place elsewhere in the Middle East, notably in Egypt and Palestine.

In December 1914 Britain had proclaimed a protectorate over Egypt, which in theory had previously been under Turkish suzerainty. London had gained a wide degree of political manoeuvre by deposing the Khedive, Abbas II Hilmi, and replacing him by his more moderate uncle, Sultan (later King) Husain Kamil. During 1915 the British took further steps to extend their influence in this strategically and geopolitically vital region by concluding agreements with the Sharif of Mecca and with Ibn Saud, whom London now recognized as ruler of Nejd. Having established this wide sphere of influence, however, London thought it advisable to compensate its Entente allies. Accordingly, in May 1916, the Sykes-Picot Agreement recognized Russian claims to the border territories of Turkish Armenia and northern Kurdistan, and French pre-eminence in western Syria and the Lebanon to the Damascus-Homs-Hama-Aleppo line. Britain was to be preeminent in the coastal region of Palestine and in the Mesopotamian areas of Basra and Baghdad. An intermediate zone was to be divided into a French sphere in northern Syria and the rest of Mesopotamia, and a British sphere in the rest of Arabia and what is today Jordan.

These power political arrangements were extremely difficult to reconcile with London's previous commitments to the Sharif of Mecca. To some extent the British negotiators on the spot may have exceeded their brief from Whitehall, given the wish of many for a vast British Arab Empire.

The Sykes-Picot Agreement contained one source of particular controversy. It was decided that the province of Jerusalem should be under international administration. Not only was this considered a useful buffer between two potentially predatory allies, London and Paris; the British were also influenced by the fundamentalist religious veneration of the Holy Land common to Lloyd George, Balfour, Smuts and others; a wish to place the region holy to Judaism, Islam, and Christianity alike in a special category; and the Zionist sympathies of several influential men in British life.

By early 1917, however, the new government of Lloyd George had become increasingly dissatisfied with the future of British interests in Palestine as defined by the Sykes-Picot agreement.

The movement to establish a Jewish homeland in Palestine had been gaining in strength since the Russian pogroms of the 1880s, and at this point Chaim Weizmann, a brilliant chemist and statesman-diplomat who later became first president of Israel, took up the cause of Zionism in Britain. He produced telling arguments that a favourable British attitude would influence American Jewish sentiment in a pro-Allied direction. In addition, the time for Zionism was ripe in 1917.

The British campaign in Palestine was moving to a climax, and on 2 November 1917, Arthur Balfour, British foreign secretary, wrote a letter subsequently known as the Balfour Declaration, to the president of the British Zionist Federation, Lord Rothschild, stating that:

'His Majesty's Government views with favour the establishment in Palestine of a national home for the Jewish people, and will use their best endeavours to facilitate the achievement of this object, it being clearly understood that nothing shall be done which may prejudice the civil and religious rights of existing non-Jewish communities in Palestine, or the rights and political status enjoyed by Jews in any other country.'

As a result of this policy, when Britain was granted a mandate over Palestine in the postwar peace settlement, Jewish emigration proceeded apace. Later, even when the British washed their hands of the matter and the Arabs looked on with hostility, The Jews continued to stream back to their ancient home, to emerge at last as a sovereign nation.

The campaign in Egypt and Palestine opened early in the war. In February 1915 a Turkish force of 20,000 under the German Colonel (subsequently General) Baron Kress von Kressenstein attacked the Suez Canal, the vital lifeline of the British Empire, after a march across the Sinai Peninsula. Fire from British and French warships foiled the Turks' attempt to cross the canal itself, though the British were as yet unable to follow the enemy's retreat because of lack of sufficient camel transports and fears that an insufficiently planned attack would result in a reverse, which would lower British prestige throughout Islam. In any event, the Turks had shown that a large number of troops could cross the practically waterless Sinai despite the obstacles.

Fears that the failure of the Allied campaign at Gallipoli would leave Egypt increasingly vulnerable were widely entertained, though they proved exaggerated. In 1915 and 1916, however, the British were harassed by raids on the part of the

Opposite: British transport crossing the Sakultutan Pass, December 1917.

Chaim Weizmann at a banquet of the Zionist Commission in Palestine.

Advanced headquarters of the 1st Corps and the 7th Division among captured trenches on the Palestine Front. On the left is Captain Kermit Roosevelt, the son of Teddy, who later joined the American army in France.

wandering Senussi sect. Perhaps the most important effect of this was that Kitchener worried over the Senussi revolt to the point of preoccupation. Eventually, nonetheless, the tribal uprising was put down.

The western border of Egypt thus secured, the British were free to advance across Sinai into Palestine. It was hoped thereby that the Arab revolt initiated under the Hashemite Sharif Husain in the Hejaz would spread, and that Husain's bid for independence would be backed by an advance on the Hejaz Railway. On 10 June 1916, although Mecca, the Muslim holy city, was captured, Feisal, one of Husain's sons, failed in his attempt to take the venerated city of Medina, which was also the chief Turkish garrison.

As the British advanced, Kress and his Turkish forces once more gave trouble, but in spite of this by 9 January 1917 the British forces had reached Rafah, on the then Palestine-Egyptian frontier. Now they prepared to attack Gaza, the historic gateway into Palestine itself. In March British Empire forces under Lieutenant General Sir Archibald Murray's deputy, Major General Sir Charles Dobell, were committed against the Turkish garrison town. In this as in other desert campaigns, water supply was a major problem, and access to the wells of Gaza thus became vital.

On 26 March, in thick sea-fog, the British surrounded Gaza. The later progress of the fight for the town was marred by much bungling. A ridge south of Gaza itself, captured at high cost, was abandoned by mistake. Other errors abounded. A second attack in mid-April failed completely, and because of the latter debacle, General Sir Edmund (later Viscount) 'the Bull' Allenby replaced Murray as commander of forces in the area. Allenby, the ebullient hero of Arras, soon raised the flagging British morale, and with his reinforced divisions planned to attack along the Turkish fortified areas extending from Beersheba, a railhead and gateway to what is now the Negev Desert, to Gaza and the coast. A seaborne landing was considered unsuitable because of the unfriendly coastal terrain and the turbulence of the waters just offshore; in any case, losses elsewhere from German U-boats meant that ships could not be spared for such a task.

The Gaza operation went unexpectedly well for the British. It was notable for the eight tanks used, the only ones thus employed outside the Western Front during the war. Beersheba fell on the first

day of fighting to mounted Australians with bayonets drawn. For some reason the defending Turks failed to destroy Beersheba's wells, which they might have known were indispensable to their enemy. After the fall of Gaza on 7 November, Allenby struck north, his forces reaching the middle of the Palestinian coast on 16 November, where they occupied the important town of Jaffa.

Next Allenby moved eastwards into the Judaean Hills, the time-honoured protectors of Jerusalem. There he ran into considerable opposition from troops under Falkenhayn. Despite all setbacks, the British superiority in strength proved itself. After assaults around Nebi-Samweil (Samuel) to the northwest and Bethlehem to the south, Jerusalem received the latest of its conquerors on 9 December. In this, Allenby was fulfilling the Prime Minister's wish of having 'Jerusalem as a Christmas present to the British nation', one which Lloyd George calculated would impress other belligerents and neutrals alike.

As he entered Jerusalem, Allenby surrendered to the invisible and enchanted spell which surrounds the Holy City. He had tried his best to direct fighting away from Jerusalem's priceless treasures of three faiths. The conquering general entered the Holy Land's eternal capital on foot, for Lloyd George had particularly instructed that Jerusalem be occupied with reverent if impressive humility. At the end of December Falkenhayn made a costly attempt to retake the city, but he was unsuccessful.

Soon afterwards Lloyd George urged a blow that would drive Turkey to sue for peace, believing that this could be done by means of the Palestine campaign. Yet Allenby and his advisers doubted that Turkey would capitulate without a German cave-in in the West.

Early in 1918 considerable flooding caused a hitch in Allenby's plans. By March, however, he was able to move against Amman, later the capital of Transjordan and subsequently Jordan, where his objective was the destruction of the Hejaz Railway. Yet lack of sufficient striking strength vitiated the project, and a further attack on 11 April was beaten off by the enemy. Now, despite Lloyd George's hopes, more than 60,000 British Empire troops had to be recalled from Palestine to meet the needs of the Western Front, where the German spring offensive was under way. In the meantime the Turkish troops, in contrast to British soldiers, became increasingly ragged and laid low by typhus and malaria. In Constantinople, Enver and his Young Turk party had completely lost interest in Palestine because of the opportunities for Pan-Turanian aggrandizement which the Brest-Litovsk settlement had provided.

The next major battle in Palestine was that at Megiddo, not far from Haifa, on 19 September. Allenby's planned 'battle of annihilation' was given an eerie quality by being staged on the site of the Biblical Armageddon, where according to Revelations 16:16 armies from all five continents would foregather at the end of the world in an apocalyptic clash. Once Megiddo had fallen, the British struck out across the Plain of Esdraelon and the Jezreel Valley to the River Jordan, while other British troops took Nazareth and almost captured the German commander, Liman von Sanders, who had replaced Falkenhayn in March 1918.

The Turks had for a long while been harassed

Turkish machine-gunners strike back in Palestine.

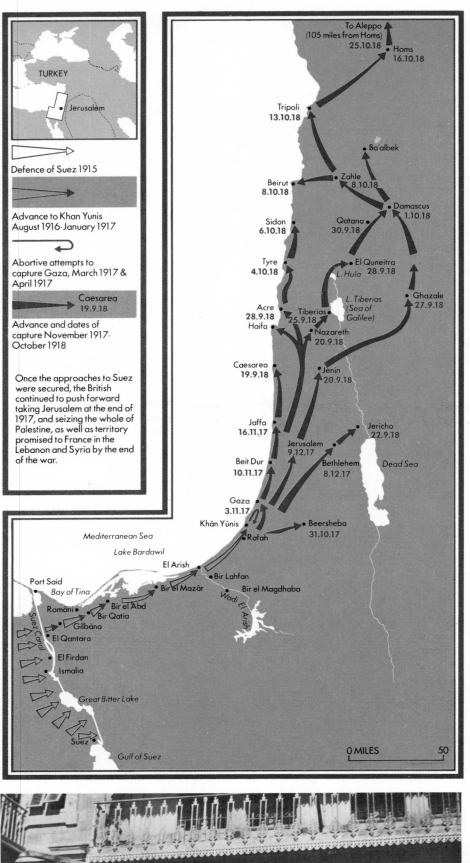

TURKEY

Jerusalem

Defence of Suez 1915

Advance to Khan Yunis
August 1916-January 1917

Abortive attempts to
capture Gaza, March 1917 &
April 1917

Caesarea
19.9.18

Advance and dates of
capture November 1917-
October 1918

Once the approaches to Suez
were secured, the British
continued to push forward
taking Jerusalem at the end of
1917, and seizing the whole of
Palestine, as well as territory
promised to France in the
Lebanon and Syria by the end
of the war.

To Aleppo
(105 miles from Homs)
25.10.18

Homs
16.10.18

Tripoli
13.10.18

Ba'albek

Beirut
8.10.18

Zahle
8.10.18

Sidon
6.10.18

Qatana
30.9.18

Damascus
1.10.18

Tyre
4.10.18

El Quneitra
28.9.18

L. Hula

L. Tiberias
(Sea of
Galilee)

Ghazale
27.9.18

Acre
28.9.18

Tiberias
25.9.18

Haifa

Nazareth
20.9.18

Caesarea
19.9.18

Jenin
20.9.18

Jaffa
16.11.17

Jericho
22.9.18

Jerusalem
9.12.17

Beit Dur
10.11.17

Bethlehem
8.12.17

Dead Sea

Gaza
3.11.17

Khân Yûnis

Beersheba
31.10.17

Rafah

Mediterranean Sea

Lake Bardawil

El Arish

Port Said

Bay of Tina

Bir Lahfan

Bir el Mazâr

Bir el Magdhaba

Romani

Bir el Abd

Bir Qatia

Wadi El Arish

Gilbâna

El Qantara

El Firdan

Ismalia

Great Bitter Lake

Suez

Gulf of Suez

Suez Canal

0 MILES   50

Left: Lawrence of Arabia.
Bottom left: General
Allenby enters Jerusalem,
December 1917. **Right:**
The charge of El Maghar
before the fall of Jerusalem.

by blows to their communications from forces
under the legendary T. E. Lawrence. These
included raids on the Hejaz Railway in order to
disrupt the line and tie down as many Turks as
possible to defend it. Lawrence's Arabs had also
staged an important diversionary attack on
Deraa, a major railway junction, prior to
Megiddo.

By late September the destruction of the
Turkish armies in Palestine proper was complete.
Now, moving north into Syria, the victorious
forces effortlessly captured Damascus on 1 October, and Homs fell some sixteen days later. Aleppo
fell on 26 October. In any case the Ottomans'
death knell had sounded with the collapse of
Bulgaria on 30 September, for thenceforth the
Turks were cut off from their German ally and
became susceptible to Allied attacks on Turkey-
in-Europe. On 30 October, at Mudros, an
armistice with Turkey was reached. The Turkish
campaign was over, at a cost of 92,500 British
Empire battle casualties in Mesopotamia alone.

Collapse in the West

After 'Germany's Black Day' on 8 August, the
German position, as we have seen, went from bad
to worse. To the dispassionate onlooker, it was
only a question of time before the Reich gave in.
Indeed, among the Central Powers themselves,
Emperor Karl of Austria-Hungary recognized
this instinctively when he said that *Der Schwarze
Tag* had disturbed Vienna far more than the
earlier Austrian defeat on the Piave – for the
latter had been expected; a major reversal for
the mighty German Army was another matter.
Yet Ludendorff's last hope was that he might
stand behind the Hindenburg Line with its complex of trenches, tunnels, and wire-tangled
obstacles to afford him a breathing-space.

At the same time American troops continued
to arrive in France in droves; and soon the fresh-
faced youths were given the task of reducing the
Saint-Mihiel salient, which had been created four
years earlier during the initial German offensive.
The United States First Army under General

Above: The bombing of
El Afuleh. **Left:** Gotha
GV. Engine: 2X 260 hp
Mercedes. Span: 77ft. 10in.
Length: 40ft. 7in.
Maximum speed: 87 mph.
Armament: four 7·92mm
machine guns. Bomb load
1300 lbs.

John Pershing was quick to rise to the occasion. The importance of the operation was obvious, since the salient stood in the path of the main rail communications between Paris and the French eastern border. In addition, the area included important iron resources at Briey and Metz.

Although they did their best, by this time the Germans were too exhausted to defend Saint-Mihiel properly; in any case, as a defensive position it was valueless. Previous to the American attack on 12 September, Berlin had ordered a withdrawal from the salient and the removal of whatever heavy materials and equipment could be taken along. After a dispute between Foch and Pershing as to the details of deployment of the American forces, it was decided that the Saint-Mihiel operation would have the limited objective of taking the base of the salient, from which the Americans would move into the Meuse-Argonne region for the final offensive against Germany.

On 12 September the Battle of Saint-Mihiel began. The First Army under Pershing was joined by the French Second Colonial Corps and British, Italian and Portuguese units. While the Americans broke through from the south, the French struck repeated blows at the tip of the salient; and by the end of the second day the troops' mission had been accomplished in the face of patchy resistance. Luck was against the Germans, for the Allies had even been aided initially by fog. On 16 September the operation ended, the Allies having taken 15,000 prisoners and 450 guns at a cost of barely 7000 casualties.

By this time the British cabinet, hitherto dubious of Foch's view that the war could be ended in 1918, and remembering the disastrous effects of Haig's hyper-optimism at Passchendaele, was now won over by the continuing Allied run of successes. Even so, the cabinet warned Haig that further heavy British casualties 'would have grave effects' on public opinion, for British losses in the last three weeks of August alone had been about 115,000.

Now, as Foch once more took the offensive, he was anxious to prevent as far as possible an orderly German retreat and especially a 'scorched earth' policy with regard to communications – for if this occurred the resultant chaos would certainly delay an Allied victory. Thus Foch concentrated on capturing the vital railway junctions of Aulnoye and Mézières, for if these could be taken the German retreat might well degenerate into confusion. To gain this objective, Foch decided to deploy a mainly British force eastwards to Aulnoye, and a chiefly American force north to Mézières. It was considered easier to take Mézières than Metz, which was the strongest fortress in Europe.

The Allies were full of that confidence which flows from superiority in men and the scent of victory. Two hundred and twenty Allied divisions faced 197 German divisions, but whereas all the German units were under strength and only a quarter were effective fighting units, the 42 American units were at full strength and contained twice the infantry of other divisions.

Under the rallying-cry *Tout le monde à la bataille* ('Everyone in the fight'), the Allied advance to the Rhine began on 26 September, when Pershing's

Left: On the road to Damascus. The Allied conquest of Syria was a walk-over. **Right:** American troops move in caution near St. Mihiel. **Far right:** US phosphorous bombs in action. **Below:** One of Lawrence's Arab patrols on the march.

Left: A sixty-pounder in a barrage at dawn. **Right:** Mule just hit by a shell splinter. **Opposite left:** German flame-throwers could only stop the tanks temporarily. **Opposite right:** A 340mm rail gun in action. Rail guns were one of the most destructively powerful and mobile weapons of the war. **Opposite bottom:** An advanced dressing station near Cambrai.

Below: A French truck brings back wounded.

First Army drove towards Mézières. Next day the British First and Third Armies entered the affray and pushed towards Aulnoye. Further British and French units came in on the twenty-ninth, while the previous day the Belgian armies thrust towards Ghent. A massive and co-ordinated Allied drive was under way, to the accompaniment of the feeling that soon, despite the misery of succeeding years, all would once again be well.

The final Allied offensive can be classified into four groupings: the operation in Flanders, that in Cambrai-Saint-Quentin (western pincers movement), that of the French centre sector, and the Meuse-Argonne (southern pincers) operation. The first part of this plan was effected by the end of October; the second in the first eleven days of November.

In the Meuse-Argonne sector the American First and French Fourth Armies, the latter commanded by General Gouraud, went into action after a mass northward movement of 500,000 men fifty miles from Saint-Mihiel had been carried out smoothly. The Germans had taken care to fortify the region with innumerable strong defences in depth. An additional defensive protection was the Argonne Forest itself.

The initial Franco-American penetration was quite successful, though in places the advance bogged down amid strong German resistance characterized by merciless bursts of machine-gun fire from snipers in thickets. The Allies were further delayed by the terrain, scarred and pitted as it was from previous battles. Thus the operation became increasingly difficult and costly as October wore on, and the Americans were cramped by their hasty preparations, difficulties in communications, and by sheer congestion from their own numbers of troops in the field. However, an offensive on the Meuse by Bullard's American Second Army was helpful, and at the end of the month the Argonne Forest had been cleared and the French had pushed forward to the Aisne.

On the Cambrai-Saint-Quentin front the British and French were faced with overcoming a series of strong defensive positions in the path of their objective, Aulnoye. For example, there existed deep canal entrenchments which could

not be bridged by tanks, in addition to mazes of barbed wire cluttered about the region. Yet, even though the Anglo-French attacks were slower than anticipated, by the twenty-eighth the German lines had broken. At this point Ludendorff, his nerve collapsing, advised Hindenburg that Germany had definitely lost the war. As he pointed out, even if the Western Front held by some miracle, the Bulgarian collapse had made possible an eventual Entente invasion from the southeast. Thus Hindenburg had to tell Berlin that 'an immediate armistice' was necessary 'in order to avert a catastrophe', and on 4 October Berlin and Vienna sent notes to President Wilson suggesting an armistice.

Ludendorff in particular seems to have held to a naïve and utterly misplaced faith in Wilson's willingness and ability to influence the Entente into peace negotiations on the basis of Wilson's Fourteen Points. (It appears that Ludendorff had never read these!) In any case, the new and more representative German government formed on 3 October with Prince Max of Baden as Chancellor was maintained only by the support of the Centre (men such as Erzberger), Progressives, and Majority Socialists (Scheidemann and others), all of whom were insisting on ending the war on practically any terms. Although Ludendorff raged that Germany's quagmire of troubles was all the fault of the Left, he was shrewd enough to ask the Kaiser to include in the new government 'those circles . . . to whom we owe chiefly our present position . . .'. The Left was thus to bear the onus of peace-making with Germany's unbending opponents; and in future this section of German political opinion was to be pilloried collectively as 'the November criminals'. The forces of reaction had nothing to lose, as it was obvious that the Allies would not negotiate with a militarist clique. Rather, Ludendorff and his coterie would bide their time, and await the aftermath of disillusionment with the peace settlement.

We must now return to the chronicle of military events. In the western pincers operation, an extensive artillery bombardment had been needed to weaken the German defences. In the Saint-Quentin sector, 25,000 tons of metal spewed

forth in the form of a million shells. A side effect
was that supplies of food and ammunition to the
German troops were interrupted, and among the
inexperienced troops who were of necessity now
being used, morale was wrecked. As the Allied forces
swarmed across the Saint-Quentin Canal, the shattered Germans took to their heels; then the Allies
pushed forward once again. Between 27 September
and 9 October, a desperate battle ensued for Cambrai, and by the latter date the Germans had been
driven from the town. The Hindenburg Line
cracked definitively on 5 October, and Ludendorff
hastily fell back to the Selle River.

From 17–20 October the British and French
attacked the new German lines, but met the kind
of stubborn resistance put up by a cornered
animal. Despite this, the Germans were overcome
and the Allied drive moved inexorably forward.

In Flanders the Belgian offensive, commanded
by King Albert, opened in pouring rain; yet
despite the hampering effect on communications,
Ypres Ridge had fallen by 1 October. Moreover,
Ludendorff had had to withdraw large numbers
of troops from the area because they were needed
more desperately further south, and by the end of
the month King Albert's forces stood on the
Schelde. Belgian revenge for the humiliation of
1914 was at hand.

In the French centre sector, the main objective
was passive: the prevention of German withdrawal to the remaining fronts. All went rather
well, and the close of October saw the Germans
losing everywhere. By now German morale was at
vanishing point, for besides the collapse of the
other Central Powers, Germany herself was in
turmoil. On 3 November sections of the fleet
mutinied at Kiel. Meanwhile workers' uprisings
broke out in a number of places, in the hope that
if the war were ended by revolutionary upheaval,
some kind of socialist democracy would be
established. At the same time the Establishment
propaganda machine continued to acclaim German retreats as withdrawals to improved defences, though Ludendorff, of course, knew the
stark truth. He had decided that his best course

Left: An American
company moves up for the
kill. **Above:** Men of the
20th Manchesters resting by
tank which slipped down a
railway embankment near
Cambrai.

was to pull back to the Meuse, hoping thus to gain time for concessions from the Allies through negotiation – a further example of the total lack of realism of his thinking, given the Allied position of strength and the vengeful fury of much of their populace and not a few of their leaders.

In the meantime, by 12 October Berlin had been driven by its dire circumstances to accept that the detailed meaning and interpretation of the Fourteen Points as a basis for an armistice was to be left to the enemy. On 14 October, after a German submarine had sunk the *Leinster* with the loss of four hundred aboard, Wilson sent a fierce note to Berlin railing against German 'acts of inhumanity, spoilation and desolation'. In desperation to secure some kind of settlement before internal social revolution got out of hand completely, on 20 October Berlin assured Wilson

that Germany had rid herself of that 'arbitrary power' against which the American president had preached.

On 25 October Ludendorff suddenly decided that conciliation had gone too far. He denounced the negotiations with America as taking place in intolerable conditions. The only result was that next day he was replaced by Gröner. Then, on 27 October, came news that Vienna intended to sue for peace. It seemed that Germany's position was now hopeless enough for her to take what terms she could get. As Scheidemann of the MSPD (Majority Socialists) put it: 'Better a terrible end than terror without end.' However, this cut both ways, for the slogan was also used by those who called for a *Götterdämmerung*-like apocalypse rather than submission to dishonourable defeat.

By now the decline in morale and the resent-

Opposite top: British awaiting attack. Opposite centre: Attack on the Aisne. Left: The German Crown Prince flees from Germany on a Dutch steamer: 10th November 1918. Below: Armistice 1918.

Left: German 77mm gun, Model 1896. Crew: 6. Calibre: 77mm. Range 17,500 yds.

Left: French 77mm gun, Model 1897, Crew: 5, Calibre: 77mm. Range: 17,500yds.

ment of the German population against continued fighting had reached their peak. The Kaiser became a scapegoat for the general feeling of impotent fury at the course of events, and the feeling grew that only by ridding themselves of the Kaiser and his concomitant autocracy could the German people hope for justice at Allied hands. In consequence, on 9 November Wilhelm II was forced to abdicate, though he signed the formal instrument of abdication only in exile on the twenty-eighth, and Prince Max was succeeded as Chancellor by Friedrich Ebert, the SPD leader. Thus the son of a saddler presided over the demise of the Hohenzollern dynasty. At 2:00 p.m. on the ninth a republic was proclaimed. On the advice of Hindenburg, next day the ex-Kaiser slipped away to refuge in neutral Holland, to the chagrin of the many among the Allies who wanted to try Wilhelm II as a war criminal.

In the meantime the last phase of the Allied offensive had swung into operation. It was marked by an American and French push to the Meuse and the Mézières-Sedan positions, by 7 and 10 November respectively. In the west, British forces attacked south of Valenciennes, seeking to break the Germans on the Schelde. After fierce fighting the Germans caved in; indeed, their collapse soon spread throughout the line. Just before the armistice of 11 November, Canadian forces reoccupied Mons, the scene of so much action in 1914.

Armistice 1918

The armistice with Germany had not been easy to arrange. The Allies had objected to peace with Berlin on the basis of the Fourteen Points, in the formulation of which they had not been consulted, and the meaning of which was unclear and confusing in several places. Colonel House finally provided an authoritative commentary on the meaning of Wilson's declaration, and at length the Allies agreed to the Fourteen Points as a basis of negotiation subject to two reservations: Point 2, relating to freedom of the seas, 'is open to various interpretations, some of which they could not accept.' Thus the Allies, led in this instance by Lloyd George, reserved to themselves 'complete freedom' of action in this regard. Moreover, they argued that the clauses dealing with the restoration of the territories which Germany had invaded must be interpreted to mean that Germany would pay compensation for damage to Allied civilians and their property.

After much additional haggling over details, the armistice terms were prepared and made ready for signature. On the evening of 7 November Matthias Erzberger, the German Secretary of State, arrived at Marshal Foch's headquarters at Rethondes in the forest of Compiègne to sign for Germany. Accompanying him were Count von Oberndorff, Major General von Winterfeldt, and Captain Vanselow of the German Navy. The Allied signatories were to be Foch and Admiral Sir Rosslyn Wemsyss, the British First Sea Lord.

As he faced the German delegation, Foch was at his most adamant. Quickly he intimated that he would not argue about terms. As he stated baldly: 'Do you ask for an armistice? If so I will make known to you the conditions on which it may be

obtained.' Then, in reply to a formal German request, General Weygand, Foch's Chief of Staff, read out the armistice terms. The Germans were to have seventy-two hours in which to accept or reject them. Erzberger wanted fighting to cease immediately because, he explained, continued chaos in Germany would merely feed the appetites of Bolshevism. Foch refused. He also rejected Germany's request that the Allied blockade be raised, while the promise nevertheless to allow Germany supplies was very badly kept until the following spring, when goods arrived in quantity after the vehement humanitarian protests of the British General Plumer.

At 4:05 a.m. on 11 November, Germany signed an armistice which the Allies thought would render impossible further hostilities even after a period of retrenchment. Erzberger said that some parts of the agreement were impracticable, and stated, 'A nation of seventy millions suffers but does not die.' Foch replied curtly and enigmatically: '*Très bien.*'

At 11:00 a.m. a general cease-fire was sounded. The Great War was over. Ahead lay a peace settlement which in its bungling satisfied none of the Great Powers fully, and was eventually to result in World War II.

Among the main terms of the armistice were the following:

1. Germany was to evacuate immediately all occupied territory, Alsace-Lorraine included. All German troops were to withdraw behind the frontiers of 1 August 1914. Allied troops were to enter the territory thus evacuated without hindrance.

2. The left (west) bank of the Rhine was to be evacuated by German military forces. The Mainz, Coblenz, and Cologne bridgeheads were to be handed over to Allied troops. A neutral zone was to be established on the right (east) bank.

3. Vast quantities of matériel were to be surrendered to the Allies.

4. All Allied prisoners were to be repatriated, without immediate Allied reciprocity with regard to German prisoners.

5. All German submarines were to be surrendered; but the Allied blockade would continue.

6. 'Annulment of the treaties of Bucharest and Brest-Litovsk and of the supplementary treaties.'

7. 'Reparation for damage done.' Details included the return of securities or valuables removed from the invaded territories, and 'restitution of the Russian and Rumanian gold yielded to Germany or taken by that power. This gold to be delivered in trust to the Allies until peace is concluded.'

On 1 December Allied occupation forces entered Germany itself, thus initiating a presence which was to last until 1930. By this time the German Army had concocted a number of excuses to shift the blame for defeat away from itself. At first it was said that Germany had asked for an armistice in order to free its civilians from the starvation due to the Allied blockade, and in order to end the endless bloodletting of the battlefield. Later, however, the main emphasis shifted to a sinister tale that betrayal and double-dealing at home had undermined Germany from within – the 'stab-in-the-back' theory.

In truth Germany surrendered and accepted the onerous armistice terms because she had reached the end of her tether. Revolutionary ferment at home would soon rapidly have overcome even those troops at the front who would have been willing to fight on. Probably from the purely military point of view, Germany could have held out until the spring of 1919, for even with American participation the Allies were in no condition to advance indefinitely. Yet everywhere among the Central Powers food and petrol were running out – and if an army travels on its stomach, it also travels on wheels. Thus Germany held out until she could do so no longer. Then she gave in after a tremendous battle of endurance. Ironically, however, it was probably this ability to endure the unendurable, coupled with the absence of actual large-scale fighting and destruction on German soil itself, which fed the legends of Germany's betrayal by others and which shortened her collective memory to allow another world war to break out within a generation.

Victory in Italy

We noted earlier the paradox that the Italian defeat at Caporetto in late 1917 pulled the nation together as no other event throughout the war had done. This was fortunate, for the following spring, the involvement of the rival belligerents on the Western Front made it necessary for each to ask his ally to stage a diversion in and around northern Italy. Germany hoped that, if an Austrian offensive could knock Italy out of the war, Vienna's troops could be brought to bear on the West before the Americans arrived to shore up the enemy. Foch, guessing Austria's intentions, asked Italy to strike first. However, Diaz, the Italian supremo, thought the idea inadvisable; but to mollify the French he sent two Italian divisions to the west.

Meanwhile Austria proceeded with her plans. Conrad was brought to command on the Trentino, and Boroević on the Piave. After a diversion lasting two days, on 15 June 1918 the main Austrian offensive began. Conrad's forces at first made gains, which nonetheless were reversed the

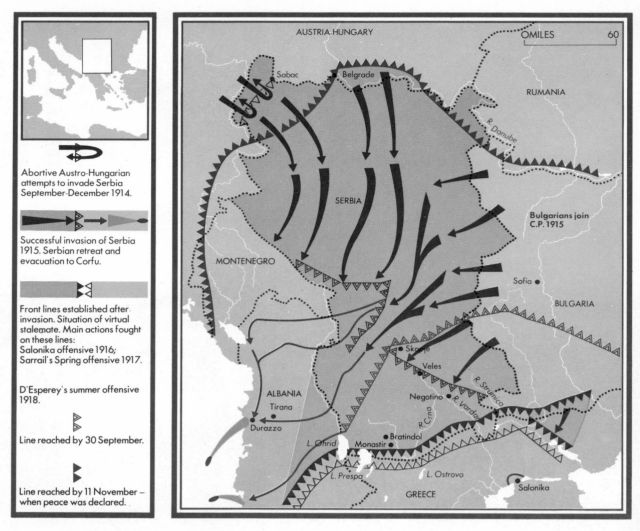

Abortive Austro-Hungarian attempts to invade Serbia September-December 1914.

Successful invasion of Serbia 1915. Serbian retreat and evacuation to Corfu.

Front lines established after invasion. Situation of virtual stalemate. Main actions fought on these lines:
Salonika offensive 1916;
Sarrail's Spring offensive 1917.

D'Esperey's summer offensive 1918.

Line reached by 30 September.

Line reached by 11 November – when peace was declared.

next day. Boroević also achieved some successes, but the battle as a whole failed because of difficulties of communications in the region, personality differences between the two Habsburg commanders, and the excellence of the Italian defence. By 24 June Boroević's forces had once more retreated behind the Piave; but Diaz still refused to take Foch's advice and fall upon the tired-out Austrians, for his own armies were in no fit state to do so at present, and he preferred to bide his time until his men were stronger and better equipped and until reserves were in greater supply. In addition, Diaz thought that the war would not be settled before the spring of 1919. Thus he could afford to wait for the propitious moment. Moreover, it was possible that now in desperation the Central Powers would throw their full weight against their weakest link – Italy.

Right: Poster appealing for the Ludendorff Fund for War Wounded, which started in May 1918.

Events elsewhere, however, began to change this picture. In September 1918 Franchet d'Esperey took the offensive in Macedonia, and rapidly Bulgaria went under. On 26 September Sofia requested an armistice. Diaz was impressed, and when the major Central Powers, Germany and Austria-Hungary, themselves applied for an armistice on 4 October, the Italian supremo saw clearly that his country had better act swiftly, lest peace be concluded and the lack of a final Italian offensive be held against Rome at the conference table. Furthermore, the Italian Prime Minister, Orlando, now stepped in, urging Diaz by telegram, 'Act at once!'

Despite the dissenting voices of the Treasury Minister, Nitti, and others, the offensive became an increasingly obvious answer as October wore on and Austria-Hungary weakened. Still, the Habsburg commanders were determined to fight on, regardless of what was happening at home, in the hope that their forward positions at the conclusion of an armistice would favourably influence the peace settlement – a hope which proved utterly vain, but which filtered down to the Austrian troops and made their last defence a truly heroic one. At the same time Italian front-line forces, reserves and preparations for battle were still quite inadequate. Political considerations, however, now overrode military ones.

On 24 October the Italians went into action on the Grappa, their superiority in arms counterbalanced by their inferiority in numbers and by the Austrian dexterity in using their ample and deadly supply of machine-guns. A piece of extreme bad luck had also intervened: the sudden flooding of the Piave had delayed a coordinated thrust there, and for a few days the men of the Grappa operation were left on their own. The Austrian counterattack of 27–28 October was particularly bloody, but by the twenty-ninth action on the Grappa had deadlocked, and conditions on the Piave had by now become such as to enable bridges to be thrown across. So far, Italy had lost 24,000 fatalities or casualties; nearly 13,000 more Italians were to fall in the next few days.

On the Piave, after a mediocre start on 26 October, by the twenty-eighth the Italian Eighth Army under Caviglia was plunged into the midst of battle. Now the Austrian lines gave way under successive Italian hammerblows. The Habsburg armies were shattered, while at home efforts at peace moves had been following one upon

another in dizzying succession. On the night of 30–31 October the battle turned into a jumble of encounters in which Italians cut off, outfought, killed or captured series after series of Austrian pockets of resistance. By 3 November the Italians had landed at Trieste. In the evening an armistice was signed near Padua. The Battle of Vittorio Veneto (named for the site of the Austrian headquarters) found Italy triumphant, while Austria's last strength had drained away with the loss of 30,000 dead and wounded and of 500,000 men as prisoners.

A Raemaekers' cartoon of the Kaiser and the Crown Prince in their new role in Holland. They claimed they were visiting the Netherlands for 'an indefinite period'.

Maxim machine gun on infantry carriage. Crew: 4. Calibre: 7·92mm. Range: 3000 yds.

Versailles: The Lost Peace

With the signing of the November armistice, it might have been thought that peace had come at last to the war-ravaged peoples of Europe and afar. For some, however, peace was not yet to be; indeed, at this very time, revolutionary turbulence was sweeping Germany and Hungary as part of the seismic shock engendered by the Central Powers' defeat while Moscow waited in the wings, gloating that the world revolution was imminent.

However, both the German and the Hungarian revolutions misfired. Their eventual successors were the liberal but in many respects ineffectual Weimar regime in Germany, and the reactionary regency of Miklos Horthy in Hungary, whom the break-up of the Habsburg Empire had left in the unenviable position of being an admiral without a seaport at his disposal. For a time half of Europe trembled on the brink of chaos or shook with fear in anticipation of the effects of the coming new order. Yet European institutions survived; the

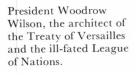

President Woodrow Wilson, the architect of the Treaty of Versailles and the ill-fated League of Nations.

Premier Clemenceau, the 'Tiger' of France. He wanted to impose a harsh peace on Germany for the sake of the millions of men who died or were injured in the war.

Prime Minister David Lloyd George discusses terms with Arthur Balfour. He mediated between Wilson and Clemenceau at the Paris Peace Conference while ensuring Britain of large new territorial gains in the colonial world.

Lloyd George arrives in Paris and is greeted by General Wilson and Marshal Foch.

tidal wave passed. However, to a great degree the whole of the 1918–19 peacemaking process was carried out in the shadow of revolution and the consequent desire of the victors to shield themselves from its effects.

The Treaty of Versailles was signed on 28 June 1919, exactly five years after the Sarajevo assassinations, in the *Galerie des Glaces* (Hall of Mirrors) of the Palais de Versailles, where the German Empire had been inaugurated in 1871 in the heady aftermath of Prussia's victory over France. In the middle of the Galerie, the plenipotentiary delegates were gathered round a horseshoe table, in front of which – 'like a guillotine', as Harold Nicolson wrote in his dairy – was the table for the signatures. In addition, the Hall of Mirrors was filled with over a thousand seats for members of delegations and other distinguished guests.

As Wilson and Lloyd George slipped into their seats, Clemenceau glanced to right and left, then signalled for silence. Over an awed hush, the French Prime Minister commanded, '*Faites entrer les Allemands*' (Bring in the Germans).

Through a door at the end of the vast hall emerged the German delegates, Müller and Bell. Their faces were ashen with emotion. After the Germans were seated and Clemenceau had declared the session open, Müller and Bell quickly rose to their feet, anxious to sign and complete the ordeal, only to be motioned to sit down again. After further preliminaries the two Germans at last were led to a small table where, at 12:03 p.m. precisely, they put their signatures to the treaty. As other delegates formed a queue to approach the table and sign, a thunderous salute boomed forth outside, and in the distance the cheering of the Parisian crowd could be heard.

In a surprisingly short period the signing was completed. '*La séance est levée*,' said Clemenceau. According to Nicolson, Müller and Bell were 'conducted like prisoners from the dock, their eyes still fixed upon some distant point of the horizon'. The ceremony was over, the delegates had dispersed. But the story of Versailles had hardly begun. The Treaty of Versailles, 200 pages in length, comprised 440 articles. Its main provisions are summarized below:

Germany was required to surrender Alsace-Lorraine, its borders limited to those in existence in 1870, to France; most of West Prussia and Posen (Poznań) and much of East Silesia and East Prussia to Poland; and part of Upper Silesia (Teschen) to Czechoslovakia. In addition she was to yield Moresnet, Eupen and Malmédy to Belgium and Memel (Klaipeda) to Lithuania. As a result of a plebiscite held in Schleswig, the northern region returned to Denmark and the southern region remained with Germany. On the Baltic Sea, the German city of Danzig was to be created a free city under the League of Nations; although France had wanted Poland to annex Danzig outright, she managed to have the city wrested forcibly from the Reich. Germany was to lose all her colonies, and the Reich 'acknowledges and will respect strictly the independence of Austria', as Article 80 of the treaty forbade a German-Austrian union (*Anschluss*). Plebiscites were to be held to determine the fate of Upper Silesia, as well as Allenstein

(Olsztyn) and Marienwerder (Kwidzýn) in East Prussia. (As a result, almost all of the latter two territories remained with Germany, but in the final settlement the smaller and richer part of Upper Silesia passed to Poland.) These changes caused Germany to lose about 13·5 per cent of its territory and economic potential, and about 10 per cent of its population.

The Versailles Treaty contained many other provisions. Germany was forbidden to fortify a large section of the Rhine. The Allied occupation of the Rhineland was to proceed as described earlier. The German army was to consist of not more than 100,000 officers and men, the navy of not more than 15,000. There was to be no German air force. The General Staff as such was abolished, and no staff college was to be maintained. Conscription was forbidden.

The most controversial part of the treaty concerned Article 231, the so-called war guilt clause. This stated that:

The Allied and Associated Governments affirm and Germany accepts the responsibility of Germany and her allies for causing all the loss and damage to which the Allied and Associated Governments and their nationals have been subjected as a consequence of the war imposed on them by the aggression of Germany and her allies.

Such was the Treaty of Versailles, a treaty which satisfied few men except the rulers of the succession states of Central-East Europe. Otherwise the settlement was too harsh for the British government, but too soft for the French. Versailles was not Utopian enough for Wilson, yet too Utopian for some cynics. The Germans rejected the entire concept of a *diktat* (dictated peace), which underlay the peace conference.

The Great War was the most destructive conflict which the world had yet seen. Its toll of lives was so vast as to defy imagination. Civilian deaths, apart from the influenza pandemic, amounted to at least 9,000,000, though some writers have set the figure at more than 12.6 million. Military loss of life is calculated at over 8,000,000, broken down as follows:

Germany	1,770,000 to 2,000,000
Russia	1,700,000
France	1,360,000
Austria-Hungary	1,100,000 to 1,200,000
Great Britain	760,000*
Italy	460,000 to 650,000
Turkey	325,000 to 375,000
British Empire	250,000*
United States	110,000 to 126,000

* Total 1,010,000.

If we include figures for wounded, prisoners and missing, total military casualties were about 37,500,000 – over 22,000,000 for the Allies, over 15,000,000 for the Central Powers.

It has been estimated that the total economic cost of the war was £75,077,000,000 (over $375 billion), of which the Allied governments spent £7,852,000,000 and the Central Powers £13,476,000. The price paid in physical devastation was greatest on French territory: 1,875 square miles of forest destroyed, along with 8,000 square miles of agricultural land and about a quarter of a million buildings.

These are cold statistics, and the reader may not sense from them the disillusionment that percolated downwards as ordinary people realized slowly the horrendous price which they had paid for a reordering of the world's affairs which was proving unsatisfactory at best. Plenty of men and organizations were waiting on the sidelines to harness and exploit this sentiment. The heirs to this fathomless disappointment, this harvest of broken dreams, were Fascism and Communism; pacifism and nihilism; anarchism, fatalism, escapism or sheer apathy. No one can understand how the world drifted into World War II almost in spite of itself without remembering the dejected legacy of World War I.

Protection troops of the newly-appointed Workers' and Soldiers' Council march down the Unter den Linden.

WORLD WAR II
Ronald Heiferman

CHAPTER ONE
Between the Wars

At the end of the Great War the victorious Allies assembled at Versailles to build a new world order. After four years of bloody brutal conflict in which empires perished, more than ten million lost their lives, and the lives of countless additional millions were disrupted, the delegates to the Paris Peace Conference convened to make the world safe, to provide a better future for the young or yet unborn. Never had there been a better opportunity to create a new political equilibrium. Never has such an opportunity been lost so pathetically.

The historian Harold Nicolson, himself a delegate to the Paris Peace Conference, suggested shortly after the conference adjourned that future historians would, with some justifications, conclude that the delegates to the conference were stupid men who had arrived in Paris determined that a wise and just peace should be negotiated, but who left the conference conscious that the treaties imposed on their enemies were neither just nor wise nor workable. The reason for the debacle was more clearly articulated by Charles Seymour, another historian also present at Paris, who explained the failure of the conference in the following terms:

The Peace Conference, representing the democracies, reflected the mind of the age; it could not rise measurably above its source. That mind was dominated by reactionary nostalgia and a traditional nationalism . . . It was not so much the absence of justice from the Paris Peace Conference that caused the ultimate debacle; it was the failure to make the most of what justice there was.

When the Allied delegates assembled in Paris, revenge was in the air, and all their lofty rhetoric could not mask their true intent. The Central Powers had caused the war and they (especially), would pay the price for that calumny. Unlike the deliberations at Vienna after the Napoleonic Wars, a century earlier, the vanquished would have no voice at the peace conference, would not participate in the creation of a new world order, and would not be returned into the family of nations until proper retribution had been made. Indeed, the conference ultimately proved little more than a punitive device to extract a pound of flesh from the defeated, and produced not a lasting peace, but the seeds for a future war.

To be sure, some justice was administered in Paris. As empires toppled, subject nationalities were granted independence and national goals and aspirations were formally recognized. Yet even here the delegates to the conference were selective, preferring to mete justice out to those people who had lived under the domination of the vanquished while failing to deal with those who sought the same rights and equality, but happened to fall under the hegemony of the victors. The Czechs, Hungarians, and Poles realized their independence; the Burmese, Chinese, and Vietnamese did not. It remained for the next war to settle their fate.

When the conference adjourned, a treaty of peace had been imposed on Germany and a League of Nations had been created. Beyond this, little had been accomplished. The treaty provided reparations for the victors, the League a forum for the idealists among them. The rest of the convention's agenda remained untouched. Wilson's vision of a new world order would never be achieved.

The Rise and fall of the Weimar Republic

For the German people the Paris settlement was a shock from which they never quite recovered. The Weimar Republic was forced to accept an ignominious end to a war which it had not initiated, and to acknowledge a huge indemnity for the destruction brought about by this war; foreign forces would occupy German soil and her armed forces would be dismantled. These were bitter pills to swallow for a people who as late as the summer of 1918 expected that they would win the war, and who had not seen allied forces in Germany at any time. It was no wonder, then, that the Germans reacted with digust to the peace which had been thrust upon them. The Allies had been just, but it was justice without mercy.

The fragile Weimar government attempted to fulfill Germany's obligations under the treaty in good faith, but the combination of revenge abroad and hostility at home was more than it could handle. The Republic had been born in chaos and represented the will of a minority of the German population. From the very beginning, conservatives and monarchists refused to accept its legitimacy while radical socialists and communists rebelled against its authority.

That the Weimar Republic survived at all was due to the genius of its leaders and not its institutions. Thanks to the efforts of Walter Rathenau and Gustav Stresemann, the government lived through the Sparticist revolt and the Kapp Putsch and re-established Germany's position in the world community, while attending to pressing domestic problems such as inflation and economic stabilization. By 1929 many of these problems

Opposite: Inflation almost destroyed Germany in 1923. These banknotes, worth billions of marks, might have been enough to have purchased a loaf of bread.

Above: Unable to maintain any sort of a large standing army, the German General Staff was forced to train with these wooden tanks during the years of the Weimar Republic.
Below: Hitler and Ludendorff join forces in an attempt to overthrow the Weimar Republic in 1923.

had been solved or solutions were near at hand. Then came the economic chaos of the Great Depression.

The depression, which had disastrous effects in America and throughout Western Europe, proved fatal to the Weimar Republic. Just as it appeared to be winning greater support from the public and the press, the floor fell out from under it; ironically, Stresemann, the architect of Ger-

many's economic reconstruction, died in the same month, October 1929, when the New York stock market crashed. This coincidence was most unfortunate for the government since Stresemann was, perhaps, the only moderate political leader capable of holding the Weimar coalition together while attending to the problems posed by the new economic disaster in Germany. With his death the coalition rapidly collapsed.

The impact of the depression in Germany was profound, bringing an immediate end to the renewed prosperity of the late 1920's. In 1930 over three million Germans were out of work; two years later the number of jobless workers was over six million. Payment of reparations, always a sore point in Germany, could not be continued and the Allies responded to this failure by sending troops into the Saar valley in order to punish the German government.

With the nation in economic dislocation and its most able defender dead, the Weimar government struggled to maintain its existence. In September 1930 Chancellor Heinrich Brüning, Stresemann's successor, was forced to call for new elections. By this time the depression had become severe, and the conservative-moderate *bloc* in the Reichstag was replaced by radical delegates from the left and right. The Communist Party increased its share of the vote from 3,263,000 in 1928 to 4,600,000. The National Socialist tally increased even more, from 810,000 in 1928 to 6,410,000 in 1930. As a result the conservatives and moderates no longer constituted a majority.

Rather than permit the creation of a communist government, President Hindenburg permitted Chancellor Brüning to remain in office and the country was governed by presidential decree from 1930 to 1932. So long as Brüning had the support of Hindenburg and the leaders of the army, the system worked well, for however much the leaders of the non-authoritarian parties in the Reichstag disliked the arrangement, they dared not cause the defeat of Brüning's government for fear of a Nazi accession to power or, on the other hand, a communist victory. Brüning was forced to resign in May 1932 only after leaders of the army refused to support him, and even then a moderate government was assured by the appointment of Franz von Papen as chancellor. Papen, who

continued to rule through presidential decree, hoped to factionalize the Nazi party and forge a new conservative coalition in the parliament. To this end, he called for an election in July 1932.

The election resulted in an increase of Nazi strength in the Reichstag, 230 National Socialist delegates being returned as opposed to 108 in 1928. Undaunted, Papen dissolved the new Reichstag and called for yet another election, hoping that the popularity of the Nazis had peaked and that their treasury had been drained by the election campaigns of July. When the new Reichstag convened in November, the Chancellor's predictions proved to have been correct, for the Nazis won two million fewer votes than four months before and lost thirty-four seats in the Reichstag. No sooner had the election been concluded, however, than his resignation was demanded by the very men who had persuaded

Hindenburg to appoint him in the first place. By this time, December 1932, the President was ill, and tired of the schemes of the Nazis' the conservative opponents. After the brief and unsuccessful chancellorship of General Kurt von Schleicher, Hindenburg finally agreed to allow Adolf Hitler to form a new government.

With Hindenburg dying, Hitler quickly moved to consolidate his power. In March 1933 he persuaded the Reichstag to pass an enabling act granting him unfettered power to legislate and conclude treaties for four years. During the following months, opposition parties were dissolved and anti-Nazi officials were dismissed from the bureaucracy. When Hindenburg died on 2 August 1934, Hitler assumed the office of the presidency as a result of a popular plebescite and the Nazi revolution began in earnest.

Having eliminated his political rivals, Hitler

Above: French troops occupied the Ruhr Valley when Germany was unable to pay reparations to the Allies.

Below: Early Nazis who tried to overthrow the State in the Beer Hall Putsch in 1923.

turned his attention to rivals within the National Socialist movement, purging them from the party in a brief reign of terror. Ernst Röhm, leader of the SA, was killed during the night of 29–30 June, and Gregor Strasser, a leading party organizer and leader of the left-wing clique within the movement, met the same fate. How many of Hitler's associates were murdered during the purge remains unknown but when it was completed, he emerged as the unchallenged leader of the Nazi movement.

Hitler was now able to turn his attention to the creation of a Nazi state. Labor unions were abolished, strikes were forbidden, and special courts were established to arbitrate labor-management disputes. Economic development plans and programs were immediately initiated and public works projects on a massive scale commenced to solve the problem of unemployment. In less than three years these plans bore fruit: unemployment declined from over six million in 1932 to less than a million in 1936; salaries and fringe benefits for workers increased; and the average German worker enjoyed a standard of prosperity unknown since the depression. Whatever their political views no one could deny that the Nazis had engineered the economic recovery of their country. As a result, many thinking Germans joined the Nazi bandwagon, and by 1936 Nazism had become a genuine mass movement.

Europe moves toward war

Once established at home, Hitler attended to the revision of foreign policy. His diplomatic objectives had originally been stated in *Mein Kampf* in 1924, and included union with Austria and other Germanic peoples in central and eastern Europe, and the creation of an area of expansion to include western Russia and the Ukraine. Although he repudiated *Mein Kampf* on occasion for political reasons, Hitler never really wavered from his original goals.

Although he recognized that conflict with the Soviet Union and France was inevitable, Hitler hoped to avoid a confrontation with Great Britain or the United States, since his aspirations did not include the creation of a vast overseas empire for Germany. Thus he was careful to pacify these democracies as much as was possible without sacrificing the attainment of his other goals. During the early years of the Third Reich, he tried to appease France as well; as long as Germany's army and navy remained small, it would be imprudent to risk confrontation with the western allies, even the French alone. It was imperative that Germany's armed forces be increased and re-equipped, and this could never be accomplished if the Allies believed that Germany intended waging another war. This being the case, he was careful to speak only of his interest in peace and to discuss only those aspects of the conditions regarding the disarmament of Germany that reasonable men could not deny needed readjustment.

While the rebuilding of Germany's armed forces went on in secret and in violation of the provisions of the Treaty of Versailles, Hitler was not yet ready to repudiate the treaty unilaterally,

Opposite: Former Chancellor von Papen, General von Blomberg, Hitler and Goebbels at a youth demonstration honoring President von Hindenburg in Berlin. **Above:** Leaders of the New Order enjoy the opera in Berlin. Watching *Die Meistersinger* (left to right): Goering and his wife, Rudolf Hess, Frau Goebbels, Hitler, Frau Hess, Goebbels and von Blomberg. **Left:** The Schützstaffeln (SS) destroyed the SA in the Night of the Long Knives and soon replaced it as Hitler's elite guard and leading para-military force.

Below: Hitler reviews the SS in 1938.

Above: The Hitler Youth mobilized for the supreme national effort to create a Greater Reich. **Above right:** Mass rallies were held in Nuremberg to drum up enthusiasm for the New Order.

nor was he unwilling to negotiate changes in its provisions. Although the French remained intransigent with regard to any alteration of Germany's military status, the British government was more willing to acknowledge that it was time that the treaty be revised. Anxious about French military supremacy on the continent and sympathetic to the reasonable nature of Hitler's proposals, they agreed that there was justice in Hitler's criticism of the peace settlement and in 1935 entered into bilateral arms agreements with the Third Reich. This provided a sanction for the rearmament of Germany which had already taken place and recognized publicly what Hitler had long been stating privately, that since the disarmament provisions applied to all signatories, the failure of the victorious allies to adhere to the spirit and letter of the treaty obviated any German obligation to do the same. The French protested, but it was too late to reverse the course of events. In 1936 German forces re-occupied the Rhineland and, for all effective purposes, the Treaty of Versailles was null and void.

Throughout the mid-30's tensions increased as fascism in Italy, Nazism in Germany and the military dictatorship in Japan grew more aggressive. In October 1935 Mussolini launched a campaign against Ethiopia. His success there encouraged him to send troops, planes and supplies to the Spanish fascists when they rebelled against the Republican government in 1936, a venture in which he was soon joined by Germany. Russia promptly moved to support the Spanish government, and the Spanish Civil War, which lasted until 1939, was to prove a testing ground for new weapons and techniques which would be used to great advantage in the larger conflict to come.

As none of the western democracies saw fit to take any effective action to stop these campaigns, Hitler was encouraged to press for a political union with Austria and territorial concessions from the Czech government. Seizing upon the Wilsonian principle that people of common background, culture, and language should be governed by their peers, the Fuehrer took Austria by force

in March 1938 with hardly a word from the Allies. Chamberlain did nothing to prevent the Anschluss because he thought it reasonable that Germans should be governed by Germans; the assumption was that the Austrians were Germans and their relationship with the Third Reich was an internal matter which should be decided without outside interference. The French did nothing because they had no commitment to come to Austria's rescue and were beset by political chaos at home, and the Americans were still clinging to their isolationist policies. Phase one of the plan to create a greater Germany had been achieved; it was now time for phase two, the annexation of the Sudetenland.

The rationale for demanding that the Czech government cede the Sudetenland to Germany was even more convincing than the explanation offered for the seizure of Austria. After all, millions of German-speaking people lived under Czech sovereignty and were demanding union with the Fatherland: in asking that their land be annexed to Germany, Hitler was only speaking for an oppressed minority. The Czechs were in a better position than the Austrians to resist Hitler's demands. Their army was large and well equipped, and the French and the Soviets were pledged to come to their assistance in the event of

Right: After keeping his supporters waiting for often more than an hour, the Fuehrer entered the stadium to be greeted by a tumultuous ovation.

an attack. The British, although under no treaty obligations to rescue Czechoslovakia, were known to oppose German military intervention, or so the Czechs believed. Thus, when Hitler began to rattle his sword in May 1938, the Czech army was partially mobilized and the Prague government prepared for war.

Since Hitler's generals were opposed to a military confrontation with the Czechs, the Fuehrer agreed to a suggestion made by Mussolini and convened a four-power summit conference in Munich on 29 September 1938. Again France and Britain remained unprepared to actively oppose a re-armed Germany and accepted his position, agreeing that some ten thousand square miles of Czech territory should be annexed by Germany. In return Hitler disowned any further territorial aims in the country and the British Prime Minister, Neville Chamberlain, returned to London hailing the conference as a harbinger of 'peace in our time'. His optimistic words, however, failed to reassure the Czechs, who had been forced to sit by and watch the great powers dismember their country. Their pessimism proved to be well justified, for in less than a year, in March 1939, Hitler swallowed up the rest of the small country; not to be outdone, Mussolini took Albania three weeks later.

The English people, who had been told repeatedly that Munich was a final settlement, felt that their government had been made fools of, and Chamberlain's own confidence in appeasement was severely shaken. When he heard rumors of German troop movements near the Polish border in March he wrote to that country, promising that if their independence was threatened, 'His Majesty's Government and the French Government would at once lend them all the support in their power'. It was an empty gesture, since Britain had no means of fulfilling her bargain, and was hopefully intended to incline Hitler toward a policy of moderation. In fact Hitler used it as an excuse to repudiate the German non-aggression pact with Poland of 1934 and the Anglo-German naval agreements of 1935; in August 1939 he shocked the world by signing a non-aggression pact with Russia. Britain responded by signing an Anglo-Polish treaty of mutual assistance, but it was too late. With his eastern front secure, Hitler was free to move troops into Poland over the issue of Danzig and the Polish Corridor. Great Britain declared war on Germany at 11 a.m. on 3 September 1939 and the French unhappily followed suit at 5 p.m.; belatedly, the two governments began leisurely to prepare for battle.

Above left: The Nuremberg rallies were often used to demonstrate Germany's new armed might. **Above:** Austrians rejoice in Salzburg when Germany annexed their country in the Anschluss of 1938.

Below left: German troops cross the Ludendorff Bridge to re-occupy the Rhineland in 1936. The Allies could have stopped them if they had tried. They didn't. **Below:** Hitler signs the Munich Pact which sealed the fate of Czechoslovakia. Behind him (from left to right) Chamberlain of Great Britain, Mussolini, and Premier Daladier of France.

Right: Neville Chamberlain returns from Munich with a scrap of paper which he thought guaranteed 'peace in our time'.

Japan's rise to power

Japan, unlike Germany, had attended the Paris Peace Conference as a member of the victorious allied coalition. Indeed, the war had been more profitable for Japan than for the other Allies. With a minimal commitment of manpower, the Japanese had annexed German leaseholds in China early in the war and consolidated their position during the remainder. When the armistice was signed on 11 November 1918, Japan was the paramount outside force in China and her economy was still in high gear, responding to the economic vacuum created by the pre-occupation of the European powers in the war against Germany. It might well be said that no country was so ill prepared for the coming of peace as Japan in 1918.

With the war over, Japanese activities in China would once again come under the jealous scrutiny of the Western powers whose governments and businessmen hoped to re-establish the pre-war equilibrium in China. This boded ill for the Japanese but well for the Chinese, who hoped to use the peace conference as a forum in which they might secure redress of their grievances from Japan with the aid of the Western powers, particularly the United States. When the conference convened, the Japanese delegation soon found itself justifying Japan's position in China and defending this position from a joint Sino-American attack. This they did successfully, but not without cost.

The Japanese, rightly or wrongly, believed that consideration of their actions at the peace conference was inappropriate and prejudicial, since the other victors were not asked to justify their own colonial policies and economic interests. As a member of the Allied coalition whose annexations of German leaseholds in China had been approved by the other allies in 1915, Japan found it difficult to understand their belated concern with the well being and sovereignty of the Republic of China in 1919, and attributed this interest to economic gain and racial prejudice. Although China's advocates could not force Japan to return her territory in China to the Chinese government, the Japanese did not view the outcome of the peace conference with much favor. On the contrary, government leaders in Tokyo saw the abortive challenge to Japan's position in China as an indication that the honeymoon with the Western allies would soon end, forcing a re-evaluation of diplomatic policies and alliances. This new mood contributed in no small way to the development of Japan's foreign policy from 1919–1937.

The re-adjustment of Japan's policy in China was a major topic when the Nine-Power Conference was convened in Washington in the winter of 1921–1922. Although ostensibly called to implement naval arms limitations, China was one of the most important topics at the conference and, under considerable pressure from the western powers, the Japanese government finally agreed to return Tsingtao most of their rights in Shantung to the Chinese, reluctantly accepting the United States' 'open door' policy.

From 1921 to 1928 the Japanese pursued a conciliatory policy toward China and the Western powers which paralled the advent of democratic government at home. This policy came to an

寧鐵路 醫院

abrupt end in 1928 when the renaissance of Chinese nationalism threatened to curtail Japanese commercial interests in China. Under the government of Prime Minister Tanaka the Japanese reverted to a tougher policy and even intervened militarily to protect Japanese interests. Nevertheless, the Japanese stopped short of wholesale military intervention in the hope that they might strike an arrangement with Generalissimo Chiang Kai-shek which would guarantee Japan's position in China.

If nothing else, Chiang Kai-shek was pledged to the proposition that special foreign interests and privileges in China would have to end, and in this regard he was no more sympathetic to the Japanese than to the West. While China remained divided and beset by warlordism, the anti-imperialist policy of the Kuomintang threatened no one. But with the establishment of the Nationalists in Nanking in 1928, their anti-imperialist stance could no longer be dismissed. While the Chinese Nationalists were in no position to force a readjustment of the unequal treaties on the Western powers or Japan, it would not be long until Chiang might feel secure enough to force the issue. Furthermore, it appeared likely that if such a readjustment were demanded, at least one of the powers, the United States, would stand behind the Nationalist government, if for no other reason than to insure the sanctity of the open door doctrine. Rather than wait for this to happen, the Japanese chose to act before it was too late.

Failing to extract concessions from the Chinese government, the Japanese resorted to force to insure their position in China. In 1928 officers of the Kwantung army assassinated Chang Tso-lin, the warlord of Manchuria, whom they considered incompetent and uncooperative. Although no friend of the Chinese Nationalists, Chang was a threat to Japanese expansion in Manchuria, a mineral-rich area vital to the development of heavy industry in Japan; although his murder was not ordered by the government in Tokyo, no effort was made to discipline the officers involved for fear that this might damage the prestige of the army. Government leaders were hardly appalled by the deed, for the mood of the nation had changed considerably since 1921, as had the situation in China.

The action of the Kwantung army in Manchuria reflected this change and gave rise to other heavy handed efforts to secure Japanese control in the province, culminating in the Manchurian Incident of 1931.

The Manchurian Incident created a war psychosis in Japan and resulted in the rapid Japanese occupation of China's three northeastern provinces and the creation of the Kingdom of Manchukuo in 1932. Faced with a *fait accompli* and the loss of three provinces, the Chinese government took its case against Japan to the League of Nations which appointed the Lytton Commission to investigate the matter. By the time the commission published its findings and reported to the League in 1933, Japan's presence in Manchuria had been cemented and there was nothing the League could do to extract concessions from the Japanese, who walked out rather than face its condemnation in 1933.

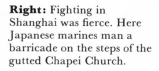

Right: Fighting in Shanghai was fierce. Here Japanese marines man a barricade on the steps of the gutted Chapei Church.

The Chinese protested and the League condemned, but the Western powers did nothing to prevent the Japanese from annexing Manchuria. Only the United States responded to Japan's aggression but even this response was limited to a verbal slap on the wrist. Try as he might to throw some weight behind his denunciation of the Japanese, Secretary of State Henry L. Stimson knew full well that Congress and the American people were in no mood to engage in anything more than a verbal debate. His non-recognition policy angered Japanese leaders but it in no way inhibited their policies in China. In fact, it moved Japan further out of the Allied coalition which had survived the Great War.

Rebuffed by the Western powers and the League of Nations, the Japanese developed a new Asian policy based upon the notion of pan-Asianism and the creation of a Japanese sphere of influence throughout Asia. As the only Asian country to successfully industrialize and come to grips with the problem of modernization, the Japanese came to view themselves as benevolent and paternalistic leaders of the Asian world and proposed to lead an anti-colonial coalition against the European powers and the United States. Although a formal program to achieve this end was not articulated until 1938, Japanese interest in the Asian world increased markedly from 1928–1938, and no opportunity was lost to advance Japanese goals and priorities in the decade prior to the war. On the other hand, there is no evidence to suggest that Japan's leaders were unwilling to

Left: Japanese troops advance warily through a town in North China. By early 1939 the forces of the Empire of Japan had swept Chiang Kai-shek's Nationalists from most of coastal China.

consider a rapprochement with the Western powers and the United States if this could be achieved without losses in Manchuria and elsewhere.

Any chance for a rapprochement with the Western powers was all but smashed when Japanese forces invaded China in 1937. More than any other single act, the invasion of China nullified diplomatic efforts to avoid a confrontation. Whatever the original merits of the response to renascent Chinese nationalism, the invasion of China proved costly and futile to the Japanese. The China incident lasted more than seven years, occupied the attention of nearly a million Japanese troops and strained Japanese-American relations almost to a breaking point. The Chinese Nationalists did not collapse in the face of the Japanese invaders but retreated to the interior of China where, together with Chinese Communist forces in northwest China, they resisted Japan until September 1945.

What were the origins of the Second World War? German dissatisfaction with the terms of the Treaty of Versailles, certainly, and the economic disaster brought on by the depression. The Japanese desire for growth in the Far East and subsequent American pressure were other factors, as were expansionist policies by Russia and Italy. But no one could have foreseen that three separate wars caused by these factors, the German-Polish war, the Sino-Japanese war and the Russo-Finnish war, would mushroom, overlap and turn nearly the entire world into a battlefield.

Left: Shanghai burns after Japanese bombers wiped out the northern part of the city.

CHAPTER TWO
Blitzkrieg (September 1939-June 1940)

On 1 September 1939 German armies crossed the Polish frontier and launched an attack which immediately shattered the fragile interwar peace. Britain and France had anticipated that Poland would be Hitler's next target; indeed, German forces had hardly sealed the fate of the Czech government in March when Mr Chamberlain, speaking on behalf of the British government, offered Poland his pledge of support. This the Poles were only too ready to accept, despite the fact that there was little the British could do to nullify the effect of Hitler's first blitzkrieg. Both in Warsaw and in London, it was vainly hoped that this new 'tough line' would deter Hitler from using force in Poland if and when diplomatic means failed. The somewhat less enthusiastic French declaration of support for the Poles which followed shortly after Chamberlain's statements simply served to reinforce this view and, unfortunately, gave the Polish government false confidence in its ability to withstand the Nazi onslaught.

While heads of state were making ever more ominous statements, an abortive attempt was made to solve the Polish problem through diplomacy. The Germans, made bold by their triumph at Munich and confident of the unwillingness of the other European powers to go to war on Poland's behalf, lost little time after Munich in presenting their bill of particulars to the Polish government; their demands included the return of Danzig to German control and the right to build a major highway and rail facility across the Polish Corridor to East Prussia. In effect, Hitler and his associates were seeking to nullify one of the most unpopular provisions of the Treaty of Versailles through negotiation and consent. When such consent was not easily forthcoming from the Poles, Hitler turned his attention to their British and French allies.

If Hitler assumed that his solution of the Polish question would be as easily foisted upon the British and French as the dismemberment of Czechoslovakia, he was gravely mistaken. Mr Chamberlain, the architect of appeasement in 1938, had suddenly 'acquired a spine,' a fact which caught both the French and the Germans off guard. Although Chamberlain had chosen not to respond with force over the Czechoslovakian *débâcle*, his almost unqualified support of the Polish government in 1939 marked the end of appeasement. Unfortunately this change was temporarily overlooked by Hitler, who continued to perceive the new situation in old stereotypes until continued rebuffs forced him to look elsewhere for allies in the Polish affair.

With Mr Chamberlain forcefully condemning Germany's appetite for territory with the French following reluctantly behind, Hitler turned toward the Soviet Union for help in solving the Polish question. Such an approach, though compelling because of the seeming intransigence of Chamberlain and Daladier, was nonetheless difficult given the deep and mutual distrust felt by Hitler and Stalin. Thus, although preliminary discussions of a Nazi-Soviet *détente* were initiated in April 1939, no agreement was reached until the end of August. It is quite possible that even after this prolonged period of negotiation an agreement might not have been reached were it not for the Molotov's arrival at the Foreign Ministry in Moscow and, especially, Stalin's frustration over the slow progress of Anglo-Russian deliberations.

Any guarantee of Polish sovereignty was meaningless without Soviet compliance. This point was not altogether lost on the British and French, but neither party was enthusiastic about seeking Russian support. Some of their reluctance to court Stalin reflected the Poles' strong distrust of any arrangement that might permit the Soviets military passage through their territory, and in addition, British and French military leaders tended to underestimate the Red Army's ability to effectively counter German units in the event of an attack on Poland. They preferred, instead, to rely on the ability of the Polish army to withstand a German onslaught until their own forces could be mobilized and sent to Poland's rescue. Thus, there appeared to be little need for bringing the Soviets into a tripartite pact to preserve the sovereignty of Poland, and in fact, the first gesture toward an entente was to be made by the Soviets and not the Anglo-French allies despite the fact that such an agreement was far more in the interest of England and France than of Russia.

The Russians revived the notion of a tripartite anti-Nazi pact shortly after the fall of Czechoslovakia, presenting it formally on 16 April 1939. Though an alliance between Russia, England, and France would have certainly given Hitler reason to pause and might well have avoided the dismemberment of Poland, neither Chamberlain nor his French colleague, Daladier, were particularly enthusiastic. Their lack of response placed the architect of the proposal, M. Litvinov, under great pressure. Litvinov was an outspoken proponent of the western alliance, a staunch anti-fascist, and a Jew, and so long as he remained

Above: On 17 September the Russians moved into Eastern Poland to secure their part of the infamous bargain struck in the Molotov-Ribbentrop Pact.

Russia's Foreign Commissar a Nazi-Soviet agreement was unlikely. Unfortunately, Stalin grew tired of the rebuffs of the British and the French and on 3 May 1939 replaced Litvinov with Vyacheslav Molotov. Molotov was more sympathetic to the fascist regimes in Germany and Italy and lost little time in altering Soviet foreign strategy; under his stewardship, Russo-German negotiations began in earnest, culminating in August 1939 with the Nazi-Soviet pact.

The German Foreign Ministry was not slow to take advantage of the Anglo-French failure to accept the Soviet initiative. Even before Molotov replaced Litvinov, new discussions of German-Russian relations had been initiated in Berlin and Moscow; though the Soviet press still seemed to echo the anti-fascist line so commonly found in England and the United States, German diplomats sensed that Stalin was growing restless and resentful at the way he was being treated in London and Paris and advised the Fuehrer to press for a rapprochment with Moscow. The advent of Molotov gave rise to redoubled efforts toward that end, but the path was still difficult and there is no reason to believe that at this point the conclusion of a Nazi-Soviet pact was inevitable. If

such had been the case, it would not have taken so long for Molotov to cement the arrangement. Clearly, the dallying of Chamberlain and Daladier was as much responsible for the announcement of 23 August 1939 as the assurances Hitler's associates gave to Stalin prior to the signing of the pact.

The Nazi-Soviet Pact provided for the fourth partition of Poland as well as for Soviet annexation of Latvia, Estonia, and Finland. Even more important, it provided time and a temporary breathing space which was advantageous for both countries. That this was its main purpose can be easily demonstrated, both by later events and contemporary evidence. Though Churchill might well say that 'only totalitarian despotism in both countries could have faced the odium of such an unnatural act,' neither Hitler nor Stalin had any illusions about the true nature of the agreement. Indeed, one might well wonder which dictator abhorred the pact the most! Whatever the answer, it is clear that both men were far more pragmatic than their opposite numbers in the west.

The pact between Germany and the Soviet Union made war certain, and there was little the British and French could do except to reaffirm their pledges to Poland and prepare for the inevitable. Though Chamberlain made one last diplomatic move to avert hostilities, it was an empty gesture and was understood to be so by both sides: it was now only a question of when and where the war would begin.

The invasion of Poland

German forces crossed the Polish border early in the morning on 1 September 1939; by the end of the month, Poland had ceased to exist. The speed and ease of the German victory was a monument to the ruthless efficiency of their 'blitz' and the hopelessly inadequate defense offered by Polish forces and their allies. Contrary to popular opinion at the time, the Germans possessed neither numerical superiority nor an absolute technological advantage over their enemies in this first battle of the European war. As Basil Liddell Hart points out, the German army was hardly more ready for war in 1939 than its adversaries; in numbers alone, the Polish army had ample forces (thirty active divisions, ten reserve divisions and twelve cavalry brigades) to contend with and hold the German strike force (48 active divisions and six reserve divisions) until help arrived from England and France. What the allies lacked was an appreciation of the fact that new developments in mobile equipment had revolutionized modern warfare. Nowhere was this more pathetically manifested than in the defensive deployment of Polish forces.

The Polish command was hopelessly antiquated in its military strategy and the pattern of its forces. Though the Polish government might eventually muster as many as 2,500,000 men, its army had few armored and motorized divisions and were very short of anti-aircraft and anti-tank guns. The cavalry, the pride of the Polish forces, could not resist Germany's mechanized units; like many other horse-minded soldiers, Poland's commanders had virtually ignored the lessons of the American Civil War and the First World

War and persisted in the illusion that cavalry charges could repel tanks and armored vehicles. They paid heavily for this belief.

In anticipation of a possible German attack, Polish forces were deployed along the long and virtually open frontiers with Germany and Czechoslovakia, a strip approximately 3500 miles long. A third of her forces were located around the Polish Corridor, a smaller number in Silesia, and the rest were thinly scattered along the southern border with the exception of a reserve force in the Lodz-Warsaw area. Although it would have been wiser to avoid this concentration of forces in the forward areas, the economic importance of the Silesian coalfields and patriotic attachments the recently acquired Corridor dictated the deployment of forces in these areas. Had the Poles assembled their forces further to the east they might have been able to resist the German offensive more successfully, but national pride would never have allowed this abandonment of the forward lines. Nor did Poland's military leaders see their deployment of forces as a liability; on the eve of the invasion, they continued to remain confident in their ability to resist until their western allies could mobilize and take counter measures to relieve the pressure.

Poland's topography was perfectly suited for the German assault, the Polish plain providing the invaders with a large area across which their mechanized mobile forces could rapidly advance. The blitzkrieg, based upon the deployment of a highly armored and mobile striking force of tanks, self-propelled guns, and truck transports, rapidly broke through Poland's front lines, wrecking command areas and cutting off supplies. With inadequate means of transportation and supply, Polish forces along the frontier could not offer a coordinated defense against their enemies nor, since railway lines from the front to the interior were savagely and successfully knocked out by the German air force, could they be quickly moved to the rear to engage in delaying action. Marching on foot or riding on horseback, large numbers of Polish troops were almost instantly trapped behind German lines as German mobile units raced toward the east.

The cavalry, upon which Polish leaders had pinned their defense, proved entirely ineffective in stopping German tanks. Despite the heroic Polish cavalry men who rode against German Panzer divisions, the heavy equipment would not be stopped by swords and lances; the use of horsed cavalry in modern warfare was unequivocably proven to be inadequate defense against the new technology of death.

Within two days German forces had sealed off the Polish Corridor and were converging on the cities of Cracow and Lodz. The German attack force, consisting of two army groups (Bock's army group in the north and Runstedt's in the south), might have advanced even further were it not for the somewhat orthodox policy of restraining the mobile forces until infantry units could catch up to them. However, as the German commanders realized how confused and inadequate the Polish defense was, even this restraint was abandoned; by 6 September Cracow, the old imperial capital, had fallen and the Polish army

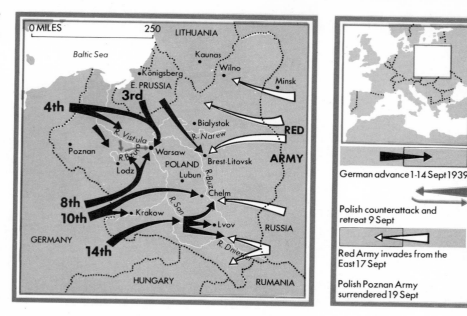

German advance 1-14 Sept 1939

Polish counterattack and retreat 9 Sept

Red Army invades from the East 17 Sept

Polish Poznan Army surrendered 19 Sept

was in retreat. On 8 September, German forces reached the outskirts of Warsaw.

The speed of the German advance (some 140 miles within the first week) caught the Poles off-guard, but it was not until 10 September that Marshal Smigly-Rydz ordered a retreat toward southeast Poland where a more prolonged defense might be prepared. By this time most of the Polish forces had been captured behind enemy lines or were spent in the brave but useless offensive actions that had been ordered prior to the call for retreat. This failure to call for an early retreat and the insistence on launching useless counter-attacks exacted a price in men and material which far exceeded any possible benefits. Though Polish forces fought bravely and won the grudging admiration of their enemies on the battlefield, the stubbornness and over-confidence of their leaders was not easily overcome; by the end of the second week of the campaign, the Polish army had ceased to exist as an organized force.

On 17 September, as the Germans pressed their attack on Warsaw and the remnants of Poland's army retreated toward the southeast, Russian forces struck across the eastern border. This attack sealed Poland's fate, although the Warsaw garrison continued to hold out until 28 September. By 5 October organized resistance had collapsed, the fourth partition of Poland had been accom-

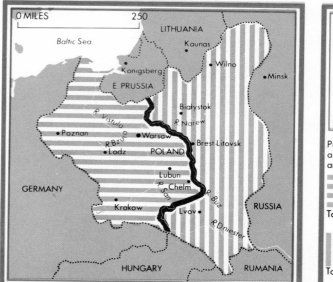

Poland is divided according to a secret pact between Germany and Russia:

To Germany

To Russia

plished, and the terms of the Nazi-Soviet Pact had been fulfilled; as its critics had predicted as early as March, the guarantee of aid from the Western allies had proved virtually meaningless. Churchill declared on 1 October that the heroic defense of Warsaw shows that the soul of Poland is indestructible, and that she will rise again like a rock . . ., but words of praise were of little consolation to the Polish people.

The 'phoney war'

Sitzkrieg followed blitzkrieg. After the dismemberment of Poland the war entered a brief quiescent stage when, except for the 'winter war' in Finland, no new fronts were opened for eight months. The 'phoney war,' as the American press called it, was a time for reflection on both sides. In Berlin, London and Paris statesmen sought to analyse the implications of the German victory in Poland while generals planned future actions and contemplated the strategies of their adversaries.

In Berlin the momentum of the Polish campaign had not excited the German general staff as much as it had fired the imagination of their Fuehrer. Although Hitler had temporarily revived the hope of a new European peace conference to avoid prolonged world conflict, he also hastened to plan for an early offensive in the West, and once his peace bid had been rebuffed (9 October) he presented the plans to his military lieutenants. Almost to a man, they balked at his suggestion of an early offensive against the British and French, but the Fuehrer persisted in his belief that such an action would forestall a longer and more costly campaign in the future. Fearing that the marriage of convenience with the Soviets would evaporate now that both parties had achieved their immediate aims in Poland, Hitler insisted that peace would have to be forced on the English and French before the Russians joined them in a plot against Germany.

Hitler's bold plans for a confrontation with England and France frightened his military advisers. Although the German press had changed the Polish conquest from an event to a legend, the generals knew better than the reading public the difficulties of repeating such a triumph against the Western allies. England and France, after all, were far more formidable foes than Poland; though they had remained virtually paralysed as the Germans swept through Poland, they could hardly be expected to do the same while their own territory was violated. In addition, the revelation of the strategy of blitzkrieg could not have been expected to go unnoticed. The preparations that were surely being made in London and Paris would prove extremely costly in the event of an attack – or so the generals thought.

On paper, the hesitation of the German General Staff appears to have been well founded. Even with the elimination of Polish forces on the east, the Germans would face superior numbers on the western front; the French alone could mobilize a total of 110 divisions to which the British might add four to six divisions at the start of the conflict with more to follow. The German generals, with a potential mobilization of 98 divisions of which as many as 36 were unfit for combat because of insufficient training and/or equipment, were understandably wary, also knowing that the French army was fully their

equal and actually possessed a numerical superiority in tanks, long-range guns, and artillery pieces. Only in the size of her air force did Germany possess an advantage over her enemies.

If the generals doubted their commander-in-chief, their troops and the German people stood behind their leader. Realizing this, Hitler grew increasingly impatient with his military advisers; he chastised them for their lack of confidence and aggressive spirit and ordered the preparation of an offensive plan. Although Brauchitsch, the Commander-in-Chief of the Army, and Halder, the Chief of the General Staff, continued to harbor reservations about the wisdom of the scheme, they finally complied with his command after failing to persuade him to change his mind.

The offensive in the west was supposed to commence in mid-November 1939, but had to be postponed several times due to meteorological conditions. The original plan, drafted by Halder and other of the older generals, was closely reminiscent of the Schlieffen Plan of 1914, calling for the main German attack to proceed through Central Belgium with a secondary and lighter thrust in the area of the Ardennes. This plan, reluctantly drafted at Hitler's insistence, was sharply criticized by some younger officers who feared it was too obvious; fortunately for them and the German army, a German liaison officer carrying a copy of the plan landed in Belgium on 10 January 1940 when his plane went astray on a flight from Münster to Bonn. Fearing that it had fallen into Allied hands, Hitler scrapped the old plan and commissioned a new one.

The architect of the new plan was Erich von Manstein, Chief of Staff of Rundstedt's army and a critic of Halder's original scheme. Collaborating with Guderian, an expert in tank warfare who had participated in the blitz of Poland, Manstein proposed a reversal of the earlier plan. Whereas Halder had called for a primary attack in central Belgium, Manstein proposed a major assault through the Ardennes with diversionary actions in central Belgium, along the Maginot line, and in Holland. Such a move through the 'impenetrable forest' would catch the allies off-guard, thus permitting the main German force to rapidly break through weakly held French lines and head toward the Channel coast, cutting off the Belgians, British, and French in the process.

Manstein's plan was a bold one, and his departure from orthodox strategy was resisted by the General Staff, who not only held that such a scheme was impractical, but also resented the personal manner in which Manstein had pressed his case. Nevertheless, their opposition went unnoticed; Hitler insisted upon its implementation and ordered a spring offensive. So pleased was he with the whole idea that he later claimed credit

J.U. 88–A4 Length: 47 ft. 1½ in. Span: 65 ft. 10½ in. Maximum speed: 293 m.p.h. Armament: 2 × 13 mm., 3-4 × 7.9 mm.

for the victory in the west, reducing Manstein to the status of the only general who had understood him when he raised the idea of an attack through the Ardennes.

Norway and Denmark fall

Preparations for the western offensive were temporarily interrupted by the German invasions of Denmark and Norway in April 1940. Unlike the previous Polish campaign, these ventures were ad hoc affairs, hastily improvised in response to the German navy's fear of a British action in Norway; this would preclude Germany's use of the long Norwegian coastline, facilitate the British blockade of Germany, and cut off the flow of iron ore from northern Sweden upon which the German steel industry was dependent.

On 19 February 1940 Hitler reluctantly ordered the completion of plans for seizing Norway; a decision undoubtedly precipitated by the British search and seizure of a German vessel in Norwegian territorial waters on 16 February. The Altmark affair, more than any other argument or incident, convinced the Fuehrer of the validity of Admiral Raeder's arguments for a preventive strike against Norway. Norwegian neutrality would inevitably be violated by the British. Was it not, therefore, wise for Germany to strike first? Hitler could hardly dispute this judgement; the bold action of the Royal Navy and the seeming compliance of the Norwegian government demanded effective countermeasures.

While Chamberlain and Daladier debated possible pre-emptive measures in Scandinavia, the German strike force under the command of General Falkenhorst completed its preparation for the invasion; aided and abetted by traitors such as Vidkun Quisling, the Germans were ready to launch their offensive at the beginning of April. Curiously enough, the Allies also planned

Below: German infantry moves into Norway behind a Panzer.

Far left: Finnish soldiers defend their untenable border when Russia invaded Finland in the Winter War of 1939–40. Russia hoped to secure its northern flank against its ally Germany, but the Red Army received a nasty shock when the Finns refused to roll over and play dead. **Center left:** Grand Admiral Raeder (center) charts the course for the German Navy, which was effectively blockaded almost from the outset of the war. **Left:** German mortars in action against Norwegian mountain troops.

Left: The *Graf Spee* was scuttled in the River Plate in Argentina after having been chased and trapped. The *Graf Spee* wreaked havoc with British shipping in both the Atlantic and the Pacific. Its destruction virtually eliminated German sea power outside the North Atlantic.

German invasion of Denmark and Norway, started 9 April 1940

14.5.40

German advance and dates of capture

15.4.40
8.6.40

Allied landings, (top date) and later withdrawals, (bottom date)

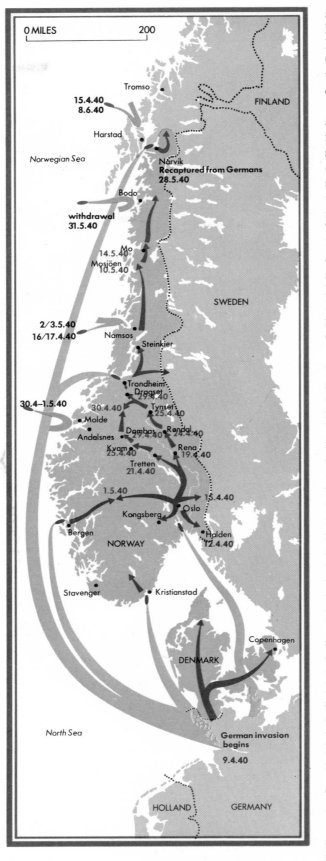

0 MILES 200

Tromso

15.4.40
8.6.40

Harstad

Norwegian Sea

FINLAND

Narvik
Recaptured from Germans
28.5.40

Bodo

withdrawal
31.5.40

14.5.40 Mo

Mosjöen
10.5.40

SWEDEN

2/3.5.40
16/17.4.40

Namsos

Steinkier

Trondheim
Driveset

30.4.40
Tynset
25.4.40

30.4–1.5.40

Molde

Dombas
29.4.40

Rendal
24.4.40

Andalsnes

Kvam
25.4.40

Rena
19.4.40

Tretten
21.4.40

1.5.40

15.4.40

Kongsberg

Oslo

Bergen

NORWAY

Halden
12.4.40

Stavenger

Kristianstad

Copenhagen

DENMARK

North Sea

German invasion
begins
9.4.40

HOLLAND

GERMANY

arrival of German bombers over Copenhagen later that morning left little room for doubt as to Hitler's intentions. Shortly after 7:00 a.m. King Christian X accepted the German terms and by the end of the day, Denmark was under German occupation.

The invasion of Norway commenced one hour after German troops had crossed the Danish frontier. The Norwegian government was presented with the same alternative as the Danes – capitulate without resistance or suffer the consequences of a German blitz. Indeed, even as this ultimatum was being delivered by the German minister, forces were being landed at Narvik, Trondheim, Bergen, and Christiansted and had begun moving toward Oslo. Despite these intimidations, the Norwegian government refused to accept Hitler's conditions. Although all major Norwegian cities were in German hands by noon, King Haakon VII and his government successfully escaped from Oslo and resistance to the German occupation began that afternoon.

With the evacuation of the monarchy, Vidkun Quisling was installed as head of the Norwegian government. His designation, contrary to German expectations, did not eliminate resistance but increased it. Meagre Norwegian army forces, buoyed by hastily improvised and somewhat indirect assistance from the British navy, attempted to stand against German units north of the capital. At the same time, frenzied preparations were being made in London to engage the German fleet off the Norwegian coast and launch relief efforts at Narvik and Trondheim. When finally mounted, these operations were ineffective and were rapidly halted by the Germans. Although resistance had not yet ceased when the western offensive was launched on 10 May 1940, the Norwegian affair was settled for all intents and purposes by the end of April.

The invasions of Denmark and Norway were a smashing success for the Germans, insuring their continued access to iron ore from Sweden and the use of air bases from which allied shipping in the North Sea might be attacked. For the British, the affair was a disaster of the first magnitude which could not be easily erased, even by their naval victory over the German fleet. For the people of Denmark and Norway, the long winter of German occupation had begun.

The Western offensive

Germany's western offensive began on 10 May 1940 with simultaneous thrusts into Belgium and Holland. At dawn, while German diplomats informed their Dutch counterparts that an invasion was being launched to preclude a similar Franco-British move, German airborne units were dropped behind Dutch lines and the Luftwaffe attacked military installations and airbases. Four days later (14 May 1940) the Dutch surrendered.

The speed of Germany's conquest of the Netherlands was the direct result of the deployment of large numbers of paratroopers, the first major airborne assault of the war. The Dutch were not unprepared for a German attack, but they had expected that attack to come on the ground and prepared accordingly. The defensive plans devised at the Hague called for the consolidation of the

some action in this area at that very time but the end of the Russo-Finnish War and the fall of the Daladier government forced its postponement. Thus, when the Germans struck, they were barely a step ahead of their adversaries.

On 9 April 1940 at 4:00 a.m. Falkenhorst's army crossed the Danish frontier. Shortly thereafter, the German ambassador presented the Danish foreign minister with his government's case: the Danes might capitulate immediately and accept the German occupation as a 'friendly necessity' or they would be forced to capitulate. If this message was not sufficiently clear, the

Top: German heavy machine-gun on Norway's coast. **Bottom:** Wrecked shipping in Narvik Bay after an attack by British warships in the First Battle of Narvik; 10 April 1940.

Above: German paratroops land in Holland on the first day of the Blitzkrieg in the West: 10 May 1940. **Above right:** German troops moved quickly across Dutch canals to successfully trap the Dutch Army. **Opposite top left:** The center of Rotterdam was wiped out on 14 May 1940, ironically after the Dutch had capitulated. **Opposite top right:** German forces streak through Flanders and the towns which were so heroically defended by the Allies in the War of 1914–18.

Right: German troops enter the port of Rotterdam even while the city was burning. **Far right:** Belgians welcome British armored vehicles as they pass forward to the front.

Dutch forces behind the Grebbe-Peel line if the Germans crossed the border. Since the Dutch-German border was over 200 miles long, it was useless to consider making a stand there; only the eastern lowlands would be flooded to slow the German advance while 'fortress Holland' was being consolidated. Here, in Amsterdam, Rotterdam and the Hague, the Dutch army proposed to make its stand. Although the possibility of an airborne assault had been considered, it was ruled out as being too impractical and beyond the capability of the German army. Thus, when it was actually launched, the Dutch were caught completely off guard and could do little to defend themselves.

That an airborne assault on Holland might strain German resources was true; when the invasion was launched on 10 May there were only some 4500 trained parachute troops in all of the German army. Of these, 4000 were deployed in Holland. There was little margin for error but the benefits to be derived from such a surprise proved well worth the risk involved. As it happened, only 180 of General Student's 4000 men were killed or wounded; by seizing important bridges, investing the major urban centres, and capturing enemy airfields intact, they cleared the way for the conventional support troops, who followed to mop up the operation and dispose of the Dutch. Germany's double blow on fortress Holland and the frontier was more than the Dutch could handle; French relief from the south under General Giraud came too late, and in any case could not have turned the tide. There was no alternative but to sue for peace.

After the conquest of Holland the Germans were free to concentrate on the campaign in Belgium and the attack through the Ardennes. In Belgium, things were going according to plan. Fort Eben-Emael had been effectively neutralized by a small contingent of airborne forces while the few other airborne units that were left after the invasion of Holland were landed west of the Albert Canal, securing important bridges to allow German ground forces to advance westward and southward. By the second morning of the invasion (11 May 1940), a general retreat was

ordered by Belgian commanders. At about the same time, British and French reinforcements arrived on the scene.

The German breakthrough across the Albert Canal and the Meuse was of far less import than the rush of British and French forces into Belgium to counter the German advance. By throwing the best and most mobile part of their army into Belgium, the Allies had left the Germans free to launch their attack through the Ardennes, safe in the knowledge that by the time Allied forces could be redeployed against them, their own would be well on the way to the Channel coast.

While German Army Group B pushed rapidly into northern Belgium occupying the attention of 36 Allied divisions in the process, Army Group A traversed the Ardennes, crossing the French frontier on 14 May, the same day that the Dutch surrender was accepted. Meeting little resistance from the weak French units guarding this sector between the end of the Maginot Line and central Belgium, German armored units quickly broke through and headed toward the coast. After some initial hesitation over the implications of too rapid progress, the green light was given to Panzer commanders Guderian, Hoth, and Reinhardt who immediately raced westward. By

Above: Stukas in a Norwegian fjord. **Right:** A German destroyer in a fjord near Narvik. **Below right:** A German minesweeper in Norwegian waters.

Below: The German attack on Norway was swift and decisive. **Below right:** A dying French soldier is assisted by the man who shot him. **Opposite:** German infantry was not stopped by Holland's river barriers.

20 May, Guderian's units reached the Channel and turned northward heading for the important ports through which British forces would have to be evacuated if a total disaster was to be averted. The situation was bleak for the Allies. Unless effective countermeasures could be launched immediately, large numbers of men would be lost and the German occupation of France would be completed in short order.

There were few alternatives open to Allied forces: the men now isolated by Army Group B in Belgium might strike south in an effort to link up with the remainder of their forces or they could evacuate the continent. The latter course was anathema to the French, and General Gamelin issued an order for a strike to the south on 19 May, one day before German forces reached the Channel coast. But, on that same day, Gamelin was removed as Commander-in-Chief of French forces and replaced by General Weygand who immediately cancelled his predecessor's order pending further consideration. With no directions from command headquarters, the Allied armies were virtually paralysed and lost any chance to salvage the situation.

Fortunately for the British Expeditionary Force, Weygand's vacillation was paralleled by a similar lapse on the German side. Although Guderian's forces were within ten miles of Dunkirk, the only port from which the expeditionary force could possibly be evacuated, the Fuehrer insisted that he pause short of this target. Why this decision was made remains one of the unsolved mysteries of the war, but whatever the reason British commanders lost little time in taking advantage of the situation.

On 25 May, General Lord Gort, Commander-in-Chief of the BEF, decided to pull his forces back to the sea and evacuate the continent. It had become abundantly clear that the situation was deteriorating rapidly and that Weygand's new call for a counter-offensive was little more than wishful thinking. The French could refuse to save their forces through an evacuation, but the British commander would not waste his men in a vain effort to save face for his French colleagues; with German forces only ten miles from Dunkirk, there was no time to lose.

The British War Cabinet cabled its approval of Gort's request to 'retire' his forces on 26 May. One day later, the plan to evacuate the continent

Above: The Germans reach the Channel coast, and the BEF is trapped.
Above right: Weary British Tommies who did not escape from Dunkirk.
Right: British soldiers used their rifles against attacking enemy aircraft during the last days of the siege of Dunkirk.

by sea was approved. This approval came just in time, for on that same day the Belgian government, its forces broken and backed to the wall, sued for peace and a cease-fire was proclaimed. With the Belgians disposed of, the Germans could turn their full attention on the Franco-British forces; any further delay in issuing the evacuation order would have doomed the British force, and even as it was, the retirement to Dunkirk was more a race than an orderly retreat. Only Hitler's temporary hesitation saved the day.

The 'miracle of Dunkirk' was facilitated by earlier plans to evacuate British forces from the continent if necessary. Operation Dynamo, the preparation of a flotilla of British ships both large and small to rescue stranded units of the BEF, was initiated on 20 May, a week before the actual evacuation was authorized. Although it was originally conceived as a modest action to rescue small groups who had been cut off as the army pushed south, the early preparations made it possible to rescue the entire expeditionary force when it became clear that an Allied counterstroke could not succeed.

When the operation began, not even the most optimistic officer was ready to believe that over 300,000 men could be successfully evacuated from the continent. If one-fifth of this number could be carried across the Channel before the Germans took vigorous measures to stop the exodus, the Admiralty would count itself fortunate. But the period of grace was to last considerably longer than had been anticipated. Although the pace of evacuation remained slow for the first two days due to confusion and lack of sufficient vessels to ferry forces across the Channel, the Germans did not strike at Dunkirk until 29 May. This first air strike failed to destroy the port and evacuation

German artillery mops up, attacking the Maginot Line from the rear. The French gun emplacements could not turn around, and the long fortress wall was captured intact.

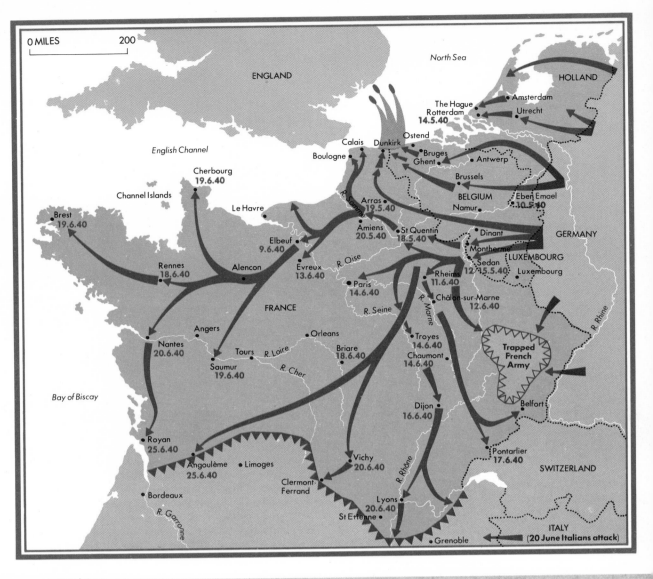

Below: The infantry
played a vital part
supporting the Panzers in
the Battle of France.
Right: A Panzer moves
swiftly through open
country after the break-
through at Sedan.
Far right: A brave
proclamation by General
de Gaulle: 'France has lost
the battle. But France has
not lost the war!' **Below
right:** De Gaulle alone
refused to co-operate with
the Germans.

0 MILES   200

North Sea

ENGLAND   HOLLAND

The Hague•   •Amsterdam
Rotterdam   •Utrecht
14.5.40

English Channel   Calais Dunkirk Ostend
                    Boulogne•   •Bruges •Antwerp
                              Ghent•
Cherbourg   •Brussels
19.6.40   BELGIUM   Eben Emael
Channel Islands   Arras•   Namur   **10.5.40**
                    Le Havre• **19.5.40**
Brest•   Amiens •St Quentin   •Dinant   GERMANY
19.6.40   Elbeuf• **20.5.40** **18.5.40**   Montherme•
                 9.6.40   Sedan   LUXEMBOURG
          Rennes•   Evreux•   R. Oise   **12 15.5.40** •Luxembourg
          18.6.40 Alencon **13.6.40**   Rheims•
                              •Paris   **11.6.40**
       FRANCE   •Angers   **14.6.40** R. Seine Châlon-sur-Marne
                                                    12.6.40   R. Rhine
                         •Orleans   R. Marne   Trapped
Bay of Biscay   Nantes•   Tours• R. Loire   Briare• Troyes•   French
                   20.6.40   **18.6.40** **14.6.40**   Army
                        Saumur• R. Cher   Chaumont•
                        19.6.40   **14.6.40**   •Belfort

                    Royan•   Dijon•
                    25.6.40   **16.6.40**
              Angoulème• •Limoges   Pontarlier•
              25.6.40   Clermont- Vichy•   **17.6.40** SWITZERLAND
          •Bordeaux   Ferrand   **20.6.40**
                                    Lyons•
      R. Garonne   St Etienne• **20.6.40**   ITALY
                                  Grenoble•   (**20 June Italians attack**)

Right: 'What General
Weygand called the Battle
of France is over. The
Battle of Britain is about to
begin.'

continued until 2 June when daylight movement
out of Dunkirk harbor had to be suspended due
to heavy German raids. By this time, thanks to
the efforts of the men who manned the ships of the
motley naval task force and the Royal Air Force,
some 224,000 British forces and 95,000 French
forces had been evacuated when the operation
was ended. Many of these men were to see action
against Germany again, when their good luck
would contribute to Germany's downfall, but
for the moment Hitler had triumphed.

The departure of the British Expeditionary
Force sealed the fate of the remaining French
forces. Weygand had already lost some 30
divisions apart from the units evacuated to
England and could count on only 49 divisions;
the Germans, who had more than 130 divisions,
quickly overran French resistance. Weygand
was proposing the negotiation of a cease-fire even
before the French government left Paris on 9
June, but the Reynaud cabinet would not hear it.
From their retreat in Tours they ordered Weygand
to stand fast, while the Prime Minister urgently
appealed to the United States for aid. This was

Left: Hitler ecstatically celebrates the fall of France near the railway carriage in which Germany was forced to sign the surrender in 1918. Hitler saw to it that the French surrender in 1940 took place in exactly the same spot.

not forthcoming and when Paris fell on 14 June a cabinet crisis was precipitated, resulting in Reynaud's resignation on 16 June. By this time, Italy had joined Germany, having declared war on 10 June, and the situation looked absolutely hopeless. Not even Churchill's profound rhetoric and emotional appeals could persuade French leaders to hold fast. On 16 June a new cabinet was formed by Marshal Pétain who immediately begged Hitler for an armistice and cease-fire; his request was granted four days later.

The battle for France ended on 25 June 1940 at 1:35 a.m. when the armistice agreements with Germany and Italy became effective. Six weeks after the beginning of the western offensive, Hitler had realized most of his goals. It remained only to arrange a compromise with the British or, failing that, to force them into submission. It was indeed a dark hour for England, left alone to champion the cause of democracy. Although Churchill would state that 'We shall defend our island home . . . until the curse of Hitler is lifted from the brows of mankind . . . ,' he could not be sure that they would triumph in the end.

Left: Marshal Pétain, hero of Verdun, formed a new cabinet to conclude an armistice with Hitler.

Right: Germans sunbathe on the Channel coast.
Opposite top left: The advance through the Low Countries met little effective opposition.
Top right: A triumphal German parade down the Avenue Foch in June 1940.
Opposite left: French aircraft destroyed on the ground. The Germans quickly established their supremacy in the air.
Opposite right: After the last ship had left, the Germans broke into Dunkirk at last.

CHAPTER THREE

The Battle of Britain

Above: Hermann Goering, who was chosen to mastermind Operation Sealion.

Below: Winston Churchill atop the White Cliffs of Dover speaking to infantry manning it: July 1940.
Below right: Germans practice landing on beaches in preparation for Operation Sealion. **Opposite:** Spitfires cruise in formation at 300 mph between cloud layers at 6000 ft.

The fall of France would have opened the way for an immediate invasion of England had it not been for two facts. First, adequate preparations for an aerial and seaborne invasion of the British Isles had not been made prior to the launching of the western offensive. Second, Hitler hesitated to order the preparation of such an offensive, hoping that a peaceful settlement of Anglo-German differences might be reached despite the events of September 1939–June 1940.

The mounting of an assault on England involved an effort for which the German army and navy had made little preparation. The army had few if any troops trained for seaborne landing operations and the navy had few if any transports to carry the men across the Channel. Neither the General Staff nor the Admiralty had seriously considered plans for such an operation before the fall of France, nor had they been prodded to do so by Hitler; more important still, there was little enthusiasm for such a venture. The military leaders of the Reich had prepared only for continental war. In their minds, a crossing of the Channel could only be undertaken as a last resort and even then they were not willing to guarantee the result. Only the Luftwaffe seemed anxious to initiate the conflict, but Goering could not persuade his peers or the Fuehrer to take immediate action.

Hitler continued to cling to the notion that he could reach a compromise with Churchill. Even after the British Prime Minister refused to accept his proposal that England recognize German hegemony on the continent in return for German recognition of the sanctity of the Empire, Hitler appears to have been reluctant to force an invasion of England. His military advisers were only too happy to follow his lead in the matter, hoping that Churchill's stubborness would give way and a rapprochment could be reached; they dallied for almost a month after the fall of France before ordering the preparation of a comprehensive scheme to invade England, and even then discussed the operation with little enthusiasm.

The German plan, 'Operation Sealion,' was finally commissioned on 16 July 1940, but was not ready for consideration until the end of the month. As presented to the chiefs of staff, it called for a hurried accumulation of shipping from Belgian, French, and Dutch ports to transport Rundstedt's Army Group A across the Channel for landings near the Thames estuary along the southeast coast. Following the initial landing of some 10 divisions plus one airborne unit in this area, the second and main force would be ferried across the Channel. This would be the major part of the operation, necessitating the requisition of thousands of ships both large and small to transport several hundred tanks and other armored vehicles plus an additional 17 infantry divisions. Once landed, these forces would join up with the first wave, isolate London, and cripple British resistance. If carried out, the operation would be by far the most complex and difficult the Germans had undertaken.

The original target date for launching Operation Sealion was set for mid-August 1940 at the insistence of the Fuehrer, who was growing increasingly angry at Churchill's intransigence. However, since actual preparations for the maneuver were not begun until the last week in July, the sheer magnitude of the task of assembling hundreds of thousands of men and thousands of transports for the venture defied Hitler's timetable and the military and naval commanders involved were forced to ask for a postponement until September. Reluctantly, Hitler acceded to their appeals and the invasion was pushed back some two weeks; in the meantime the Luftwaffe was told to go ahead and soften the British for the eventual kill.

Goering's anxiety to annihilate the Royal Air Force as soon as possible delighted his peers in the other services; they continued to be sceptical about the whole affair and were only too happy to have the Luftwaffe prepare their way. Admiral Raeder was frightened enough at the possibility of having to engage the British fleet while ferrying thousands across the Channel, and if Goering could neutralize the RAF in advance of the effort, his task would be much easier. If, on the other

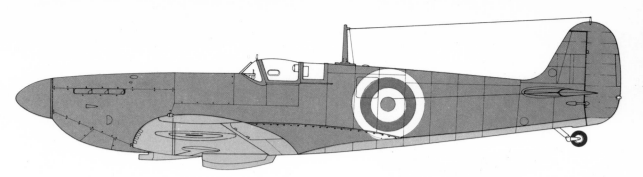

hand, the Luftwaffe failed to carry out Goering's mission, the Fuehrer might think twice and cancel or drastically alter the operation. In any event, by encouraging the Luftwaffe to 'carry the ball,' the resources of the army and navy remained intact, at least for the moment.

When Hitler issued his order on 5 August authorizing massive air strikes against England, Goering was more than ready to respond; by the beginning of August, he had already gathered a force of nearly 2700 aircraft for this purpose. Like his colleagues in the Admiralty and on the General Staff, Goering placed little faith in Operation Sealion but he was anxious to employ his aircraft not simply in support of the objections of the operation, but in a total effort to prove the supremacy of air power in modern warfare. During the months of the Luftwaffe attack on England this was to cause considerable friction between the Air Marshal and the heads of the other services who feared that Hitler might continue to insist on the execution of Operation Sealion whether Goering had correctly followed his orders and prepared the ground for them or not. The bickering and confusion continued until the operation was superseded by the invasion of the Soviet Union and proved to be of indirect but immense aid to the British, who were spared the worst consequences of the attacks by Goering's frequent changes of tactics and targets.

At the start of the Battle of Britain, the Luftwaffe possessed a numerical superiority over the Royal Air Force. Numbers, however, proved to be somewhat misleading; although the Germans had more bombers and dive bombers, the two sides were nearly equal in numbers of fighter aircraft. Germany's slight edge at the outset was more than compensated for by the superior output of British aircraft plants which were eventually able to build planes faster than they were destroyed. It was the fighter and not the bomber which held the key to victory or defeat in this encounter, and here the British had one great advantage: their nimble Spitfires and Hurricanes did not have so far to fly. The German Bf 109, like its British counterparts, only had a radius of action of about 125 miles, and thus, after leaving

a fuel margin for combat, could barely cover the distance from Calais to London and back. Even to do this much required a fairly inflexible routing plan, which greatly aided the British defenders. What the RAF did lack as the battle progressed was not aircraft so much as trained pilots. Had RAF training schools been producing more pilots, or had there been a larger reservoir of trained men available at the beginning of the battle, the situation would have been far less critical for the British.

The first phase

Although German aircraft had appeared over England in July, the Battle of Britain was not begun in earnest until 13 August 1940, when the Luftwaffe launched the first in a series of concentrated attacks on British fighter bases and radar installations. Such attacks were to last until the middle of September when tactics and targets were changed and a second phase of the battle began.

The raid on 13 August was the largest aerial attack to that date; over 1400 aircraft were sent aloft over England and German pilots were instructed to destroy the forward bases of the Royal Air Force southeast of London. This was to be the first in a series of four raids, to be launched on consecutive days, with which Goering hoped to destroy the aerial defense in the greater London area, thus opening the way for uncontested German bombardment of British naval and merchant marine targets. The success of Operation Sealion would depend upon the accuracy of the Air Marshal's predictions.

Adlertag, or 'Eagle Day' proved to be somewhat disappointing for the Luftwaffe and its commanding officer. The weather co-operated with the British defenders and this plus the early warning radar system allowed them to 'scramble' into the air and meet the attacking German fleet before that armada could successfully unload its cargo of bombs and explosives. By the end of the afternoon the Luftwaffe had managed to seriously damage only two of the forward bases at a cost of 45 of their aircraft. The RAF lost only 13 planes, managed to prevent the destruction of all but two

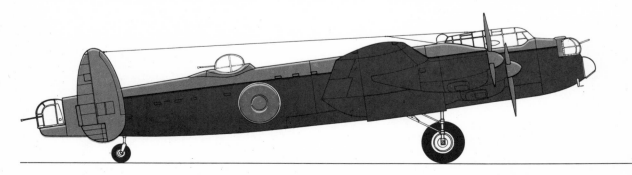

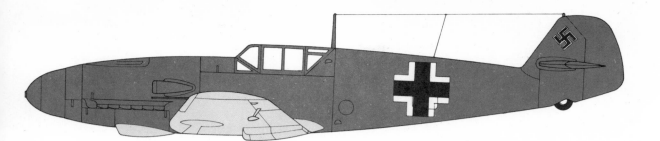

M.E. 109 F.I. Length:
29 ft. 8 in. Span: 31 ft.
6½ in. Maximum speed:
369 m.p.h. Armament:
4 × 7.92 mm. machine guns,
1 × 20 mm. cannon.
Weight: 4440 lbs. empty.

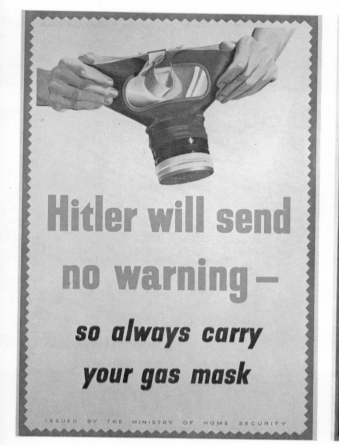

Below: At first the
Luftwaffe concentrated on
bombing airfields. The outskirts of major cities,
however, did not escape.

Right: Bombing continued throughout the day and night. Here a mobile YMCA canteen gives tea to men on a gun site.
Far right: WAAF's plot the Battle of Britain at radar control.

Right: "Never in the field of human conflict have so many owed so much to so few". **Right center:** The other side. German pilots plan another bombing raid on Britain. **Far right:** Members of the Luftwaffe relax before take-off.

Right: Hawker Hurricanes of the RAF. **Far right:** Me-110 sinks slowly into the Channel.

fighter bases and, most important, kept the Germans from destroying the radar installations that dotted the coastline. That night, however, the Luftwaffe returned and succeeded in attacking several aircraft plants, thereby exposing the RAF's inability to combat night attacks as efficiently as those flown during daylight hours. Such night flights, therefore, were to become increasingly common and devastating.

The Luftwaffe launched another massive attack on 15 August, the largest raid to be mounted by Goering during the battle for Britain. Over 1800 aircraft, including Scandinavian based units, took part in this effort to destroy RAF fighter bases in southeast England, but these bases were not the Luftwaffe's only target. Goering and his subordinates also hoped to destroy installations in the Midlands and Yorkshire while RAF units from these bases were sent south to aid Fighter Groups 10 and 11, who were protecting the southern approach to London and the Channel coast. If the plan was successful, England's fighter defense would be incapacitated in one stroke and the Luftwaffe would be able to bomb military and naval targets with impunity.

The sheer number of aircraft in the German armada dwarfed the resources of the British defenders and Germany might well have scored a dramatic victory were it not for the early warning provided by British radar installations and aircraft spotters, and the superb co-ordination of RAF units by Air Vice-Marshal Keith Park, the commander of Fighter Group 11 and his counterpart in the north, Air Vice-Marshal Leigh-Mallory, commander of Fighter Group 12. By the time German task forces arrived over the Channel coast, British units were already in the air and what they lacked in numbers was more than compensated for by their spirit, and the information they had received from flight headquarters.

In the north the Luftwaffe was badly mauled. There a fleet of over 100 bombers accompanied by 35 fighters attempted to attack airfields near Newcastle and in Yorkshire, but met with little success. Savage fighter resistance and effective anti-aircraft fire cost the invaders over 15 aircraft while little damage was done to British bases. A second attack by some 50 bombers met with better luck later in the day and managed to circumvent RAF defenses in the north, destroying at least one

Above: The Dornier "Flying Pencil", used to raze Rotterdam, was turned on British cities.

base in the process; on the run back to Denmark, however, RAF pilots downed at least 10 of the 50 with no loss to themselves. Such losses proved the vulnerability of bombers without adequate fighter cover, a fact which the Luftwaffe was slow in comprehending. In any case, 15 August marked the first and last major attempt to destroy British bases north of London.

In the south, the RAF was less successful in turning back the German attackers. Faced with far greater numbers of enemy aircraft than their colleagues in the north and with more bases to defend, about the best that Fighter Groups 10 and 11 could do was to soften the German blow by engaging the enemy wherever and whenever possible; even this might not have sufficed were it not for the fact that the two German airforces sent over southern England, Luftflotten 2 and 3, had not adequately coordinated their efforts. Thus, although confusion at the radar stations caused by the sheer number of German planes threatened to deprive the RAF of the time they needed to prepare their defense, the Luftwaffe's inability to deliver a single well coordinated attack insured that the RAF could at least hold its own. By the end of the day the Luftwaffe had not succeeded in its major goal of eliminating England's southern aerial defense. Thirty-nine British planes had been lost and several bases were badly damaged, but the RAF still flew. Churchill might well say of this encounter that: 'Never in the field of human conflict was so much owed by

so many to so few.' Unfortunately, however, there was still more to come.

The loss of 75 planes on 15 August did not stop Goering's campaign against British bases. On 16 August yet another attack was launched and almost 1700 planes were sent over England. Based upon intelligence reports which estimated current British strength at no more than 300 planes, Goering remained confident that the end of the RAF was near. He was so confident, in fact, that he suspended attack on British radar sites on the grounds that the few aircraft left to the RAF could hardly benefit by such installations, and that by using all of his aircraft against the bases instead of diverting some to the radar sites, he could hasten the collapse of England's aerial defense, guaranteeing absolute German air supremacy within a matter of weeks. Neither of these assumptions proved to be correct.

Although British losses had been heavy during the first days of the Battle of Britain, they were not nearly as high as German leaders believed; thus, the German raiders suffered heavier losses than were necessary in their raids of 16 August and later because they were not prepared for the stiff resistance they encountered. During the first three weeks of August alone, Germany lost over 450 planes, an average of about 150 per week. During the weeks to come, this number was to increase considerably.

Despite the heavy losses suffered by the Luftwaffe, Goering still pressed the attacks on British fighter installations, and by the beginning of September they were beginning to bear fruit. Although British morale was buoyed up by exaggerated reports of RAF successes, the almost daily pounding of their facilities by Goering's air force was not without grave consequences. During the month of August the RAF had lost 359 planes while many more were damaged on the ground, and the loss per week had increased rather than decreased by the beginning of September. Since the aircraft production schemes introduced by Lord Beaverbrook had not yet reached the point where replacements exceeded losses, the situation looked bleak as summer drew to a close. Had Goering not been diverted to another course of action early in September, the RAF might well have been destroyed.

The campaign against the forward bases of the RAF was brought to an abrupt end by the British bombing attack on Berlin on 25 August. This attack, itself precipitated by the accidental bombing of London the night before, had a

Below: Grey Tube Shelter: by Henry Moore.
Opposite: Old Bailey in ruins during the Blitz.

enthusiasm for the campaign against RAF installations. Ironically, their attitude was even beginning to affect Goering who appeared to be wavering just as the effort was on the brink of success. When he and his commanders met at the Hague on 3 September, it did not take them long to persuade him to abandon the first phase of the offensive in favor of a new course of action. The main advocate was Field Marshal Albert Kesselring whose Luftflotte 2 had borne the brunt of the original attack plan; having sustained extremely heavy losses, his advocacy of the bombing of London was not difficult to understand, as it afforded the Luftwaffe an easier target and promised the collapse of British resistance at an early date. With his own commanders clamoring for a change of tactics and Hitler demanding revenge for the British raids over Berlin, Goering had little choice but to accept their suggestions.

The attack on London

Once the new plan was agreed, the Germans lost little time in beginning raids on London; on 7 September, the same day that Hitler had ordered Goering to seek reprisals, the first was launched; while Goering and Kesselring watched from the cliffs at Blanc Nez a thousand planes (almost 400 bombers and slightly more than 600 fighters) were sent against England. Arriving over the Channel coast in the late afternoon, the German fleet met little opposition and was able to unload its cargo of bombs over the docks, central London, and the East End. By the end of the afternoon, much of the city was in smoke and over 1600 Londoners were either killed or injured.

As if the daylight attack of London was not enough, the Luftwaffe returned that evening to continue its devastating work. Over 250 bombers maintained 'a slow and agonizing procession over the capital' which lasted from early in the evening until 4 a.m. the following morning. With in-

Top: Night raids on London began to intensify by September 1940.
Above: This bus fell into a bomb crater. **Opposite: top:** Damage from air raids became increasingly severe. This is the City looking down from St. Paul's.

Right: Kesselring and Goering watch from the cliffs near Calais as a thousand German planes were sent against England.
Opposite bottom: Field Marshal Albert Kesselring wasn't smiling so broadly after 15 September.

stunning effect on the people of Berlin and their leader, as did renewed bombings of the German capital during the last days of that month. An infuriated Hitler, speaking before the German people on 4 September, vowed to repay the British in kind. 'The British,' he said, 'drop their bombs indiscriminately on civilian residential communities and farms and villages. . . . If they attack our cities, we will rub out their cities from the map. . . . The hour will come when one of us two will break and it will not be Nazi Germany.' Three days later, on 7 September 1940, Goering was ordered to begin the blitz on London. Although countless thousands would suffer in England's largest city, the RAF would be spared.

Hitler's order initiating the Blitz on London was welcomed by Goering's lieutenants in the Luftwaffe who did not share the Air Marshal's

adequate numbers of anti-aircraft guns to protect the capital and few if any aircraft equipped for night fighting, there was little that could be done to resist the attack; only one plane was shot down and much of the city was aglow with flames.

From 7 September to 3 November, the Luftwaffe attacked London nightly. At first there was little that the British could do to protect themselves, but as they grew accustomed to the raids more adequate precautions were taken. People took to the underground railway stations, evacuation was stepped up, anti-aircraft installations were increased, and the RAF began to master the technique of night fighting. Soon after the start of the blitz the Luftwaffe was forced to discontinue daylight bombing runs, and even the nightly raids over the capital became increasingly costly as anti-aircraft gunners became more and more

accurate with their weapons. Most important, the abandonment of daylight raids prevented the Luftwaffe attacking military and naval targets whose destruction was absolutely necessary if Operation Sealion was to be launched before winter. That possibility, however, seemed increasingly remote as the campaign over London was obviously not succeeding.

Fourteen September was Operation Sealion's target date, and on the French side of the Channel, all was ready. British reconnaissance aircraft confirmed the presence of thousands of barges and other seagoing vessels. It remained only for Goering to destroy London and the RAF and the invasion of England could begin, but since neither of these tasks had been accomplished the operation had to be postponed yet again. Although Hitler remained confident that the attacks

on London would succeed, Goering and his associates were under pressure to produce signs of progress. If more time was lost, weather would indefinitely postpone the venture; if the RAF was not quickly neutralized, they would inevitably strike back. There was little time to lose.

Goering and Kesselring decided to make an overwhelming effort to destroy London, and that effort, launched on 15 September 1940, proved to be a major turning point in the Battle of Britain. On that day 1000 aircraft were sent over the British capital. The weather was good, the time was right, the Luftwaffe was ready. But so too was the RAF: this was to be their finest hour.

The fact that the raid took place in daylight nullified the Luftwaffe's numerical advantage over the Royal Air Force, and German bombers, even though accompanied by five fighter aircraft per bomber, did not succeed in breaking through the British defenses. Luftwaffe formations were broken up, scattered, and doggedly pursued by RAF pilots. The battle raged all day and took every plane the British could muster; the sky above London was a 'bedlam of machines,' but by day's end the attack had been repulsed. The Germans lost 60 planes, most of them bombers, at a cost of 26 aircraft to the RAF, once again, proving the value of the early warning system. Had it not been for this and the skilful coordination of the defense by Air Chief Marshal Sir Hugh Dowding, the Luftwaffe raid might indeed have been successful. As it was, not only was the RAF still intact, but it was soon able to take the offensive, hitting the landing craft that the German navy had assembled for Operation Sealion.

destroy British morale and humble Mr Churchill.

Night time raids had become almost commonplace and by the beginning of October the residents of London were dug in and resigned to suffer more of the same. The Germans however, had a new surprise in store for them; on 15 October and every night thereafter, incendiary bombs were added to the Luftwaffe's manifesto. Londoners had become accustomed to seeking shelter when the Luftwaffe approached, but now they were forced to leave their basements and take to the roofs. The incendiary bombs were far more destructive than the more conventional high explosive bombs, as they set fire to the structures they hit instead of just pulverizing them. Fires were difficult to control in the midst of an attack and even the organization of civilian fire brigades and spotters could not contain the destruction wrought by these weapons. By the end of October, fire bombings were extracting a greater and greater toll. Each night the Luftwaffe destroyed the homes of thousands, hundreds were maimed, and business and government were disrupted. Despite these and other horrors the people of London stood fast, and with them stood their government and their monarch.

On 3 November, for the first time in nearly two months, no air raid alarms sounded in the British capital. After nightly ritual of Luftwaffe attacks the silence must have seemed strange indeed, giving rise to conjecture as to what the Germans might be up to next. Did this mark the end of the Battle of Britain or was there more to come? Would the Germans return to London or

Raids spread to the provinces

The Luftwaffe's failure on 15 September sealed the fate of Hitler's plans for invasion. The weather had already begun to turn cold, turbulent conditions in the Channel were predicted for the rest of the month, and most important of all, the Luftwaffe had failed to destroy the RAF or significantly devastate other military and naval targets. On 18 September, the craft assembled in French coastal ports were dispersed lest additional losses be suffered from RAF attacks and on 12 October the campaign was officially postponed until the spring of 1941.

The death of Operation Sealion effectively eliminated the threat of invasion but the aerial harassment of England was to continue for another three months. If Goering could not succeed in defeating the RAF, Hitler would still attempt to

Above: The center of Coventry was obliterated.
Right: Sir Hugh "Stuffy" Dowding, whose RAF was able to take the offensive by mid-September. His quiet, even taciturn manner camouflaged an intensity and stubbornness which Goering discovered at his cost.

Above: Barrage balloons
were extensively used.
Right: Battle of Britain
1940: by Paul Nash.

"..... but of course it mustn't go any further!"

CARELESS TALK COSTS LIVES

Above: Stirlings over Britain. These were among the first RAF bombers to be used against German targets.

were other cities to be subjected to the blitz? The answers to these questions came soon.

A new phase in the air war over England was initiated on 14 November when German bombers attacked Coventry. Failing to obliterate London, Goering and his lieutenants had decided to change policy and refocus the German attack on provincial cities and industrial installations. The capital had been too large and 'vague' a target to destroy, but the provincial cities might be more efficiently devastated. Also, attacks on munitions facilities, especially aircraft plants, would decrease or destroy their capacity to provide replacements and new equipment for the RAF which was daily becoming bolder in its defense.

The attack on Coventry destroyed much of the center of the city and took the lives of over 400 of its residents. Other cities were also to be attacked during this phase of the battle. Birmingham was struck from 19–22 November, and Bristol, Liverpool, and Southampton were attacked the following week. Glasgow, Leeds, Manchester, Plymouth, and Sheffield were added to the list during the

first weeks of December and, of course, London was not forgotten. Thousands lost their lives as a result of these attacks; tens of thousands were made homeless; commerce and industry were disrupted. But British resistance was not destroyed.

The end of the Blitz
At the start of the new year (1941), there was no sign that England had been humbled by the Luftwaffe. The program of raids over provincial cities and munitions works had been no more successful than previous attacks on London and RAF installations. The German offensives had, perhaps, caused more damage than was publicly admitted at the time but the Luftwaffe had failed in achieving its main objectives, the destruction of the RAF and the breaking of British morale. Although attacks over England would continue for several months, the major blitz was over. Bad weather and faltering enthusiasm would soon abort the entire venture and, having failed to defeat England, the Fuehrer would look to the east for new satisfaction.

Left: Spitfire, symbol of the Battle of Britain.

CHAPTER FOUR
The Invasion of Russia

The cancellation of Operation Sealion opened the door to a German invasion of the Soviet Union, a prospect which Hitler had viewed with increasing enthusiasm as the Battle of Britain dragged on with no victory in sight. The notion could not be considered seriously as long as there was any chance that Goering might succeed in his mission of humbling England, but when it became apparent that the Luftwaffe's efforts were in vain, the Fuehrer was quick to revive the scheme to refocus the thrust of Germany's offensive posture from England to Russia.

As had been the case so often in the past, Hitler's enthusiasm for a new military venture was not shared by his military advisers who remembered only too well the difficulties imposed by fighting a two front war from 1914–1918. That experience had been a sobering one which none of the senior officers wished to repeat. There was hardly an officer of any consequence willing to take the risks involved in an invasion of the Soviet Union, and members of the General Staff were agreed almost to a man that such a scheme would result in a disaster which would dwarf the fate suffered by Napoleon's armies a century earlier. Their personal pleas might not suffice to dissuade the Fuehrer from such a venture, but he could hardly refute cold facts – or so they thought.

The generals argued against an invasion of Russia with candor and vigor but their position, unfortunately, did not prevail. Hitler had long been critical of his senior officers' conservation and bitter over their past opposition to his plans. Had they not opposed the invasions of Poland, the Low Countries, and France? Had they not privately predicted that these ventures would bring only disaster? The success of these operations despite the opposition of the older generals had convinced Hitler that his judgement on military matters was superior to that of his advisers, who were tied to the past and fearful of initiating bold new programs. Arguments against an invasion of Russia were dismissed as militarily and politically naive: Hitler would once again have his way.

To those who predicted doom and disaster should Germany invade the Soviet Union, Hitler issued a stern rebuke. The generals were reminded that the Nazi-Soviet *détente* was never meant to be permanent; it was a temporary expedient, designed to buy time while Germany disposed of the Western powers. Once this was accomplished, it was only a question of which partner acted first to annul the agreement. The Soviets had already indicated their intentions vis-à-vis Germany by their occupation and annexation of Lithuania, and their territorial demands in Rumania. If Germany did not act quickly, Stalin's forces would be well entrenched on the eastern border

Opposite: Russians parade on Red Square before moving up to the front. **Left:** Nazi troops paddle across the Russian border. This is one of the first pictures of the invasion of Russia, 22 June 1941.

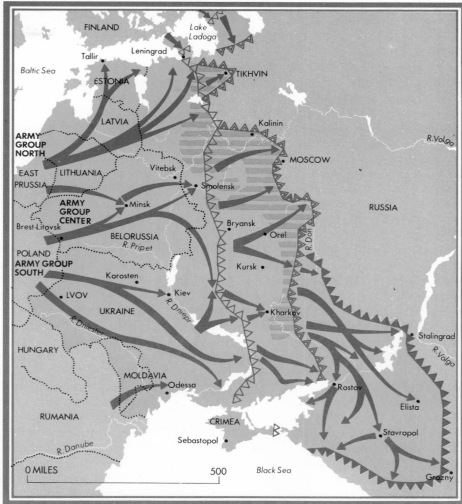

within easy striking distance of the heartland of the country. Those who refused to recognize this were blind to reality; their blindness could not and would not be tolerated. In the end, the generals were left with no alternative but to follow Hitler's direction.

Preparation for the invasion

Having failed to deter the Fuehrer from invading Russia, it became the unhappy lot of the General Staff to prepare plans for such an invasion; the assignment was given to General Paulus in October 1940. Although details of German operations in the Soviet Union were to be worked out by the general, the Fuehrer insisted on three things. First, the Wehrmacht was to destroy Russian forces in the western part of the Soviet Union. Second, following its success, German armies were to push eastward, establishing a defensive line stretching from Archangel to the Volga to provide territorial insurance against a Russian counterattack. Third, preparations for the invasion were to be made in a manner that would not excite Soviet suspicions. This dictated the most discreet movement of men and munitions as well as close cooperation with the Foreign Ministry, which was to maintain the facade of *détente* while military preparations were completed.

An outline for the attack on the Soviet Union was ready at the end of November, tested in a series of war games, and presented to Hitler on 5 December. The plan called for a three-pronged attack aimed at capturing production centers in the Ukraine, the Donetz basin, and the cities of

Axis Powers advance into Russia

22 June–1 Sept 1941

1 Sept–5 Dec 1941

Reoccupied by Russians during counterattack, 6 Dec 1941–April 1942

Further advance in the South 28 June–18 Nov 1942 (Regaining some of the ground lost in 41/42 winter campaign)

Opposite top: Stukas on a Luftwaffe base in Bulgaria.
Bottom: Hitler's Panzers met with success after success in the first weeks of Operation Barbarossa.
Left: German progress towards Moscow was as swift as the infantry could march.

Leningrad and Moscow. By dividing their forces and sweeping rapidly into European Russia, the Germans would overcome the Red Army before adequate defenses could be prepared. Since the number of men available for the invasion was small compared to the resources of the Red Army, speed and surprise were essential if the Soviets were to be overwhelmed before they could mobilize. Quality would make up for quantity. What the Wehrmacht lacked in numbers would be more than compensated for in the efficient and fast execution of the plan. By such daring action Germany would win her greatest victory of the war, taking hundreds of thousands of prisoners, and capturing Russia's agricultural and industrial resources intact. If all went well, a German victory would be a *fait accompli* by December 1941. Hitler, needless to say, was excited by the prospect of presiding over the dismemberment of the Soviet Union and quickly gave his approval to the plan prepared by Paulus and the General Staff, ordering all necessary preparations to commence on 18 December 1940. It was now up to the diplomats to do their part while the preparations were completed. This was no simple task.

Soviet leaders were not blind to the possibility of a German attack but preferred, for the time being, to preserve the Nazi-Soviet pact, for Russia needed time to prepare for war; while the diplomats dallied, Russian factories could continue to produce guns, tanks, and planes. Since it was unlikely that Hitler would strike before the successful conclusion of the Battle of Britain, there was no reason not to respond to German diplomatic feelers. When Molotov was invited to Berlin in November 1940, Stalin was only too happy to accept the invitation. Little did he realize that his willingness to extend the *détente* with Germany played right into Hitler's hands.

While men and munitions were readied for the invasion of Russia, Soviet diplomats were lulled into thinking that Hitler wished to preserve the status quo with Stalin. German-Russian discussions were pursued in an atmosphere of 'mutual trust and mutual understanding' while the Wehrmacht was preparing for war. Diplomats might gloat over the atmosphere of the summit but it was the German military which had won a victory in this matter. Never had deception been more brilliantly practiced.

A new German-Russian treaty was signed on 10 January 1941 embodying the results of the Berlin negotiations, and to the world, and many in Germany, all seemed well between Hitler and Stalin. Nothing could have been further from the truth; convinced that Stalin did not expect the Germans to attack Russia, Hitler reached the point of no return on the invasion of Russia.

Operation Barbarossa begins

Operation Barbarossa was launched on 22 June 1941. At 0400 that Sunday morning German forces crossed the Russian frontier. In the north an army group under the command of General Leeb crossed from East Prussia into Lithuania. In the south a second army group under the command of General Rundstedt moved from Lwow toward Galicia. In the center, a third group under the command of General Bock moved across northern Poland toward the Russian border. The long awaited invasion of the Soviet Union had begun.

As Hitler had expected, the Russians were unprepared for the German attack. Although units of the Red Army had been moved into the Baltic states and the western provinces just weeks before the attack, they were not deployed systematically. Such forces as there were on the German frontier were thinly spread over a large area. When the three German army groups initiated action, these forward units were easily overrun and could not be rescued, due to the distance between them and the rest of the Russian forces, scattered anywhere from 60 to 380 miles away in the hinterland. With little effective resistance from the Red Army, German forces were able to race eastward at a pace never dreamt of by Hitler and Paulus. Even the most whole-hearted advocates of the operation were stunned at the speed and facility of the Wehrmacht's advance.

Germany's military leaders had reason to be impressed by the results of the first day's activities against the Soviets. Within twenty-four hours, 10,000 prisoners had been taken, the Luftwaffe had destroyed or disabled 1200 Russian aircraft, and German mechanized units had moved fifty miles into Russian controlled areas of Poland. It was an unmitigated triumph for the Germans and in succeeding days they were able to press on further, repeating the feat of the first day. By the beginning of July few in Berlin doubted that Hitler would feast in Moscow at Christmas.

Success posed certain problems for Hitler's lieutenants, who were divided over whether to alter the original plan of invasion and race toward Moscow and other interior points, or maintain the original program which called for a slower eastward advance and the encirclement of Russian armies in the western part of the Soviet Union. Tank experts, like Guderian, wanted to take advantage of the momentum to rush eastward, driving as deep as space and time would permit, thus repeating in Russia the program which had been so successful in France. More conservative strategists urged restraint. They advised Hitler to use tank forces in support of infantry action until the bulk of Russia's western armies were defeated, promising the capture of tens of thousands of prisoners when the encirclement of Soviet forces was completed. To the chagrin of the tank experts, Hitler chose to accept the more orthodox approach.

The decision to abide by the original plan of invasion proved to be of greater benefit to the Red Army than to the Wehrmacht because it allowed the Russians to finally respond to the invasion while German forces were still tied up on the fringe of the Soviet Union, far removed from the important urban centers and rear grouping areas of the Russian army. Although the Germans would exact a heavy price in men and material from Russian forces, Stalin could rally the nation while forward units of the Red Army tenaciously held out against overwhelming odds. Losses would be heavy by orthodox standards, but in the end Germany's resources would be strained long before Russia's were depleted.

On 3 July, after a silence of nearly two weeks, Stalin spoke to his nation. All Soviet citizens were called upon to defend their motherland and make whatever sacrifice was necessary to defeat fascist aggression. If the Red Army was forced to retreat, nothing of value would be left for the Germans; the Soviet citizenry would pursue the same scorched earth policy against the invader as their forefathers had used a century before. Hitler would reap no easy victory in Russia.

Stalin's refusal to succumb in the face of adversity led him to risk losses that other men would never have considered. If Soviet citizens were prepared to sacrifice themselves in the defense of mother Russia, members of the Red Army could be asked to do no less. Field commanders were instructed to hold positions regardless of cost, so that even when surrounded and clearly defeated, Russian forces continued to fight on, their stubborn resistance slowly blunting the German advance. The proverbial doggedness of the Slav was well illustrated by the Russian conscripts, who seemed to have 'an illimitable capacity for obedience and endurance'; the Germans might outflank and outmaneuver their adversaries, but they would not outfight them.

This stiff opposition, and the changing weather, began to have a serious effect on the morale of the German troops; although the Wehrmacht had made great headway during the first two weeks of the Russian campaign, the pace and progress of the invasion were gradually slowed down. In the north Leeb's army group had raced through the Baltic states but was stalled before Leningrad. In the south Rundstedt was encountering particularly heavy resistance from the Soviet Fifth Army and had to call on Bock's central army group for reinforcement. The diversion of elements of Bock's army to the south crippled the advance on Moscow by depriving it of armored and mechanized units. This was most unfortunate, since it was Bock's group which had the greatest chance for an early victory. The capture of the Soviet capital would have paralyzed Russian communications and severely affected Russian morale, but for the Fuehrer, the most important task of the Wehrmacht was to conquer the

Left top: German troops hit the dirt as a Russian shell explodes in front of them. **Left center:** The first raids of the Luftwaffe on Russian territory went almost unopposed.
Left: Wounded members of Russia's suicide squads. They were purposely left behind when the Russians withdrew in order to hamper the Nazi advance. Few came out alive.
Right: When winter set in suffering for civilians and soldiers alike was severe. This child was among the many evacuated from Leningrad prior to the siege.

Crimea and the Donetz basin, thereby severing Russia's pipelines from the Caucasus. Only after this was accomplished could the assault on Moscow be resumed with full force.

Hitler's diversion of resources to the southern sector proved even more fortuitous to the Russians than his refusal to alter the original invasion plan. Had Bock pressed on toward Moscow, there is little doubt that the city would have fallen into German hands by the end of the summer, but with the movement of armored units south to aid Rundstedt, it was doubtful whether the offensive in the central area could be resumed before the onset of autumn; by that time weather conditions would make such a drive increasingly difficult and Russian reserves from the far eastern provinces would be mobilized and ready to defend the Soviet capital. The specter of being trapped in front of Moscow at the onset of winter was not a pleasant one for the German field commanders and their superiors on the General Staff, and it is not surprising, therefore, that most senior German officers favored disregarding the situation on the southern front and pressing on toward Moscow at full speed and with full strength. If Hitler viewed Moscow as 'a geographical expression only,' his commanding officers were of another mind. So serious was the breach over this matter that Brauchitsch and Halder were prepared to tender their resignations if the advance on Moscow was not continued, but even this threat was not sufficient to change Hitler's mind. In the end, Brauchitsch and Halder chose not to resign, apparently concluding that such a move would serve no useful purpose.

The argument over Rundstedt's reinforcement wasted five weeks; it was not until 21 August that the matter was finally resolved, and by then conditions were considerably more unsatisfactory for a German advance than they had been at the beginning of the summer. Rains had washed out many secondary roads and primary roads were clogged with men and equipment. The advent of cold weather was near and the movement of supplies was becoming increasingly more difficult. Resistance was stiff and victory was still far from sight. Although a triumph of sorts would be achieved in the south, its cost would be far more than the net gain it yielded.

The attack is deflected

Hitler's order of 21 August was unequivocal. The major part of Bock's armored forces were sent south under General Guderian; they joined forces with General Kleist's mechanized units 150 miles east of Kiev, completing the encirclement of Russian forces in that city by 16 September. How many Russians were killed or captured in the Kiev pocket remains unknown. The Wehrmacht claimed to have captured over 600,000 men, while the Soviets acknowledged the loss of 527,000. Whichever figure one chooses to believe, Russian losses were staggering, but if Stalin paid heavily for his determination to hold Kiev, the Germans paid even more.

Rundstedt's double envelopment of the Kiev pocket was a smashing tactical success but it did not prove decisive. Despite an unparalleled loss of men and equipment, the Red Army showed no sign of succumbing to the Wehrmacht. Four Soviet armies may have been lost at Kiev but they would quickly be replaced by fresh units from the east, while the Germans enjoyed no equal availability of manpower reserves. Although they might exact casualties from the Soviets at the rate of 10:1 or higher, the Germans could ill afford the losses they were suffering to say nothing of the time wasted in the south. The Kiev encirclement was not completed until the end of September; winter was fast approaching and there was little time to resume the offensive in the north. The 'brightness of the Germany victory' was overshadowed by his somber prospect.

With the defeat of the Soviet Fifth Army, Guderian's armored forces were returned to Bock, and the northern offensive was resumed at the beginning of October. Although tanks, trucks and other heavy equipment were in poor condition as a result of Guderian's rapid movements south and back again to the northern front, Bock's reunited forces were able to repeat Rundstedt's triumph in the north. Moving rapidly along the Minsk-Moscow road, German forces once again enveloped a huge Russian force, this time around Vyasma some 150 miles west of Moscow. The Vyasma encirclement netted another 600,000 Russian captives and was even a greater tactical success than Kiev, but it was not completed until the end of October. By

this time the weather was rapidly worsening and Russian reinforcements had arrived from the far eastern provinces to defend Moscow.

The German command was divided as to what to do following the Vyasma encirclement. Bock, Brauchitsch and Halder pressed for continuing the German offensive. Bock believed that Russian morale would collapse in the face of an assault on the capital while Brauchitsch and Halder were fearful of the repercussions of a failure to take that city. Thus, for personal and quite varied reasons, the three men urged Hitler to move on, knowing that he would not forfeit his chance to capture Moscow if there was the slightest possibility that this could be accomplished before hard winter forced an end to the fighting. There was little hope, therefore, for the advocates of strategic withdrawal, particularly when the commander of the army in the field wished to press on. At a command meeting early in November, it was decided to continue the campaign. Whatever the price, the Wehrmacht would make one last effort to take Moscow.

Hitler might order his armies to advance on Moscow but he could not alter weather con-

Above: Winter turned the German offensive into retreat.

Below: German troops await the onslaught at Smolensk. **Below right:** The Waffen-SS served as a formidable spearhead in Operation Barbarossa.

ditions which continued to remain poor. The offensive could only be resumed after a break in the weather in mid-November, and even then the going was slow. Communications and supply lines were overextended, mechanized vehicles were short of gasoline and lubricants, and troops lacked adequate clothing and rations. Although efforts were made to alleviate these problems by airlifting clothing and supplies, the shortages remained a hard fact of life and every mile that the Wehrmacht advanced became more difficult to endure.

While German forces trudged on toward Moscow plagued by heavy snows and below-freezing temperatures, the Red Army was digging in in front of the city. The defense of the capital was coordinated by General Georgi Zhukov, one of the most capable officers in the Red Army. Recognizing the precarious position of the Germans, Zhukov carefully husbanded his resources, planning to hold his men back until the Wehrmacht reached the suburbs of Moscow, when he would launch a counter-offensive. Short of arms and ammunition, the exhausted German forces would

be easy prey for the Russians who would then surround them and inflict heavy casualties on their ranks. The encirclement of German forces near Moscow would dwarf German victories at Kiev and Vyasma, forcing Hitler to abandon the entire Russian campaign. It was with cautious optimism, therefore, that Zhukov awaited the arrival of the Wehrmacht. He did not have long to wait.

Advance units of the German army reached the suburbs of Moscow on 2 December. Two days later Zhukov launched his counter-attack. Exhausted and half starving, German troops were too spent to retaliate, but Hitler refused to allow an immediate and general withdrawal. He preferred, instead, to replace his field commanders and assume personal command of the entire operation. Bock and Brauchitsch were dismissed, Leeb resigned, and Guderian was transferred. Having eliminated those officers responsible for the disaster in Russia, he himself would try to salvage the situation.

In the fear that a general retreat would quickly degenerate into an unadulterated rout, the Fuehrer would only permit short local withdrawals; troops were to fall back on their supply dumps, turning these into fortified 'hedgehogs'; proper clothing and supplies were to be rushed to the eastern front by the Luftwaffe so that the survivors of the battle could hold their positions until they were reinforced the following spring. Until then, when another campaign would be launched to pacify the Soviet Union, the men of the Wehrmacht would have to endure hardship and heroic sacrifice without question.

Although those who survived the winter of 1941 suffered greatly, Hitler's decision to stand fast rather than withdraw from Russia was a correct one. No disorderly retreat took place, the Wehrmacht was spared the fate of Napoleon's Grand Army of 1812, and the Germans were in a strong position for launching another attack the following spring. Nevertheless, there was little cause for celebration in Berlin. About 750,000 German troops had been captured, killed or wounded in the Soviet Union by the end of 1941, many of them in the effort to take Moscow. Hitler's goals, the capture of the Caucasus, Leningrad and Moscow, had not been achieved. Victory was as far from sight at the beginning of the new year as it had been in June when the invasion was originally launched. Operation Barbarossa had failed.

Failure of the operation

Hitler blamed the failure of Operation Barbarossa on the weakness and vacillation of his generals, but it was he who was responsible for the Russian debacle. Although his military advisers had underestimated Russia's resources and the quality of the Red Army, they still foresaw possible disaster; Hitler had forced the invasion on them despite their vigorous objections. Once the attack was initiated, he refused to abide by their suggestions, preferring to rely on his own judgement. When field commanders suggested a rapid push on Moscow in August, Hitler disregarded their opinion and ordered the transfer of forces from the central zone to the south. When some officers

suggested withdrawing to a winter-line at the end of October, Hitler ordered the advance on Moscow to continue regardless of the cost in men. The conflict between the generals and the Fuehrer not only contributed to the near disaster in Russia, but tainted the relationship between Hitler and the General Staff in future campaigns. Hitler's strategy may have been correct in 1940 but his judgement had tragic consequences for the fate of the Russian campaign.

Above: Men of Hoth's relief force who fought to within 50 miles of the Stalingrad pocket. They were hurled back by a Soviet counter-offensive.

Below: Hitler's thrusts into Russia pushed the endurance of his troops to the limit.

CHAPTER FIVE

America Moves Towards War

Events in Europe and the Far East did not go unnoticed in the United States. Americans roundly condemned Japanese agression in Manchuria and China, viewed with disfavor the advent of the Third Reich and the remilitarization of Germany, and watched with disgust as the Czech crisis was resolved at Munich. Thinking Americans agreed that these and other incidents in the interwar period boded ill for the future but there was less agreement over the appropriate response to such crises. Some, perhaps a majority, believed that strict neutrality and non-interference in the affairs of other nations was the best course for their government to pursue. Others, a vocal

Below: The Great Depression was the primary concern of Roosevelt's first Administration. Here unemployed demonstrators run through Union Square in New York pursued by police.

minority, strongly urged greater American participation in the world community, hoping to thwart aggression by lending the military might and moral support of the United States to those governments which supported democracy. Still others were too deeply caught up in the throes of the Depression to worry about events abroad. Such was the state of public opinion in the United States on the eve of war.

President Roosevelt was an internationalist by virtue of his education, family background, and personal convictions. He was also a shrewd politician, and as such he sensed that most Americans were primarily concerned with setting their own house in order. His election in 1932 and re-election in 1936 were based upon domestic issues and programs; he had received no mandate from the American people to cure the world's ills, nor had Congress prompted him to play the role of mediator between the forces of good and evil. Whatever his own views, the President had to accept these realities and act accordingly.

During Roosevelt's first term (1933–1937) the United States did little to alter the course of world affairs beyond participating in several abortive disarmament conferences. During his second term (1937–1941) even less was done to exert a positive influence in the world community. As the mood grew more somber in Europe and the Far East, the United States seemed to retreat deeper and deeper into its isolationist cocoon. When Italy attacked Ethiopia in 1935, the Congress of the United States responded by passing a neutrality act calling upon the President to refrain from taking any action which might offend either of the belligerents. When civil war broke out in Spain in 1936, Congress restated its commitment to neutrality and expressly forbade the shipping of arms to the republican government in Madrid or its fascist rivals. A third and more comprehensive neutrality act was passed in 1937. It retained previous bans on shipments of munitions and advances of cash to belligerent nations and added additional restrictions which prohibited American nationals from travelling on belligerents' vessels or selling non-military supplies to such nations except on a cash and carry basis.

At first, given the mood of Congress and a majority of the American people, Roosevelt had little choice but to accept the limitations imposed upon him by the legislature, but as tensions increased in Europe and China the President grew increasingly restive and impatient with his colleagues. If Congress could not be persuaded to abandon or modify its isolationist stand, the executive might still articulate America's moral outrage over the misdeeds of the dictators. If the United States could not lend its physical support to sister democracies, the least she could do was to lend them moral support. It was clearly time for the United States to adopt a more constructive policy and Roosevelt felt ready to define it.

Speaking to an audience in Chicago on 5 October 1937, Roosevelt pleaded for a more affirmative foreign policy. Peace-loving nations, the president stated, would have to stand together if law and order were to prevail in the world. Isolation or neutrality would not provide immunity from a disease of the mind and soul.

The Italian invasion of Ethiopia evoked little concern in the United States.

Likening the world situation to an effort to combat a deadly epidemic, Roosevelt called for strong measures, suggesting a political quarantine of those who threatened world peace lest their cancer spread to all members of the family of nations. Those who lived in peace and in accordance with international law must find a way to make their will prevail else they would soon fall prey to the forces of evil. Although the American people wanted to keep out of war, Roosevelt warned that non-involvement would not insure peace. There was no guarantee the United States could remain aloof from war indefinitely.

Reaction to Roosevelt's 'quarantine speech' was less than enthusiastic. Isolationists called the President a warmonger. Critics of his domestic policies and programs charged that he was using the international crisis as a smoke screen to draw attention away from the failure of his political programs at home. The rest of the people remained apathetic, failing to see the relevance of the President's message. Try as he might, Roosevelt could not change the temper of the times. So strong had the partisans of isolation become that even his forceful personality could not effectively counter their influence. As crisis followed crisis, the American people seemed supremely confident that they would escape the conflagration. The President did not succumb to this illusion.

Isolationism remains paramount

By 1938 Roosevelt was convinced that a European war was imminent. Unlike many others, he placed little faith in the appeasement of dictators as a means of preserving the peace. 'Peace by fear', the President stated, 'has no higher or more enduring quality than peace by the sword'. This remark proved to be prophetic; the Munich conference provided no solution to Europe's ills, for no sooner had Hitler been placated by Chamberlain and Daladier than he escalated his demands, taking the rest of Czechoslovakia by force and threatening Poland. Could there by any doubt that war was inevitable? For Mr Roosevelt it was only a matter of when and where.

Germany's invasion of Poland in September 1939 hardly took the President by surprise. As England and France declared war on Germany, Roosevelt delivered his strongest condemnation of fascist aggression to that date. Speaking to the American public in one of his radio 'fireside chats', he promised to maintain American neutrality as long as was possible, but told his audience that neutrality was a political policy which ought not to affect their state of mind. Free men could not applaud aggression. If government could not act, the citizen was free to articulate his moral outrage; in fact, it was his obligation to do so.

While Roosevelt implored Americans to speak out against what he considered international banditry, he assiduously abided by the neutrality legislation then in effect, hoping that mounting public reaction to events in Europe would force the Congress to modify the statutes. Unfortunately the advent of war in Europe did not result in a coalescence of public opinion in the United States. On the contrary, the differences between the isolationists and internationalists seemed to widen; those who opposed intervention in world affairs saw the war as further proof of the need to stand aloof from the quarrels of others, and while the President tried to rally the nation to action, they redoubled their efforts to maintain her isolation.

The America First Committee was the isolationists' response to the war in Europe. A

Below: Ethiopian troops, often armed with little more than spears, fought bravely when the Italians invaded. **Below right:** The Italian army enters Addis Ababa – 1936. It took almost a year to subdue Ethiopia.

A column of Italian tanks moves towards the Ethiopian capital.

coalition of diverse groups and individuals, the organization sought to prevent Congress from altering neutrality legislation through a nation-wide propaganda campaign of immense proportions. Led by public figures such as Charles Lindbergh, the Committee succeeded in rallying to its banner almost all isolationist groups. Until the Japanese attack on Pearl Harbor, members of the organization spread their gospel with zeal, idealism, and energy but met with only partial success.

Roosevelt did not adequately anticipate the strength of isolationist sentiment and was at a loss as to how to respond to it. Had Hitler immediately followed the invasion of Poland with subsequent moves into France and the Low Countries, the issue of German aggression would have been clearer and the threat to international order would have been more universally understood by Americans. As it happened, however, there was a lengthy pause between the rush into Poland and the resumption of the blitz in April 1940; although the 'phoney war' was only a lull before the storm, at the time many Americans believed that the deadlock might become permanent. If this were the case, a world conflict was hardly inevitable. As long as the situation remained static, there was little the President could do, and he was forced to accept the need to proceed cautiously.

Support for the Allies

The fall of France ended America's complacency, for even the isolationists could not deny that Hitler's victory in France and the pending battle for Britain posed a threat to the United States. If England suffered the same fate as France, the United States would stand alone. For most Americans, the fall of France was a catastrophe of the first magnitude, and they prepared to

follow the President's lead; only the most unrestrained isolationists remained sceptical.

Roosevelt quickly pressed for changes in neutrality legislation and subsequent aid to Great Britain. Speaking at the University of Virginia in June 1940, he outlined his view of America's new responsibilities and how he proposed to prepare for them:

'In our American unity we will pursue two obvious and simultaneous courses; we will extend to the opponents of force the material resources of this nation, and, at the same time, we will harness and speed up the use of those resources in order that we ourselves in the Americas may have equipment and training equal to the task of any emergency and every defense.'

Soon after his speech in Virginia, Roosevelt submitted a series of special messages to Congress outling his plans to strengthen the defenses of the United States and aid Great Britain. At a time when the world was 'threatened by the forces of destruction', the president proposed an immediate mobilization of America's resources and a major revision of the neutrality laws so that she could commence aid to her British allies without delay. This time Congress was willing to follow Roosevelt's lead and passed enabling legislation with a speed and vigor reminiscent of the first days of the New Deal. By summer's end, huge sums had been appropriated to modernize America's armed forces and one by one provisions of previous neutrality acts were amended or altered to permit her to become the 'arsenal for the world's democracies.'

To insure that his program would not assume a partisan character, Roosevelt appointed leading Republicans to cabinet and sub-cabinet positions. 1940 was an election year and having decided to

Below left: A patriotic ceremony in honor of Mussolini in Addis Ababa – 1937. **Below:** Japanese invasion of China Proper in 1937 aroused little initial sympathy in the US.

run for an unprecedented third term, the President did not wish to see his foreign policy become a campaign issue. Although he realized that diehard isolationists would keep the issue alive, Roosevelt believed that the majority of the American people supported his policies regardless of their party affiliation. By bringing into his administration such nationally prominent Republicans as Henry L. Stimson, Secretary of State during the Hoover Administration, and Frank Knox, Republican vice-presidential nominee in 1936, Roosevelt hoped to build a coalition which would survive the election.

The plan succeeded, and the election of 1940 did not become a referendum on foreign policy. The Republican presidential candidate, Wendell Willkie, shared many of Mr Roosevelt's convictions on foreign policy matters; he was a strong advocate of military preparedness and aid for the Allies, and his criticism of Roosevelt's administration was almost entirely limited to its domestic programs. For his part, the President did not campaign energetically, making few speeches and remaining in Washington D.C. during most of the campaign period. When the votes were tallied, Roosevelt had won a third term by a comfortable majority; the isolationists had lost their last chance of effectively checking America's movement toward intervention.

With four more years in the White House ahead of him, Roosevelt could now concentrate on implementing his programs. Among his first items of business was arranging aid for the British who, at the very moment the election was concluded, were under daily attack from the Luftwaffe. The United States had already made arrangements to send England surplus stocks of guns and ammunition left over from the First World War, and in addition Mr Roosevelt had concluded an Anglo-American agreement, which permitted the exchange of some fifty old destroyers for leases on naval bases in Britain's American colonies. Now, with his election victory fresh behind him, the President proposed a far more ambitious program to make munitions and supplies available to the Allies.

Speaking to the Congress in January 1941, Roosevelt outlined his proposal:

'I ask this Congress for authority and funds sufficient to manufacture additional munitions and war supplies of many kinds, to be turned over to those nations which are now in actual war with aggressor nations.

Our most useful and immediate role is to act as an arsenal for them as well as for ourselves. They do not need manpower. They do need billions of dollars worth of the weapons of defense.'

In return, Roosevelt proposed to receive compensation in kind, or property, or any other manner deemed satisfactory by the President.

A Lend-Lease bill was submitted to the Congress shortly after the President's address. Needless to say, it was the subject of considerable controversy, but its opponents could not muster sufficient votes to defeat it; on 11 March 1941, it became law and immediately thereafter over seven billion dollars was appropriated for its implementation. According to the provisions of the legislation, military equipment could be

Above: Charles A. Lindbergh, hero in the 1920's for having flown the Atlantic single-handed, was one of the leaders of the America First Committee. **Bottom:** He visited Germany in 1936. Although he was not a Fascist himself, Lindbergh and others like him honestly felt that the war in Europe was none of America's business.

Above right: Japanese soldiers pause for a meal on their way southward. **Right:** Roosevelt could not stop the Japanese conquest of China by speeches alone. **Far right:** He declared American neutrality and promising the American people that their boys 'would not be sent to any foreign war', he won an unprecedented third term in 1940.

Below center: Lord Beaverbrook (center) stated Britain's need to administrators of the Lend-Lease Act. Left of Beaverbrook, Lord O'Brien and Edward R. Stettinius, later Secretary of State; to his right William S. Knudsen and W. Averill Harriman, Lend-Lease Administrator in London. **Below far right:** Churchill aboard HMS *Prince of Wales* on his way to Newfoundland.

shipped with a minimum of red-tape to those who opposed fascist aggression. Although most of the funds were initially committed to Great Britain, aid was also extended to the Soviet Union, Nationalist China and some 35 other nations.

The passage of the Lend-Lease Act moved the United States one step closer to war, for although the bill by no means called upon the American government to sever diplomatic ties with Germany, Italy, or Japan, the coordination of vast amounts of aid to those who opposed these powers forced the United States to enter into planning arrangements with them. Such discussions laid the foundation for the grand alliance which emerged after the attack on Pearl Harbor.

An outline of the alliance mentioned above was first worked out in August 1941 when President Roosevelt met Prime Minister Winston Churchill at sea off the Newfoundland coast in what might well be called the first of the wartime summit conferences. As a result of this meeting, Roosevelt's concept of an 'Atlantic Charter' was embraced by Churchill and the two men committed themselves to creating a world order in which democratic nations would unite to quash aggression and maintain the peace. Though not technically a declaration of war, the Newfoundland communiqué was a clear statement of America's intent to aid the Allies which strained beyond belief the veneer of American neutrality. This message was not lost on Hitler.

America becomes a de facto belligerent

Having arranged to send supplies to Great Britain and other nations, the United States was soon involved in an effort to insure that such equipment reached its destination. German submarine attacks on allied shipping exacted a heavier and heavier toll in the months following the passage of the lend-lease program; the Soviets were not equipped to wage anti-submarine warfare; and England's navy was already committed to other operations. If the goods were to arrive safely, the United States would have to assume some of the burden of organizing and protecting convoys.

Although Roosevelt was quick to accept the challenge of supporting allied shipping, he and his advisers realized full well that participation in the convoy system would move America closer to war and thus invite the wrath of the isolationists. Nevertheless, the need to move supplies across the Atlantic was far more critical than the political consequences of a further American commitment and the President did not hesitate to take all

Krupp's submarine production kept Allied shipping busy.

appropriate measures to achieve this end. In April 1941 American forces were stationed in Greenland with the agreement of the Danish government. From air bases in this northern wilderness, American pilots patrolled the north Atlantic tracking the movement of German submarines and providing aerial cover for allied convoys. Three months later American forces were stationed in Iceland and assumed similar assignments.

Of course, America's protection of allied shipping was bitterly denounced by the Axis powers as an act of war. Although Roosevelt might distinguish between patrol and convoy activities, Hitler did not. By escorting allied merchantmen across the Atlantic, the United States Navy was directly contributing to the war against Germany, and this could not be tolerated.

German U-boats began to attack American ships in May 1941 but attacks remained sporadic until the end of August when American naval vessels were more regularly engaged while 'on patrol'. The President reacted strongly to these attacks, warning that if German or Italian vessels of war entered waters whose protection was deemed vital to America's security, they would do so at their own peril. American commanders were instructed to attack any and all German U-boats in the north Atlantic security zone. By these actions, Roosevelt attempted to place the burden of responsibility on German's shoulders and alert the American public to what lay ahead.

With Roosevelt's decision to attack Axis warships in the north Atlantic if they fired upon American vessels, the last pretence of American neutrality was abandoned. It remained only for

Far left: A U-boat returning to its French port after a successful mission. **Top left:** A beleaguered Henry L. Stimson kept war production up before Pearl Harbor. **Left:** Secretary of the Navy Frank Knox, Cordell Hull, Secretary of State, and Henry L. Stimson, Secretary of War, leave a meeting of the Senate Foreign Relations Committee after a discussion on the Lend-Lease Act.

the President to ask Congress to repeal remaining neutrality legislation to make this official and this he did at the end of October, declaring that: 'We Americans have cleared our decks and taken our battle stations standing ready in the defense of our nation that only the thinnest of lines separated the United States from war with the Axis.

Roosevelt's proposal was vigorously discussed in the Congress and might have stalled there were it not for renewed German attacks on American ships early in November. With American vessels and men under attack, Congress could hardly dally over the administration's legislation, and despite a valiant effort by the isolationist lobby, the last of the neutrality statutes was repealed in November, permitting the President to order armed American merchantmen to participate in the convoys and trade with nations already at war.

The Undeclared War

With the repeal of the neutrality statutes, the United States entered into an undeclared war with the Axis powers in Europe, a situation which satisfied neither the isolationists nor the interventionists. Although the President had moved the United States closer to his own foreign policy goals, the nation remained divided. Isolationists demanded an immediate reversal of the policies which had carried the nation to the brink of war while interventionists called for a declaration of war so that American support of Allied forces in Europe could be more efficiently achieved. The situation remained static until 7 December 1941 when Japan decided the matter with her attack on Pearl Harbor.

Left: German U-boats sank many American supply ships in 1941.

311

CHAPTER SIX
The Road to Pearl Harbor

While Germany and the United States moved closer to war, Japanese-American relations were also rapidly deteriorating. For thirty years, the two nations had pursued contradictory policies in Asia but had somehow managed to avoid an armed conflict. As Roosevelt began his third term as president, however, the crisis in China was rapidly undermining this state of peaceful co-existence.

Japan's effort in China seemed as far from completion in 1941 as it had in 1937 when the Sino-Japanese war was initiated; yet the Japanese remained steadfast in their determination to humble the Chinese. This was a policy which Mr Roosevelt could not and would not accept. Since 1899, the United States had consistently supported an 'open door' policy which called upon all nations to recognize and insure the political and territorial integrity of China; Japan's policies violated this dictum and threatened to disrupt the balance of power in Asia, but how to go about changing them remained a problem.

For several decades, the United States had responded to Japanese aggression in China with verbal reprimands. When the Japanese presented the Twenty-One Demands to the government of Yuan Shih-k'ai in 1915, William Jennings Bryan, Mr Wilson's Secretary of State, condemned this action. When the Japanese invaded and annexed Manchuria in 1931, Henry L. Stimson, Mr Hoover's Secretary of State, denounced Japan's

aggression and announced that the United States would refuse to recognize the state of Manchukuo which the Japanese had created out of China's three northeast provinces. When the Sino-Japanese War was launched in 1937, Cordell Hull, Mr Roosevelt's Secretary of State, deplored Japanese brutality and lawlessness. These verbal attacks had little or no effect except to exacerbate the enmity between the two countries; force was the only language that the Japanese might have understood, and this the American government was not prepared to use.

As a result of their previous experience with American leaders, Japanese officials had come to expect a weak response to their activities in Asia. They could hardly feel threatened by the pious platitudes of American administrators, however humiliating their verbal harangues might be. Still, America's readiness to condemn Japan's policies remained irritating; Japanese leaders found it difficult to understand American moral outrage over the attempt to found a new order in Asia when the United States had been doing the same thing for decades in the Americas. If other nations were asked to recognize America's 'special interest' in Latin America and the Caribbean, was it illogical to expect recognition for Japan's 'paramount interest' in China?

Had America's interest in China been simply economic, the United States and Japan might have reached a reasonable understanding, but

Above: Japanese atrocities were commonplace in their war with China.

Opposite: Japan's march through China in 1937–38 was relentless. **Left:** China, 1938 – some effects of the bombardment of Wuchang.

America's commitment to the Chinese was emotional as well as pragmatic. To be sure, the 'open door' policy had originally been designed to secure a fair share of the China market for American merchants. But over fifty years, Americans had come to see this policy as a moral commitment as opposed to an economic expedient. For many, China appeared to be America's special responsibility in the world, and the American people built up a genuine, if patronizing fondness for the country, finding contact with the Chinese adventurous, exhilarating and rewarding in material and spiritual terms. Unfortunately, the Japanese did not share this enthusiasm, nor did they view America's role in China as one of a benign ally. To their mind, the United States was merely another Western power seeking to exploit the people and resources of Asia without regard for the needs of the area, while Japan represented a different, truly 'Asian' ideal which her neighbors would fully accept once their initial reluctance had been overcome.

As long as America's response to Japan was limited to verbal chastisement, the danger of a Japanese-American confrontation remained minimal. However, after Japanese forces escalated their activities in 1937, many Americans demanded stronger action to curb Japan's aggressive appetite; a suggestion which, if followed, would markedly increase tension between the two countries. For the Japanese there could be no turning back if their new order in Asia, the 'Greater East Asia Co-Prosperity Sphere', was to be achieved. For the United States, there was no way to stop the war in China short of forcefully intervening or initiating economic sanctions, neither of which was an attractive alternative for the Roosevelt administration. Nevertheless some action had to be taken.

Economic sanctions against Japan

Although the United States viewed Japanese activities in China with contempt, the Roosevelt administration reacted cautiously, hoping to restrain Japan without inviting retaliation. Some of China's friends had already mounted a boycott of Japanese goods and hoped to persuade the government to follow their lead by embargoing shipments of scrap iron and gasoline to Japan. Although the President made it quite clear that he was sympathetic to the idea of the boycott, the only action that was taken in 1937 was to hint to the Japanese that a boycott might follow if they did not alter their course.

The State Department attempted to articulate the stand of the administration and convey the feeling of the American people to the leaders of Japan. Joseph Grew, United States Ambassador to Japan, bluntly told his Japanese counterpart of the hardening attitude in the States in 1937. In 1938 the Department of State suggested a 'moral embargo' on the sale of aircraft and other munitions to the Japanese. In 1939 this suggestion was broadened to include the shipment of gasoline and other petroleum products. Still, at the time of the outbreak of war in Europe, the embargo was not official nor was any effort made to enforce it. Its effectiveness, such as it was, depended on

Above left: Japanese troops scale the walls of Kaifeng. **Above:** By 1939 the Japanese found great difficulty in pushing westward to the new Chinese capital of Chungking.
Left: The Cabinet of Prince Konoye (third from left). War Minister Tojo (left of Konoye, in uniform) discouraged Konoye's attempts to avoid war with America.

personal moral judgement and commitment rather than a government regulation. This being the case, it could not succeed, and it was only after the advent of war in Europe that the administration would commit itself to more positive policies.

On 26 January 1940 the Japanese-American Treaty of Commerce lapsed and was not renewed. This allowed the Roosevelt administration to prohibit, except under licence, the export of certain materials to Japan; in July the President used his discretionary power to prohibit the export of certain crucial materials including petroleum products, steel, and scrap metals, except as directed by the White House. Although his proclamation did not specifically limit such action to Japan, it was clearly intended to bring pressure on the Japanese government and was supplemented by additional restrictions in the months that followed. Slowly but surely, the screws were being tightened around the Japanese in an effort to alter their policies in Asia.

The imposition of economic sanctions on Japan posed a fundamental problem for her leaders. Japan's military and civilian industries were dependent upon the importation of large quantities of raw materials from the United States and other Western powers. Without American petroleum it would be difficult to pursue the Sino-Japanese war, to say nothing of projects elsewhere in Asia. Japan's petroleum reserves were limited, and as the war in China was as far from solution in 1940 as it had been in 1937, it would have to cease if the United States put a complete embargo on the export of petroleum products or alternative sources of this vital product were not found.

If the American government had not unrealistically insisted that Japan relinquish the fruits of her aggression, the Japanese might have chosen to extricate themselves from China and modify if not forsake their plan to create a new order in Asia. Since there was no possibility that the Roosevelt administration would seriously consider a compromise, there was no way for the Japanese to get out of China and still maintain face. Humiliation was not a palatable alternative for Japan's leaders who, in their rejection of American demands, were then forced to find new sources of raw materials.

Japan's alternative to a retreat from China was to accelerate the creation of the Greater East Asia Co-Prosperity Sphere. The Japanese had already taken advantage of the European war to occupy the northern part of Vietnam with the reluctant permission of the Vichy government. It was a relatively simple step to extend this occupation to the rest of that country and arrange for similar concessions from other hard pressed colonial powers, namely the Dutch and the British. If the Japanese gained access to the resources of the Indies and Malaya, the effect of America's embargo would be greatly reduced if not nullified.

The Japanese had attempted to obtain larger quantities of petroleum products from the Dutch East Indies even before the United States levied embargos on such products, but it was not until after the German occupation of Holland that the issue was forcefully pressed. By this time, shortages of gasoline and lubricants had become acute and the Japanese government faced the unhappy prospect of having to use reserve stocks for daily needs if another source for these products could not be found. Luckily for the Japanese, the German blitz against the Netherlands succeeded at precisely the moment when their dilemma was greatest, providing an opportunity to reopen negotiations from a position of strength.

During the autumn and winter of 1940–41, several Japanese missions visited the Indies in an attempt to come to new arrangements with Dutch colonial authorities. The Japanese proposed, in essence, that the Dutch supply petroleum products to Japan without restriction and allow Japanese interests to explore and develop as yet untapped oil fields. This the Dutch were unwilling to do, despite the fact that they were hardly in a strong bargaining position and so the authorities in Batavia made only minimal concessions to the Japanese, giving them as little as possible in order to delay a confrontation until assurances of assistance were received from England and the United States. As negotiations were pursued with the Japanese parallel discussions were held by British, Dutch, and American officials; the Dutch were quite willing to follow Washington's lead in limiting the export of petroleum products to Japan, but could only do so if the United States and Great Britain were willing to come to the colonial governments' assistance in the event that the Japanese decided to press their demands by force instead of at the conference table.

But although the United States was not eager to see Japan supplied with high octane aviation fuel and other petroleum products, the Roosevelt administration was unwilling to commit itself to the defense of the Indies in the wake of a Japanese attack. The British, for their part, were somewhat more inclined to support the Dutch, but preoccupation with the defense of their own colonial empire prevented them from committing themselves in the absence of a similar American pledge. Thus, although both powers agreed that Dutch participation in the petroleum embargo was useful and necessary, neither government would make the promises which were absolutely prerequisite for such an agreement as far as the Dutch were concerned. In the end, whatever policy the colonial authorities in Batavia chose to adopt, they would face the Japanese alone.

In the absence of guarantees of assistance from the United States and Great Britain, Dutch leaders agonized over their response to the Japanese. After careful deliberation, it was decided that some oil and low octane fuel would continue to be sent to Japan but that the colonial government would not meet Japan's demands for high octane aviation fuels. Although the Dutch hoped that such a compromise would not overly provoke the Japanese, they could not be sure what Japan's response would be.

The tough attitude of Holland's colonial officials surprised the Japanese, who returned from Batavia to Tokyo almost empty-handed. Japan's leaders felt certain that the Dutch refusal to accede to their demands indicated a secret agreement with England and the United States to expand the embargo of petroleum products in

Far left: While she continued to negotiate, Japan's military buildup went on unabated. **Left:** T. V. Soong, China's Minister of Foreign Affairs, and Cordell Hull, American Secretary of State. The US sent considerable amounts of lend-lease aid to Chungking before Pearl Harbor. **Above:** Major-General Jonathan Wainwright with MacArthur in the Philippines. They faced the Japanese onslaught of 7 December 1941. **Below far left:** Japanese troops march through Osaka on their way to the front in China. **Below left:** General Douglas MacArthur was appointed by FDR to assist the Philippine army.

return for Anglo-American protection of the Indies. This, however, was not the case at all; the Indies government had chosen to confront its fate with no external pledges of support.

The failure of Japanese diplomacy

Having failed to gain their ends through diplomacy, Japanese leaders faced an agonizing decision. They could force the issue by invading the Indies or shift their diplomatic efforts to break the embargo from the Dutch to the Americans. Neither alternative was attractive. An invasion of the Indies would be acceptable only if there was a reasonable chance that the oil wells and refineries in the islands could be captured intact; if they were destroyed as a result of a scorched earth policy before the conquest of the Indies was completed, that conquest would be in vain. A new diplomatic offensive, on the other hand, would be far less costly than taking military action but there was no indication that the American government would be more pliable than it had been in the past. This was the dilemma facing the Japanese government at the beginning of the summer of 1941.

For the moment, it was decided to try diplomacy again. In an effort to appease the United States, Admiral Nomura Kichisaburo, a well known proponent of Japanese-American rapprochement, was appointed the new Japanese Ambassador to the United States. It was hoped that his presence in Washington would reassure the American government and people of Japan's sincere desire to avoid war and facilitate the initiation of new discussions of the situation in Asia. Nomura was instructed to inform the Roosevelt Administration that Japan would not employ force in the Pacific if the United States moved toward re-establishing normal economic relations and helped the Japanese to settle the China incident by pressing the Chinese Nationalists to make peace.

Nomura lost little time in articulating the position of his government and reopening conversations with the Department of State. For his part, Secretary of State Cordell Hull responded to Nomura's suggestions with several counter-proposals. Hull suggested that no progress could be made toward solving Japanese-American differences unless both powers recognized four basic principles: respect for the political sovereignty and territorial integrity of all nations in Asia; an agreement that neither party would interfere in the internal affairs of the nations of the area; an acceptance of the 'open door' principle which provided that all nations have an equal opportunity to develop their commerce in the area; and a renunciation of the use of force in altering the status quo. Only after both powers pledged themselves to abide by these guidelines could substantive discussions begin.

This response was hardly satisfactory, at least in so far as Nomura's superiors in Tokyo were concerned. The Japanese government wanted an end to restrictions on American trade with Japan, not a lecture on morality and international law. Once again, diplomacy seemed to fail. The Roosevelt administration still refused to consider the normalization of economic relations between

Far left: Japanese soldiers leave Tokyo on their way to the Pacific. **Left:** Admiral Nomura Kichisaburo became the new Japanese Ambassador to the United States in 1941.

the two countries unless the Japanese agreed to accept the principles which Hull advanced, a position which was totally unacceptable as the Japanese had no intention of retreating from China or anywhere else in the Far East.

Japan prepares to fight

Japanese-American relations reached a low point at the end of July, following Japan's occupation of southern Indochina, when in response to new crisis, President Roosevelt issued an executive order freezing Japanese assets in the United States and bringing all trade between the United States and Japan to a virtual halt. After months of vacillation, the administration had determined that no further Japanese aggression would be tolerated. It was at this point that the last diplomatic effort was made to avert hostilities.

Early in August, Premier Konoye Fuminaro proposed a meeting with Roosevelt in a final attempt to avoid war. The president rejected this proposal, informing Japan's Ambassador to the United States that Japan would have to stop her military advances before any such meeting could take place. With this rejection the Hull-Nomura discussions were doomed and war became in-

Left: Kurusa and Nomura, Japan's peace envoys to the US. **Right:** General Tojo Hideki, who replaced Konoye as Japan's Premier on 18 October 1941.

evitable; although Japanese-American negotiations continued in Washington, they were little more than a facade designed to buy time while both sides prepared for war.

In Japan, operational plans were drawn for an invasion of the Dutch East Indies, Malaya, and the Philippines, and a general mobilization was commenced. At the same time, the Japanese navy began to practice for an attack against American military installations in Hawaii, a plan which had been discussed as early as January 1941 but which now was being most seriously considered. In the United States, preparations for war were also being made. Factories were being rapidly retooled to produce munitions and other necessities of war and the Conscription Act of 1940 was being implemented for the first time. Slowly but surely, both sides were reaching the point of no return.

As it became apparent that Ambassador Nomura was getting nowhere in his discussions with the State Department, the Japanese high command pressed the government for a decision on the matter of war with the United States. After weeks of indecision, an Imperial Conference on 6 September decided to face the issue squarely. Diplomacy was to be given one more month to find a solution to the Japanese-American crisis; if by the beginning of October a solution had not been found, Japan would use force.

On 18 October the Konoye government was forced to resign and General Tojo Hideki became Prime Minister. Now the die was cast; Tojo's government was committed to war, and its plans were approved at a second Imperial Conference on 5 November. It was agreed that one last proposal would be submitted to the United States which would have to be accepted by 25 November. Should the Americans reject it, which seemed probable as it was simply a restatement of Japan's old position, war would follow almost immediately with simultaneous attacks on Pearl Harbor, Manila, and Singapore.

A special Japanese envoy, Kurusu Saburo, arrived in Washington on 17 November. His instructions were simple: he was to present Japan's last offer to Secretary of State Hull and keep the negotiations going until such time as he was ordered to return home. Unknown to him, this would give the Japanese navy time to prepare the attack on Pearl Harbor while maintaining the ruse of diplomacy until the very last moment. No one believed that the Americans would seriously entertain this 'new' proposal, but discussion of it would buy a little more precious time.

The Tojo government were correct in assuming that the United States would not accept this last proposal for settling Japanese-American conflicts through diplomacy. Responding to Kurusu's bid, Hull offered a counter-proposal which, although not an ultimatum, was a denial of everything the Japanese had attempted since 1915. As such, it was completely unacceptable and so, on 1 December 1941, an Imperial Conference made the final decision for war with the United States. The discussions in Washington, however, were to be continued until the attack was ready to be launched.

The War in the Far East Begins

Japan's decision to go to war was hardly a secret to the Roosevelt administration. Thanks to the deciphering of Japanese diplomatic codes, it had long been known in the United States that the hour of confrontation was drawing near. What was not known, however, was when and where the attack might take place. Although American military installations in Hawaii appeared to be a possible target, Roosevelt's advisers believed that the Japanese would strike first against British and Dutch bases or, if they chose to hit the United States, would attack the Philippine Islands rather than Hawaii. In any case, the United States needed more time to prepare for war, and thus it was just as vital for her as for Japan that the Hull-Nomura conversations be continued as long as possible.

The State Department washed its hands of the negotiations at the end of November but kept the discussions formally alive so that the army and navy would have more time to prepare for the imminent clash with Japan. They did not have long to wait. On 6 December Nomura and Kurusu were alerted to expect a lengthy message from Japan, severing diplomatic relations with the United States, which was to be presented to the Department of State the following day. By late evening, the message was received and was being decoded and translated. Unknown to the Japanese, it had also been intercepted by American intelligence authorities.

Thirteen of the fourteen points in Tojo's cable had been received and sent to Roosevelt before midnight on the 6th. Upon reading the despatch, there was little doubt in his mind that war would soon follow, but there was still no indication as to when or where. Neither the President nor his advisers expected the attack to follow the very next day nor did they anticipate that Pearl Harbor would be the Japanese target. But the next morning Roosevelt learned that the decision to terminate diplomatic relations was to be presented to the State Department at 1:00 p.m. that afternoon; thinking that the hour of this presentation might be significant, a cable was sent to American commanders in Hawaii warning of the danger of possible attack. It arrived in Hawaii at 7:33 a.m. and was being delivered to military authorities when the attack on Pearl Harbor began Japan's envoys were received at the State Department shortly after 2:00 p.m., by which time Hull had already received reports confirming the Japanese attack. After a bitter denunciation of Japan's duplicity, they were abruptly dismissed; the time for discussion was over.

Right: Nomura and Kurusu (with hat) leave the White House after conferring with Roosevelt on 27 November. By this time Japan had already sent her fleet steaming toward Pearl Harbor.

Above: *Aircraft Maintenance Aboard a Carrier* by the Japanese artist S. Arai.
Left: Japanese planes on their way to "a rendezvous with destiny".

CHAPTER SEVEN

Days of Infamy: Pearl Harbor, the Philippines, and Singapore

As Japan's military leaders prepared for war with the United States and the other colonial powers in Asia, they realized that they could never defeat the United States, Great Britain, and the Netherlands decisively; about the best they could hope for was a temporary victory based upon the neutralization of Allied naval forces in the Pacific and the seizure of certain territories, especially the mineral rich colonies of Malaya and the Dutch East Indies. Beyond this, a permanent solution to the Asian crisis would have to be reached through diplomacy.

Plans for an attack against the colonial powers had been prepared months before 7 December 1941 but it was not until 6 September that the proposal was formally presented to the Supreme War Council in Tokyo. This plan, conceived and articulated by Admiral Yamamoto, called for Japanese forces to launch a four phase attack against the Western allies immediately following the collapse of diplomatic efforts to settle the China tangle. During the first and second stages of the offensive, some six divisions would invade Malaya, Siam, and Burma while another three and one-half divisions would overrun Hongkong and the Philippine Islands. Phase three would see Japanese forces seize American bases in the Pacific, and in the final stage of the operation land forces would complete the occupation of British Malaya and the Dutch East Indies.

To achieve these goals, it was essential that Japanese naval superiority in the Pacific remain

Below: Japanese pilots warm up the engines of their Zero's on the flight deck of the aircraft carrier *Akagi*. Their objective – Pearl Harbor. **Opposite top:** Wheeler Field, Pearl Harbor. 0800 hours, 7 December 1941. **Opposite bottom:** The US fleet around Ford Island in Pearl Harbor was like a flock of sitting ducks.

unchallenged. This, in turn, meant that the American fleet at Pearl Harbor had to be neutralized before it could offer an effective counter-stroke to the Japanese offensive; the Japanese would have to launch a surprise attack on fleet headquarters similar to the British raid against the Italian fleet at Taranto in 1940. Japan's leaders understood this and accepted the risks involved, ordering preparations for the pre-emptive strike to be set in motion.

Anticipating the collapse of negotiations with the United States, a vast armada was gathered and committed to 'war games' off the coast of Japan late in September. The strike force, consisting of four fleet carriers, two light carriers, two fast battleships, three cruisers, a flotilla of destroyers, eight tankers, and a number of submarines, was ready for action against the United States when the Hull-Nomura conversations collapsed at the end of November. In fact, it was under way before Hull had replied to Japan's ultimatum of 25 November, though had the negotiations succeeded at this point the fleet could still have been recalled.

The Attack on Pearl Harbor

Little was done by American authorities to bolster the defenses of military installations at or near the naval base at Pearl Harbor, for although intelligence reports indicated that some form of attack was imminent, the time and place remained unknown. Most senior officers expected

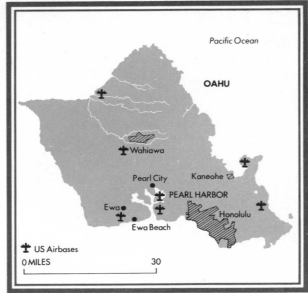

in all, reached Oahu shortly before 0800, whereupon the strike force divided into several attack groups. Fighters were deployed to destroy parked aircraft at Wheeler Field and Kanaohe, high-level bombers were sent over Hickam Field, and torpedo planes and dive-bombers flew over Battleship Row at Pearl Harbor. At 0750 Japanese pilots were ordered to attack, and shortly thereafter, all hell broke loose.

Thanks to last minute intelligence reports from Japanese operatives in Honolulu the night before the attack, the Japanese pilots knew precisely where to find their prey and lost little time in carrying out their mission of destruction. Within ten minutes two American battlewagons had been sunk and hundreds of sailors killed or injured; by 0830 90% of the damage of the attack had already been inflicted. American servicemen scrambled out of bed, away from the breakfast

the Japanese to attack the Philippine Islands rather than headquarters of the Pacific Fleet, and the only preparations against a surprise attack that were taken at all were initiated by Admiral Thomas C. Hart, commander of the Asiatic Fleet in Manila. The Hawaiian command remained unprepared for an attack until the very morning of 7 December 1941.

The Pacific Fleet had good reason to remain unprepared for a surprise attack, for the movement of Japan's strike force offered no clue as to its ultimate destination. In charting the course to Hawaii, great care had been taken to avoid normal shipping routes and land-based reconnaissance aircraft. Although this dictated passage through the northern Pacific with its foul weather, and necessitated refuelling at sea, Japan's fleet moved unmolested and undetected toward its target, arriving some 490 miles north off Oahu on the evening of 6 December 1941.

By 0600, on 7 December, the fleet had reached its flying-off position 275 miles north of Pearl Harbor at 0600 7 December 1941. Although it was still dark and the ships of the task force pitched badly in the swell, the first planes were aloft and on their way to Pearl Harbor before 0700. As Japan had anticipated, the entire American fleet, less four carriers, was in port and there were no indications that the command was expecting any action that day. However disappointed they might have been at the absence of the aircraft carriers, the commanders of the Japanese task force could hardly have asked for a more fortuitous situation.

The first wave of Japanese aircraft, some 190

Mitsubishi A6M5 Zero
Length: 29 ft. 8$\frac{11}{16}$ in.
Span: 39 ft. 4$\frac{7}{16}$ in.
Maximum speed: 331.5 m.p.h. at 14,930 ft. Range: 1675 miles. Armament: 2 × 7.7 mm., 2 × 20 mm., 2 × 60 kg. bombs. Weight: 6164 lbs. max.

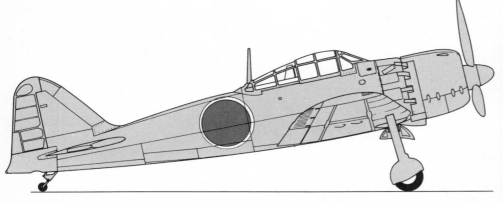

324

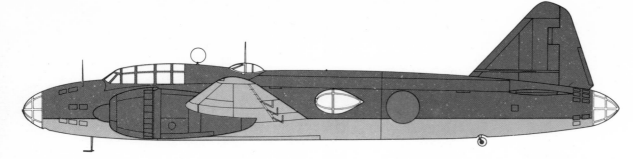

Mitsubishi G4MI. Length:
65 ft. 7$\frac{13}{32}$ in. Span:
82 ft. $\frac{1}{4}$ in. Maximum
speed: 266 m.p.h.
Armament: 4 × 7.7 mm.,
1 × 20 mm. Crew: 7.
Weight: 14,991 lbs. empty.

table, or out of church, but it was already too late to save the fleet.

Battleship Row was an easy target for Japanese bombardiers; the eight battlewagons of the fleet were moored to massive quays a short distance from the shore, completely unprotected against torpedo attack. The *Arizona* was attacked first and was torn apart by torpedo and bomb explosions within several minutes. Next, the *Oklahoma* was attacked and before 0800 a call to abandon ship was sounded. Within the next twenty-five minutes, five of the remaining battleships, *California*, *Maryland*, *Pennsylvania*, *Tennessee*, and *West Virginia*, were badly damaged or destroyed; only the *Nevada* managed to get under way before the end of the attack, and even she was hit by bombs and torpedoes. The Japanese attack force had accomplished its most important mission, the neutralization of the Pacific Fleet, in only thirty minutes, and had also inflicted heavy

Below: Most American planes were never able to take off.

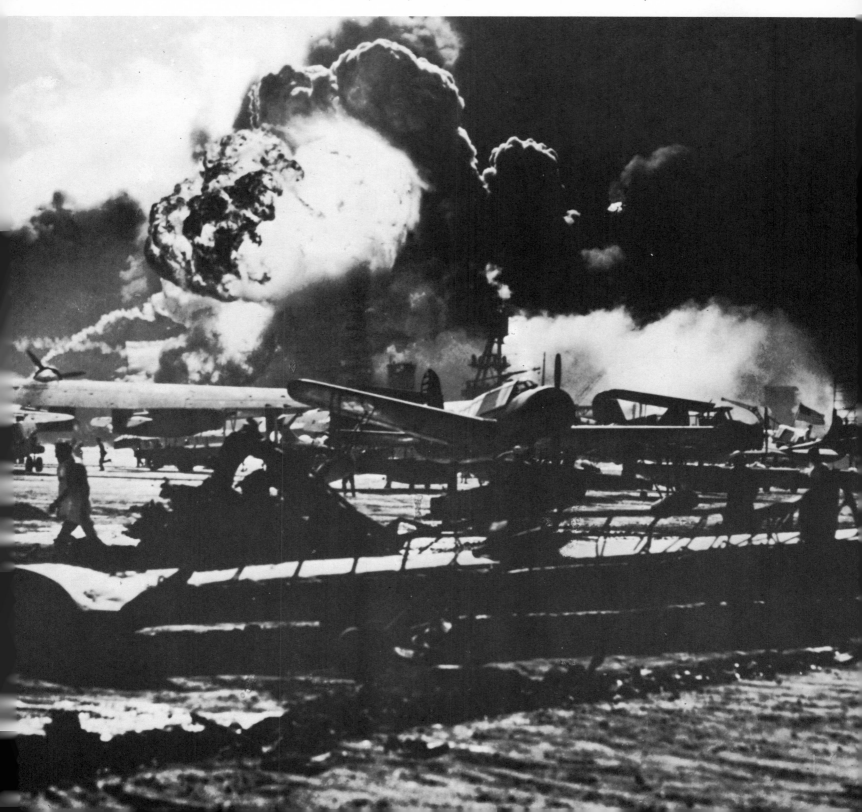

Above: Japanese invaders just before the attack on Luzon.

losses on American air units and installations. In short, the attack was a tactical success.

As morning wore on, the Japanese armada retreated and American officials surveyed the destruction wrought by their savage attack. In a little more than two hours, Japan had mauled the fleet, destroyed American air strength, and killed over two thousand men.

The Philippines Fall

News of the Japanese attack at Pearl Harbor reached the Philippines eight hours before Japanese forces invaded the Islands. Realizing that an attack was probably imminent, the senior military commanders, General Douglas Mac-Arthur and Admiral Thomas Hart, immediately alerted all units to prepare for action. Defensive preparations had already begun, thanks to a warning from the War Department on 27 November, but were still incomplete when news of the disaster at Pearl Harbor reached Manila at 0230 on 8 December (0830, 7 December, Hawaiian time); however one may feel about the abilities of MacArthur and Hart, there was nothing they could do to successfully defend the Philippines. For decades, critics of American colonial policy in Southeast Asia had warned of the difficulties of defending the Islands in the event of attack, but even as war approached Congress refused to appropriate enough money to allow for the establishment of an adequate insular force. The eight-hour notice of possible attack might just as well have come eight minutes before the strike; the battle for the archipelago was lost even before it was begun.

Japanese planes began their attack in the Philippines at 0530, 8 December 1941, sinking a sea plane tender off the coast of Mindanao. Six hours later, Formosa-based bombers attacked American bases on Luzon, destroying dozens of fighters and several B-17 bombers at Clark, Nichols, Iba, and other air fields near Manila. Although warnings were received at Army Air Force headquarters at least forty-five minutes before the attack, nothing was done to evacuate the aircraft before the Japanese reached Manila; Japanese pilots found their targets parked like sitting ducks on the runways and, with no anti-aircraft fire to distract them, proceeded to

Below: Admiral Thomas Hart.

Above left: Back to Bataan – the 4th Marines retreat to the peninsular redoubt. **Above:** Japanese tanks enter Manila after the American withdrawal. **Far left:** The Japanese close in on the beleaguered American perimeter. **Center left:** An anti-tank company holds the line at Bataan. **Left:** Thousands of American and Philippine troops were captured only to face the "Death March" to prison camp or death. **Far left:** The men on Corregidor resisted to the last. **Center left:** The Japanese breakthrough at Bataan forced the Americans back to the island of Corregidor.

Left: The Japanese land on Corregidor.

Right: From left to right: USS *West Virginia*, severely damaged; USS *Tennessee*, damaged; USS *Arizona*, sunk. **Far right:** The USS *California* settles slowly into the mud. **Below:** The battleship *Arizona* was the first to be attacked.

annihilate America's air force in the Philippines. Not only had the Far Eastern Air Force been destroyed just as the Pacific Fleet had been neutralized at Pearl Harbor, but the Asiatic Fleet, such as it was, was badly mauled and important dock and repair facilities in the port of Manila were destroyed.

Japanese forces were landed in northern Luzon (Aparri) on 10 December and in the following weeks additional forces were carried into other ports on the island. Without aerial or naval strength Admiral Hart could no nothing to stop these amphibious operations; the fleet at his disposal was too small even to harass them. With absolute control of the air over Luzon and complete superiority at sea, Japanese forces made rapid headway as the new year approached.

This hopeless situation gave American commanders little choice but to withdraw from Manila to safer quarters. On 21 December Navy command moved to Corregidor and on Christmas Eve General MacArthur was forced to withdraw his forces to the Bataan Peninsula under heavy bombardment. What remained of the Asiatic Fleet was sent to Java and preparations were made to evacuate the leaders of the Philippine Commonwealth to the United States.

By withdrawing to the Bataan Peninsula and Corregidor, MacArthur hoped to be able to hold out against Japan until reinforcements could be brought to Luzon. This proved impossible and although American forces and their Filipino comrades fought bravely, it was soon necessary to abandon even these fortresses. On 11 March 1942, MacArthur reluctantly left the Islands for

Australia, leaving General Jonathan Wainwright in command of army forces on Bataan. Wainwright held Bataan until 8 April when he finally had to evacuate to Corregidor. There the remnants of MacArthur's army and a few Marine units held out for another month but finally, on 6 May 1942, Wainwright surrendered Corregidor and all armed forces in the archipelago to the Japanese. America's inability to hold the Philippines had cost tens of thousands of lives and untold billions of dollars and was a disaster. Although MacArthur had vowed to return and liberate the Islands, it would take him nearly three years.

Malaya and Singapore are Occupied

On 8 December 1941 Japanese forces invaded British Malaya, crossing the Siamese frontier and landing at Kota Bahru. Unlike the Americans who were completely unprepared for the attack on Pearl Harbor, the British actually traced the movement of Japanese forces from Indochina to the Malay peninsula. Nevertheless, despite the fact that they had at least two days notice of the movement of men and ships from Saigon and Camranh Bay, they chose to wait and see what the Japanese would do before implementing their plans to defend Malaya and Singapore. This delay proved to be a tragic mistake.

Plans for the defense of Malaya and Singapore had been prepared years before, and relied on the ability of the Royal Navy and Air Force to repel any amphibious landings or assaults from the Siamese border. On paper and in the minds of

Below: The British C-in-C in Malaya, Sir Robert Brooke-Popham.

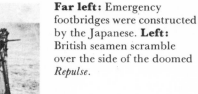

Far left: Emergency footbridges were constructed by the Japanese. **Left:** British seamen scramble over the side of the doomed *Repulse.*

Far left: Japanese troops mop up in Kuala Lumpur. **Left:** General Sir Archibald Wavell (left) took over command of the Allied Forces in the Southwest Pacific. Rear Admiral Thomas C. Hart (center) and Major-General George Brett, Deputy Supreme Commander (right) confer with Wavell.

Far left: HM ships *Prince of Wales* and *Repulse* after being hit by Japanese torpedos. A British destroyer moves off in the foreground. **Left:** The abject surrender of Singapore was a stain on British honor and a death blow to the Allied defense of Southeast Asia.

Left: Japanese troops march toward the Raffles statue in Singapore.

those who prepared the plan, there was no doubt that the British could defend their colony if the fleet was reinforced and adequate numbers of aircraft were despatched to bases in the colony. Unfortunately, when Japanese forces struck, British air strength was barely half that required by the plan and the fleet was hardly on a par with Japanese naval forces in the Pacific. Whether or not the British would have been able to hold the line against Japan with their forces at full strength will never be known; as it was, the Navy and the RAF could not hope to deter Japan's advance through Southeast Asia.

When the Japanese launched their attack, British forces in Malaya were commanded by Air Marshal Sir Robert Brooke-Popham. He based his defense of the colony on the assumption that the Japanese would make their main thrust across the Siamese frontier and, with this in mind, hoped to deploy British forces in a defensive line across the Kra Isthmus. With proper advance notice (at least thirty-six hours), additional forces could be sent across the border to capture the port towns of Singora and Patani before the enemy could land; at the very least, British forces could close the roads and railway lines between Singora and Jitra in Malaya, thus slowing if not stopping the Japanese advance. In any case, however, the British commander refused to close the Siamese ports or to implement the Jitra alternative until the Japanese first violated Siam's neutrality.

While one may sympathize with British unwillingness to be branded an aggressor, waiting for the Japanese to make the first move cost precious time which allowed them to gather too much momentum. By the time Brooke-Popham was ready to respond to Japanese violation of the frontier on 8 December it was already too late to close the ports or to employ the Jitra alternative effectively. British forces made a valiant attempt to hold the line in northern Malaya, but the Japanese were able to break through their line within four days of the initial attack, forcing them into hasty retreat.

Even more important than Brooke-Popham's failure to seize the initiative in northern Malaya was the destruction of the *Prince of Wales* and the *Repulse* on 10 December. Both battleships had joined the fleet 2 December and were being deployed under the command of Admiral Sir T. S. V. Phillips, Commander-in-Chief of the Eastern Fleet, when they were sunk after a two-hour bombardment by Japanese planes. The loss of these mainstays of the fleet sealed the fate of Malaya and Singapore as, without effective naval resistance, Japanese forces were moved ashore in large numbers where they quickly solidified Japan's hold on the peninsula and pushed south toward Singapore.

By mid-January 1942 the Japanese had reached the State of Johore and were preparing to attack Singapore. By this time command of British forces had been transferred to General Sir Archibald Wavell who hoped to be able to hold Jehore until he was strong enough to launch a counterattack, for unless Johore was successfully defended, Singapore would fall, and it would not be long before Japan invaded the Dutch East

Above: The Japanese victory parade after their conquest of the Philippines.

Below. The Japanese push through Malaya was devastating. **Below right:** The Japanese moved swiftly down the Malay Peninsula by bicycle.

Indies. This decision to make a stand in Johore and Singapore necessitated the rapid withdrawal of all British forces north of Kuala Lumpur, thus leaving the Japanese free to travel on the roads leading south. The latter were able to move much faster than their adversaries, and as a result were poised to attack Wavell's forces in Johore before the reinforcement from the north was complete.

On 8 February 1942 two Japanese divisions attempted to cross the straits from the mainland to Singapore in the dark of night. By the next morning, 13,000 Japanese troops were ashore, and there was little that could be done to save the city. Unlike Bataan and Corregidor, Singapore did not offer its defenders a position of natural strength or a fortress from which to resist the invaders; even the naval base could not be held since its defenses were useless against an attack from the mainland. Although British forces fought on for a week following the first Japanese crossing, their effort was in vain, and Singapore fell on 15 February 1942.

The Sun Sets on the British Empire

In less than three months the Japanese had occupied Malaya and were ready to complete their conquest of what remained of the colonial empires in Southeast Asia. Like the Americans,

Left: British surrender at Singapore. Below: British retreat through the jungles of Malaya.

the British had underestimated the capability of Japanese forces and had based their defense on obsolete principles and strategy. Assuming that Japan would be deterred by the presence of a strong American fleet in the Pacific, the British government did little to provide for an adequate defense of Malaya by bringing the fleet at Singapore up to full strength; thus, when the United States Pacific Fleet was destroyed at Pearl Harbor, all chances of successfully defending the empire were lost. The loss of Singapore shattered British prestige in Asia and, although she would avenge this loss some years later, Britain would never be able to re-establish her prewar position.

CHAPTER EIGHT
The Battle for Burma

The Japanese attack on Pearl Harbor shattered the illusion of neutrality which had characterized the diplomatic situation between Great Britain, the United States and Japan before 7 December 1941. With Japanese forces attacking the Philippines and Malaya, it would only be a matter of time before they crossed the Burmese border and preparations for defense were hastily begun. General Wavell, commander of British forces in Burma, believed that the colony could be defended with a minimum of outside aid, asking only that the Chinese commit one and one-half divisions to its defense and that lend-lease supplies destined for China be used in Burma if necessary.

For the Chinese, even more than for the British, the defense of Burma was absolutely vital. The closing of the Haiphong-Yunnan railroad soon after the Japanese occupation of Indochina in 1940–1 left the Burma Road as China's only link with the outside world. This road which wound its way some 750 miles from Lashio in Burma to Kunming in China, was literally China's jugular vein; if the Japanese succeeded in closing it, her ability to resist would be greatly diminished. Chiang Kai-shek, therefore, was willing to do anything that might facilitate the defense of Burma, though for the moment, the British did not call for his assistance.

Rangoon Falls to Japan

The Japanese launched their first raid on Rangoon on 23 December 1941, expecting no resistance over the city, and retreated quickly when units of the Royal Air Force and the American Volunteer Group (Flying Tigers) at-tempted to block their path. Nevertheless, the raid was costly to the combined British-American force for, although they managed to wreck at least ten Japanese aircraft, the defenders lost nine of their own planes; this was a loss of major proportions since the British and their American allies only had fifty-seven planes at their disposal, thirty-six of which were antiquated and hardly suitable for combat against modern Japanese fighters.

More important, perhaps, than the loss of nine planes was the effect of the bombing on the people of Rangoon. Fires raged throughout the city, thousands were killed or wounded, and many shorefront warehouses were damaged or destroyed. Although British volunteers cleaned up efficiently and attended to the needs of the injured, they could not prevent the exodus of Burmese and Indian coolies to the countryside; by Christmas 1941, all activities in the city had ground to a halt, resulting in shortages of fuels and other essentials, and martial law had to be imposed to prevent looting and rioting. As Japanese raids continued the main railroad station was knocked out, lend-lease equipment was destroyed in warehouses along the waterfront, and thousands more Burmese and Indians fled the city. By 1 January 1942, the devastation of Rangoon was virtually complete.

On 20 January 1942, after almost a month of bombing raids against Rangoon and other sites, Japanese forces crossed the Thai border into southern Burma, their purpose being to cut the link between Rangoon and Kunming. Moving straight across country they easily defeated the

Left: The Japanese move swiftly through Burma. **Right:** Japanese bombs and the British scorched earth policy reduced most of Rangoon to rubble.

British, Burmese and Indian troops in their path; on 23 February, Japanese forces ambushed Indian forces near the Sittang Bridge, crossed the Sittang River, moved past Pegu, and turned south toward Rangoon. The city was now seriously threatened and AMMISCA personnel prepared to move lend-lease supplies northward or destroy them at the docks and warehouses so that they would not fall into Japanese hands. As the Japanese moved toward the city, goods were moved out at a rate of a thousand tons per day, but even at this accelerated rate of shipment there was not enough time to move all the lend-lease supplies north to China. Much of the equipment was either given to British forces or destroyed, but when the Japanese captured Rangoon on 6 March 1942, they still found almost 20,000 tons of lend-lease supplies intact in warehouses.

The fury and rapidity of the Japanese advance into Burma far exceeded anything that its defenders had anticipated. As the Japanese drew near to Rangoon, Wavell hastily requested the additional aid from China that he had refused at the beginning of February. Despite the ill will between the Chinese and the British which had resulted from Wavell's original rebuff. Chiang Kai-shek responded to his later request and Chinese forces began to move across the Sino-Burmese border on 28 February.

Shortly after the Japanese captured Rangoon, Chinese forces were massed in Toungoo and points north while British and Indian units were concentrated in Mandalay, Prome, and Yenangyaung. Wavell hoped to hold those cities and cut the road from Rangoon to Mandalay; if the Japanese could be held south of Prome and Toungoo, the oil fields at Yenangyaung which were China's major source of crude oil would be protected and a new road could be built from Assam to Burma linking the Indian ports of Calcutta and Chittaging to Yunnan province. Once the new road was completed, lend-lease supplies would once again be funnelled into China.

The Allies Retreat

After taking Rangoon, Japanese forces moved northward along the Sittang and Irrawaddy rivers toward Prome and Toungoo. As they moved north, they were harassed by RAF and AVG pilots flying out of a base at Magwe, some 200 miles north of Rangoon, but a series of massive raids against the installation on 27 March by some 200 bombers forced its abandonment. The RAF retreated into India while the AVG moved north into China; Allied air strength in Burma had been almost totally destroyed, leaving the Japanese in complete control of the skies over southern Burma. The loss of air cover and the absence of adequate aerial reconnaissance left the British and Chinese easy prey for the Japanese who had secured information about Allied troop movements from Burmese nationalists.

The Japanese began their attack at Toungoo on 19 March and took the city within a week. As they prepared to march north from their new stronghold, General Joseph Stilwell, Commander-in-Chief of American forces in the China-Burma-India theater and Wavell's lieutenant in the

Top: A living bridge in the Burmese jungle. **Far left above:** Japanese armor met little effective Allied resistance. **Far left:** Banzai! Japanese victory in Burma was complete. **Left:** Burmese women give water to their new masters.

defense of Burma, sought to persuade the Chinese forces in the area to mount a counterattack. Failing in this, he persuaded British commanders to take up the idea, with disastrous results. The Japanese easily routed the few forces the British has mustered in the area, and moved on immediately to take the city of Prome.

Japanese victories at Toungoo and Prome checked the Allied plan to cut the Rangoon-Mandalay road, and soon they were advancing northward, threatening Yenangyaung, Mandalay and Lashio. As total victory became an increasing reality, steps were taken to evacuate these important centres; the British prepared to destroy all stores, equipment and supplies which might be of use, including the oil rigs and depots at Yenangyaung.

Lashio, the southern terminus of the Burma Road, fell to the Japanese on 29 April 1942 along with 44,000 tons of lend-lease supplies destined for China. With the closing of the Burma Road, the only land routes open to China were the old silk highway across Sinkiang province from Russia and the ancient caravan trails across the Himalayas and through Tibet from India, neither of which were much use for transporting large quantities of goods and supplies. To reach the borders of Sinkiang, American and British supplies would have to be moved through crowded Russian ports and over the inadequate and over-burdened Russian railroads for thousands of miles, after which they would have to be transferred to trucks and pack animals and moved thousands of miles more to the war front in China. The caravan trails through Tibet offered a much shorter route but only pack animals could negotiate the mountain trails; the trip was slow, and heavy equipment could not be carried. Thus, the fall of Lashio represented a crushing blow to the Chinese from which they might never have recovered were it not for the establishment of the air lift over the Hump. At the time the loss of the Burma Road seriously hampered all Allied operations in China and Burma.

The 'Flying Tigers'

With the fall of Lashio, Allied forces retreated rapidly toward China. During this retreat, the American Volunteer Group played an important role. AVG planes flying from bases in China were the allies' only source of reconnaissance and intelligence and its pilots provided valuable air cover for the retreating Chinese and British armies. The men of the AVG also prevented a Japanese advance from Burma into Yunnan by destroying the northern portion of the Burma Road and many of the bridges across the Salween River.

AVG reconnaissance missions were inaugurated in March 1942. Although the pilots in the group disliked such missions, considering them a waste of resources, the switch from combat missions to patrol and reconnaissance was dictated by shortages of fuel and equipment; since Chennault's mercenaries had no bombers at their disposal, they could not undertake offensive raids against Japanese bases in Thailand or Indochina. In the lull between battles AVG pilots were assigned to patrol missions, but as the retreat of Allied forces

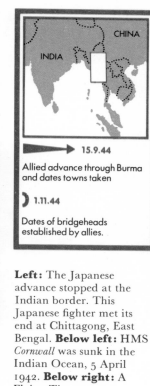

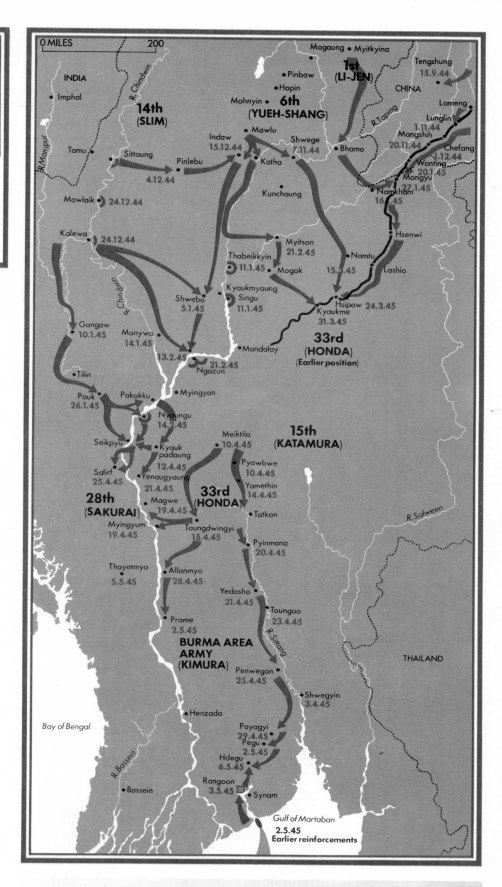

Left: The Japanese advance stopped at the Indian border. This Japanese fighter met its end at Chittagong, East Bengal. Below left: HMS *Cornwall* was sunk in the Indian Ocean, 5 April 1942. Below right: A Flying Tiger.

Map legend

→ 15.9.44

Allied advance through Burma and dates towns taken

◗ 1.11.44

Dates of bridgeheads established by allies.

Map labels

INDIA

CHINA

0 MILES 200

Imphal
Tamu
R. Manipur
R. Chindwin
14th (SLIM)
Sittaung
Pinlebu 4.12.44
Mawlaik 24.12.44
Kalewa 24.12.44
Gangaw 10.1.45
Monywa 14.1.45
Tilin
Pauk 26.1.45
Pakokku
Myingyan
Nyaungu 14.2.45
13.2.45
Ngazun 21.2.45
Seikpyu
Kyauk padaung 12.4.45
Salirf 25.4.45
Yenaugyaung 21.4.45
28th (SAKURAI)
Myingyum 19.4.45
Magwe 19.4.45
Thayetmyo 5.5.45
Allanmyo 28.4.45
Taungdwingyi 15.4.45
Prome 2.5.45
BURMA AREA ARMY (KIMURA)
Henzada
Bay of Bengal
R. Bassein
Bassein
Shwebo 5.1.45
Indaw 15.12.44
Mawlu
Katha
Kunchaung
Kyaukmyaung 11.1.45
Singu 11.1.45
Thabeikkyin 11.1.45
Myitson 21.2.45
Mogok 15.3.45
Mandalay
Mohnyin
6th (YUEH-SHANG)
Pinbaw
Hopin
Mogaung • Myitkyina
1st (LI-JEN)
Tengshung 15.9.44
CHINA
Lameng
Lunglin 1.11.44
Bhamo
Shwege 7.11.44
Namtu
Lashio
Hsenwi
Namkham 16.1.45
Mangshih 20.11.44
Wanting 1.12.44
Mongyu 20.1.45
27.1.45
Chefang
Hsipaw 24.3.45
Kyaukme 31.3.45
33rd (HONDA) (Earlier position)
R. Taping
R. Salween
15th (KATAMURA)
Meiktila 10.4.45
Pyawbwe 10.4.45
Yamethin 14.4.45
Tatkon
33rd (HONDA)
Pyinmana 20.4.45
Yedasho 21.4.45
Toungoo 23.4.45
R. Sittang
THAILAND
Penwegon 25.4.45
Shwegyin 3.4.45
Payagyi 29.4.45
Pegu 2.5.45
Hdegu 6.5.45
Rangoon 3.5.45
Synam
Gulf of Martaban
2.5.45 Earlier reinforcements

toward the Chinese border was stepped up, AVG pilots resumed limited combat activities.

The Allied evacuation to China necessitated the destruction of bases and supplies in Burma; in order to prevent the Japanese from crossing the Salween into China, the bridges across the river and roads leading to these crossings had also to be destroyed. Strafing and bombing raids carried out against the advancing Japanese armies were equally important, and optimum use was made of the limited number of planes left in the AVG.

To maximize the use of available aircraft and minimize equipment losses, AVG units were scattered over several bases in China; strikes against the Japanese were launched from many bases and planes were never immediately returned to the base from which they had taken off. Thus the Japanese were kept off balance by the group's total mobility and consistently overestimated the numbers of planes available to their enemies. Undoubtedly, had they realized the real strength of the AVG, they would have taken even bolder steps in the Burma campaign.

In retrospect, the performance of the American Volunteer Group in Burma was impressive. Despite shortages in supplies and equipment, failing morale, and the deteriorating situation of the allies in Burma, the men of the group performed bravely and as effectively as circumstances permitted. Nevertheless, by the end of April, Japanese forces reached the Salween River, completing their occupation of Burma.

The rôle of Burmese nationalism

The speed of the Japanese conquest in Burma and the ease with which they rallied to their banners indicated the weakness of the British colonial system. British efforts to persuade nationalist leaders to resist Japan failed dismally because these men saw little profit in remaining true to their colonial masters; the failure of the British to promise independence in return for active Burmese participation against Japan insured that such cooperation would not be forthcoming. In contrast, the Japanese held out the prospect of independence and participation as equal members in the Greater East Asia Co-Prosperity Sphere, and these promises of a better tomorrow were enough to win the support of most Burmese leaders.

Right: Airdrop to guerrilla teams in southeast China.

The successful occupation of Burma was the result of a period of several decades during which the Japanese assiduously cultivated their interest and image in the country. Capitalizing on their victory over Russia in 1905, Japan attempted to make a psychological impact on all the peoples of Asia including the Burmese and, although such efforts were subdued until the 1930's, there can be little doubt that pro-Japanese sympathizers had increased markedly in the area. In Burma, interest in things Japanese grew steadily until by 1930, when the Japanese government consciously sought to increase its influence in Burma, there was already a small but influential group of Burmese Japanophiles.

To facilitate expanded Japanese activities in Burma, particularly contacts with the nationalist movement, several Japanese military and civilian officials were dispatched to the colony. Among them was Colonel Suzuki Keiji, a man who soon became the chief of Japanese cadres operating in Burma. He was to establish contacts with anti-colonial elements and help them to equip and train a nationalist army which might later support Japanese action in Burma. As a result of his efforts, several dozen young nationalist leaders were sent to Japan where they were trained in the art of warfare; upon their return to Burma, these men formed the nucleus of the Burma Independence Army which fought with the Japanese against Britain from December 1941–May 1942.

Participation of the Burma Independence Army in the Japanese invasion and occupation of Burma transformed what might have simply been an exchange of one colonial master for another into a liberation campaign, and Burma welcomed the Japanese, seriously believing in their willingness to die for her freedom. Swept off their feet by the speed of Japanese victories, all segments of Burmese society welcomed the Japanese invaders.

This enthusiasm also benefited the nationalist movement, which was able to mobilize a large segment of the population as a result of Japan's victories against the colonial regime. Operating under the protective umbrella of the Japanese army, the leaders of the Burma Independence Army established their authority in the villages and hamlets. For the first time in fifty years,

Headquarters, 14th Air Force, China. Chinese and Americans load bombs.

foreigners did not rule the country, though the period in which the BIA operated independently was to be very short.

Despite the eagerness of Burmese nationalists to declare the establishment of independence and self-rule, Japanese military authorities refused to sanction any such move. Independence was to be postponed for at least a year; a military administration would govern the country, re-establish law and order, and define the new administrative apparatus which would govern the country until independence was granted. Japan did not pledge independence until 1 August 1943, and even after this formality Burmese independence was more imaginary than real.

Realities of life Under the Occupation

Japanese influence and prestige, at its high point during the first days of the occupation, declined steadily thereafter, for the reality of Japanese rule proved to be far different from the benefits Burma had expected to derive from their presence. Although most Burmese had refused to see Japanese shortcomings prior to the invasion, the severity and brutality of their conduct was soon manifestly clear to all. Understanding little about the character and traditions of the Burman majority and other ethnic groups, the Japanese tried to remold them in their image, under-

taking a moral conversion that was doomed to failure. Pan-Asianism could not bridge the important differences between their cultures and habits; the Japanese, with little regard for Burmese traditional values, mistakenly assumed that Burma was ready to adopt Japanese culture, and when it did not, responded with brutality.

Burmese hopes for equality within the Great East Asia Co-Prosperity Sphere were never realized. Having come to expect inferior treatment and racist attitudes from the British, the Burmese nationalists looked for better treatment from the Japanese, especially since much of their propaganda in the prewar period had been based on the promise that they would treat other Asian peoples with dignity and equality. The reality proved altogether different and soon, repelled by the frequently boorish, patronizing and uncivil attitude of Japanese officers in Burma, even the most ardent Japanophiles recognized the ill treatment they were receiving from the occupiers. Ultimately the Japanese lost considerable support in Burma as a result of their lack of sensitivity and appreciation of the indigenous culture. Their expectation of 'filial piety' from other Asians was never realized because these people soon learned that Japanese interests and their own did not coincide. The Japanese conquest began the drive forward to independence in Burma.

Below: An American mechanic introduces Chinese recruits to the P-40.

CHAPTER NINE
Stalemate in China

By the time of the German invasion of Poland in September 1939, the Sino-Japanese War had become a stalemate. Although the Nationalist armies had been depleted in the first months of the war, the Japanese were unable to force Chiang Kai-shek and his lieutenants to surrender. Ensconced in their southwest retreat, the Chinese Nationalists stubbornly resisted all Japanese offers of appeasement and negotiation, and it seemed that neither diplomacy nor warfare could settle the China Incident.

With the advent of war in Europe, the situation worsened for Chiang Kai-shek. What little aid had been forthcoming from the Soviet Union ceased while the British and French, fearful of Japanese retaliation against their colonial empires in Asia, went out of their way to avoid provoking a conflict. Translated into specific terms, both colonial powers agreed, under threat of force, to close the lifelines from Free China to the outside world, namely the Haiphong-Yunnan railroad and the Burma Road. Although the British later re-opened the Burma Road, the situation after 1939 was far more critical for the Chinese than it had been in the two preceding years. Were it not for belated assistance from the United States in 1941, the Chinese Nationalist regime might have succumbed to Japan; even this aid was of a marginal nature, limited to surplus weaponry and equipment and tacit American support from Claire Chennault's Flying Tigers, a unit of American volunteer airmen and mechanics.

The Japanese attack on Pearl Harbor changed the nature of the war in China. For the first time in four years, China had allies. Within days after the Japanese attacks on Pearl Harbor, Malaya, and the Philippines, the Allied powers, of which China was now one, established the China-Burma-India theater of war and designated Chiang Kai-shek as supreme commander of the war effort in China. Optimism replaced pessimism in Chungking as the Chinese Nationalists looked forward to taking revenge.

The Allies enter the war in China

At first the creation of the China-Burma-India theater and the designation of Chiang Kai-shek as the commander of Allied forces in China solved few problems and actually created additional headaches for the Chinese and their American allies. From the beginning in January 1942, the two sides pursued contradictory courses which resulted in hostility, recriminations, and a legacy of bitterness and frustration. The Chinese wished

China to be the major theater of war against Japan, while the United States and Great Britain had other ideas, seeing China only as a holding action, a second priority sideshow. To complicate matters further, personalities in the CBI clashed even more than policies, contributing to the near collapse of the alliance. Nowhere was this more clearly illustrated than in the relationship between Chiang, the commander of Allied forces in China, and his lieutenant and chief-of-staff, General Joseph Stilwell, United States Army.

General Stilwell was despatched to China on 5 January 1942, charged with the command of American forces in the CBI and the reorganization of Chinese forces. A one-time military attache in Peking and fluent in Chinese, General Stilwell could have been an effective liaison between China and the United States. Although his superiors knew that he was not a diplomat, they hoped that his knowledge of China and the Chinese might enable him to rally dissident political factions and increase the capability and efficiency of the Chinese army. Unfortunately, this was not to be the case.

His experience in China had made Stilwell distrustful of the leadership of the Kuomintang, and he insisted that Chiang give him *carte blanche* as his chief-of-staff to reorganize Chinese forces. This the Generalissimo refused to do for, although he appreciated the need for a strong, effective army, he feared the political repercussions that a reorganization was likely to yield. Above all, Chiang wished to preserve his command intact and hold his forces in reserve for the postwar battle with the Chinese communists which he believed was inevitable. Thus it was necessary to negate Stilwell's schemes, particularly the re-organization of the army and its commitment in a second Burma compaign.

Had it not been for the presence of another American officer in China, General Claire Chennault, Chiang might have been forced to accommodate his chief of staff. Chennault, however, provided him with an alternative by his very presence and strong advocacy of an aerial strategy, which required little commitment of Chinese manpower and promised fast and cheap results. The Chennault plan, needless to say, was far more attractive than Stilwell's proposals; more important Chennault, who shared the Generalissimo's dislike of Stilwell, was successful in winning Chiang's personal approval.

The substance of Chennault's proposal, which was advanced by Chiang to President Roosevelt

Opposite top: Curtiss P-40s of the Flying Tigers attack enemy positions in South China.
Opposite bottom: Anti-British cartoon depicts the Indian nationalists driving out a defeated Churchill.

later in the war, was outlined in a series of memoranda from Chennault to Stilwell in the fall of 1942. Shortly after assuming command of the China Air Task Force, on 16 September, Chennault submitted a statement outlining his views on the potential of China-based air power. His objectives for the CATF were sixfold: (1) to protect the air supply route over the Hump; (2) to destroy Japanese aircraft in China in large numbers; (3) to damage and destroy Japanese military and naval bases in China and encourage Chinese resistance; (4) to disrupt Japanese shipping along the Yangtze and Yellow rivers and the China coast; (5) to damage Japanese bases in Thailand, Indochina, Burma, and Formosa and to interest Japanese air concentrations being ferried from Chinese bases across Indochina and Thailand to Burma; (6) to destroy the efficacy and morale of the Japanese air force by destroying rear depots and aircraft production facilities in Japan. To accomplish these ends, Chennault requested additional aircraft, operational independence, and an increased share of supplies flown over the Hump.

Vinegar Joe's Response
Stilwell responded less than enthusiastically to Chennault's proposals. Although he was not

opposed to the aggressive spirit of Chennault's memo, Stilwell urged moderation in light of shortages of equipment and problems of supply. Chennault's plan, according to Stilwell, went well beyond the capability of his tiny force; to bring it within the realm of possibility would require equipment and supplies which could not be obtained at the time, given priorities in the CBI and the capacity of the air lift from India to China. Stilwell refused to release the supplies necessary for the scheme and rejected Chennault's proposal to separate the CATF from the 10th Army Air Force Command in Delhi.

Chennault never accepted Stilwell's reservations about the potential of air power in China and lost no opportunity to criticize his military judgement. In a letter to Roosevelt, dated 8 October 1942, Chennault presented his case against Stilwell directly to the commander-in-chief, maintaining that Japan could be defeated by effective use of air power and requesting authority to build and command an enlarged and independent air force in China. This, Chennault predicted, would bring about an early victory.

If his objectives were to be reached, Chennault deemed it essential that he have complete freedom of action and direct access to Chiang Kai-shek and the Chinese government. The military task of defeating Japan was a simple one which had been complicated by an unwieldy and illogical military organization and men who did not understand aerial warfare and its potential. At the end of his note, Chennault summed up his plan:

'Japan must hold Hongkong, Shanghai, and the Yangtze valley. They are essential to hold Japan itself. I can force the Japanese to fight in the defense of these objectives and I am confident that I can destroy Japanese aircraft at the rate of between ten and twenty to one. . . . My air force can burn up Japan's main industrial areas and Japan will be unable to supply her armies in her newly conquered empire in China, Malaya, and the Dutch East Indies with the munitions of war. The road then is open for the Chinese army in China, for the American navy in the Pacific, and for MacArthur to advance from his Australian stronghold all with comparatively slight cost.

My entire above plan is simple, it has been long thought out. I have spent five years developing an air warning network and radio command service to fight this way. I have no doubt of my success.'

Disagreement between Chungking and Washington
Roosevelt received Chennault's proposal enthusiastically and passed it along to the Department of War for consideration. The circulation of the letter at the Pentagon caused a major military scandal. It was already well known that Chennault and Stilwell disagreed over questions of strategy in the CBI, particularly regarding Stilwell's plan for a land invasion of Burma, but Chennault's note revealed the depth of their differences and forced Stilwell's supporters to respond immediately to Chennault's scheme lest the President agree.

In general, military leaders at the Pentagon reacted cooly to Chennault's air plan. General Arnold, head of the Army Air Force, informed General Marshall, Chief of Staff of the United

Below: Lieutenant-General Hap Arnold inspects P-40's with Chennault.

Left: From left to right:
Field Marshall Sir John
Dill, Chennault, Arnold,
Vinegar Joe Stilwell and
Clayton L. Bissell visit
Flying Tiger headquarters
in Chungking.

States Army, that he was opposed to seeing the China Air Task Force turned into an independent air force under Chennault and dismissed the plan as unrealistic because of the logistical problem of supplying such an operation. Although Arnold was willing to concede that Chennault was an excellent tactician, he agreed with Stilwell that Chennault did not understand the logistics of supply and recommended, therefore, that the CATF be kept under the command of the 10th Air Force in India.

Marshall shared Arnold's view and discussed his reservations about the plan with Roosevelt in December 1942. By that time, however, Roosevelt was leaning increasingly toward Chennault's position and informed Marshall that he believed that Chennault should receive an independent command in China and that he should be immediately given a force of one hundred planes with which to begin the bombing of Japanese military bases and shipping in China. If for no other reason than for its psychological effect on the Japanese, the President favored Chennault's aerial strategy.

Roosevelt's increasing tendency toward implementation of Chennault's plan reflected the tremendous influence of the China Lobby in Washington. This group, which included in its inner circle such presidential intimates as Harry Hopkins, Henry Wallace, and Lauchlin Curry, consistently promoted the scheme and presented Roosevelt with regular appreciative evaluations of the man himself. Although Stilwell had considerable support from General Marshall and other military leaders, his stock at the White House steadily declined and he and his supporters were placed on the defensive, attempting to justify their policies in the face of increasing criticism from Chennault's proponents and the press.

In part, Stilwell's problem reflected the difficulty of his mission, for his assignment was undoubtedly the most delicate diplomatic mission thrust on a professional soldier during the war. Stilwell served in several roles in China, being at one and the same time commanding general of American forces in the CBI theater, Chief-of-Staff of the Chinese army, director of the lend-lease program in China, and American representative to the Southeast Asia Command. Such a multiplicity of duties doomed Stilwell from the outset but most disastrous of all was his position as Chiang Kai-shek's Chief-of-Staff.

Stilwell was not the sort of man the Chinese situation required. He had difficulty in handling other nationalities tactfully and could not cope with the overwhelming political problems he faced in China. Had his been solely a military command, he might have been successful, but he was not as much a strategist as a diplomat, and his temperament was not suited to the role.

When Chennault proposed his air plan in September 1942, Chiang Kai-shek quickly became its principle adherent. In a cable to Roosevelt on 9 January 1943, the Generalissimo expressed his support in the following manner:

'The remarkable potentialities of an air offensive in China have already been demonstrated by a small and ill-supported force. I believe that an early air offensive is feasible, since, owing to the peculiar tactical conditions which prevail here, neither the supply, material, and personnel requirements are such as to embarrass the United Nations air efforts elsewhere. The return, I predict, will be out of proportion to the investment, and by further weakening the Japanese air arm and striking at the seaborne communications with their new conquests, an air offensive in China will directly prepare for the ultimate offensive we are looking for.'

In the same cable, Chiang expressed his reservations about Stilwell's plan for an invasion of Burma to reopen the Burma Road and announced his unwillingness, at that time, to commit large numbers of Chinese troops to the effort.

As might have been expected, Stilwell did not accept Chiang's position without protest, but mounted a propaganda campaign of his own through his associates at the Pentagon. He suggested to Marshall that if Chiang did not accede to his demands voluntarily, a *quid pro quo* policy toward the Generalissimo should be adopted and military aid to the Chinese withheld until Chiang agreed to cooperate. It was Stilwell's belief that China's total dependence on the United States gave the latter sufficient leverage to force the Kuomintang into accepting his views, views which were shared by most high ranking officers at the Pentagon.

Stilwell firmly believed that strong-arm tactics were the only way of dealing with the Chinese, and in his notes to Marshall, he repeated this view many times. Logic, reason, and persuasion would do no good. Pressure was the only effective technique in dealing with the Generalissimo. 'In dealing with him,' said Stilwell, 'we should exact a commitment for everything we do.' This view was shared by other American officers in China but, unfortunately for Stilwell, not by the president's intimates in the White House.

Stilwell's *quid pro quo* policy was pursued with a tactlessness which eventually cost him his position. His acid comments on Chiang Kai-shek and his

government, which were as well known in Chungking as at the Pentagon, aroused an emotional reaction from the Kuomintang which destroyed any remaining influence Stilwell had at the White House where Roosevelt's advisers were openly critical of him and suggested his recall. Whatever good will existed between him and the generalissimo evaporated in the debate over Chennault's plan. Chiang had little trouble in making Stilwell position untenable, particularly in so far as Roosevelt had refused to agree to the *quid pro quo* formula. Turning his nearly total dependence on the United States into a position of political strength by taking advantage of the important role that Roosevelt had assigned to China in the defeat of Japan, Chiang Kai-shek used his diplomatic talents to persuade Roosevelt to support Chennault's proposal and increase aid.

The arguments continue

President Roosevelt ultimately accepted Chiang Kai-shek's suggestion that Chennault be given an augmented force and an independent command in China. In March 1943, he decided to overrule his military advisers and prepared a cable to the generalissimo announcing his intention to place Chennault in command of a new air unit in China. In explaining his decision to General Marshall, Roosevelt pointed out that Stilwell did not fully appreciate the potential of air power in China or Chiang's commitment to the Chennault plan. Moreover, in so far as the maintenance of good Sino-American relations was involved,

Opposite: The Burma Road was the lifeline of the Nationalist China until 1942, when Japan seized Lashio. **Above:** After the Burma Road was cut, the only link between India and China was by air. Here British and Indian troops load supplies to be carried "over the Hump".

Roosevelt felt that he had no choice but to submit to Chiang's request. At the same time, he warned Marshall that Stilwell was using the wrong approach in dealing with the generalissimo and might have to be removed if he continued to treat Chiang as one might the Sultan of Morocco.

Chennault was promoted to the rank of major-general on 3 March 1943 and placed in command of the newly created 14th Army Air Force, formerly the CATF, on 11 March. According to the President's instructions, he was to be given complete control over all aerial operations in China; Stilwell was informed that he was not to interfere with Chennault in any manner that was likely to anger Chiang Kai-shek. Although Stilwell was to continue to direct the air ferry over the Hump, he was to allocate sufficient tonnage to Chennault to facilitate his operations while, at the same time, leaving enough free for land operations in China and Burma.

At the request of Chiang Kai-shek and General Marshall, Chennault and Stilwell were summoned to Washington in April 1943 to present their proposals to the Allied leaders assembled for the Trident Conference. Chennault presented his case on 30 April, Stilwell on 1 May. Roosevelt reacted positively to Chennault but postponed a final decision until he had heard Stilwell's objections. At this meeting, Stilwell outlined his objections to Chennault's plan, his methods of operation, and Chiang Kai-shek's failure to honor his commitments.

Stilwell did not deny that opportunities for aerial attacks on Japanese bases and shipping were real nor that the results of such attacks would be impressive. He did fear, however, that once Chennault's attacks proved sufficiently damaging, the Japanese would launch a major attack against the bases of the 14th Air Force. Unlike Chennault, Stilwell was not optimistic about the ability of the Chinese army to stop this advance. Should Chinese resistance falter, the Japanese would surely push on to Kunming and Chungking would be left virtually defenseless. Only a well trained and equipped land force could hold these centers; the Chinese did not constitute such a force. This being the case, Stilwell suggested that the first priority in China should be the reorganization of the Chinese army followed by an offensive to reopen the Burma Road. Only after these two goals were achieved would Chennault's plan become feasible.

Stilwell then told Roosevelt that reorganization of the Chinese army could not be completed until Chiang Kai-shek agreed to cooperate. He suggested that the president remind Chiang of the

reason for the American presence in China and of his agreement to furnish manpower and accept assistance in training these men. He also suggested that Chiang be requested to use regular military channels in dealing with American forces in China; this would mean that in dealing with Chennault, Chiang could not bypass Stilwell's command, nor would Chennault be allowed to willfully bypass his superiors and disobey orders. Above all, Stilwell believed, as he had consistently stated in the past, that Roosevelt must use a strong hand in dealing with the Generalissimo. As he put it to the President:

'The only short-cut to Japan is through China. The Chinese know this and are disposed to extract from the situation every possible advantage. Unless we are prepared to accept infinite delay, they must be held to their commitments as fully as we are holding ourselves to ours.'

The President makes his decision

Having listened to the arguments, Roosevelt decided in favor of Chennault's proposal for an aerial offensive against Japan. In making this decision, the President was influenced by both political and military factors, overruling the objections of his military advisers because he believed it promised a quick victory over Japan. Stilwell's plan to reoccupy Burma, on the other hand, would require a major commitment of American, British, and Chinese manpower and take considerably longer to execute. Since the British did not view the liberation of Burma as a matter of high priority and Chiang Kai-shek was unwilling to commit his forces to such a campaign unless the other allies did the same, Roosevelt dismissed Stilwell's plan as impractical.

Politically, the President felt bound to support Chiang Kai-shek, and placated the Generalissimo by supporting Chennault. Once again, fear that the Chinese might pull out of the war and make a separate peace with Japan prevailed over reason and logic. Since the War Department wished, above all, to keep China in the war, even Chennault's critics at the Pentagon recognized that Roosevelt had little alternative other than to accept the Chennault plan if only to bolster the morale of the Chungking regime.

As might have been expected, Chennault and the Chinese hailed Roosevelt's decision while Stilwell and Marshall decried it. Unfortunately the promises made so freely could not be fulfilled, resulting in increased tension between Chennault and Stilwell, Chiang and Roosevelt. As Stilwell put it, 'it was fatal to promise anything.'

CHAPTER TEN

Chess in the Desert: The Desert War 1940-1943

The Italian government entered the war on 10 June 1940. Although Mussolini's belated decision to join Hitler presented no additional danger to the Allied position in Europe, which had already collapsed, it did pose an immediate threat to Britain's position in Africa and the Mediterranean. The British garrison in Egypt was small and there was little possibility that reinforcements could be sent, given the disaster that had recently befallen British forces in France. With an Italian force of half a million men facing them across the Libyan frontier, the British garrison of 50,000 in Egypt hardly appeared capable of defending Suez against the Axis. In addition, Italy's participation in the war closed the sea route through the Mediterranean to Alexandria; supplies and reinforcements had to be sent via the Cape of Good Hope into the Red Sea, a long and circuitous route which added to the difficulty of maintaining an efficient supply operation.

British forces in the Middle East were commanded by General Sir Archibald Wavell. Rather than wait for the Italians to strike the first blow, he was determined to take the offensive and waited only four days after Italy's entry into the war to move against Italian border positions in Cyrenaica. On 14 June 1940 British forces struck at Fort Capuzzo, capturing this border post in one day but abandoning it the next. Thus began a series of raids across the border which lasted for over a month and netted some 3500 Italian casualties at a cost of only slightly more than 150 men to the British.

After a month of successful raids against their installations, the Italians moved cautiously across the western desert toward the British position at Mersa Matruh. On 13 September they captured Sidi Barrani where they established a chain of fortified camps; in the following weeks, however, they made no effort to push on to Mersa Matruh, allowing Wavell to bring in reinforcements which had been rushed to North Africa on Churchill's orders. Strengthened by the arrival of these reinforcements, which included three armored regiments, Wavell again decided to take the offensive.

Wavell's offensive was an unmitigated triumph and almost led to the destruction of the Italian army and the collapse of Italy's position in North Africa. Although British forces were outnumbered by more than two to one, and by three to one in tank power, they succeeded in thoroughly mauling their adversaries and inflicting heavy losses in manpower and equipment. The speed and ease with which the Italians were pushed back

Opposite: Italian troops move forward into the fray.
Above and overleaf: Masses of Italian prisoners march back, in some cases guarded by only one soldier.
Right: Benito Mussolini commanded over a half million troops in Libya.

surprised the British command which, unfortunately, had made no provisions for a sustained offensive and lost the opportunity to obtain an overwhelming victory. Nevertheless, they did succeed in pushing as far west as Tobruk, capturing that port city on 21 January 1941. By the end of the month, the British had taken over 125,000 prisoners and paused to regroup before pursuing the offensive into Tripolitania.

British forces resumed their push westward early in February, hoping to capture the city of Benghazi and complete their conquest of Cyrenaica. Aerial intelligence reported that the Italians were preparing to abandon Benghazi in favour of a stronger position at the Agheila bottleneck, and the British field commander, General Richard O'Connor, quickly altered his plan to proceed along the coast road and diverted part of his force across the desert in an effort to beat the retreating Italians to El Agheila. On 5 February, this force established a blocking position at Beda Fomm and waited for the Italian army, which reached the cross-road on the following day. The retreating Italian force was considerably larger than the British garrison, but the British were comfortably dug in and were able to destroy most of the Italian armor as it tried to pass through the bottleneck. At the end of the day, 120 tanks were disabled and 20,000 prisoners of war were taken. This was nothing short of amazing considering that the British force at Beda Fomm numbered only 3000 men. As Anthony Eden had said of an earlier battle, 'never has so much been surrendered by so many to so few'.

After the victory at Beda Fomm, O'Connor prepared to complete the destruction of the Italian army in North Africa. Much to his horror and the regret of his superiors in Egypt, the offensive was not permitted to go any further. On 12 February Churchill cabled Wavell and instructed him to withdraw most of the British forces in Cyrenaica so that an offensive in Greece could be mounted. O'Connor was confident that he could go on to capture Tripoli but his appeals were of no avail. The Prime Minister was committed to the Balkan offensive and there was no changing his mind. Accordingly, 50,000 British troops were landed in Greece in March and the North African campaign came to an abrupt end.

The Greek diversion was a disaster. On 6 April German forces invaded Greece and shortly thereafter the British had to evacuate their forces in a move reminiscent of Dunkirk. Twelve thousand

Above left: The Italian retreat in the desert was even swifter than their advance.
Above: General Sir Archibald Wavell chatting with the Commander of the Desert Forces, Lieutenant-General Richard O'Connor.

Opposite: British forces moved swiftly through Cyrenaica. **Left:** The Italian invasion of Greece met with initial success.

Right: The Italian invaders were soon slowed by Greek partisans and the Greek Army. **Below:** A storm trooper barks his orders during the Greek campaign. **Below right:** The Wehrmacht was forced to move into Macedonia to save the Italians from humiliation. **Opposite: center:** A Panzer column enters Salonika. **Opposite bottom:** Fortified by German support in Greece, the Italians moved to the attack once again. **Overleaf:** The Luftwaffe over Athens.

men were lost and, more important, the opportunity to annihilate the Italian army in Cyrenaica was lost as well. By the time that the withdrawal of British forces to North Africa was completed in late April, the Italians had regrouped in Tripolitania and were reinforced by the arrival of additional units, including a small German force under the command of General Erwin Rommel.

Rommel had distinguished himself as commander of the 7th Panzer Division in the French campaign; on 6 February 1941 he was summoned by Hitler to lead a small German force to the rescue of the Italians in North Africa. He flew to Tripoli on 12 September and immediately took charge of the defense of Axis forces in the desert. Although technically the inferior of several of the Italian officers and immediately responsible to the Italian command, Rommel was the architect of Axis participation in the desert war from his arrival until 1943 when the Axis position in Africa collapsed. His career in Africa was to become legendary.

It would be several months before Rommel's men and equipment arrived in Tripoli. However, finding that the British had depleted their strength in Cyrenaica and showed little inclination

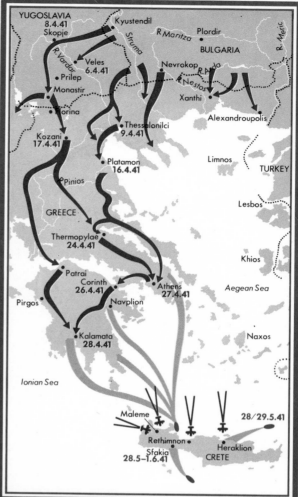

YUGOSLAVIA
8.4.41
Skopje
Kyustendil
R Maritza
Plordir
R Meric
BULGARIA
R Vardar
Struma
Veles
6.4.41
Nevrokop
R Nestos
Prilep
Monastir
Xanthi
Florina
Thessalonilci
9.4.41
Alexandroupolis
Kozani
17.4.41
Platamon
16.4.41
Limnos
TURKEY
PPinios
GREECE
Lesbos
Thermopylae
24.4.41
Khios
Patrai
Corinth
26.4.41
Athens
27.4.41
Aegean Sea
Pirgos
Navplion
Naxos
Kalamata
28.4.41
Ionian Sea
Maleme
28/29.5.41
Rethimnon
Heraklion
Sfakia
CRETE
28.5–1.6.41

8.4.41
German Invasion and dates of capture

German parachute and airborne landings in Crete 20 May, 1941

British evacuation

to revive the offensive against the Italians in Tripolitania, Rommel decided to assume the offensive himself. Massing what forces were available and constructing a fleet of dummy tanks mounted on Volkswagen chassis in order to confuse the British as to his actual strength, Rommel disregarded his orders to wait until May and began his first offensive on 2 April.

Rommel's ruse worked. With only fifty tanks and two divisions of Italian infantry, he crossed into Cyrenaica and quickly overwhelmed British forces there. Benghazi fell on 3 April, Michili on the fourth. By 11 April, all British forces except the garrison at Tobruk were evacuated to Egypt. In nine days, Britain's fortunes in North Africa had been reversed. As the late Sir Basil Liddell Hart so aptly observed, the British paid a heavy price for forfeiting the golden opportunity of February 1941.

On 11 April 1941 Rommel ordered the investment of Tobruk, the last British garrison in Cyrenaica, and the siege began on the following Monday, 14 April. Although their forces had been routed in Cyrenaica, the British command was determined to hold Tobruk at all costs; this decision was reinforced by Churchill's insistence

that the defense of the port was absolutely vital if Rommel's advance toward Egypt was to be halted. Accordingly, General Leslie Morshead, commander of the 9th Australian Division which held the city, was instructed to hold out as long as was humanly possible or until reinforcements could be brought in by sea.

The Axis army repeatedly failed to pierce Tobruk's defenses. This undoubtedly reflected the weakness of Rommel's forces rather than the strength of the defenders but was sufficiently disheartening to his superiors in the Italian command, who insisted that the campaign be halted. When Rommel refused to listen, the Italians pressed their case with General Halder in Berlin. Halder was sympathetic, for he feared that to push the offensive in North Africa further might require reinforcement of Rommel's forces; this he could not think of doing in light of the anticipated invasion of Russia. General Paulus was despatched to Africa to 'head off this soldier gone stark mad', but Paulus sanctioned Rommel's scheme and persuaded Halder to do likewise.

The attack on Tobruk was resumed on 30 April but proved no more successful than the first assaults. Although Rommel's forces were able

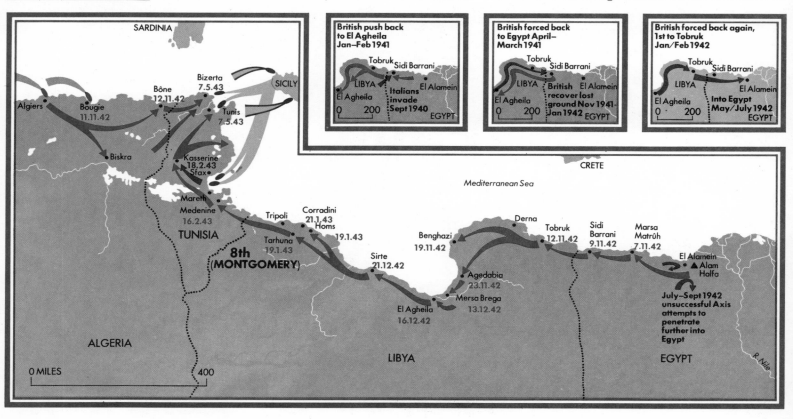

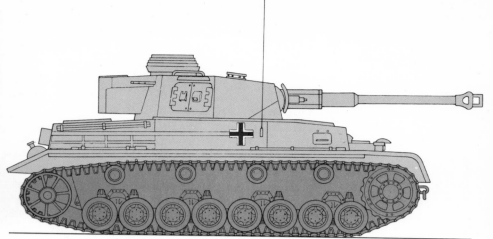

to breach the outer defenses of the city, they were not strong enough to break through the intense artillery barrage coming from inside the port. After four days the attack was broken off; although German and Italian forces continued to lay siege to the city, for the moment, it remained in British hands.

The failure to take Tobruk did not dent Rommel's determination to push on toward Egypt; on the contrary, it seemed to reinforce it. To do so, however, would require more men and equipment than the general could muster, and he therefore requested that the General Staff send him an additional four Panzer divisions as soon as possible. Unfortunately, the invasion of the Soviet Union was still occupying the minds of the Nazi command in Berlin; even had Hitler and Halder been willing to send such a force to North Africa, it is doubtful whether the Italians would have accepted a large German presence in their African empire. Rommel's requests were refused, and in so doing the General Staff forfeited the chance for a German victory in North Africa. Although this might not have seemed obvious in June and July 1941 when Rommel's request was first made, it proved fateful the following year

when German fortunes in the desert war were gradually reversed.

If the German command was hesitant to comply with Rommel's requests, the British government had no reservations about the need to reinforce Wavell's forces in Egypt. After the abortive Greek campaign, Churchill and his advisers badly wanted a victory in North Africa, and the British, despite critical shortages of arms and equipment, quickly assembled a large convoy in April and sent it to Egypt by the end of the month. Rather than waste time sending the convoy around the Cape of Good Hope, Churchill ordered the Navy to run the ships through the Mediterranean, a risky but considerably shorter route. The mission was successfully concluded on 12 May; one ship carrying some sixty tanks was sunk by a mine near the coast of Sicily, but all the others delivered their cargo of 238 tanks intact.

Wavell took the offensive in May. Knowing that Rommel's forces were short of supplies and gasoline, Wavell ordered Brigadier W. H. E. Gott into Cyrenaica with orders to overrun the enemy's border positions and push on to relieve Tobruk. The attack began on 13 May and might have been successful had not Rommel reversed the initial

Above: PZKW IV. Length: 21 ft. 9 in. Width: 9 ft. 5½ in. Maximum road speed: 24.9 m.p.h. Range: 130 miles. Armament: 1 × 75 cm. L/43, 2 × 7.92 mm. MG34 machine guns. Crew: 5 Weight: 23.2 tons.
Opposite far left: After the conquest of Greece, Crete was next. German paratroops prepare for the initial attack. **Opposite center:** Masses of German parachutists descend upon Crete. **Opposite right:** By mid-June 1941 the Germans made it impossible for the Allies to unload supplies in Crete. **Above left:** After the German conquest of Crete the RAF continued their challenge.
Below left: Rommel enjoyed initial success as the Afrika Korps raced toward Egypt. **Below:** General Erwin Rommel flew to Tripoli in September 1941 to take command.

German-Italian retreat and called for a counter-attack against Gott's positions. At the end of the month, the British retreated to Egypt and the Germans occupied the Halfaya pass and other positions near the border.

The Defense of Suez

Having chased the British back into Egypt, Rommel fortified his border positions so that they would have to break through strong anti-tank batteries before gaining access to the coast road leading to Tobruk. With his tanks outnumbered by four to one, this was his only chance to stop Wavell, for he knew that once the British reached the coast road it would be impossible to halt their advance. He therefore deployed his limited forces in order to create a bottleneck which would stall the British until reserves could be brought up from the west.

Rommel did not have to wait long to test his defenses. Undaunted by the failure of 'Operation Brevity' in May, Wavell mounted an even larger attack in June. The new plan, 'Operation Battleaxe', was even more ambitious than the first offensive and aimed to destroy Rommel's forces in North Africa by means of a three-stage assault on German-Italian positions in Cyrenaica. During the first phase of the attack, British forces would assault enemy strongholds at Halfaya, Sollum, and Capuzzo. During phase two, an additional force would lunge toward Tobruk, taking the city and clearing German forces from the area. In the last phase, the British forces joined by the garrison at Tobruk would push toward Tripolitania, eventually driving German and Italian forces from the continent. The plan was a bold one upon which Churchill was staking his political fortune. There could be no defeat if Wavell wished to continue his command of England's forces in the Middle East.

The British attack was launched on 14 June 1941. As Rommel had hoped, the enemy's armored units were unable to pass through Halfaya without sustaining heavy losses. Of the tanks that attacked the German position, only one was able to pass through the bottleneck without being destroyed. The British had better luck, however, at Fort Capuzzo where they encountered no anti-tank batteries and captured the stronghold in short order. This might have given Wavell cause for optimism were it not for the destruction of a second British armored column at Hafid ridge where Rommel had established another battery of anti-tank guns. British losses at Hafid were even greater than at Halfaya; by the end of the first day almost half of Wavell's tanks had been lost.

Never one to wait for his opponent's next move, Rommel, whose strength remained undiminished, took the offensive on 15 June and attempted to recapture Fort Capuzzo. To facilitate his counter-attack, Rommel called upon the German-Italian force laying siege to Tobruk to send an armored column to his assistance. Although he failed to recapture Capuzzo, the presence of an enlarged German force seizing the offensive was enough to disrupt the momentum of the British who were forced to switch to the defensive if they were to escape Rommel's flanking moves. After four days,

Above: The British moved forward to defend Tobruk. **Left:** The British took Tobruk easily in January 1941. **Left center:** Italian prisoners captured before Tobruk. **Bottom left:** British tanks negotiated some rough country in the defense of Tobruk. **Right:** South African troops, one poised with a hand grenade, search for the enemy. **Far right:** Tobruk remained in British hands and by June 1941 they moved to the attack. **Bottom right:** A British convoy risks the dangers of the Mediterranean.

the British scrapped their offensive. Once again, the desert fox had outwitted his adversaries.

Following the collapse of 'Operation Battleaxe', Churchill removed General Wavell from command of England's African forces replacing him with General Sir Claude Auchinleck. The Prime Minister refused to accept Rommel's victory and remained convinced that with a properly aggressive commander, British forces would succeed in destroying the Afrika Korps. In Auchinleck, Churchill believed he had found his man.

Auchinleck shared Churchill's view that a victory over the Axis allies was possible but he did not share the Prime Minister's impatient wish for a victory before the end of the year. In fact, he insisted that the men and equipment lost in June be replaced before a new offensive was launched; otherwise he would resign his commission. Churchill could hardly argue with such an ultimatum nor could he afford another defeat since his prestige at home had reached a low ebb. He was forced to bide his time and provide the men and supplies necessary for launching the next offensive, 'Operation Crusader'.

Operation Crusader
Preparations for Operation Crusader took the better part of four months during which time a vast muster of planes, tanks, and artillery pieces were sent to North Africa. When Auchinleck opened the campaign in November 1941 he possessed an unprecedented numerical superiority in men and equipment. British air strength was nearly three times that of the Axis, tank strength was over two times greater, and in manpower British forces outnumbered their German and Italian adversaries by tens of thousands. According to all indices, the British had an easy victory in sight.

The plan for Operation Crusader, however, had one fatal flaw: it called for the division of British forces into several attack groups, reasoning that the dangers involved in spacing out the troops were a small price to pay for the element of speed and surprise that such a deployment would allow. Auchinleck hoped to pin the Germans and Italians down in their fortified positions near the coast while simultaneously racing toward Tobruk and destroying Rommel's armored divisions. Britain's absolute numerical superiority seemed to ensure the plan's success as long as communication between the various fronts could be maintained, but as Rommel himself recorded in his diary, that superiority was neutralized by the deployment of troops which enabled him to play havoc with one unit at a time.

British forces crossed the Egyptian frontier on 18 November and, catching Rommel by surprise, penetrated rapidly into Cyrenaica. By the morning of the 19th Auchinleck's forces had reached Trigh el Abd and were pushing west to Tobruk; By night fall they were at Sidi Resegh, twelve miles southwest of Tobruk's defense perimeter. Hastily, Rommel rushed forces between the port and the airfield and, in the absence of reinforcements to Sidi Resegh, were able to keep the British from linking up with the garrison in Tobruk. Hampered by lack of reconnaisance aircraft and shortages of fuel, however, he was able to do little more than hold while Britain continued to advance on other fronts.

Rommel did not have a clear picture of British positions until 21 November; even then he continued the encirclement at Sidi Resegh, bringing up men and tanks to supplement German units in the area. When the British garrison in Tobruk tried to break out of the port and link up with the force at Sidi Resegh he effectively prevented the maneuver and immediately struck Sidi Resegh itself, taking the stronghold on 23 November. Three thousand British troops were killed or captured, but 70 tanks were lost as well. Although the victory at Sidi Resegh was a tactical triumph it proved to be a strategic error for which the Germans would pay heavily in the months that followed.

Encouraged by his victory, Rommel once again assumed the offensive. In a bold effort to outflank his opponents he sent his mobile forces on a race toward the border, intending to relieve the German-Italian border garrisons and mop up isolated British pockets in the process. His break for the frontier upset the equilibrium of the British attack and threw their command into a panic.

Before the British knew what had happened, German forces had advanced perilously close to the Egyptian frontier. By 25 November Rommel's army was poised to cross the border.

On 26 November the British recovered their composure and launched a counter-attack across the frontier. Italian forces failed to break through and reinforce his meagre army and Rommel had no choice but to order a fast retreat lest his men be caught between two British forces, one advancing west across the frontier, the other moving eastward from Tobruk. By the evening of 27 November, Rommel's forces had fallen back to a position south of Tobruk. Both the German counter-attack and Operation Crusader had failed, at least for the moment.

As Rommel and the Afrika Korps retreated, the British pursued them relentlessly. Commonwealth forces broke through to Tobruk on 27 November; on the following day they continued their drive, but could not manage to annihilate the Afrika Korps before it joined the rest of Rommel's forces on 29 November. Even then, the British far outnumbered the Germans and might have completed their destruction had they continued to press their drive. They did not, and as a result Rommel was once again able to take offensive action, isolating a unit of New Zealanders between Tobruk and Belhamed. By 1 December they were overrun. Rommel had triumphed again.

Rommel's ability to turn defeat into victory discouraged British field commanders, but General Auchinleck refused to give up the offensive. Sensing that Rommel could ill afford the loss of men and equipment however stunning his victories, Auchinleck determined to turn the desert war into a campaign of attrition. Therefore, he refused to abandon Operation Crusader and persisted in his design to carry the war to the Germans. Tired and demoralized men would be replaced by fresh troops. Battered and worn out equipment would be replaced as well. Time and patience would prevail.

While the British command pondered over its position, Rommel was also taking stock of his situation. He had succeeded in blunting Operation Crusader but only at substantial cost to himself. Since he could not expect reinforcements until the new year (1942), he had no choice but to withdraw German and Italian forces to Tripolitania where they would be safe from British attack. Accordingly, the siege of Tobruk was abandoned on 7 December and all Axis forces

Left: Hitler wished Rommel luck before he left for North Africa. For over a year Rommel had more than his share. (Note the autographed picture of Mussolini in the background).

were ordered to retreat to the Mersa Brega bottleneck. The retreat was completed in January 1942, not without heavy losses inflicted on slow moving infantry forces, largely Italian, by British units.

Scarcely had Rommel retreated to Tripolitania when fresh supplies and reinforcements arrived. On 5 January 1942, a task force of six ships landed several dozen tanks and other equipment which enabled Rommel to consider resuming offensive action against the British later that month. It did not take much to persuade him of the necessity to re-establish the Axis position in Cyrenaica; on 21 January he moved eastward.

Rommel's newest offensive irritated the Italians, but by the time Italy's Minister of War arrived at Rommel's desert headquarters to protest, the campaign was under way and the Axis forces had pushed well into Cyrenaica. The offensive was a *fait accompli* and showed every sign of being successful. Nothing could be done to abort the drive and whatever objections the Italians held evaporated in the face of the promising situation in the desert. In any case, Rommel was not about to court the Italian command. He had better things to do.

By 25 January Rommel's forces had taken the port of Benghazi and British forces had been withdrawn to Derna and Michili. The capture of Benghazi was significant because of the large stock of weapons and ammunition left behind by

Left: As the Afrika Korps swept into Egypt they seemed to be invincible.

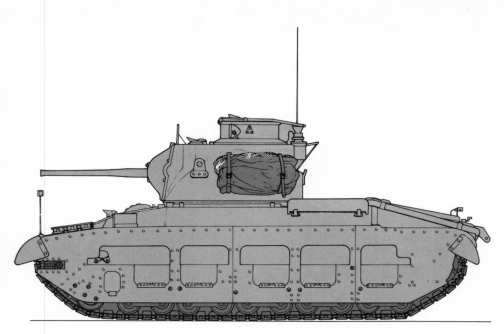

to take Tobruk for two years, with little success.
In less than a fortnight in June, he succeeded.

After the fall of Tobruk British forces retreated
rapidly into Egypt. Had the Desert Fox had his
way, he would have moved after them immediately, but his superiors hesitated to carry the
offensive into Egypt. In fact, the day after Tobruk
fell, Rommel was ordered to suspend the offensive,
and it was only as a result of his direct appeals to
Hitler and Mussolini that these orders were
countermanded. Rommel, who had been promoted to the rank of Field Marshal as a reward
for his triumphs in the desert, was a favorite of
the Fuehrer who used his good offices with
Mussolini to have Marshal Bastico's orders
annulled, but he did not receive permission to
march into Egypt until 24 June. By this time the
panic in the British command had subsided.

Rommel crossed the frontier into Egypt immediately. There was little resistance along the
coast road, as the British had wisely decided to regroup east of Mersa Matruh; Rommel's forces
were able to move within less than one hundred
miles of Alexandria by 30 June, reaching El
Alamein by the end of that day.

Rommel's rapid thrust made it necessary for the
British to prepare to evacuate Alexandria lest
the fleet and government offices in the port fall
into German hands. Accordingly, the fleet left
the city on 2 July with orders to withdraw through
the Suez Canal into the Red Sea. Government
offices were abandoned in the expectation that
Rommel would reach the outskirts of the port on
the following day. Fortunately for the British,
these precautions proved unnecessary.

Despite the initial success of the thrust into
Egypt, Rommel's forces were tired and their
equipment and supplies were almost exhausted.
Repeated attempts to pass the Alamein line failed,
and on 7 July the Germans were no better off than
they had been on the 2nd while the British were
preparing to launch a counter-offensive. This
attack was initiated on 8 July and within a week
Rommel's army was on the verge of collapse. By
20 July, the situation had become so critical that
Rommel was forced to consider a retreat; in fact,
with no ammunition and only a small number of
operating tanks, disengagement was a foregone
conclusion.

Rommel opted to disengage but not to retreat.
He hoped to remain west of the Alamein line
until reinforcements could be sent so that he could
resume his offensive. Since the British had broken
off their counter-attack, there was little reason to
withdraw to safer positions. His reinforcements

the retreating British. With these and the new
equipment that reached Tripoli at the beginning
of the month, Rommel was able to press on with
his offensive and soon his troops were astride the
Gazala line less than fifty miles west of Tobruk.
There the offensive stopped momentarily to await
the arrival of additional Italian forces.

Rommel did not outflank the Gazala line until
26 May, feigning an attack on the stronghold
while moving his forces around the position in an
attempt to move back to the coast road just before
Tobruk. This maneuver failed when the Germans encountered British armored units equipped with the Grant tanks. Rommel's forces were
trapped for two days, cut off from their supply
caravan which was stuck just west of the British
position at Gazala. Had the British moved swiftly,
they might have trapped Rommel then and there
but, rather than move mechanized units in to
tighten the noose around Rommel's neck, the
British chose to soften the German force by aerial
bombardment before they moved in for the kill.
This gave Rommel time to take stock of the
situation and make one last effort to break out of
'the cauldron' before it was too late. Typically,
he turned near defeat into victory when his forces
broke the back of the British position at Gaza on
13 June and captured the stronghold on the
following day.

With Gazala neutralized, the Axis army moved
quickly toward Tobruk. The city, its garrison of
35,000 men, and a vast stock of supplies were
taken on 21 June with little difficulty and surely
consistuted one of the worst disasters to befall the
British during the entire war. Rommel had tried

arrived early in August, and by the end of the month the Afrika Korps was again ready to attack.

Rommel launched his second attack against Alamein on 30 August, hoping to catch the British by surprise by moving out under cover of darkness. Thanks to aerial reconnaisance and the artful positioning of mines in the desert, however, the British were prepared. On 31 August Allied aircraft made a debilitating raid on the Afrikan Korps, inflicting heavy losses. Rommel refused to call off the offensive; instead he ordered the main body of attack to concentrate on the British position at the Alam Halfa ridge where they could take the enemy by surprise. This attack could not be completed, however, for the Afrika Korps ran out of fuel. With only a day's ration of gasoline left, Rommel reluctantly abandoned his position on 3 September and withdrew toward the frontier.

No effort was made to block Rommel's retreat, for Montgomery refused to move until his forces regrouped and new supplies and equipment arrived. Thus, despite heavy pressure from Churchill, it was seven weeks before the British began their pursuit of the Afrika Korps. Montgomery and Alexander were determined to wait until the odds were overwhelming in their favor before launching 'Operation Lightfoot'.

Operation Lightfoot began on 23 October 1942, by which time British forces had been increased until they represented a numerical superiority of men and equipment hitherto unprecedented in the desert war. With these odds in their favor, capable leaders in Montgomery and Alexander, absolute command of the air and an increasingly more efficient intelligence operation, it seemed only a matter of time before Rommel was forced off the continent.

On the other hand Rommel's armies, short of fuel, food, and supplies, were anything but ready for battle. Moreover, Rommel himself was desperately ill and had to leave the front to seek medical treatment in Germany shortly before the offensive began. His replacements, Generals Stumme and von Thoma, were able men but neither had any experience in desert warfare, both having arrived in Africa via the Russian front. Earnestness proved to be no substitute for experience and ability and, as the British pressed

Below: German 8.8 cm. Flak Gun. Range horizontal: 16,200 yds. Range vertical: 35,100 ft. Traverse: 360°. Rate of fire: 15–20 rounds per min. Crew: 11.

the offensive, Rommel, was ordered from his sick bed back to the desert.

When he arrived near the Alamein line on 25 October, the situation was already critical. British aircraft, flying almost uncontested missions, had bombed and strafed German positions for several days, inflicting reasonably large losses on the Axis army and demoralizing the men. The Germans were short of ammunition and shells, and could do little to stop the advance of British infantry units. Only the carefully laid minefields, planted before the attack on Rommel's orders, slowed the British advance, and even these could be navigated.

For four days the Axis forces stalled Montgomery's offensive, but not without sustaining heavy losses, especially of tanks. By 28 October Rommel had only ninety tanks left on the front line while Montgomery possessed nearly eleven times that number. Even the perpetually optimistic Rommel could not deny that this was a bad omen. Sick and downhearted, he prepared himself for the worst. Although he refused to give one inch of unnecessary ground to his adversaries, he realized that once the British pierced his defenses. there would be no stopping them. Preparations were made for a strategic retreat, and when, by the end of the last week in October, it appeared that further resistance was useless, the Germans fell back to more easily defended positions.

Rommel had never encountered the wrath of Hitler nor had the Fuehrer ever intervened to countermand his orders. But when the German and Italian forces prepared to abandon their positions near the Alamein line, Hitler ordered the Desert Fox to hold them at any cost. Always the Fuehrer's obedient servant, Rommel temporarily suspended the order to retreat, but this did not stop him trying to change Hitler's mind. He did not succeed, unfortunately, until 4 November, by which time the Afrika Korps had been further decimated. Had the British moved less cautiously, they might have finished their enemies then and there.

Once retreat was ordered, the Afrika Korps quickly evacuated their forward positions, outrunning British efforts to cut them off. When Allied forces reached Fuka on the coast road, the Germans had already passed through the city and only those tanks which had run out of fuel, largely older Italian vehicles, were captured. The bulk of Rommel's mobile force was well on the way to Mersa Matruh and passed through that bottleneck a day before British forces arrived. By 7 November, Rommel's forces had arrived at the Halfaya pass; they were almost destroyed by British aircraft, but thanks to excellent traffic management most units had escaped by the time night stopped the RAF attacks.

Rommel's forces reached Fort Capuzzo in Cyrenaica on 11 November but were in no condition to take up a defensive position; instead they were ordered to continue the flight westward. Although Rommel had managed to elude Montgomery and a final encounter was still some weeks away, the retreat had taken a heavy toll. Tens of thousands of German and Italian forces were captured along with many of the weapons of those

Top right: The Afrika Korps bombarded British positions at El Alamein.
Center right: The Luftwaffe made a supreme effort to break the British lines of defense. **Right:** Rommel and von Thoma ponder their fate at El Alamein. **Below:** The Commander of the Afrika Korps, General Ritter von Thoma, surrenders to Montgomery: 7 November 1942.

who had managed to escape. The fact that British losses had also been high, some 13,000 men wounded or killed, was little consolation, as Rommel could ill afford the loss of even one able bodied man or piece of equipment.

As the end of November neared, Rommel's army reached Mersa Brega and passed through the Agheila bottleneck where, for the first time in the campaign, defensive positions were prepared. When British forces arrived on 26 November, they encountered heavier resistance than they had since the first weeks of the campaign and were held for two weeks by Rommel's forces supplemented by three Italian infantry divisions newly arrived from Tripolitania. They finally broke through on 14 December, but even so, the British army did not enter Tripolitania until after the beginning of the new year.

As 1943 dawned, the Axis powers faced an unprecedented crisis in North Africa. Montgomery's forces threatened Rommel from the east and the Anglo-American expedition in Algeria and Tunisia threatened the Axis position from the west. Rommel's forces could not possibly be sufficiently increased to meet these demands and he begged his superiors to allow him to evacuate the continent before his forces were completely destroyed.

Once again his appeal was temporarily rebuffed; Mussolini hesitated to give up Italy's African empire while Hitler, for his part, was unwilling to admit that he had been defeated in the desert. When Marshal Bastico refused to assist him in evacuating the troops, Rommel personally appealed to the Fuehrer in Berlin flying there after his unsuccessful discussions with the Italian commander. Hitler refused to compromise, flying into a rage when Rommel suggested that the situation was lost in Africa, but Mussolini proved somewhat more pliable. Rommel had a long conference with Il Duce on his way back to Tripolitania; although the Italian dictator would not hear of a retreat from Africa, he did agree that the German-Italian army should be moved nearer to the Tunisian frontier. Upon his return to Tripoli, Rommel hastily carried out his plan, and the game of chess in the desert was moved to Tunisia.

Above: The 1st Household Cavalry round up thousands of prisoners.

Below: Squadron of Ju-52s flying convoy across the Mediterranean from German bases in Italy to bolster the sagging defenses of the Afrika Korps.

CHAPTER ELEVEN

Operation Torch: Defeat of the Axis Powers in North Africa

Soon after the United States entered the war, Allied leaders met in Washington to consider co-ordination of the effort against the Axis powers. Although it was the Japanese attack on Pearl Harbor which occasioned America's entry, Roosevelt agreed with Churchill that the first task of the Allies was the defeat of Germany. What remained to be determined was just how the United States might contribute to the Allied effort in 1942. Here, the two statesmen disagreed.

Churchill proposed that the United States commit its forces to a campaign in North Africa, nicknamed Operation Gymnast by British military planners. According to this proposal, first presented to the Americans at the Arcadia Conference in December 1941, the United States would start an offensive in North Africa, landing forces in Algeria and coming to the relief of the British Eighth Army in Cyrenaica. Together, the British and American armies would crush Rommel's forces and drive the Axis powers off the African continent. Having accomplished this, the Anglo-American allies would move on to Sicily, from Sicily to the Italian boot and from there to Germany, eventually forcing Hitler to capitulate.

Roosevelt did not share Churchill's enthusiasm for a venture in North Africa. To begin with, American officers did not favor a war in the desert and criticized the plan for Operation Gymnast as being both too risky and relatively ineffective. Marshall and other senior American officers proposed instead a landing along the French channel coast. Such a plan would have the virtue of stunning the Germans and stimulating French resistance and the eventual defection of the Vichy regime. It would also satisfy Stalin's demand that the Allies open a second front in Europe to reduce Nazi pressure on the Soviets. For the moment this latter plan prevailed, and it occupied the attention of Allied planners until the summer of 1942 when the situation in Cyrenaica dictated a return to Churchill's original proposal.

By the beginning of July 1942 Rommel's forces had carried their offensive into Egypt and were attacking El Alamein. Had it fallen, the road to Alexandria would have been open to the Germans and it would only have been a matter of time before the Suez Canal was threatened. In this critical situation Churchill could not possibly consider going ahead with the preparations for Operation Sledgehammer, the cross-channel crossing, and advised Roosevelt to this effect on 8 July, suggesting in the same cable that the

Left: Lieutenant-General Dwight D. Eisenhower, who helped lead Operation Torch. **Below:** Major-General Charles Ryder commanded the forces which were to land at Algiers. **Below right:** Lieutenant-General George S. Patton and Ike after the landing at Casablanca.

United States carefully reconsider the now-abandoned Gymnast scheme. His argument failed to convert Marshall and the other American chiefs of staff but the President, sensing Churchill's desperation, found it impossible to refuse his comrade and overruled his military advisers, ordering them to prepare an acceptable version of the Gymnast plan.

Since there was no changing Roosevelt's mind, Marshall and his lieutenants set to work on a new plan for the invasion of North Africa by American forces, presenting their proposal to the President on 24 July. The new plan, codenamed Operation Super-Gymnast, was reminiscent of the original British proposal, but sought to restrict the area of operations in which the American army would be involved and maintain the integrity of the American command as opposed to integrating the forces of the Anglo-American allies under a joint command. Although precise details of the operations were yet to be worked out, Roosevelt quickly endorsed the proposal and forwarded it to Churchill who did the same, requesting only that the offensive be renamed Operation Torch.

With the approval of the President and Prime Minister in hand, British and American officers met to finalize plans for the operation. It was generally agreed that the offensive could not be launched before October 1942 with the Americans preferring a date in November. A greater problem was the definition of the scope of the landings and where they should take place. Marshall and his

associates wished to proceed cautiously, limiting American landings to Casablanca and points west of this city in Morocco. The British, however, wished to have American forces landed on the Mediterranean as well as the Atlantic coast of North Africa and pushed for simultaneous American landings in Morocco and Algeria. They argued that if the Americans did not move boldly, German and Italian forces would be rushed into Tunisia, giving the Allies little if any chance of seizing this area before the Axis powers cemented their position there. Equally important, British commanders felt that once the Germans understood the scope of Allied operations, they would lose no time in overrunning French-controlled Algeria and Morocco, having little faith that the Vichy forces in North Africa would stand fast with the Third Reich. Thus, if the Allies did not seize Algeria before the Germans, there would be no chance of pinning Axis forces between the converging Americans in the west and British in the east.

Eisenhower's Compromise

In August General Eisenhower proposed a compromise. According to his proposal, which was submitted to Allied leaders on 9 August, American forces would be landed in Algeria as requested by the British, but would not be landed east of Algiers where they would be exposed to attack from German-Italian aerodromes and installations. As in the original American proposal, there would also be a landing near Casablanca.

Eisenhower's proposal represented a concession to the British but they continued to balk at the idea of wasting American forces at Casablanca when they could be used to take more important points east of Algiers and closer to Tunisia. Vigorously pressing their case, the British persuaded Roosevelt of the soundness of their scheme and he, in turn, ordered General Marshall to proceed with plans for an expanded venture in North Africa. Marshall told Eisenhower to reconsider his proposal and continue his conversations with British planners until a satisfactory agreement could be reached. This he did, but it took until the middle of August to come to an agreeable arrangement, and even then there was still disagreement over a landing along the Atlantic coast of Morocco.

On 21 August Eisenhower proposed that the landing at Casablanca be eliminated, as the only way to placate the British. His superiors, however, refused to sanction the change, pointing out to Eisenhower and Roosevelt that if the United States placed all of its eggs in one basket by restricting the operation to Algeria, there was a very real danger that the Germans would close the supply line through the Straits of Gibraltar either by forcing General Franco to seize Gibraltar or by shelling the Straits. If, on the other hand, a bridgehead was established at Casablanca, supplies would be moved overland if necessary.

Marshall's argument was hard to refute and Roosevelt was inclined to support his chief-of-staff on this matter. Although he continued to disagree, there was little Churchill could do but accept the American plan lest more time be wasted. He gave his tentative approval on 5 September, and on the 15th, after agreement had been reached on the locations of the Allied landings and the approximate numbers to be landed at each spot, the plan was finally approved by both sides.

The final Allied plan for Operation Torch called for a three-pronged landing in North Africa. An American force under the command of Major General George S. Patton would land near Casablanca. A second American group under the command of Major General Lloyd Fredendall would land at Oran. The third landing party, a joint Anglo-American force under the command of Rear Admiral Harold Burroughs and General Charles Ryder would be set down near Algiers. The target date for the operation was set for 8 November.

The transport of the Allied armies presented a major problem for the British and American navies and called for the closest cooperation and coordination. Patton's army, some 25,000 men, would be ferried across the Atlantic by an armada under the command of Rear-Admiral H. Kent Hewitt. The other landing parties were to be dispatched from England, but would have to pass through the Straits of Gibraltar in order to reach their targets. This would be no simple feat since the Italian navy had the potential to contest the passage if it took too long. There was also the matter of several hundred slow-moving and relatively unprotected supply vessels which were vital to the success of the effort.

To coordinate this herculean naval effort, Eisenhower chose the commander of the British Mediterranean Fleet, Admiral Sir Andrew Cunningham. It would be his responsibility to move ships quickly through the Straits while keeping the Italian fleet at bay. This was a difficult assignment, but one which Cunningham was perfectly capable of carrying out.

The Allied convoys left England on 22 October and rendezvoused just west of Gibraltar on 5 November, passing through the Straits during that night without incident, since the Italian navy did not dare challenge Cunningham's Mediterranean Fleet. Altogether, over 250 merchant ships and transports had arrived safely in the Mediterranean by the morning of 6 November, all according to plan. By 7 November, all Allied units were in position and ready for the landing the following morning.

The Allies were partially dependent upon the cooperation and good will of Vichy French authorities in North Africa for the success of Operation Torch. With their cooperation, the landings would surely succeed; without it, they might be a disaster. It was imperative, therefore, that an effort be made to discover the sentiments of French officials in the colonies before plans for the landings were finalized. This mission fell to Robert Murphy and General Mark Clark.

Murphy was the top-ranking American diplomat in North Africa, tactful, trustworthy, and a friend of many of the Vichy leaders. In short, he was the perfect man to inform the French of the Allies' intention without, at the same time, revealing the full details of their plan of operation. As Roosevelt had anticipated, he fulfilled his mission

brilliantly. While the Anglo-American attack was being prepared, Murphy met secretly with military leaders of the Vichy colonial governments in North Africa, seeking out those who were sympathetic to the Allies and soliciting their blessing for the venture. When he was convinced that a sufficient number of these men would support the Allied landings, Murphy suggested that a ranking Allied officer be sent to join the underground discussions. General Mark Clark, Eisenhower's deputy commander, was chosen for this mission and was carried to Algeria aboard a British submarine, to join Murphy and the French leaders on 21 October, the day before the first British convoy left for Gibraltar.

After a series of mishaps trying to land, Clark met Murphy and General C. E. Mast on 22 October. Mast was the commander of French forces in Algiers and a subordinate of General Juin, commander of French forces in Algeria. According to Murphy, Mast was one of the most reliable of the Vichy generals and was sympathetic to the Allied cause; indeed, it was he who suggested to Murphy that Clark be sent to North Africa in the first place. Clark found Mast a decent fellow and generally agreed with Murphy's estimate of the man, but he refused to tell the French general anything more than was necessary

to prepare him for the landing; Murphy was authorized to fill in details of the size and scope of the operation once the offensive had been launched. Such caution was understandable, but proved unfortunate in the long run since Mast, ill informed of the mechanics of the landings, was caught off guard when they finally began, which caused him no small amount of embarrassment and seriously jeopardized his position.

In their conversations, Clark, Murphy and Mast spent much time discussing the question of leadership among the Vichy community in North Africa. While it was known that many Vichy officials and officers were secretly ready to support the Allies, particularly the Americans, an endorsement of Allied effort by a prominent French leader would help convert some of the more cautious colonials, who this man might be, however, was difficult to determine. Mast's superior, General Juin, might have been chosen to lead the French defection from the Axis camp, but he was considered rather bland and given to vacillation. General de Gaulle might have been considered for the 'assignment', but he would never have been accepted by the senior French officers or Roosevelt. This left only two alternatives, General Giraud or Admiral Darlan.

Since Admiral Darlan had been a sympathetic

Right: American troops disembark from assault boats and land on a North African beach.

out immediate incident in the early hours of the morning of 8 November 1942. Despite problems with the weather and the general's pessimism about the navy's ability to deliver his forces safely, all went well. The landings were made at several points along the Moroccan coast with the main group coming ashore at Fedala, fifteen miles north of Casablanca. Thanks to the confusion of French authorities as to the time, place, and scope of the attack, there was little resistance along the beaches; Patton's men and equipment were unloaded and a beach-head was easily established. Some confusion did result, not from hostile action by the French, but rather from the difficulty of moving heavy equipment along the beach and onto the main coast roads. Nevertheless, Patton's forces were ready to roll toward Casablanca the following morning.

The landing at Oran was considerably more difficult than at Casablanca, Arzeu, Les Andalouses and Mersa Bou Zedjar. Eventually the assault party was repulsed at great loss of life for the invaders. Nevertheless, it was only a matter of days before General Fredendall's forces reached the port and the French officially surrendered the city on 10 November.

The landings near Algiers proved the most difficult of all. Although there was no initial resistance, thanks to the orders of General Mast, he was relieved of his command when news of the operation reached his superiors, and forces collaborating with the allies were replaced by loyal troops. It was necessary, therefore, to negotiate with Vichy authorities if the city was to be taken without bloodshed and once again the task fell to Robert Murphy. Since General Giraud's appeal for cooperation had fallen on deaf ears, Murphy had no choice but to seek the support of General Juin, hoping that he in turn would convey the hopelessness of resistance to Admiral Darlan,

supporter of Hitler and the Third Reich, Churchill and Roosevelt had little faith in him, and public opinion in England and the United States would not have tolerated an alliance with such a man. By process of elimination, General Giraud was the only viable candidate to lead the defection; whatever his vices, at least he had not been an enthusiastic Nazi supporter and in fact he was known to be plotting a revolt against German rule in France.

Having decided to seek Giraud's assistance, it was necessary to bring the general to North Africa for consultation with French leaders and Allied diplomats. This was no easy task since the general's political activities were being closely monitored and he was under regular surveillance by French and German authorities. Nevertheless, on 7 November he was carried by submarine and sea plane to a rendezvous with General Eisenhower on Gibraltar; he was to be dropped in Algeria when the landings began the next morning.

Patton's army landed near Casablanca with-

commander-in-chief of Vichy's armed forces. Fortunately, Darlan happened to be in Algiers and Juin was able to hastily arrange a meeting between the two men.

When Murphy informed the admiral of the size and scope of the Allied landings he was furious, but agreed to send a radio message to Marshal Petain seeking permission to negotiate. At approximately 0800, Petain answered Darlan's message, authorizing the admiral to make whatever arrangements were necessary to preserve the French position in Algeria. Darlan, always a realist, swallowed his pride and entered into serious discussions with Murphy which quickly resulted in an order for French forces to quit their resistance in Algiers pending a final agreement for a ceasefire throughout French North Africa.

Giraud reached Algiers on 9 November and joined the discussions between Murphy and Darlan that afternoon. Murphy, who was also joined by General Mark Clark, pushed hard for an early ceasefire agreement, but the two French officers seemed more interested in quibbling over which one of them was authorized to lead French forces in Africa. Darlan contended that Giraud's very presence in Algeria would excite the German-Italian command, inviting their intervention in Algeria and leading to a rapid build up of Axis forces in Tunisia. Although the Allies preferred to deal with Giraud, Clark and Murphy could hardly refute Darlan's argument and did not wish to risk his prediction coming true if Giraud called for the ceasefire. Giraud was scuttled and Darlan became the Allies' chief compatriot in North Africa.

Darlan issued an order for a ceasefire throughout French North Africa on 10 November and cabled a message to this effect to Pétain. Pétain privately approved of the action but could not publicly sanction it lest the Germans take

Top left: Eisenhower was apparently in no mood to take orders from Admiral Darlan (center); Major-General Mark Clark stands to the right of Darlan.
Center left: The American occupation of North Africa was not always as easy as this picture would indicate.
Left: The landings at Oran met considerable opposition. Here an American sniper is looking for trouble.

Left: Operation Torch: personnel and equipment unload near Oran.
Below: General Giraud proved to be far more acceptable to the Allies than Darlan.

Right: American tanks move in to Tunisia to close the circle around Rommel.

punitive action against the Vichy régime; to placate the Germans, therefore, he countermanded Darlan's order and transferred command of French forces in North Africa to General Noguès, a 'more reliable officer'. In reality, however, Darlan's order stood and a ceasefire was achieved in Algeria; in other parts of French North Africa, the situation remained confused.

Pétain's charade may have been designed to quiet the Germans but they were not fooled by the masquerade. When Pétain refused Hitler's request to allow German and Italian forces to move into Tunisia to forestall an allied thrust into that colony, the Fuehrer ordered German forces to occupy the area by force if necessary. German commanders lost little time in carrying out the order; on 9 November, they had crossed the Libyan border and by the end of the month almost 24,000 Axis troops occupied the area. They arrived just in time, for the Allies were ready to launch their drive into Tunisia in the middle of the month.

Had the French cooperated wholeheartedly, the Allies would have been able to push into Tunisia two days after the first landings in Algeria. Except for a small commando force

landed at Bone on 12 November, however, the Anglo-American attack force did not commence operations in Tunisia until 15 November when British and American paratroops were dropped west of Tunis to gain control of forward air bases and military installations. On succeeding days, Allied forces were dropped east of Tunis in an effort to trap the Axis garrison in the city and prevent its further reinforcement.

Rather than wait for additional troops, Axis forces in Tunis were placed on the offensive immediately and sent out along the Tunis-Algiers road to clear French troops from the highway before they defected to the Allies. By striking quickly and feigning strength, the German-Italian forces surprised their new enemies and made remarkable headway considering their actual numbers. Parallel assaults were launched east of Tunis, resulting in the occupation of the strongholds of Sousse, Sfax, and Gabès and guaranteeing the Axis a safe passage from Tripolitania to Tunisia. By the end of the month, General Nehring's army controlled most of northern Tunisia and was in an excellent position to defend it against Allied assaults from the east or west.

Above: A Gurkha detachment faces the enemy on the Tunisian Front.
Left: President Roosevelt was escorted through Casablanca by Eisenhower when Morocco and Algeria had been secured.

For their part, the Allies preferred to proceed cautiously in Tunisia. The original timetable had already been modified and Eisenhower agreed with General Anderson, commander of Allied forces in the Algiers area, that there was no reason to rush into Tunisia until they were at full strength and the Royal Air Force was fully prepared to support British and American ground units. Although the push had begun on 15 November, they did not feel ready to make a major effort to dislodge the Germans until the end of December. By that time, however, Axis forces in Tunisia were estimated at over 35,000 and a new commander, General von Arnim, had been sent to Tunis. This increase in the enemy's strength and the onset of bad weather forced yet another postponement. For the moment, Tunisia would remain in Axis hands.

The Fall of Tunisia

The Allied push into Tunisia was resumed in February 1943. In actual numbers, the Axis army in Tunisia, which included the remnants of Rommel's Afrika Korps, was five times the size it had been at the beginning of November 1942, but many of the soldiers in this army had been exhausted in the desert war in the east and tank strength in the mechanized units was well under par. Although equipment and supplies were once again being received, Axis commanders had little to be happy about; they were faced on two sides by hostile forces and had nowhere to retreat. Tunisia was the last Axis beachhead on the continent.

Although he was tired and ill after managing the retreat from Cyrenaica, Rommel understood that if the Axis command waited until Allied armies converged on Tunis, it would be too late to salvage a position in North Africa. There was no choice but to strike again before the Allies could mount their final assault; Rommel contended that the best place was west of Tunis where Allies forces were most vulnerable. However, his own forces were preparing to bar Montgomery's entrance from the east. General von Arnim controlled the western sector, and it would be up to him to launch the pre-emptive strike.

Von Arnim was less than enthusiastic about launching an offensive but he could not deny that it was necessary. Consequently, although he ordered an attack in the west, he did so half-heartedly, holding a good part of his tank strength in reserve for future encounters. The result was predictable. The Anglo-American advance was slowed but not stopped, and it soon became clear that the Allies might turn von Arnim's drive into a rout. Rommel, who was already fuming at his colleague's reluctance to engage the Anglo-American forces, was forced to join the fray in order to preserve the Axis position in northern Tunisia.

By 17 February Rommel's forces, except for a

This plane was among the hundreds destroyed by the Allies when the Desert Campaign neared its conclusion in Tunisia. **Below left:** British infantry move through a wired position on the Mareth Line. **Opposite above:** Rugged terrain did not prove insuperable for these American Rangers. **Opposite below:** German artillery digs in to defend Tunis after Rommel's departure. **Bottom:** Breakthrough on the Mareth Line sealed the fate of the Axis in North Africa.

few small garrisons adjacent to the Libyan frontier, were being moved westward. It was the Desert Fox's intention to push through the Kasserine Pass and break through to the coast road near Bone before the Allied army captured that position and moved on Bizerta. To succeed, however, he needed the cooperation of von Arnim and the Italian command, neither of whom looked upon such a bold venture with pleasure. In fact, von Arnim was absolutely opposed to the plan. Since there seemed little hope in discussing the matter with him, Rommel appealed directly to Mussolini in the hope that Il Duce would accept the risks involved in order to salvage a victory in North Africa. As he had hoped, Mussolini gave him the 'green light' on 18 February, placing him in command of all Axis forces in Tunisia.

Rommel wasted no time; on 19 February, Axis forces were ordered to the Kasserine Pass, taking it two days later. As the Axis drive continued, Thala was taken from American forces 22 February. But Rommel had no time to rejoice over these triumphs, for Montgomery's forces were threatening German positions near the Tunisian border. The western offensive had to be broken off so that he could rush back to stop the Eighth Army. Rommel's forces reached the Mareth Line at the end of February, but it was already too late to prevent Montgomery entering Tunisia. Realizing that the situation was hopeless, Rommel begged his superiors to prepare for an evacuation. When they refused to consider it, he took a long overdue sick leave, leaving Tunisia on 9 March 1943. Although he could not have salvaged the Axis position in Africa by his

Above: General von Arnim is taken into custody: 14 May 1943. **Opposite:** French and Tunisians cheer the Allied victory in North Africa: Tunis, May 1943.

Below: Allied troops in action during the street fighting in Tunis: 7 May 1943.

continued presence, there seems little doubt that Rommel might have been able to engineer a German Dunkirk had he chosen to remain. Without him, although Axis forces fought bravely to hold their positions, they were decimated when Tunisia finally fell to the Allies.

After Rommel's departure, the defeat of Axis forces was swift. On 20 March Montgomery's forces attacked the Mareth Line, forcing the enemy to withdraw to the west. On 10 April the Eighth Army captured Sfax. On 12 April Sousse was taken and the southern defenses in Tunisia were abandoned as the Axis army retreated to the north where they attempted to maintain a blocking position near Enfidaville. Here they held Montgomery for awhile but in the west, the situation was rapidly deteriorating.

By the end of April, American forces under the command of General Omar Bradley were ready to deliver the *coup de grace* to the remnants of Rommel's once-proud African army. Pushing across rear areas to the north of the front, Bradley's II Corps had captured Bizerta and Tunis by 7 May. Within days after the fall of these ports, German forces in northern Tunisia surrendered. Only the Cape Bon Peninsula remained in Axis hands. Had Hitler and Mussolini followed Rommel's advice, this area might have been the staging point for a retreat to Sicily. Instead, the remaining 250,000 troops were ordered to hold their ground and fight to the death. Actually, German and Italian units surrendered in large numbers until, by the end of the war in the desert, a quarter of a million men had surrendered to the Allies. On 12 May 1943 the Axis empire in North Africa came to an end.

CHAPTER TWELVE
The Allies Return to Europe: Sicily and the Italian Campaign

As the North African campaign drew to a close, Allied leaders met at Casablanca from 14–24 January 1943 to decide upon the next steps to be taken in the war against the Axis powers. It would only be a matter of months before converging Anglo-American forces trapped the Germans and Italians in Tunisia, forcing the Axis partners to abandon the continent. The Allies could then either pursue the enemy across the Mediterranean or discontinue further action in that area and launch a cross-Channel attack. Both options were attractive and each had its supporters, but after considerable discussion it was decided to opt for the former plan and invade Sicily.

The decision to attack Sicily before attempting a cross-Channel invasion of France was based upon the assumption that if pressure was taken off Axis forces in the Mediterranean, they could be withdrawn from the Italian peninsula and sent to France where they would make the Channel crossing that much more difficult. If by a small investment of manpower the Allies could tie up these units in Italy, the risks of failure in France would be greatly diminished. Thus, the Sicilian campaign was not merely a continuation of the North African conflict, but a diversion which would permit the Allies to build up their strength for the Channel crossing in 1944. As such, it had the unanimous support of Churchill, Roosevelt, and their military advisers.

General Eisenhower, as Supreme Commander of Allied forces in North Africa, was chosen to coordinate the Italian campaign, but the actual planning and execution of the operation was to be the joint responsibility of Generals Montgomery and Patton. The date for 'Operation Husky' was not set immediately but all agreed that it could not possibly take place until the summer. As it happened, the North African campaign ended on 12 May and the Allies did not launch the invasion of Sicily until 10 July, a delay of two months.

The final plan for Operation Husky was largely the work of General Montgomery and called for a joint Anglo-American assault. The Eighth Army was to land along the southeast coast of Sicily, take the port of Syracuse, and push on toward Messina. Patton's newly activated Seventh Army was to land at Gela, Licata, and Scoglitti, where they could protect Montgomery's flank and push toward Palermo.

To carry the Allied armies across the Mediterranean to Sicily, a vast armada of ships and landing craft gathered off the coast of North Africa. Operation Husky was to be the first major Allied amphibious assault of the war; in fact, it was the largest operation of its kind in the entire conflict, including the Normandy landings. All told, 478,000 men (250,000 British troops and 228,000 Americans) were moved from North Africa to Sicily during the first weeks of the campaign. They were carried on troop transports but put ashore in new landing craft, including LST's (landing ship-tank), LCT's (landing craft-tank) which carried equipment, LCI's (landing craft-infantry) and (LCVP's (landing craft-personnel and vehicles). Over 2500 vessels were employed in the operation and the Allied armies were landed in an area less than 100 miles wide.

Allied commanders prepared for stiff resistance to the landings, knowing that there were 230,000 Germans and Italians on the island. But in fact, except for some difficulty encountered at Gela where the Hermann Goering division supported by two Italian units put up a fight, the landings were made without incident. By 12 July all Allied beachheads were secured and the two armies were ready to proceed toward their targets.

To reach Messina, the Eighth Army had to pass through Catania or move around Mount Etna, an active volcano which dominated the valley below. It was here, at Catania, that the Axis forces offered their heaviest resistance, attempting to block the road to Messina until the rest of their army could be evacuated to the Italian peninsula.

Opposite: Domination of the central Mediterranean was crucial to a successful Allied invasion of Italy.

Allied troops landing by sea

22.7.43

Allied advance and dates of capture

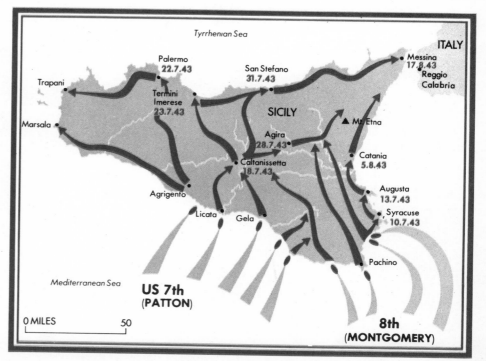

Frustrated, Montgomery tried to send some of his men around Mount Etna, hoping to outflank the enemy and break through to the coast behind their rear lines. This was both wise and necessary, but by using his own forces to make the run, Montgomery was usurping Patton's position. Never one to play second fiddle without protest, Patton was not going to allow the British to upstage his army. If Montgomery did not need the Second Army's assistance, it would be used for other purposes like the capture of Palermo. Accordingly, Patton's forces and General Bradley's II Corps drove north and west respectively, capturing Palermo on 22 July and Marsala the following day. These were the first American victories of the war and Patton, ready to take advantage of the high morale of his men, eagerly pressed on toward Messina, hoping that he could beat Montgomery there.

Patton encountered heavy resistance in his drive along the northern coast road from Palermo to Messina, and Montgomery also met stiff opposition. Catania did not fall to the Eighth Army until 8 August, almost a month after the landings, and heavy casualties were inflicted on both sides. Nevertheless, once Catania fell, the end was in sight. With Patton's armies rushing eastward along the northern coast road and Montgomery's forces pushing northward along the eastern coast road, the Axis command had no choice but to evacuate their forces. This was accomplished by the morning of 17 August; later that day, Patton's forces entered Messina.

In many ways, the Allies had won a pyhrric victory in Sicily. To begin with, a good part of the Axis garrison, some 100,000 men, were safely ferried to Italy along with their equipment and tanks. Although an almost equal number of forces were left behind and were taken as prisoners of war, these were freshly conscripted Sicilian units and not the hard core veterans of the German or Italian army. Although Axis losses (dead and wounded) were estimated at 24,000, the Allies lost a similar number so that the campaign could hardly be called an unmitigated triumph. Nevertheless, the tide of war seemed to be definitely turning. If the Axis had achieved a moral victory, the Allies had a physical victory and the stage was now set for carrying the war across the Straits of Messina into Italy proper.

As Allied forces pushed toward Messina, a political crisis brewed in Rome. The loss of North Africa and the impending defeat in Sicily forced Italian leaders to reconsider their position before Allied forces reached the Italian mainland and occupied their country as conquerors. Accordingly, the Fascist Grand Council was convened on 24 July to consider what was to be done, and arrived at a swift answer. On 25 July King Victor Emmanuel was restored to full power, the Parliament was reconvened, and Mussolini was forced to resign, to be replaced as Prime Minister by the aging Marshal Pietro Badoglio.

Needless to say, the Germans viewed the palace revolution in Rome with alarm. Despite Badoglio's assurances that Italy would continue to participate in the war, Hitler believed that if the Allies offered the Italian government peace with some honor, Badoglio would not hesitate to abandon the Axis. He was quite correct; immediately after Mussolini was deposed, the Italians entered into secret negotiation with the Allies in the hope of arranging a surrender on favorable terms. Badoglio even let it be known that he would be willing to join the Allies against the Germans if participation would give Italy the status of a co-belligerent and a position of influence at the peace conference after the war.

Hitler did not intend to tolerate this defection; Rommel and a German army were ordered to

occupy northern Italy in anticipation of the surrender, and an attempt was made to rescue Mussolini and establish him at the head of a rival Italian government loyal to the Axis. Both of these measures were completed in August 1943, weeks before the Badoglio government signed its military armistice with the Allies on 3 September. When the Allied invasion of Italy was launched in earnest six days later, the Germans were ready to seize Rome and push south to prevent the rapid movement of Allied forces toward the Austrian border. Badoglio took no effective measures to resist this incursion, and as a consequence, the Allies paid a heavy price for Italy.

Across to Italy

Units of the Eighth Army were ferried across the Straits of Messina on the evening of 3 September 1943, landing near Reggio on the toe of the Italian peninsula. Resistance was light and although retreating German forces attempted to destroy bridges, highways, and tunnels in the path of the advancing Allies, they made rapid headway. Taranto, site of a major Italian naval base, was taken on 9 September. Bari, an important harbor on the Adriatic, was seized several days later. By 17 September the Eighth Army had secured a firm hold on southern Italy. In the north, however, the Allies were not faring nearly as well.

The operation in southern Italy and along the Adriatic coast had been designed as a primarily diversionary maneuver. The major thrust of the invasion was to take place on the west coast near the port of Salerno, from which point Allied armies would seize control of air fields in the area and proceed north along the coast road in an effort to break through to Rome. After the signing of the armistice with the Badoglio regime, Allied commanders did not anticipate much resistance and hoped to attain their goal in a matter of weeks.

When General Clark's Fifth Army landed at Salerno on 9 September, however, they immediately encountered fierce resistance from German units and gun positions located in or near the port. The Germans had not been fooled by the activities of the Eighth Army in southern Italy. They fully expected a major Allied assault along the west coast; the obvious advantages of such a landing site were as clear to the Germans as to the Anglo-American command, and the Nazis had lost no time in preparing their defense.

By 10 September the Allied landings had been completed, but not without sustaining heavy casualties along the beaches and in the push for the coast road. Although Salerno was taken by the evening of 10 September, the Germans had done an efficient job of destroying useful installations and gutting the air fields surrounding the city so that they could not be used to launch aerial attacks on retreating German forces which were preparing a new line of defense near Naples.

In pushing inland and north from the beaches, American forces encountered even stiffer resistance than they had in attempting to land. German artillery positions were well placed in the hills above the coastal plain and helped to pin down the invading forces near the beaches. German ground forces had also encircled the Salerno area and

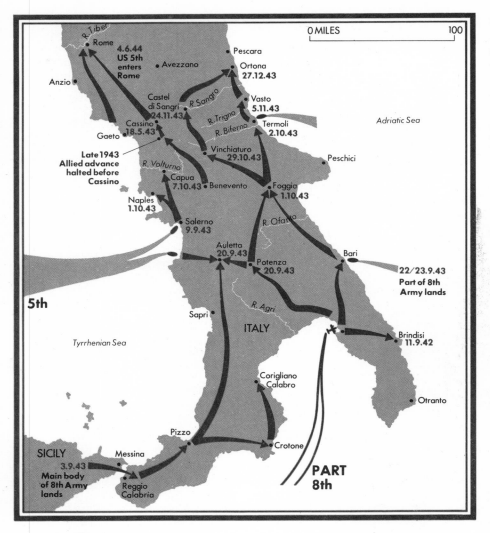

Allied troops landing by sea

Allied troops landing by air

3.9.43

Allied advance and dates of capture

resources to prepare additional defensive positions in the north. Dislodging the Germans required such a tremendous expenditure of manpower and was so frustratingly slow, that Allied leaders began to wonder whether they would reach Rome by the end of the year as planned.

When the Allies crossed the Volturno in mid-October the Germans retreated to the Gustav line, a defensive position astride the Liri, Sangro, Rapido, and Garigliano rivers, and here they held the Allies at bay until the spring of 1944. For every inch the Allies advanced, they sustained heavy losses. Something drastic had to be done to break this stalemate, or the contest might go on indefinitely and endanger the long awaited cross-Channel offensive.

At Churchill's insistence, Allied commanders prepared an amphibious assault around the end of the German position at the Gustav line. General Patton had employed similar techniques on a smaller scale in the Sicilian campaign with good result, and the Prime Minister and some of his military advisers hoped that the same results could be achieved in Italy, despite the fact that a similar proposal had been introduced earlier but had been dismissed as too risky.

'Operation Shingle', as the plan was known, called for the landing of two divisions at Anzio, sixty miles north of the German's main defensive positions. Once landed, these divisions would push south, attacking the Germans' rear along the Winter line while the Fifth and Eighth armies pushed through the front. If all went well, a breakthrough would be achieved, German units would be trapped between two advancing Allied armies, and the long delayed push toward Rome could be resumed with all speed. If the attempt failed, two divisions might well be lost on the beaches, but this was a risk that had to be taken. Preparations for the landings began in January 1944.

As preparations for the Anzio assault were completed, General Clark ordered the Fifth Army to attack the enemy stronghold of Cassino in order to divert their attention. Reinforced by units of the Eighth Army and the Free French Expeditionary Force, commanded by General Juin, the battle for Cassino started on 12 January 1944 with simultaneous attacks on German positions along the Gustav line. Clark wanted Allied forces to be ready to break through Cassino when the VI Corps landed at Anzio on 22 January so that he could link up with the landing force before the Germans had time to patch the hole in their defensive wall. Had the scheme worked, the Allies would have soon been on their way to Rome.

During the first three days, the attack on enemy positions near Cassino went relatively smoothly; by 15 January French forces had taken Sant' Elia and the American II Corps was ready to cross the Rapido river. The X Corps had already crossed the Garigliano and established a beachhead on the other side of the river. At this point, however, the Allies suffered reverses. First, the Americans were not able to cross the Rapido. The Germans who had laid mine fields on the northern bank of the river and had pill boxes constructed in the hills overlooking it forced the Americans to abandon the crossing after sustaining heavy casualties.

counter-attacked wherever Allied lines were most vulnerable. With the sea at their backs, American forces had to fight very hard to preserve their beachhead and the breakthrough to the coast road and the interior was considerably delayed, allowing the Germans to prepare their next defensive position before the Fifth Army was able to break through the ring around Salerno.

Allied forces did not reach the Volturno River north of Naples until the first week in October. By this time, the Eighth Army had seized the Axis air field at Foggia and was moving west to the aid of the Americans, in the hope that through a joint assault the Allies could break through the German line on the Volturno and speed on toward Rome, some 100 miles to the north. The capture of Rome with its air fields and communications facilities would be a genuine triumph and a great morale booster, and hence every effort would be made to take the Eternal City as quickly as possible. But the Allies were also sure that Hitler would spare no effort to deprive them of this victory and that the march toward Rome would be difficult. Even so, they did not realize just how difficult it would be.

The distance from the Volturno to Rome was relatively short but the path was difficult to traverse and easy to defend. Aside from the narrow marshy coastal plain, the area west of the coast road was mountainous and impossible for heavily mechanized units to pass through. On the other hand, such terrain provided unlimited opportunities for defensive positions and permitted the enemy to harrass advancing Allied forces with a minimum investment of manpower and equipment. This allowed the Germans to use their

Second, the beachhead on the northern bank of Garigliano could not be expanded due to heavy German counter-attacks. It was only through sheer luck and dogged resistance that the Americans managed to hold on to this position at all.

Given these unexpected reverses, General Clark ordered his forces to move north of Cassino and try once again to cross the Rapido while the French assaulted Monte Cassino. The crossing was completed at the end of January but the attempt to move beyond the river failed after two weeks of intensive fighting. It proved impossible to dislodge the Germans from their hilltop bunkers and machine gun emplacements and

Above: Mussolini, captured by Skorzeni, was flown back to Germany.
Below left: Italian anti-US poster. **Below:** Partisans and Americans talk with captured German officers near Milan.

I DELITTI INUMANI DEI "GANGSTERS PILOTI" RADIANO PER SEMPRE GLI STATI UNITI DAL CONSORZIO CIVILE

Victory in Italy was dearly bought. This tank was knocked out by a 75-mm gun and its crew paid the supreme penalty.

Allied prisoners captured near Anzio are marched through the Piazza Venezia in Rome.

American forces were withdrawn from the area on 12 February, to be replaced by fresh troops from the New Zealand Corps.

The New Zealanders had no better luck than the Americans or the French. Although Allied aircraft bombed German positions atop Monte Cassino, completely destroying the old and famous monastery, Commonwealth forces failed to break through and capture Highway 6 which would lead the Allies to Rome. In fact, the bombing strikes helped the Germans hold the area, since the rubble provided an additional obstacle course for the Allies to overcome. When it became obvious that there was little point in continuing

what was essentially an impossible mission, the effort was broken off and the attempt to take Monte Cassino was postponed until March. As February drew to a close, Germany's defensive positions remained intact.

The Allies' failure at Cassino had grave consequences for the landing party that had been put ashore at Anzio on 22 January. The landing had been conceived as an outflanking maneuver which would permit the Allies to break through German defenses in a simultaneous assault on rear and frontal enemy positions. But when the attack at Cassino failed, the invaders found themselves trapped along the coast with no place to retreat but the sea. What had started out as a relief expedition was now in need of relief.

Ironically, the actual landing had been carried out without incident, but it was not long before the Germans isolated VI Corps near Anzio and counter-attacked. Although the Americans were only forty miles south of Rome and might well have seized the Eternal City by surprise, this was not within the scope of their operation. Failing to receive orders to the contrary, General Lucas kept his forces in place where they were soon surrounded by German units rushed in from northern Italy and Yugoslavia at the order of Marshal Kesselring. Here the Americans were contained until May.

Hitler was infuriated by the audacity of the Anzio landing and was determined that the Allies

be given no quarter. Referring to the Allied offensive as an 'abcess', the Fuehrer told Kesselring that the situation should be treated as if it were a medical crisis, through radical surgery. This Kesselring was only partially successful in achieving. The Allied landing party was driven back to the beaches, but there they stubbornly held out until late in May when a breakthrough was finally achieved at Monte Cassino. Operation Shingle may have failed, but no thought was given to evacuating Anzio if the position could be held.

In the long run, Hitler's obsession with turning back the Allied landing party at Anzio proved fortuitous, for while German forces were concentrated in this area no effort was made to reinforce their position along the Gustav line. When the Allies resumed their attack the lack of an adequate reserve force hampered German efforts to keep them at bay. In launching the new attack, Allied commanders were careful to avoid concentrating their forces at Cassino. General Alexander preferred, instead, to deploy his troops along a broader front; units of the Eighth Army were withdrawn from positions along the Adriatic coast and despatched to assist the Fifth Army. Together, they were to attack German defensive positions over a thirteen mile front stretching from the sea to the Liri valley. If all went well, a hole would be punched in the German position somewhere along the line, the American garrison at Anzio would be relieved, and the Allies would gain coastal Highway 7 which led to Rome.

The Fifth Army concentrated its attack in the hills since previous attacks along the coast had proved costly and unproductive. At the same time, the Eighth Army resumed the attack on German defenses near Cassino, hoping to ford the Rapido

below the city. A third effort, an attempt to scale Monte Cassino, would be undertaken by the newly arrived Polish Corps. The battle was to begin on 11 May.

The Germans had not thought that the Allies would renew their offensive nor had they prepared for an action along such a wide front. As a result, although the early action was heavy and not immediately successful for the Allies, they were finally able to break through the German line. By 17 May French forces, which had supplemented the Poles in the attempt to take Monte Cassino, had succeeded in dislodging the Germans from positions near the base and in the foothills of the mountains, and on the following day Polish forces reached the summit. For the Poles, this was a significant breakthrough and one which was fraught with poetic justice. Like their French compatriots, they found that revenge was sweet.

With Monte Cassino and the surrounding area in Allied hands, the Germans were forced to abandon the Gustav line on 23 May. They withdrew to Rome where a brief but unsuccessful attempt was made to establish another defensive position in front of the city. To his credit Marshal Kesselring refused to destroy the city in order to block the Americans' advance. On 4 June the capital was declared an open city and American forces entered it later that day. The capture of Rome was an achievement of tremendous importance and symbolized more graphically than any other victory to that date the collapse of the Axis. Although the sequel to the march into Rome was slow and frustrating, with the Germans grimly holding on in northern Italy for six more months, Hitler was unmistakenly on the defensive, retreating from Italy and trying to defend France.

When the tables turned, Italians cheered the Allied entry into Rome after it was declared an open city.

CHAPTER THIRTEEN
Operation Overlord

Below: Planning Operation
Overlord – left to right:
Eisenhower, Air Chief-
Marshal Leigh-Mallory,
Air Chief-Marshal Tedder
and Montgomery.
Opposite top: A German
Kampfgruppe marching to
take up their positions along
the Atlantic Wall.
Opposite center:
American Flying Fortresses,
newly arrived in Britain,
soon to be used against the
factories of the Ruhr.
Opposite bottom:
American airmen shortly
before D-Day.

In January 1944 General Dwight D. Eisenhower returned to London to take charge of the mightiest fighting force in Western history. The directive from the Allied Combined Chiefs of Staff was simple. The principal paragraph read, 'You will enter the continent of Europe and, in conjunction with the other Allied Nations, undertake operations aimed at the heart of Germany and the destruction of her Armed Forces.' The destruction of the German forces was the paramount principle; the occupation of land was important only in so far as it would help to achieve this goal.

Even before the United States entered the war American planners had concluded that, in the event of war with the Axis powers, Germany would have to be defeated first. Not only was she industrially far more powerful than Japan, but the Allies would find it easier to mass forces for a concentrated attack against her. Any offensive mounted against the Japanese would have to be conducted almost solely by the United States.

The 'Japan First' viewpoint, however, was not without its advocates and, especially after the attack on Pearl Harbor on 7 December 1941, found increasingly vocal support. But the black days immediately after the attack found Allied forces reeling backward, trying desperately to slow the Japanese advance. Meanwhile, the Germans had been stopped short of Moscow and, with the winter of 1942 setting in, Russian partisans were strangling German communications and supply lines. Thus while in the Pacific Allied

forces were steadily being driven out of Asia, in the West the Germans appeared to be an easier target, wedged in between British and Russian threats.

Keeping Russia in the war was imperative, but it was necessary to assure her that, contrary to appearances in those last days of 1941, she was not carrying on the war with Germany alone. To the Russians, anything other than a direct attack on Germany would be unpalatable, but especially a front in the Pacific where the Soviet Union was not even a belligerent. Thus from 1941 to 1943, the goal of defeating Germany first became more urgent.

Although British and American planners were in agreement over the need to defeat Germany before Japan, they could not decide where and when the offensive should take place. As early as 1942 General George C. Marshall had planned a cross-channel invasion (code name 'Roundup') but the British had balked. In 1942 the British would have had to bear the brunt of the responsibility and provide most of the manpower, which they could not afford to do at a time when their forces were hard-pressed in North Africa.

The Russians, desperately holding off the Germans, were not favorably impressed with Allied gains in the Mediterranean, for they failed to see how it would materially relieve the pressure on their front. Winston Churchill, however, continued to advocate the 'soft underbelly' of Europe approach, arguing that these operations would knock Italy out of the war and stop the attacks upon British convoys that were trying to continue the lifeline through the Mediterranean to the Suez Canal. Control of the Italian bases would undermine if not completely remove the Luftwaffe as a threat to Allied shipping in the Mediterranean, and German forces might have to be diverted from other fronts to replace the Italian troops that would be lost.

American thinkers, however, felt that the application of Allied resources to what was essentially a side show would mean diverting badly needed and meager supplies to a painfully slow, grinding war that would not yield immediate dividends either in the early defeat of Germany or the relief of the Russian front. As a compromise, the invasion of Sicily and the subsequent Italian campaign were launched.

The slow but steady progress in Italy permitted the Combined Chiefs of Staff to turn once again to the planning of a cross-channel invasion. Such an operation had in the meantime attained a new sense of urgency. The Russians had smashed the Germans at Stalingrad and were on the offensive for the first time. Their demands for a coordinated attack on two fronts would not be satisfied by the diversionary Italian front.

On the German side, since the failure to capture Moscow in the fall of 1941, the unpleasant prospect of having to fight a two-front war had become a reality by 1942, first with the Allied North African invasion and then with the Italian campaign. Allied progress in Italy pointed out their vulnerability in the West and now, for the first time since Dunkirk, Adolf Hitler set about defending that flank.

The task of defending land which had already been conquered in the West appeared to be far more difficult than the original *blitzkrieg*. Since the invasion coastline, which stretched in a mighty arc from Norway to Greece, had been penetrated by the Allies in Italy, Allied superiority in air and naval forces could assure a safe cover for landings anywhere. The coasts of Denmark and Norway appeared especially vulnerable; landings via the North Sea south into Germany was also a possibility. As a matter of fact, German intelligence agents flooded higher headquarters with reports of prospective landings in the vicinity of the Franco-Spanish border as well as in southern France.

Logic, however, dictated that a direct invasion across the English Channel could be best supported from England and this possibility came to receive the most urgent attention in Germany. The strengthening of fixed fortifications along the Channel coast and the reinforcing of the garrisons manning these structures claimed the highest priority; responsibility for the project was given to Field Marshal von Runstedt.

The Atlantic Wall

The nucleus of the coastal defense system was the Atlantic Wall, built under the auspices of a Nazi labor organization called Todt. The quality and quantity of the fortifications was hardly uniform, being strongest in Holland and the Pas de Calais area, reasonably strong in Normandy and Brittany, with the stronger areas connected by structures which were little more than field earthworks.

The acerbic von Runstedt was appalled by the concepts and quality of the fortifications, and even more bitter about the men that were assigned to hold them. The Russian front had drained most of the divisions of their best fighting men, and many were under strength, woefully under-equipped and demoralized. Large numbers of the troops consisted either of older men, convalescents from the Russian front, or captured foreign prisoners of war (most notably Russians) from earlier campaigns. According to von Runstedt, of the sixty nominal divisions assigned to defend the West, no more than fifteen could be considered to be first-line units.

It is always difficult to take a hostile shore by direct assault and the task is increased tenfold when the enemy has long anticipated such an attack and is doing his utmost to strengthen his defenses. Though Allied bombing raids had taken their toll of German aircraft the enemy had

British women serve tea to American servicemen during the build-up before D-Day.

General von Rundstedt was appalled by the quality of the coastal fortifications.

the shortest distance across the English Channel, being only some 20 miles from Dover, but intelligence reports indicated that the Germans were rushing reinforcements into this area as fast as they could and were rapidly improving the fortifications. The Caen area, though farther away, appeared to be less well-fortified and more removed from enemy supply and troop concentrations. Moreover, it was within range for most of the fighter cover that the Allies considered vital to the success of the operation.

Thus it was decided that the landing operation (now given the code name 'Overlord') be conducted in Normandy. Plans called for an initial assault wave of five divisions with two more in reserve. Once the landing had been successfully concluded, the five-division force should be strong enough to pick a soft spot on the wide beach for a breakout toward Paris.

The initial responsibility for planning such an invasion in the early days of 1943 had been British, but as American manpower had begun to predominate, an American, General Dwight D. Eisenhower was appointed Supreme Commander with a British deputy, Air Chief Marshal Sir Arthur Tedder. The field commander of the entire assault was Lt. Gen. Omar Bradley. The assault forces would be composed of American, British and Canadian forces.

One major restriction placed upon selecting a date for the operation was the shortage of landing craft. Though priority was given to Overlord and landing craft were gathered in from all over the world to the protests of their commanders, the original plan to invade in May 1944 had to be postponed until June so that more vessels could be produced. In the meantime, the Allied command had to contend with an increasingly impatient Soviet Union on the need to open a second front.

Plans called for an airborne assault to precede the actual landing; this required a moonlit night for parachute and glider landings. At the same time, the Allied command needed a period of relatively low tides so that landing craft could avoid the thousands of steel barricades on the beaches. Furthermore, the navy wanted to approach the shore under cover of darkness, yet have at least an hour of daylight to bombard shore defenses. This combination of requirements fixed the alternate dates to a period between 5 and 7 June, or about the 20th of the month. The latter date was discarded since it meant further delay. Thus, 5 June was picked as the date and 0630 as the time.

Ironically, the Germans had also guessed that the attack would take place either at Pas de Calais or in Normandy. Pas de Calais was considered more likely since it was the closest point to Britain and also because it was near the launching sites of the V-1 and V-2 rockets that would soon be creating havoc in England. With the erratic intuition that he sometimes seemed to possess, Adolf Hitler had personally picked Normandy as a likely place. This was transmitted to von Runstedt, but while the Field Marshal agreed that Normandy offered a possible site, he persisted in the belief that it would afford only a feint designed to draw German forces away from the main assault at Pas de Calais.

responded to the growing threat in the West by increasing fighter aircraft production. Most of the factories were beyond the reach of Allied fighter escort range in 1943 and early 1944 and Allied bombers were being lost at an alarming rate.

The effectiveness of strategic bombing in World War II has been the center of much controversy; it is sufficient to state that its results were overrated. The role of enemy fighter interdiction against a landing operation was the cause for great anxiety, and the choice of a landing site depended in part upon the ability of Allied airpower to maintain its superiority until the beachhead could be successfully established.

Another consideration in choosing a landing site was the need to establish supply lines to the assault troops once they had gained a foothold. It was known that the major ports would be destroyed in the event of Allied attack and thus the attacking forces would have to depend on protected beaches for reinforcement and supply.

The coast of western Europe offered a number of prospective landing areas from Holland to Bordeaux. The limited range of fighter air cover precluded Denmark or the German coastline on the North Sea, and other considerations such as restricted exits from beach areas, the ease of German counterattack and supply problems gradually reduced the number of areas to Pas de Calais and the Normandy coast between Caen and Cherbourg. The Pas de Calais area offered

The possibility of a secondary or diversionary attack in support of the main attack did, of course, exist. The Allied Combined Chiefs of Staff had formulated an operational plan called 'Anvil' to be launched simultaneously against the southern French coast. But though it was to be a supporting attack, the landing craft it required would take equipment away from Overlord. Eisenhower hung on to the idea for weeks, but finally, when he realized that Overlord would be seriously undermined, the Supreme Commander reluctantly decided to postpone Anvil.

The German high command in the west at this time suffered from a difference in opinion between von Runstedt and his chief subordinate, Field Marshal Erwin Rommel, who commanded Army Group 'B', the organization charged with the defense of the coastline itself. The controversy centered around the commitment of the mobile reserve of some ten tank divisions which constituted the chief hope of shattering any Allied landing.

Rommel was convinced that the only time to smash the Allied effort was at the beach areas and therefore he argued for placing the tanks as near the coast as possible. Though von Runstedt agreed with the need to shake the Allies loose from whatever toehold they could gain as soon as possible, he was afraid of using his reserves prematurely, before the actual size and disposition of the Allied attack could be discerned.

Above: Artillery being loaded into LCTs for the attack on Normandy.
Left: Ike gives final instructions to US paratroopers, just before they board their airplanes in the first assault of the invasion of Europe.
Below left: 'Synchronize your watches'.

Below: Scharnhorst Length: 741½ ft. Beam: 98½ ft. Draught: 24½ ft. Maximum speed: 31½ knots. Armament: 9 × 11 in., 12 × 5.9 in., 14 × 4 in., 16 × 37 mm., 38 × 20 mm., 6 × 21 in. torpedo tubes, 4 aircraft Crew: 1800. Displacement: 32,000 tons.

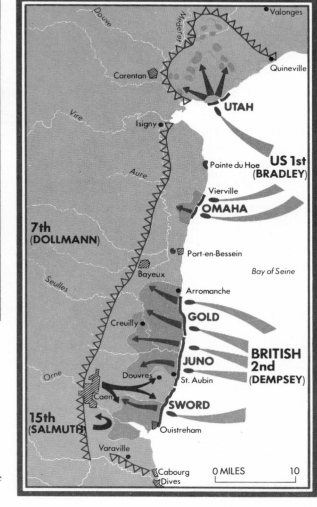

Top left: US paratroops practice for a training drop.
Top right: RAF base jammed with Dakotas.
Far left: 'This is the Enemy', a piece of American propaganda which possibly drew its inspiration from the films of Erich von Stroheim.
Above left: A German warning which almost came true for the Americans.

The relations between the aging and haughty von Runstedt and the Fuehrer had never been cordial, whereas Rommel was the hero of the African campaign. Due to his direct influence with Hitler, he was able to inject his personal view into von Runstedt's overall plan. The result was a rather fatal compromise; the tanks were placed neither close enough to have an immediate effect upon the landing nor far enough away to be able to respond flexibly to changing situations. Furthermore, four of the ten divisions were scattered in the general reserve for south and southwest France. Control of the divisions was divided between the two commanders. When the Allied attack began, there was neither sufficient power to push the Allies into the sea, nor enough to form a significant counterattack.

The German analysis of the situation was confused by the Allies' efforts at deception. Throughout southern England phony camps were assembled with false unit designations; radio traffic simulated an army commanded by General George S. Patton, and as the invasion date drew near – movement in and out of the staging area became increasingly restricted. British agents deliberately sought to confuse German commanders by planting false information, aided in their task by disagreement between German intelligence and the Nazi political command Postwar reports show that when the all-Nazi secret service under Himmler tried to assess invasion data, they made over two hundred guesses, all of which proved incorrect.

Actually the German side was not alone in being deceived. Nazi efforts to build up the 'invincibility' of the Atlantic Wall were at least partially effective in creating the impression that the Pas de Calais area was heavily fortified. This was true, but the extent of fortification was greatly exag-

Previous page: Thousands of reinforcements and pieces of equipment poured into Normandy when the beachhead was secured.
Left: British Commandos attack Sword Beach.

Bottom: Caen was the crucible of Normandy. Its seizure insured Allied victory in France.
Below: MA–A2 Sherman Length: 19 ft. $5\frac{7}{16}$ in. Width: 8 ft. 7 in. Maximum road speed: 29 m.p.h. Armament: 1 × 75 mm., 1 × .30 machine gun, 1 × .50 machine gun. Crew: 5. Weight 31.8 tons.

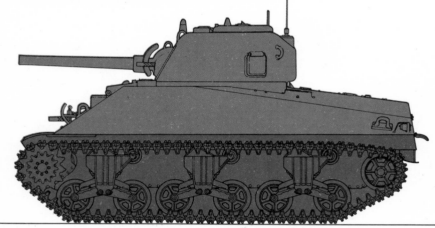

gerated. This in turn helped influence the Allied decision to invade Normandy instead.

An operation involving such vast numbers of men in a wide area created many security problems, and there were a number of incidents that could have compromised the plans. Loose-mouthed officers and freak accidents gave the planners nightmares. One hot day in May, copies of a top-secret document were actually blown into the streets of London. Frantic staff officers recovered all except one, and a few agonizing hours passed before it was discovered that a passerby had picked it up and given it to a Horse Guard.

The crucial factor upon which the entire operation depended was the weather, since men and ships would have to move at least three days before the actual D-Day. Should a sudden change occur prohibiting landing operations, the lead elements would have gone too far to be recalled. On 1 June, to the horror of the high command, the skies turned ominously grey. The next day, weather forecasts predicted high winds and low visibility for June 5, 6 and 7. At a meeting on 3 June, the chief meterologist advised the Supreme Commander to postpone the operation. For Eisenhower, those were heavy hours. A postpone-ment of this sort was sure to undermine the physical status and morale of the troops at sea. Furthermore, there would be no way to avoid letting the troops out on leave, and the chances of secrecy would be practically impossible. In practical terms, postponing the invasion meant almost 30 days of keeping a secret that was

Vergeltungswaffe Eins (V-1)
Length: 26 ft. Span:
17 ft. 6 in. Maximum speed:
410 m.p.h. Range: 150
miles. Armament: 1870 lbs.
warhead. Weight: 4800 lbs.

The British landing on Juno Beach. Some men never made it and their bodies had to be carried out of the water.

no secret to almost 150,000 men. The effect of a delay were not limited to immediate problems. It would also mean reducing the time available for a summer campaign in France and would restrict the use of the channel ports before stormy weather arrived.

The Germans relaxed during the bad weather, realizing that the chances of invasion were considerably less promising. Rommel made plans to return to Germany to celebrate his wife's birthday on 6 June. Most of the senior commanders were scheduled to attend a paper war exercise to test out anti-invasion plans. But at a meeting on 4 June, Eisenhower was told that a

temporary break in the weather might occur on the 6th. It was at best a fifty-fifty chance, but the next definite break would not be toward the end of the month, and besides, there was the commitment to the Russians to consider. Reluctantly, Eisenhower gave the order to proceed.

In the dark, British and American paratroops preceded by special Pathfinder teams and followed by glider troops dropped into Normandy. Their mission was to seize and secure bridges and other vital points behind the coastal defenses to delay German attempts to reinforce the shore garrisons. Due to errors in judgment and wind conditions, many were dropped a considerable distance from

Below: Normandy prisoners pour into Britain.

their intended zones, but these highly trained men exploited local situations wherever they could, disrupting communications, ambushing German couriers and generally creating confusion. Cut off from each other, the Germans could not effectively assess the extent of the penetration.

Some 2700 vessels loaded with men and equipment crossed the English Channel. At dawn German coastal watchers saw the armada deploy with fascinated horror; shortly afterward, the heaviest bombardment of the war commenced. Overhead, Allied aircraft flew a total of 25,000 sorties. There were almost no German aircraft in operation on 6 June over the beaches while in England, on average, an aircraft took off every 3.5 seconds.

The landing zone was divided into five main areas. Two on the west flank, code named Utah and Omaha, were American responsibilities. The remaining three, named Gold, Juno and Sword, were to be occupied by British and Canadian troops. The first assault wave at Omaha numbered 34,000 troops with 3300 vehicles; a second wave of 25,000 men and 4400 vehicles followed. Behind Omaha, the brush covered ground rose steeply to about 150 feet, and here the Germans concentrated their heaviest forces; soon the landing was considerably behind schedule, creating a serious follow-up problem due to the anticipated change in the weather. The beach was littered with wrecked landing craft and disabled tanks, and the congestion of men and equipment created problems in evacuating casualties.

The landing at Utah Beach went 2000 yards beyond the landing point, but it was a disguised blessing, for the obstacles at that point were far less formidable. Quick thinking exploited the situation and men were fed into the area, thereby avoiding the heavier losses that might have been suffered at the original point of landing.

Despite such difficulties, however, by mid-morning over 18,000 Americans were on Omaha alone, and the Germans had failed to mount a single serious counterattack. By late afternoon Omaha and Utah beaches were linked by a thin sliver of American troops who had made their way through German defenses via a narrow country road.

The British assault began a half-hour after that of the Americans. The landing procedure was similar, but the British had improvised a number of devices to penetrate minefields and bridge shell craters. A number of tanks were equipped with revolving drums attached with short lengths of chain. Acting as a flail, they cleared a path through German minefields for the infantry. The British later were subjected to the only two major German attempts at armor attacks, both of which failed, thus depriving the enemy of their last tank reserves.

The Germans first suspected that a major operation was about to develop after intercepting a large number of coded BBC messages to the French underground. Based on these reports, German forces near Paris went on conditional alert but the men in Normandy were not warned at all.

The first overt signs of invasion activity occurred when reports arrived at von Runstedt's head-

quarters of parachute landings. Attempts to get a clear picture of the situation were negated by the disruptive tactics of the paratroops, and at least in the beginning, much of the activity was dismissed as nuisance tactics.

Once the front-line troops on the coast were hit, the paratroops saw to it that, in effect, the coastal area was isolated from the rest of France and thus from reinforcement. Feeble armor attacks failed because the von Runstedt-Rommel compromise had deprived them of sufficient striking power; without sufficient armor, little could be done about reinforcing the coast until more troops arrived, but Allied air superiority saw to it that few would. The Luftwaffe was effectively shot out of the air in the preparatory air strikes before the invasion. Then, without any enemy to contend with, Allied fighters strafed and bombed every bridge, railway line, marshaling yard and road within range so that nothing could move on the surface.

The Germans had only one other source of troops and that was the Fifteenth Army in northern France, Belgium and Holland. But the notion that Pas de Calais was the main site of an invasion and that Normandy was a diversion died hard. The Allied tactics of deception had done their work, and the Germans continued to believe that there was another army under Patton still in England awaiting embarkation.

After two weeks von Runstedt finally became convinced that Normandy was the main attack but Berlin continued to believe that Pas de Calais would be attacked and refused to release the troops in northern France. Hitler did not change his mind until August, and by then it was too late. With no troops to reinforce the Normandy area, there was little that could be done to patch the break other than to cling desperately to the ground still occupied. Cherbourg and other ports held and inflicted casualties upon Allied forces, but the end was inevitable.

Top left: American Liberty ships were deliberately scuttled off the beaches to provide makeshift breakwaters during the first days of the invasion.
Top center: Not every American made it to the cliffs overlooking Omaha Beach. **Above:** Once the beaches were secured, the Allies clambered over the chalk cliffs to penetrate the interior. **Left:** Two days after D-Day; the beaches were well under control, and an unceasing flow of troops and supplies reinforced combat units.

CHAPTER FOURTEEN
The Russian Front: 1942-1944

Operation Barbarossa ground to a halt in December 1941 and for three months the Russian front remained calm. Although Hitler had failed to achieve a quick victory over the Soviet Union, he remained committed to continuing the struggle against the Russians, using the winter interlude to prepare for a new offensive in the spring of 1942. The Soviets also took advantage of the lull to prepare an offensive of their own.

As it happened, the Soviets struck first. Underestimating the strength of the Germans and overestimating their own capacity, the Russians launched a three-pronged offensive in March 1942: in the Crimea, an effort was made to relieve the siege of Sevastapol; in the north, an effort was made to restore communication and transportation links between Moscow and Leningrad; and in the south, a major campaign was undertaken to recapture Kharkov and re-establish Soviet control of the Donetz basin. All three efforts failed.

The Russian campaign in the Crimea was quickly turned back by German forces and as many as 100,000 Soviet troops were taken prisoner. Far from relieving the siege of Sevastopol, the collapse of the Russian offensive insured that the city would fall, and fall it did on 1 July after a long and bitter confrontation in the suburbs. With the loss of Sevastopol, Russian hopes to re-establish a strong position in the Crimea faded.

The Soviets met with no better luck in their effort to reopen lines of communication between Moscow and Leningrad and relieve the siege of the latter. In fact, the battle for Leningrad proved an even greater disaster than the Crimean offensive. Leningrad had been isolated by German forces during the winter months in an effort to starve the city into submission; though Russian efforts to break the siege had failed repeatedly, a whole army being lost in January 1942 in an effort to cut through German lines, the Soviet commander in the city would not surrender. Except for those who endured the Battle of Stalingrad, few have ever sustained more hardship or suffering than the defenders of Leningrad. During the winter months of 1941 the death rate soared to several thousand per day for want of food, shelter, and proper clothing, while the Germans continued their unmerciful shelling of the city. Unless the siege was soon lifted, the city would surely be destroyed.

Stalin could not permit the slaughter in Leningrad to continue without making one last effort, and Russian forces massed near Moscow in preparation for a march to the west. The offensive was to begin in May with General Andrei Vlasov

Above: Marshal Timoshenko hoped to push the Wehrmacht back into the Ukraine.
Opposite top: The Russian campaign in Crimea was quickly turned back, these three were among almost 100,000 Soviet troops taken prisoner.
Opposite bottom: German soldiers examine a T-34 captured when the Soviet Crimean front collapsed.

Russian T34-76. Length: 21 ft. 7 in. Width: 9 ft. 10 in. Maximum road speed: 32 m.p.h. Armament: 1 × 76 mm., 2 × 7.62 mm. machine guns. Crew: 4 Weight: 27 tons 16 cwt.

commanding the relief army. He fared no better than his colleagues in the Crimea. After an initial breakthrough, Vlasov's army was encircled and, without adequate reinforcements and supplies, was destroyed in front of Leningrad. Residents of the former Russian capital, however, continued to hold fast, refusing to surrender to the Germans. They paid dearly for their bravery; by year's end the population had been reduced to less than a million, one-third the prewar population of the city.

After the failures in the Crimea and Leningrad, the southern offensive remained the Soviet's only hope, and here they mounted their largest effort, massing an army of hundreds of thousands of men and the best equipment available. The Russian army in this area was under the command of Marshal Semen Timoshenko, who hoped to crush German positions south of Kharkov and push the Wehrmacht back into the Ukraine and from there into Poland. The campaign started on 12 May 1942 with a successful dash through German positions south of the city. It was five days before the Germans could recover their equilibrium and counter-attack, but by then Soviet lines were overstretched, forming a corridor seventy miles long which the Germans attacked on 18 May. By 23 May what had appeared to be a Russian victory was turned into a disaster; German forces surrounded Timoshenko's army, capturing over 240,000 men and most of their equipment, and inflicting a defeat even greater than that suffered in front of Leningrad.

Having disposed of the Russian offensives, the Germans were ready to launch one of their own. Hitler intended bringing the Caucasus under German control. To achieve this, German forces were redistributed so as to permit the continuation of the 1941 campaign in the southern sector. Forces in Leningrad and Moscow were placed on the defensive so that Army Group South could be reinforced prior to the new campaign.

Army Group South was divided into two com-

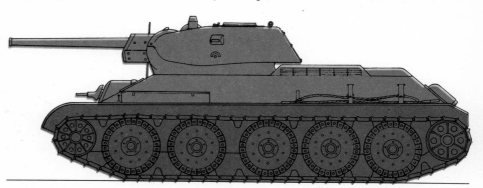

General von Kleist's Fourth Army took the Maikops oilfields by 9 August 1942.

Chuikov was determined to hold the bridgeheads along the Volga.

ponents, Army Group A, under the command of General List, and Army Group B, under the command of General von Bock; Army Group A was to strike for the Caucasus while Army Group B secured its left flank. To bolster these forces, additional troops from the satellite countries (Hungary, Italy, and Rumania) would be despatched to the Russian front where they would assist Army Group B in maintaining the long and vulnerable line stretching from Voronezh to Stalingrad. The scheme was a bold one and perhaps beyond the capacity of the Wehrmacht to fulfill, but Hitler would hear of nothing less than a total seizure of the southern region. Rather than argue with their leader, the German generals once again fell in with his plans.

The German offensive was to begin in June and Russian forces, still retreating after their defeat in May, were not able to offer effective resistance to the Wehrmacht's advance. Army Group B moved easily toward the Donetz and Don basins, and it was only when von Bock's forces reached Veronezh at the beginning of July that the Soviets mounted a counter-attack.

The Stalingrad Slaughter

The Soviet commander at Veronezh, General Vatutin, was under orders from Stalin to prevent the Germans from marching north to Moscow at any cost. Had Hitler permitted von Bock to engage Vatutin, as he originally wished to do, the battle would have undoubtedly been one of the bloodiest and most costly of the war in the Soviet Union. Fortunately Hitler would not permit such

a diversion because he realized only too well that this would delay the race for the Caucasus; since he had no immediate intention of pressing an attack on the Soviet capital, a confrontation with Vatutin's forces be of little value. Von Bock was overruled and later dismissed, and the original plan proceeded apace.

While Army Group B raced toward the Don north of Stalingrad, mechanized units from Army Group A pressed an attack on Rostov, further south. Assisted by units from von Bock's command which had been ordered south at the insistence of the Fuehrer, General von Kleist's Fourth Panzer Army took Rostov on 28 July and proceeded toward the Maikops oil fields; these were taken by 9 August, although the Soviets destroyed much of the equipment in the fields as they retreated to the east. By 22 August German forces reached Mount Elbrus and continued their march east, heading toward the oil fields at Grozny and Baku. It appeared at the beginning of September that Hitler's goals might well be achieved, but the momentum of the offensive was soon slowed as problems of supply increasingly plagued List's army. Dismissing List and replacing him with General von Kleist did not improve the situation. Ironically, although the Germans had struck deep into the heartland of the Caucasus and captured the oil fields so important to their war effort, they were short of petroleum products and could not continue their rapid advance due to the scorched earth policy of the retreating Soviets. Until the rigs and equipment in the Maikops fields could be repaired and replaced, all gasoline and oil for Army Group A had to be carried overland from the west, a difficult if not impossible task. By the end of September they were forced to stop the offensive several hundred miles short of their objective.

The diversion of General Hoth's tank corps to the Caucasus delayed the movement of Army Group B south to Stalingrad, and von Kleist was not able to swing south from Veronezh until the beginning of August. By this time the Soviets had recovered from their earlier defeats and were preparing to defend Stalin's namesake against the invaders. When the Germans reached the outskirts of the city at the end of the month, the stage was set for the greatest contest of the war in Russia.

General Paulus's Sixth Army reached the suburbs of Stalingrad on 23 August and succeeded in penetrating the outer defenses of the city, establishing a bridgehead to the north, on the

Volga. That evening the Luftwaffe launched a massive raid on Stalingrad, killing thousands of people and destroying most of the wooden buildings in the city. Paulus predicted the imminent capture of the city on the morning of 24 August, but far from creating a mentality of surrender, the Luftwaffe raid strengthened Russian resistance. The citizens of Stalingrad refused to bow before the German invaders; rather than have a foreign army occupy their city, they took to the streets, constructing barracades at every intersection from the rubble left by the air raid of the night before. For an army used to rapid movement across an unobstructed plain, the makeshift defense of Stalingrad proved an insurmountable obstacle, with each block a fortress, each house an enemy camp. In Stalingrad Germany's arsenal was neutralized as mechanized warfare gave way to house to house fighting.

Stalled outside the city center, Paulus called for reinforcements, leaving the protection of his flank to troops from the satellite countries, the most unreliable under the German command. For the moment, this seemed the wisest thing to do, but it was to have profound consequences in November when the Russians launched their counter-attack. For the moment, however, even this extra strength did not permit the capture of the city.

Paulus renewed his attack toward the end of September. By this time, German air raids had further reduced the city to rubble; there was hardly a major building which had not suffered some damage and what the bombers failed to destroy, artillery barrages wrecked. By all standards resistance should have been destroyed, but the people of Stalingrad continued to struggle on, manning their barricades and the factories which continued to produce the materials necessary to keep the effort alive.

Paulus succeeded in driving a corridor across the city to the Volga by the end of September, cutting the defending garrison in two as a result. Nevertheless, the fighting remained intense, with gains being measured in inches. Although a good part of the city was in German hands by the middle of November, the Russians continued to hold on, General Chuikov's forces stubbornly clinging to their bridgeheads along the Volga with their backs to the river.

Paulus hoped to deliver Stalingrad to Hitler as a Christmas present, but unknown to him, the Russians were preparing to launch a counter-attack. While Chuikov's forces tenaciously clung

Top: General von Manstein was ordered to relieve the German front.
Above: Rokossovsky commanded one of Zhukov's three armies defending Stalingrad.

Paulus could not retreat, but the Italians could, and did in December 1942.

to their positions, keeping awake by taking alcohol and benzedrine, General Zhukov was quietly massing a huge force north of the city along the Don. By mid-November he was ready to launch his counter-attack.

Zhukov's forces were divided into three armies under the command of Generals Golikov, Vatutin, and Rokossovsky. A fourth army under the command of General Yeremenko waited south of the city. On 19 November the Russians struck, surrounding the Sixth Army in a classic trap and catching Paulus completely by surprise. He hastily cabled Hitler for permission to withdraw from the city, but the Fuehrer refused to sanction a retreat, commanding Paulus to take Stalingrad or perish in the attempt.

Although he was adamant about refusing to allow a retreat from Stalingrad, Hitler recognized that General Paulus would have little chance of salvaging the situation if German forces did not relieve Zhukov's siege of the Wehrmacht garrison. Accordingly, he commissioned General von Manstein to gather a relief force, Army Group Don, to break through to the city and restore the German front. At the same time, Goering was ordered to supply Paulus's forces by air until ground contact could be re-established by von Manstein.

Despite his optimistic prattling, Goering could hardly supply the minimum daily needs of Paulus's forces in Stalingrad let alone do more. This failure made it even more essential that von Manstein break through to the city, but he could not begin his mission until rail and road communications were repaired; this was not done until the middle of December, by which time winter was setting in and the relief effort was threatened by the cold weather. Despite these obstacles, von Manstein moved toward Stalingrad on 12 December, getting to within 25–30 miles of the city by the end of the month. There his army was stalled and prevented from linking up with the rest of the Sixth Army by Russian forces which had had time to dig in around the city.

Ever the loyal soldier, Paulus made no attempt to break out of the Russian encirclement. To do so would have meant disobeying Hitler's order. Since the Fuehrer showed no sign of reconsidering his previous order to stand fast, Paulus kept the Sixth Army in the city until the new year. When General Rokossovsky offered him a chance to surrender on 8 January 1943, he refused. A second offer was similarly dismissed on 24 January after Paulus failed to persuade Hitler to

Il-2 Shturmovik. Length: 38 ft. ½ in. Span 48 ft. ½ in. Maximum speed: 251 m.p.h. Armament: 2 × N-37 or 2 × P37 Anti-tank cannon.

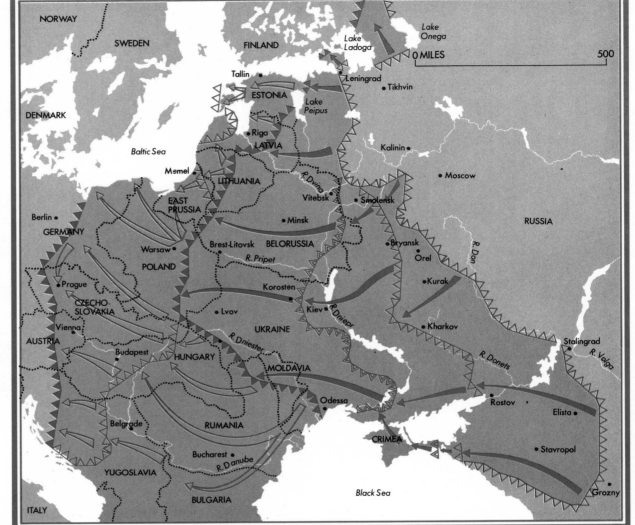

Limit of Axis Powers advance by Nov 1942

Ground reoccupied:

By 24 Aug 1943

25 Aug–23 Dec 1943

24 Dec 1943–29 Aug 1944

Advances made:

29 Aug 1944–20 Dec 1944

By May 1945

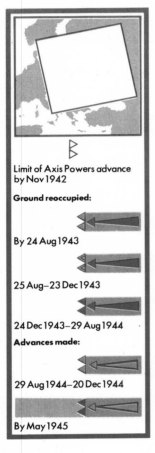

Below: Haggard and exhausted, the Germans fought on. **Bottom:** General von Paulus after his capture.

save his army. Although he warned the Fuehrer that further resistance was useless, Hitler remained adamant, replying: 'Surrender is forbidden. The Sixth Army will hold their positions to the last man and the last round . . .'.

The Sixth Army held on in Stalingrad until 31 January when Paulus, who had just been rewarded for his obedience by being promoted to the rank of Field Marshal, surrendered to the Russians when they captured his bunker. After more than four months, the battle for Stalingrad was over. In the effort to hold the city, the Germans sustained 72,000 deaths, 42,000 wounded, and 107,000 taken as prisoners of war. Rarely have so many been sacrificed for the whim of one man; rarely have a people fought so bravely for their city and their homes.

Stalingrad was one of the most decisive battles of the war. Before the battle, Germany's fortunes had reached a high point, but after the surrender, 'the paths for Hitler and his legions led only to the grave'. Churchill expressed the significance of the battle most succinctly:

This crushing disaster to the Germans ended Hitler's prodigious effort to conquer Russia by force of arms and destroy Communism by an equally odious form of totalitarian tyranny.

With the surrender of the Sixth Army in Stalingrad, the German offensive collapsed. Army Group A was pulled out of the Caucasus and the remnants of Army Group B and von Manstein's Army Group Don were regrouped in order to prevent the Russians from turning the retreat into a rout. In the north, the tide had also turned. A Russian offensive had succeeded in reopening part of the rail line between Moscow and Leningrad, and it was only a matter of time before the seige of Leningrad would be lifted. Only in the Crimea were the Germans able to hold their positions.

The victory at Stalingrad seemed to inspire the Red Army, which lost no time in pursuing the Germans to the west. By 7 February Soviet forces had captured Kursk, the original starting point of the German offensive in the Caucasus; two weeks later, they captured Kharkov. Although von Manstein managed to rally German forces and

Far left: Deployment of German armor near Kursk, the biggest tank battle in history. **Left:** German Pzkw-111 Specials advance through steppe grass set on fire by Russian shells.

Manstein was faced with an immediate Russian counter-offensive after Kursk.

German troops at Stalingrad, November 1942.

The Soviet triumph at Stalingrad was the most decisive battle of the war in Europe.

retake the latter, the German position was much diminished when the spring thaw made it impossible to continue the confrontation.

During the lull in the battle (April–July 1943), both sides reinforced their armies. Russian forces were strung along a long front stretching from Orel to Stalingrad with a bulge in the Kursk area. German forces occupied a smaller area along the Donetz river. For once, the Russian position was more exposed than the Wehrmacht's, inviting a German attack when the war was renewed in July. Zhukov and his associates expected the Germans to attack at Kursk and made preparations accordingly.

Struggle at Kursk
Von Manstein's Kursk offensive was the last German initiative of the war in Russia. The Germans amassed a large force equipped with the newest tanks and supported by a Luftwaffe armada of almost one thousand planes. The battle

began on 4 July 1943 with an assault on Russian positions near the Kursk bulge. Although the German Porsche and Panther tanks were far superior to Soviet armored vehicles, Russian tank reserves far outnumbered von Manstein's vehicles; even though the Germans inflicted losses on the Soviets at a rate approaching 2:1 tanks, the Red Army could still afford to sustain losses at this rate better than the Wehrmacht. After a week of direct confrontation, which involved as many as 3000 tanks at the height of the battle, the Germans were forced to call off the battle lest Zhukov's forces destroy what was left of the German army. On 13 July von Manstein was forced to sound the call to retreat. This time, even Hitler was forced to accept the inevitable and concur with his field commander. With the crisis brewing on the western front, he could ill afford to sacrifice what remained of Germany's armies in the Soviet Union.

After their defeat at Kursk, German forces were

The Big Three of the Teheran Conference: Stalin, Roosevelt and Churchill.

pushed back to the Russian border, but not before a last ditch attempt to hold strongpoints in the Soviet Union east of the Dnieper line. Hitler stubbornly clung to the belief that something might be salvaged from the Russian debacle. Although he recognized the need to withdraw German forces from the Kursk area, he would not accept von Manstein's advice to retreat rapidly to the Dnieper River, preferring to replace him with a 'more aggressive' commander, General Walter Model. However, by the time von Manstein was removed in February 1944, the situation was hopeless.

Had Hitler followed von Manstein's advice, it might have still been possible to prepare adequate defensive positions along the Dnieper, but by waiting till November to authorize a retreat to the river, he forfeited whatever chance the Germans might have had to establish a strong position. On 6 November, the Russians took Kiev and were pressed west toward Zhitomir, an important rail junction and German communication center. As winter approached, the Germans were still retreating; in January von Manstein was fighting in the Pripet marshes while further south, the Soviets pushed toward the Black Sea. On February 7, Nikopol fell to the Russians. The following week, they took Krivoy Rog. By the end of February, the Germans had been chased back to the Bug River, and when Model arrived to take command of what was left of the German army in the south, the Wehrmacht had been pushed back across the Pruth River into Rumania.

On the northern front, in January 1944, Russian forces crossed Lake Ilmen and moved north across

The Russian sacrifice equalled the German challenge.

Below left: General Model took command of a shattered German army in the South. **Below:** Silent testimony to the Soviet victory.

the adjacent swamps, while other Russian units established a beachhead just west of Leningrad at Oranienburg. By the end of the month, both groups converged on Leningrad forcing the Germans to abandon their 900-day siege of that city. The Germans were chased from Leningrad to the Luga River, from the Luga to Lake Peipus, and from Lake Peipus to Lake Pskov where they maintained a defensive position until May 1944.

With the Caucasus lost and the northern front deteriorating, it was only a matter of time before the Germans were forced to retreat from the Crimea. The Seventeenth Army had successfully withstood Soviet assaults on the Crimea but soon even this force had to be withdrawn, in April 1944.

At the Teheran Conference (November 1943),

Stalin agreed to launch an offensive against Germany in 1944 that would coincide with the long awaited invasion of France. He kept his word; as Anglo-American forces were ferried across the Channel and established their beachheads along the Normandy coast, the Red Army prepared to carry its drive against the Germans into eastern Europe and Germany's satellite states. Two and a half weeks after D-Day in France, the Soviets struck in Belorussia.

For this new offensive Stalin's commanders massed more than 100 divisions. The Germans, with a line of defense stretching from the Gulf of Finland to the Black Sea, were ill prepared to contain such a force, and when the Soviets struck the Wehrmacht caved in and collapsed. By the

Right: Russian poster encourages Soviet troops to drive out the German invader. **Opposite top:** A German soldier crushed by tanks during retreat. **Opposite left:** Russian soldiers dance in the streets of Lvov in the first days of its liberation. **Opposite bottom:** German Panzer forces lost their numerical superiority to the Russians in the southern sector of the front.

ВОИНЫ КРАСНОЙ АРМИИ!
КРЕПЧЕ УДАРЫ ПО ВРАГУ! ИЗГОНИМ НЕМЕЦКО-
ФАШИСТСКИХ МЕРЗАВЦЕВ С НАШЕЙ РОДНОЙ ЗЕМЛИ!

end of June the Germans were pushed back to a line stretching from Riga to Rumania but even this was too wide a front to defend. When Zhukov moved against General Busch's Army Group Centre in Belorussia, Hitler ordered Busch to stand fast at all costs, defending German positions to the last man. This policy was to have disastrous consequences.

The Soviets punched a 250-mile hole through Busch's line, moved forces through the hole and trapped Army Group Center. Busch could not escape from the encirclement and when the battle was over on 28 June the Germans had lost 350,000 men, an even greater number than were lost in the Battle of Stalingrad. They could ill afford to sustain such a defeat, for their forces were already spread paper thin. With the loss of Army Group Center, there was little chance of stopping the Russians; it could only be a matter of time before they reached the German border.

By the end of July the Soviets had taken Brest and Lublin, and were poised on the outskirts of Warsaw; Army Group North had been isolated in Estonia and Russian forces were ready to take Riga, while to the south, Lvov had been taken by General Koniev on 27 July, his forces marching north toward Warsaw during the last days of the month. The Russians could have taken Warsaw at the beginning of August but preferred instead to wait until the beginning of September, by which time the Germans themselves had dealt with Polish underground forces and razed the city.

Stalin's failure to relieve the Poles in the liberation of their capital excited the anger of the other Allied leaders but served Soviet interests; by the time Russian forces entered the city, the Germans had done their dirty work for them. There was little love lost between the Russians and the Poles and Stalin's refusal to press the attack against the Wehrmacht did nothing to improve this relationship. His explanation that the strength of the German counter-attack precluded an early move into the capital pleased few and satisfied no one. Nevertheless, Stalin was quite willing to postpone the defeat of Germany in order to extract a pound of flesh from the Poles; there would be time enough to tighten the noose around Hitler's neck.

CHAPTER FIFTEEN

The Tide Turns in the Pacific

Within six months after their attack on Pearl Harbor, the Japanese had succeeded in creating a Greater East Asia Co-Prosperity Sphere through force. Their original plans called for a defensive strategy, to cement their gains and protect against an eventual Allied counterattack. Understandably, however, Japanese leaders (especially in the navy) were reluctant to give up the initiative they had grasped so boldly and so successfully achieved.

Although the attack on Pearl Harbor had been a success in many ways, the American carrier force had not been incapacitated. It was entirely possible for the United States Navy to use these ships in an attempt to block further Japanese efforts and to eventually augment them for a strike against Japan itself. Unless and until this remnant of the American navy was destroyed, Japan's position in the Pacific would not be secure. Consequently, the ranking officers of the Japanese Navy proposed to expand the Pacific naval offensive in a final effort to neutralize the United States fleet. Specifically they proposed to extend Japan's defense perimeter through a campaign in

the area of the Coral Sea and a second attack on Midway Island, and lure the United States Navy into a battle in the Aleutians where it could be destroyed once and for all. After considerable debate, the Imperial Government approved the plan in April 1942.

The Battle of the Coral Sea was to be a combined aerial, land, and naval effort. Japanese ground and aerial units were assembled at Rabaul in New Britain while the fleet gathered off the island of Truk in the Caroline Island chain. On 3 May 1942 Japanese forces were landed on Tulagi, a small island in the Solomon chain, taking the island with no difficulty as its Australian garrison had already been withdrawn. Thanks to intelligence reports, the Allies were prepared for the attack; having deceived the Japanese at Tulagi into assuming that they would have an easy victory, what remained of America's Pacific Fleet prepared to do battle.

Admiral Nimitz had ordered his forces southward from Pearl Harbor as soon as he discovered that the Japanese were up to something. His fleet,

Admiral Chester W. Nimitz, US Commander-in-Chief, Pacific (CINCPAC).

Task Force 16 as seen from the flight deck of the USS *Enterprise* in the Coral Sea.

B.17.F. Length: 74 ft. 8.9 in.
Span: 103 ft. 9.38 in.
Maximum speed: 325
m.p.h. Armament:
7 × .30 machine guns,
9 × .50 machine guns.
Weight: 35,728 lbs. empty.

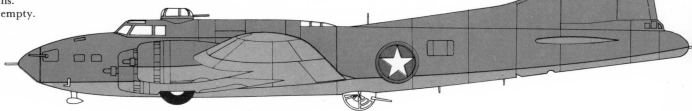

limited to two aircraft carriers (*Lexington* and *Yorktown*) and several cruisers, was steaming toward the Solomons when the Japanese landed at Tulagi but was still far from the area. *Yorktown* did not get near enough to the Coral Sea to launch an attack on Japanese ships until the following day, 4 May, and even this effort failed; planes from the *Yorktown* sank only one Japanese destroyer. Indeed, *Yorktown* was lucky to escape Japanese retaliation after having revealed its presence.

By 7 May the two fleets were converging and Japanese search planes spotted the Americans. They immediately opened fire, sinking a tanker and its destroyer escort. On the mistaken belief that a carrier and a cruiser had been sunk, the Japanese commander, Admiral Takagi, continued to stalk the Americans, sending several dozen planes aloft from his flagship. Of the twenty-seven planes that were sent, twenty did not return. Meanwhile, the Americans were also searching in the dark for their Japanese counterparts.

Planes from the *Yorktown* went out on the evening of the 7th to attack Japanese forces in the Port Moresby area. Although Admiral Fletcher was mistaken in believing that he would find the major part of the Japanese fleet in this area, the raid was not a complete loss since the light carrier *Shoho* was sunk in the fray.

Battle of the Coral Sea

On 8 May the two sides met in strength, and the Battle of the Coral Sea was decided in a contest which lasted the whole day. When they met that morning, both sides were more or less evenly matched. The Japanese task force consisted of two carriers, *Zuikaku* and *Shokaku*, four heavy cruisers, and six destroyers. The American fleet consisted of two carriers *Lexington* and *Yorktown*, five cruisers, and seven destroyers. Japan's carriers housed 121 aircraft, the American's 122.

The Battle of the Coral Sea was decided by aircraft, not by artillery barrages or naval man-

euvers; as such, it was the first major naval encounter in history in which air power played the major role. Neither fleet saw the other; neither fleet fired upon the other. Guns were aimed at enemy aircraft not enemy ships. Still, the toll in ships lost was heavy: when the battle was over, two American aircraft carriers were disabled, one beyond repair (*Lexington*) while the Japanese lost the *Shokaku*, which was disabled after several direct bomb hits. More important, perhaps, was the loss of aircraft. Here the Americans fared better than the Japanese, destroying almost all of the planes on the *Shokaku* and *Zuikaku* while losing only seventy-six of their own.

After the battle both sides limped away, nursing their wounds. Although neither had won a clear-cut victory, the Americans had some consolation in the fact that they had been able to thwart Japan's efforts to capture Port Moresby and cut the supply line from Hawaii to Australia. This was no small accomplishment, since they were still reeling from the earlier Japanese strike against Pearl Harbor. If nothing else, the experience in the Coral Sea was a leavening one for the United States, giving the commanders and men of the Pacific Fleet new confidence to pursue their enemy. In that sense, along with the Battle for Midway, the Battle of the Coral Sea marked a turning point in the Pacific War.

While the Battle of the Coral Sea was still in progress, the Japanese prepared to take Midway Island. According to the plan for this venture, approved by the Imperial Military Headquarters on 5 May, a huge armada was to be assembled off the coast of Japan and converge on Midway early in June. The Japanese task force consisted of almost two hundred ships, including eight carriers, eleven battleships, twenty-two cruisers, sixty-five destroyers, and twenty-one submarines plus twelve troop transports and 600 planes. Another task force of eleven ships (three troop transports, two light carriers, two heavy cruisers, and four

P.51.D. Length: 32 ft. 2⅝ in.
Span 37.03 ft. Maximum
speed: 401 m.p.h.
Armament: 6 × .50
machine guns.

battleships) was to be dispatched to the Aleutians where the Japanese hoped to divert and trap the American fleet.

American intelligence reports, however, saved the day once again; Admiral Nimitz received decoded communications between Tokyo and the Japanese fleet, learned of Japan's plan to seize Midway and took appropriate measures to prevent it. No effort was made to engage the Japanese off the Aleutians. Nimitz husbanded his resources and prepared to send the Pacific Fleet to the Midway area.

Although Nimitz knew where the Japanese planned to strike, his major concern was how to cope with the vast armada assembled for that purpose. There were only two carriers available for the battle, *Enterprise* and *Hornet*, and even the addition of the *Yorktown* after its rapid repair did not alter the situation very much, since the Japanese task force had at least eight carriers, to say nothing of the eleven battleships in the armada. The Pacific Fleet had no battleships thanks to the destruction wrought by the attack on Pearl Harbor six months earlier. In contrast with the even balance of forces in the Battle of the Coral Sea, the Battle of Midway was a contest between two grossly disproportionate fleets. That the United States held its own was due to the foreknowledge of the Japanese plan and the skillful deployment of limited resources.

The American fleet was ordered to a station north of Midway, out of the range of Japan's carrier-based reconnaissance craft. Thus, the Japanese approached Midway and prepared to launch their attack, completely unaware of the presence of the three American carriers. Nimitz, on the other hand, had been able to follow the movement of the Japanese armada through intercepted messages and reconnaissance aircraft based on the island. As the Japanese fleet drew near to the point of attack, the Americans moved in to launch an attack of their own.

On 4 June Admiral Nagumo ordered 108 carrier-based aircraft to attack military installations on Midway. An additional 100 planes were sent aloft to search for and destroy any Allied aircraft sighted in the area. The first raid was devastating and the admiral immediately ordered a second attack aimed at knocking out aerodromes on the island. Shortly after Japanese fighter-

Top: The destruction of the aircraft carrier USS *Lexington:* 8 May 1942.
Above: Last stages of the destruction of the *Lexington.* All hands abandoned ship and not a man was lost.

Survivors from the *Lexington.*

Top: The Japanese scored a direct hit on the USS *Yorktown*. Above: Fleet Admiral Ernest J. King, Commander-in-Chief and Chief of Naval Operations. Right: The deck of the sinking *Yorktown*.

bombers were refueled and sent up to carry out this second strike, American ships were spotted some 200 miles northeast of Midway.

At first Nagumo believed that the American force was limited to two cruisers with a destroyer escort, but later reports confirmed the presence of at least one aircraft carrier in the group. This presented a problem. With most of his carrier-based aircraft flying over Midway, Nagumo could do little to counter an American attack on his ships unless he changed course; to do so, however, would jeopardize the raid over the island. In haste, Nagumo chose to risk sacrificing the Midway raid in favor of saving his task force. This choice proved to be correct, for at the very moment when the admiral ordered his fleet to change course, the Americans were zeroing in on him with dive bombers from their carriers. When the first group of American planes reached the area where Nagumo's task force was supposed to be, it was not there; by the time the Japanese fleet was spotted, Nagumo was ready to attack.

The first wave of American dive-bombers was practically destroyed, the Japanese shooting down thirty-five of the forty-one planes. A second attack proved more successful. Two minutes after the last of the six surviving aircraft left the vicinity of Nagumo's task force, thirty-seven more planes, launched from the *Enterprise* and *Yorktown,* found their mark. Not suspecting the presence of more than one American aircraft carrier, Nagumo and his lieutenants had assumed that the worst was over and were totally unprepared for the second wave of attackers. Nagumo's flagship, the carrier *Akagi*, was hit and the ship was abandoned shortly thereafter. The carriers *Kaga* and *Soryu* were also hit and destroyed. Only the *Hiryu* remained intact, and she was able to retaliate by sending planes to destroy the *Yorktown* before she was destroyed. By day's end, the Americans had mauled Nagumo's fleet with the loss of only one major ship.

The destruction of Nagumo's carriers ended the attack on Midway. Although his superior, Admiral Yamamoto, considered recalling the Japanese task force in the Aleutians and engaging the American fleet, this idea was quickly abandoned; on 5 June the Battle of Midway was called off, and the Japanese fleet steamed off to the west. Thus ended the most important naval confrontation of the Pacific War.

The victory in the Battle of Midway proclaimed a momentum which Allied military leaders were anxious to exploit. Although the defeat of Germany still had the highest priority, Nimitz and MacArthur were eager to take the offensive if a plan could be devised which would not hamper the effort in Europe. Both men were agreed that the time was right for launching a counter-offensive, but how this could be done, where it would take place, and who would command the venture remained unresolved questions.

Nimitz, reflecting the position of the Navy, was eager to have his service play the major role in any new offensive. He was supported by Admiral King, Commander-in-Chief of the United States Fleet, who had been reluctant to accept the importance of Roosevelt's 'Germany first' strategy which placed the Navy in a supporting but

Admiral Nagumo, Japanese commander in the Battle of Midway.

Below: Japanese aircraft carrier *Hiryu* off Midway; it was the only one remaining intact after the battle.
Bottom: General Douglas MacArthur of the US Army, Commander-in-Chief of Allied Forces in the Southwest Pacific, on an inspection tour.

secondary role. General MacArthur, on the other hand, was anxious to avenge the earlier defeat of the Army, and would hear of no plan in which his forces did not play at least an equal role with those under Nimitz's command.

To avoid protracted debate about jurisdiction over the proposed counteroffensive, a compromise was worked out by the Joint Chiefs of Staff and presented to Nimitz and MacArthur on 2 July. According to this plan, the offensive would be carried out in three stages. During phase one Nimitz would be responsible for the occupation of the eastern Solomons, particularly Tulagi and Guadalcanal, and the Santa Cruz Islands. Phase two would see MacArthur's forces completing the occupation of the Solomons and landing along the New Guinea coast. In the final phase MacArthur's forces would advance to Rabaul, Japan's major base in the southwest Pacific.

Like most compromises, this satisfied no one. MacArthur balked at the over-cautiousness of the scheme. Nimitz resented the role assigned MacArthur's forces during the second and third stage of the operation. Nevertheless, they had no choice but to accept the compromise if there was to be any positive action in the Pacific theatre; their superior officers would not tolerate a prolonged conflict between egocentric field commanders.

While Allied leaders ironed out the details of the counter-offensive, American intelligence reported a Japanese build-up on Guadalcanal, including the construction of an air strip at Lunga Point. If the Japanese succeeded in fortifying the island, it would be difficult if not impossible to execute the American offensive. It was necessary, therefore, to commence action immediately and to focus attention on Guadalcanal as opposed to other islands in the Solomon and Santa Cruz chains. Nimitz modified his plans and prepared to land Marines on the island as soon as possible.

Responsibility for coordinating the landings on Guadalcanal was given to Vice-Admiral Robert Ghormley and Rear Admiral Frank Fletcher. Major General Alexander Vandegrift commanded the 1st Marine Division which was to make the landing on 7 August. On the morning of the 7th, the fleet gathered off Guadalcanal and began an all day bombardment of supposed Japanese installations on the island. Some 10,000 Marines were put safely ashore later in the day. The landing was unopposed since the majority of the Japanese troops on the island were construction workers who fled into the jungle before the Marines' advances. A simultaneous landing on Tulagi proved equally successful.

The Japanese responded to the American landing by attempting to reinforce their own garrison on Guadalcanal. Admiral Mikawa, commander of the Japanese garrison at Rabaul, immediately sent a task force of seven ships (five heavy cruisers, two light cruisers) to survey the situation and engage the American force under Admiral Fletcher's command. The Japanese successfully navigated the 'Slot' between the chains of the Solomons and surprised the American fleet off Savo Island on the evening of 7 August, sinking four American cruisers and badly damaging a fifth before withdrawing. Although they failed to follow up this triumph by attacking troop

Left: US Marines clamber down the side of a transport as they approach Guadalcanal. **Right:** The Japanese underestimated the size and ferocity of the US Marines in Guadalcanal.

ships further south, the destruction of a substantial part of Fletcher's task force forced the Americans to withdraw their ships and aided the reinforcement of Japanese forces on Guadalcanal.

The Japanese underestimated the size of the American force on Guadalcanal, and consequently did not adequately reinforce their own garrison on the island, although they could have done so at the time. It was believed that the Marine force landed near Lunga Point numbered no more than 2000 men and that 4000 Japanese troops in addition to the garrison of 2200 already on the island would be sufficient to dispose of the Americans. Thus two troop convoys carrying approximately 3000 men were despatched from Rabaul on 17 August. When they landed near Lunga Point on the 18th, they were decimated by the Americans who outnumbered them several times over. A second Japanese landing several days later was hardly more successful.

The Japanese command at Rabaul was also anxious to lure the remnants of Admiral Fletcher's task force into a naval confrontation. When the second band of reinforcements left Rabaul on 19 August, their troop convoy was accompanied by a large force of carriers and battleships. Mikawa intended using one of the carriers, the *Ryujo*, as bait in the hope that Fletcher would pursue the craft into a trap from which there would be no escape. Fortunately Allied intelligence once again came to the rescue and what had been planned as an American rout was turned into a modest victory for the Allies.

Admiral Ghormley plotted the movement of the Japanese task force, moving three carriers (*Enterprise*, *Saratoga* and *Wasp*) south of Guadalcanal. The *Ryujo* was sighted and destroyed on 24 August and two additional Japanese carriers were seen; when they launched their planes, the Americans were prepared. The Japanese lost over eighty planes in the effort to sink the task force while only one American ship, the *Enterprise*, had

been hit when the engagement was broken off on the evening of the 24th.

After the disastrous attempt to dislodge the Americans from Lunga Point, Japanese authorities stepped up the effort to reinforce the remaining Japanese forces on Guadalcanal. The 'Tokyo Express' brought reinforcements to the island on a regular nightly basis during late August and September; by the beginning of October, the Japanese had brought their troop strength on Guadalcanal to over 22,000 and numerically were just about equal to the Marine garrison.

The Japanese launched a second offensive against the Americans on 24 October, this time moving overland through the dense jungle and tropical forest. The result, however, proved no different from their first attempt. After sustaining heavy casualties, the attack was broken off pending further reinforcement. A third attack was beaten back early in November. This was the last Japanese land offensive on Guadalcanal; by the end of November their forces had been depleted while the Americans had been steadily reinforced and now enjoyed a numerical superiority which permitted them to take the offensive. Although the Japanese stubbornly continued to fight, they were short of supplies and suffering from malaria. It would only be a matter of time before they were cleared from the island.

More important than the fighting on Guadalcanal was the naval confrontation between the United States and Japan in the waters surrounding the island during October and November. On 26 October the two fleets clashed in the Battle of the Santa Cruz Islands. Two weeks later they met again in a three-day battle (13–15 November) which has become known as the Naval Battle of Guadalcanal. Both navies sustained heavy losses in these contests but on balance, the United States Navy emerged victorious. Rather than risk another confrontation with the Americans, the Japanese government ordered the evacuation of

Guadalcanal on 4 January 1943. After more than four months of struggle and the loss of over 25,000 men and more than a dozen capital ships, the Battle for Guadalcanal was over.

The New Guinea Campaign

Having disposed of the Japanese in the southern Solomons, it was MacArthur's turn to shoulder the burden of the counter-offensive. While the battle for Guadalcanal was still in progress, his American and Australian forces had begun a campaign in the Papuan peninsula of New Guinea to prevent the Japanese from seizing Port Moresby, thus interrupting Allied supply lines and disrupting industrial production in Australia. This contest, a prerequisite for the assault on Rabaul, was still in progress when the Battle for Guadalcanal ended. Until it was concluded, there could be no pressing on with the counter-offensive.

To reach Port Moresby, the Japanese would have to either take the city through an amphibious operation or advance across the Owen Stanley mountains from Lae and Salamaua. Since an attempt at the former had been repulsed in July 1942, the Japanese were forced to adopt the latter approach, i.e., a trek through the mountains. Although the peaks were high and the terrain rugged, the Japanese succeeded in crossing the mountains through narrow foot paths, and on 12 August they took Kokoda and its small airstrip. From Kokoda they tried to seize Allied installations at Milne Bay but were pushed back instead to the Buna-Gona area.

A joint Australian-American force sought to dislodge the Japanese from their foothold on the northern coast of Papua in November, but the Japanese had dug in and built bunkers out of earth reinforced with sheet iron or steel drums. Although they lacked supplies, food, and medicine, they were able to keep the Allies at bay for over two months. MacArthur was so distressed by this that at the end of November he personally

ordered a change in the Allied command in this area in the hope that more spirited commanders would end the engagement so that the Allies could get on with the assault on Rabaul. Still, the Japanese were able to hold their position until the beginning of 1943; the last men were withdrawn on 22 January.

With Guadalcanal and the Papuan peninsula secured, the Allies could move on to Rabaul, Japan's major station in the southwest Pacific. In the compromise plan of 2 July 1942, the Joint Chiefs of Staff had proposed that the assault would follow immediately upon the seizure of the Solomons and the neutralization of Japanese positions in New Guinea. Although New Guinea had been partially secured by the end of 1942, of the Solomons, only Guadalcanal was controlled by the Allies. So before the attack on Japan's primary base could begin, the offensive in the Solomon Islands would have to be completed. The fierce resistance put up by the Japanese in Guadalcanal and New Guinea had shown, however, that this part of the campaign would take longer than had been anticipated and require a greater expenditure of force than had been originally allotted. In short, it was necessary to rewrite plans for the completion of the offensive.

In plotting a revision of their scheme the Joint Chiefs of Staff again encountered the problem of securing the cooperation of both the Army and Navy. Neither MacArthur nor Admiral Halsey had enough men to execute the scheme alone, nor would a one-track approach to Rabaul have been in the best interests of the Allies. Even if MacArthur or Halsey could have engineered an attack without the cooperation of the other, a two-pronged assault with the eventual convergence of Allied forces on Rabaul would confuse the Japanese and had a greater chance of success.

Operation Cartwheel, the revised plan for the attack on Rabaul, called for a dual effort. General MacArthur's Southwest Pacific forces were to

Seen from the flight deck of the USS *Enterprise* during the Battle of Santa Cruz: US destroyer rips off a round of anti-aircraft fire to protect the rear of the *Enterprise*.

attack and take the Trobriand Islands, the Lae-
Salamaua area in New Guinea and the western-
most portion of New Britain, the island on which
which Rabaul was located. Meanwhile, Admiral
Halsey's South Pacific force was to seize the rest of
the Solomon Islands, particularly Bougainville,
from which they would be ready to attack New
Britain. Both ventures would require amphibious
assaults supported by aerial drops, following which
new airfields would be hacked out of the jungle.
The terrain would be difficult, the weather uncooperative, and the risk of malaria and other
tropical diseases immense.

Preparations for Operation Cartwheel began
in March 1943, but the offensive was not launched
until 30 June, when forces commanded by Halsey
and MacArthur landed simultaneously at Wood-
lark, Kiriwina, Nassau Bay (New Guinea), and
New Georgia. The Trobriands were taken with
no difficulty but MacArthur encountered stiff
resistance when the landing party at Nassau Bay
pushed on toward Lae and Salamaua. It was two
weeks before the Americans could link up with
Australian forces pushing toward Salamaua from
the south, and even then the Japanese were not
easily dislodged. It was only through a ruse that
MacArthur succeeded in throwing the Japanese
off balance and this involved the capture of Lae.
Salamaua was not taken until 16 September, but
from that point on, the New Guinea campaign
proceeded as planned.

Admiral Halsey's South Pacific force encountered equally stiff resistance in the campaign in the Solomons. The landings at New Georgia were carried off without incident, but the Americans soon came under heavy fire from the Japanese defenders. The purpose of the landing in New Georgia was to capture the Japanese airbase at Munda Point, from which American aircraft could then be sent over Bougainville. A direct assault on the air base had been ruled out as too dangerous, so Halsey and his lieutenant, Rear Admiral Richard Kelly Turner, proposed a series of landings followed by an overland trek to the Munda Point base, a difficult task due to the rugged terrain and dense jungle cover. Munda Point did not fall to the Allies until 5 August, thirty-six days after the first landings were made.

New Georgia was secured by mid-August, but the campaign had proved more costly and time-consuming than the Joint Chiefs had anticipated. If the Japanese continued to offer as much resistance as they had in New Georgia and New Guinea, the offensive would drag on indefinitely and Allied casualties would soar. Shortly after the New Georgia campaign was concluded the Joint Chiefs unveiled a new scheme.

The alternative plan called for Allied troops to leapfrog over or around the fiercely defended Japanese bases. By substituting a flexible policy the Allies would gain valuable time and save lives. Japanese bases which they had passed would not prove menacing, as the garrisons would be isolated; once the Allies established forward air bases in front of the sites, they could be neutralized through aerial attack.

Leapfrogging was begun immediately and proved so successful that the principle was ultimately applied in the decision to skip over the Japanese base on Rabaul in favor of a less costly landing elsewhere. But this decision was not made until the end of 1943, and in the meantime the Allies faced some hard fighting, particularly on Bougainville, where they landed at the beginning of November.

The Bougainville landing was made at Empress Bay on 1 November. Halsey intended building a bridgehead deep enough to allow construction of an air field which could be used to attack Japanese bases at Rabaul and elsewhere in the South Pacific, and then to neutralize the Japanese garrison on the island. Although the Japanese had as many as 55,000 men on Bougainville, they were located at the southern end of the island and did not pose an immediate threat to the landings; when Halsey's Marines tried to expand their perimeter, however, they met with strong resistance.

Bougainville was too close to New Britain for the Japanese to accept the American landing lightly, nor could they permit Halsey to supplement his original landing force unmolested. Accordingly on 2 November, the day after the first landing, a Japanese task force of seven ships was sent to the area to prevent the landings. Halsey ordered Admiral Spruance to engage this task force, and on 5 November Spruance's Fifth Fleet attacked the Japanese, forcing them to abandon the waters between Rabaul and Bougainville. From then on the Japanese Navy did not menace the Allied operation on Bougainville. Although Japanese forces continued to occupy the southern portion of the island, they were unable to dislodge the Americans from their beachhead which had been expanded to a ten-mile wide enclave by the end of the year.

After Bougainville, Operation Cartwheel entered its final phase. Rabaul had been the original goal of the Allied advance, but as the year ended, the Chiefs of Staff decided that successful operations elsewhere had neutralized Rabaul and that it would not be necessary to attack the installation. Instead, a minor landing would be made to secure an air field on the western tip of New Britain and the Allies would increase their forces on New Guinea in order to clear out the remaining Japanese pockets on that large island.

Divisions of the United States Sixth Army landed in western New Britain at the end of December and quickly succeeded in establishing a beachhead and constructing an airfield. The Japanese, whose forces were concentrated on the other end of the island, hardly resisted the landings. Additional units of the Sixth Army were then ordered to New Guinea where they made landings at Saidor on 2 January 1944 and linked up with Australian forces on the island. The Huon Peninsula was cleared by the end of April and the Japanese were in retreat. At this point, with New Guinea secured and Rabaul neutralized, Operation Cartwheel was complete.

Next, Allied leaders began to plan an attack on the Philippines. The Admiralty, Marshall, and Gilbert islands had been successfully occupied, Truk and Rabaul neutralized. Only some cleaning up chores remained in the southwest Pacific. MacArthur believed that he could complete these by the end of the summer and begin an invasion of Mindanao, the largest of the southern Philippine islands, by November 1944. He was particularly anxious to return to the islands to avenge the humiliation suffered by the Americans and their Filipino comrades some two years earlier. It was with pleasure, therefore, that he prepared for the attack.

Above left: Paratroops and C-47s pave the way for one of the leapfrogging campaigns on the north coast of New Guinea. **Far left:** Australian patrol in the jungle of New Guinea. **Below:** US soldiers fire into a Japanese dugout near Buna.

CHAPTER SIXTEEN
Defeat in Southeast Asia

By the end of May 1942, six months after the war began with the West, the goals that the Japanese high command had set for itself had all been accomplished. On the Allied side, however, the picture was thoroughly depressing. All but the French had lost their empires in Southeast Asia and with these, substantial amounts of natural resources that would be sorely needed to fight the war ahead. When Allied leaders decided on a Europe first strategy, they made an initial defeat in Asia inevitable.

Almost immediately after their first defeat, the colonial powers began to plan for the reconquest of their former territories. The British were primarily concerned with the recovery of Burma as part of an overall plan to recover their empire. On this basis, all of Burma would have to be recaptured and used as a base to attack Thailand, Malaya, and finally the Netherlands East Indies. To the Americans, however, this plan meant moving away from one of their major goals, the supplying of Chinese Nationalist armies. As an alternative, they suggested a more modest drive through north Burma in order to sustain Chinese forces and enable them to launch coordinated land and air attacks on the Japanese. These basic differences in strategic thinking were to plague Allied planners throughout the war.

With only limited measures available for Southeast Asia, the British, despite their strategic priorities, could make no more than a tentative stab eastward on the Arakan front in 1942. The backbone of this thrust was formed by the very troops that had already been defeated in Burma, since the few reinforcements allocated to Southeast Asia were still in India, untrained in jungle warfare. The drive could not be sustained; the Burma Road remained closed, and China was completely isolated except for one remote route to Russia. The airlift over the 'Hump' kept China in the war but was insufficient to meet her needs.

Plans for establishing a Southeast Asia Command (SEAC) had been laid during the Casablanca Conference in January 1943 and the Washington meeting (code name: 'Trident') in May of the same year, but it was not until the Quebec Conference between Winston Churchill and Franklin D. Roosevelt in August that a commander was designated and the command officially confirmed. Since Southeast Asia was considered to be a British responsibility it was agreed that an Englishman would command with American representation, and Lord Louis Mountbatten was appointed Supreme Commander.

The American representative to SEAC was Lieutenant General Joseph Stilwell. He wore several hats. As a member of Mountbatten's staff, he was Deputy Commander of SEAC. He was also Commanding General in the China-Burma-India theatre of operations (CBI) with command of all American forces in the region, Chief of Staff to Generalissimo Chiang Kai-shek, thus commanding all Chinese forces in Southeast Asia, and in addition he managed Lend-Lease aid to China. When General Slim became commander of the British 14th Army (subordinate to the 11th Army commanded by General Sir George Giffard), Stilwell's forces should have come under the command of Giffard, if not under Slim. But Stilwell, in his capacity as the commander of Chinese and American forces and as Chief of Staff to Chiang refused to do so. As Deputy Supreme Commander of SEAC, he was second only to Mountbatten himself; eventually his area of operations in northern Burma was organized into the Northern Combat Area Command (NCAC),

Above: Lord Louis Mountbatten, Supreme Commander of Southeast Asia Command.

Left: Lieutenant-General Sir William Slim.

Opposite top: The Japanese conquest of Burma was complete by mid-1942. **Opposite far left:** The British destroyed most of the major bridges in Burma before they evacuated. **Opposite right:** Vinegar Joe Stilwell, US representative to SEAC, enjoying his breakfast of C-rations on Christmas morning in Burma, 1943.

Merrill's Marauders enter Burma, accompanied by Burmese volunteers.

Brigadier Orde Wingate, whose Chindits penetrated deep behind Japanese lines in Burma.

but it operated as a quasi-autonomous command, dependent upon the 14th Army for logistical and administrative supply and keeping Slim advised of its activities, but retaining near-independent freedom of action.

Meanwhile the Japanese were building up their organization and strength. By November 1943, the Japanese Army, Southern Region had the following formations under its command: the Burma Area Army, based in Rangoon with four divisions under 15th Army and two others on the Arakan front under 28th Army; the Siam Garrison Army (Bangkok) with two divisions; and the 25th Army in the Netherlands East Indies with seven divisions. In addition the Indo-China Garrison Army in Saigon had approximately three divisions, while the 3rd Air Army provided air support (approximately 400 aircraft) for the entire region, with headquarters in Singapore and one of its two divisions located at Rangoon and Moulmein.

Assuming that a Japanese division numbered 10,000 men, there were at least 60,000 combat troops deployed in Burma alone with another 100,000 men in the Southeast Asia operational area. Four of the six divisions in Burma had participated in the original conquest of the country. Now, though each had contributed units to Pacific campaigns, they were still in first-class fighting condition and had the psychological advantage of facing enemies that they had defeated before.

Mountbatten and Slim had a monumental task before them – that of getting the defeated troops into fighting trim. The retreat across Burma into India had obviously weakened the men physically, but the psychological effects were probably worse. Tired, hungry, beset with the constant fear of being cut off by the enemy, the troops had replaced an earlier contempt for the fighting qualities of the Japanese with respect. The Japanese infantryman seemed almost super-human, able to survive in the jungle, outflank the British, live on a bag of rice, slip into friendly lines to snipe or to stab and then disappear. The short-range Arakan offensive in mid-1943 merely served to accentuate the difficulties in trying to defeat an experienced enemy in impossible terrain. In addition, the British commanders had to contend with a serious tropical disease problem, especially scrub typhus, which resulted in a number of fatalities.

In November 1943 plans were made to start offensive operations against the Japanese in Burma in late 1943-early 1944. Basically SEAC's job was to tie up as many Japanese troops as possible to prevent their employment in the Pacific, and to reopen land routes to China. At first the Combined Chiefs of Staff had favored a companion amphibious assault, but their landing craft were withdrawn to Europe to support the Italian and Normandy operations.

On land, the Allied plan called for an attack on the central front in Arakan accompanied by a northern thrust by Stilwell's Chinese and a newly arrived American formation, later to be known as Merrill's Marauders. Stilwell's group would link up with an attack southward from China by Chinese forces to open the Ledo road to Yunnan. This two-pronged attack once again reflected the basic difference between British and American thinking. To the Americans, the northern advance was vital for securing the route to China. To the British, the job would be better performed by the central front attack which would lead to the well-established old Burma Road while helping to secure Mandalay and Rangoon and getting back all of Burma for the British as well. The result was, of course, a compromise.

Wingate's Chindits

The narrative would be incomplete without mentioning the Long Range Penetration Groups (LRP) of the remarkable Brigadier Orde Wingate. Wingate, who had given the Italians an extremely hard time in Ethiopia, advocated the landing of large forces behind enemy lines, there to harass their lines of communications and disrupt their logistical network. He had already led one raid in 1942, but the group was not evacuated by air and had to make it out in small groups; over one-third of the original force did not survive. Militarily it had been a failure, but psychologically it had made the Japanese nervous about rear area security.

Now, with increased air transport capability and improved techniques, Wingate was ready to try again, but he received only a tepid response despite Mountbatten's personal enthusiasm. Field Marshal Slim had reservations because he was convinced that the Japanese, unlike the Italians would not be bullied into a withdrawal. If they fought back, a force deep in enemy territory would have to evacuate by air prematurely, thereby disrupting other plans, or be gradually annihilated. Also, the mere act of transporting Wingate's *Chindits* would use more aircraft and fuel than Slim considered reasonable for the expected dividends. In the end Wingate was granted an airlift but not as many men as he had wanted. Nevertheless he eventually got 12,000 men into Burma where they acted as flank security for Stilwell's NCAC attack as well as disturbing the enemy's peace of mind.

The Americans had a counterpart for Wingate. The 5307th Composite Unit, variously known as the 'Galahad' Force, the 5307th Provisional Regiment and 'Merrill's Marauders' (after their commander, Brigadier General Frank Merrill), were Stilwell's Long Range Penetration Group, but they entered Burma by land. It was a gallant force of volunteers; by the end of the war, casualties from combat and illness made it virtually non-existent as a fighting outfit.

Meanwhile the Japanese were doing some assessing of their own. The first *Chindit* operation in 1942, while not quite alarming them, had pointed out disturbing possibilities for the future, and the first Arakan campaign, abortive as it was, at least proved that the British were thinking about

Left: The RAF drops supplies to the Chindits in northern Burma. **Below:** Members of Wingate's Jungle Penetration Force. **Bottom:** Gurkhas and men of the West Yorkshire Regiment advance under cover of forward tanks.

425

Burma. The war in the Pacific was not going well. First Guadalcanal, then Attu in the Aleutians, Tarawa, New Guinea and other south and central Pacific Islands had fallen to American forces. The sea battles of Midway and the Coral Sea had turned back the once-invincible Japanese Navy and the island garrisons in the Pacific were becoming more and more difficult to supply and reinforce. The interior shipping lanes of the Outer Zone were coming under increasing enemy interference.

Clearly the oil-producing southern regions had to be preserved under Japanese control, sea communications from these regions to the Home Islands had to be kept open at all costs, and the American offensive in the Pacific had to be contained. There was not much that the Imperial land forces could do in Southeast Asia about the last two objectives, but if Burma was to be a shield for the oil-producing regions, it must be kept intact.

One look at a map of eastern India would reveal the importance of the Imphal-Kohima region of Assam province as a logical staging area for any British offensive; an attack should be launched elsewhere to confuse them and draw off troops from Imphal. Ironically, since the British also considered a multi-front attack into Burma, the respective British and Japanese offensives in the Arakan may be seen as mutually diversionary.

So, at the very end of November 1943, the British launched a two-pronged attack. In Arakan they met dogged resistance; once again, Japanese had to be dislodged individually from foxholes and tunnels. The process was slow, painful and bloody, but the British now held several advantages. First, they had found that in the areas where tanks could be employed, Japanese tanks were no match for the American and British models. Second, the Allies had achieved air superiority and cleared the skies of the enemy. Now it would be Japanese that would have to hide from strafing planes. Third, improved air supply techniques meant that British troops no longer needed to rely on roads. Last, the British had finally learned not to be upset when encircled by the enemy. They would merely sit tight, wait for air supply and let the enemy wear itself out.

Despite all these advantages, some have termed the British effort an 'avoidance of defeat' rather than a victory. A superior force had found that it took over a month to reduce an enemy strongpoint about 80 square miles in area. The Japanese had holed up in tunnels and previously prepared positions and it took the bayonet and flame-thrower to get them out. By 1 February 1944, when the last enemy redoubt had been reduced, there were already signs of a Japanese counter-offensive. On 4 February 1944 the Japanese 28th Army, led by General Sakurai, attacked the Arakan front. Progress was good and the 7th Indian Division found itself surrounded, but instead of withdrawing as in the past, the 7th held its position and relied on air supply; the Japanese, optimistically expecting to break through British lines and feast on captured stores, had only brought a ten-day supply of food. The climax came on February 14 when the Japanese launched an all-out attack, including the use of night infiltrators

Top left: Moving toward Kohima through dense jungle. **Left:** A formation of RAF Thunderbolt fighters make a sweep over Burma.

and suicide squads. It was a waste of brave men, for the 7th continued to hold. By 24 February they had been joined by the 5th Indian Division, and another division (26th Indian) was closing in on Japanese remnants. By the beginning of March, the British had resumed their offensive on the Arakan front and were advancing toward the east.

For the first time in the Burma campaign the Japanese had been defeated in a setpiece battle, with over 5000 casualties in February 1944 alone. The British had failed to retreat as they had in the past, and when their positions could not be easily overrun, the Japanese supply system's failings came back to haunt them.

The Japanese invasion of Assam carried with it political hopes as well as military ones. It was no secret that the British were having trouble with Mahatma Gandhi, and it was hoped that the advance to Imphal would not only ruin British plans for retaking Burma, but would create further problems by the establishment of a Japanese-sponsored Indian state under Sri Subbhash Chandra Bose.

The Indian National Army
Bose had sought refuge in Nazi Germany and attempted to raise a National Army there. In 1943 he arrived in Singapore, where he established his *Azad Hind* government and raised an *Azad Hind Fouj* (Indian National Army) from the Indian prisoners taken during the earlier Malayan and Singapore campaigns. Apparently he was quite successful, for two divisions were organized and sent to the Imphal front with the Japanese 15th Army in 1944. They did not, however, see much service due to internal dissension and Japanese distrust; eventually they were withdrawn, and in the later British drive toward Rangoon many were captured or surrendered.

The British realized that Imphal would be an important Japanese target for it would be useful, not only as a forward base for the invasion of India, but as a means of isolating China and Stilwell's forces in northern Burma. General Slim planned to draw the enemy onto the large plain in front of the city where his superior armor and air power could be used to best effect; consequently, the Japanese attack on Imphal was not only anticipated, but actually desired as a chance to destroy several enemy divisions.

The Japanese were expected to follow their usual tactics and try to surround Imphal; this expectation was reinforced when the Japanese 33rd Division cut the road south of the city a week before the main attack began. But in the north the Japanese 31st Division, instead of turning toward Imphal, launched a major attack on Kohima and isolated it from the rest of the Imphal line. Kohima was vital to the British because it was only a stone's throw from Dimapur, a stop on the Bengal-Assam railway which carried all their supplies and reinforcements to the front. Luckily, whether through lack of knowledge or simply inflexibility, the Japanese did not go on to take Dimapur although it was virtually undefended.

Instead, the battle settled down to a bloody personal conflict which was often resolved in hand-to-hand combat. Soon, despite air lifts, the food supply in the city was down to two weeks'

reduced rations with a one-week supply of gasoline; ammunition too was nearly exhausted. The Japanese, however, were in an even more precarious situation. Their offensive troops travelled lightly, hoping to exist on captured stores, and their supply lines could not support a sustained offensive. Air transport just kept the British alive and gradually the balance tipped in their favor. By April 1944 they were able to launch local counterattacks; by mid-May the defenders of Kohima were able to break out of the encirclement; and by the end of the month Imphal was free as well.

Even with all hope for victory gone, the Japanese hung on grimly, so that every hole had to be cleared, every 'dead' man confirmed. The Japanese command did not actually acknowledge its failure until mid-July, and the last Japanese soldier did not quit Indian soil until mid-August. They left behind 53,500 of the 84,300 men that had started the offensive, among them 30,000 or more killed or wounded. The British forces had 16,700 casualties, one-quarter of which occurred at Kohima.

Aside from general Japanese weaknesses, such as their supply and intelligence systems, the fact that the British did not fall for the diversion and thus had ample time to deal with the Arakan threat and then send troops to the relief of Imphal, presented the Japanese with an impossible inferiority in manpower and weapons. The Japanese penchant for continuing to use the same tactics and carry on with missions that were no longer valid resulted in a needless waste of lives. But one of the most important intangible factors was the new spirit of the Allied side. They had found out that the Japanese, tenacious and formidable, could be defeated.

While this fighting was going on, Stilwell's Chinese and Merrill's Marauders were finding the going rough in the north. Nevertheless, in August 1944, the key city of Myitkyina fell. Its capture facilitated an air route to China without the hazards of the Hump, provided a waterway to support the central Burma front, and moved the Allies a step closer to opening land routes to China.

With India's safety insured, there came a discussion as to future strategy which once again centred on two alternatives. The first plan called for a continued drive through central Burma toward Mandalay; the other entailed an amphibious landing near Rangoon. Due to requirements in Europe, however, which showed no signs of lessening despite the successful landing at Normandy, the second plan (code name 'Dracula') was cancelled.

Although the Japanese were steadily pushed back, there was no rout; instead they contested the advance wherever possible and staged a number of fierce counterattacks. But Allied air power was too much for them; only a few individual snipers stayed behind until they were killed.

As SEAC proceeded into Burma they faced political as well as military problems. Some members of the Burma Defence Army (BDA), a nationalist group organized by the Japanese, had contacted the British underground organization, Force 136, in 1944. At the end of the year the question of supplying them with arms arose and was opposed by some members of Mountbatten's staff on the grounds that they were suspected of having some contact with Communist groups. Mountbatten himself, however, saw no point in discriminating between the BDA and other minority groups that were already being supplied by the British; he finally sent them

Above left: The Japanese ambushed this armored column in Burma in early 1945. **Above:** The complex river systems of Burma did not stop the British drive north.

Opposite: Bombs from a RAF Liberator head down toward Japanese Headquarters at Kyaukse. **Left:** The largest floating Bailey bridge, constructed by the 14th Army.

429

On the road to Mandalay . . .

weapons on an individual rather than a group basis with the proviso that his action implied no future political commitment. He also insisted that it be made clear to the Burmese people that their liberators were the British, Indians, Americans and Chinese – not the BDA.

In one of the most extraordinary ruses of all time, some 5000 members of the BDA left Rangoon on 16 March 1945, ostensibly to help the Japanese fight the British; on 28 March they rose in revolt and renamed themselves the Burma National Army (BNA). They served with little significance during the rest of the war.

The Japanese, now forced to tighten their perimeter, were being pushed back toward the southern tip of Burma, near Pegu. The honor of forcing down along approximately the same route as the original invasion fell to the 17th Indian Division, first to feel the Japanese fury in 1942, now webbed into one of the world's finest fighting forces. Mandalay fell to the British in March and Rangoon was recaptured on 3 May. Japan surrendered on 15 August 1945, after two atomic bombs were dropped on her cities, and on 13 September formally signed the surrender agreement with SEAC at Singapore.

Opposite left: Welsh soldiers before the un-damaged Bahe Pagoda, January 1945. **Opposite center:** Operation "Nipoff" – General Ichida directs the repatriation of Japanese soldiers in Rangoon. **Left:** Japanese staff officers arrive in Rangoon to discuss surrender arrangements.

CHAPTER SEVENTEEN
The Defeat of Germany

The Allies had gained a secure foothold on Europe after the Normandy landings, but there was still bloody fighting ahead. Twenty days after the landing on the beaches, the port of Cherbourg was taken following four days of combat; the Germans had systematically destroyed every port facility, but skilled Allied engineers were able to return them to full use by August. Meanwhile, two gigantic artificial harbors called Mulberries were towed across the Channel and badly needed supplies flowed over them to the expanded beachheads.

By 26 July the Allies had broken out of Normandy and were enveloping the rest of France in a series of moves which, despite vigorous counterattacks, the Germans were unable to contain. On 15 August Operation Anvil the invasion of southern France, was begun near Cannes against relatively light German resistance. While these forces headed north to link up with the Normandy troops the French underground, the *Maquis,* offered valuable assistance. Within two weeks Marseilles, Toulon and Nice were liberated. In their turn, the Normandy forces caught the bulk of the German forces in France in a huge pocket, taking 50,000 prisoners and killing 10,000 Germans. The way to Paris was open.

The liberation of Paris was a sensitive issue. It was not directly essential to military operations, and its relief would mean the expenditure of valuable fuel and ammunition, but it was a symbol to the people of France. In the city itself, as the news spread that the Allies were getting closer, the people were preparing for an uprising against the German garrison.

General Eisenhower was reluctant to move toward the city, but his hand was forced when, on 19 August French underground forces launched general attacks against the German garrison. It was feared that unless Allied forces moved toward the city to relieve the Maquis, they would be annihilated by the Germans and the civilian population would suffer bitter reprisals.

The German garrison commander, General von Choltitz, was in a dilemma. He had received orders from Hitler to defend Paris to the death; if he could not hold the city, he was to reduce it to ashes. The task was extremely distasteful to him and in the end, through underground intermediaries, he agreed to surrender to the Allies. The French General LeClerc and his Second Armored Division were chosen to be the first Allied unit to enter Paris after four years of German occupation and the next day, 26 August,

Charles de Gaulle walked proudly down the boulevards of Paris past ecstatic crowds. The celebration lasted three days, but then the enemy threatened to counterattack; American troops marched in parade formation right from the city streets into combat.

Since the beginning of the Normandy invasion, the Germans had lost over 500,000 men including 200,000 bottled up in by-passed areas. The remnants of formations still in condition to fight now headed back toward the Siegfried Line, which was in effect the last major German defensive barrier. The Allies, with over two million troops on the continent, pushed forward with a series of spearheads, cutting off German positions as they forged ahead. Their advance was swift; Brussels was liberated on 3 September and Antwerp on the following day. Grown over confident, the Allies tried a bold gamble to shorten the war by trying to outflank the Siegfried Line using airborne troops.

In what turned out to be the biggest airborne operation of the war, over 20,000 men were

Captured German soldier is marched into captivity during the street fighting which preceded the liberation of Paris.

433

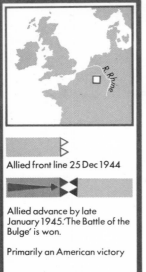

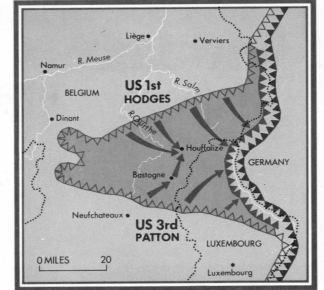

Above: Generals Patton and Bradley. Patton's 3rd Army saved the day for the Allies at Bastogne. **Top right:** Bastogne held and the German attack ground to a halt.

25 pdr. Gun. Range: 13,400 yds. Armament: 3.45 in. caliber $24\frac{1}{4}$ lbs. shell. Crew: 7. Weight: $1\frac{1}{2}$ tons. 1460 lbs.

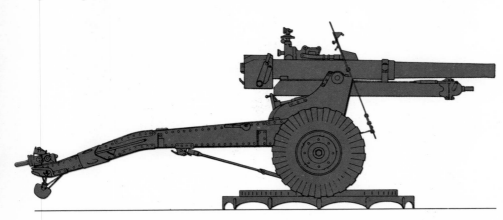

dropped into Holland on 17 September 1944, the Americans in the vicinity of Eindhoven and Nijmegen and the British further north at Arnhem. Their mission was to seize key communications centers and secure bridges across the Maas and Waal Rivers. The Americans made good progress, though with some difficulty. But at Arnhem on the Lower Rhine, 8000 British paratroops ran into serious trouble. The Germans had evidently prepared for such an airborne assault, and the paratroops in the sky were shot as easily as clay pigeons. Once on the ground, they found their relief forces bogged down by bad weather.

For nine days and nights the British paratroops were steadily decimated by the furious German bombardment. Food began to run short, and ammunition was rationed. Eventually, the high command gave up and ordered them to break for their own lines. Of the 8000 men, barely 2000 escaped. In terms of the larger picture it was no disaster, but in view of the loss of large numbers of highly trained airborne troops, it was a minor catastrophe. It also showed that the Germans were still willing to fight and would have to be ground into defeat.

After the Nijmegen–Arnhem operation, a disagreement occurred between General Omar Bradley and Field Marshal Montgomery. Montgomery wanted a single concentrated attack toward the Ruhr north of the Ardennes forests, but General Bradley felt that American firepower, especially Patton's mobile Third Army, could best be utilized in a two-pronged attack, one north toward the Ruhr, one south toward the Saar basin. This would force the enemy to divide

his dwindling forces against two major attacks. Eventually, Bradley won his point, and the offensive did indeed proceed on two fronts. But the November weather intervened to slow down American mobility, and the campaign began to drag despite vigorous local attacks.

As the momentum of the offensive began to slacken, the Allies were faced with the problem of replacing the men lost since the landings. Some infantry divisions were attacking with only three-quarters of their authorized combat strength, since due to administrative difficulties, replacements were slow in reaching the front-line units. Then, on 16 December 1944, the Germans launched their last counter-offensive on the western front. The Battle of the Bulge was about to begin.

The Battle of the Bulge

Even as Hitler was recuperating from the bomb blast in the Wolf's Lair, the idea of a counter-offensive on the western front was being conceived. Planning began in September 1944 when the Germans quietly started to mass over 250,000 men. This was a pitiful number compared to the Wehrmacht when the war began, and the men could not measure up in quality to the original soldiers, but it was still a sizable force, stiffened by fanatical SS units, well-equipped, dedicated Nazis. Coupled with it were some 1000 tanks, the last armored reserve in the West, or anywhere else for that matter.

Von Runstedt was brought out of retirement to command this counter-offensive, but the plan was really Hitler's own brainchild. 'Operation Autumn Fog' was to collect all available men and supplies for one powerful strike in the Ardennes; they would penetrate Allied lines, break into open country and drive toward Antwerp. The attack would be made when bad weather was forecast, so that Allied aircraft would be restricted.

In early December Hitler called a conference to finalize plans for the operation. Gone was the self-assured and arrogant Fuehrer of the old days. He was visibly hampered by the bomb injuries, and seemed nervous, with his left hand twitching from time to time. When he spoke, he was hesitant, but his determination to defeat the West was unshaken.

The professional officers gathered to hear the plan were not unanimous in their reactions. General von Manteuffel questioned the distant objective of Antwerp with the forces available, and von Runstedt continued his contempt and distrust of the Austrian corporal, though he was entrusted with the plan's execution. But the surviving generals had largely been cowed by the purges after the bomb plot and Hitler was adamant.

A major cause for concern was air cover, and here Hitler seemed to be dealing in fantasy. In answer to a question, he claimed that the Luftwaffe was 'being deliberately held back. Goering has reported that he has 3000 fighters available. . . . Discount 1000 and that still leaves 2000'. It is doubtful if by that time the entire Luftwaffe had even half of that number in operational planes of all types.

On the Allied side, there had been reports of movement of the Sixth SS Panzer Army toward Cologne with another group slightly to the rear. The openness of these movements led Allied intelligence officers to speculate on the possibility of a feint and a major attack against what must be, in light of restricted German resources, a limited objective. An attack on Antwerp, in view of the distance, was considered too ambitious; it was estimated that the Germans had suffered over 100,000 casualties in November, not counting prisoners, and it was assumed that von Runstedt would probably husband his remaining manpower to try to blunt the Allied drive toward the Rhine.

The Ardennes sector was held by two fresh, untried American divisions in the north and two veteran, but badly mauled divisions in the south. It was considered to be generally unsuitable for tanks, being closely wooded with narrow, circuitous roads all but impassable in snow. The two new divisions were assigned to this area because it was considered to be a 'quiet' sector where the green troops could gain some battle experience fairly easily. The two veteran divisions were here to 'rest' from their ordeal in the Huertgen Forest a month before.

On 16 December 1944 when the German counter-offensive smashed into them, the impact upon the Americans was something like that at Pearl Harbor. In less than forty-eight hours penetrations, some more than fifteen miles deep, were made in Allied lines across a fifty-five mile front. The first blows swept away unsuspecting outposts; stubborn pockets of resistance were by-passed. To add to the confusion, the Germans employed troops disguised as American soldiers speaking perfect 'American' English. Though the tactic ultimately failed, it caused Americans at the front anxious moments and stragglers and strangers wandered at their own peril.

The operation gained momentum in the center, taking advantage of bad weather and Allied confusion over German objectives. For a while, it was reminiscent of the early Blitzkrieg days and a deep cut, some 45 miles wide and 65 miles deep, was gouged out of the Allied positions. But despite the stunning blows, Allied troops fought back everywhere. The lines buckled, but the Germans never were able to break completely through the defenses. In the center, they struck for the town of Bastogne in Belgium, a key road center in the southern Ardennes. Bastogne would give the Germans three different approach routes, but if it was retained by the Allies it would be an ideal jumping off point to smash the German attack. An American armored division, the 10th, fought a delaying action, trading lives for time; eventually von Runstedt was able to outflank them, but by that time the 101st Airborne Division was solidly entrenched in the city center.

Bastogne was surrounded, but resisted valiantly; German artillery pounded it with merciless accuracy, but the paratroops grimly held on. Even as they expended their energy against this one lone town and division, they themselves were being squeezed on both sides of the bulge, and as the weather began to clear, 5000 Allied aircraft ranged over the entire area to destroy anything German that moved. Despite the fact that by December 26 the German attack ground to a halt, Hitler continued to throw in new divisions, most of them filled with ill-trained recruits.

By January 1945 it was clear that the bold gamble had failed. The Russians had started a gigantic offensive against the Germans and Hitler was forced to transfer all available forces to the eastern front. Within a month, all the ground gained had been lost.

If his goals had been limited, Hitler could conceivably have delayed the Allied drive toward the Rhine, though in 1944 Germany did not possess the power to defeat the Allies permanently. But by striving for the long-distance objectives of Antwerp and the other Channel ports without sufficient strength, the Germans squandered away any reserve that might have been used against either the Russian offensive or subsequently in the defense of Germany beyond the Rhine. As it

Above: Benito Mussolini hangs by his heels in Milan.

Scraping the bottom of the barrel, Hitler called upon children to defend his crumbling regime.

was, the Battle of the Bulge achieved a one month delay, but left the road into Germany from the West a wide thoroughfare.

The counter-offensive left 120,000 Germans killed, wounded, captured or missing; over 1000 planes and 500 tanks were destroyed as well. The Americans sustained nearly 80,000 casualties. Though British troops were involved in the north, it had been primarily an American show, and it had put to rest once and for all the Hitler myth that Americans could not withstand pressure.

On New Year's Day, 1945, Adolf Hitler went on the air to give the German people renewed pledges of ultimate victory for the Reich and destruction for 'defeatists'. He repeated the vow that Germany 'will never capitulate', and called upon the German people for continued sacrifice for 'survival, . . . culture, . . . for prosperity'. As he spoke, British, American and Russian armies totalling more than 10 million men were pressing in upon the German nation. In the east three Russian thrusts headed for Berlin, Czechoslovakia was invaded, and East Prussia was isolated. These moves forced the transfer of all available forces from the West at top speed, but most of the men were already exhausted from the Ardennes offensive. From the air Allied bombers pulverized the German armament industry.

Across the Rhine

The shortage of manpower had now put older men, sub-teen striplings and infirm males into uniform as the Germans desperately sought to build up the Rhine defenses. The western Allies headed for the Rhine, sweeping up the last pockets of German resistance, and the Germans made ready to demolish all the bridges across this last major defensive barrier in the West. While the British and Americans brought up river crossing craft, the Americans had not had to cross any body of inland water under hostile fire since the American civil war. No one had successfully crossed the Rhine into Germany since Napoleon in 1805. All the bridges were supposedly blown up and the Germans sat and waited on the east side of the river where the steep ground gave them excellent observations and fields of fire.

Then on 7 March 1945, the Allies had a lucky break. A small American patrol approached the ancient medieval town of Remagen, located between Bonn and Coblenz, and found that the bridge was largely intact, despite the fact that explosive charges had been placed on it. Indeed one had already exploded. The small group hurried across under fire and reported the situation. As quickly as possible, more Americans were fed across; engineers reinforced the bridge so that tanks and trucks could cross, and within 24 hours more than 8000 men were on the other side. Two more emergency bridges were built alongside, and the Rhine was crossed.

The Luftwaffe tried unsuccessfully to destroy the bridges from the air. One more span did eventually collapse sweeping a number of Americans to their death, but the Rhine had been nullified as a defense. Eighteen days later, all Allied offensive forces were across. Germany proper was defenseless.

After clearing the Rhine barrier, the Allies

Left: Civilians flee for safety when German snipers open fire on de Gaulle and his staff as they entered the Notre Dame. **Left center:** General Dietrich von Choltitz surrenders in the Gare Montparnasse. **Left lower center:** Warm welcome for British soldiers in Paris. **Bottom left:** Brussels gave the Allies an equally enthusiastic welcome.

Right: Small bands of Germans caused crowds to panic in the Place de la Concorde, even after they surrendered the city. **Below:** Hitler and Mussolini view the devastation caused by the explosion of a bomb in the Fuehrer's conference room **Below center:** German prisoners and Belgian collaborators were locked in cages in the Antwerp Zoo. Here a German joins his comrades in the lions cage. **Below right:** Soldiers of the Waffen SS during the breakthrough at the Bulge.

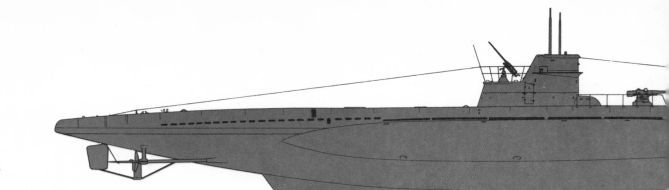

Right: VII C 'U' Boat
Length: 220¼ ft. Beam:
20¼ ft. Draught: 15¾ ft.
Maximum speed: 17/7½
knots. Armament:
1 × 3.5 in., 1 × 37 mm.
A.A., 2 × 20 mm. A.A.,
5 × 21 in. Torpedo tubes,
14 × torpedo. Crew: 44
Displacement: 769/871 tons.

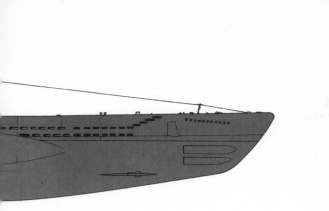

General Jodl signs the unconditional surrender of the Third Reich.

encircled the industrial heartland of Germany, reducing the Ruhr valley to a hollow shell with intensive bombing raids. Once more Hitler ordered his troops to stand and fight to the death; once more they were encircled or outflanked. By 1 April 1945 the entire Ruhr area had been enveloped, trapping German forces in an 80-mile circle. More than 400,000 were taken prisoner.

Twenty-one German divisions had been devoured by the Allied juggernaut and the Third Reich was buckling in the center, while to the south, another Allied Army thrust east into Germany. Mannheim fell on 29 March, Nuremberg on 20 April and Munich on 30 April. Thirsting for revenge, Free French forces overwhelmed Stuttgart and Karlsruhe near the Swiss border. But the fastest moving of all was Patton's Third Army. His precision machine was a military wonder: engineers cleared minefields and barriers while tank-infantry teams followed close behind and artillery pulverized resistance ahead. Supporting units kept the equipment repaired and replenished. Few Germans could stand in the way, and his advance guard closed in on Czechoslovakia on 23 April.

On 12 April 1945 President Franklin D. Roosevelt died. If Hitler rejoiced over his death, he found in the successor, Harry S. Truman, an equally relentless enemy. In a short speech Truman called for the 'unconditional surrender' of Germany.

British and Canadian troops swung north into Holland, toward the German coast. In the east Vienna fell on 13 April as on both fronts Allied armies scooped up thousands of dazed German soldiers. The streamlined, efficient Wehrmacht was a thing of the past; animal-drawn transport cluttered the roads, and fighting units were scattered or simply disappeared. Then on 25 April 1945 small American and Russian patrols faced each other curiously at the town of Torgau on the Elbe River, some 75 miles south of Berlin. The confrontation was soon built into a full-fledged linkup slashing Germany in two.

That same day, Benito Mussolini attempted to escape into Switzerland with his mistress. Allied armies were converging upon Milan and the erstwhile dictator was now a broken man, frightened and despised. A group of Italian Communist partisans came upon him and, in a burst of machine-gun fire, ended the life of the man who had 'made Italian trains run on time'. His corpse along with those of his mistress and a number of other Fascists were publicly displayed in Milan and then buried in a potter's field.

Yet Hitler continued to believe that salvation was imminent. He now planned to direct the defence of northern Germany from Berlin while assigning Heinrich Himmler to defend the south. The Russians were rapidly approaching Berlin from the east and the city was studded with pillboxes and minefields, but the Nazis continued to scrawl slogans on the walls declaring their intention to fight to the death.

Allied airpower seemed about to pound the city into dust. Russians attacked from the east, northeast and southeast and their artillery crashed into the metropolitan heartland. German citizens cringed in terror, but the Nazis rounded up every able-bodied male from twelve to eighty for a last-ditch stand. By 23 April Russian forces held the center of the city and on 2 May 1945, all formal or organized resistance ceased.

There has been much speculation over the eventual fate of Adolf Hitler. As the Allies moved through Germany, the top Nazi leadership had begun to disintegrate. Some, like Goebbels, would commit suicide rather than face Allied retribution. Others, such as Goering, would be captured and then cheat the executioner by taking their own lives. More, such as Martin Bormann, would never be found. Some would even seek to find their own accommodation with the Allied authorities, as in the case of Himmler.

But the Fuehrer himself steadfastly refused to leave Berlin for any other sanctuary or headquarters. Almost to the end, he continued to study war maps, call conferences, and move nonexistent armies about. More and more he lapsed into fits of rage over the incompetence of subordinates or the 'ingratitude' of the German people. His health had been steadily deteriorating during the last days until he looked like some grim caricature out of a nightmare. He was bent and stooped and his left leg dragged, both souvenirs from the bomb plot; he was pale and hollow-eyed and ate less and less, becoming reluctant to leave his dank bunker and suffering from loss of sleep.

As one of his final acts, Hitler expelled Goering and Himmler from the Nazi Party and named Admiral Karl Doenitz to be the next leader of the Third Reich. On 15 April 1945 his mistress Eva Braun appeared at the bunker. They were married on 29 April with Russian artillery shells and rockets as their marital symphony. Although the facts have not been completely proved, it is generally accepted that on 30 April Hitler shot himself, while Eva Braun took poison. The bodies were burned in the courtyard, but the remains have never been found.

Admiral Doenitz attempted to continue as the head of government by offering to surrender to the Western Allies only. This was rejected, and on 7 May 1945 Nazi Germany unconditionally surrendered. The European phase of World War Two came to an end.

General Jodl signs the unconditional surrender of the Third Reich.

Opposite top: Frankfurt-am-Main was wiped out. **Opposite bottom:** The Anhalter Station in Berlin, like the rest of the city, was heavily hit. **Below:** Red flag over Berlin.

CHAPTER EIGHTEEN
Japan Subdued

Before MacArthur could begin his drive to liberate the Philippines, he still had to do some cleaning up in the Southwest Pacific. In April 1944 Allied forces took Hollandia in Dutch New Guinea. In May they pressed on to Biak and Wakde. Wakde was taken two days after the first Allied landings (19 May) but Biak proved more difficult. Allied forces were landed on the island on 27 May but it was not secured until the end of August, although an Allied air base had been constructed a month before the battle was over.

The battle for Biak would have been more difficult still if the Japanese had not decided to cancel a planned assault on Allied forces in the area in favor of sending what remained of the Japanese fleet against them in the Philippine Sea where landings on Saipan and Guam were imminent. The Saipan landing had actually begun while Biak was still being contested, on 16 June. When Allied leaders learned that Japan intended to engage Admiral Spruance's task force, the Guam landing was postponed and the US Navy prepared to meet the Japanese in one of the last major contests in the naval war in the Pacific.

The Battle of the Philippine Sea began on 19 June 1944. Unlike previous naval engagements in the Pacific, the American task force outnumbered its Japanese rival by more than two to one ships. More important, the American group that engaged the Japanese in the Philippine Sea was well seasoned. Whereas the Japanese had sustained heavy losses in personnel and equipment, particularly aircraft, by the summer of 1944, which forced them to rely on improperly trained seamen and fliers, the United States task force was experienced and able. The battle, therefore, proved to be an uneven match. By the time the Japanese retreated on 21 June, they had lost at least three carriers and more than 300 aircraft, a loss that the Imperial Japanese Navy could ill afford to sustain.

After the defeat of the Japanese fleet the capture of Saipan was only a matter of time. Had it not been for the fierce resistance of the Japanese garrison on the island, the Marines would have wrapped things up in a few days but as it happened, the campaign took several weeks. The Japanese did not surrender until 8 July and even then pockets of resistance still had to be cleaned out. Perhaps the term 'surrender' is misleading since the commander of the Japanese force on Saipan, General Yoshio Saito, ordered his men to fight to the death and fought to his own death beside them. Given this suicidal resistance and the

General Douglas MacArthur led his forces through a series of amphibious landings along the northern New Guinea coast in preparation for his conquest of the Philippines.

difficult terrain of the island, the Marines sustained unusually heavy losses before the island was secured with 3400 dead and over 14,000 wounded. Japanese casualties have been estimated at more than 24,000, one of their worst disasters of the war. Tojo was forced to resign as Premier shortly after this dreadful toll was announced in Tokyo.

The neutralization and conquest of Saipan had hardly been completed when the Allies attacked Guam and Tinian. Following a massive bombardment of Japanese installations, Guam was invaded on 21 July, and Tinian on 24 July. Both campaigns were efficiently and rapidly completed; the Stars and Stripes flew over Tinian by 3 August, and Guam was subdued by the 10th. Army engineers and Seabees lost no time in constructing and expanding air bases on the two islands, giving the Allies bases within easy flying time from Formosa and the islands from which to launch their B-29 strikes. For Japan, the end was near.

'I Shall Return'

The successful conclusion of the Marianas campaign opened the way for MacArthur to return to the Philippines. The only unsettled question was whether the thrust through the Philippines should be part of the major effort to subdue Japan or given second priority. For once, all major commanders in the Pacific theatre were in agreement; MacArthur was joined by Admiral Halsey and other senior naval officers who argued against a diversion of Allied efforts to China or Formosa. The campaign in the Philippines was quickly given top priority.

MacArthur's plans were already made when the Joint Chiefs gave their official blessing to the venture; all that remained to be done was to co-ordinate with the Navy and fix a date and place for the invasion. MacArthur and his associates had originally considered Mindanao the most likely target of an Allied attack on the islands of Leyte and Luzon. Morotai, Peleliu, and Ulithi, with their bases and refueling stations had to be captured first, however. The scheme was submitted to the Joint Chiefs in late August and was immediately approved.

By mid-September Morotai and Ulithi were in Allied hands, but Peleliu there was tough fighting and heavy resistance. Although the major landing target, an air field, was secured on 12 October, the island was not cleared until the middle of November. Nevertheless, MacArthur would not be deflected from his primary goal; re-occupation of the Philippines. Preparations

for the invasion of the Philippines went on without interruption, and the Allies were ready by mid-October.

On 20 October 1944 America returned to the Philippines when units of the United States Sixth Army were landed in Leyte. The Japanese responded by sending what was left of their Combined Fleet to stop them. Four days after the Leyte landing the two sides met in the final major naval engagement of the Pacific war, the Battle of Leyte Gulf.

The Japanese divided their fleet, sending one group north through the Surignao Strait to Leyte Gulf, and another south from San Bernadino. If all went according to plan, the two halves of the fleet would converge upon the American task force in the gulf and suicide pilots, *Kamikazes,* would destroy American troop ships and their escorts. Surprise was essential, but on 23 October Admiral Kurita's Center Task Force was spotted by American submarines as it was moving south through the Palawan Passage Strait. When Kurita reached the Sibuyan Sea the following morning, Admiral Mitscher was waiting. American aircraft sunk a battleship, the *Musashi,* three cruisers, and several smaller ships, and he was forced to withdraw. Japan's Southern Force fared little better.

On 25 October ships of the United States Seventh Fleet opened fire on the Southern Task Force as it tried to move from the Strait of Surigao into Leyte Gulf. The Seventh Fleet was deployed in a fifteen-mile line blocking the entrance into the Gulf, and the Japanese could reach it only by steaming through the American line. This they declined to do, although Admiral Mishimura made a more concerted effort to breach the line than did his partner, Admiral Shima. The Japanese lost several destroyers in the contest but managed to withdraw from the battle area with no additional losses.

Encouraged by the withdrawal of the Center Task Force, Admiral Halsey was anxious to pursue the retreating Japanese to find and attack Admiral Ozawa's decoy fleet which had been sent south from the Japanese Islands to draw the Americans away from the Philippines. With Kurita in retreat and the Seventh Fleet engaging the Southern Task Force, Halsey felt it was safe to leave the escort carriers of the Seventh Fleet near the San Bernadino Straits while his Third Fleet sought out Ozawa's task force. This proved to be a great mistake; no sooner had Halsey's task force left Leyte Gulf than Kurita appeared with his fleet. By the time Halsey got word of this, he was 150 miles north of the area and could have done little to rescue the fleet carriers even if he had thought such a mission possible, which he did not.

Although Kurita's reappearance was alarming, Halsey had overestimated the damage done to the Japanese armada in the contest off the Palawan Passage on the 24th, and did not think it presented any danger which American naval forces in the Gulf of Leyte could not handle. Unfortunately he was mistaken. When Kurita appeared in front of the carriers of the Seventh Fleet on 25 October, he had four battleships, a half dozen heavy cruisers, and several destroyers under his command, while the Americans could

Above: Homage to the Emperor before certain death. **Right:** Kamikaze attacks on American ships caused considerable damage **Center right:** One or two direct hits by Japanese suicide planes could put an aircraft carrier out of commission. **Bottom right** USS *Franklin* lists badly after having received a direct hit.

Left: Tons of equipment and thousands of men reinforced the invaders of Luzon. Below left: The first wave of invaders heads toward the beaches of Luzon.

CHINA

Equator

NEW GUINEA

Japanese held areas until August 1945

19.2.45

Allied (U.S.) attack and date of attacks

muster only six carriers and their destroyer escorts. By the end of the day one American carrier and two destroyers had been laid to rest. But at least the carrier fleet was not annihilated, so the incident was not an unmitigated disaster for the Americans.

While Admiral Sprague battled Kurita's task force, Halsey found and engaged Admiral Ozawa's fleet 200 miles northeast of Luzon. Here the Americans more than made up for their losses further south; planes from American carriers flew hundreds of sorties and when the battle was over, four Japanese carriers lay at the bottom of the Pacific. Had Halsey not belatedly sent a small task force under Admiral Lee to the rescue of the Seventh Fleet carriers in Leyte Gulf, Ozawa's force would have been completely decimated. Nevertheless, the Japanese sustained heavy losses in the Battle of Cape Engano which, at this stage of the war, they could ill afford.

Back to Bataan

With the Imperial Navy neutralized, Japan's only hope of maintaining her position in the Philippines was to foil the American invasion effort. This would be no easy task, for their only advantage lay in the topography of the area and their fierce determination to resist to the last man if necessary. While this would not suffice in the end, it would considerably delay the capture of Leyte, forcing MacArthur to re-assess his plans for using the island as a jumping-off point in the attempt to recapture Luzon.

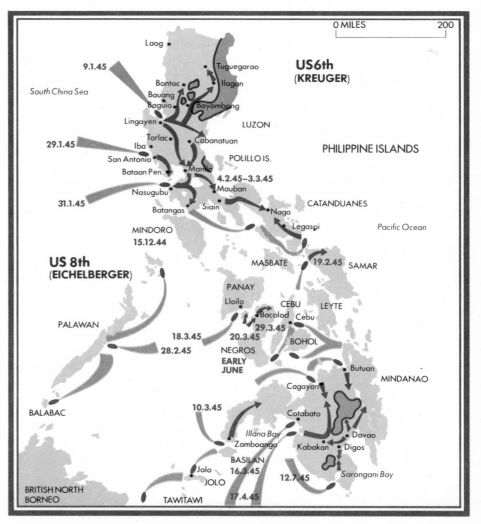

American troops move into the devastated Intramuros section of Manila.

MacArthur reads the proclamation of the liberation of Leyte.

spring. While the mopping-up progressed on Leyte, the major action of the Philippine campaign, the invasion of Luzon, began. On 9 January American forces landed in the Lingayen Gulf.

Although the landing of the Sixth Army at Lingayen was easily accomplished, General Yamashita, the commanding general of Japanese forces in the Philippines, could not permit the landing party to proceed inland without contest. Japanese forces were deployed in front of the landing sites to resist the four American divisions put ashore during the first day of the Allied offensive, but the effort failed. While I Corps of the Sixth Army pushed the Japanese into the mountains of the Gulf, other units raced south toward Clark Field and Manila.

The Sixth Army encountered heavy opposition as it pushed toward Manila. Thanks to the establishment of air fields on Mindoro the Allied were able to check the effectiveness of Japanese air power over Luzon, but the going on the ground was extremely tough. The distance between the landing sites on the Lingayen Gulf and Manila was only 110 miles, but it took over a month to cover. True to their tradition, the Japanese fought bravely and often to the last man; since there were about 170,000 Japanese on Luzon, General Krueger's advance was necessarily slow.

As Krueger's forces pushed toward Manila, MacArthur prepared to seal the escape route through the Bataan Peninsula by landing a second Allied force close to that area on 29 January. A third force was airlifted and dropped 40 miles south of Manila on 31 January. Together, the three groups proceeded toward Manila, converging on the city, at the beginning of February by which time General Yamashita had abandoned it. Although Japanese army forces had been withdrawn to the mountains, the Manila was still defended by units of the Japanese Navy under the command of Admiral Iwabachi, who refused to obey Yamashita's order declaring Manila an open city and continued to resist the Americans for another month. With several thousand men under his command, Iwabachi turned the battle for Manila into a house to house confrontation, resulting in great damage to the city during the final stage of the campaign. By 4 March, when the city was finally cleared, much of it had been destroyed.

The capture of Manila marked the end of Japanese control in the Philippine Islands. Within weeks, the Bataan Peninsula was cleared and Corregidor was retaken. By the beginning of April Allied shipping was using the port of Manila again, and military leaders were considering their next move against Japan. Although isolated pockets of Japanese resistance were not eliminated until August 1945, shortly before the war's end, they presented no clear or present danger to the American position in the Philippines. MacArthur had returned.

Iwo Jima

It had originally been thought that once the Philippines were subdued the Allied would carry the war to Formosa and/or the China coast, but the success of the Philippine venture encouraged military planners to consider a direct attack

Soon after the initial landings on Leyte, the Americans encountered additional obstacles. Rain-soaked roads proved unable to bear the weight of heavy armored vehicles which quickly bogged down in the mud, and airfields proved unusable for much the same reason. While the landing force was stuck in this mire, the Japanese were able to reinforce their garrison on the island; by the middle of December 45,000 men had been put ashore.

MacArthur and Halsey had intended using Leyte as a major site for air bases from which Japanese installations elsewhere in the Philippine Islands could be attacked, but this plan had to be modified. Carriers of the United States Third Fleet were ordered to stations in the Gulf of Leyte so that these attacks could be launched using carrier-based as opposed to land-based aircraft. This posed two problems which had not been originally anticipated. First, the carriers were themselves targets for Japanese *kamikaze* squadrons, and second, carrier-based aircraft were necessarily smaller than land based bombers, carried smaller payloads and were less effective.

There was no way to protect against *kamikaze* attacks. Suicide pilots, sealed into their aircraft, and determined to crash their planes which were loaded with bombs into Allied ships, presented a threat hitherto unheard of in modern warfare. The Third Fleet suffered the loss of two carriers and several other ships before Halsey ordered part of it to withdraw to the Caroline Islands at the end of November. By that time, however, things were going better on Leyte and the Americans considered plans for the invasion of Luzon.

Leyte was finally secured on 25 December 1944, although the Japanese continued to resist the Americans in isolated pockets until the following against the Japanese home islands. Such a move would end the war more rapidly at a minimal cost in men and equipment, and the plan was generally well received by MacArthur, Halsey and their associates and quickly accepted by the Joint Chiefs of Staff.

The Joint Chiefs felt that if an attack on Japan was to be successful the Allies would have to capture Iwo Jima, Okinawa, and the Bonin Islands first. With these bases secure the Allies could launch a major aerial bombardment of the Japanese islands, pulverizing the major cities with their powerful B-29 bombers and destroying any remaining industrial capacity.

Iwo Jima was to be the first target, and even before Manila was captured, preparations were made for the invasion of this small volcanic island. The head of the American force assigned to capture Iwo Jima was to be Admiral Spruance, the new commander of the Fifth Fleet which for this venture included three Marine divisions. The date for the landing was set for 19 February 1945.

From 8 December 1944 to 19 February 1945, Allied aircraft bombed Japanese installations on Iwo Jima daily in order to soften Japan's defenses on the island. This represented the single most prolonged bombing action of the war but the results did not seem to justify the effort; when the Marines landed on 19 February, they found most of the Japanese positions intact and the Japanese garrison ready and willing to engage them. Although Iwo Jima had been considered a relatively easy target, it was to prove to be one of the most costly and difficult battles for the Americans in the Pacific war.

Iwo Jima had not been a major Japanese station and until the summer of 1944 would have been relatively easy for the Allies to take. By September 1944, this situation had changed. As it became clear to the Japanese that the Allies would soon be pressing their homeland, the Japanese garrison on Iwo Jima was quickly reinforced to a strength of approximately 25,000 men, for Japan's military leaders understood as clearly as the Allies the value of the island as a long-range bomber base. Every effort was made to prepare for the American attack, including the construction of an elaborate network of caves and tunnels which would be difficult if not impossible to destroy.

When the Americans landed, they were greeted by mortar fire and an almost constant artillery barrage. Unlike earlier amphibious operations in which the Allies were able to establish a beachhead and quickly fan out to attack their targets, the Marine attack force at Iwo Jima was pinned down on the beaches and sustained exceptionally heavy losses (2500 killed or wounded) on the very first day of the operation. Nor was the first day an exception; in the slow march from the beaches to the inner island, losses continued to be very large. Even with the aid of aerial reconnaisance and naval bombardment, the Americans could not dislodge the Japanese from their fortifications without incurring heavy casualties.

Iwo Jima was not secured until 26 March 1945. During the nearly six weeks that the attack was in progress, the Marines sustained 26,000 casualties. Nearly one-third of the American forces were

Wounded marine is evacuated from Iwo Jima.

killed or wounded; of the approximate 25,000 Japanese, 21,000 lay dead when the campaign ended and only a few hundred prisoners were taken alive. The remaining several thousand Japanese troops took to the hills where they held out until the end of May. All in all, almost the entire Japanese garrison was lost, making this one of Japan's worst defeats of the war.

By the beginning of April, American bombers were flying regular missions from their new bases on Iwo Jima. The Allies had achieved their goal but they paid a high price for it, and the fierce resistance on Iwo Jima gave Allied military commanders food for thought about the invasion of Japan proper. If the Japanese could fight so hard for a tiny volcanic island, what might the Allies expect when they landed in Kyushu or Honshu?

Okinawa

While the Battle for Iwo Jima was still in progress the Allies prepared to invade Okinawa, largest of the Ryukyu Islands, on 1 April 1945. Okinawa was even more strategically important than Iwo Jima, located mid-way between Japan and Formosa only 360 miles from the China coast. Its large size, approximately 480 square miles, would make it difficult to secure and require an even larger effort than the Iwo Jima campaign in which the Americans landed 80,000 men. Nevertheless, if Okinawa was captured, the door would be open to Japan itself. Conversely, if it was not taken, it would be difficult, if not impossible, for the Allies to press the war to the Japanese islands. In short Okinawa, the Allies believed, would be one of the most crucial operations of the war.

To insure success the American command massed a huge invasion force consisting of four

Top: Midget submarines in a wrecked drydock at Kure.
Above: The American fight against fanatical opposition was relentless.
Opposite: The Japanese fought to the bitter end.
Opposite bottom: Raising the flag on Mount Suribachi—a costly victory on Iwo Jima.

Army divisions and three Marine divisions, a total of over 280,000 men. Accompanying the troop ships and guarding them from aerial attack was a task force under the command of Admiral Mitscher, consisting of a fast carrier group plus some escort craft. Supporting the United States Navy was a British task force under the command of Admiral Sir Bruce Fraser which included two battleships, several heavy cruisers and four additional aircraft carriers. Never had the Allies massed a larger armada in support of an amphibious operation.

The Japanese also steeled themselves for the contest. Their garrison on the island numbered slightly over 100,000 men dug into caves and other sturdy defenses and supported by hundreds of gun emplacements and artillery pieces. As if this were not enough, the Japanese massed over 2000 *kamikaze* aircraft for suicide attacks against the Allied flotilla. Rarely had the Allies encountered such a horrifying array.

On 1 April 1945 the first wave of American troops were landed on Okinawa. Unlike the landing on Iwo Jima, it was carried off without any overt resistance, and a five-mile beachhead was carved out within hours after the first troops sloshed ashore. By the end of the day this beachhead had been widened to almost ten miles and still there was no sign of the Japanese. Indeed, the enemy was not sighted at all until three days after the first landings.

Until 13 April American ground forces advanced with little or no difficulty but in the air and on the sea, it was a different story. *Kamikaze* pilots systematically attacked Allied ships, sinking a dozen destroyers and damaging several others. In addition, the Allied armada encountered a new obstacle, a floating suicide squad. The capital ship *Yamato* had been sent to the waters off

Okinawa accompanied by a small escort force, with only enough fuel to drive her to the scene of the battle where she was to employ at sea the same dastardly tactics used by the *kamikaze* pilots. The mission was a true sign of the desperation of the Japanese, but might have proved quite devastating if American aircraft had not spotted the battleship and followed her approach. When the *Yamato* reached the battle area on 7 April she was attacked by 280 carrier-based aircraft and sent to the bottom. The Allied fleet reigned supreme and was never again challenged. The stage was now set for the land contest.

Two weeks after the original landing, the Japanese began their counter-attack. Japanese forces were concentrated in the southern part of the island. Thus, while the Marines had little difficulty pushing into the Motobu Peninsula, their peers in the south had a very difficult time. Despite an unusually heavy and continuous bombardment of Japanese positions in the south of Okinawa, the Americans could not dislodge them from their bunkers and caves. Aerial attack and artillery bombardment proved an ineffective substitute for infantry.

For three months American Marines and infantrymen slogged their way through the hot, humid and muddy Okinawan terrain, encountering zealous and often fanatic opposition reminiscent of the suicide missions of the *kamikazes* and the ill-fated *Yamato*. The battle was finally over on 21 June 1945, by which time both sides had sustained casualties that paled those suffered on Iwo Jima. According to official reports, the Americans lost almost 50 000 men, the Japanese over 110,000. Again the Allied command had to stop and think. If the Japanese sacrificed 110,000 men for the defense of Okinawa, how many would die to defend their homeland?

The Atomic Decision

Allied leaders were not ready to invade the Japanese islands. For months American bombers flying from their new bases in the Pacific had attacked targets in Japan with the ultimate aim of demoralizing the Japanese people, destroying Japan's industrial base, and disrupting Japanese agriculture. Yet despite the fact that the Japanese had taken a terrible pounding, the Allies were still uncertain about an invasion of the home islands even though they knew that the Soviets were prepared to join them in the effort once the European war was over. If the horrendous losses suffered on Iwo Jima and Okinawa were an

indication of what would happen during an invasion of Japan, not even the presence of the Soviets would diminish the disaster that would befall the Allies. It was not unnatural, then, for Allied and particularly American commanders to welcome any feasible alternative to the loss of two million men wounded or killed in the last phase of the war against Japan. Fortunately, or perhaps unfortunately, there was an alternative the use of atomic weapons.

American scientists, aided by refugees from Nazi Germany and Fascist Italy, had long labored on the ultimate destructive device at a series of secret sites in the United States. In the spring of 1945 they had perfected this device and were ready to test it. By the time President Truman attended the Potsdam Conference in July, there was every evidence that the new weapon could be deployed against Japan, and Truman said as much without going into great detail in a conversation with Churchill in 14 July. Churchill analyzed the implications of this new development in the following manner:

'We seemed suddenly to have become possessed of a merciful abridgement of the slaughter in the East and of a far happier prospect in Europe. . . . To avert a vast indefinite butchery, to bring the war to an end, to give peace to the world, to lay healing hands upon its tortured people by a manifestation of overwhelming power at the cost of a few explosions, seemed after all our toils and perils, a miracle of deliverance.'

Whatever has been said about the use of the atomic bombs on Japan, few people at the time would have differed from the point made by Churchill that 'there was never a moment's discussion as to whether the atomic bomb should be used or not'. Whatever the moral debate triggered by the destruction wrought by these horrible devices, for the moment they offered an alternative to the loss of two million men. Allied leaders felt this was an alternative they could not afford to refuse, and plans were made to test the new weapon against Japan, to bring the Japanese government to its senses. It only remained to decide where and when the devices would be used.

Was there an alternative to the use of the atomic bombs against Japan other than a land invasion of the Japanese islands? There may have been. By the summer of 1945 Japanese leaders attempted to feel the Allies out about a possible peace settlement, using the Soviets as intermediaries. The Allies did not know how serious these feelers were because the Soviets did not convey the message clearly; nor were they necessarily better informed about the terrible damage already done in Japan. The Japanese may have been ready to concede defeat, even unconditional surrender, but some of the Allied leaders did not know this, or if they did, they chose to ignore it in favour of extracting the last pound of flesh from the Japanese. In any case, the evidence indicates that, whatever the state of informed opinion in the Allied camp, most civilian and military leaders favored use of the new weapon.

After a considerable secret debate, plans were made for use of the new weapons against Japan. On 6 August 1945 the first atomic bomb ever to be used in warfare was dropped on Hiroshima,

Top: The Japanese finally surrendered in late June after having lost over 110,000. **Center:** B–29s over Yokohama. **Above:** By mid-1945 American bombing laid waste to most of Japan's industrial machine. **Right:** The new Big Three continued the Potsdam Conference: Attlee, Truman and Stalin. **Opposite:** Hiroshima: 6 August 1945.

leveling the city and killing over 80,000 people. Three days later, on 9 August, a second atomic bomb was dropped on Nagasaki. The following morning the Japanese sued for peace.

Ironically, the Russians entered the war just as the Japanese were seeking an acceptable way to end it. Even the two atomic bombings of Japan had not resulted in a mentality of surrender among Japan's leaders. Although the Imperial Council agreed that the war must be brought to an end, the Emperor's advisers remained divided on what terms they would be willing to accept for ending the war. It was only as a result of direct intervention by Hirohito that the stalemate was resolved. Fearing that the Allies might drop more atomic weapons on Japan and continue their regular bombing raids, the Emperor announced on 14 August 1945 that his government would accept the terms for ending the war that the Allies had articulated at Potsdam. These included: 1) unconditional surrender of Japan's armed forces; 2) surrender of all territories other than the Japanese islands over which Japan had acquired control since 1895; 3) militarism would be eliminated in Japan; 4) to accomplish this, the Allies would occupy Japan.

Unconditional Surrender

Hirohito's decision was communicated to the Swiss, who immediately forwarded his message to the United States. It was received by President Truman and Prime Minister Attlee on 14 August, less than twenty-four hours after the Emperor's announcement to the Imperial Conference. Formal surrender ceremonies were held on board the *USS Missouri* on 2 September 1945. After more than seven years, the war was finally over. In accepting Japan's surrender on behalf of the Allies, General MacArthur expressed the hope that 'a better world would emerge out of the blood and carnage of the past . . .'. Considering that tens of millions of people had lost their lives in the conflict, this was surely not too much to ask.

World War II was the greatest war in history: greatest in scope and in fighting, on every continent; greatest in numbers of dead; greatest in its horror – the concentration camps, genocide, the atomic blasts, the fire raids, the Blitz – and, above all, the greatest ideological war of modern times. Wars of religion are nothing new. But wars of the modern religion, nationalism, are probably the most fierce, made all the more devastating by the 'advances' of perverted science. The war was a war of rival ideologies – fascism versus communism, democracy versus dictatorship – as well as a war between rival national myths. In the perspective of over twenty-five years, the war, if it was fought to rid the world of dictatorships, was a failure. If it was fought to suppress the economic and political might of Germany and Japan, it was also a failure. It succeeded only in weakening the democracies and economies of Western Europe for a time, which allowed the nations of the Third World to add their national myths to a world still ridden with nationalistic fervor. It is, undoubtedly, pessimistic to conclude that World War II accomplished little, and that the men who struggled in it died in vain. But perhaps that is the legacy of all wars.

Nagasaki: 9 August 1945.

451

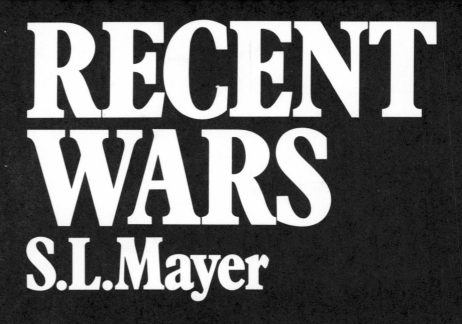

RECENT WARS

S.L. Mayer

CHAPTER ONE
The Korean War

President Harry S. Truman was at home that Saturday evening, 24 June 1950, spending the weekend away from Washington attending to some family business in Independence, Missouri. He was sitting in the library of his old frame house on North Delaware Street when the telephone rang. It was Secretary of State Dean Acheson calling from his farm in Sandy Spring, Maryland. He said, 'Mr President, I have some very serious news. The North Koreans have invaded South Korea'. Acheson told Truman that he felt that the Security Council of the United Nations should be convened at once to declare that an act of aggression had taken place. Armed aggression had indeed taken place when at 0400 Korean time an invasion force composed of 150 Russian-built T-34 tanks and seven infantry divisions crossed the 38th Parallel, the demarcation line between the two Koreas, along a 150-mile front extending across the peninsula from the Yellow Sea to the Sea of Japan. Truman decided that immediate American action might be premature, as the invasion might have been merely a border raid. When it became clear that this was no raid but a full-scale invasion, Acheson phoned Truman again at 0200 on Sunday morning. They agreed to notify the Secretary-General of the UN, Trygve Lie, and asked him to convene a special session of the UN Security Council the following day so that either economic sanctions, a blockade, military action, or a combination of all these could be taken collectively. Truman's mind shot back to the time in 1936 when Hitler's forces violated the Treaty of Versailles and militarily occupied the Rhineland, the first step in Hitler's conquest of Europe. He recalled the time in 1935–36, after Mussolini had invaded Ethiopia, when the League of Nations proved its impotence to stop the invasion effectively through weak and unenforced economic sanctions against Italy. Or the time in 1931, when Japan seized Manchuria, and the League debated and did nothing. If the League, or a group of nations intent on maintaining the *status quo*, had acted in any of these cases, or indeed, in 1938 when Austria and Czechoslovakia were threatened by Nazi Germany, World War II might not have occurred. Britain had drawn the line at Poland too late to avoid war. Truman was determined that monolithic Communism, as he perceived it, would not get away with further gains.

The postwar world proved to be a difficult adjustment for the Western Allies who had won World War II. The Yalta and Potsdam agree-ments with the Soviet Union, which effectively partitioned Europe and East Asia, were not fully adhered to by Russia, who was anxious to consolidate her hold over Eastern Europe. Although Britain and the US had much of eastern Germany most of Austria and part of Czechoslovakia in their hands at the end of hostilities in 1945, they withdrew to the sectors devised for them at Yalta in February 1945, against the advice of then Prime Minister Winston Churchill and Generals Eisenhower and Patton. Patton especially felt that the US and UK ought to continue their drives at the end of the war, so that at least half of Czechoslovakia, Berlin and Vienna were taken by them rather than the Soviet Union. But these warnings went unheeded by Truman, who had taken over the Presidency after Roosevelt's death in April, and who hoped to make the Yalta agreement and the Potsdam agreement, which he negotiated in July, work. In his view there was no need to force a split in Allied ranks. Stalin took advantage of this, and when he later refused to allow free elections in Poland, occupied by Russian troops, Truman began to think less kindly of the Soviet Union's intentions.

The Cold War

As the Soviet Union tightened its iron grip on the states of Eastern Europe over whose liberty Britain ostensibly went to war in 1939, the atmosphere characterized by the phrase 'cold war' began to emerge. When Russia attempted to achieve Communist coups in Turkey and Greece, in the latter through a protracted civil war in which Russia gave considerable assistance to the Greek Communist insurgents, Britain, for a time, and in 1947 the United States, gave military and financial assistance to the existing governments. The Truman Doctrine, under which American aid to Greece and Turkey was authorized, marked a major step away from traditional peacetime isolation toward Europe which the United States

Opposite: US Super-fortresses rain destruction on a chemical plant in North Korea.

Russian T34-85.
Length: 24 ft. 7 in.
Width: 9 ft. 10 in.
Max road speed: 32 m.p.h.
Armament: 1 × 85 mm.,
2 × 7.62 mm. machine
guns. Crew: 5.
Weight: 31.5 tons.

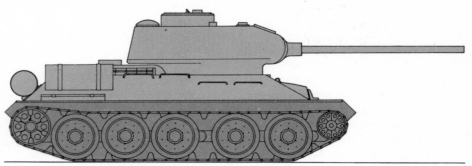

had maintained throughout its history and which Truman had vainly hoped to reinstate after World War II. Meanwhile, the states of Western Europe sought to achieve unity through alliances concluded in 1947 and 1948, while the US stepped up its economic support of the Western economies which, as a result of the war, were near collapse. The Marshall Plan, announced at a Harvard commencement ceremony by General George C. Marshall, now Secretary of State, in June 1947, hoped to aid all the countries of Europe. In the event, however, only the war-torn economies of Western Europe accepted American technical and financial assistance. Russia and its client states in Eastern Europe refused or were forced to refuse.

The threat of Communist takeover of Western Europe by one means or another was very real in the postwar period. Although revisionist historians today tend to underestimate the situation, there is little doubt that democratic, capitalist-oriented government was in real trouble in some states, particularly France and Italy, whose Communist parties were powerful, commanding a sizable minority of the vote. It is to be remembered that after 1941 the Communists were in the forefront of what underground resistance against Hitler existed in Western Europe. There was every chance that with or without Soviet aid they could achieve power democratically and if they did so, their international orientation would be directed toward Russia, not the United States. Part of the reasoning behind the containment policy of George Kennan and the Marshall Plan it engendered was the fact that unless Western Europe were helped, and quickly, the area could fall under Stalin's dubiously benign hand, thus obviating much of the sacrifice of Britain and America during World War II. How could all the lives lost by the Anglo-Americans in the war be justified if the result were the absorption of the whole Continent by a dictatorship as ruthless and an economic system as exclusive as Germany's had been?

Czechoslovakia and Berlin

The Marshall Plan, apart from being one of the most humanitarian acts in modern history, raising Western Europe from the ashes of war and the degrading deprivation that came in its wake, was successful in fulfilling America's economic and political aims. France and Italy did not go Communist in 1948 as many feared they would. The broken societies of Western Europe began to mend, while at the same time, Russia consolidated her gains in the East. The Czechoslovak coup of February 1948 removed the last democratic government in Eastern Europe when Edward Benes was removed as President and Jan Masaryk's defenestration raised cynical doubts about his death all over the world. At Munich in 1938 the Western powers helped to carve up Czechoslovakia like a feast placed before Hitler's table. In 1948 the same country, even the same people, like Masaryk and Benes, underwent a similar agony, and without a shot being fired passed once again into the hands of a foreign dictatorship. When democracy died under Klement Gottwald's Stalinism in Prague, the West became alerted to the threat Communism

General Chu Teh led Chairman Mao to victory in 1949. He was the head of all Chinese Communist fighting forces at the start of the Korean War.

posed in Europe more than ever before, but in the case of Czechoslovakia, as in 1938, did nothing. The Berlin blockade in the same year, however, evoked a more positive response, when the Americans helped to airlift food and other essential materials to the Western sectors of a city more than a hundred miles behind what was now universally called the Iron Curtain. It took over a year of daily airlifts to Berlin to convince the Soviet Union that the West meant business when it came to defending her interests in Europe, and the blockade of Berlin was dropped in 1949, the same year that the North Atlantic Treaty Organization was created. The NATO alliance pledged the United States to militarily defend Western Europe in the event of armed attack. With American atomic superiority a fact in 1949 – indeed, at the time, atomic monopoly – Russia dared not risk testing Western defenses at a time when she was trying to rebuild after suffering more than any nation at the hands of Nazi Germany. At least she dared not test American willingness to abandon traditional isolationism in the NATO pact, whose defense area lay entirely in Europe and North America. But America's willingness to support her interests in Asia were still open to question.

Communism in China

During the Chinese Civil War, which, despite the Marshall Mission, resumed with growing ferocity in 1947, the United States had not used her military strength to aid the crumbling régime of Chiang Kai-shek. True enough, something like three billion dollars worth of aid flowed into Chungking and later Nanking, but President Truman was not prepared to risk American lives for the sake of the Nationalist government. When the Communist armies of Mao Tse-tung overwhelmed the corrupt, inflation-ridden government of Chiang in 1949, forcing the remnants of his army to the island redoubt of Formosa, many critics of Truman in America charged the Democratic government with being 'soft on Communism'. In the Senate William Jenner, Joseph McCarthy, William Knowland and other right-wing Republicans felt that Truman had not done enough to aid Chiang Kai-shek. In their view, despite the NATO commitment, Truman and his Secretary of State since 1949, Dean Acheson, had 'lost' Czechoslovakia and China to godless Communism. Indeed, they further charged that Roosevelt at Yalta and Truman at Potsdam, advised by men like Alger Hiss, then under indictment for disloyalty, had unwittingly sold out American interests to Russia. Some even muttered that a degree of willingness to do so was involved. These exaggerations and simple misstatements of fact (the US never had China to lose, for example) had their effect on the American public and Truman's credibility as President. When Korea was attacked, Truman was placed in a position where inaction or something less than direct involvement by American troops would have been construed as treasonable by his opponents in the Congress and in the country. Much of what Truman did in those last days of June 1950 can be explained by the political climate in which those acts would be judged.

The Korean attack

Just before the Trumans were about to sit down to have Sunday dinner, 25 June 1950, as the noon hour approached, Truman received another phone call from Acheson. He predicated that the UN Security Council would pass a resolution calling for a cease-fire along the 38th Parallel, but that North Korea would ignore it. Truman decided to return to Washington, and within an hour his plane, the *Independence*, had left Kansas City's Municipal Airport for the nation's capital. At 7.15 pm he was back in Washington. By that time the UN, by a vote of 9-0, with Yugoslavia abstaining, agreed to the American resolution, and called on all members 'to render every assistance to the United Nations in the execution of this resolution'. But the North Koreans had not stopped their advance. After a hurried dinner at Blair House, Truman's residence while the White House was being renovated, he met with Acheson and the Joint Chiefs of Staff. There was no doubt in anyone's mind that the US should act decisively. This attack was perceived as America's 'Rhineland' – and unlike 1936, the democracies would act in the face of aggression.

An order was issued to General Douglas MacArthur, Supreme Commander Allied Powers in Japan (SCAP), to evacuate all Americans from Korea but to try to keep airports open. He was also assigned to send ammunition and other available supplies from American-occupied Japan to South Korea. The US Seventh Fleet was ordered to the Formosa Strait to prevent either a Communist Chinese seizure of the island or an attempt by Chiang to reoccupy parts of mainland China. In other words, MacArthur was ordered to isolate the war; to prevent it from spreading to other parts of East Asia. Thus, South Korea and Formosa were now included in an American defense perimeter in East Asia.

Prior to the invasion of South Korea the American defense perimeter had excluded both areas, most clearly in a speech given by Acheson in Washington on 12 January 1950. American troops had been withdrawn from the peninsula, leaving the Republic of Korea an army of 100,000, supported by a local constabulary of 48,000. There were no tanks, no fighter or bomber aircraft, no heavy artillery; only some field artillery, small arms, mortars and anti-tank guns. In short, no more than enough to delay a powerful and well-equipped North Korean Army for a few days. The North Korean Army, supplied with Russian arms and a number of Soviet military advisers, had 135,000 men, many of whom had served with the Chinese Communist army during World War II and the Chinese Civil War which had only ended a few months before. The North Koreans had 120 medium tanks (T-34's with 85 mm guns) and an armored brigade of about 6000. In June 1950 the North Korean Air Force had some forty fighters and seventy bombers: about 180 planes in all.

The Americans were, on the face of it, unprepared to defend South Korea. John Foster Dulles, later Eisenhower's Secretary of State, had visited the 38th Parallel a couple of weeks before the invasion and reported that he saw no signs of imminent attack. But MacArthur had his own intelligence team working in Korea, and there is considerable evidence to indicate that he realized that an attack would come soon. The build-up north of the 38th Parallel was considerable. It takes some time to mount an offensive such as that which was launched in late June 1950. MacArthur was yearning to resume his active military career after five years as the *de facto* dictator of occupied Japan. The attack on South Korea was a golden opportunity to once again place himself in the American headlines as a military hero. If Truman failed to respond to the attack, then MacArthur, through his right-wing contacts in the States, could charge the Democrats with weakness, and place himself in a position to try once more for the Presidency, his long-term aim. His abortive candidacy never got off the ground in 1948. Perhaps in 1952 things would be different whatever Truman did, since as a (presumably) conquering hero, MacArthur could also run either against Truman or another Democratic nominee, while at the same time pre-empting General Eisenhower's expected candidacy. Eisenhower, after all, had been MacArthur's second-in-command in the Philippines before the war. Ike claimed that he had taken dramatic lessons from MacArthur during those years. There was little love lost between these men, and even less between the President and MacArthur, who had never met but viewed each other with mutual and growing suspicion. Now that the war had come and Truman had reacted, MacArthur was named US

Below: US M-4 tanks of the 2nd Infantry Division engage Chinese Communist forces in North Korea in early 1951. **Opposite:** US helicopter lands at 8063rd Mobile Army Surgical Hospital (MASH), Eighth Army.

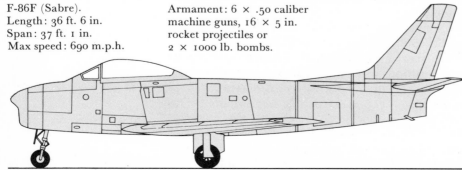

F-86F (Sabre).
Length: 36 ft. 6 in.
Span: 37 ft. 1 in.
Max speed: 690 m.p.h.

Armament: 6 × .50 caliber machine guns, 16 × 5 in. rocket projectiles or 2 × 1000 lb. bombs.

C-in-C and subsequently UN Commander. Thrilled by the challenge, MacArthur prepared for his final and most controversial campaign.

The United Nations was able to support the unilateral action of the United States because of the unusual circumstance of Russia's boycott of the organization since early in the year when the UN refused to allow Communist China to unseat the régime of Chiang Kai-shek, now lodged in Formosa. Thus there was unanimity when, after North Korea refused to withdraw, the UN recommended member states 'to furnish such assistance to the Republic of Korea as may be necessary to repel the armed attack'. With or without UN support, the US was prepared to act. However, with this vote of 27 June the US gained international support for her actions. This support, however, was to place unnecessary constraints upon American action in Korea later in the war, for the UN brief was to restore the *status quo ante bellum*. The US intention was first to repel the aggressor and then, if possible, to unite Korea under the leadership of its client, Syngman Rhee, President of South Korea. At least this was the aim of Rhee, the Republicans and MacArthur. Truman at this stage was chiefly concerned with throwing back the ever advancing aggressor, who threatened to overrun Korea.

Retreat to Pusan

But in those last days of June and increasingly anxious days of July even MacArthur was not overly concerned with the push northwards. He doubted if the few American troops available in Japan would be sufficient to stem the Red tide. By the time Truman committed the United States to action, North Korean troops were already in the suburbs of Seoul, the South Korean capital. MacArthur was ordered to use his air and naval forces south of the 38th Parallel. By 28 June Seoul fell and ROK casualties approached the 50% mark. MacArthur boarded his plane, the *Bataan*, the following day and landed twenty miles south of Seoul. When he saw the flames of the burning city and thousands of disorganized ROK troops and civilians streaming southward, he recognized that the situation was desperate. His opinion, as expressed to Truman and the Pentagon, was that without US ground troops the war was lost. But he thought the ROK forces could hold the enemy at the Han River if Washington allowed him to use two of his four Eighth Army divisions in Japan. On his way out from Tokyo MacArthur had ordered Lt-Gen Stratemeyer to bomb North Korean targets north of the 38th Parallel.

President Truman was wary about committing ground troops to the continent of Asia. He first decided that since air and naval forces could not stop the North Koreans, sufficient ground troops would be sent from Japan to facilitate an evacuation from the port of Pusan at the southern tip of the Korean peninsula. Truman did not want a wider war, and in this belief he was more than strongly supported by America's leading partner in the NATO alliance, Great Britain. American forces, depleted from the 15 million she had under arms in 1945 to about a million, were strung out thinly all over the world. The only wider war America was capable of waging was an atomic war

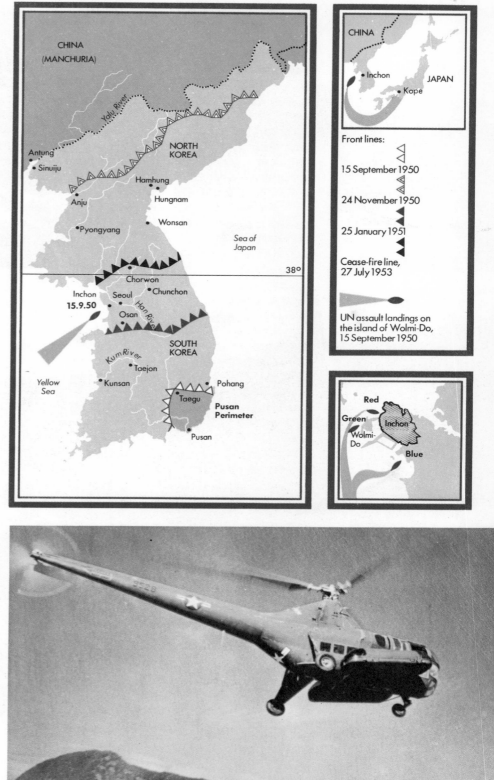

MiG-15. Length: 36 ft. 4 in.
Span: 33 ft. 1¼ in.
Max. speed: 665 m.p.h.
Armament: 2 × .23 mm.

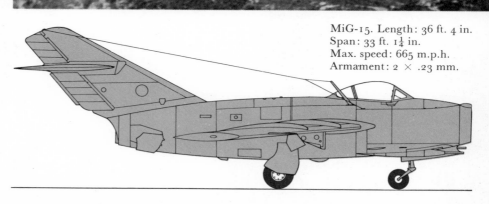

459

if the Korean conflict spread. But when the fear of a wider war subsided later in the week when it became apparent that the Korean onslaught would not have European repercussions, Truman felt more confident about committing the United States further. A naval blockade of all Korean coasts was ordered at Admiral Sherman's suggestion on 30 June as the first two companies of the 24th Infantry Division arrived in Pusan by air. Thus within a week the invasion by the Communists of an area already clearly defined by the US government as outside its sphere of interest brought the Americans inexorably into their first experiment in limited war in the post-World War II era.

Truman was careful to warn the American public that 'we are not at war'. This was called a 'police action' whose purpose it was to resist

aggression. This is why, contrary to MacArthur's advice, Truman rejected Chiang's not entirely selfless offer to send Chinese combat troops to Korea, for this would undoubtedly have provoked Communist China into entering the conflict in Korea as well as probably encouraging her to advance an attack against Formosa to complete her conquest of China. However, when Chiang's offer was rejected, this meant that American forces would have to be increased measurably in Korea. At this point Truman decided to commit all four Eighth Army divisions in Japan to Korea under the command of General Walton H. Walker. Australian troops were added to MacArthur's command, which on 8 July became CINCUNC (C-in-C United Nations Command) in addition to his title of CINCFE (C-in-C Far East), a purely American designation. MacArthur, however, considered himself to be responsible only to the President, the US Commander in Chief of all armed forces, and that Truman would deal with the UN aspects; a fine point perhaps, but one which was to be crucial in 1951.

Call for reinforcements
On the day he received his new title MacArthur asked for more men. As the Eighth Army was understrength anyway, he needed replacements merely to flesh out the force occupying Japan. But MacArthur asked for five more divisions and three tank battalions to enable him to strike 'by amphibious maneuver' behind North Korean lines. The plans for the Inchon invasion were already being prepared. This request was initially denied by the Joint Chiefs of Staff on the grounds that defense of Germany and Western Europe was paramount and that these areas ought not to be denuded for the sake of saving South Korea. MacArthur was understandably furious. All this seemed like a repetition of Roosevelt's policy of Europe-first during the 1942–44 period when MacArthur time and again asked for men and material and was refused. But at least then there was a war on in Europe. MacArthur made the best of things by adding ROK troops to American units and persuading Premier Yoshida of Japan to form a 100,000 man 'national police reserve' which could take over the burden of maintaining civil authority in Japan, thereby releasing more Americans for duty in Korea.

On the battle front, however, things were moving from bad to worse. By the beginning of July, little over a week after hostilities began, over half the ROK army had been destroyed. Korean troops were moving southward as fast as they could in a disorganized retreat. Walker's understrength Eighth Army began to filter into Pusan harbor with their recoilless rifles, their 92 medium tanks taken out of 'mothballs', and mortar and bazooka (rocket launcher) platoons, and move up to the front. Just as rapidly they were forced to retreat with the ROK's, as B-29 Superfortresses of World War II vintage began to strike against North Korean airfields and their Ilyushin light bombers. In the raids of 2–4 July over thirty North Korean aircraft were destroyed on the ground. By the end of July the air attacks were so successful that the North Korean Air Force ceased to exist as an effective unit.

Opposite left: American soldiers cover their withdrawal back to the Pusan Perimeter, July 1950. **Opposite right:** Wounded GIs during the pullback in July 1950. In some areas casualties reached the 50% mark.

Opposite: Korean refugees stream southward into the Pusan Perimeter.

The Impending Collapse

But on the ground the North Korean T-34's and the infantry swept all before them. While the 24th Division tried to hold the line of retreat along the Seoul-Taejon axis, North Korean forces advanced down the entire peninsula on a broad front. Walker, who was appointed head of military operations in Korea on 13 July, faced a desperate situation. One of Patton's corps commanders in 1944–45, Walker could only hope that the path southward could be blocked near Taejon by the 25th Infantry Division, under Major-General William B. Kean, and the 1st Cavalry Division, under Major-General Hobart R. Gay. Taejon was crucial because it commanded the road south to Pusan, which was the only conceivable evacuation point for UN forces if worst came to worst. The threat of another Dunkirk lay before

Walker if Taejon fell, with its roads radiating south and west behind the Kum River. While the Americans on the front suffered heavy casualties and fought bravely during the retreat, many asked the question, 'What is this police action?' It looked realistic enough to be war from their point of view. As the assault on Taejon began, and the Kum was crossed, the Americans dug in for the defense of the city. But 4000 men were insufficient to hold it as the T-34's entered the city on 19 July. The new 3.5 inch bazookas, just flown in from Japan, knocked out eight North Korean tanks, but Taejon was doomed. Major-General William F. Dean led the retreat from Taejon after the Communists lost fifteen tanks, but like many of his men, Dean escaped from the encirclement behind the city then put into effect by the North Koreans. After wandering around in

the hills for about a month, Dean was finally captured. He was awarded the Medal of Honor, but remained in prison camp as a guest of the People's Republic of Korea for the balance of the war.

What accounts for the initial North Korean success? First of all, the unpreparedness of their opponents and the element of surprise in the attack. Their tactics, however, cannot be underestimated. Frontal pressure would develop through infantry assault teams, supported by tanks in many instances. Then, when their opponents were pinned down, flanking forces would proceed to the rear and complete the envelopment. US tactics did not hinder the North Koreans unduly. The Americans tended to deploy near roads which ran above paddy fields which stank of human excrement used as fertilizer, which inhibited the Americans sufficiently to allow the North Koreans to complete their envelopment tactics against an enemy which was exposed and limited in their scope to some degree. The lack of experience of many of the men hindered the Americans as well.

Backs to the wall

Now the race was on for Pusan, which was being reinforced with new units. By the end of July Walker intended to hold what came to be called the Pusan Perimeter, a semi-circular enclave in the southeast corner of the peninsula. If Pusan fell the war was over, as it was the only escape route for the UN and Korea's only major deep water port. Air reconnaissance indicated that the North Koreans were moving toward Pusan at a rate of two miles an hour, night and day. By the beginning

Far left: Amphibious tractors begin the assault at Wonsan, October 1950. **Left:** The push northward after Inchon was not without casualties. South Korean women identify the bodies of political prisoners killed by the North Koreans during their retreat.

Below: Up the ladders at Wolmi-do in the first minutes of the Inchon invasion, 15 September 1950. The Marines took the peninsula in the first hour of the attack.

The 1st Marine Division prepares to land on Blue Beach, Inchon.

of August positions were taken around the perimeter. Time was needed if the forces now mobilizing in the States and being shipped from Hawaii, Tacoma, San Diego and Okinawa were to arrive before it was too late. Units from each of these points arrived by the end of August, and on 29 August nearly 2000 men from the British 27th Infantry Brigade arrived in Pusan from Hong Kong. Five armored battalions of about 69 tanks each arrived during August, and by the end of the month the UN had well over 500 tanks in the perimeter, among them M-26 Pershings and M-4 Shermans. This number gave the UN tank force superiority in the area of roughly five to one. Thus, with air superiority already established, the UN was now in a good position to hold their lines and, in time, counter-attack. During the period 18–25 August the area around Taegu was stabilized after some fierce tank battles, so that by the end of August the semi-circular defense line had held for the time being.

The lull in the fighting which had lasted for only a few days ended the night of 31 August–1 September when the North Koreans launched a new offensive, approaching within ten miles of Taegu. The British 27th Brigade, composed of units from the Middlesex Regiment and the Argyll and Sutherland Highlanders, held the line as the Americans retreated. General Walker sent in marine units which hurled back the enemy between 3–5 September, later described by Walker as the most critical point in the war. For if the front at Taegu caved in, there would have been little to stop a headlong thrust by the Communists into Pusan which would have been the end for the UN. Walker moved swiftly back and forth along the front at this time in an armored jeep, occasionally riding gun on the jeep, or flying over the area in a plane. When, on the 6th, it looked as if the lines before Taegu might crack, Walker ordered his headquarters moved to Pusan just in case the teleprinter which connected him directly with MacArthur's headquarters in the Dai-Ichi Building in Tokyo might be captured. At this stage some rich South Korean civilians were leaving Pusan for the Tsushima islands off the Korean coast. Only the knowledge that relief was coming in the form of a major amphibious assault at Inchon kept up flagging morale in Walker's camp. He told a fellow officer, 'I don't mind being shot at, but these bastards are not going to ambush me.'

After some debate with the Joint Chiefs, MacArthur's plan to invade behind enemy lines at the port of Inchon, near Seoul, was approved by the Pentagon on 29 August. Preparations were well under way by then, and MacArthur's confidence in the plan came from his knowledge of the unquestioned superiority the UN possessed on the seas and in the air. But the chances of failure were still high. The tides at Inchon were immense for the Far East. At high tide the depth of water at the coast ranged between 23 and 33 feet. At low tide the harbor was a vast mudflat stretching almost three miles out to sea. Thus, the landing craft would have to come in and depart quickly or be trapped in the sands and the mud of the harbor. Most landing craft drew 23 feet, and the LST's drew 29. Only around mid-September or mid-October would the tides be high enough to risk such a landing, and even then luck and speed were required, since there would be scarcely three hours for the whole operation of landing and safe departure. In addition, the area around Inchon was studded with reefs and shoals and small islands. Twelve foot high sea walls would have to be climbed by the marines who were to land first. The ladders needed to scale the walls would have to be carried ashore by the marines and placed against the walls after landing. In other words, this was a dangerous mission. Any slip-up would spell disaster, not only for the invasion force, but for the course of the entire war.

The Inchon invasion

Operation Chromite, as the Inchon landing was called, was set in motion even as a typhoon approached the Japan-Korea area, which could have completely thrown off the timing of the mission. An armada of some 260 ships set out from Japan on 5 September, carrying nearly 70,000 men and vessels from many countries, including New Zealand, Australia, the Netherlands, Britain, France, Canada, and the United States. Despite one of the worst storms ever experienced in the area on the 11th, the typhoon passed the main invasion force on the seas. MacArthur himself boarded the *Mount McKinley* at Sasebo on the 12th, while near Inchon a naval bombardment was already taking place. The island of Wolmi-do, connected to the mainland by a causeway, was the first objective, and after heavy shelling, was attacked in the early morning hours of 15 September. The marines arrived on the narrow

A bivouac of the 1st Marine Division in North Korea, late November 1950. Temperatures fell to minus 25°F. The Marines had to throw water cans into the fire to thaw them out.

beach, scaled the sea wall, and within twenty minutes of landing raised the American flag atop the hill dominating Wolmi-do. The whole area was secured within 90 minutes. MacArthur, watching from his flagship outside the harbor, sent a message to Vice-Admiral Struble aboard the *Rochester*: 'The Navy and Marines have never shone more brightly than this morning.' Wolmi-do had been taken without a single fatality. The first part of Operation Chromite was a success. The next tide came flowing in during the late afternoon, and two more landings on the mainland were effected as severe fighting was going on in the city of Inchon. By morning of the 16th the North Koreans were driven from Inchon. The victory was cheap in terms of lives lost. Only 196 casualties were suffered by the UN, and of these only about twenty killed. General MacArthur's courageous gamble had paid off. The American public awoke the next morning to learn that an astonishing victory had been snatched from the jaws of what had heretofore appeared to have been a desperate situation.

But the initial victory had to be followed by a swift advance toward Seoul itself, which was now turned into a fortress. MacArthur predicted that the capital would fall in five days. This time his judgement proved incorrect, for it took almost a fortnight. The North Koreans defended Seoul fiercely, and by the time they evacuated Seoul on 28 September 130,000 prisoners had been taken. The next day MacArthur went to Kimpo airfield and at midday, at a ceremony held in the hall of the South Korean National Assembly, MacArthur dramatically restored Seoul as the seat of government. A grateful President Rhee, tears flowing down his cheeks, replied to MacArthur: 'We admire you. We love you as the savior of our race.' MacArthur flew back to Tokyo that afternoon, having achieved the most remarkable triumph in a long and remarkable military career.

Across the 38th

The question now was whether and to what extent to pursue the enemy. Truman came to the conclusion that the UN could not afford to allow the North Koreans privileged sanctuary north of the 38th Parallel. On 27 September the Joint Chiefs authorized MacArthur to cross the 38th Parallel, a decision which altered the course of the war. This was no longer to be, as the UN ordered,

a war to defend South Korea against aggression. It was now a war the ultimate aim of which was to unify Korea under the government of Syngman Rhee. But although the military objective was clearly stated – the destruction of the North Korean armed forces – no UN troops were to be used in the frontier area abutting on the territory of Communist China and the Soviet Union. Under no circumstances, the Pentagon stated, were troops to cross that frontier, and the air space of China and Russia was not to be violated. MacArthur further asked the Pentagon to approve a plan to send the Eighth Army north to seize Pyongyang, the capital of North Korea, while the 10th Corps would effect an amphibious landing at Wonsan, and join the Eighth Army. This plan was approved on 1 October, the same day that

Below: General of the Army Douglas MacArthur in Korea. Behind him (left) is Matthew B. Ridgway, who succeeded him less than two months after this photograph was taken.

MacArthur asked the North Korean commander-in-chief to surrender. This was refused, despite the fact that his forces, now surrounded and being closed in upon two sides as the Eighth Army swiftly broke out of the Pusan Perimeter, were trying to regroup north of the 38th Parallel. Many of their men and much of their equipment was, of course, lost on the way, and thousands of prisoners were taken. The UN approved MacArthur's plan to strike north of the 38th on 6 October, and Chou En-lai warned from Peking that China would not stand aside if 'the imperialists' invaded North Korea. Thus the stage was set for the most controversial part of the war, at a point when MacArthur suspected that Chinese 'volunteers' had already joined the North Korean army, in order to bolster the defenses around Pyongyang. There can be no doubt that MacArthur received support for the drive north of the 38th; but how far he would go disturbed Truman, the Pentagon, and many of America's European allies.

President Truman wanted to make his position clear to MacArthur and to sort out whatever differences they had about strategy in this next phase of the conflict. Truman invited the General to meet him at Wake Island, well into the Pacific. it was almost as if one head of state were inviting another head of state to meet him at a neutral location. At least in geographic terms, Truman was meeting MacArthur more than halfway. MacArthur greeted Truman as he stepped off his plane at Wake on 15 October. Truman noted that MacArthur's cap 'had seen a good deal of use'; his open-necked shirt and ubiquitous corncob pipe were in evidence. Truman said, I've been a long time meeting you, General'. MacArthur replied, 'I hope it won't be so long next time'. This was the only time the two men would ever meet.

MacArthur assured the President that the war was virtually won. He stated that he doubted if the massive Chinese forces now assembling north of the Yalu River, the border between Korea and

China, would be used. In any event, he asserted his view that if Chinese or even Russian forces were used, they would not co-operate with each other if both nations intervened, and the UN forces would chew them up since they commanded the skies. Truman stated that he was concerned that the war might widen, and that he wanted to limit the scope and extent of the war; to end it quickly without either Chinese or Russian intervention was Truman's aim. Russia now had atomic capability. Although Truman pinned a medal on MacArthur's chest and they parted amiably, the Wake Island talks were a failure. Neither man accepted the other's point of view. Truman, for his part, was trying to warn the General that despite his regard for him as a military commander, he was the Commander-in-Chief and Chinese intervention was to be avoided at all costs. Five days after the conference the Eighth Army entered Pyongyang.

Push to the Yalu
More UN troops poured into Korea as the area south of the 38th Parallel was cleared and the Allies pressed toward the Yalu. Australian, Dutch, British, Thai, Turkish and Canadian soldiers joined the Americans and the ROK's triumphant drive. Two days after the Wake meeting, MacArthur authorized his forces to advance to within 30–40 miles of the Yalu, well above the line he had fixed in his original victory plan. On 24 October he lifted all restrictions on the movements of UN troops in Korea. This was an action in direct contradiction of orders, but the Pentagon did nothing. The amphibious landing at Wonsan went well, and another landing 150 miles to the north went unopposed. Airborne troops landed well behind enemy lines, cutting off the North Koreans' chaotic retreat. MacArthur landed in Pyongyang and declared that the war was all but over. But he and General Walker were increasingly concerned about the huge Chinese build-up in Manchuria across the Yalu. On 5 November the Joint Chiefs learned that MacArthur had ordered

Far left: Sherman tanks of the Canadian Army cross the Han River. **Center left:** A P-51 Mustang of the Fifth Air Force releases napalm fire bombs over an industrial target in North Korea. **Above:** Marines pause during the withdrawal from North Korea in February 1951. **Below left:** US Marines move forward after knocking out an enemy bunker, March 1951.

Left: Pfc John J. Allen, 25th Infantry Division, leads an attack in March 1951.

Right: A squad of the 2nd Infantry Division on patrol on New Year's Day, 1952.
Below center: The 64th Tank Battalion cross the Imjin River during the drive back to the 38th Parallel in April 1951.

the bombing of bridges across the Yalu, and the Pentagon directed him not to bomb within five miles of the frontier. MacArthur then asked if his planes could pursue the North Korean air force into Chinese air space, and this request was denied. But the Pentagon again gave in to MacArthur's *fait accompli* and merely asked him not to bomb any power plants which supplied electricity to Siberia or Manchuria. The war was inexorably escalating; and then disturbing reports trickled in of South Korean forces being ambushed by Communist Chinese troops who seemed to appear from nowhere. By the first week in November two Chinese divisions were identified as being in Korea. Communist China had entered the Korean War.

American forward units, some of which were virtually at the Yalu, had advanced far too rapidly. Their supply lines were extended. The Chinese formations began to encircle these units. Most of them were able to fight their way out of the traps, but the situation was serious. MacArthur had miscalculated. These Chinese units were tough. Their commanders were excellent, and they were battle-hardened from the long war against Japan and the Nationalist Chinese. MacArthur, who had claimed less than a month before that the North Koreans were defeated, now was forced to ask for additional arms from the States. Instead of ordering a general retreat to a viable defense line, he ordered further advances, for he figured that when the Yalu froze over in mid-winter Chinese troops could cross into Korea more easily. After inspecting the border by air, MacArthur con-

Wounded soldiers are brought to a forward aid station prior to evacuation in September 1952.

Colonel James C. Murray, USMC, and Colonel Chang Chun San of the North Korean People's Army initial maps which demarcate the boundaries between North and South Korea during the ceasefire talks, July 1953.

firmed his decision to advance. The Eighth Army slowly pushed forward, against Walker's judgement, on 25 November. The next day the Chinese commander, Lin Piao, ordered a new offensive with 200,000 men. The Eighth Army and the marines near the Chongjin reservoir were now forced to fight their way back to the coast to effect a withdrawal, which MacArthur finally approved. By the end of November the UN was in full retreat, and Pyongyang was evacuated on 5 December. MacArthur hoped to hold the line at the 38th Parallel. At this point Truman decided to hold the line at the 38th, but to withhold further massive troop movements from the US to Korea to prevent MacArthur from launching yet another offensive. MacArthur vehemently argued that unless reinforcements were sent, the UN would lose the war. The Pentagon was almost prepared there and then to relieve MacArthur of his command, and Truman later stated that he should have done so at least by December, since MacArthur had already disobeyed orders on more than one occasion. When Prime Minister Attlee visited Truman in December, he assured the British Prime Minister that the United States would not risk all-out war with China and her ally, Russia, and that a ceasefire along roughly the 38th Parallel would be the optimum alternative.

What made matters worse was the fact that the UN was unable to hold the line even at the 38th. They had to regroup at a defense line south, at a point when the Pentagon decided that no blockade of the Chinese coast should be effected, that no Nationalist Chinese troops should be used in Korea (underlining an earlier decision), and that no aerial attacks should be made on Chinese soil, including the industrial plants and military installations in Manchuria. Adding to this the decision that no major reinforcement of the UN should take place, MacArthur viewed the policy as one of accepting total defeat. There was an impasse between MacArthur and his superiors.

The death of General Walker on 23 December when his jeep crashed on an icy road brought further bad news for MacArthur. His replacement was Matthew B. Ridgway, a man loyal to the Pentagon, unlike MacArthur, and one who would report on MacArthur's actions to Washington if orders were disobeyed. MacArthur, however, had full confidence in Ridgway as a field commander, and gave him an open brief to do what he thought best. Ridgway authorized another evacuation of Seoul and the establishment of a defense line at the Han River. Ridgway instilled new enthusiasm into the UN forces. Obliged to withdraw a hundred miles south of the Han in January, the Eighth Army fought its way back to it, and by 9 February had advanced to within thirty miles of the 38th Parallel. Seoul was retaken on 14 March. MacArthur's dire predictions of total defeat were clearly unfounded.

MacArthur sacked

Truman and the Pentagon were now agreed for a variety of reasons that MacArthur should be replaced. It was a question of timing. His remarks leaked to the press criticizing Truman's conduct of the war in a 'no-win' policy received wide publicity, and he had already disobeyed orders on more than one occasion. MacArthur's letter to Joe Martin, Republican House Minority Leader, in which he concluded: 'There is no substitute for victory'. When he called for a lifting of restrictions on bombing Chinese military and industrial targets, this statement read on the floor of the House of Representatives received the widest publicity. His public communiqué of 24 March denegrated China's industrial strength and suggested that if the China coast and interior bases were bombarded, China would soon be defeated. This last example of insubordination sent Truman into a rage. He had already warned MacArthur on 6 December that he should not issue statements without clearing them with the Pentagon. Truman felt he had no choice but to replace him. The London *Daily Telegraph* published an interview with MacArthur where he restated his views: 'The true object of a commander in war was to destroy the forces opposed to him. But this was not the case in Korea. The situation would be ludicrous if men's lives were not involved.' From 6–9 April Truman held meetings with members of his Cabinet and the Joint Chiefs. The decision was made and on 11 April Truman relieved MacArthur of his command, replacing him with Matthew Ridgway, who had helped cut the ground from under MacArthur's feet through his reports direct to Washington. After 52 years of distinguished military service, Douglas MacArthur's career was at an end.

The public reaction within the States and around the world was shocked and uncomprehending. Rage at the sacking of America's great military hero resounded throughout the country and even impeachment of President Truman was suggested. MacArthur arrived in San Francisco to a tumultuous greeting, and MacArthur for President was heard throughout the country. He was given the opportunity to address Congress in a televised broadcast on 19 April, where MacArthur delivered his most famous address in which he presented his plan for winning the war in Korea:

1. Intensification of the economic blockade of China.
2. Impose a naval blockade on China's coasts.
3. Remove impositions on aerial reconnaissance of China's coasts and Manchuria.
4. Allow Nationalist China to help in the fight against Communist China.

He repeated his argument that 'in war . . . there can be no substitute for victory.' Interrupted many times during his 34-minute address, MacArthur concluded:

'I am closing my fifty-two years of military service. When I joined the army even before the turn of the century, it was the fulfillment of all my boyish hopes and dreams. The world has turned over many times since I took the oath on the Plain at West Point, and the hopes and dreams have long since vanished. But I still remember the refrain of one of the most popular barrack ballads of that day which proclaimed most proudly that "Old soldiers never die, they just fade away". I now close my military career and just fade away – an old soldier who tried to do his duty as God gave him the light to see that duty. Goodbye.'

There was not a dry eye in the Congress or the country when MacArthur concluded his speech. His popularity was at its height, but as he toured the country it rather rapidly diminished with his presidential hopes, as the country began to realize that he had defied his commander-in-chief, had disobeyed written orders, and that insubordination could not be tolerated of any general by any president.

Back in Korea the war began to wind down in its intensity, although to any man in the field it did not seem that way. Two Communist spring offensives, the first in late April and the second in late May 1951, pushed the UN back, but Seoul held, and by July all ground lost in the spring had been recovered. Indeed, the UN pushed across the 38th Parallel in all areas except that surrounding Kaesong in the extreme northeast corner of South Korea. It was in July that the first peace talks were held at Kaesong between North Korean and Chinese generals and representatives of the UN forces. As sporadic and often quite intense fighting continued on the front line, the talks moved to Panmunjom and continued there for the next two years. A war of attrition along a fixed front ensued during this period, as the American public became increasingly frustrated at the failure to end the Korean conflict, which ceased to capture the imagination of the American people after MacArthur was recalled and chances of outright victory were gone. MacArthur was not even invited to the peace conference later in 1951 in which the official American occupation of Japan ended and the war with Japan officially came to an end. When the final armistice took place on 27 July 1953, roughly along the lines reached two years before, a sense of relief and frustration were the inevitable results. South Korea's independence had been secured, and to that extent the war had been worth fighting. But the legacy of the MacArthur-Truman controversy was to hang over the United States long after both men had left the political and military stage. The Korean War was the UN's first war and America's first experiment in limited war. Although fighting has taken place along the truce line since 1953, no major conflict has as yet broken out over Korea. The Korean conflict, then, showed Russia and China that the US would defend what it construed to be its interests in Asia. This bolstered the credibility of NATO and the other bilateral treaties the US was making in 1951 with the ANZUS Pact, the Philippine and Japanese defense treaties negotiated during and after the Korean War, not to mention the SEATO Pact of 1954.

The Problem of Limited War

But the lingering question which MacArthur raised was to plague American policy in Asia in the future. All wars are to some extent or another limited. MacArthur was right in arguing that the UN need not have worried about an all-out war with China, since, for China's part, she was already fighting one. As long as the UN troops did not invade China itself, and this was not MacArthur's intention, the UN need not have worried about a Russian intervention, despite the fact that Russian planes and pilots were already in action in Korea. Neither of the two superpowers wanted a world war in the 1950's, and this explains why there was none despite numerous provocations on both sides. Lin Piao, the Chinese Communist commander claimed that he would never have made the attack in Korea if he were not assured that Truman would restrain MacArthur's freedom of action in the Korean War. Thus, by limiting the war unnecessarily, partly to allay the fears of America's allies in Europe, notably Britain, Korea was not unified by the UN. One cannot sustain a war and conscription of civilians in a democracy for very long without a clear-cut goal which is consonant with the ideals and general aims of that democratic society. Americans were willing to fight for the independence of Korea if there was some chance that the war could be won. Once it became clear that this would not happen, the American people lost interest in the war, and a sense of frustration not unlike that expressed by MacArthur was experienced. But the feeling that America was fighting a war with one hand tied behind her back, which the Korean War engendered, would be felt all the more dramatically by the American public during the 1960's when the United States became ever more deeply involved in the Vietnam controversy.

CHAPTER TWO
The Vietnam War

Of all the types of war fought by men over the centuries, two are worst: guerrilla war and civil war. The war that had been going on continuously in Vietnam and Indo-China since World War II had the worst aspects of both. A civil war between hill tribesmen and lowland agriculturalists, country versus town, Christian against animist against Buddhist, Communist versus bourgeois opportunist, the hope for freedom against the promise of dictatorship – the war in Vietnam is all of these. Sinicized for over two thousand years, Vietnam has felt the heel of the Chinese and European invader and has adjusted its way of life to both. Conquered by Imperial France

under Napoleon III, a conquest which was completed by the Third Republic, Indo-China kept largely to its indigenous, langorous and individual life style during the French occupation. Some industry was built up in the north along the Red River; rubber plantations were created by the French, and in Saigon, the Paris of the Far East, great tree-lined boulevards and smart clubs and restaurants reminded settlers and planters on a spree that a French presence endured in Vietnam. But this atmosphere, pleasant and decadent, was superficial. Behind the sophisticated French mask lay the faces of millions of peasants and hill tribesmen virtually untouched by European civilization. When Japan conquered Indo-China after France itself fell to the Wehrmacht, the French presence remained, while Japanese soldiers called the tune. But when the conquest of Japan appeared imminent in 1945, jockeying for power for the Vietnamese themselves ensued. Ho Chi Minh, a longtime Communist, an ascetic and enigmatic figure, had organized a guerrilla organization during the war for this purpose. His dream was a unified, independent Indo-China under Vietnamese Communist domination. He hoped for American support for his cause. It was not forthcoming, as the French supported his rival, the aristocratic and indolent Bao Dai, who tried to set up an alternative government before the Japanese troops were evacuated.

The situation became confused after the Japanese capitulation. Vietnam had two rival governments, and the British and Nationalist Chinese forces moved into coastal Vietnam to take the Japanese surrender. Within a few months they slowly withdrew in favor of the French, who hoped to reconquer their colony while paying rather transparent lip service to Vietnamese ideals of nationalism and independence (*doc-lap*). The Viet Minh, the army of Communist Vietnam, was led by a brilliant strategist, Vo Nguyen Giap, who correctly assessed the dilemma facing France:

Below: Guerrilla fighters march forward during the early stages of the Vietnam War. **Right:** Bao Dai in his regalia as Emperor of Annam in 1938. He became the French champion of Vietnamese independence at the end of the Second World War.

'The enemy will pass slowly from the offensive to the defensive. The blitzkrieg will transform itself into a war of long duration. Thus, the enemy will be caught in a dilemma: he has to drag out the war in order to win it and does not possess, on the other hand, the psychological and political means to fight a long, drawn-out war . . .'

Giap's assessment of how the war in Vietnam would be fought was right on the mark. The French grossly underestimated the strength of will of the Communists to fight for Vietnamese independence, and they discounted the degree to which nationalist sentiments would attach themselves to the Viet Minh when a credible, non-Communist nationalist alternative failed to appear. Bao Dai was not a credible nationalist figure. A former Emperor of Annam under French protection before the war, amiable enough and a charming ladies' man, Bao Dai had the taint of European influence on him which he was unable to shake off. He was fond of French ambiance and the Côte d'Azur in particular. The French played Bao Dai off against Ho Chi Minh, who initially was prepared to do a deal with the French to gain some degree of legitimacy, but Ho tired of this game when the French began to re-assert their authority over Indo-China in 1946. By the end of that year Giap's forces numbered some 50,000 armed largely with equipment begged, borrowed or stolen from the Chinese, French, British and Americans. The French military authorities considered this motley army with irregular equipment to be no match for the trained, well-equipped legions of the French Empire, many of whom had considerable combat experience in World War II. They were too strong not to be used; but not strong enough to prevent the Viet Minh from trying to solve the problem by force. Perhaps compromise was impossible. All that was needed was a spark to set Vietnam alight for decades.

The Haiphong Incident

The Haiphong Incident, 20 November 1946, provided that spark. A French naval boat, having stopped a Chinese junk loaded with contraband, brought it to the port of Haiphong. Local Vietnamese forces opened fire as both ships anchored. The sound of gunfire caused the Viet Minh in the port to cross barricades erected by the French, thereby cutting off French units from each other. About 23 French soldiers were killed. On 22 November a French burial detail was ambushed by the Viet Minh, and six more French soldiers were killed. The French commander in the area, General Valluy, decided that Viet Minh ought to be taught a lesson, and French troops issued an ultimatum to the Viet Minh to evacuate the Chinese quarter of Haiphong which they occupied. The French moved in, and fighting broke out, as thousands of Vietnamese civilians streamed out of Haiphong for the countryside. The French cruiser, the *Suffren*, anchored offshore, noticed the fighting, and opened fire on the city. Over 6000 Vietnamese were killed by the gunfire, the street fighting, or were trampled to death in the panic. On 19 December, despite conciliatory moves by both sides to avoid a general war, a rumor was spread among French circles that uprising was about to take place in Hanoi. At 2000 hours the electric power plant was blown up, and waves of Viet Minh militia killed or abducted nearly 600 French civilians in the northern capital. Within hours every French garrison in the country was under attack. The Vietnam War had begun.

The Viet Minh, which launched this all-out war, were greatly provoked by French arrogance, but they hoped for a quick victory. All major cities in the country were under Communist fire. The coup was meticulously planned and executed. The French turned to Bao Dai as a nationalist alternative to Ho Chi Minh, and the Americans supported him as a Western puppet. But Bao Dai was unwilling to play this role, as he wanted an independent if European-oriented Vietnam as much as Ho wanted a Communist and neutralist, independent Vietnam. The French wanted to re-establish their colony, an aim which the Americans opposed. In the confusion, Ho and the French turned to armed conflict as the only way to solve this dilemma. The French cleared the cities of the Viet Minh, but it took months before Hué, the old imperial capital of Vietnam, was cleared of the Communists. Ho's popularity in the country increased as the French came to realize that a purely military solution to their problem was impossible. Too late they decided to create a quasi-independent Vietnam under French influence, and Bao Dai played along with them when France officially recognized the independence of Vietnam in 1948. But the French definition meant merely autonomy, as France still retained some measure of control and, of course, continued to fight the Viet Minh. But the military initiative had passed into the hands of Ho Chi Minh just as the political initiative already had done. Ho seemed to be the true representative of Vietnamese independence, as he was tied to no foreigner. It seemed as if the mistake made by the Americans in tying Chiang Kai-shek too closely to them in China after the war was being repeated by the French in Vietnam.

De Lattre arrives

As guerrilla warfare intensified, the French maintained their control over the cities and the chief railways and ports, while the Viet Minh began to tighten their net in the northern countryside. French morale was flagging, and to support it, a new High Commissioner and Commander-in-Chief of Indo-China was appointed: General Jean de Lattre de Tassigny, who combined the political and military roles. Autocratic, an aristocrat to his buttonholes, he shored up French morale by preventing the withdrawal of French families from Indo-China and by taking a strong and spirited hand at a moment when spirit was lacking on the French side. Having gone into the struggle overconfidently, Giap had defeated the French badly in early 1950 so that the whole area of northern Tonkin from the coast to the Laotian border, as well as the territory adjacent to China, except for the enclaves of the major cities was under Communist control. The army was despondent, having been beaten in battle by an ill-trained and poorly equipped guerrilla force. The politicians in Paris blamed the soldiers. The soldiers blamed the politicians. De Lattre was sent to end this bickering. Above all he was a born leader of men, a man not to be questioned easily. His arrival in Saigon on 17 December 1950 restored confidence almost at once.

Giap, flushed with recent success and reinforced with arms from Communist China, decided to strike in the Red River Delta, the heartland of what territory remained to France in northern Tonkin. If the link between Hanoi and Haiphong could be severed, the war in the north was won. The French built up their forces in the north and repelled this attack in early 1951. The French victory was due entirely to de Lattre, whose authority was unquestioned and whose resolve was iron. De Lattre asked the hill tribes to wage counter-insurgency against the Viet Minh. His use of napalm against the enemy surprised them and threw them back throughout the north. De Lattre was convinced he was leading a crusade against Communism, in line with NATO policy and the war in Korea. He was also keen to protect the huge French investments still extant in Indo-China. They owned all the rubber plantations, all the mines, the shipping, two-thirds of the rice and most of the banks. French finance backed the war, even if the French public was tiring of it. Victories were needed, and victories were provided by de Lattre.

Giap, defeated in the Delta, turned to consolidating the Viet Minh hold over the northwest, especially the area close to the Laotian border. By 1952 the Viet Minh were once again on the road to victory. De Lattre, deathly ill, had to return to France in December 1951, and he died of cancer in Paris in January 1952. If anyone could have won for France it was he. Now he was gone and the Viet Minh moved to the offensive once more. US aid began to pour into Vietnam, which the French both needed and resented, while a native Vietnamese force was being created to fight the Viet Minh as French financial resources and public patience wore thin. Henri Navarre was appointed C-in-C in Indo-China to replace de Lattre, and he issued a report which indicated that French forces were over-extended and tied down in hopelessly defensive positions. The local Vietnamese forces were being trained to take over

French officers captured by the Viet Minh at the battle of Nghialo, October 1952.

these defensive positions, while America urged France to take action or make a truce, as US aid since 1950 amounted to about $500 million annually. The US reluctantly agreed to supply more material so that the French forces could take the offensive while the Vietnamese took over the static positions. One string attached to American aid was the promise of real independence to Laos, Cambodia and Vietnam, which the French set into motion. In order to block a Viet Minh incursion into Laos, and to defeat them in their strongest area, Navarre decided to seize and hold a forward base near the Laotian frontier, Dien Bien Phu, as a sign of strength which was necessary to maintain morale among his troops and to show Paris and Washington that the French were capable of winning.

Dien Bien Phu

The gamble to hold Dien Bien Phu was the undoing of France in Vietnam. Of little strategic significance in itself, Dien Bien Phu controlled routes into China and Laos and had two airfields in the area surrounding it so supplies could be airlifted to the fortress. The French controlled the hills around the plain. Giap felt that if he could win a victory there, the heart would go out of the French determination to stay in Southeast Asia. In the second week of March 1954, Giap began his attack on Dien Bien Phu. First, he planned to overrun the three outlying French defensive areas, and then begin an all-out assault on the positions surrounding the airstrip and the village. The first phase began on 13 March, and the three outlying posts were soon lost, at a great cost in lives to the Communists. But the French did not count on the ability of the Viet Minh to transport heavy artillery and anti-aircraft guns across the mountainous terrain of northwest Tonkin. The Viet Minh were able to concentrate their fire, and many French planes bringing in supplies were brought down. Giap surrounded the French redoubt, and while the French were hungry for more ammunition, the Viet Minh brought up more of their own. The Communist guns died down on the 26th, lulling the French into a false sense of security. On the afternoon of 30 March, the massive Communist assault began. The major assault had taken further territory at a great cost in lives to the Vietnamese, and French defenses around Dien Bien Phu held. By mid-April 50,000 Viet Minh were in place around the village, and more artillery was brought in through the mountains. The 16,000 French troops, including units from the élite Foreign Legion, were hopelessly trapped. The French begged the Americans for more aid, which was not forthcoming. Giap began his final assault on Dien Bien Phu on 1 May at all points along the perimeter, and regardless of casualties, the Communists advanced. Navarre realized that he had miscalculated, but all too late. On 7 May at about noon the Viet Minh 308th Division broke through into the heart of French defenses. Soon after the French raised their white flags. The news of the fall of Dien Bien Phu reached Geneva where the international conference to discuss the future of Indo-China and Korea had just begun. The Vietnamese National Army, on which so much hope had been

placed, was starting to break down. The French day in Indo-China, after almost a hundred years of interrupted occupation, was done.

At Geneva the French had to accept the inevitable, and began to make plans for their withdrawal from Indo-China. The ball was placed firmly in the Americans' court. Would they replace the French and continue the struggle, or allow the whole of Indo-China to fall into Communist hands? Their decision was to permit a partition of Vietnam, giving the territory above the 17th Parallel to the government of Ho Chi Minh, while South Vietnam would be reconstructed along with an independent Laos and Cambodia, the three successor states being protected by the newly-formed SEATO Pact. Ngo Dinh Diem was chosen as the leader of South Vietnam, a Catholic mandarin of aristocratic and authoritarian bearing. Bao Dai was summarily dropped, and elections were promised to unite the whole of

Far left: Viet Minh forces brought most of their equipment up to the siege of Dien Bien Phu by bicycle.
Below left: The assault on Dien Bien Phu, 1954.

Below: Ho Chi Minh, whose long stated object was the conquest of the whole of French Indo-China.

Vietnam under one government by 1956. As the Americans began to pour aid into their new protégé's capital, Saigon, they realized what the French already knew. If elections were held Ho Chi Minh, the acknowledged nationalist leader, would win hands down. The elections were never held. Instead, while Giap re-equipped his forces and began to send men into South Vietnam down the Ho Chi Minh Trail through the mountains and jungles of Laos, the South Vietnamese Army was built, retrained and re-equipped with American arms and advisers.

Escalation in the South

By 1958 infiltration of the South had reached a dangerous point. The hard core of guerrillas in the South numbered perhaps 5000, but these figures were soon to double. The threat to major cities in the South was growing. By 1959 about a third of the countryside in the South was controlled by the Viet Cong, the guerrilla organization equivalent to what had been the Viet Minh in the North. While Diem's forces outnumbered the Communists by seven or eight to one, the quality of government forces was poor. The Communists held the initiative, even more so because they were Southerners themselves, not North Vietnamese regulars sent in to help, although obviously there were even a few of these at this stage acting in an advisory capacity to the Viet Cong. By late 1960, after the American Presidential election which put John F. Kennedy in power, a major attempt to overthrow Diem was launched. On the morning of 11 November three paratroop battalions of the South Vietnamese forces seized key government centers in Saigon and prepared to attack Diem's palace. The Americans knew of the coup plan but did nothing to warn Diem. That evening Diem agreed to step down but secretly moved troops loyal to him around the capital, from which they retook the city's strong points. The failure of the coup and the flight of its leaders to Cambodia did nothing to dispel the feeling, widespread in Washington and Saigon, that Diem was simply not the man to champion Vietnamese nationalism or to prevent a Communist takeover of the South. When President Kennedy took office the US still had only a small number of advisers assisting the efforts of the Army of the Republic of Vietnam (ARVN). Kennedy urged Diem to undertake land reform while immediately beefing up the American presence in Saigon.

Kennedy began to lose his nerve about events in Indo-China almost as soon as he took office. The situation in Laos had deteriorated to the point where large parts of the country, chiefly the highlands along the Vietnamese border, had fallen to the Pathet Lao, the Communists in Laos, aided and abetted by North Vietnam. Kennedy went on television to prepare the American people for a possible US military intervention on the part of so-called democratic forces in Laos, but changed his mind soon after, when he accepted the fact that the logistics of supplying a non-government in a non-country with weapons and men hundreds of miles from a major port made a defense of Laos unrealistic. His recent failure in the Bay of Pigs fiasco in Cuba made it

imperative that yet another blunder of an interventionary nature would be disastrous for his presidency. It was at this point that the US decided to help create a 'neutralist' government in Laos, abandoning Eisenhower's policy of resisting the Communists obdurately. This meant that if the US was to take a stand in support of pro-Western elements in Indo-China, it would have to be in South Vietnam. And the US seemed to be stuck with Diem. Vice-President Lyndon B. Johnson's visit to Saigon convinced the South Vietnamese that some attempt at land reform was the only way to pacify the Americans. It was, in fact, the only realistic way to help the South Vietnamese help themselves to remain independent of Hanoi.

The Fall of Diem

But whatever land reform took place was done halfheartedly. The guerrillas continued to make progress, while organized opposition to Diem faded for a time. The US increased its aid and its advisers, who numbered some 16,000 by 1963, while Buddhist and other opposition to Diem began to be felt. The South Vietnamese had the

choice between the rigors of Communist terrorism and the decadent hand of French-educated elitism represented by Diem which was only less stultifying because of its inefficiency. The most far reaching land 'reform', if that is the operative word, was the concept of strategic hamlets. This plan, inspired by the Americans after a model used by the British to defeat Communism in Malaya, forced the evacuation of certain parts of the countryside into fortified villages which were defensible. In a Vietnamese context the village, the land around it and the people living in the village and from the land were inextricably entwined. Although the plan had some military merit, it displaced too many people, creating disorientation among the peasants and a decided disinclination to support those who moved them out of their traditional homes. Only middle-class elements actively supported the strategic hamlet idea, since their position was shored up by it. But the vast majority of people in Vietnam were cultivators; peasants. Although a good idea from a short-term military standpoint, this scheme did more to undermine Diem's and therefore the Americans' position than any other. By 1963

opposition to Diem and his poisonous brother, Ngo Dinh Nhu, a megalomaniac and drug addict to whom Diem had given considerable power, was massive, even in pro-Western circles in Saigon. On 1 November Diem and Nhu were overthrown with American concurrence, and both were killed by their captors. Now Kennedy was faced with an even more difficult problem. Which South Vietnamese leader had the charisma to save the demoralizing situation in Saigon? For all his faults, Diem was respected by many peasants, and had the wholehearted support of the Christian community, some 15% of the population. Those who were to step in his place – Duong Van Minh, Air Vice-Marshal Nguyen Cao Ky, and General Nguyen Van Thieu – were military men. Diem, at least, was a traditional mandarin and was held in some esteem if only for that reason. He was an integrative factor in a disintegrating society. He would not be replaced easily.

Perhaps Madame Nhu, who survived the coup, and whose excesses helped cause it, found some measure of satisfaction when President Kennedy was killed just three weeks after her husband was assassinated. The new President, Lyndon Johnson,

Top: An F-104 drops a 750-pound bomb on a target in the Mekong Delta, August 1965. **Opposite:** Skytroopers of the 1st Cavalry Division are affected by the sound of their own mortar fire during a search and destroy mission. **Far left:** A petroleum depot near Hanoi is hit in June 1966. The USAF was permitted to bomb all around the Vietnamese capital but not the city center.

Above left: General William Westmoreland. **Above:** A 'Black Scarf' of the 1st Battalion, 2nd Infantry, fully equipped with rifle, smoke, axe and machete. **Left:** A marine tank arrives at Da Nang in 1965 when the Americans began to reinforce a deteriorating military situation in South Vietnam.

a rough Texan imbued with the Hispanic obsession with *machismo*, had long felt that Kennedy should not 'play around' with the Communists in Vietnam. An arch-hawk, Johnson could not accept the fact that the United States were unable to handle the North Vietnamese. Immediately on taking office, Johnson began to take steps to escalate the war dramatically. The military situation in Vietnam was deteriorating badly, but America, stunned by the death of Kennedy, was unready for full commitment to a war in Vietnam in an election year. Barry Goldwater, Johnson's Republican opponent in the 1964 election openly declared that the US should intervene fully. Johnson covered his real intentions until the election was over, where he won a landslide victory. General Nguyen Khanh ruled Vietnam for a time, backed by General William Westmoreland, ramrod straight, a West Pointer, a Southerner with a square jaw jutting defiantly forward. They would have to hold the line until after the elections. Meanwhile Johnson started to convince his Cabinet and advisers, mostly old Kennedy hands, that the US should fully enter the Vietnam War.

The Tonkin Gulf Incident

His opportunity came during the election campaign when the USS *Maddox*, actually some thirteen miles from a North Vietnamese island in the Tonkin Gulf, was attacked by North Vietnamese PT boats, returned the fire and hit one of them. Johnson claimed the ships were thirty miles offshore, and therefore had a right to be there. Johnson ordered that the *Maddox* and its companion ship, the USS *C. Turner Joy*, return to the area four days later on 3 August 1964. The ships were challenged again. What actually happened in the Tonkin Gulf is still not altogether clear, the obfuscation a deliberate gesture on the administration's part. Later Johnson suggested the incident may never have taken place. But the immediate result of the incident was LBJ's request of the Congress that they give him the power to wage aerial war on North Vietnam and a blank cheque to increase massively the numbers of American troops in Vietnam. This Tonkin Gulf Resolution was passed by Congress, which thereafter relinquished its power to curb the President's war-making capacity.

Under pressure from men like General Curtis LeMay, who believed that wide-scale bombing won the war for the Allies in World War II, Johnson began massive bombing of military targets in both South and North Vietnam, and later stepped up this campaign in Operation Rolling Thunder which was supposed to bomb North Vietnam into the Stone Age. Hanoi and Haiphong were carefully excluded from this saturation bombing effort. These were, perhaps, the only two targets worth destroying.

Saturation bombing had even less effect on Vietnam than it had on Germany, a far more highly industrialized and urbanized country and therefore more susceptible to strategic bombing attacks. By the end of President Johnson's Administration more bombs were dropped on Vietnam than the US dropped in World War II, and under Nixon's first four years two and a half

million tons more. The US dropped about two million tons of bombs in the years 1941–45. But all of this came to nought. The war in Vietnam could not be won in the air, despite the fact that for most part North Vietnam had no air cover and until the end little in the way of effective anti-aircraft artillery. Communist infiltration was a matter of subversion of confidence in the South, so that peasants would acquiesce in the takeover of their villages. The only way to track down these infiltrators was by going out into the villages, the jungles, the trails and the hills of Vietnam and winkling them out one by one. Once the American elections were over Johnson began to step up the numbers of troops in Vietnam to do just that.

US intervention

The fear that the régime in the South would crumble in the autumn of 1965 caused Johnson to increase American involvement. LBJ felt that if he allowed Vietnam to go the way of China and Eastern Europe his entire domestic program would never pass Congress. 'They won't be talking about my civil rights bill, or education or beautification. No sir, they'll push Vietnam up my ass every time', Johnson elegantly put it. But it turned out that they (the Congress) and the country did that anyway, and hundreds and hundreds of thousands of Americans were sent to defend a country which wouldn't defend itself and fight for a cause which never seemed clear even to those who supported it.

But how many combat troops were needed, Johnson asked General Maxwell Taylor. In early 1965 75,000 was considered the right figure. By July it was 125,000. Johnson told the American people that some 50,000 might be required, but at the time he said it he had already upped his private estimate to 200,000. As Marine and regular army units poured into Vietnam in 1965, Johnson reluctantly accepted the fact that the US was taking over the war, not just merely helping out an ally. The analogy of appeasement and Munich and Hitler was again raised, despite the fact that even Ho Chi Minh in his wildest imagination thought only of taking over Indo-China, not Asia or the world. The question of Vietnam's value to the United States was not asked in Cabinet circles. Paramount in the minds of Johnson's advisers – McGeorge Bundy, Walt Rostow, Robert MacNamara and the rest – was the domino theory, once mooted by Eisenhower.

The domino theory held that if South Vietnam fell to the North, then so would Laos and Cambodia, then Thailand, Malaysia, Indonesia and so on, until, at the very least, the Communists would be in Australia or San Francisco. If Communism were a monolithic international conspiracy, this might have been the case. But Communism had never been monolithic, and with Russia and China competing for North Vietnam's favor, while Ho Chi Minh tried to play each off against the other to maintain his own independence from both, the domino theory seemed only to make sense in Indo-Chinese terms. If Ho won in the South, surely Laos and Cambodia would fall under North Vietnam's influence. Whether or not this mattered to American and Western interests was never seriously debated at

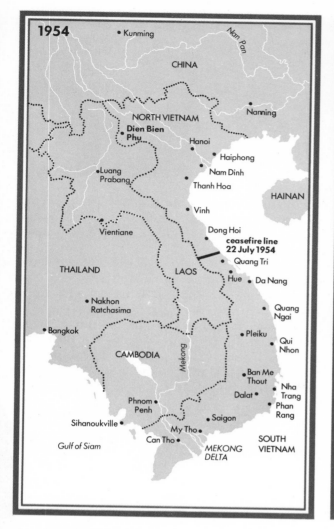

1954

TODAY

Areas of communist advances in Indo-China

Below: A flight of B-52s hit a target 25 miles from Bien Hoa, an important US air base in South Vietnam: 1 December 1966. Several times more bombs fell on Vietnam than were dropped by all forces in World War II.

the time. For Johnson it was a matter of pride to win in Vietnam where Kennedy had failed to win; to prove his own *macho* (or masculinity) was stronger than his predecessors, his critics, or his opponents in Hanoi. This was Johnson's, and America's tragedy.

In Too Deep

By 1967 the Communists were closer to victory than ever. American bases proliferated the coast of South Vietnam and the US presence there neared 500,000. At each stage of the escalation General Westmoreland kept talking about 'the light at the end of the tunnel' and repeated that his last request would be sufficient, only to later argue that only 100,000 more men would be enough. As Johnson repeated these platitudes and examples of wishful thinking to the American public, they began to seriously question the wisdom of going into Vietnam in the first place. But too late, far too late. America found herself in a similar position to France in the early 1950's, stepping up the war effort while the political position of her leadership crumbled under criticism of the war at home. North Vietnam began to send regular troops into the South to support the insurgency. As the ratio between guerrillas and their opposition narrowed, Johnson felt obliged to keep the ratio at from eight up to ten to one, the ratio required for victory. Russia and China supplied North Vietnam with arms, and many American weapons found their way into Communist hands through pilfering of US supplies or, more often than not, the South Vietnamese selling the weapons the US gave them to

the Communists through the black market.

Black market activities and the very presence of so many Americans in a poor, underdeveloped country torn by decades of war played a major role in subverting the entire societal structure and economy of South Vietnam. A prostitute could make more in a good day than a professor could make in a month. A hawker of stolen PX goods in a street stall could make more money than a worker or farmer. As Communist activity in the country stepped up, a mass flight to the cities occurred which broke up families and sapped the will of the Vietnamese people to care who won the war. Vietnamese currency became so inflated by the introduction of comparatively rich Americans with their PX's, NCO clubs and R and R (Rest and Recreation) centers that the most profitable business in the South was catering to their needs. Bars on Tu Do Street in Saigon thrived, teeming with GI's, prostitutes and pushers of marijuana and other, more lethal drugs. In 1968 alone an estimated $250 million went into the black market. Meanwhile, the US balance of payments deficit soared as the US had the only economy in the Western world that was on anything like a wartime basis. US inflation was exported to Europe and Japan as the vicious spiral escalated with every increase of the war effort. As government platitudes to the public masked a growing despair in circles surrounding Johnson, riots and demonstrations of all kinds spread from American campuses to the streets, where anti-war manifestations were joined by civil rights riots which grew in ferocity and destruction. The US was losing the Vietnam War at home.

The Tet Offensive

But in the jungles and villages of steaming South Vietnam, the Communists needed another decisive victory, another Dien Bien Phu, to put an end to American determination to remain in the war. At three o'clock in the morning of the first day of the Vietnamese New Year, Tet, 31 January 1968, the American Embassy in Saigon was invaded by Viet Cong. In those early morning hours almost every important American base was under attack by the National Liberation Front, the South

Vietnamese Communists. Eleven NLF battalions entered Saigon, while simultaneously around the country some 84,000 troops moved on major cities and bases.

The ARVN and the Americans were taken completely by surprise, and while the Communists tried to seize the South and destroy the American sense of security in the cities, measures to counterattack were launched. At the same time North Vietnamese forces crossed the so-called demilitarized zone at the 17th Parallel and pushed south to the US Marine outpost at Khe Sanh. The American military reckoned that Khe Sanh

Above: President Johnson with Ellsworth Bunker, US Ambassador to South Vietnam, at Camp David. The Vietnam War destroyed the career of LBJ.
Above right: Men of the 4th Marines on a search and destroy mission. They had to move quickly to catch the Viet Cong.

Above: Headstones of some of the victims of the Tet Offensive in 1968. **Below:** Infantrymen leap from a UH-1D helicopter during an assault from their base camp in the highlands.

NONE BETTER

Right: A minesweeper from the 4th Infantry Division on Highway 19 during the American withdrawal in 1970. **Far right:** Men of the 25th Infantry Division return to fire support base Jamie in 1970. These bases helped to cover the American withdrawal.
Below right: Members of the Peoples Self-Defense Force learn how to defend their hamlet as part of the Vietnamization policy.
Below: The reality of a search and destroy operation: heat, mud, water and danger.
Opposite above: An M-42 twin 40 mm. self-propelled automatic weapon protects the An Lao Valley.
Opposite below: Deforestation of the Vietnamese jungle was an ill-conceived plan. With the tops of the trees burned off, it was thought that the Viet Cong could be more easily spotted. Actually new undergrowth quickly sprouted up which provided even more effective cover for the Viet Cong.

would be their Dien Bien Phu and reinforced it, while the North Vietnamese simply went past the coastal town and moved into Hué, the old imperial capital. Like a wounded animal, the US and ARVN forces responded with a ferocity not yet experienced in the war. American planes strafed and bombed large population centers indiscriminately, destroying whole cities like Kontum City, My Tho and Ben Tre. Hué suffered the worst of all, the beautiful city on the Perfume River reduced to rubble as US Marines fought for weeks to drive out the Viet Cong. Communist forces were soon pushed out of Saigon and other major centers, but the fight for Hué riveted American public attention to Vietnam as never before in the war. Civilian dead in the Tet Offensive numbered 165,000; two million more refugees streamed into the ruined cities. By March Hué was also cleared and the results of Tet became clear to both sides. As a military venture, a go-for-broke gesture to win the war at a stroke, the Communist offensive was a dismal failure. Their best units destroyed, their carefully hoarded supplies near exhaustion, the Viet Cong and NLF were in no position to mount another offensive for years. But as a political gesture, the Tet attack was a stunning success.

President Johnson's credibility reached new lows at the moment when he planned to launch his re-election campaign. Although the US had ironically won a great victory over Communist forces, the US had been humiliated. Pressure to step down as President mounted in the country as anti-war demonstrations continued. In a primary election in New Hampshire, Senator Eugene McCarthy, an anti-war Democrat, did surprisingly well, and the popular brother of President Kennedy, Robert Kennedy, belatedly announced his intention to run for the Democratic nomination

An M-48 tank patrols an area near Highway 19 in the An Khe area.

486

for President against Johnson. On 10 March Westmoreland informed Johnson that he would need 206,000 more men in Vietnam, when the American presence already stood at over half a million. Johnson was then told that America would be forced to devalue the dollar if a further escalation were contemplated.

On 31 March Johnson decided not to run again. He knew he was beaten, not so much on the battlefield as politically. No candidate could run and hope to win on the promise of four more years of war. The public, disillusioned with Democratic war policies for the past eight years and shattered by the assassinations of Martin Luther King, the black leader, and Robert Kennedy, turned reluctantly to the familiar Richard Nixon, Eisenhower's Vice-President and candidate for President in 1960. Rioting by blacks, anti-war riots and the usual political demonstrations common to an American election year vied for headlines, as US and ARVN forces tightened their grip in South Vietnam. For the first time in memory the Communists were on the defensive, just at the moment when America lost its will to fight.

Vietnamization

But the war was far from over. Nixon announced a policy of 'Vietnamization' of the war, which was a cover word meaning a slow American withdrawal from Indo-China while the ARVN was trained and equipped to maintain its newly-won positions. General Creighton Abrams, Westmoreland's successor, cleared villages once under NLF control; dangerous roads were cleared of snipers and ambushers. Under US pressure President Thieu ordered a full mobilization of South Vietnamese youth for the first time in the war. Some 400,000 more men were recruited for the ARVN, which by 1970 stood at over a million. About half the young able bodied males of the South were in the armed forces. The US gave the ARVN the new M-16 rifles, rocket launchers, helicopters, tanks and F-5 bombers which previously had been kept in American hands. But the Vietnamization policy accelerated the social upheaval of South Vietnam which the war and the American intervention had brought, thereby creating conditions in the long run which would play into the Communists' hands.

Despite continuing American troop withdrawals, after the overthrow of neutralist Norodom Sihanouk in Cambodia, Nixon gave in to the Pentagon's request to attack North Vietnamese bases in Cambodia in April 1970. Although thousands of tons of North Vietnamese equipment was destroyed in the Cambodian incursion, the public reaction in the US to this raid was violent. Congress opposed this apparent re-escalation of the war and Nixon was obliged to withdraw US troops from Cambodia in July. The attack probably set the Viet Cong back about a year, but it also encouraged the American public and the Congress to urge Nixon to step up the American withdrawal from Indo-China.

A similar and less successful operation against Viet Cong bases in Laos was launched in February 1971, but ARVN casualties were so great that the operation was halted later in the spring. Meanwhile the US Air Force continued to bomb targets south and north of the 17th Parallel. By 1972 the US still had over 100,000 men in Indo-China; the Viet Cong and Pathet Lao position in Laos had strengthened to the point where about three-quarters of the country was in Communist hands. Communist activity in South Vietnam began to increase again. 1972 also saw another election victory for Nixon on a withdrawal program. In 1973 the last American troops left Indo-China with the South Vietnamese government still in control of the situation.

The agreements ending the active American role in Vietnam in 1973 called for the establishment of a government of national conciliation. It was widely assumed that although complete 'Vietnamization' of the war had taken place, the American government would still supply arms to South Vietnam and Cambodia. The Watergate scandal, culminating in the resignation of President Nixon on 9 August 1974, weakened the will of Congress to support the presidential policy of sustaining the Saigon and Phnom Penh regimes. Prior to his leaving office Nixon's hands had been tied when Congress forbade the President from using US forces in, over and around Indo-China without its expressed permission. This meant that unless a continuous supply of arms flowed into South Vietnam, the Viet Cong as well as the Khmer Rouge in Cambodia could expect no further interference in the war by the United States. As Congress whittled away at the funds supplied to America's allies, it was only a matter of time before one last, big push would be attempted to win Indo-China for Communism.

The final push began in the early spring of 1975. Phnom Penh, already surrounded by forces of the Khmer Rouge, was besieged, and the USAF continued to bring in a trickle of supplies and food. The seizure of Phouc Binh, northwest of Saigon, by the Communists in January 1975 had failed to bring the expected US reaction: a resumption of bombing or additional supplies to Saigon. Knowing that the US was not going to support South Vietnam any further in any tangible way North Vietnam's 968th Division made a feint attack on Pleiku. The following day, 5 March, President Thieu of South Vietnam sent his 23rd Division to defend the fortress in the Central Highlands. By 15 March Thieu realized that he had been duped. He was unable to hold either the Central Highlands or the coast near the demilitarized zone. He ordered the ARVN Rangers, one of his crack units, to evacuate Kontum and Pleiku and to withdraw to the coast.

Morale began to collapse in both Saigon and Phnom Penh as airborne units of South Vietnam were withdrawn on 17 March from Quang Tri near the 17th Parallel to defend Saigon, while in Cambodia the Mekong River, a source of contact and supplies between South Vietnam and Phnom Penh, was cut by the Khmer Rouge. A domino effect took place as city after city, base after base which had held out for years, were given up without a fight: Quang Tri on 19 March, Huè, the old imperial capital on 26 March and the city and major air base of Da Nang on 30 March. Panic-stricken refugees struggled to reach ships that would take them to the safety of the south.

In Cambodia President Lon Nol left for an 'indefinite visit' to Indonesia as the Khmer Rouge closed in. By the first week in April the entire coastline of South Vietnam was in Communist hands down to Nha Trang. A hurried evacuation of Americans from Phnom Penh by helicopter to waiting aircraft carriers off the Cambodian coast or to air bases in Thailand was successfully completed on 12 April just before the unconditional surrender of Cambodia to the Khmer Rouge. By this time only a truncated South Vietnam remained in government hands, chiefly Saigon and its environs and the port of Vung Tau, choked with thousands of small craft bringing in an estimated two million evacuees from the coastal cities which had been seized.

The will to defend Saigon slipped away from the government. Units of the ARVN 18th Division and the Rangers tried to hold the vital airfield at

Bien Hoa near Saigon, but the fall of Xuan Loc after an intense battle made it clear that further fighting was futile. One of the most difficult maneuvers in warfare is strategic withdrawal. The ARVN was unable to carry out this strategy, and the retreat turned into a rout.

By mid-April pressure was being put on President Thieu to resign, but when he finally did, his replacement served only for two days. As their armies closed in around Saigon, a new President for South Vietnam was chosen: Duong van Minh, 'Big' Minh, who had previously taken power after the fall of Ngo Dinh Diem in 1963. He had always favored a negotiated solution.

The evacuation of Americans, newsmen, other foreigners and a few thousand Vietnamese who had served the Americans was stepped up. Communist shells hammered Saigon airport and the rush to get out was fierce. Sensing that their hour of triumph had come, the Communists refused to negotiate with 'Big' Minh, and in the last hours, as Communist forces entered the capital, the airlift was completed, saving the remaining Americans and newsmen, but leaving hundreds of thousands of helpless Vietnamese.

On 30 April Saigon fell, left largely undefended by members of the ARVN, who shed their uniforms to avoid recognition. Saigon was renamed Ho Chi Minh City. The Communist victory was complete. 'Big' Minh agreed an unconditional surrender. Over a hundred thousand refugees were in evacuation camps in the Philippines and Guam, expecting to be relocated in the United States. After thirty years of war, Indo-China was in Communist hands.

CHAPTER THREE

The Middle East Wars 1948-1973

Below: A boatload of Jewish immigrants arrives in Haifa harbor, July 1946. The flood of Jewish immigrants to Palestine after the Second World War threatened the Arab majority in the British Mandate. **Opposite Left:** Jewish terrorists blew up the King David Hotel. **Opposite right:** Units of the Israel Defense Army secure the Negev Desert during the first Arab-Israeli Conflict in 1948.

Perhaps the most outrageous example of genocide in any period of history took place during World War II when many millions of non-combatants were systematically slaughtered by the Third Reich for a crime which they committed at birth: being what they were. Hundreds of thousands of gypsies, whose colorful folk customs paraded around Europe for centuries, were exterminated. Millions more Poles, Russians and other Slavs met the same fate in Hitler's gas ovens, concentration camps and crematoria. But Hitler's pet hate-symbol, the Jews, suffered most of all. Rough estimates indicate that something in the number of six million Jews met their deaths in Nazi extermination camps, although it is difficult to accurately assess genocide of this magnitude. Hitler boasted toward the end of his life and the war he brought

to Europe that he would always be remembered as the man who rid Germany and Europe of its Jews. He was only partly correct; he did not exterminate them all, not because of inefficiency, but because the end of the war came too suddenly to complete the extermination process which began in earnest in 1941, and which he accelerated as the war neared an end. Hundreds of thousands of Jewish refugees, most of whom began their lives in Eastern Europe, found themselves liberated but with no place to go. There was little enthusiasm either on their part or on the part of their original countries, Poland, Rumania, the Soviet Union, Hungary, Czechoslovakia and Rumania, to have them back. Nazi anti-semitism was matched and at times exceeded in Eastern Europe, for something like three-quarters of the

German Jews escaped the war with their lives, if often with little else. The victorious allies were faced with a problem: what was to be done with the Jews?

For over fifty years, especially in Eastern Europe, the movement called Zionism tried to convince European Jews that their only true home was in Palestine, the land of their forefathers who had been dispersed some 1900 years before. During World War I Palestine was taken from the Ottoman Empire by the British, and became a League of Nations mandate under Britain in 1919. The British encouraged Zionism through the Balfour Declaration of 1917, which promised a 'national homeland' for Jews in Palestine. At the time only about 5% of the population of the area was Jewish. As more Jews drifted into Palestine during the interwar period, Arab spokesmen in Palestine protested. In 1922 the British promised to limit the numbers of Jews allowed to enter the mandate, and again in 1939 restated their position but raised the limit to permit refugees from Nazism to emigrate to Palestine. The British needed to maintain good relations with the Arabs for many reasons, but the strategic position the Arabs held in the defense of the lifeline of Empire, particularly the Suez Canal area, made it vital for Britain to stay on the good side of the Arabs lest the area fall into German hands through Arab subversion of the Anglo-French hegemony over the Middle East. This policy paid off during World War II, for while Hitler tried to make

contact with certain Arab leaders and sometimes succeeded, the Arabs largely supported the Allied cause when the Desert War reached its most intense period during 1941–43. Supplies of oil continued to flow from the Middle East to Great Britain throughout the war through the Suez Canal and around the Cape of Good Hope.

The Creation of Israel

Straddling the issue was to prove more difficult after the war, and pressure to open Palestine to hundreds of thousands of Jewish refugees became intense. The Labour Government was torn between sympathy for the refugees and British interests in the Arab world which became all the more important when the decision was reached to abandon the Indian Empire in 1947. Suez and oil were the chief British interests, and the Jews came second. Thus in 1947 the British prepared to abandon their mandate while at the same time preventing more Jews from entering Palestine. The United Nations, seeing no easy way out of the impasse, decided to partition Palestine, leaving the Jews with a large area in the Negev Desert, which at the time was largely unpopulated, and an unviable series of frontiers with the Arab part of Palestine based on the heavy concentration of Jews in certain parts of the country. Both Arabs and Jews prepared themselves for the inevitable struggle for territory once the British left Palestine. At midnight of the evening of 14–15 May 1948, the British mandate came to an end, and the first

Top: Israeli troops plunge into the Gaza Strip in the 1956 Suez War. **Above:** British paratroops during the assault on El Gamil. **Left:** David Ben Gurion. **Bottom left:** Israeli forces reach the outskirts of Gaza on 2 November 1956. **Center:** French tanks patrol the streets of Port Said during the Suez War. **Right:** French troops during the landing at Port Fuad.

Arab-Israeli war broke out.

A state of Israel had been declared under Chaim Weizmann, supported by the United States, which sent considerable economic, monetary and military aid to the new state. The Arabs, for their part, felt betrayed. The British had consistently promised that Palestine would never become more than half Jewish, and now half the country had been given over to Israel. Egypt, Syria and Jordan attacked the Israelis, whose military prowess had been underestimated by both the British and the Arabs. By the end of the year, after intense and sporadic fighting on all fronts, the Israeli frontiers now included the area up to Jerusalem and half of the city holy to Muslims, Christians and Jews alike. Truce lines were drawn in 1949 which confirmed the military realities. Well over half of Palestine was now in Israeli hands.

The early 1950's were a period of reassessment for the Arabs. While Israel had become a Jewish state which discriminated against Arabs still left in it, hundreds of thousands of Arab refugees, many of whose families had lived in Palestine from time immemorial, fled from Israel to parts of Palestine still unoccupied by Israeli armies; the Gaza Strip, belonging to Egypt, and the west bank of the Jordan River, which belonged to the Hashemite Kingdom of Jordan. This flight was encouraged by the Israelis, who burned Arab homes and killed many civilians in the intensity of their struggle for independence.

Hatred of Arabs in Israel intensified, and the feeling was mutual. Treatment of Palestinian Arabs became the *cause célèbre* of Muslim nations all over the world, but few other than those immediately affected – Syria, Jordan and Egypt – paid more than lip service to the cause of those displaced by the Jews. European sympathies were on the side of the Jews. After all, Western Europe and the United States could have allowed emigration of Jewish refugees into their countries after the war, but they had refused. Zionism was championed by the Western nations because of the guilt they shared in covert anti-semitism, which was the cause of Zionism in the first place, and because their propaganda in World War II directed against Germany largely centered around German overt racism and anti-semitism. In America it was politically expedient to champion the Jewish cause, since the most populous state at the time, New York, had about four million Jews, and the nation itself had five and a half million, most of whom regularly gave donations to Israel through charities, buying Jewish bonds, and by pressuring the US government by various means to supply arms and grants to Israel.

The revolution in Egypt in 1952 which overthrew the corrupt régime of King Farouk eventually brought Gamal Abdel Nasser to power, a superb orator and a man who had aspirations of being a leader of all Arab peoples. Egypt had been within the British sphere of influence since 1882, and even after independence had been granted to Egypt, British troops still policed the Suez Canal,

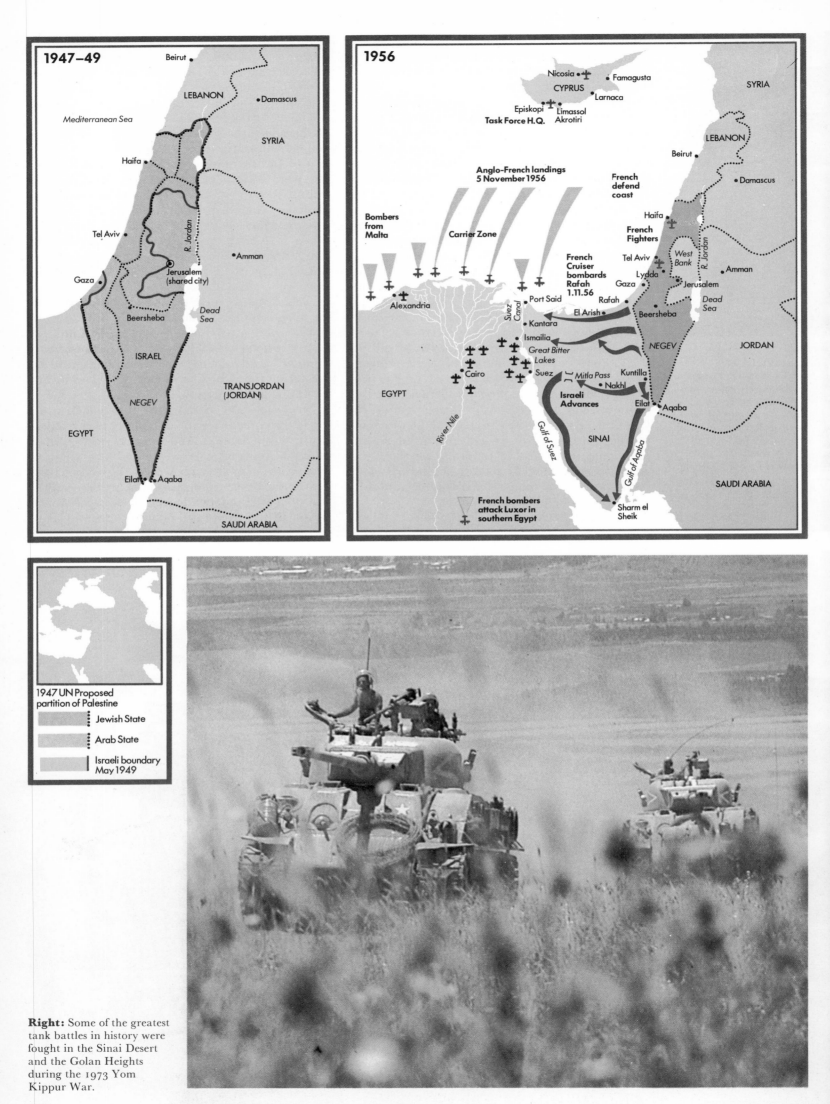

1947–49

Beirut

LEBANON

Damascus

Mediterranean Sea

SYRIA

Haifa

Tel Aviv

R. Jordan

Amman

Jerusalem
(shared city)

Gaza

*Dead
Sea*

Beersheba

ISRAEL

NEGEV

TRANSJORDAN
(JORDAN)

EGYPT

Eilat • Aqaba

SAUDI ARABIA

1956

Nicosia • Famagusta

CYPRUS

Larnaca

SYRIA

Episkopi • Limassol
Akrotiri

Task Force H.Q.

Anglo-French landings
5 November 1956

French
defend
coast

LEBANON

Beirut

Damascus

Haifa

Bombers
from
Malta

Carrier Zone

**French
Fighters**

Tel Aviv

*West
Bank*

R. Jordan

**French
Cruiser
bombards
Rafah
1.11.56**

Lydda

Amman

Gaza

Jerusalem

Alexandria

Port Said

Rafah

Beersheba

*Dead
Sea*

*Suez
Canal*

El Arish

NEGEV

JORDAN

Kantara

Ismailia

*Great Bitter
Lakes*

Kuntilla

Cairo

Suez

Mitla Pass

Nakhl

**Israeli
Advances**

Eilat • Aqaba

EGYPT

River Nile

Gulf of Suez

SINAI

Gulf of Aqaba

SAUDI ARABIA

**French bombers
attack Luxor in
southern Egypt**

Sharm el
Sheik

1947 UN Proposed
partition of Palestine

Jewish State

Arab State

Israeli boundary
May 1949

Right: Some of the greatest
tank battles in history were
fought in the Sinai Desert
and the Golan Heights
during the 1973 Yom
Kippur War.

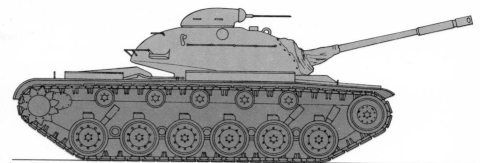

M-48 M2. Length: 23 ft. 1 in. Width: 12 ft. 4 in. Max. road speed: 32 m.p.h. Armament: 1 × 90 mm. cannon, 1 × .5 caliber machine gun. Crew: 5. Weight: 46 tons.

Far left: The Suez Canal, goal of the Israeli offensives of 1956 and 1967. **Left:** General Moshe Dayan, hero of the 1956 and 1967 Arab-Israeli Wars. **Below:** Israeli tanks cross the Suez Canal on dam-like bridges during the final withdrawal of their forces as agreed in the Kilometer 101 talks after the Yom Kippur War. Similar bridges were constructed during their breakthrough across the Canal during the war.

and British interests remained paramount in Cairo and Alexandria. It was precisely this influence which Nasser hoped to challenge and break.

In 1954 Nasser negotiated a deal with the United States to have them finance the building of an Aswan Dam, which was supposed to bring prosperity and power to large parts of Egypt. John Foster Dulles scotched the deal, and Nasser turned to the Soviet Union, which welcomed Nasser and the opportunity to build the dam with open arms. Although British forces left the Suez in 1954, they still maintained a base in Ismailia, so they could re-enter Egypt if they so desired. When the US refused to give Nasser military aid without strings in 1955, Nasser began to encourage guerrilla activity inside Israel and moved closer to the Soviet bloc, which was anxious to become involved in the Middle East in order to fill the obvious power vacuum that the US and the UK were leaving. The arms deal which Nasser struck with Czechoslovakia convinced the new British Prime Minister, Anthony Eden, that Nasser was an evil force who had to be checked early. Invidious comparisons were made between Nasser and Hitler. Eden likened Nasser to the German dictator, who had been encouraged by appeasement in the 1930's. Thus, Nasser's power had to be checked at once lest he seize further influence in the Middle East.

This comparison, in retrospect, seems absurd. Nasser repeatedly tried to buy arms or obtain arms grants from the US and UK, but was refused because of their support of Israel. If Nasser was to appear as a credible champion of Arab interests, and latterly the interests of the Palestinian Arabs, he needed to challenge Israel. The US took a more sanguine view of Nasser, which infuriated both Eden and the Israelis. Israel, in order to stop an increase in Nasser's military strength, considered invading the Sinai peninsula, part of Egyptian territory, late in 1955. By 1956, however, they were able to get support for this pre-emptive strike from Britain and France, who collaborated with Israel in a plot to invade Egypt. Nasser nationalized the Suez Canal in 1956, which had been owned by an Anglo-French company, and Britain

Egyptian soldiers discarded their clothing during their disorganized retreat from the Sinai Peninsula in the 1967 rout.

and France, which had already lost parts of their vast colonial empires, wanted to regain lost prestige and assert their independence from the Americans by consorting with Israel. The US was having an election in November 1956 and wanted no part of anything which smacked of a neo-colonialist display of force, particularly since the United States was trying to maintain and increase its position in the Middle East, above all in Saudi Arabia and the oil-producing states of the Persian Gulf.

The Polish and Hungarian revolutions of October 1956 were an unexpected fillip to the Anglo-French-Israeli plans. The Soviet Union would be tied down with these events, and was obliged to send troops into Hungary in November. All of these dramatic occurrences would allow the invasion forces to continue their preparations in secret with most of the world's press concerned with events in Eastern Europe. Feeling that neither the US nor the USSR would interfere, hopes rose in London and Paris that a swift slapping down of Nasser could proceed successfully,

The Suez War

On 29 October 1956 the Israeli part of the invasion began. Border posts were quickly seized, and with the help of 36 Mystères of the French Air Force, Israel started to plunge across the Sinai Desert toward Suez. President Eisenhower, astonished by the attack, asked Britain and France to condemn this aggression in the UN, which they, of course, refused to do. Britain began to activate its plans to retake the Suez Canal 'temporarily', the same phrase used by Gladstone when Egypt was occupied by Britain in 1882. According to the plans laid beforehand, Britain was to begin bombing Egyptian airfields on 31 October, 36 hours after the Israeli attack began. Despite some delays in activating the plan, Israeli planes already had taken command of the skies over Sinai by that time. French ships were already in place along the Israeli coast, and the Israeli paratroops who landed at the strategic Mitla Pass were not overtly exposed. As the flow of oil from the Middle East abruptly came to a halt, the Egyptians began to sink ships in the Suez Canal. Thousands of Egyptian prisoners were taken by the Israelis in the Sinai and Israeli troops entered the Gaza Strip. By 5 November Gaza was taken, while opposition to the attack began to rise within Britain and France, whose leaders began to waver in their resolve to persevere in the attack. After having attacked Egyptian airfields for some days, on the morning of 5 November British and French paratroops began to descend on Port Said. A wave of landings hit the coast that afternoon, and American infuriation with the Anglo-French attack rose dramatically. Eisenhower asked Britain and France to stop in no uncertain terms, and for a few days a diplomatic revolution had taken place. For a change, America and Russia were on the same side, both demanding that the invasion cease. By the following day fighting between Israel and Egypt had virtually come to a halt, and British and French armored columns had progressed to within 75 miles of the city of Suez. The United Nations called for a ceasefire, with the US and the Soviet Union in agreement.

The selling of sterling on world money markets had reached epidemic proportions, and the US Treasury informed the Bank of England that it could expect no support of sterling from the US as long as the invasion of Egypt continued. Nikita Khrushchev warned Britain and France that unless the attack stopped within 48 hours, they could expect an atomic attack on London and Paris. Actually, the American threat carried more weight than the Russian, as few expected Russia to mend the rift between America and her allies in NATO and risk a third world war over Egypt. American nuclear superiority was such that if the Russians had made their threat good, Russian cities would have been wiped out at once.

Whatever the motivation, the threats from Washington and Moscow, the cutoff of oil, the hostility of virtually every country in the world, as well as intense hostility from the opposition parties within their countries and significant parts of the parties in power, Britain and France decided to call it a day. A ceasefire and eventually a withdrawal was agreed on the 7th. Britain and France had suffered an unprecedented humiliation, and it took more than a year before relations with the US were put on a firm footing. Anglo-French forces withdrew by December, and Israeli troops, now in possession of Sharm-el-Sheik at the foot of the Gulf of Aqaba and the whole Sinai Peninsula, were obliged to withdraw as well. The last attempt at a revival of imperial power by Britain and France had been a total failure, although the completion of the conquest of Egypt probably would not have taken more than a couple of days had the Americans not withdrawn their support of the pound.

UN troops were placed in the Gaza Strip and along strategic points at the Israeli-Egyptian frontier in 1957. The whole affair might have succeeded if Britain and France had taken Eisenhower and Dulles into their confidence, but it was the manner and secrecy in which the invasion was carried out that caused the US to abandon its European allies. British and French motorists soon learned that their countries could not attack an Arab state with impunity, as shortages and even rationing of petrol in Britain continued for months after the Suez War. The Suez Canal was blocked for almost a year. Eden, whose health was poor even before the attack, soon collapsed and resigned in favor of Harold Macmillan. The Fourth French Republic, which had already suffered defeat in Indo-China, was shaken to its roots, and was replaced two years later by the Fifth Republic of Charles de Gaulle. But Israel had shown the Arabs and the Egyptians in particular that her armed forces were formidable and vastly superior to whatever any combination of Arab states possessed.

During the years after the Suez War British and French influence in the Middle East rapidly declined, as the British continued to wind up their imperial operations in Africa and Asia and the French under de Gaulle rid themselves of virtually all of theirs, including Algeria, after a vicious guerrilla war which lasted almost twenty years. American influence, because of her support of Israel, was being overshadowed by that of the Soviet Union, who, in the wake of the Suez War,

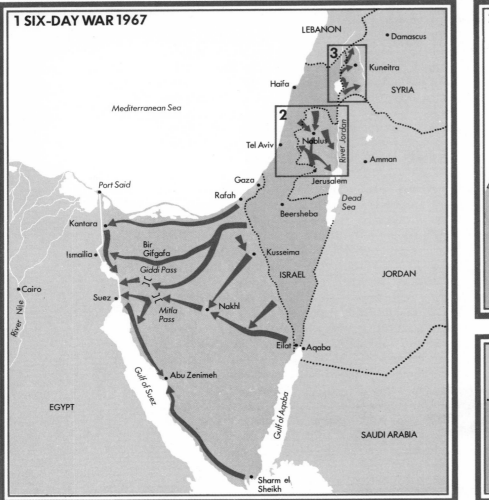

1 SIX-DAY WAR 1967

LEBANON

Damascus

Mediterranean Sea

Haifa

Kuneitra

SYRIA

Tel Aviv

Nablus

River Jordan

Amman

Port Said

Gaza

Jerusalem

Dead Sea

Kantara

Rafah

Bir Gifgafa

Beersheba

Ismailia

ISRAEL

Giddi Pass

JORDAN

Cairo

Kusseima

River Nile

Suez

Mitla Pass

Nakhl

Gulf of Suez

Eilat

Aqaba

Abu Zenimeh

Gulf of Aqaba

EGYPT

SAUDI ARABIA

Sharm el Sheikh

Megiddo

Sandala

Tulkharm

Kalkilya

Nablus

Tel Aviv

WEST BANK

Damiya Bridge

ISRAEL

Ramallah

JORDAN

River Jordan

Latrun

Jericho

Allenby Bridge

Jerusalem

Bethlehem

Dead Sea

Massada

Golan Heights

Kuneitra

Darcara

ISRAEL

Almago

Boutmiya

Sea of Galilee

El Al

SYRIA

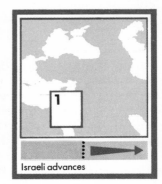

Israeli advances

T-55. Length: 28 ft.
Width: 10 ft. 9 in.
Max. road speed: 34.4
m.p.h. Armament:
1 × 100 mm. cannon,
1 × 7.62 mm. machine
gun. Crew: 4.
Weight: 35 tons.

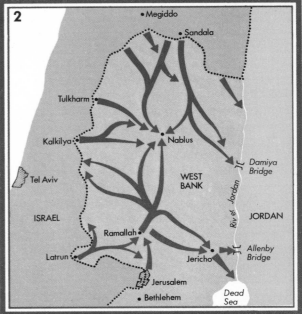

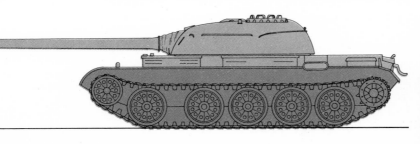

became the chief supplier of arms to the militant Arab states including Egypt. American influence was greatest outside Israel in the conservative oil-rich sheikdoms of the Persian Gulf and above all in Saudi Arabia, which was threatened by Nasser's growing influence in Yemen. King Hussein of Jordan was perhaps closest to Britain, despite the fact that British control of the famed Arab Legion had long since passed. Nasser forged a union with Syria, the United Arab Republic, but it soon broke up when Syria realized that it would be the junior partner. By 1966 Syria, of all the Arab states, had drawn the closest to Russia, which supplied her with tanks, planes and all sorts of military equipment and economic aid. But despite border activity on the part of Palestinian liberation groups which were loyal to no state and only to their own cause, the situation in the Middle East remained relatively quiet.

Israel's economic growth, thanks to American aid, was phenomenal, and immigration of Jews to Israel from the Afro-Asian world was stepped up to the point where oriental Jews almost outnumbered Jews of European origin in Israel. But skirmishes along Israel's borders with Syria and Egypt increased in the spring of 1967, and finally Nasser asked the UN forces within his territory to leave forthwith. This was a warning to Israel that Egypt might try out the heavy Russian armor and aircraft she now had in her possession. When Nasser announced the closure of the Straits of Tiran to Israeli ships and ships carrying strategic goods to Israel on 23 May 1967, Israel began to prepare for another pre-emptive strike against her neighbors.

The Six-Day War

With Jordan, Syria and Egypt ranged against Israel, all with powerful air forces and ground troops, and the latter two well equipped with Russian tanks (Jordan had mostly US and UK armor), Israel faced a real problem in deployment. If she waited for war to come, and she felt that this was inevitable, she would be faced with an attack on three sides. If, however, Israel struck first, where would the first strike come? For the first hours of the pre-emptive strike would bring the might of the other two states upon her. Israel was outnumbered on every count; men, planes, armor. The plan devised by the Israeli General Staff, under the leadership of General Moshe Dayan, was very like that which Hitler used to attack Holland in 1940. Destroy the Egyptian air forces on the ground by attacking them from their blind side – the west – rather than across the Sinai Desert where an attack would be expected. The time of 0845 Egyptian time (0745 Israeli) was perfect, as it was the moment after the usual dawn readiness alert. Egyptian flight crews would be breakfasting, and the ground mist, which was normal for that time of year, would have cleared by 0800. Under a cover of 40 Mirages, the first wave of attacking Israeli Mystères hit nine Egyptian airfields in small groups on the morning of 5 June 1967. The Israeli aircraft flew very low over the sea to avoid the radar screen. Just at the moment of attack the aircraft climbed so as to be visible on the Egyptian radar, so that the pilots would scramble to their planes, just in time to be destroyed on the ground. The Israelis allowed for about four runs at the airfields in the

Above: Israeli forces surround Jerusalem in the Six-Day War. Jordanian defenses were overrun and forced to retreat to the east bank of the Jordan River.

Opposite left: Israeli forces begin their advance into Egypt after suffering initial losses of territory during the Yom Kippur War. **Opposite right:** Victorious Egyptians raise their flag on the eastern bank of the Suez Canal for the first time in six years in the first days of the Yom Kippur War. **Opposite bottom:** More tanks clashed in the Sinai Desert in 1973 than at El Alamein in 1942.

ten minutes allotted to them, for their fuel consumption dictated that they could have no more than ten minutes in the attack. Furthermore, anti-aircraft fire would become too intense after the first strikes were made.

Destroyed on the Field

After the first attack, the anti-aircraft fire appeared with each successive wave. But the damage was done. Only eight MIG-21s of the Egyptian Air Force reached the skies, and only two Israeli Mirages were lost in the attack. But further waves of Israeli aircraft, each following the other in ten-minute intervals, descended from the cloudless skies. This kept up for 80 minutes, and at 1000 hours three more Egyptian airfields were hit. By 1035 the job had been done. The Egyptian Air Force had been wiped out. All 17 Egyptian airfields had been attacked, and over 300 planes destroyed. Israel gambled everything on this surprise attack and it had paid off. With command of the skies in Israeli hands, Israel could now turn her air forces toward Syria and Jordan, while panzer groups swept aside demoralized Egyptian armor as they moved across the Sinai Desert to the Suez Canal. By 1145 the Syrian Air Force began its attack on Israeli territory while Israeli bombs pounded Jordanian air strips. The attack on Jordan began at 1215, and within twenty minutes the Jordanian Air Force was wiped out. Israel lost only one plane over Jordan. As Iraqi troops pushed into Jordan to help their reluctant Arab ally, Israeli planes pounded away at them for the balance of the day. Meanwhile Syrian airfields were hit at 1215, the same time as the attack on

Jordan. In 25 minutes most of the Syrian Air Force had met with a similar fate. It had been a busy day. In the first four hours of the Six-Day War Israel had won it by her daring gamble in the skies.

On the second day of the war Israel was briefly surprised by a Lebanese air attack, but it was insignificant and Lebanon, reluctant to make war anyway, did not fight thereafter. Mopping up operations occurred over Egyptian territory when the remainder of their air forces challenged the Israelis, and after the second day there was hardly any opposition to Israel in the air. The victory in the air was the key to victory on land, as it gave the Israeli tanks and troops sufficient air cover and reconnaissance to proceed without difficulty. On the first day Israeli tanks crossed into Sinai on three major fronts. Russian T-34's, T-54's and T-55's were excellent weapons, and faced the Israeli tank commanders, Israel Tal, Ariel Sharon and Avraham Yoffe, all Brigadiers with Pattons and Shermans at their disposal. Supported by paratroop brigades, these *Ugdas* or task groups swept through the disorganized and unprotected opposition.

The Gaza Strip was sealed off and taken on the first day. By the end of the second day of fighting, thanks to the Centurions of the Yoffe *Ugda*, the Egyptians had withdrawn to the central ridge in Sinai, which meant that half the desert had been relinquished. This advance continued into the third and fourth day, and although the Egyptians made some counter-attacks against the force crossing the desert near the sea and another near the Mitla Pass, Israeli air power smashed the

Israeli armor seized the Sinai Desert in the Six-Day War against little effective Egyptian opposition.

Egyptian armored units so that Egypt had the choice of withdrawing across the Suez Canal, which some one hundred tanks did, or being attacked by Israeli tanks and planes in the desert and destroyed. By the end of the fourth day the whole of the Sinai Desert up to the Suez Canal, including Sharm el Sheikh, was in Israeli hands. Although Egypt started the war with twice the number of tanks and men Israel possessed, air power and the element of surprise won the day.

Fight for Jerusalem

On the Jordanian front things went almost as well. The worst fighting took place in Jerusalem, half of which was controlled by Jordan. Fierce building by building, hand-to-hand combat took place. By the third day not only Jerusalem but the entire West Bank of the Jordan River had fallen to Israel. Jordanian troops, deprived of air cover, fought bravely, unlike so many of the Egyptian units which in the chaos of retreat quickly capitulated, but the leadership of Jordanian General Riad is open to question. His retreat across the Jordan was mismanaged, but the loss of Jerusalem was a mortal one to Jordan and the entire Arab cause. In three days King Hussein had lost the richest part of his Kingdom, and he was relieved when Israeli forces stopped at the Jordan River, which they could easily have crossed.

On the Syrian front Israel was prepared to hold the line as their troops advanced elsewhere, but after the first four days when Egypt and Jordan had clearly lost, Israel turned her attentions to the strategic Golan Heights, which commanded both the approaches to Damascus as well as Israeli territory, since 1948 in Syrian hands. Brigadier Elazar started the advance on the fourth day, but on the fifth, when most of the Israeli Air Force was freed from duties on the other two major fronts, it pounded away at Syrian field positions. By the end of the day, after heavy fighting, much of the territory on the heights had been taken. But many Israeli tanks were lost on the fifth and sixth days. Syrian lines held despite the severe air attacks upon their positions, and Israeli high command admitted later that it lost more men in the two major days of fighting in Syria than on the other two fronts combined. But the Golan Heights belonged to Israel, and her air force declined to press further when the Syrians retreated to defend their capital, Damascus.

After six days of fighting Israel had over doubled its territory. It had won on every front with apparent ease, with the loss of only 778 soldiers and 26 civilians. Many of the Palestinian Arabs were now within Israeli territory, although 150,000 of them fled across the Jordan. Taking into account Israel's Arab population before the war of some 300,000, Israel now had about 1,385,000 Arabs under her flag. There were only 2,365,000 Jews in Israel. The Jews of European origin who helped found the country in 1948 and which, by and large, ruled it, were now outnumbered by roughly a 3:1 ratio. Israel had stunned the world with its resounding victory, but the problems imposed by the magnitude of that victory in the Six-Day War were to prove more than a burden in the years to come.

Egypt and Syria were drawn even closer to the

An Egyptian soldier surrenders after his unit was overwhelmed in the Six-Day War.

USSR in the years after the Six-Day War. Their armor and air forces were re-equipped, and new missiles were installed near the Suez Canal, now the border between Egypt and Israel. Nasser, despite the loss of a good deal of his territory and all of the prestige of his armies, offered to resign, but the Egyptian people rallied behind him. The UN and the US tried to force Israel to withdraw as they had done in 1957, but without success. A war of attrition began on Israel's new frontiers with Egypt and, to a lesser degree, Syria in 1969, which grew in intensity with each passing year. Israeli hopes that the death of Nasser on 28 September 1970 would bring a new policy and a détente were soon dashed by Egypt's new President, Anwar Sadat. In order to maintain his credibility as Egypt's leader, Sadat could ask no less than an Israeli withdrawal, which Israel was unwilling to make. As time went on Sadat could not remain in power without challenging Israel at the first opportunity. Until then the war of attrition continued, and the sporadic fighting often was intense, costing many lives.

The uneasy truce

By 1973 the uneasy truce was not expected to last much longer. Most observers expected another Israeli pre-emptive strike as more missiles and other arms flooded into Egypt and Syria. The United States was unwilling to allow Israel to lose the superiority which she had proven in 1967, but conversely the US was anxious to make a lasting peace in the Middle East which could only be accomplished by Israel's relinquishing some of her new-won territory. It was an impasse, which the Soviet Union exploited to her favor by rushing more arms to the Arabs, placing the US is a position in which she had to increase her arms to Israel or face the ultimate collapse of her protégé. After the riots in Cairo in 1972, Sadat knew that he could not wait too long if he was to maintain his support among his people.

Meanwhile the Palestinian Arab situation was getting worse. There were now something like two million of them, 600,000 of whom were lodged in refugee camps. The Israelis began to incorporate parts of formerly Arab Palestine into their country. The annexation of the Old City of Jerusalem, until the Six-Day War part of Jordan, was especially provocative to all Muslim states, as the Holy Places of Islam were now officially part of Israel, along with the Wailing Wall, which has equally emotive connotations to Jews all over the world. Palestinian guerrilla groups of varying degrees of fanaticism attacked Israeli athletes at the Munich Olympics in 1972. Israeli planes all

over Europe and Israeli tourist and airline offices and embassies were threatened, and Israeli citizens or prominent Jews living abroad were kidnapped, killed or menaced. The desperation of the Palestinian Arabs' plight was obvious. They were pawns to the national interests of the various Arab states. Their cause, which was ostensibly championed by these Arab countries, was secondary to them, and the Palestinians knew it. Now the whole of Palestine was in Israeli hands. The problem between Jew and Arab would not be settled until the situation of the Palestinians was resolved.

Meanwhile the Russian presence in Egypt continued to build up. Some 40,000 Russians, advisers and their families, were present in Egypt along with the missiles they installed. After realizing that neither Russia nor America was keen to have another war break out in the Middle East, and knowing that his position in Egypt depended on another war soon, Sadat ordered all Soviet military personnel to leave Egypt at once on 17 July 1972. Egypt took over the SAM sites and the airfields rebuilt by the Russians. Dissatisfaction with Sadat in the army and among the students was stilled by this dramatic announcement. But Sadat's diplomatic initiatives in the following months were as inconclusive as

ever. By spring 1973 Sadat made it clear that only another war could help clear the diplomatic log-jam which made concessions on either side of a significant nature virtually impossible.

Israel was complacent in the years after 1967. Always contemptuous of the Arabs, the Israelis were convinced of their invincibility. The victory in the Six-Day War was, in a way, their undoing. Overconfidence led to inadequate preparations for a pre-emptive strike on the Arabs' part, which was by now considered an unthinkable possibility. By the summer King Hussein was won over to a policy of an attack against Israel, which the Syrians had never opposed. This time Egypt would be supported to the full by the conservative members of the Arab bloc, including Saudi Arabia and the Gulf States. As Egyptian armor, now equipped with T-62 tanks, massed near the Suez Canal in September, the Israelis were not worried. Maneuvers were held every autumn. Although Dayan issued warnings that similar build-ups were occurring on the Syrian frontier near the Golan Heights, Israeli attentions were turned toward Vienna, where a Jewish refugee agency had been closed after it had been threatened by Palestinian Arabs. The last Cabinet meeting before the holiest day in the Jewish calendar, Yom Kippur, dealt with this Schonau incident.

Israeli forces advance into Syrian territory on the Golan Heights in the final stage of the Six-Day War.

Overleaf: Thousands of Palestinian refugees streamed across the Jordan into DP camps after Israel took over the rest of Palestine in the Six-Day War.

The Yom Kippur War

Yom Kippur, the Day of Atonement, 6 October 1973, found most Jews in Israel in their synagogues. Over 700 Syrian tanks attacked the Golan Heights while Egyptian units swept across the Suez Canal into Sinai, taking the Israelis totally by surprise on the day when even most Israeli soldiers were not on duty. The afternoon of the 6th and that evening, Egyptian forces crossed the Canal at three key points, bringing with them heavy armored units. The first line of Israeli defense, the Bar-Lev Line, was soon taken. As air raid warnings were heard in Jerusalem, a stunned Israeli public became aware that the fourth Arab-Israeli War was in progress. The radio broke its traditional holy day silence at 1440, and soldiers on leave were pulled from their synagogues to return to the fronts. Syrian thrusts on the Golan Heights threatened to cut Israeli forces in half, and their early capture of Mount Hermon enabled the Syrians to range their artillery against Israeli positions. By the third day of the war the Golan front seemed to stabilize, but Egyptian forces continued to pour into Sinai. This was to be no Israeli rout as in 1967. Complacency had given way to terror, as Israeli civilians feared that this time their presumed armed superiority might be in doubt. By 12 October, the sixth day of the war, the three Egyptian bridgeheads across the Suez Canal had widened into a broad front controlling the whole west bank of the canal.

When Israel swept across Sinai in 1956 and 1967 there were only three ways to get through to the Suez Canal: the Mitla Pass, the Gidi Pass, and the Khatmia Pass. The alternative was the northern route across the top of the desert between the Sea of Sand, impossible for tanks to penetrate, and the Mediterranean. The Egyptian armored legions faced the same choice if they were to drive Israel out of Sinai. Saad Shazli, the Egyptian Chief of Staff, urged a further push into Sinai, preferably along the northern route, since the three key passes were heavily defended. As Russia airlifted new supplies to the Syrians, they began to fall back from their newly-won positions, but when the Israelis penetrated Syria as far as Saasa, the second line of Syrian defense held fast, protecting the road to Damascus.

The first week of the war ended inconclusively, with Syria on the defensive in the north, but Egypt holding their western bank of Suez. On Sunday, 14 October, one of the greatest tank battles in history took place near the Israeli defensive position guarding the Gidi and Mitla Passes. Something like 2000 tanks fought bitterly, compared with the 1600 which fought at El Alamein in 1942. Super-Shermans, similar to those used by Montgomery at Alamein, were used by the Israelis, while the Egyptians were equipped with T-34's, used at Kursk in 1943, and the more modern T-55's and T-62's. But the Centurions and Pattons the Israelis also had were superior in desert warfare to the Russian equipment because of their range of fire. The greater comfort the American tank gave to the crew in comparison with the Russian models became an important factor in the torrid heat of the Sinai Desert. By the evening of 14 October the major Egyptian thrust had been broken. Israeli lines held. It was now time to move to the counterattack.

Battle of Chinese Farm

General Arik Sharon discovered a gap between the Egyptian Second and Third Armies west of the canal, and on 15 October decided to try to break through this gap, while one of his three armored brigades made a diversionary move to the west. His Third Brigade pressed the advantage, and then swung north of the Great Bitter Lake, around it, and then southward to expand the bridgehead. On the night of 16 October the Egyptians moved down to cut off this daring thrust in the Battle of Chinese Farm. They were too late. The Israeli forces withstood this assault, and were not cut off. The bridgehead held, and with this battle the tide of the war turned in favor of Israel. Meanwhile the oil producing countries, encouraged by Egypt, decided to raise the price of oil by 70%, using petroleum as a lever to force the United States and Western Europe to wring concessions from their protégé. Nixon responded by putting his troops in Europe on full alert and sent massive military aid to Israel, some of it airlifted from Europe. Russia, seeing her policy of détente with the West crumbling, urged Egypt to quit while they were still ahead. While Israeli ground troops contined to destroy the missile sites west of the canal which had hampered her ability to knock out the Egyptian air force as she had done in 1967, the Egyptian Third Army found

After the 1967 War the whole of Jerusalem, including the Wailing Wall, the last remnant of Solomon's Temple, was in Israeli hands. General Dayan's prestige was at its height after his triumphs in 1967.

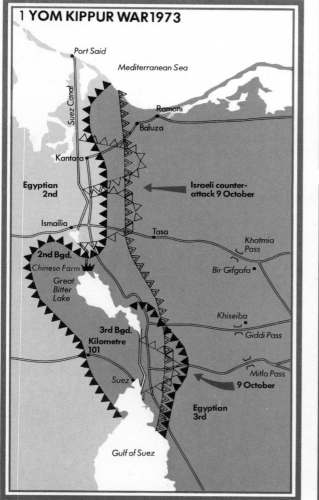

1 YOM KIPPUR WAR 1973

Port Said
Mediterranean Sea
Suez Canal
Ramani
Baluza
Kantara
Egyptian 2nd
Ismailia
Tasa
Khatmia Pass
Israeli counter-attack 9 October
2nd Bgd.
Chinese Farm
Great Bitter Lake
Bir Gifgafa
Khiseiba
Giddi Pass
3rd Bgd.
Kilometre 101
Mitla Pass
Suez
9 October
Egyptian 3rd
Gulf of Suez

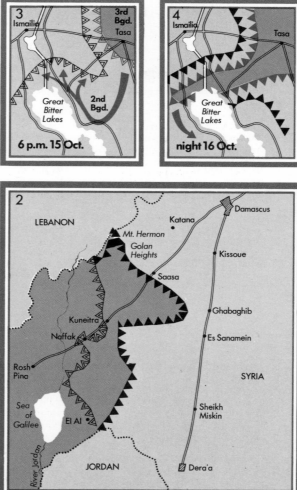

3 Ismailia — 3rd Bgd. Tasa — Great Bitter Lakes — 2nd Bgd. — 6 p.m. 15 Oct.

4 Ismailia — Tasa — Great Bitter Lakes — night 16 Oct.

2 LEBANON — Katana — Damascus — Mt. Hermon — Golan Heights — Kissoue — Saasa — Ghabaghib — Kuneitra — Es Sanamein — Naffak — Rosh Pina — Sea of Galilee — El Al — SYRIA — Sheikh Miskin — River Jordan — JORDAN — Dera'a

Egyptian bridgeheads

6–7 October 1973

9–12 October 1973

23–24 October 1973

Syrian advances

9 October 1973

11 October 1973

itself trapped near the town of Suez by the Israeli sweep around the Great and Little Bitter Lakes.

When the final ceasefire came into effect on 24 October, Israeli forces were deep into Egypt, only 60 miles from Cairo. But the Egyptians still held part of the area east of the canal. Henry Kissinger, President Nixon's Secretary of State, had forged a truce, but the Yom Kippur War ended inconclusively. Although Israeli armed forces held more territory on the Syrian front than they ever had before, and now had territory west of Suez, some territory east of Suez had been forfeited to Egypt. It was a victory for Arab morale. The Western world had discovered its dependence on Arab oil. The Arab states, after 25 years and four wars, had achieved unity and with it, impressive strength. Above all, it became clear to Arab and Jew alike that wars of this kind could never bring about the desires each of them harbored: on Egypt and Syria's part, revenge for past defeats; for Israel, security for her ever-expanding frontiers.

In the uneasy peace which followed the Yom Kippur War, Sadat and his Persian Gulf supporters who embargoed the shipment of oil to the United States, realized that in the crunch Russia would never help the Palestinian Arabs, nor would she allow Israel to be utterly destroyed if this meant nuclear confrontation with the United States. In the months after the war, Russian influence in the Middle East waned, as Henry Kissinger successfully brought all the Arab states, including a reluctant Syria, perhaps the most militant and anti-Israeli of all, into the American camp. It looked as if the Yom Kippur War might be the last in the series of wars plaguing the Middle East ever since Israel's creation. But until the vexing problem of the Palestinian Arabs was solved and the Israelis retreated to more realistic frontiers, no permanent peace in the Middle East could be reached.

This violent century

The wars fought after the two world wars only pointed up the fact that major confrontation of the 1914–18 and 1939–45 type was senseless in the nuclear age. While wars will continue as they always have, for they will exist as long as human pride and human conflict of any kind exist, it is to be hoped that they remain localized as the wars in Korea, Vietnam and the Middle East have been. The modern superpowers, the Soviet Union and the United States, are unlikely to go to war as long as credible defenses remain on both sides of what used to be called the Iron Curtain. While struggles may continue for spheres of influence, major nuclear war between these two powers is improbable. But with the proliferation of nuclear weapons among many countries, it is not unlikely that nuclear war of some type may break out in future. If the wars of the 20th century teach us anything, it is this: wars never turn out the way those who waged them thought they would. The goals they sought were distorted; the achievements both more and less than what was expected. In the 20th century war accelerates change. In a world greatly changed since 1900, not always for the better, let us hope that violent change as this volume has described is not often repeated during the last three decades of this violent century.

Index

Acknowledgements

The publishers would like to thank John Batchelor for the armament illustrations, and are also grateful to the following individuals and organizations for their kind permission to reproduce the pictures which appear on the pages shown:

Associated Press: Pages 252/3, 274/5, 293, 296/7 (bottom), 312/3, 314/5, 317 (top, top left), 331 (top center), 335, 354 (bottom left), 358 (top left, center), 367 (center), 371 (left), 375 (bottom), 399 (bottom), 411 (bottom left), 446 (bottom), 456/7, 482 (top left), 490 (inset) 494

Australian War Memorial: Page 420 (bottom)

Bapty: Pages 20, 44 (top left), 97, 116 (top left), 124 (top right), 141 (top), 149 (bottom), 302 (bottom right), 342 (bottom), 382, 411 (bottom right)

Bundesarchiv: Pages 183 (top), 235 (top center), 236, 286 (bottom right), 287 (bottom)

Camera Press: Pages 418 (right), 432, 460/1, 489 (bottom)

Canadian War Museum: Page 466 (top)

Central Press: Pages 306 (bottom left), 403, 487 (bottom)

Daily Telegraph: Pages 492 (bottom), 493 (top left), 496 (center right)

Rene Dazy: Pages 472/3, 475, 476/7

Fox Photos Ltd.: Pages 262 (top left), 262/3, 270/1, 285 (bottom)

Hultons/Radio Times Picture Library: Page 178 (bottom), 249 (top left)

Robert Hunt Picture Library: Pages 14 (top left, top center, top right, bottom), 15 (left, right), 16, 17, 18 (left, right), 19 (bottom), 21 (top, bottom), 22/3, 24/5, 26, 27, 28, 29, 30, 32 (top, left, right), 33, 34 (bottom left, bottom right), 35 (top right, bottom left, right), 36 (top, bottom), 37, 39 (bottom right), 40 (top, bottom), 41, 42, 44 (top right), 44/5, 46/7 (top), 46 (bottom), 48 (top, bottom), 49 (top, bottom), 50/1, 52 (top, bottom), 54/5, 54 (bottom), 55 (bottom), 56, 62/3 (top center, bottom), 63 (above right), 65 (top left, right, bottom left, right), 66 (bottom), 68 (top, bottom), 69 (top, bottom), 70, 72/3, 74/5, 79 (bottom), 80 (left, center, right), 81, 82/3, 84/5, 84 (bottom), 85 (bottom), 91 (top right), 92 (top, bottom), 93, 96, 98 (bottom), 99 (top, bottom), 100, 101, 103, 104/5, 106 (top, bottom), 106/7 (top, bottom), 107 (top, bottom), 108, 109 (top right, bottom), 110/11, 112, 113 (top, bottom), 115 (bottom), 116 (bottom left), 117 (top right, bottom), 118 (top), 118/9, 112/3 (top, bottom), 124 (top left), 124/5, 125 (top), 126 (top right), 128 (top left, right, bottom), 129 (top, bottom), 132 (bottom), 133 (top), 135, 136, 137 (top, bottom), 140, 143 (top, bottom), 144 (top, bottom), 145 (top, bottom), 146 (top left), 153 (top, bottom), 154, 156 (top), 157 (top left, right, bottom), 158/9 (top, bottom), 161, 165 (top, bottom right), 166 (top, bottom), 167 (top left, right), 168/9, 169, 172 (top, bottom left), 173, 174, 175, 176, 177 (top left, bottom), 178 (top left, right), 179, 180 (top, bottom), 181 (top), 182 (top), 184/5 (top), 184 (bottom), 187 (top, bottom left, center), 192 (top, bottom), 193 (top, bottom left, right), 194 (top left), 194/5 (bottom), 195 (top right), 196 (top, bottom), 197 (top, bottom), 200 (bottom), 201 (top left, right, bottom), 203 (top left, bottom left), 204 (top, center), 205 (top, bottom), 206/7, 207, 208 (top left, right), 210/11, 211, 213 (top, bottom), 216/7, 225 (top), 228 (bottom), 232 (bottom), 235 (top left, bottom), 237, 238 (top center, bottom), 240, 242, 247 (top, center, bottom), 248 (top left, top right, bottom), 249 (bottom right), 250, 256, 258 (bottom), 259, 265 (top), 266 (top left), 266/7, 268 (top center, bottom center, bottom left), 269, 272/3, 273 (top left, top right, bottom), 276, 277 (top left, right, bottom left, right), 278 (top, bottom right), 281 (top right), 282 (top, center), 282/3 (top), 284 (top), 286 (center), 288/9, 290 (top), 292, 294 (top, bottom), 295, 296/7 (top, center), 298/9, 302 (top, bottom left), 303 (top, bottom), 306 (top, bottom right), 307 (top, bottom left, right), 308 (top left, center), 309 (bottom left), 310/11, 313 (left, right), 315, 316 (top, bottom), 318, 319 (bottom, top left), 321 (bottom), 326 (bottom right), 330 (top, top right), 332 (top, bottom), 332/3, 333 (bottom, right), 334, 336 (center bottom), 336/7 (bottom), 350, 351 (bottom), 353 (bottom), 354/5, 354 (bottom right), 355 (bottom), 356/7, 359 (bottom left), 361 (center right), 362/3, 365 (top, bottom), 366 (bottom left), 368 (top, top center, bottom center), 369 (bottom), 379 (bottom left, bottom right), 384 (center left), 385 (top), 387 (top, bottom left, right), 388 (bottom), 389 (top), 391 (top), 392 (bottom), 394 (center left), 402 (top, bottom), 404 (top), 405 (top, center, bottom), 407 (top left, right, center, bottom), 409 (top, bottom left), 411 (top), 421, 422 (bottom left), 434 (top right), 437 (top), 440, 442 (bot-

tom center), 447 (top), 452, 454, 458 (bottom), 459 (bottom), 460 (top left), 460 (top right), 462 (left), 462/3, 463 (center), 464/5 (all), 466/7 (bottom), 467 (all), 468/9, 470, 478/9, 481 (bottom), 482 (top right), 483 (top right), 482/3, 485/6, 487 (top left and right), 487 (center), 489 (top right), 490 (center), 498/9

Imperial War Museum: Pages 1, 19 (top), 34/5, 34 (bottom right), 35 (top left, center right), 38/9, 38 (bottom), 39 (center, bottom left), 47 (bottom), 57 (left, right), 58/9, 60, 61, 62 (top left), 63 (top center, right), 66 (top), 76, 77, 78 (top; bottom), 79 (top), 80 (bottom right), 86/7 (top, bottom), 88/9 (top), 88 (center left, right), 89 (top, bottom), 90/1, 91 (top left), 94/5, 98 (top), 102 (top), 109 (top left), 114, 115 (top), 117 (top left), 120/121, 126 (top left, center), 126/127, 127 (top left, right), 130/131, 132 (center), 133 (bottom), 134, 139 (top, bottom), 141 (bottom), 142, 146 (top right), 146/7, 147, 148 (top, bottom), 149 (top, bottom right), 150, 150/1, 151 (top, center, bottom), 152, 153 (bottom), 155 (top, center bottom), 156 (bottom), 158/9 (top), 159, 160 (top, bottom), 162/3, 163, 164/5, 165 (bottom left, middle), 170/1, 172 (bottom right), 177 (top right), 181 (bottom), 182/3, 184/5 (bottom), 186, 187 (bottom right), 188, 189 (top, center, bottom), 190 (top left, right), 191 (top left, right), 194 (top right), 195 (top left), 198, 199 (top, bottom), 200/1, 202 (top center, bottom), 203 (bottom right), 204 (bottom), 208 (bottom), 209, 212, 214, 218/9, 220, 222 (top, bottom), 223, 224 (top, bottom), 225 (bottom), 226, 226/7, 227 (top right), 228 (top left, right), 229 (top left, right, bottom), 230/1, 231, 232, 232/3 (top, bottom), 234 (top left, right), 235 (top right), 238 (bottom center), 239 (top), 244 (top), 251, 252, 252/3 (top), 265 (bottom), 266 (top right), 267 (top left, right, bottom), 270 (top left, right), 271 (top), 274 (bottom), 278 (bottom left), 279, 281 (top left), 282/3 (center, bottom), 283 (center), 284 (bottom), 287 (top), 289 (bottom), 290 (bottom), 291 (top left, right), 297 (bottom right), 300, 301 (bottom), 309 (bottom right), 310 (top), 311 (top left), 314 (top), 320, 326 (top), 328 (top), 330 (bottom left, center right, bottom right), 330/1, 331 (top), 336/7 (top), 338/9 (top, bottom), 339, 340, 345 (top), 346, 347, 351 (top), 352/3, 352 (bottom), 353 (top), 355 (center), 358 (top right), 359 (top left), 360/1, 360 (top, center, bottom), 361 (center left, bottom), 364, 366 (bottom right), 367 (bottom), 368 (bottom), 369 (top), 375 (center, bottom left), 377 (top), 378, 378/9, 380 (top, bottom), 381, 384 (top), 388 (top), 392 (top), 393 (center, bottom), 394/5, 398 (top, bottom), 399 (top), 406 (bottom), 408 (bottom), 415 (center), 416 (top, bottom left, right),

417 (center, bottom), 418 (left), 422 (top), 423 (bottom left), 424 (top, bottom), 425 (top, center, bottom), 426/7 (top), 428, 429 (top left, right, bottom), 430/1, 430 (bottom left, right), 431 (bottom left), 433, 434 (left), 435 (top), 436 (top, center, bottom center, bottom), 436/7, 437 (center), 442 (top center), 448 (top center), 488/9, 489 (top left), 490/1 (bottom)

Keystone Press Agency: Pages 249 (top right), 406 (top), 423 (top), 426/7 (bottom), 448 (bottom), 490/1 (top and inset bottom), 491 (bottom right), 497, 500, 501, 504

Library of Congress: Pages 245 (top), 249 (bottom left), 317 (bottom), 359 (bottom right)

Novosti Press Agency: Pages 301 (top, center), 404 (bottom), 408 (top), 409 (bottom right), 410

Opera Mundi: Pages 367 (top), 411 (top)

Parismatch: Page 474

Paul Popper: Pages 67, 102 (bottom), 275 (bottom), 331 (bottom center)

Popperfoto: Pages 493 (top right and bottom), 496 (left and bottom right), 502/3

Search: Page 12

Südd Verlag: Pages 244 (bottom), 283 (bottom right)

Ullstein: Pages 254 (top, bottom), 258 (top), 260/1, 262 (top right), 263 (top), 286 (bottom left), 439 (bottom)

United Press International (U.K.) Ltd.: Pages 304/5, 309 (top right), 311 (center right), 390, 409 (top)

U.S. Airforce: Pages 308 (top right), 321 (top), 333 (top), 342 (top), 344, 391 (bottom), 395, 400, 420, 438 (bottom), 448 (bottom center), 449

U.S. Army: Pages 281 (bottom), 309 (top), 311 (top right), 317 (top right), 326 (top center right), 327 (top center left, right), 326/7 (bottom), 341, 370, 371 (right), 373, 374 (top), 374/5, 375 (top), 376, 377 (bottom), 379 (top right), 384 (bottom left), 384/5, 387 (bottom right), 391 (center), 393 (top), 394 (bottom right), 400/1, 401 (top left, right), 421 (bottom), 422 (bottom right), 434 (left), 435 (bottom), 437 (bottom right), 438 (top), 439 (top), 442 (top), 446 (top), 450

U.S. Coastguard: Pages 396/7, 443 (top, bottom), 445

U.S. Marines: Pages 326/7 (top), 441 (top, bottom), 442 (top center), 447 (bottom), 448 (top)

U.S. National Archives: Pages 202 (top left), 202/3, 206 (top, bottom), 214/5, 227 (center), 238 (top), 245 (bottom), 246, 308 (bottom), 322, 323 (top, bottom), 324/5, 326 (bottom left), 327 (bottom center left, top right), 328/9, 348/9, 419, 420 (bottom)

U.S. Navy: Pages 318/9, 329 (top), 412/3, 413, 415 (top, bottom), 417 (top), 444 (top, bottom)

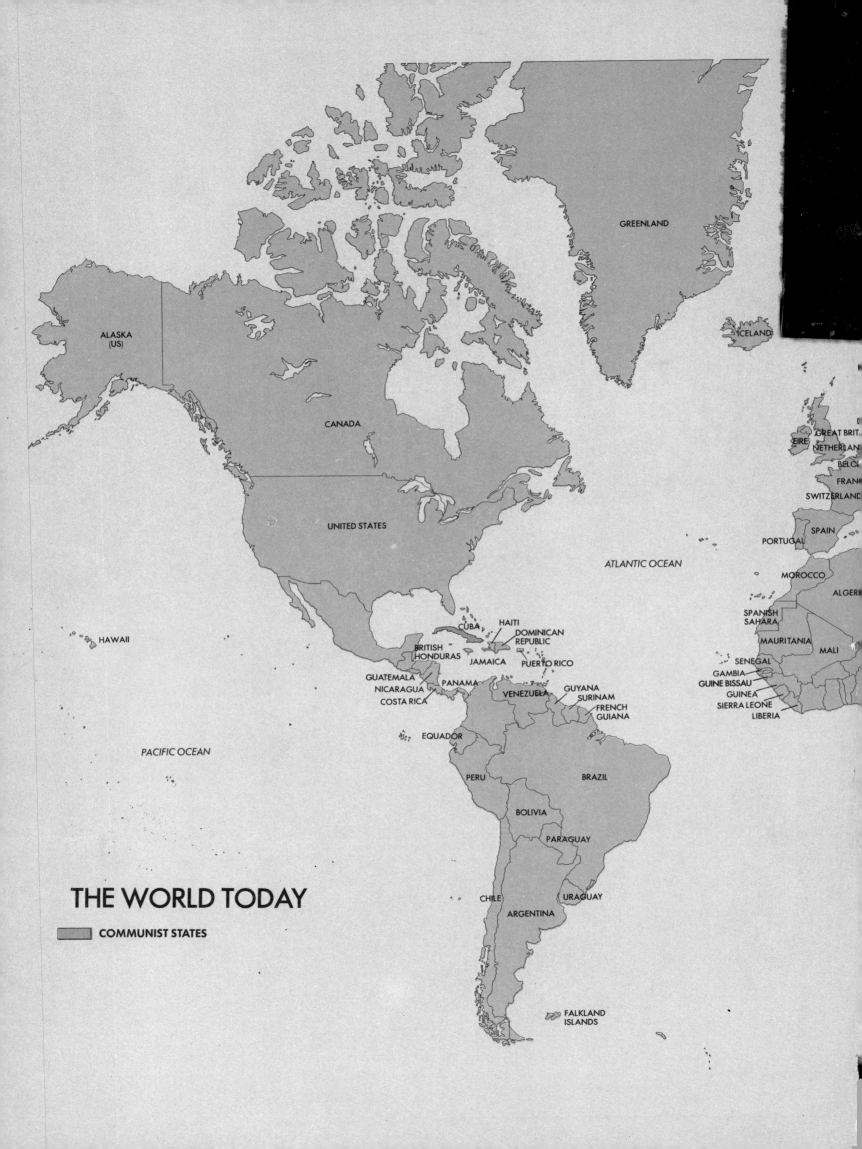

THE WORLD TODAY

COMMUNIST STATES

ALASKA
(US)

CANADA

UNITED STATES

HAWAII

GREENLAND

ICELAND

ATLANTIC OCEAN

PACIFIC OCEAN

CUBA
HAITI
DOMINICAN
REPUBLIC
BRITISH
HONDURAS
JAMAICA
PUERTO RICO
GUATEMALA
NICARAGUA
COSTA RICA
PANAMA
VENEZUELA
GUYANA
SURINAM
FRENCH
GUIANA

EQUADOR

PERU

BRAZIL

BOLIVIA

PARAGUAY

CHILE
URAGUAY
ARGENTINA

FALKLAND
ISLANDS

EIRE
GREAT BRIT.
NETHERLAN
BELG.
FRANC
SWITZERLAND

PORTUGAL
SPAIN

MOROCCO
ALGER

SPANISH
SAHARA

MAURITANIA
MALI

SENEGAL
GAMBIA
GUINE BISSAU
GUINEA
SIERRA LEONE
LIBERIA